A COMPANION TO URBAN ECONOMICS

Blackwell Companions to Contemporary Economics

The *Blackwell Companions to Contemporary Economics* are reference volumes accessible to serious students and yet also containing up-to-date material from recognized experts in their particular fields. These volumes focus on basic bread-and-butter issues in economics as well as popular contemporary topics often not covered in textbooks. Coverage avoids the overly technical, is concise, clear, and comprehensive. Each *Companion* features introductions by the editors, extensive bibliographical reference sections, and an index.

Already published

1   *A Companion to Theoretical Econometrics* edited by Badi H. Baltagi
2   *A Companion to Economic Forecasting* edited by Michael P. Clements and David F. Hendry
3   *A Companion to the History of Economic Thought* edited by Warren J. Samuels, Jeff E. Biddle, and John B. Davis
4   *A Companion to Urban Economics* edited by Richard J. Arnott and Daniel P. McMillen

A Companion to Urban Economics

Edited by

RICHARD J. ARNOTT
Boston College, Massachusetts
DANIEL P. McMILLEN
University of Illinois at Chicago

Blackwell
Publishing

BLACKWELL PUBLISHING
350 Main Street, Malden, MA 02148-5020, USA
9600 Garsington Road, Oxford OX4 2DQ, UK
550 Swanston Street, Carlton, Victoria 3053, Australia

First published 2006 by Blackwell Publishing Ltd

First published in paperback 2008 by Blackwell Publishing Ltd

1   2008

Library of Congress Cataloging-in-Publication Data

A companion to urban economics / edited by Richard Arnott and Daniel McMillen.
p. cm. — (Blackwell companions to contemporary economics ; 4)
Includes bibliographical references and indexes.
ISBN 978-1-4051-0629-0 (hardcover : alk. paper) ISBN 978-1-4051-7968-3 (paperback : alk. paper)
1. Urban economics .   I. Arnott, Richard.   II. McMillen, Daniel P.   III. Series.
HT321.C625 2006
330.9173′2—dc22
2005033631

A catalogue record for this title is available from the British Library.

Set in 10/12pt Book Antique
by Graphicraft Limited, Hong Kong

For further information on
Blackwell Publishing, visit our website:
www.blackwellpublishing.com

Contents

List of Figures

List of Tables

Notes on Contributors

Alex Anas is Professor of Economics at the State University of New York at Buffalo. He has published articles and books on land use, transportation, housing markets, agglomeration, traffic congestion, employment dispersal, and urban sprawl issues. His research has been supported by grants from the National Science Foundation, the Departments of Transportation and of Housing and Urban Development, the Fannie Mae Foundation, and the Environmental Protection Agency. He is currently developing a computable general equilibrium model that is suitable for testing the effects of a variety of policies on urban form and metropolitan economies.

Richard J. Arnott is Professor of Economics at Boston College, Massachusetts. His recent research focuses on the economics of urban transportation (Alleviating Urban Traffic Congestion, with Tilmann Rave and Ronnie Schöb). He has extensive editorial experience, including serving as an Editor for *Regional Science and Urban Economics*, the *Journal of Economic Geography*, *Public Economics: Selected Papers by William Vickrey* (Cambridge University Press, 1994), and *Economics for an Imperfect World: Essays in Honor of Joseph E. Stiglitz* (The MIT Press, 2003).

Timothy J. Bartik is a Senior Economist at the W. E. Upjohn Institute for Employment Research, a nonprofit and nonpartisan research organization in Kalamazoo, Michigan. Since coming to the Institute in 1989, he has focused on research on state and local economic development policies, local labor markets, and urban poverty. He is the author of numerous research articles in scholarly journals, as well as two books: *Who Benefits from State and Local Economic Development Policies?* (W. E. Upjohn Institute, 1991) and *Jobs for the Poor: Can Labor Demand Policies Help?* (Russell Sage Foundation, 2001). He is currently working on a book on preschool education and state economic development.

Marcus Berliant is a Mathematical Economist at Washington University in St Louis, who works primarily in urban economics and public finance. He received the Emerson Excellence in Teaching Award in 2003, and Outstanding Faculty Mentor Awards in 2000 and 2002 for his work with graduate students, and was elected a Fellow of the Regional Science Association International in 2005. Uncle Marcus is fond of dogs and his graduate students, 32 of whom have completed their doctorates and one of whom is now his boss.

Glenn C. Blomquist is the Carl F. Pollard Professor of Health Economics and Professor of Economics and Public Policy at the University of Kentucky in Lexington, Kentucky. His research deals with valuation of risks to human health and safety, valuation of urban and environmental amenities, benefit–cost analysis, and public policy. He has published in journals such as the *Journal of Political Economy*, the *American Economic Review*, the *Journal of Urban Economics*, the *Journal of Risk and Uncertainty*, the *Journal of Health Economics*, and the *Journal of Environmental Economics and Management*. His work has been published by the Brookings Institution and the National Academy of Sciences, and he has received grants from the National Science Foundation, the US Environmental Protection Agency, and the Urban Institute.

Nancy E. Bockstael is a Professor in the Department of Agricultural and Resource Economics at the University of Maryland. She has written extensively on environmental valuation, the effects of land use on the environment, and the effect of regulations on the spatial pattern of land-use change. She has published in numerous journals, including the *American Economic Review*, the *Economic Journal*, the *Review of Economics and Statistics*, the *Journal of Environmental Economics and Management, Regional Science and Urban Economics*, the *Journal of Economic Geography, Land Economics*, and the *American Journal of Agricultural Economics*, and is a Fellow of the American Association of Agricultural Economists.

Jan K. Brueckner is Professor of Economics at the University of California, Irvine, and serves as Editor of the *Journal of Urban Economics*. He has published widely in urban economics, local public economics, housing finance, and industrial organization.

Gerald A. Carlino is currently a Senior Economic Advisor and Economist in the Research Department of the Federal Reserve Bank of Philadelphia. He is an Associate Editor of the *Journal of Regional Science*. He has taught at the University of Pennsylvania, the University of Pittsburgh, the University of Missouri, and Florida International University. His research interests include the role of local economies in innovation, regional economic growth, and regional business cycle models. He has published in the *Journal of Regional Science*, the *Journal of Urban Economics, Regional Science and Urban Economics, Urban Studies*, the *Review of Economics and Statistics*, and the *Journal of Monetary Economics*. He has authored the book *Economies of Scale in Manufacturing Location* (Martinus Nijhoff, 1978).

Bradford Case is an Economist with the Research and Statistics Division of the Federal Reserve Board of Governors in Washington, DC. His research interests include estimation of value indices for residential and commercial real estate, mortgage default modeling, portfolio-level mortgage credit risk, and consumer credit issues. He has published in the *Journal of Real Estate Economics*, the *Journal of Real Estate Finance*, and the *Review of Economics and Statistics*, among others.

N. Edward Coulson is Professor of Economics at The Pennsylvania State University. He has published widely on a variety of topics in professional journals such as the *American Economic Review*, the *Journal of Urban Economics*, *Real Estate Economics*, the *Journal of Labor Economics*, the *Review of Economics and Statistics*, and others. He is on the Editorial Board of the *Journal of Urban Economics* and in January 2006 became Co-editor of *Real Estate Economics*. He has been a visiting scholar at the Federal Reserve Bank of Philadelphia, the New Economic School in Moscow, Russia, and elsewhere.

Robert H. DeFina is a Professor of Economics in the Sociology Department of Villanova University, Pennsylvania. His teaching and research interests include macroeconomics, poverty, and income inequality. He has published his work in numerous journals, including the *Review of Economics and Statistics*, the *Journal of Money, Credit, and Banking*, the *Journal of Macroeconomics*, the *Journal of Labor Economics*, the *Journal of Urban Economics*, and the *Review of Income and Wealth*.

Gilles Duranton is an Associate Professor in the Department of Economics at the University of Toronto. A Philip Leverhulme Prize winner in 2003, his research interests are both theoretical and empirical. On the theory side, he is interested in the modeling of urban system and the micro-foundations of agglomeration economies. His empirical work is concerned with the measurement of location and concentration in continuous space, the estimation of urban increasing returns, and the identification of spatial externalities. He also served as consultant on regional and urban policy for various European governments.

Randall W. Eberts is Executive Director of the W. E. Upjohn Institute for Employment Research. His research focuses on labor market analysis and employment program evaluation, with particular emphasis on issues related to urban markets. He has held positions at the University of Oregon, Texas A&M University, the Federal Reserve Bank of Cleveland, and on the President's Council of Economic Advisers. He received his PhD in economics from Northwestern University.

William A. Fischel is Professor of Economics and Patricia F. and William B. Hale '44 Professor in Arts and Sciences at Dartmouth College, New Hampshire, where he has taught since 1973. He is the author of *The Economics of Zoning Laws* (Johns Hopkins University Press, 1985), *Regulatory Takings* (Harvard University Press, 1995), and *The Homevoter Hypothesis* (Harvard University Press, 2001). He is currently working on a book about the economics of school districts.

David Geltner is the George Macomber Professor in the MIT Department of Urban Studies & Planning, and Director of the MIT Center for Real Estate. He is co-author of the graduate textbook *Commercial Real Estate Analysis & Investments* (South-Western/Thomson, 2001), Academic Advisor to the National Council of Real Estate Investment Fiduciaries, and a member of the Real Estate Investment Committee of the Ohio State Teachers Retirement System. He has published numerous articles on real estate investment and performance measurement, and is a former Editor of *Real Estate Economics*.

Franz Hubert holds a chair for Management Science at Humboldt University, Berlin. His research interests are in the fields of contract theory and industrial organization.

Keith R. Ihlanfeldt is Director of the DeVoe L. Moore Center, DeVoe L. Moore Eminent Scholar, and Professor of Economics at Florida State University. His articles have appeared in such journals as the *American Economic Review*, the *Quarterly Journal of Economics*, the *Review of Economics and Statistics*, and the *Journal of Law and Economics*. Currently, he serves as an Associate Editor or on the Editorial Board of a half dozen economic and public policy journals.

Robert P. Inman is the Mellon Professor of Finance and Economics, Wharton School, University of Pennsylvania. His scholarly research focuses on political economy, fiscal policy, and urban economics, and has been published in leading economics research journals, law reviews, and collected essays. He has served as an advisor on matters of fiscal policy to the National Research Council, the US Treasury, the US Departments of Education and Housing and Urban Development, the Federal Reserve Banks of New York and Philadelphia, the Republic of South Africa, and the Central Bank of Sri Lanka.

Elena G. Irwin is an Associate Professor in the Department of Agricultural, Environmental, and Development Economics at Ohio State University. Her research interests include land use, urbanization, sprawl, residential location, and coupled human–environment systems. She is currently the co-director of the Exurban Change Project and Ohio State University's Biocomplexity Project on Coupled Natural–Human Interactions in Large Lake Ecosystems, which is supported by the National Science Foundation.

Matthew E. Kahn is Professor of International Economics at the Fletcher School at Tufts University, Massachusetts. His research focuses on environmental and urban issues. He is the author of *Green Cities: Urban Growth and the Environment*, to be published by the Brookings Institution Press in 2006.

Yoshitsugu Kanemoto is Professor of Economics at the University of Tokyo. He is widely published in the fields of urban economics, contract theory, and public economics, in such journals as *Econometrica*, the *Journal of Urban Economics*, the *Journal of Labor Economics*, and the *Review of Economic Studies*. He is a member of many advisory boards of the Japanese government, including the Council for Transportation Policy (MLIT), the Commission on Policy Evaluation and Evaluation of Independent Administrative Institutions (MPHPT), and the Advisory Committee for Natural Resources and Energy (METI).

Marvin Kraus is a Professor of Economics at Boston College, Massachusetts, where he has been on the faculty since 1972. His research in urban economics has been in land use and transportation, with a particular focus on optimal pricing and investment in urban transportation.

Anne Laferrère is affiliated with INSEE, the French National Institute of Statistics and Economic Studies, and CREST (Centre de Recherche en Économie et Statistique). She is currently a Country Team Leader of SHARE (Survey on Health Aging and Retirement in Europe) and has mostly worked on intergenerational transfers and housing.

Courtney LaFountain is an Assistant Professor of Economics at the University of Texas at Arlington. She has published papers in the *Journal of Urban Economics* and *Public Choice*. Her research interests include urban economics, public finance, and corruption.

David Le Blanc is a Senior Housing Economist at the World Bank, where he has been since 2003. His primary research interests are in housing and household economics, and his recent work focuses on housing subsidies, informal housing, and housing policy reforms in developing countries.

Robin Lindsey has worked at the University of Alberta since 1982, where he is a Professor of Economics. His academic specialties are transportation economics and industrial organization, and his current research interests include traffic congestion and road pricing. He has been a visitor at the University of British Columbia, the University of California, Irvine, the Free University of Amsterdam, the Université de Cergy-Pontoise, and the Hong Kong University of Science and Technology.

Stephen Malpezzi is Professor, and Wangard Faculty Scholar, in the Department of Real Estate and Urban Land Economics, as well as an associate member of the Department of Urban and Regional Planning, of the University of Wisconsin-Madison.

John F. McDonald is Professor Emeritus of Economics and Finance and Director of the Center for Urban Real Estate at the University of Illinois at Chicago, where he was Senior Associate Dean for Academic Affairs and Research in the College of Business Administration at UIC from 1999 to 2004 and Interim Dean of the College during 2004–5. He was President of the Illinois Economic Association during 1993–4, and served as North American Editor for *Urban Studies* from 2001 to 2005. Currently, he is Editor of the *Journal of Real Estate Literature*, Fellow of the American Real Estate Society, and a consultant to Real Estate Research Corporation.

Daniel P. McMillen is Professor of Economics at the University of Illinois at Chicago, and a member of the Institute of Government and Public Affairs. His publications have appeared in such journals as the *Review of Economics and Statistics*, the *Journal of Urban Economics*, *Regional Science and Urban Economics*, the *Journal of Business and Economic Statistics*, and *Real Estate Economics*.

Arthur O'Sullivan is the Robert B. Pamplin Jr Professor of Economics at Lewis & Clark College. He is the author of *Urban Economics* (McGraw-Hill/Irwin), currently in its sixth edition. His research has been published in the *Journal of Urban Economics*, the *Journal of Public Economics*, *Regional Science and Urban Economics*, the *Journal of Law and Economics*, and the *Journal of Environmental Economics and Management*.

André de Palma has taught at Queen's University, Northwestern University, the Free University of Brussels, and the University of Geneva. He is currently Professor at the Université de Cergy-Pontoise and at the Ecole Polytechnique, and also a Senior Member at the Institut Universitaire de France. His main areas of research are transportation economics and industrial organization, and he has published more than 130 articles and two books in these fields. His recent interest is risk analysis – which he plans to apply to transportation. He is a partner of adpC, and the author of the dynamic transportation planning software METRO-POLIS, which is currently distributed by PTV.

Nathalie Picard has an undergraduate degree in mathematics and two graduate degrees in economics. Since 1998 she has worked at the Université de Cergy-Pontoise, where she is an Assistant Professor of Economics. Her academic specialities are microeconometrics and public policy evaluation. Her current research interests include the economics and econometrics of individual behavior in risky environments.

Steven Raphael is Associate Professor of public policy at the University of California, Berkeley. His research focuses on urban labor markets, the economics of racial inequality, and the economics of crime.

Piet Rietveld is a Professor in transport economics at the Vrije Universiteit Amsterdam. He has published in numerous journals in transport and regional science. He has an interest in themes such as transport pricing and transport policy, as well as the interrelationship between transport infrastructure and urban development.

Stuart S. Rosenthal is a Professor in the Economics Department at Syracuse University and Senior Research Associate in the university's Center for Policy Research. He has written widely in urban economics, housing finance, real estate markets, and local public economics. His research has appeared in leading economics journals and has been supported by numerous institutions, including the US Department of Housing and Urban Development, the John D. and Catherine

T. MacArthur Foundation, the Ford Foundation, and the Kauffman Foundation. He serves on the Editorial Boards for several scholarly journals and has also served as an advisor to the New York Federal Reserve Bank. He is a Fellow of the Homer Hoyt School of Advanced Studies in Real Estate and Urban Economics.

Miki Seko is Professor of Economics at Keio University, Japan. Her research on topics relating to housing has appeared in the *Journal of Housing Economics* and *Real Estate Finance and Economics*. Her research interests are in housing demand and policy. Currently, she serves on the Editorial Boards of four real estate and urban economics journals.

Melissa Sills is a graduate student and research assistant at the University of California, Berkeley. Her primary research interest is economic demography. She has also co-authored several reports on welfare and poverty.

William C. Strange is RIOCAN Real Estate Investment Trust Professor of Real Estate and Urban Economics at the University of Toronto's Rotman School of Management. His research has concerned urban economics, local public economics, and investment under uncertainty. His work has been published in a wide range of journals, including the *American Economic Review*, the *Review of Economics and Statistics*, the *Journal of Urban Economics*, the *Journal of Public Economics*, and the *Journal of Economic Dynamics and Control*.

John Douglas Wilson is Professor of Economics at Michigan State University. His research spans the fields of urban economics, public economics, and international trade, including numerous articles on tax competition among independent governments. He is now Editor-In-Chief of *International Tax and Public Finance*.

Anthony M. Yezer is a member of the Department of Economics of The George Washington University, where he directs the Center for Economic Research. He teaches courses in regional economics, urban economics, microeconomics, and the economics of crime. He has been a Fellow of the Homer Hoyt School of Advanced Studies in Real Estate and Urban Economics since 1991, and served as an expert witness for the Federal Trade Commission testifying in connection with the trade regulation rule governing Consumer Credit Practices. His research interests have included the measurement and determinants of credit risk in lending, the effects of regulations on credit supply, and fair lending.

Yves Zenou is a Professor of Economics at the Research Institute of Industrial Economics, Stockholm, and a Research Fellow at the Centre for Economic Policy Research (CEPR) and the Institute for the Study of Labor (IZA). His research interests cover urban economics, labor economics, public economics, and development economics, and consist in better understanding social interactions between agents in the context of education, crime, and labor. He has published his research in such journals as the *Economic Journal*, the *Journal of Economic Theory*, the *Journal of Development Economics*, the *Journal of Labor Economics*, the *Journal of Public Economics*, the *International Economic Review*, and the *Journal of Urban Economics*, among others.

Preface

By definition, urban economics is the economics of cities. But what does this mean? In the United States, almost 80 percent of the population lives in urban areas, and in Europe the proportion is almost as high; the urbanization rate is lower in the rest of the world, but is increasing at a rapid rate, so that while the world's urbanization rate was only 30 percent in 1950 it is projected to be 61 percent in 2025 (O'Sullivan 2003, p. 7). The proportion of economic activity that occurs in cities, as measured by value added to national product, is even higher. Furthermore, most kinds of economic activity occur in cities; agriculture and the natural resource industries are the major exceptions. Thus, the bulk of the economic activity that is studied in macroeconomics, labor economics, industrial organization, financial economics, and so on occurs in cities. How, then, does one draw the line between what is urban economics and what is not?

Some intellectual historians study the evolution of subjects, such as economics, fields, such as urban economics, and subfields, such as urban labor economics. An issue arises in the forum of public debate that is taken up by the academic community. If existing bodies of thought are ill suited to discussion and analysis of the issue, there is an incentive to develop a new line of thought. Depending on the importance of the issue and how long it remains in the public spotlight, as well as the quality and fecundity of the new line of thought that has been developed to address it, a new field or subfield may develop, which may subsequently blossom, wither away, or be absorbed by another field.

What is urban economics and what is not is the outcome of such an evolutionary intellectual process. Urban economics became an identifiable field in the 1960s in the USA, as the result of concatenation of three developments. The first was the importation from Western Europe of spatial economics/location theory into US economic thought. The migration of largely Jewish academics from Germany and Eastern Europe during the interwar period transformed many fields. Economics in the Anglo-Saxon tradition pays scant attention to space. Almost all the major contributors to the history of spatial economic thought (Ponsard 1983) have been Continental economists, Johann von Thünen being the best known and most influential. This development by itself gave rise to regional science. The second development was the transportation and land-use studies of the 1950s. Neither of us knows the exact impetus for these studies, but one must have been concern for the impacts on the location of economic activity of the massive urban highway-building programs of that decade, which spurred post-war suburbanization. In any event, these studies led to heightened awareness of, and interest in, the intra-metropolitan location of economic activity, and the relationship between transportation and land use (Hoover 1963). The third develop-ment was the social unrest of the 1960s: the Civil Rights Movement, the War on Poverty, the Great Society, and the urban riots, all of which focused attention on the problems of the inner city and particularly of the black ghetto. One imme-diate impact was an explosion of interest in urban studies on college campuses and a sharp increase in research funds to study the urban economy. Fortuitously, the intellectual foundations for urban economics had already been laid. Von Thünen's theory of agricultural land use had been adapted by Alonso (1964), Muth (1961, 1969), and Mills (1967) to develop a theory of urban land use. The 1960s was also the decade of the general equilibrium revolution in applied microeconomics. The hallmark of general equilibrium theory is its focus on the economy as a whole rather than on pieces of it. The outcome was a general equilibrium model of the urban economy – the *monocentric city model* – that per-mitted the simultaneous treatment of urban land use, transportation, housing, and government.

The period from the mid-1960s to the mid-1970s was the Golden Age of urban economics. Many of the best and the brightest economics professors and gradu-ate students in the USA turned their attention to the urban economy. The result was the rapid development of a core body of urban economic theory that remains the cornerstone of the field to this day, and accounts for why the field endured when public and government interest in urban problems flagged in the subsequent decades.

Urban economics *per se* remains predominantly a North American field. Outside North America, each country has its particular intellectual history with respect to the study of the urban economy. After Americans, Japanese urban economists from a regional science background have contributed most to the development of the field, especially in the area of urban location theory. The United Kingdom has strong traditions in housing, transport, and land-use eco-nomics, but those fields never become integrated under the rubric of urban economics as they did in the USA. Scandinavia has a strong tradition in local public finance, and British, Belgian, and German economists have been dominant in game-theoretic location theory.

Although urban economics started out as a body of applied microeconomic theory, even in its early days it had a strong empirical orientation, and since then the field has become increasingly empirical. Many other bodies of theory have been captured by mathematical economists and have become increasingly abstract, abstruse, and axiomatic. But this has not happened in urban economics. A prox-imate reason is that the leading theorists have aimed in their modeling to explain what they observe on a day-to-day basis in the cities in which they live and work; perhaps the familiarity of the subject matter has attracted theorists with an empirical bent. Urban economics has become increasingly empirical in another sense of the word; more and more of the work that is done in the field estimates and tests econometric models using large microdatabases. This emphasis on empiricism has occurred in many fields in economics. The root cause is the tremendous increase in computing power that has occurred during the past 30 years, which has made routine the econometric analysis of large microdatabases. This in turn has led to the collection of more and more microdata, to the rapid development of econometric theory, and to the widespread diffusion of econometric competence. American and, to a lesser extent, British economists have been in the vanguard of this major reorientation of economics. In urban economics, the American preeminence has been compounded by more and better data being available on almost every subject than in other countries.

Thus, urban economics has been more successful than most other microeconomic fields in achieving a healthy balance between theory and empirical work and a good interaction between them in the spirit of the scientific method.

American parochialism is infamous, and unfortunately extends to urban economics. Because the urban economic textbook market is largest in the USA, all the leading textbooks are written with the American student in mind and pay scant attention to the urban experience and policies of other countries. The leading international academic journals publish articles that are methodologically innovative; a study of a particular urban problem that follows the method of a US study done a decade earlier is rarely deemed worthy of publication. Because American urban economists have so much better data and are generally so much better trained in empirical work than urban economists elsewhere, the bulk of empirical studies published in academic urban economic journals deal with the US experience. This is unfortunate because it conveys the impression that the US experience is universal. In some ways it probably is, and in other ways it probably isn't, but without cross-country comparisons, which are made difficult by inconsistent data definitions, it is not possible to tell. This parochialism is particularly evident and particularly unfortunate in policy analysis. US policymakers could learn much from the policy experience of other countries, but do not because existing studies are rarely sufficiently innovative or of sufficiently high quality to merit publication in the international journals. American parochialism is not as much of a problem in urban economic theory. Mainstream microeconomic theory is the same across the world, and all that is required to do theory is paper, pencil, and a brain. There is nonetheless a US bias. The empirical regularities that urban economists build their theories around are usually empirical regularities for the US urban economy. Americans also tend to be the agenda setters, though this is less of a problem in urban economic theory than in many other areas of theory.

An unfortunate result of US dominance of the field and US parochialism is that the academic establishment in many countries resists urban economics. This is particularly evident in the UK, where urban transport, housing, environmental, and land-use economics evolve largely independently, without the benefit of the conceptual integration that urban economics offers.

By 1990, urban economics was in danger of becoming an intellectual backwater. Practically useful work was being done and understanding of the urban economy was steadily improving, but little innovative theory was being formulated and most of the empirical work was derivative from other fields, especially labor economics. As a result, there was little interest outside urban economics in the work being done in the field. That has changed due to another concatenation of developments, principally the reformulation of international trade theory and public policy issues that have arisen out of European Union. International trade theory was the first field in applied microeconomic theory to "go g.e." – to apply the model of competitive general equilibrium *à la* Arrow–Debreu. An impressive intellectual edifice was constructed explaining patterns of trade based on comparative advantage due to difference in factor endowments. Courses in international trade focused on theory, to the virtual exclusion of empirical work. Predictably, the theory provided little insight into contemporary trends, such as the development of multinational corporations and the increasingly large proportion of international trade that was *intra*-industry, and little guidance for policy. That changed with several complementary theoretical developments in the late 1970s and the 1980s – models of international trade combining different combinations of ingredients, including product differentiation/monopolistic competition, oligopoly, increasing returns to scale, and transport costs, in addition to the traditional differential factor endowments. At the same time, many theoretical physicists laid off in the post Cold War disarmament were looking for other problems to which to apply their skills. One skill that many theoretical physicists have that most economic theorists lack is expertise in nonlinear, dynamical systems. Using what he learned from theoretical physicists concerning self-organizing systems, Paul Krugman developed a dynamic international trade model with monopolistic competition (that entails a form of increasing returns) and transport costs. This model has subsequently been adapted in many ways, and has given rise to a new field, the "new economic geography." Development of the model was stimulated by interest within Europe concerning the implications for regional development of the lowering of trade barriers that has accompanied European integration. Would all footloose economic activity be attracted to some center of economic gravity, with residents of peripheral regions becoming hewers of wood and drawers of water? Or would an altered pattern of regional specialization emerge? Much as in urban economics a generation earlier, the excitement of developing a new body of theory and applying it to issues at the top of the policy agenda has attracted many of the best and the brightest young economists in Europe to the field.

This new line of research has revitalized urban economics. Why? One reason is that urban economics has traditionally been taught in tandem with regional economics. For many years, regional economics was in a sorry state, being a combination of macroeconomics writ small, as in regional econometric models, or urban economics writ large, as in the study of systems of cities, with only a small and crude body of theory to call its own. It was very much the poor cousin that urban economics brought along. That has changed, and now the regional component of urban and regional economics courses is attracting as much interest as the urban component. But the more important reason is that the new economic geography provided a new kitbag of tools that could be applied to a central problem in urban economics that had hitherto been neglected: *agglomeration*. Agglomeration, the spatial concentration of economic activity, is the very essence of urbanization. Urban economists have always recognized its central importance and paid lip service to it, but did not know how to model and analyze it. In the monocentric city model, they simply *assumed* that all nonresidential economic activity occurs at the city center. Traditional general equilibrium theory, on which modern urban economics is built, assumes *convexity*. Convexity in production implies constant or decreasing returns to scale, but with transport costs, constant and decreasing returns to scale in production, and a spatially uniform endowment of resources, economic activity would be uniformly distributed over space in backyard economies. Thus, nonconvexities in production are central to agglomeration. The new economic geography provided the tools to tackle these nonconvexities.

The new economic geography, which was originally developed as part of trade theory, and then adapted to treat regional economic development, has been adapted again to develop the broad structure of models of urban agglomeration. *The Spatial Economy* (Fujita et al. 2001) provides an integrated introduction to these literatures. These models are being applied to study the dynamics of urbanization, and the evolution of systems of cities, including their patterns of industrial specialization. Another major line of research is the microfoundations of agglomeration. Workers are more productive in larger cities. Why? Yet another major line of research has been polycentric cities. On most fronts, empirical work has lagged behind theoretical developments but is quickly catching up.

We have still not provided a direct answer to the question posed at the beginning of the introduction: What is urban economics and what is not? But in a somewhat roundabout way, we have provided an indirect answer. Urban economics is what urban economists do, and what urban economists do reflects the field's intellectual evolution. The core subfields used to be urban land use/spatial structure, urban transportation, urban housing, and urban public finance. Urban spatial structure has continued at center stage, but its character has changed. Urban transportation continues to play an important role, but is not as prominent as it used to be. With the retreat of governments everywhere from the housing sector, much of housing economics has been absorbed into real estate economics and taught in business schools. Urban public finance is less studied than it used to be, since fiscal federalism is now focusing on issues of European integration. New characters have joined the cast. Urban pollution, urban labor markets, urban crime, urban macroeconomics, which had only bit parts three decades ago, are now featured in more episodes. And urban agglomeration and urbanization, which were merely talked about at the beginning of the series, are the new hero and heroine.

The thumbnail history of urban economics over the past four decades outlined above is reflected in the North-Holland Handbook Series on Regional and Urban Economics. Volume 2, the first to be dedicated to urban economics and published in 1986, focused primarily on the theoretical developments of the 1960s and

1970s; volume 3, entitled *Applied Urban Economics* and published in 1999, covers primarily empirical contributions; and volume 4, entitled *Cities and Geography*, and hot off the press, provides 1,000 pages of essays surveying the rapid progress of the new economic geography.

When Blackwell approached us about editing *A Companion to Urban Economics*, our immediate reaction was "Not another set of review articles." We were reviewed out and expected that our colleagues were too, and saw little to be gained from putting together a pale imitation of the admirable North-Holland series. Then we thought about our experiences teaching urban economics. Commercial publishers are understandably, though rather distastefully, concerned with the bottom line. Their concern with maximizing market share results in the "dumbing down" of most undergraduate textbooks. Standard urban textbooks are generally interesting, stimulating, and very well written, providing very good coverage of the field, and are systematically updated to reflect recent developments. But, they are written for second-year students who have only studied principles of economics, not intermediate micro theory and not econometrics, and who on average are less intellectually sophisticated than upper-level undergraduate, master's, and professional students. Additionally, standard undergraduate textbooks are also used in urban economics courses in other countries, where students typically specialize earlier and are better trained technically. There are no graduate textbooks in urban economics. There are a number of excellent, specialist books on which very sound PhD courses can be constructed, when supplemented by journal articles, but these books assume knowledge of economics and of mathematics at the PhD level.

We therefore started thinking that a Blackwell *Companion to Urban Economics* could somehow fill this large gap between urban economics at the sophomore level and at the PhD level. But what about the format? Review articles are very useful for the specialist, but by their nature are often rather superficial, touching on a large breadth of material, and quite often dull. They typically cover too much material for a single lecture, and are not designed to train a student to "think like an economist" or to expose her to how urban economists do urban economics or to develop technical skills. Also, most of the essays in the North-Holland Handbook Series provide excellent reviews; some, but not all, are too advanced for use in pre-PhD courses. We therefore chose as our format a collection of essays, each of which could form the basis for a stimulating and challenging lecture to a class of intellectually lively upper-level undergraduates. In the USA, students at this level have typically had an introductory econometrics course and have studied basic calculus, but by the standards of economics majors in other countries are not technically well trained. Their relatively weak technical training is, however, offset by development of those traits that make for the successful academic economist: curiosity in how the world works, skills in conceptualizing how it works, a well-developed critical sense, and a strong skepticism of received wisdom. We envisioned a representative essay as covering relatively few topics but covering those well. An essay might discuss a particular issue in urban public policy at a high level of conceptual sophistication, indicating what models might be applied in thinking about the policy, what the empirical literature has to say about the magnitude of the policy's various effects and its degree of confidence in these magnitudes, what groups are hurt and helped by the policy and are likely to favor or oppose it, and what notion of social justice is appropriate in evaluating the policy. A theoretical essay might instead discuss how an urban economic theorist goes about constructing a model to address a particular phenomenon, how he chooses, in light of his knowledge of the empirical literature, what essentials to focus on and what inessentials to assume away in order to make a complex reality conceptually tractable, and how he then goes about putting the model through its paces. An empirical essay might lead a student through the process of estimating a crucial parameter, explaining how to deal with data deficiencies, how to specify the estimating equation, and how to avoid the common econometric pitfalls.

In choosing subject areas to be covered, we attempted to achieve balance, to have the essays reflect the distribution of current interests within the field, but made no attempt to be comprehensive. We suggested general subject areas to authors and conveyed our vision for the essays, but made little attempt to influence their choice of topic or their treatment of it. The result is a rather eclectic collection of essays, in terms of both approach and technical level. This is entirely appropriate, since instructors will have an opportunity to pick and choose in accordance with their tastes and teaching methods.

In deciding whom to invite to write the essays, we had three considerations in mind. We wanted the essays to be lively, stimulating, and well written. We also leaned toward up-and-coming stars rather than senior leaders in the field, who are chronically overcommitted and who right now are suffering from exposition fatigue. Finally, to make the book more appealing to non-US readers and also to combat the American parochialism of the field, we leaned toward experts from outside North America.

Our organization of the essays into subfields is quite standard: urbanization, urban land use/spatial structure, housing/real estate, urban transportation, urban public economics, urban labor markets and macroeconomics, and urban quality of life. At the beginning of subfield's set of essays, we provide a brief introduction that aims only to place the essays in the context of the corresponding literature.

Perhaps more than any other field of economics, urban economics studies the quotidian – what we encounter every day in our journeys to work, in the errands we run, and in the neighborhoods in which we live. Attempting to explain what we all observe and experience accounts for the field's strong empirical bent. At the same time, the subject matter is The City, a physical manifestation of civilization in all its glory and disgrace. We hope that the essays in the *Companion*, taken as a whole, convey not only the technical accomplishments of the field, but also its fascination.

RICHARD J. ARNOTT AND DANIEL P. McMILLEN
December 2005

Bibliography

Alonso, W. 1964: *Location and Land Use*. Cambridge, MA: Harvard University Press.

Fujita, M., Krugman, P., and Venables, A. 2001: *The Spatial Economy: Cities, Regional, and International Trade*. Cambridge, MA: The MIT Press.

Hoover, E. 1963: *The Location of Economic Activity*. New York: McGraw-Hill.

Mills, E. 1967: An aggregative model of resource allocation in a metropolitan area. *American Economic Review*, 57, 197–210.

Muth, R. 1961: The spatial structure of the housing market. *Papers and Proceedings, Regional Science Association*, 7, 201–20.

—— 1969: *Cities and Housing*. Chicago: The University of Chicago Press.

O'Sullivan, A. 2003: *Urban Economics*. New York: Irwin/McGraw-Hill.

Ponsard, C. 1983: *History of Spatial Economic Theory*. New York: Springer-Verlag.

Urbanization

Urbanization

The essays in part I deal with different facets of urbanization. *The Concise Oxford Dictionary* defines urbanization as "rendering urban" or "removing the rural character of a district." In everyday usage, the term connotes the dynamic process whereby a district undergoes the transformation from being rural to being urban. The term is here used somewhat more broadly. Urban economists define a city as a spatial concentration of economic activity. Accordingly, "urbanization" covers *description* of the spatial pattern of economic activity over space, and *explanation* of that pattern as well as of the *evolution* of that pattern.

Imagine an economy on a large, homogeneous plain in which transportation is costly and in which all firms produce under constant or decreasing returns to scale. Such an economy exhibits a uniform distribution of economic activity over space. Since each household produces everything it consumes in its own backyard, we may refer to such an economy as a *backyard economy*. There are no benefits from spatially concentrating economic activity but there are costs, in particular transportation costs. While an uneven distribution of resources over space gives rise to a nonuniform distribution of economic activity over space, this factor can explain only a fraction of the high degree of spatial concentration of economic activity observed in today's service- and knowledge-based economies.

There is broad agreement among economists that at the present time the dominating trade-off determining the spatial structure of economic activity is between *transport costs* and *increasing returns to scale in production*. Consider an economy that produces a single good in factories that exhibit increasing returns to scale and are operated by separate firms. If transport costs are high and the degree of increasing returns to scale small, market areas – the area to which a single factory distributes its output – are small, while if transport costs are low and the degree of increasing returns to scale large, market areas are large. In such an economy, each firm will recognize that it has market power within its market area and that the size of its market area depends on the pricing policy of the firms whose market areas border on its own, as well as its own pricing policy. *Spatial competition theory* describes how the economy's equilibrium is determined, taking into account the strategic or game-theoretic interplay between firms. Now add another good, so that there are now two industries. If firms in the two industries operate completely independently, there will be an overlapping pattern of market areas, with the firms in the one industry having larger market areas than those in the other. But the two sets of firms do not operate independently. For one thing, a firm in industry A likely uses the output of the closest firm in industry B in its production process, and vice versa. This by itself gives the two firms an incentive to locate closer to one another than they otherwise would, so as to reduce transportation costs. But the firms would then have to compete more intensively for the land and labor in their common market area, which would give the two firms an incentive to locate further from one another than they otherwise would. One can imagine adding more industries to the model, and getting a rich pattern of industrial location, with each firm in some industries operating in its own specialized city and each firm in other industries co-locating with firms from other industries. Such a model would be empirically unrealistic in two important respects. First, firms within a particular industry would be spatially dispersed, whereas in fact firms within the same industry are often spatially concentrated. Second, firms would tend to be large, to exploit scale economies in production. That may have been the case in economies in which manufacturing predominated, but not is not the situation today. Economists have reconciled theory and observation by developing models in which economies of scale operate at the level not of the individual factory but of an industry within a city (*localization economies*) or of the city (*urbanization economies*). Since these economies of scale operate externally to the individual firm, they are referred to as *external economies of scale*. And since, by hypothesis, they form the basis for today's large urban agglomerations, they are also referred to as *agglomeration economies*. Each firm faces a horizontal average cost curve, but the level of the cost curve falls as the size of the industry–city, or simply city, in which it is located increases.

Rapid progress has been made in measuring the various sources of external economies of scale that have been hypothesized. The earlier work measured localization economies (by industry) and urbanization economies, aiming partly to determine which are more important. More recent work, which makes use of very detailed microdatabases, recognizes that the magnitude of the cost-reducing benefits a firm receives from another firm being located nearby depends on the distance between the two firms, and attempts to measure the rate at which these benefits fall off or attenuate with distance. This is just one of the strands of empirical literature that have developed out of the new economic geography, which was mentioned in the introduction. Volume 4 of the North-Holland Handbook series, entitled *Cities and Geography* (Henderson & Thisse 2004) provides an up-to-date review of this burgeoning literature; and the *Economics of Agglomeration*, by Masahisa Fujita and Jacques-François Thisse (2002), provides an overview of the current state of theory on the subject. Two essays in this part treat facets of the recent empirical work on external economies of scale, "The Micro-Empirics of Agglomeration Economies," by Stuart Rosenthal and William Strange, and "Human Capital Externalities in Cities: Identification and Policy Issues," by Gilles Duranton.

Urbanization, in the more colloquial usage of the word, is the topic of the other two essays in this part. An outstanding debate in the urbanization literature is what spurred development of the first cities, all of which appeared in today's Middle East. Many explanations have been put forward, though none has been modeled with precision. Animal husbandry and the domestication of wild grains permitted a nonnomadic, sedentary lifestyle, and presumably incremental technical progress in agriculture in due course made feasible an agricultural surplus that could be used to feed city dwellers. But since agriculture *per se* is not characterized by increasing returns to scale, on a large homogeneous plain these developments would lead to more efficient agricultural production but not cities. Even though most of the cities developed alongside rivers, transport costs would have been high. There must therefore have been some sizeable source of economies of scale to give rise to cities rather than scattered settlements. Various sources have been suggested: defense, offense, religious public goods, political administration, marketplaces, grain storage, hydraulic infrastructure (e.g., irrigation and the control of flooding), education (for writing and adding), and culture. In "The First Cities," Arthur O'Sullivan discusses what light current archaeological evidence casts on the debate.

The broad history of urbanization in Western Europe since the beginning of the Industrial Revolution should be familiar to all readers; Bairoch (1988) provides a particularly magisterial account. Though it has distinct phases, the picture it paints is of a seemingly inexorable rise in urbanization, population, and prosperity. We should not, however, forget the sobering experience of the Dark Ages, when Western Europe retrogressed: the splendor that was once Rome crumbled into disrepair and became overgrown in weeds; population fell, with the vast majority living in isolated subsistence agricultural communities; trade dried up; and most of the glorious intellectual achievements of Ancient Greece were lost – some forever, some for a millennium, until they reentered Europe from North Africa via Spain in the late Middle Ages.

Outside Western Europe, modern urbanization has been compressed in time. Except in centrally planned economies, which were able to resist market forces, it seems that the *qualitative* process of urban development has been much the same everywhere. Despite this, huge disparities in income and wealth remain between the less developed countries, particularly those in Africa, and developed countries. Stephen Malpezzi's essay, "Cross-Country Patterns of Urban Development," documents both the similarities in process and the disparities in outcomes.

The aim of the *Companion* is not to give a comprehensive review of the literature but, rather, to provide a collection of stimulating and challenging essays to supplement available textbooks. Nevertheless, we regret that some important branches of the literature have not been covered, and one in particular, the *description* of spatial structure. We need to describe spatial structure well before we can explain it well. Most description of spatial structure is based on data collected for administrative units – wards, school districts, zip codes, cities, metropolitan areas, regions, and countries. Such data are much better than no data, but we could do so much better using modern technology. Put a thin sliver of an onion ring under a microscope, and gradually increase the level of resolution. At some levels of resolution, there is a blur, but at other levels a visual structure emerges, and the pattern of this structure is different at different levels of resolution. The situation for the spatial distribution of economic activity is analogous. Census microdata can now be obtained at the block level, and modern satellite imaging collects spatial data down to the resolution of a meter. So we could perform the microscope exercise on spatial economic data, except of course at a considerably larger scale. In principle, we could infer much about the forces shaping the spatial structure of economic activity by identifying the levels of resolution at which well-defined structure is observed and by describing the structure at these levels of resolution. To do the latter, we need to describe spatial structure, which is the job of *spatial statistics*. The field of spatial statistics has been developing rapidly, with urban economists contributing greatly to the work done by econometricians and geographers.

Bibliography

Bairoch, P. 1988: *Cities and Economic Development*. Chicago: The University of Chicago Press.

Henderson, J. V. and Thisse, J.-F. (eds.) 2004: *Handbook of Regional and Urban Economics*, vol. 4: *Cities and Geography*. Amsterdam: North-Holland.

Fujita, M. and Thisse, J.-F. 2002: *Economics of Agglomeration: Cities, Industrial Location, and Regional Growth*. Cambridge, UK: Cambridge University Press.

CHAPTER ONE

The Micro-Empirics of Agglomeration Economies

Stuart S. Rosenthal and William C. Strange

1.1 INTRODUCTION

Economics is the study of the allocation of scarce resources. Urban economics focuses on the allocation of resources across space. In considering this sort of resource allocation, a striking fact becomes apparent immediately: economic activity is highly concentrated. More than 75 percent of Americans live in cities as they are defined by the US Census Bureau, and yet these cities occupy only 2 percent of the land area of the lower 48 states. This story is not unique to the United States. Capital and labor are highly agglomerated in every developed county, and they are increasingly agglomerated in the developing world.

It is not just aggregate activity that is agglomerated. Individual industries are concentrated too. The top panel of Figure 1.1, for instance, presents the density of employment in the wine industry (SIC 2084). As is well known, most of the country has little employment devoted to wine production. The most significant exceptions are California, Eastern Washington, and New York State, especially in the Finger Lakes region. The forces contributing to the spatial concentration of wine industry employment in these regions are not hard to grasp. All three regions have climates that support the growing of grapes. Because grapes are perishable, wine makers locate production facilities close to the source of the grapes in order to reduce transportation costs.

If the location of the wine industry seems easily explained, the bottom panel of Figure 1.1 presents more of a challenge. It shows the spatial concentration of the software industry (SIC 7371–3, 7375). Although this is an activity that could

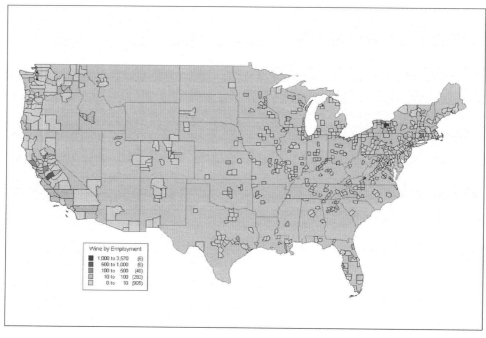

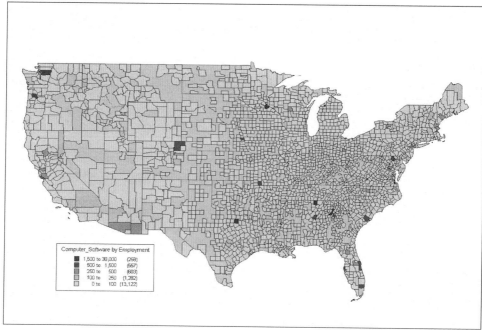

Figure 1.1 Employment in the wine (SIC 2084) and computer software (SIC 7371–3, 7375) industries.

seemingly take place anywhere, it is clear from the figures that it does not. Once again, most of the country has little employment in these industries, while a relatively small number of counties account for a large fraction of software development. Moreover, these counties are not randomly scattered across the USA. Instead, they are disproportionately located in California (Silicon Valley), Washington State (Microsoft's headquarters), the Northeast (especially around Boston), and a small number of other areas around the country (including Minneapolis, Austin, and the research triangle area of North Carolina).

The macro pattern in the bottom panel of Figure 1.1 repeats itself in Figure 1.2, a map of the location of software producers in the vicinity of San Francisco (top panel) and Boston (bottom panel). As can readily be seen, in both metropolitan areas, activity is highly concentrated in a few places. Yet there is no material input that is analogous to grapes. Something is going on that is leading to this kind of geographical concentration.

It is tempting to speculate that the nature of high-technology production contributes to the spatial concentration of software development. Perhaps, ideas flow more readily when engineers have opportunities to interact. This may well be the case, but it does not seem to offer an explanation for Figure 1.3. Here, we present the spatial concentration of employment in the carpet manufacturing industry, both for the country overall (top panel) and for the area centered around the northwest corner of Georgia. Carpet manufacturing is a mature industry with a well-established technology. This industry clearly is not as dependent on new ideas as is software. Carpet production does require raw materials, but the materials are easily transported, unlike grapes. Despite this, in the top panel it is clear that carpet production is heavily concentrated in the Southeast of the USA, especially in the vicinity of the northwest corner of Georgia. Moreover, as with software development, spatial concentration at the macro level is mirrored at a more refined level of geography. In the bottom panel of Figure 1.3, carpet manufacturing is heavily concentrated in the northwest corner of Georgia. Clearly, something beyond locating near raw materials or some sort of high-technology learning from neighbors is taking place.

This chapter will consider the evidence on the forces that lead to agglomeration. These forces are usually referred to as agglomeration economies, although they are also known as external economies of scale. Economies of scale arise when an increase in the scale of activity reduces the long-run cost per unit of output produced. *External* economies of scale exist when long-run average cost falls in response to an increase in the size of a city or the size of an industry in a city. In contrast, *internal* economies of scale arise when average cost at a given factory declines in response to an increase in the level of activity at the factory. In the discussion to follow, we will focus on the agglomeration of industries that are at least somewhat footloose, such as software or carpets, rather than industries where some locations have natural advantages, such as the wine industry.

The chapter will consider a number of key questions. Are agglomeration economies restricted to individual industries such as software and carpets, or are their effects comprehensive, extending across all activities? Are the effects highly localized, as appears to be the case with software and carpets, or do the effects

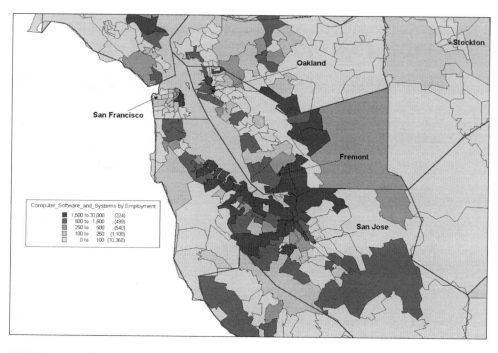

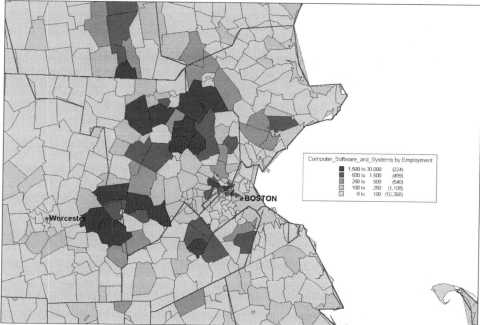

Figure 1.2 Employment in the computer software industry (SIC 7371–3, 7375), San Francisco and Boston.

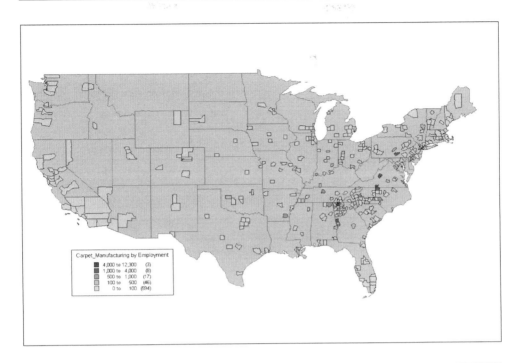

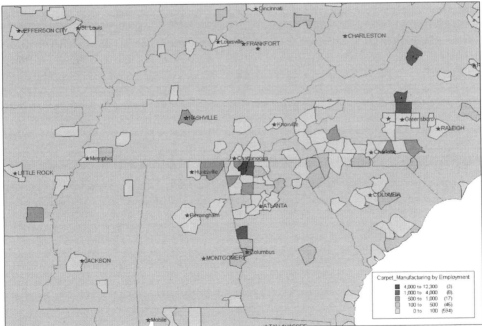

Figure 1.3 Employment in the carpet industry (SIC 2273).

operate at a larger geographical scale? Does the effect of agglomeration differ for large and small firms? The empirical literature on agglomeration economies has gone a long way to answering these questions.

Another set of questions has only recently begun to be answered. These questions concern the sources of agglomeration economies. In his classic textbook, Marshall (1920) identifies three sources: input sharing, labor-market pooling, and knowledge spillovers. An example of input sharing is when an apparel manufacturer in New York is able to purchase a great variety of relatively inexpensive buttons from a nearby company that specializes in button manufacturing. An example of labor-market pooling is when a software company in Silicon Valley can quickly fill a position by hiring one of the many skilled programmers already present in the Valley. Similarly, a skilled programmer in the Valley can more easily find a new position without having to relocate. In both instances, labor pooling reduces search costs and improves match quality, providing valuable benefits for employers and workers. An example of knowledge spillovers is when the software company's programmers can learn the tricks of the trade from random interactions with other programmers in Silicon Valley. What is the evidence on these sources? As of now, the answers to this question are suggestive rather than conclusive.

In discussing the measurement of agglomeration economies, this chapter also addresses methodology. The literature sometimes involves very precise structural econometrics. A good example of this is the estimation of the parameters of a production function describing how inputs are turned into products and services. These estimates are very tightly linked to economic theory, and they require highly refined data that is not always available. Because of limitations on data, other empirical papers on agglomeration economies employ reduced-form methods. This involves estimating relationships that are implied by the connection between agglomeration and productivity; for instance, the relationship between city size and growth. This kind of estimation can provide useful insights into agglomeration, even if it does not provide precise estimates of underlying structural parameters, as with the estimation of a production function.

The rest of the chapter begins with a discussion of the oldest debate on agglomeration: whether the effects depend on city size or only on the size of the own industry. Section 1.3 then considers the geographical scope of agglomeration economies, while section 1.4 considers the sources of agglomeration economies. Section 1.5 considers the role of industrial organization and local culture. Section 1.6 concludes by considering the relevance of the evidence on agglomeration economies for public policy toward innovation, productivity, and local economic development.

1.2   LOCALIZATION AND URBANIZATION

The oldest debate on agglomeration economies concerns whether they are related to the concentration of an industry or to the size of a city itself. The latter effect is known as an "urbanization economy," where city scale impacts productivity. The former is known as a "localization economy," where it is the size of a firm's own industry that matters. The idea that industrial localization can increase productivity goes back to Alfred Marshall:

> When an industry has thus chosen a locality for itself, it is likely to stay there long: so great are the advantages which people following the same skilled trade get from neighborhood to one another. The mysteries of the trade become no mysteries; but are as it were in the air, and children learn many of them unconsciously . . . Employers are apt to resort to any place where they are likely to find a good choice of workers with the special skill which they require . . . The advantages of variety of employment are combined with those of localized industries in some of our manufacturing towns, and this is a chief cause of their continued economic growth. (Marshall 1920, p. 271)

The idea that a city's size or its diversity directly contributes to agglomeration economies is often attributed to Jacobs (1969), although the idea predates her work. Marshall, for example, also recognized the value of urban diversity, both as a way to achieve domestic complementarity and to reduce risk:

> On the other hand a localized industry has some disadvantages as a market for labour if the work done in it is chiefly of one kind, such for instance as can be done only by strong men. In those iron districts in which there are no textile or other factories to give employment to women and children, wages are high and the cost of labour dear to the employer, while the average money earnings of each family are low. But the remedy for this evil is obvious, and is found in the growth in the same neighbourhood of industries of a supplementary character. Thus textile industries are constantly found congregated in the neighbourhood of mining and engineering industries, in some cases having been attracted by almost imperceptible steps; in others, as for instance at Barrow, having been started deliberately on a large scale in order to give variety of employment in a place where previously there had been but little demand for the work of women and children . . . A district which is dependent chiefly on one industry is liable to extreme depression, in case of a falling-off in the demand for its produce, or of a failure in the supply of the raw material which it uses. This evil again is in a great measure avoided by those large towns or large industrial districts in which several distinct industries are strongly developed. If one of them fails for a time, the others are likely to support it indirectly; and they enable local shopkeepers to continue their assistance to workpeople in it. (Marshall 1920, pp. 273–4)

It is not hard to see evidence consistent with both of these effects. Silicon Valley is a well-known concentration of industry, in this case the computer industry, broadly conceived. Although the cost of labor and land in the Valley is very high, firms continue to do business there. This is entirely consistent with the idea of localization economies. One can find a good example of urbanization economies several hundred miles to the south, in Los Angeles. Los Angeles does not have a single dominant industry in the way that Silicon Valley does. Film and television production have a high profile, but they are only a small part of a diverse local economy, which also includes employment in high-technology industries such as aerospace and old industries such as apparel. The broad range of activities taking place in Los Angeles, coupled with its large size, is presumably part of the explanation for the city's continued growth. Jacobs (1969), for instance, attributes Los Angeles' success in generating "new work" in the postwar period to its diverse economy. Hughes Air spawned roughly 100 spinoffs according to her estimate, including some products that bear little resemblance to aerospace, such as sliding doors. In this case, the diverse local economy created synergies between the region's booming construction industry and aircraft manufacturing. Similar arguments have also been offered as explanations for New York City's strength relative to less diverse cities such as Pittsburgh (Chinitz 1961).

Of course, economists are not satisfied with casual empiricism of this kind. To really understand agglomeration economies requires a more careful application of econometric techniques. Since agglomeration economies are by definition enhancers of productivity, it is natural to begin by looking at what we can learn by estimating a production function. Suppose that an establishment's production function may be written as $g(A)f(l,n,m,k)$. $f(\cdot)$ is a traditional production function, defined on the inputs land (l), labor (n), materials (m), and capital (k). The variable A characterizes the establishment's environment, and so allows for the influence of agglomeration.

How would one estimate a production function? The first requirement would be to measure the various inputs, including employment, land, capital, and materials. Labor inputs are perhaps the easiest to measure, since many data sets provide counts of workers, hours worked, and proxies for skill level (e.g., education). Data on purchased materials are available in some data sets, but data on materials produced internally typically are not. Few data sets make available measures of land use and the stock of capital. Since omitted variables may bias the estimates obtained in a regression, finding a way to control for these inputs is a fundamental challenge when estimating production functions.

The second requirement is to control for agglomeration, the variable A introduced above. Several approaches have been taken. One is to include a measure of the city's population to capture urbanization economies and a measure of the employment in a particular industry to capture localization economies. This is a common approach. It is not, however, the only reasonable approach. Researchers have, for instance, also looked at urban diversity directly and at a city's specialization in a particular industry, as measured by the share of employment in that industry rather than the level.

Despite the challenges, a number of researchers have estimated production functions in order to evaluate the impact of agglomeration. Taken together, the conclusion from these studies is that doubling city size seems to increase productivity by an amount that ranges from roughly 3 percent to 8 percent (for a review, see Rosenthal & Strange 2004). Nakamura (1985), for example, considers the influence of agglomeration in Japan, while Henderson (1986) examines the effect of agglomeration in the USA and Brazil. Both estimate production functions separately for manufacturing industries, specifically Standard Industrial Classification (SIC) "two-digit" industries. Urbanization is proxied by total employment in the city. Localization is proxied by employment in the industry. While there is evidence of urbanization economies in several industries, there is evidence of localization economies in more. Some industries exhibit no evidence of external economies at all. Nakamura summarizes his work as finding that a doubling of industry scale leads to a 4.5 percent increase in productivity, while a doubling of city population leads to a 3.4 percent increase. Henderson finds almost no evidence of urbanization economies and substantial evidence of localization. In related work, Moomaw (1983) finds evidence of both. Overall, these studies are somewhat more favorable to the existence of localization economies than to urbanization economies. In addition, the results strongly suggest that one ought to estimate agglomeration economies separately for different industries, since there is such substantial variation across industries.

There are other ways to look for evidence of localization and urbanization economies. If agglomeration enhances productivity, labor demand will shift out. This will lead employment to grow more quickly and to higher wages. Accordingly, Henderson, Kuncoro, and Turner (1995) consider employment growth in the USA over the period from 1970 to 1987. They conduct their estimation separately for eight industries, three of which experienced rapid innovations in high technology during the period, and five that were mature industries with stable technologies. For the high-technology industries, they find that specialization of employment at the metropolitan level is not associated with faster employment growth within these industries. For the mature industries, they find a positive effect of specialization. This result is parallel to that of Duranton and Puga (2001), who use French data to show that while new industries evolve in diverse "nursery" cities, they move to specialized ones after reaching maturity.

Glaeser and Mare (2001) look at wages instead of growth. They find that wages are higher in larger cities – an urbanization effect. This urban wage premium is larger the longer a worker has stayed in a large city. Even when the worker moves to a smaller city, some of the urban wage premium remains. This seems to suggest that cities foster knowledge spillovers, a topic discussed further in section 1.4.

Finally, Rosenthal and Strange (2003) examine the location decisions of new plants in a model of plant births. The intuition is that if agglomeration enhances productivity, additional plants will be drawn to agglomerated areas. The key findings are that diversity attracts new arrivals, and that localization economies are more important than urbanization economies for the six industries studied.

It is important to recognize that in all of the studies discussed above it is difficult to be certain about causality. Agglomeration causes workers to be more productive. But skilled workers may also be drawn to urban areas, both because of higher urban wages and also because of consumption amenities associated with urban life (e.g., theaters, restaurants, etc.). This complicates efforts to identify the impact of agglomeration on productivity. In studies that estimate production functions, this has proved especially challenging. Henderson (2003) addresses this issue by using econometric methods that rely on "instrumental variables," variables that are correlated with the agglomeration measures but that are exogenous to the dependent variable being analyzed. A similar approach is taken in Glaeser and Mare's (2001) analysis of urban wage rates. In studies that examine employment growth, economic conditions from up to 20 years in the past have been used to explain future patterns of growth (e.g., Glaeser, Kallal, Scheinkman & Shleifer 1992; Henderson, Kuncoro & Turner 1995). The motivation for this is that deeply lagged previous conditions are exogenous to future growth in employment. In birth studies (Rosenthal & Strange 2003), a similar approach has been used, evaluating the location decisions of new arrivals based on the previous spatial distribution of economic activity. The assumption here is that entrepreneurs take as given the existing economic landscape when choosing where to locate a new establishment. It should be emphasized in conclusion that despite the challenges associated with identifying a causal effect of agglomeration, a clear consensus has emerged: agglomeration economies enhance productivity.

1.3   GEOGRAPHY

The productivity studies reviewed in the last section took particular and narrow approaches to geography. Most of them used political boundaries to define the extent of a city. This amounts to assuming that all firms in New York benefit from all other firms in the city. Whether the firm is nearby or far away makes no difference. The patterns in the lower panels of Figures 1.2 and 1.3 for software and carpet manufacturing strongly suggest that, at least for these industries, this is not the case. Instead, the patterns in these figures indicate that firms tend to be drawn to locations where activity in their industry is most concentrated. Although not conclusive by itself, this is consistent with the idea that firms benefit much more from own-industry activity in the immediate area than from activity farther away.

In a recent paper, Rosenthal and Strange (2003) examine this issue as part of their effort to provide a micro-level analysis of the geographical scope of agglomeration economies. The paper takes advantage of geocoding software and data that place firms in zip codes, the same as used in Figure 1.2. This makes it possible to measure total employment and own-industry employment within a certain distance of an employer. Using these measures, it is possible to calculate the effects of the local environment on the number of firm births and on these new firms' employment levels for six industries (computer software, apparel, food processing, printing and publishing, machinery, and fabricated metals). Some of the results of this estimation are presented in Figure 1.4.

The figure graphically shows that agglomeration economies attenuate with distance. The level of employment chosen by newly arrived firms increases when employment increases in the firm's industry within 1 mile of the firm's zip code. In the case of software, for example, the presence of 100 additional existing software employees within 1 mile of a given zip code attracts new firms that add a total of 1.2 new software workers to that zip code in the following year, everything else equal. On the other hand, the influence of existing employment in the own industry just 5 miles away has a much smaller effect, as does employment

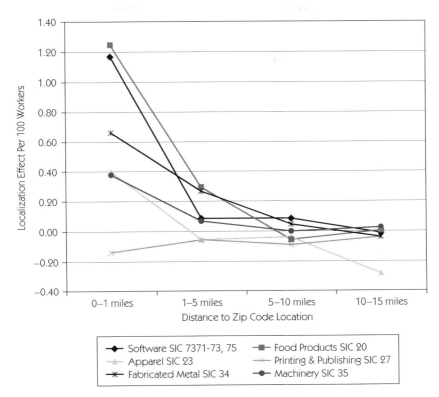

Figure 1.4 Localization effects. The localization effect measures the number of additional employees that a zip code's new establishments would hire in response to the presence of an extra 100 workers in the same industry at various distances from the zip code.
Source: Rosenthal and Strange (2003)

farther out, beyond 10 and 15 miles. This pattern holds for computer software, food processing, apparel, machinery, and fabricated metals. Interestingly, it does not occur for printing and publishing, suggesting that this industry may be less sensitive to localization economies or that printing and publishing firms serve local markets.

These results are consistent with anecdotal evidence about industrial concentration. Silicon Valley is a hotbed of productivity in the computer industry, as well as in other related fields. A number of explanations have been offered to account for this. Some of them involve learning, where knowledge is a kind of local public good. Perhaps the most famous example of this is Steve Jobs's visit to the Xerox Corporation's Palo Alto Research Center, which is credited with suggesting a number of ways in which Apple could improve its products, including the mouse and the object-oriented operating system. This kind of knowledge spillover depends crucially on physical proximity, as Tom Furlong of Digital Electronics Corporation notes:

> Physical proximity is important to just about everything we do. I have better rela-
> tionships with Silicon Valley companies than I have even with my own company . . .
> because I can just get in the car and go see them . . . You never work on the same
> level if you do it by telephone and airplane. It's very hard to work together long
> distance. You don't have a feel for who the people are, they are just a disembodied
> voice. (Saxenian 1994, p. 157)

Thus, even in the industry most responsible for the so-called "death of distance," proximity matters.

Of course, nothing in these results directly supports the interpretation that agglomeration economies exist because of knowledge spillovers. There are many other potential explanations. The next section deals with this issue by looking at the sources of agglomeration economies.

1.4   THE SOURCES OF AGGLOMERATION ECONOMIES

It is not hard to see that understanding the sources of agglomeration economies is fundamentally important. Communities around the world look at the success of Silicon Valley, and would like to enjoy that kind of success themselves. It is also not hard to see that becoming a Silicon Forest (Portland and Seattle) or a Silicon Desert (Phoenix) requires more than just silicon and wishful thinking. It requires a critical mass of computer industry activity. And achieving this re-quires that the benefits of an agglomeration be available. But exactly what are these benefits?

There are many candidates. We will focus on the three that were identified by Marshall (1920): knowledge spillovers, input sharing, and labor pooling. The concentration of software depicted in Figures 1.1 and 1.2 is consistent with the presence of knowledge spillovers. In fact, the relationship between agglom-eration and innovation is not particular to software. Looking across industries, Audretsch and Feldman (1996) show that innovations are highly concentrated spatially and that innovative industries are more likely to be geographically con-centrated. Jaffe, Trajtenberg, and Henderson (1993) provide even more direct evidence. They show that an innovator is 5–10 times more likely to cite a patent from a firm in the same metropolitan area than from another firm elsewhere in the country, controlling for industry characteristics.

Input sharing involves local outsourcing. Suppose, for example, that an apparel manufacturer makes use of specialized buttons. If these buttons are produced under increasing returns to scale and transportation is costly, then the presence nearby of another apparel producer may allow both to purchase their buttons more cheaply. Evidence of local input sharing is provided by Holmes (1999). Central to his analysis is "purchased input intensity," which is equal to an industry's purchased inputs divided by sales. This measure captures the degree of outsourcing in an industry. Holmes finds that more concentrated industries have a higher value of purchased input intensity, which is consistent with the presence of input sharing. For instance, the pantyhose industry is concentrated in North Carolina, where 62 percent of the industry's employment is found. The purchased input intensity among pantyhose firms in North Carolina is 53 percent, compared to 40 percent input intensity among pantyhose firms throughout the USA. This pattern is repeated for other concentrated industries.

A third benefit of agglomeration is labor-market pooling. This occurs when firms are able to acquire specialized labor by locating near other firms in the same industry. Krugman (1991) has argued that the carpet industry, as highlighted in Figure 1.3, benefits from this. Pooling labor reduces risk for both workers and employers alike by reducing search costs and enhancing the match quality between workers and jobs. For example, if a carpet producer in a remote area were to fail, workers who had developed industry specific skills might have to relocate in order to find comparable jobs. This would not be the case, presumably, in the northwest of Georgia, where carpet manufacturing reigns. In effect, agglomeration offers workers a sort of insurance. The converse holds for employers. If a key employee were to leave a company in an outlying area, the firm might find that individual difficult to replace. This would not be the case in areas where skilled individuals are plentiful.

Costa and Kahn (2001) provide particularly compelling evidence of one aspect of labor pooling, better matches between workers and employers in large cities. They show that couples in which both individuals have a college degree or more – referred to as "power couples" in the paper – have increasingly located in large metropolitan areas since 1970. This coincides with the dramatic increase in female participation in high-skilled occupations that took place during that period. Factors driving the locations of power couples are then analyzed by comparing their location decisions to those of other individuals and couples, both with and without college degrees. This enables Costa and Kahn to allow for the possibility that individuals seek out big cities for a variety of reasons, including a taste for urban amenities, marriage markets, and employment opportunities. The results indicate that power couples have increasingly gravitated toward big cities at least in part because it is easier for both individuals to find high-skilled work.

Recent research has considered the influence of all these sources of agglomeration economies as part of a single model. This work involves analyzing the variation in agglomeration between industries as a function of industry attributes that serve as indicators of the potential importance of the three benefits of agglomeration just discussed: knowledge spillovers, input sharing, and labor pooling. The basic strategy is to regress an industry-specific index of agglomeration on proxies for the importance of agglomeration economies, where each industry is an observation. In Rosenthal and Strange (2001), for example, proxies for the importance of agglomeration economies include measures of how innovative the industry tends to be – as reflected in the pace of new product creation – and the use of both manufactured and service inputs. The model also includes variables that proxy the importance of labor-market pooling, including the degree of labor specialization in the industry as measured by the number of managers per production worker, and the educational characteristics of an industry's workforce.

Additional controls are also provided to address the importance of transport costs and natural advantages, since these factors also contribute to agglomeration for reasons unrelated to external economies of scale. Recall, for example, our discussion of the wine industry in Figure 1.1. The regressions are carried out using four-digit SIC manufacturing industries as observations, a total of 459 manufacturing industries in all.

The results of this analysis suggest that all of the factors discussed above contribute to industrial agglomeration. The evidence is strongest for labor-market pooling, with proxies having a positive impact on agglomeration at the state, county, and zip code levels of geography. The proxies for knowledge spillovers also impact agglomeration positively, but only at the zip code level. Reliance on manufactured inputs or natural resources – factors that cause industries to be sensitive to shipping costs – positively affect agglomeration at the state level but have little effect on agglomeration at lower levels of geography. The same is true for inventory–sales ratios, a proxy for the perishability of output, and a further indicator of the importance of shipping costs, as with grapes in the wine industry. In contrast, reliance on service inputs reduces state-level agglomeration. Taking all of these results together, an interesting pattern emerges, with industry attributes sensitive to shipping costs (reliance on manufactured inputs, reliance on natural resource inputs, perishability of output) influencing agglomeration at the state level, knowledge spillovers impacting highly localized agglomeration, and labor impacting agglomeration at all levels of geography.

When the evidence reviewed above is taken as a whole, it is clear there is support for a range of different agglomerative forces. This means that any policymaker hoping to gild his or her community with silicon cannot simply rely on one sort of incentive to attract the necessary critical mass. An industry cluster requires a number of different characteristics in order to succeed. The next section takes this story one step further, by looking at the role of a city's organization and culture in the building of a productive local business environment.

1.5   INDUSTRIAL ORGANIZATION

The issue is this: one can find locations that are similar in their local knowledge, labor market, and input market characteristics that diverge in their economic performance despite this similarity. The idea is due to Saxenian (1994). In her comparison of the differences in performance between Silicon Valley and Boston's Route 128, she argues that local technological capabilities are not the fundamental source. The primary cause is instead the differences in local industrial organization and culture. The key difference is that Silicon Valley is in some sense more entrepreneurial than Route 128. This point is made by Jeffrey Kalb, an entrepreneurial refugee from the Digital Electronics Corporation:

> There's a fundamental difference in the nature of the industry between Route 128
> and [Silicon Valley]. Route 128 is organizes into large companies that do their own
> thing . . . It's very difficult for a small company to survive in that environment . . . The

Valley is very fast-moving and startups have to move fast. The whole culture of the Valley is one of change. We laugh about how often people change jobs. The joke is that you can change jobs and not change parking lots. There's a culture associated with that which says that moving is okay, that rapid change is the norm, that it's not considered negative on your resume . . . So you have this culture of rapid decisions, rapid changes, which is exactly the environment that you find yourself in as a startup. (Saxenian 1994, pp. x–xi)

This seems to be a compelling difference between Boston and Silicon Valley.

In order to understand whether this kind of difference manifests itself across the USA, and in industries that are not as cutting-edge as the computer industry, Rosenthal and Strange (2003) look at firm births. Two tests are carried out. First, the local concentration of existing own-industry employment is partitioned according to the size of the establishment in which a local employee works. This allows the estimation of different agglomerative effects for a worker in a small firm compared to a worker in a large firm. The idea is that the small firm is likely to be more open to interacting with its neighbors, with a greater external effect being the predicted result. The second approach involves partitioning the data by whether the employee works at a subsidiary establishment or at an independent establishment. The latter is presumably more open, while the former is presumably more closed.

The results of this estimation are partly consistent with Saxenian. Adding an additional employee at a small firm typically has a positive effect on births and new firm employment. Adding the employee at a large firm typically does not. To the extent that small firms are more open, this result is consistent with Saxenian. The performance of the subsidiary/nonsubsidiary variable is unexpected. In this case, an extra worker at a subsidiary establishment has a larger effect on the attraction of new own-industry arrivals. This is not consistent with Saxenian, suggesting as it does that corporate establishments may have larger effects on the productivity of neighbors. In some sense, this may imply that the quality of the interactions with nearby employees of subsidiary plants is greater than those of nearby independent plants. However, the reason for such quality differentials remains to be explored.

1.6   CONCLUSION

This chapter has considered the measurement of agglomeration economies. Because it has also considered innovation, economic growth, and productivity, it is natural to conclude by discussing the policy implications of the research covered by the chapter.

The area of policy to which this research speaks most directly is local industrial policy. Some places are wealthy, having high incomes and low unemployment rates. Others are not. In the USA, federal, state, and local governments have all taken steps to help the country's poor places. There are at least two forms that such policies have taken: policies to improve the economic environment in a general way and policies designed to attract particular industries or even particular firms. This is not the place to discuss general policies such as the provision of physical infrastructure, the protection of person and property, the moderation of taxes, or improvements to education. All we can say is that there is evidence that these sorts of general policies can be successful in promoting prosperity.

The most important thing to remember when considering policies to attract specific industries or firms is that there appear to be strong forces at work leading to agglomeration. This is clear from the maps with which the chapter began. This should comfort a government trying to retain firms who are already located in an industry cluster. For instance, New York's Mayor Bloomberg is, as of this writing, not responding aggressively to threats from firms who are considering relocating outside of the city. Thus far, this has not led to a commercial exodus (*The Economist*, March 13, 2004). On the other hand, the evidence that agglomeration matters should worry a government attempting to attract firms to a less developed location, since it suggests that it is not easy to get an industry to locate somewhere it would otherwise not. At the very least, the existence of agglomeration economies means that in order to attract any firms at all, it may be necessary to attract a critical mass.

Unfortunately, this may not be easy to do. As noted earlier in the chapter, there are many different aspects of a location that may matter to firms. A well-intentioned policy could easily fail because it neglected to attend to one or two of these. Also, industries differ, and the environment that helped the software industry grow in Silicon Valley, or the carpet industry in Georgia, may not help some other industry in some other place. Finally, it may not be possible to duplicate elsewhere the circumstances that led to a successful agglomeration in another place. This appears to be the lesson of attempts to recreate a Silicon Valley type cluster in northern New Jersey (Leslie & Kargon 1996). This is not to say that government policy has never contributed to the formation of clusters. It certainly has, but the formation of clusters has been a side-effect rather than the primary goal of the policy. For instance, defense procurement helped the chemical industry to grow in nineteenth-century Germany and various high-technology industries to grow in California after World War II. All of this suggests to us that specific policies designed to foster agglomeration or attract industries are risky to say the least. Ultimately, government must tread carefully, or its efforts may amount to attempting to develop a wine industry in the desert.

Acknowledgments

We are grateful for the financial support of the Connaught Fund at the University of Toronto, the Social Sciences and Humanities Research Council of Canada, and the Kauffman Foundation.

Bibliography

Audretsch, D. B. and Feldman, M. P. 1996: R&D spillovers and the geography of innovation and production. *American Economic Review*, 86(3), 630–40.

Chinitz, B. 1961: Contrasts in agglomeration: New York and Pittsburgh. *American Economic Association Papers and Proceedings*, 51, 279–89.

Costa, D. L. and Kahn, M. E. 2001: Power couples. *Quarterly Journal of Economics*, 116, 1,287–315.

Duranton, G. and Puga, D. 2001: Nursery cities: urban diversity, process innovation, and the life-cycle of products. *American Economic Review*, 91, 1,454–77.

Economist, The 2004: The mystery of Michael Bloomberg. March 13, p. 36.

Glaeser, E. L. and Mare, D. C. 2001: Cities and skills. *Journal of Labor Economics*, 19(2), 316–42.

——, Kallal, H. D., Scheinkman, J. A., and Shleifer, A. 1992: Growth in cities. *Journal of Political Economy*, 100, 1,126–52.

Henderson, J. V. 1986: Efficiency of resource usage and city size. *Journal of Urban Economics*, 19, 47–70.

—— 2003: Marshall's scale economies. *Journal of Urban Economics*, 53, 1–28.

——, Kuncoro, A., and Turner, M. 1995: Industrial development in cities. *Journal of Political Economy*, 103, 1,067–85.

Holmes, T. J. 1999: Localization of industry and vertical disintegration. *Review of Economics and Statistics*, 81(2), 314–25.

Jacobs, J. 1969: *The Economy of Cities*. New York: Vintage.

Jaffe, A. B., Trajtenberg, M., and Henderson, R. 1993: Geographic localization of knowledge spillovers as evidenced by patent citations. *Quarterly Journal of Economics*, 108(3), 577–98.

Krugman, P. R. 1991: *Geography and Trade*. Boston, MA: The MIT Press.

Leslie, S. W. and Kargon, R. H. 1996: Selling Silicon Valley: Frederick Terman's model for regional advantage. *Business History Review*, 70(4), 438–75.

Marshall, A. 1920: *Principles of Economics*. London: Macmillan.

Moomaw, R. L. 1983: Is population scale a worthless surrogate for business agglomeration economies? *Regional Science and Urban Economics*, 13, 525–45.

Nakamura, R. 1985: Agglomeration economies in urban manufacturing industries: a case of Japanese cities. *Journal of Urban Economics*, 17, 108–24.

Rosenthal, S. S. and Strange, W. C. 2001: The determinants of agglomeration. *Journal of Urban Economics*, 50, 191–229.

—— and —— 2003: Geography, industrial organization, and agglomeration. *Review of Economics and Statistics*, 85(2), 377–93.

—— and —— 2004: Evidence on the nature and sources of agglomeration economies. In J. V. Henderson and J.-F. Thisse (eds.), *Handbook of Urban and Regional Economics*, vol. 4: *Cities and Geography*. Amsterdam: North-Holland.

Saxenian, A. 1994: *Regional Advantage: Culture and Competition in Silicon Valley and Route 128*. Cambridge, MA: Harvard University Press.

CHAPTER TWO

Human Capital Externalities in Cities: Identification and Policy Issues

Gilles Duranton

2.1   INTRODUCTION

The case for corrective economic policies as stated in Econ101 is relatively straightforward. In some instances, there is a wedge between the *private* costs (or benefits) resulting from some choice made by an economic agent and the *social* costs (or benefits) accruing to society. Such a wedge occurs when markets fail to mediate properly some economic interactions; that is, when there is an *externality*. In such a case, the privately optimal decision made by the agent does not lead to a socially optimal outcome. For instance, investors underinvest when they cannot appropriate all the positive returns from their investments. Firms overproduce goods, whose production damages the environment at no cost to them, and so on. Pigou's (1920) ingenious solution to this type of problem is to impose a tax (or a subsidy) so that the private and social costs are made equal. In other words, whenever there is an externality, an appropriately chosen Pigovian tax or subsidy can make agents *internalize* the external effects of their choices so that the privately optimal decision leads to a socially optimal outcome.

After exposing the details of this argument, the Econ101 textbook typically points out that such taxes and subsidies are difficult to implement empirically because of their informational requirements. Then the textbook usually ends the discussion on this topic and turns to something else. From a policy perspective, however, this is where the real work ought to start. In this chapter, the objective is to show how in practice economists attempt to identify such externalities. With this in mind, this chapter will analyze the case of one set of externalities: those pertaining to the market for human capital and education. Human capital externalities are of particular interest to urban economics, as shall be made clear below.

The rest of this chapter is organized in the following way. Section 2.2 shows why human capital externalities in cities matter. Section 2.3 outlines a simple theoretical model and shows how it has been estimated empirically. Section 2.4 highlights a first set of criticisms to the standard approach. Section 2.5 discusses crucial issues of model identification and shows how they matter for policy purposes. Section 2.6 describes alternative approaches for the estimation of human capital externalities in cities. Finally, section 2.7 concludes.

2.2   WHY STUDY HUMAN CAPITAL EXTERNALITIES?
WHY IN AN URBAN CONTEXT?

Among all the externalities that economists have been thinking about, human capital externalities are "special" in two respects. First, they are potentially of formidable importance for a number of reasons. Such externalities provide a strong justification for subsidies to education. If the private returns to education are only half the social returns, the optimal Pigovian policy is a 50 percent subsidy to education. If, instead, the social returns are essentially equal to the private returns, no subsidy is needed. Given that most developed economies spend up to 10 percent of their income toward education and training (broadly construed), the numbers at stake are very large. It is worth noting, however, that human capital externalities are important beyond the issue of the optimal split between public and private expenditure for education. As argued by Lucas (1988) and his followers, *human capital externalities could constitute the fundamental engine of growth and development.* If this were the case, governments could draw on education policy to speed up economic growth. Moreover, since Marshall (1890), human capital externalities are also accepted as one of the main reasons to justify the existence of cities. This is because human capital externalities may arise predominantly from direct (or face-to-face) interactions between people, which are themselves expected to be highly distance sensitive.

The second reason why human capital externalities are special is that they are particularly difficult to identify. To repeat, we speak of an externality when market prices fail to reflect the true social costs and benefits of an action. Unfortunately, most of the data collected around the world consist of simple measurable characteristics of economic agents or of recorded market transactions. Since prices and quantities only reveal private costs and benefits, *externalities, by their very nature, leave no obvious paper trail by which they can be tracked or measured.*

This being said, with some externalities, social costs and benefits may be measured indirectly without too many conceptual difficulties. For instance, the costs of urban congestion can be measured by counting how many people are stuck in traffic jams and estimating how much time is wasted there. The mechanism at play is relatively simple: by taking the road at peak hours, I slow down everybody else and I do not take this into account when entering my car. The social cost of traffic congestion is the cost of the time wasted by people stuck in traffic jams plus that of an increase in pollution. Admittedly, measuring these costs precisely is by no means an easy task, but it is still feasible. Urban congestion is a reasonably well-circumscribed problem, with regard to which transport economists have made very significant advances.

Human capital externalities are much more problematic, because the mechanism at play is far less obvious. As shown below, there are many mechanisms that can generate human capital externalities. These mechanisms call for different policy prescriptions. In some extreme cases, subsidizing education may even be counterproductive. The fact that the social costs and benefits of education have many dimensions complicates the matter even more. Human capital externalities can be thought of having a positive effect on productivity and wages as well as criminal behavior or even voting outcomes. In what follows, the discussion will be restricted to the effects of human capital externalities on wages and earnings.

To look at human capital externalities, the starting point of existing research is the following. Positive human capital externalities imply that *measures of aggregate human capital should matter in the determination of outcomes over and above individual characteristics.* In the absence of experiments on the issue, there are two main avenues for research: cross-section or time series analysis. Time series analysis does not appear to be particularly appropriate. Isolating the effects of an increase in education on aggregate output and confronting this to the private returns to education may be a hopeless task because of the incredibly large number of confounding factors that may affect changes in aggregate output over time. Instead, most research focuses on cross-section analysis conducted either at the cross-country or at the subnational level. Cross-country analysis is made very difficult by the large number of institutional factors that may affect the outcomes of different countries. The second major problem is that comparing education data across countries is also very difficult. Subnational analysis seems "easier" to conduct because in many countries labor-market data sets are of good quality and have become widely available. Such data typically records individual wages, education, and location for large samples of workers across a given country.

Among existing subnational units, cities are of particular interest for two reasons. First, as highlighted above, human capital externalities may be at the root of the existence of cities. These externalities are thus expected to manifest themselves strongly at this level of analysis. Second, urban areas when properly defined provide economically meaningful economic units of analysis as opposed to arbitrarily defined administrative regions or states. Note, however, that by conducting the analysis across cities we give up on any attempt to measure country-wide human capital externalities. This may not be a serious issue when looking at wages or crime (which may, to a large extent, be determined locally), but it is potentially more problematic when we are interested in voting behavior.

2.3   THE STANDARD APPROACH TO THE ANALYSIS OF HUMAN CAPITAL EXTERNALITIES IN CITIES

Consider an economy with workers (subscripted i or j) living in cities (subscripted a). The *social* output of worker i with human capital h_i and living in city a is given by

$$y_i = (A + B_a)h_i, \tag{2.1}$$

where A is a technological parameter independent of location and B_a is a city-specific parameter. At the same time, the earnings of this worker are

$$w_i = Ah_i + D_a. \tag{2.2}$$

A straightforward comparison of equations (2.1) and (2.2) shows that workers do not receive the full value of their social product. Worker i cannot appropriate the part of her social output given by $B_a h_i$. At the same time, however, this worker benefits from being in city a and receives D_a as part of her earnings. This latter quantity will receive different theoretical interpretations in what follows. For the time being, it is convenient to think of it as the part of the external output of the other workers in the same city that accrues to worker i. Put differently, *there is a reciprocal externality within cities: workers do not receive the full surplus that they create, but instead receive part of the surplus created by the others.*

Note that the specification of equations (2.1) and (2.2) is additive rather than multiplicative. This is mostly for simplicity and does not matter here (it does, however, in empirical work, where multiplicative specifications are preferred because they fit the data better). It is also useful to bear in mind that empirically we can only observe the wage w_i, some proxy for human capital h_i, and a few aggregate variables relating to city a, but not the social output y_i.

To finish the description of the model, assume that the cost of human capital, h_i, is

$$C_i = c_i h_i^\alpha, \tag{2.3}$$

with $\alpha > 1$. The cost shifter, c_i, can vary across individuals to reflect their differences in intrinsic abilities. Note that in a static context this cost may be interpreted as both a cost of acquisition and maintenance of human capital.

At the free-market equilibrium, the investment in human capital of worker i is chosen so as to maximize $w_i - C_i$. After simplification, we find equilibrium investment to be equal to the following:

$$h_i = \left(\frac{A}{\alpha c_i}\right)^{1/(\alpha-1)}. \tag{2.4}$$

The socially optimal human capital investment is, instead, such that it maximizes $y_i - C_i$. It is given by

$$h_i^* = \left(\frac{A + B}{\alpha c_i} \right)^{1/(\alpha - 1)}.$$ (2.5)

The optimal Pigovian tax is to subsidize the returns to human capital in equation (2.2) by offering worker i an amount B_a per unit of human capital. Equivalently, one may subsidize the cost of acquiring human capital by a fraction $B/(A + B)$ so that the worker faces a cost of acquiring human capital equal to $C_i = Ac_i h_i^\alpha/(A + B)$ rather than equation (2.3).

What are human capital externalities about in this model? The standard story about human capital externalities in cities is eloquently summarized by Lucas (1988): "Most of what we know we learn from other people. We pay tuition to only a few of these teachers, either directly or indirectly by accepting lower pay so we can hang around them, but most of it we get for free, and often in ways that are mutual – without a distinction between student and teacher." Indeed, to write this chapter I have read and benefited freely from a nice survey on human capital externalities in cities by Enrico Moretti (2004b), from whom I borrowed the above quote. To write this chapter, I also built on previous work conducted with Sylvie Charlot (Charlot & Duranton 2004). Again, she did not receive any direct compensation, despite contributing to this chapter indirectly. Arguably, such external effects take place across the board, in many industries and not only academia.

To be more precise about human capital externalities in an urban context, assume that worker i's human capital directly benefits N other workers in the city by an amount bh_i. This "interaction group" of N workers with whom worker i interacts is assumed to be a representative sample of workers in city a. At the same time, worker i also benefits from the human capital investment made by all other workers in the interaction group. With our notations, summing across all workers j who are part of the interaction group of worker i, this implies $B_a = bN$ and $D_a = \Sigma \, bh_j = bN\bar{h}_a$, where $\bar{h}_a$ is the average human capital in city a and N is the (unknown) size of the interaction group. Equation (2.2) can thus be rewritten in the following manner:

$$w_i = Ah_i + bN\bar{h}_a.$$ (2.6)

This equation (as well as many closely related specifications assuming different functional forms) can be estimated by means of regression analysis. The data needed for this exercise must be at the individual level. This data must contain the wage of each worker, a set of human capital characteristics (such as schooling, but also labor-market experience, etc.), and possibly further individual controls. To estimate equation (2.6), a set of aggregate (i.e., city-level) characteristics is also needed. Average schooling (or the fraction of university graduates) in the city is of course of particular interest here. The size of the interaction group may be taken as constant across cites or may be expected to increase with city population. In this case, the coefficient on city population can also be informative about the extent of human capital externalities.

Jim Rauch in 1993 was the first to estimate a specification with the same flavor as equation (2.6). He found that a 1-year increase in average schooling in a city would raise the expected wage of any of its workers whose education is unchanged by between 3 and 5 percent. Conversely, increasing a worker's education by 1 year and keeping average city schooling constant raises her wage by around 5 percent. He found these estimates to be robust to the inclusion of a large number of individual and city controls. Stated differently, *Rauch's key empirical result is that external returns to education are roughly of the same order of magnitude as private returns* (3–5 percent as opposed to 5 percent). Given that Rauch conducted his analysis very carefully and used a very large sample of workers, this correlation between wages and average human capital was unlikely to be accidental. It attracted a large amount of attention and was successfully replicated many times.

If we accept this finding at face value and assume a causal relationship as in the model, the policy implications are as follows: large subsidies to education are needed across the board because strong human capital externalities induce workers to grossly underinvest in their human capital. Related to this is the fact that education everywhere is heavily subsidized. In this respect, note that human capital externalities are not the only market failure mechanism justifying subsidies to education. Credit constraints, lack of insurance, and suboptimal parental investments are three other important motivations for public intervention in education. These other motives are justified by market failures surrounding the acquisition of human capital in equation (2.3). In this chapter, the focus is instead on equations (2.1) and (2.2).

So much for average city schooling, $\bar{h}_a$. What about the size of the interaction group, N? Another robust finding in the literature is that the coefficient on city population N_a (used to proxy for the size of the interaction group) in the estimation of equation (2.6) is usually positive and significant. This finding has further important implications for urban policy (for more details on this, see the chapter by Stuart Rosenthal and William Strange in this volume).

2.4   SOME POSSIBLE PROBLEMS WITH THE STANDARD APPROACH

After making sure that an empirical finding is not a coincidence by examining whether it is affected by slight changes in the specification, it is useful to envision two kinds of criticisms. They are both potentially very serious, but each has a different nature. In this section, we will be concerned with causality issues that could affect the magnitude of the coefficients within the proposed theoretical framework. In practice, this means addressing a range of relatively narrow concerns about equation (2.6). The second series of problems have to do with deeper issues about model selection; that is, whether or not we can interpret the empirical results in the light of the proposed model. These identification/specification concerns will be examined in the next section, where we will consider whether the estimation of equation (2.6) vindicates the theoretical model laid down in equations (2.1) and (2.2).

There are many potentially confounding factors that may introduce a spurious correlation between aggregate human capital and individual wages. First, it is worth noting that *workers are not assigned exogenously to cities and that some characteristics of cities and workers remain unobserved.* For instance, two observationally equivalent workers (sex, education, age, etc.) may have nonetheless very different abilities, ambition, and dedication to their work. In a systematic way, these two workers may have a tendency to choose to live and work in very different cities. Furthermore, cities experience shocks on their local economies which are very difficult to observe but nonetheless can have a simultaneous impact on wages and the skill composition of the workforce. For instance, it can be argued that the Internet boom in the late 1990s led to both higher wages and an influx of educated workers in the San Jose area.

Allowing for worker mobility, it is also natural to ask whether causality in equation (2.6) is running from high average schooling to high wages or, instead, from high wages to high schooling. Cities with high wages (after controlling for individual characteristics) may provide more education and thus enjoy more educated workers. For instance, the revenue derived from a local natural resource may be used to increase local education. Alternatively, "high-wage" cities may attract primarily more educated workers who will be able to benefit more from them. In these two cases, causality is running from high wages to high levels of human capital and not the other way round. Put differently, when any of these two arguments applies and is not dealt with, the coefficient on average education will overstate the true extent of human capital externalities.

At the same time, however, cities with good unobservable amenities may attract large numbers of highly educated workers who value these amenities more. For instance, a city with a milder climate may appeal primarily to highly educated workers who put a higher premium on such amenity. In such a city, the price of land will be higher because each worker may be willing to consume more land (e.g., to have a larger garden) and because more (highly educated) workers will be willing to live in this city. Higher land prices will in turn reduce the demand for land from firms. If labor and land are imperfect substitutes in the production function, higher land prices will imply a lower productivity of labor and in turn lower wages. Put differently, when amenities such as this are not included in the regression, the coefficient on average education will understate the true extent of human capital externalities.

To summarize, *average schooling may be suspected of being determined simultaneously with wages.* Depending on which one of the above stories applies, the coefficient on average schooling may be overestimated (as in the high-wage cities attracting highly skilled workers story) or underestimated (in the unobserved amenity argument). This type of concern has been taken very seriously in the literature. To deal with it, instrumental variables have been considered.

An instrumental variable is a variable that is correlated with the explanatory variable suspected of being endogenous but uncorrelated with the residual of the main regression. The procedure works as follows. In the "instrumental regression," the variable suspected of being endogenous is regressed on the set of instrumental variables and a predicted value is computed. This predicted value (which is determined only by a "truly" exogenous set of instrumental variables) is then used as a regressor in the main regression. The idea behind this procedure is to re-create a *ceteris paribus* whereby the effects of exogenous changes in the dependent variables can be properly assessed. In our case, a good instrument for average schooling would affect the schooling of the majority of workers in a given location without being *otherwise* correlated with local wages.

Acemoglu and Angrist (2000) argue that differences in school compulsory attendance laws and child labor laws in US states over the twentieth century provide good instruments for average schooling, at least for secondary education at the state level. In their preferred estimation, they obtain very small external returns to education. In the same spirit but using different instruments for average schooling (lagged demographic variables and the presence of land grant colleges), Moretti (2004a) shows that the share of university graduates in a city has a strong effect on individual earnings. These results are not as contradictory as they seem. The results of Acemoglu and Angrist (2000) regard mostly the supply of secondary education, whereas the regression of Moretti (2004a) contains the share of university graduates. It may well be that human capital externalities are mostly generated by university graduates rather than workers who were forced to stay in high school up to the age of 15 or 16 by legislation. It also appears that the unit of analysis (US states in Acemoglu and Angrist versus metropolitan areas in Moretti) matters a lot.

To deal with workers' unobserved heterogeneity, longitudinal data are desirable. The idea here is that there may be permanent but unobserved worker characteristics that play an important part in the story. Such unobserved characteristics are ambition, motivation, trustworthiness, self-discipline, and so on. These characteristics are usually unobserved by the statistician, but play a very important role in the labor market. If workers sort themselves according to their characteristics in a manner that is correlated with high average schooling, the coefficient on this latter variable will be biased. The effect of these permanent characteristics for a given worker is called a fixed effect. When workers are observed at least twice in the data at different periods, it is possible to estimate their fixed effects. What is needed to do this estimation is some mobility of workers across cities. Otherwise, if no worker ever moves, it is impossible to distinguish what is caused by the permanent characteristics of workers from the effect of the permanent characteristics of their cities. In short, by using a panel of workers we can condition out all the permanent characteristics of workers. However, note that using a panel of workers is not as foolproof as is sometimes claimed. Imagine, for instance, that the workers with high fixed effects tend to move to cities that are receiving a positive shock (e.g., more ambitious workers flocked to Silicon Valley at the beginning of the Internet boom). This generates a correlation between the true residual in the regression and individual fixed effects that will bias the estimates. More generally, movers may not be a random sample of the population, so that the estimation of the city effects is made with a biased sample of population.

Moretti (2004a) develops a slightly different strategy and assumes a fixed effect for each city/worker match. In this case, the source of identification is given by changes in the human capital composition of the city for "constant" workers. Put differently, his estimation strategy allows him to estimate the impact on the wage of any worker of a change in aggregate human capital around this worker. Again, estimates may be biased, since stayers may not be a random sample of the population. To get around this problem, Moretti (2004a) tries a variety of different specifications. His estimates show that a 1 percent increase in university-educated workers raise the average wage of workers whose education is unchanged by around 0.5 percent. Given that university-educated workers have a wage about 50 percent higher than those of other workers, the external returns to education implied by these estimates are again of the same order of magnitude as the private returns.

Although the evidence is not overwhelming, a few conclusions can be drawn at this stage. First, there is a strong and robust correlation between most measures of average human capital and average wages after controlling for individual characteristics. This holds across most types of subnational spatial units. Second, it also appears that, at the city level, there is a causal effect of the share of university graduates on local wages. In other words, *there is some empirical support about causality running from average human capital to average wages in cities* as stated in equation (2.6).

2.5   DEEPER PROBLEMS: IDENTIFICATION AND ITS POLICY IMPLICATIONS

In the previous section, we mostly examined "problems" that may complicate the estimation of equation (2.6) but without fundamentally questioning the assumptions made in equations (2.1) and (2.2). What we did was to assume that our basic story as told by equations (2.1) and (2.2) was true, but consider that there could be some other economic phenomena that could come into play and create some *perturbations* in the basic estimates. It could also be the case that our estimation of equation (2.6) may be "working" for reasons that have very little to do with equations (2.1) and (2.2). Put differently, it may be that we observe that average schooling in a city has a positive effect on average local wages, but the true model may be unrelated to the existence of human capital externalities of the sort postulated so far. Put yet differently, *nothing that we have done so far guarantees that we have tested "the true model."* In our case, this is particularly important from a policy perspective. This also matters a lot for our understanding of how cities tick.

Before exploring some alternatives to our basic model, let us insist more on this fundamental point. The "Standard Paradigm" in applied economic analysis was first introduced by Alfred Marshall (1895) in the third edition of his *Principles of Economics*. His analogy was as follows. It is very difficult to predict the exact movement of tides because, although tidal movements are initially caused by gravity, they are also affected by many subtle meteorological factors. However, the "tendencies" can still be predicted by using gravity, because meteorological factors only have a secondary influence on tides. As argued by Sutton (2000), from whom this argument is borrowed, some economic situations do indeed follow this analogy. Economists interested, for instance, in option pricing face a problem for which the variable to be explained (the price of options) depends on a small number of factors playing a systematic role. All of these factors can be measured. The model explaining the price of options is "self-evident" (although mathematically very difficult) since it is based on a strong arbitrage argument. Besides, the institutional rules that govern the actions of the participants are common knowledge. In this type of situation, economists are doing remarkably well at explaining the observed outcomes. To some extent, urban congestion externalities follow a similar pattern. With human capital externalities, unfortunately, model selection is a serious problem, as there are many plausible stories aside from the one given above that could explain our findings so far. (As argued by Manski (1993), this type of identification problem is pervasive in situations involving nonmarket interactions.)

2.5.1 Imperfect substitutability across workers

With respect to our model, the most obvious (and damaging) alternative is a simple story of supply and demand. Assume, for simplicity, that there are only two levels of human capital, high or low, superscripted by H and L, respectively. Let us take the human capital composition of cities as given for now. The production function replacing equation (2.1) is now of aggregate nature. Output in city a is now given by

$$Y_a = A(N_a^L)^\alpha (N_a^H)^{1-\alpha},\qquad(2.7)$$

where N_a^L is the number of low human capital workers in the city and N_a^H that of high human capital workers. In this model, there is no externality of any kind. Workers are paid at their marginal product, w_a^H and w_a^L. The average wage in the city is $\bar{w}_a = (N_a^L w_a^L + N_a^H w_a^H)/N_a^H + N_a^L$. Simple algebra then shows that, for N_a^H sufficiently small,

$$\left.\frac{\partial \bar{w}_a}{\partial N_a^H}\right|_{N_a=Ct} > 0.\qquad(2.8)$$

According to equation (2.8), when high human capital workers are scarce an increase in their supply raises average wages. This is because workers with low levels of human capital gain more than high human capital workers lose. Put differently, keeping city population constant and assuming that high human capital workers are relatively scarce, this alternative model predicts that an increase in the proportion of high human capital workers increases the average wage in the city. Hence, even in the absence of human capital externalities, an increase in the supply of high human capital workers can raise the average wage in the city.

   This competing explanation, put forward by Ciccone and Peri (2005) and Moretti (2004a), would be particularly damaging for the whole idea of human capital externalities. *There may not be any such thing as human capital externalities and all the regressions commented above would boil down to nothing more than bad estimations of production functions with imperfect substitutability.* To deal with this issue, Moretti

(2004a) runs the same regressions as before but considers only highly educated workers. Finding that the wages of highly educated workers increases with their supply would indicate that positive human capital externalities more than offset the negative effects of relative supply. He finds strong support for this. However, Ciccone and Peri (2005) propose another estimation procedure, in which they look at the effects of an increase in average schooling keeping the relative supply of the different education groups constant. Using this "constant composition" approach, they find only weak evidence of human capital externalities. To explain the divergence on this crucial point, further work is certainly needed.

2.5.2   Internalized externalities and ability externalities

Unlike the previous one, the two arguments explored in this subsection do not deny the existence of some externalities related to human capital in cities, but their policy implications differ radically from the standard prescriptions given about subsidizing the acquisition of human capital.

First, assume that equations (2.1), (2.2), and (2.3) hold, but that the human capital externality, rather than taking place in a large group (i.e., the city), takes place in a much smaller unit (e.g., a firm) that for simplicity we model as a pair. In this story, workers are randomly paired *and then cooperatively invest* in the acquisition of their human capital. Put differently, we assume that for worker i paired with worker j, we have $D_a = bh_j$. In this case, the total income of the pair is

$$w_i + w_j = (A + b)h_i + (A + b)h_j. \qquad (2.9)$$

In equilibrium, i and j cooperatively maximize equation (2.9) with respect to their choice of human capital. Since $C_i = c_i h_i^\alpha$ and $C_j = c_j h_j^\alpha$, we obtain $h_i = ((A + b)/\alpha c_i)^{1/(\alpha-1)}$ and $h_j = ((A + b)/\alpha c_j)^{1/(\alpha-1)}$. It can then be verified that this equilibrium investment is optimal. A discrepancy between social and observed private returns may be present when the returns to investment are delayed (such as in law firms or consultancies, where it takes a long time to become partner). Of course, this story may not appear to be very plausible with basic formal schooling. Typically, schooling choices are made well before workers are paired (e.g., before they join a firm). However, when it comes to training, it may be highly relevant and it may explain why firms heavily subsidize the training of their workers.

Another possible argument is that the externality may not be caused by human capital but, instead, by the innate abilities of workers. In our framework, this would mean that the externality is not in h_i but instead in $1/c_i$ (to the extent that a low c_i captures high abilities). The individual production function would then be

$$y_i = Ah_i + bN/c_i, \qquad (2.10)$$

and within the interaction group, the term D_a would be of the form $D_a = \Sigma\, b/c_j$. In this case of ability-driven externality, the investment in human capital by workers is optimal. With human capital investment given by equation (2.4), it is quite clear that in equation (2.2) there will be an apparent correlation between average human capital and individual wages. *This correlation is, however, spurious here since both individual wages and average human capital are determined by an ability externality.* Since abilities (captured by c_i) are usually not known to the analyst, we are facing a case of a missing variable bias.

A similar problem plagues the interpretation of the coefficient on individual education. Does the effect of individual schooling on wages really reflect the returns to human capital acquisition, or does it only reflect innate abilities, acknowledging that more able individuals get better degrees? Labor economics has been wrestling with this problem for a long time. The interested reader may refer to Card (1999) for a survey. However, the conclusion of Card and much of the literature on the topic is that the measured returns to educational attainment indeed largely reflect the returns to schooling and not those to ability. We may suspect that the same applies to human capital externalities. The suspicion is strong, but this is still unproven.

2.5.3 Market failures "elsewhere"

We have explored three objections so far (another complementarity, internalized externalities, and missing variable). A fourth type of objection may be made. It basically states that the model is not "precise enough" about the real economic phenomena that it attempts to capture. This matters a lot here, because policy recommendations are sensitive to the exact details of the true model.

To understand this important point note first that, from an economic stand-point, cities are best viewed as a trade-off between "agglomeration economies" and congestion costs. This argument is developed at length in Duranton and Puga (2004). These agglomeration economies (i.e., productive advantages coming from the spatial concentration of labor and capital) can be of different kinds. Alfred Marshall (1890) distinguished between the benefits from labor pooling (a large market gives firms a constant pool of skilled workers), those from input/output linkages (a large market favors the existence of specialized suppliers), and a better circulation of ideas (the famous "industry is in the air" argument). Only this last motive is directly consistent with the arguments given in section 2.3 to motivate equations (2.1) and (2.2). However, all three explanations may link directly with human capital. Put differently, it is now time to enter the micro-economic structure of equations (2.1) and (2.2) and attempt to *understand precisely how human capital externalities percolate.*

When trying to reconcile Marshall's first two arguments for agglomeration in a human capital framework, it may be argued, for instance, that having a greater number of skilled workers may facilitate matching between employers and employees. This is because a larger market for skills will make it easier for firms to find employees with the exact characteristics they require. At the same time, a large labor market will make it easier for highly skilled employees to find a job corresponding to their skills. In a different vein, with a larger supply of human capital in a city, we expect an increase in the number of specialized suppliers. A large range of specialized suppliers may again have productive benefits and raise the marginal product of all workers in the city. In short, *most mechanisms generating local increasing returns to scale can be enriched to take human capital into account and generate external effects of human capital.* Hence equations (2.1) and (2.2) need not rely on direct interactions across workers.

The external effects that appear in the matching and input/output linkages argument that are sketched in the previous paragraph are nonetheless of a nature different from those in the standard story of section 2.3, where direct interactions between workers are put forward. These alternatives may also require very different policy instruments. For instance, if the observed correlations are mostly explained by a thick (or large and liquid) local labor-market argument, it is very unclear whether the best thing to do is to encourage the acquisition of human capital or, instead, to attempt to reduce matching frictions so that workers are paid at their marginal product.

This point is further illustrated by the following example. Imagine that cities with larger shares of university graduates generate more employment in local R&D. Then assume that the successful innovations of the R&D sector cannot be fully appropriated by the inventors and benefit other firms in the same city. What is the best policy prescription: encourage the acquisition of human capital or strengthen intellectual property rights? This is far from obvious. Here again, the answer will depend on the precise microeconomic foundations of the model.

2.6 FURTHER ATTEMPTS AT IDENTIFICATION

To deal with these problems, the way forward is to identify more precisely how these externalities work. This is a very hard task because, as already argued, externalities tend to leave no paper trail. *All the approaches explored so far have only made some inference about their existence, without ever being able to observe them directly.* Only a very small number of papers have attempted to identify human capital externalities. Two main methods have been used: clever use of existing "standard" data and the use of more "exotic" data.

Patent data have been used by economists for a long time to measure innovative output. Jaffe, Trajtenberg, and Henderson (1993) start by reasserting that patents can also be viewed as inputs in the innovative process. When filling in an application for a patent, inventors must cite which other patented innovations they used in their own work. In a nutshell, patents are like academic papers: they must contain a "bibliography." The crucial difference compared with academic papers, where authors may cite liberally (and arbitrarily), is that for patents the bibliography is not done by the author but by the equivalent of an independent editor, the patent officer. For this reason, patent citations may contain valuable information about the real intellectual sources of innovations.

The null hypothesis of Jaffe, Trajtenberg, and Henderson (1993) is that the citation trail is neutral with respect to geography. In absence of "knowledge spillovers" (which may be thought of as the counterpart to human capital externalities when embodied in an innovation), we expect cited patents to be distributed like any "control group" of patents. In other words, if California accounts for 20 percent of past patents in microelectronics in the United States, we expect any new patent in this industry to quote 20 percent of Californian patents, regardless of where the new innovator is located. The key result of Jaffe et al. (1993) is that this null hypothesis is strongly rejected at three different spatial scales: the USA versus the rest of the world, between US states, and between US metropolitan areas. US innovators quote patents from the same country, state, and city much more than patents from other countries, states, and cities, even after controlling for the spatial distribution of the research output across sectors.

Taking a different direction, Charlot and Duranton (2004) exploit a unique survey recording communication practices for around 6,000 French workers in 1997 (with information about whom they communicate with and how). Their identifying assumption is very much in line with the standard story told by Lucas (1988) about human capital externalities. More educated (and more populated) cities should favor communication and in turn more communication should have a positive impact on individual earnings. The strength of the "communication" externalities can then be computed as the effects of average urban schooling (and city population) on communication multiplied by the effect of communication on earnings. Consistent with these two hypotheses, Charlot and Duranton (2004) find that workplace communication is positively associated with earnings. Furthermore, average urban schooling (and city population) is positively associated with workplace communication. Between a tenth and a quarter of the effects of average urban schooling (and city population) appear to permeate through communication externalities.

2.7   CONCLUSIONS

Given how little we know and the large number of possible channels though which human capital externalities may percolate, it is far too early to make definitive conclusions. Note, however, that the past 10 years have seen tremendous progress on the subject. The first serious paper documenting the issue was Rauch in 1993. Over the past 10 years, much has been learnt about human capital externalities in cities.

If we go back to the general argument about "how to do economics" that is raised above, it is worth noting that human capital externalities is one of these subjects where problems of model selection are very important. Progress on this type of issue is always going to be slow and tentative. When I first spoke with one of the editors (Richard Arnott) about this chapter, he encouraged me to write on this topic, but to highlight the difficulties of the topic he wrote to me: "There seems to be something special about large cities that makes them centers of culture, art, and innovation. Cities attract not just the bright and knowledgeable, but also the bold, unconventional, innovative, and ambitious. Cities are where you go to make a name, and cities are where you find access to patrons and venture capital." Capturing this type of argument theoretically through neat little models and then estimating them is certainly not an easy task.

To summarize, after 10 years of work on human capital externalities in cities, there is a strong suspicion that "something is going on" here, a weaker suspicion that such externalities may be quite large, and a hunch that direct interactions may not be everything. We are still quite a long way from policy recommendations strongly grounded in evidence. However, this should remain the final goal. From a narrow perspective, it may be argued that if only 10 percent of resources in education were misallocated (arguably a very conservative estimate), the numbers would still be huge: $70 billion would be wasted in the USA each year! This probably justifies a fair amount of research resources devoted to the topic. From a broader perspective, a successful education is clearly a life-changing experience (and often for the best, academics like to think), which certainly impacts on others around. The proper provision of education is obviously crucial, at least in this respect.

Acknowledgments

I am very grateful to Adala Bwire for her thorough reading and constructive comments on this paper. Richard Arnott and an anonymous referee also provided some useful feedback.

Further reading

This chapter is at the crossroads between several threads of literature. Here are some leads:

- On human capital externalities, the next step is certainly the survey by Moretti (2004b) in the *Handbook of Regional and Urban Economics*. This survey is much more technical than the present chapter. It discusses in depth the material in sections 2.4 and 2.5.1.
- On the empirics of agglomeration economies more generally, the chapter by Stuart Rosenthal and William Strange in this volume should be an obvious point of departure. Their more involved survey in the *Handbook of Regional and Urban Economics* (2004) is certainly the next step.
- On the theories of agglomeration, the chapter by Duranton and Puga in the *Handbook of Regional and Urban Economics* provides a comprehensive survey.

Bibliography

Acemoglu, D. and Angrist, J. 2000: How large are human capital externalities? Evidence from compulsory schooling laws. *NBER Macroeconomics Annual*, 15(0), 9–59.

Card, D. 1999: The causal effect of education on earnings. In O. Ashenfelter and D. Card (eds.), *Handbook of Labor Economics*, vol. 3. Amsterdam: North-Holland.

Charlot, S. and Duranton, G. 2004: Communication externalities in cities. *Journal of Urban Economics*, 56(3), 581–603.

Ciccone, A. and Peri, G. 2005: Identifying human capital externalities: theory with an application to US cities. *Review of Economic Studies*, forthcoming.

Duranton, G. and Puga, D. 2004: The micro-foundations of urban agglomeration economies. In J. V. Henderson and J.-F. Thisse (eds.), *Handbook of Regional and Urban Economics*, vol. 4: *Cities and Geography*. Amsterdam: North-Holland, 2,063–117.

Jaffe, A. B., Trajtenberg, M., and Henderson, R. 1993: Geographic localization of knowledge spillovers as evidenced by patent citations. *Quarterly Journal of Economics*, 108(3), 577–98.

Lucas, R. E. Jr. 1988: On the mechanics of economic development. *Journal of Monetary Economics*, 22(1), 3–42.

Manski, C. F. 1993: Identification of endogenous social effects: the reflection problem. *Review of Economic Studies*, 60(3), 531–42.

Marshall, A. 1890, 1895: *Principles of Economics*, 1st and 3rd edns. London: Macmillan.

Moretti, E. 2004a: Estimating the social return to education: evidence from longitudinal and cross-sectional data. *Journal of Econometrics*, 121(1), 175–212.

—— 2004b: Human capital externalities in cities. In J. V. Henderson and J.-F. Thisse (eds.), *Handbook of Regional and Urban Economics*, vol. 4: *Cities and Geography*. Amsterdam: North-Holland.

Pigou, A. C. 1920: *The Economics of Welfare*. London: Macmillan.

Rauch, J. E. 1993: Productivity gains from geographic concentration of human capital: evidence from the cities. *Journal of Urban Economics*, 34(3), 380–400.

Rosenthal, S. S. and Strange, W. 2004: Evidence on the nature and sources of agglomeration economies. In J. V. Henderson and J.-F. Thisse (eds.), *Handbook of Regional and Urban Economics*, vol. 4: *Cities and Geography*. Amsterdam: North-Holland, 2,119–71.

Sutton, J. 2000: *Marshall's Tendencies: What Can Economists Know?* Cambridge, MA: The MIT Press.

CHAPTER THREE

The First Cities

Arthur O'Sullivan

3.1 INTRODUCTION

This essay explores the origins of the world's first cities, which evolved in different parts of Southwest Asia. The city of Jericho developed in the Jordan Valley in the eighth millennium BC, with a population of about 2,000. Jericho had formidable fortifications, suggesting that it had accumulated wealth and was targeted by raiders. About one millennium later, Çatalhöyük (or "Çatal Hüyük") developed in present-day Turkey, with a population of about 5,000. The city produced obsidian tools and other craft products, and may have served as a regional trading center. In the second half of the fourth millennium BC, Uruk developed in southern Mesopotamia (in present-day Iraq), with a population of about 50,000. The central religious organization was the dominant force in the economy, producing a wide variety of private goods such as barley, cloth, and pottery. The offerings to the 2,400 gods doubled as payments to the managers of temple enterprises.

Our knowledge of the economic features of these cities is derived from the material that city residents left behind. Archaeologists have excavated the piles of rubble that used to be cities, uncovering city walls, buildings, household implements, tools of craft fabrication, and religious objects. In the case of Uruk, archaeologists have also discovered clay tablets with primitive forms of writing. In trying to piece together these bits of information to form a picture of life in the first cities, we must be careful not to jump to conclusions, but instead recognize the speculative nature of any conjectures. In this essay, I will try to avoid the trap that has ensnared many scholars, including one who "was not always able to control his imagination and his weakness for paradoxes." Given our limited knowledge about these early cities, many puzzles remain. In addition, future excavations may reveal other cities that developed earlier.

3.2 CONDITIONS FOR URBANIZATION

A necessary condition for the development of cities is an agricultural surplus. Urban employment diverts labor from food production, and the remaining workers must produce enough to feed themselves and city workers. The domestication of barley and wheat occurred in about 10,000 BC in the areas of Southwest Asia that were to later generate the first cities. The domestication of animals – goats, sheep, cattle, and pigs – occurred about 2,000 years later.

Jacobs's (1969) contrary view is that cities preceded the development of agriculture. She suggests that city dwellers initially consumed imports from hunter–gatherers. If imported nuts and seeds were mingled and spilled onto fertile ground, the combination of happenstance and opportunism could lead to the domestication of the most productive hybrids. If the wildest of the imported live animals were eaten first, opportunistic city dwellers could then domesticate the tamest animals. Jacobs argues that urban development caused agricultural innovation, and uses the city of Çatalhöyük to illustrate her "cities-first" theory.

As noted by Bairoch (1988), Jacobs's theory ignores "the tyranny of distance." Before the domestication of animals, food transport was costly because the human transporter consumed a large part of the load. Van de Mieroop (1997) uses the area around Çatalhöyük to illustrate the problem with Jacobs's theory. Given the low productivity of hunting and gathering and the high costs of human transport, the accessible hunter–gatherer output would not be sufficient to feed the residents of Çatalhöyük. Bairoch notes that although urban development didn't cause the invention of agriculture, it did contribute to its diffusion.

An agricultural surplus is not sufficient to generate cities. The costs of high-density living are obvious: competition for land drives up the price of land, and density causes congestion and pollution. To explain why cities develop, we must identify economic benefits that more than offset these obvious costs:

1   In a region with trade, if there are scale economies in trade services (record-keeping, transportation, finance), organizations that provide these services will generate concentrations of employment, causing the development of trading cities. Jacobs (1969) emphasizes the role of trade in the development of the first cities.
2   If there are internal scale economies in production (internal to the firm), the concentration of workers in a single enterprise will generate a city.
3   If innovation and learning are facilitated by physical proximity of individual producers, the clustering of producers will generate a city.
4   If citizens consume a public good that requires physical proximity for collective consumption, the concentration of consumers will cause the development of a city. Some examples are cities based on defense and religion. Mumford (1961) suggests that the first cities developed when earthen gods, who were worshiped at small village shrines, were replaced by celestial gods, who were worshiped at large temples administered by a priestly class.

3.3   JERICHO   •

Archaeological evidence suggests that the first city in the world was Jericho (Tell es Sultan), situated at a junction of travel routes in the fertile Jordan Valley. The site was occupied in the period 8400–7300 BC, with a population of about 2,000.

The fertile Jordan Valley had a reliable supply of water, and residents domesticated crops (barley and wheat) and animals (goats and sheep). In addition, the
spring near the city attracted wild game, providing a ready supply of gazelle and
other wild animals.

There is some evidence of trade in the area, but it appears that the volume of
trade was small. Among the city's imports were obsidian from Anatolia, green
stones from Jordan, turquoise from the Sinai, and shells from the Red Sea. There
is no evidence of production for export from the city. The likely export goods
were raw materials from the nearby Dead Sea, including salt, bitumen (for seal-
ing and adhering), and sulfur.

3.3.1 Defense: the walls of Jericho

The most startling feature of Jericho is a formidable system of defense, consisting
of a wall, a surrounding ditch, and a tower. The wall was about 7 m tall and 3 m
thick at the base, and was built with undressed stone to surround an area of
about 4 ha. The ditch surrounding the wall was 9 m wide and 3 m deep, and
presumably served as a moat to discourage assaults on the city's protective wall.
The tower was located just inside the wall, and was at least 8 m tall and 9 m in
diameter. The tower presumably served as an observation post to anticipate the
arrival of hostile forces.

The building of the fortifications involved enormous amounts of resources, both
labor and material. The walls were built of undressed stone, not formed bricks, and
the stone was transported long distances to the city site. To dig the moat, the workers
scooped out solid rock at the base of the wall, a task apparently performed with
the simplest of tools, the stone maul. There is no evidence of even simple stone
digging tools, and of course metal tools weren't available for another 5,000 years.

The presence of these massive fortifications suggests that agricultural productivity in the area was relatively high. A productive food sector freed up a large
fraction of the population to work on building and maintaining the city's fortifications, and could generate enough wealth to attract thieves. In sifting through
the rubble of several thousand years of occupation, archaeologists have not yet
found any stores of wealth that would have attracted raiders, so the nature of the
booty (goods stolen in war) remains a mystery. One possibility is a storable
agricultural product.

The fortifications also suggest the presence of persistent raiders. The city was
located at the junction of several travel routes, making it a convenient target in
the same way that modern convenience stores (Stop-and-Shop; Stop-and-Rob) are
easy targets. The city was surrounded by hunter–gatherer groups, and archaeologists speculate that these groups occasionally supplemented hunting and
gathering with stealing. At the time, the technology of war involved attacking at
a distance with bows and arrows (a range of 100 m) and slings (a range of 200 m),
and using spears and maces for close combat. The artwork dating from the time of
Jericho provides evidence of organized attacks, with warriors arranged in columns.

Given the technology of war at the time, the fortifications would have been
the appropriate response to frequent raids (Ferrill 1997). Archers could position

themselves atop the walls, allowing them to keep attackers at a distance, preventing them from scaling the wall. The methods for assaulting city walls – the battering ram and undermining – hadn't been invented yet, so the wall was an effective defense. Fending off attacks wasn't without cost: archaeologists estimate that about a quarter of the population served as defenders.

3.3.2   Why did Jericho develop?

Given our limited knowledge about everyday life in the city of Jericho 10,000 years ago, we can merely speculate about its origins. Recall that the possible reasons for urbanization are (i) trade and the resulting cluster of activities that support trade (record-keeping, transportation, finance), (ii) large-scale fabrication with large workforces, (iii) clustering of producers to promote innovation and learning, and (iv) public goods such as religion and defense that require physical proximity.

It does not appear that Jericho owes its existence to trade or large-scale production. There is no evidence that city residents fabricated tools or other craft goods. This eliminates the possibility of large workforces, and also means that the city didn't produce any products to trade with other regions. There may have been some trade in raw materials from the nearby Dead Sea, but what appears to be a small volume of trade could not have supported a city of 2,000 people.

There is not much archaeological evidence concerning religious activity. There is evidence of small shrines in individual dwellings, as well as a large building that served some public function, perhaps serving as a temple. This "temple" building had a large central room that appears to have had a ceremonial function, and annexes with domed ceilings. Among the religious objects found were figurines of a mother goddess, presumably an icon of a fertility cult. In addition, there appears to be what Kenyon (1957) labels a "Cult of Skulls." Some of the amassed skulls are covered in plaster as portraits of venerated ancestors. There is no evidence that religion was a public good requiring physical proximity, so it appears that the city does not owe its existence to religion.

Based on archaeological evidence, it appears that Jericho developed to provide a public good, defense. Given the frequency of raids, the wealth of households needed protection, and the collective provision of defense is more efficient than provision by individual households. A small group of raiders, armed with spears, maces, and bows, could overwhelm an individual household and steal their wealth. A group of households could match the personnel and weaponry of a raiding band, but would fare better by combining resources to build fortifications that discouraged attacks. Given the substantial labor cost associated with its fortifications, the residents of Jericho apparently had something to protect, but the nature of the booty remains a mystery.

3.4   ÇATALHÖYÜK

Çatalhöyük was a city of around 5,000 people in the sixth and seventh millennia BC. The city was on a 13-ha site in the Konya plain, an area that is now part of Turkey.

The city fed its residents with domesticated crops and animals, and produced a wide variety of craft products, some of which were exported to other regions.

The food economy of the city was based on simple agriculture and domesticated cattle. The domestication of cattle, which provided the bulk of meat as well as transport, contrasts with the domestication of sheep and goats by other cultures. The city grew wheat and barley on irrigated land, and also harvested legumes, nuts, fruits, and berries. The city residents hunted boar, deer, bear, and leopard for supplementary meat and skins. In addition, the residents of the city consumed dairy products and beer.

The most unusual feature of Çatalhöyük was its building architecture. Flat-roofed buildings were stuck together, with back-to-back walls. There were no ground-level entries, so people entered a house through the roof, using a retractable ladder. The small windows on the buildings were placed high in the walls, well beyond human reach. Archaeologists speculate that this architecture promoted the defense of the city. The exposed walls of the outermost buildings formed a wall around the entire city, presumably deterring small groups of raiders trying to steal the city's wealth.

3.4.1   Production and trade

The people of Çatalhöyük were involved in highly sophisticated and specialized production of products made of wood, stone, and obsidian. The black obsidian from a nearby volcano was flaked and polished to produce points (for spear-heads and arrowheads), wedges (for scraping and butchering), blades, and mirrors. Imported flint was fashioned into daggers. The city's polished stone industry produced a wide variety of products, including statuettes, perforated mace heads, stone bowls, greenstone axes, and chisels. Workers in the city processed shell and bone into ornaments and tools. Woodworkers squared oak and juniper for construction purposes, and also produced bowls, dishes, and boxes with lids.

The production of obsidian products had several stages. Itinerant workers chipped obsidian from a volcanic site about 150 km from the city and processed the raw obsidian into "cores," reducing the bulk and weight of the material. The itinerants then transported the cores to Çatalhöyük for further processing. In the city, skilled workers used pressure and punching techniques to fashion obsidian products from the cores. The itinerant workers then served as transporters and traders, exchanging obsidian products for products from other regions.

In recent experiments, workers have tried to duplicate the production process for obsidian tools in Çatalhöyük. The experiments revealed the high level of skill required for tool production:

> Recent studies indicate that pressure flaking (of blades) is a difficult and demanding practice, which requires extensive knowledge of rock flaking properties as well as good neuromuscular coordination. The latter takes several years to acquire, but allows thereafter a very high productivity . . . Consequently, pressure flaking conforms to the typical criteria one associates with the highly skilled and productive practice of a specialist. (Conolly 1999)

Conolly concludes that specialization occurred within a kin group, with some members of the extended family engaging in part-time obsidian tool production for the kin group.

One of the lingering questions about Çatalhöyük concerns the location of craft production. Archaeologists have not yet uncovered any workshops for the processing of obsidian, wood, or stone. Based on the existing evidence, it appears that production was not concentrated in workshops, but dispersed among individual homes.

There is evidence that Çatalhöyük was involved in interregional trade. The city exchanged its craft products – obsidian and stone tools, ornaments, and wood products – for resources that were not available locally. Archaeologists have discovered flint from Syria, shells from the Mediterranean, and bitumen from the Dead Sea. The city also imported wood and copper from nearby sources. Among the imported materials of unknown origins are various types of rocks, including apatite, rock crystal, and jasper.

Was Çatalhöyük isolated, or part of a system of cities? Recent archaeological work has uncovered several smaller settlements close to Çatalhöyük. In addition, there is evidence that the city's culture spread to the entire Konya plain and the outlying areas. These discoveries have led to speculation that Çatalhöyük was a sort of regional trading center, the largest city in a system of cities that traded with each other and with people outside the region.

3.4.2   Religion

The religious activities of Çatalhöyük were not concentrated in a single large temple, but distributed throughout the city in shrine rooms in individual houses. The wall paintings and plaster reliefs in the shrine rooms show a mother goddesses exhibiting unusual feats of fertility. The shrine rooms also have bucrania, sculptures of wild ox heads, complete with long horns. One object that appears in many shrines is a bench with up to seven pairs of sharp ox horns pointing upward, making for uncomfortable sitting but presumably a better relationship with the gods.

The shrines also contained offerings to the gods. These offerings included deposits of grain and legumes, new and used tools, pots and bone utensils, animal bones, bull horns, and stamp-seals. Among the obsidian tools serving as offerings were arrowheads and spear points that were too thin and fragile for use in actual hunting. High-status people were buried below the floor of the shrines, along with worldly possessions such as textiles, jewelry, mirrors, adzes, daggers, obsidian points, and clay seals.

3.4.3   Why did Çatalhöyük develop?

Compared to Jericho, our knowledge of the economic life of Çatalhöyük is much better. Nonetheless, there are gaps in our knowledge, and we can only speculate about the reasons why the city developed about 9,000 years ago.

It appears that Çatalhöyük owes its existence to its production of obsidian tools and other craft products. The production of obsidian tools required a high skill level, meaning that two phenomena were present in the industry:

1 Innovation: someone must develop the innovations that lead to a sophisticated production process.
2 Learning: the skills must be passed on to new workers.

The concentration of production in a city – with workers located close to one
another – would hasten both innovation and learning. In general, cities facilitate innovation because they bring people of different backgrounds and skills
together to exchange ideas. Cities facilitate learning because workers learn by
observation, and there are more people to observe in cities. In general, there are
benefits from physical proximity of production facilities – even if they are in
tightly packed houses rather than in factories – and Çatalhöyük may have been
the center for innovation and learning in the production of obsidian tools.

A second possible reason for cities is the provision of defense as a public good.
Given the massive fortifications of Jericho, the idea that the Çatalhöyük architecture – houses stuck together, with roof entryways and high windows – would
deter raiders seems far-fetched. But perhaps the booty-seekers in the time of
Çatalhöyük were different from the raiders who tormented Jericho. The simple
architectural fortifications of Çatalhöyük, combined with some system of organizing people to defend the city from raiders, could have in fact deterred potential
raiders. If so, defense could have been a public good that encouraged the clustering of people in the city.

3.5 Cities in Southern Mesopotamia

Starting in the middle part of the fourth millennium BC, a cluster of cities developed in Babylonia, the southern part of Mesopotamia (the area around the Tigris
and Euphrates rivers in present-day Iraq). The population of Uruk, the largest
city in Babylonia, reached 50,000 at the end of the fourth millennium BC. Other
cities, each with tens of thousands of people, developed nearby, including Ur,
Erudi, and Kish. In this essay, I focus on the economic features of these cities
from the middle of the late fourth millennium BC to the early part of the third
millennium BC.

3.5.1 The ecological setting

Babylonia had a number of rich and varied ecosystems, including alluvial plains,
rivers, and grasslands. These ecosystems were suitable for a wide variety of
food-producing activities, including farming (barley, emmer, fruit), fishing, hunting (wild pig, gazelle, wild asses), and grazing (sheep and goats for wool, hair,
and milk). In contrast to its rich agricultural resources, Babylonia lacked many
basic raw materials, including hardwood, basic metals (copper, tin, silver, lead),
and precious stones. The dry climate did not support rain-fed agriculture, but the
water from the Tigris and the Euphrates rivers was easily diverted into canals,
allowing the cultivation of lands beyond the banks of the rivers. The first
rudimentary irrigation canals date back to 5500 BC.

Given its ecological setting, Babylonia was a perfect candidate for specialization and trade. The varied ecosystems generated comparative advantages in different parts of the region, opening the possibility of specialization and gains from trade. Similarly, the combination of rich agricultural resources and limited raw materials generated a comparative advantage in agricultural goods, opening the possibility of interregional trade, with agricultural goods being traded for raw materials.

Given its many comparative advantages, it seems likely that Babylonia would eventually develop a system of specialization and trade, causing the development of trading cities. In the middle of the fourth millennium BC, however, there were two major impediments to widespread specialization and trade. First, there was no money, and exchange was based on barter, an awkward system with high transaction costs. Second, writing hadn't been invented, so there was no system of recording transactions. People involved in trade were dependent on human memory and honesty to keep track of transactions, and were presumably reluctant to trade with strangers. As a result, specialization and trade typically occurred at the kin-group or village level.

The development of cities in Babylonia in the middle of the fourth millennium BC, before the invention of writing and money, remains a puzzle. The question is: How did the Babylonians overcome the obstacles of barter and illiteracy to develop widespread specialization and trade? One possibility is that the Sumerians, who migrated to the region some time between 4000 BC and 3500 BC, brought a social system that made cities possible. The Sumerians provided the region with the dominant spoken language and a system of religion. Over the second half of the fourth millennium, Sumerian priests developed a system of recording transactions, culminating in the invention of writing in 3100 BC.

3.5.2   Religious beliefs

The Sumerian religion adopted in Babylonia was based on the belief that the gods determined the fertility of flora and fauna. The gods were responsible for all natural phenomena, with each of the 2,400 gods responsible for a piece of the natural order. For example, the crop gods included Innana, originally responsible for ripening dates, and Ashnan, responsible for the productivity of grain fields. The domesticated herd gods included Dumazi, who determined the timing of livestock births, and Lahar, who was responsible for the productivity of sheep. There were also gods for hunting, including Suagan, who was responsible for generating large and accessible herds of gazelles and wild asses. Together, the gods were responsible for ecological continuity, keeping nature working as it had in the past. The Babylonians did not ask the gods to perform miracles, but simply asked them to continue the "miracle" of nature. The role of the gods was to keep the crops growing, the dates ripening, and the wild asses running on time.

The role of humans was to provide goods to the materialistic gods, freeing them to manage the natural world. According to the Sumerian legend of the origin of humans, second-rate gods originally tilled the soil to provide for the needs of greater gods, who were busy with the tasks of nature management. When the second-rate gods tired of tilling, they persuaded the other gods to create humans to feed, clothe, and shelter all the gods. According to Bottéro (2001):

> The faithful were convinced that humans were created and put on earth for the sole purpose of ensuring, through human industry and solicitude, that the gods led an opulent and worry-free life, free to concentrate on the government of the world and its inhabitants.

In other words, the gods were not mystical beings with mysterious motives, but simply hungry managers.

People offered huge volumes of goods to the gods, and most of the goods were ultimately consumed by members of the temple staff. In other words, the goods provided to the gods were not sacrificed in the traditional sense. The gods were housed in large, luxurious temples, and were fed four elaborate meals per day. After the fully prepared food had sat in front of the statues of the gods for a while, it was distributed to the religious elite and members of the temple staff, who numbered in the hundreds. An old Sumerian saying is "the priests eat off the altar." Some members of the staff lived in the temple area, sharing the luxurious accommodation with the icons.

Of course, some of the goods offered to the gods were not consumed by humans, but were true sacrifices. For example, people provided the gods with festive clothing and precious jewelry. Resources were used in the production of icons and ceremonies. The most famous image of Babylonian cities, the ziggurat, actually came much later, in the late third millennium BC, about a millennium after the cities first developed.

3.5.3 Religious offerings as a public good

The religion of Babylon is an example of a public good, at least a perceived one. Religious contributions freed the gods to better manage the ecosystem (e.g., by bringing favorable weather), so the fertility of flora and fauna increased. A more fertile ecosystem made everyone more productive, so each person's contribution benefited everyone. In other words, the social benefit of a religious contribution exceeded the private benefit.

We can use a simple example to illustrate the public-good nature of religion. Consider a group of 1,000 people, and suppose that a religious contribution of one bushel of barley was assumed to increase each person's productivity by 1/100 bushel. The marginal social benefit of a one-bushel contribution is 10 bushels (1,000/100), compared to a marginal social cost of only one bushel. The marginal social benefit exceeds the marginal social cost, so a contribution is socially efficient. However, the private benefit of a contribution is only 1/100 bushel compared to a private cost of one bushel, so a rational individual won't voluntarily make the contribution. This is the free-rider problem: no single individual has an incentive to make a socially efficient contribution. The challenge for the religious authorities in Babylonia was to get individuals to act in the social interest. To get people to contribute, some sort of collective decision-making would be required.

Could the religious authorities solve the free-rider problem by promising an uncomfortable penalty for free riders in the afterlife? In Babylonia, an afterlife incentive program was not feasible because the people believed that everyone had the same afterlife – a long, quiet time in a bland location below the earth – regardless of their earthly behavior.

One possible solution to the free-rider problem is a sort of public sharecropping arrangement. Suppose that the religious authorities announced that each person was obligated to give 10 percent of his harvest to the gods. A potential problem with this scheme is keeping track of who contributed: in a pre-literate world without money, it would be difficult to insure that each citizen contributed the appropriate share of the harvest. Although tracking contributions might not be a problem with a small number of beneficiaries (e.g., at the village level), the Babylonian gods were responsible for ecosystem management for the entire region, so there were tens of thousands of beneficiaries.

An alternative to public sharecropping is for the religious authorities to take administrative responsibility for the economy. The temple could manage the region's land and water resources, organize production, and engage in inter-regional trade. By administering a centrally planned economy, the temple could collect the aggregate output of the economy and reserve the appropriate share for the gods. The leftover output could then be distributed to the workers and other citizens.

In the fourth millennium BC, Babylonia had a mixed economy, with a wide variety of temple enterprises as well as some private enterprise. According to Potts:

> Herding, weaving, pottery manufacture, metalworking, woodworking, stone working, agriculture, gardening, forestry, fishing, beer production, and baking, just to name the most obvious activities, all came within the purview of the temple administration, as did the distribution of rations in *naturalia* (e.g., barley, oil, wool, etc.) (Potts 1997, p. 237)

The archaeological evidence is insufficient to determine the fraction of the economy directly administered by the temple, but it is clear that the temple was the dominant force in the economy. In amassing the offerings to the gods, the temple supplemented the residuals from temple enterprises with sharecropping contributions from private enterprises.

3.5.4   Temple enterprises

In the fourth millennium BC, the temple owned and managed a large fraction of the agricultural land around the city. Some of this land was made productive by the temple's irrigation projects. There was some privately held land, including land owned and cultivated by villagers, and land owned by city dwellers who had either inherited it or received land grants as a reward for service to the temple. The temple granted land to individuals for service in farming, plowing, fishing, herding, and craft production.

· The temple operated as a sort of vertically integrated agricultural firm, being involved in every step of the production of grain. The temple hired workers to build and maintain the irrigation system, plow the fields, plant the seeds, process the grain, and store the grain for future use. These workers were paid rations in barley, oil, and wool, which they either consumed themselves or used in the barter economy to trade for other products. The temple was also involved in production on private lands, hiring workers to plow the fields and distribute seeds.

The temple also acted as a vertically integrated textile firm. Professional herdsmen, hired by the temple, raised sheep on grasslands around the city. The temple's wool office collected the wool and distributed raw wool to villagers near the city for initial processing (cleaning and fulling). Large workshops in the city transformed the processed wool into textiles, and the temple took ownership of the finished textiles.

The temple was responsible for interregional trade, with textiles serving as the main export good. Although wool is bulky and thus costly to transport, finished cloth is not, and the region had a comparative advantage in textile production. The temple exchanged textiles for copper, tin, wood, silver, and precious stones from nearby regions. The imported metals and precious stones provided the raw materials for the city's metallurgy and jewelry industries. Trading opportunities were enhanced by the location of Babylonia at the junction of trade routes linking Asia and the Mediterranean.

The temple's output – the sum of output from a wide variety of temple enterprises and contributions from private enterprises – was distributed in several ways. First, some of the output was offered to the gods and then con- sumed by temple personnel, including priests involved in rituals and others who managed the temple enterprises. Second, some of the output was distributed as rations to the workers who built and maintained the irrigation canals, worked on temple farms and workshops, and were engaged in interregional trade. Third, the temple ration was given to people incapable of working, including children and the aged. Fourth, some of the output was used in interregional trade.

Why was the temple involved in so many economic activities? The temple provided a mechanism for collective decision-making, but unlike governments in the modern world, did not confine its activities to the provision of public goods; for example, religious services and public works. Instead, the temple produced all sorts of private goods, defined as a good that is rival in consump- tion (consumed by a single person) and excludable (a person who does not pay can be prevented from consuming the good). In the modern mixed economy, private goods such as grain, cloth, and pottery are produced by private enter- prise, not a central authority. Why were things different in Babylonia?

The disadvantages of the central provision of a private good are obvious. A central authority generates a monopoly, and the lack of competition is likely to cause relatively high prices and small quantities, leading to the familiar deadweight welfare loss from monopoly. In addition, a large organization is likely to be less responsive to changing economic conditions.

In the fourth millennium BC, one advantage of temple enterprise was related to the barter system. In an economy without money or writing, people tended to trade with people they knew and trusted; that is, members of their kin group in the local village. To get people to trade beyond the kin group, there had to be a system that engendered trust, and the temple provided such a system. The temple specified the terms of trade, in particular the temple ration amount for each occupation, and also produced the goods (barley, oil, and wool) that could either be consumed by the recipient or bartered for other goods. It is possible that the temple served as a trusted broker, encouraging specialization and trade beyond the kin group.

A second possible advantage of temple enterprise results from double counting of contributions to the gods. Most of the offerings to the gods were actually consumed by temple workers, not only the people involved in religious activities, but also those involved in managing temple enterprises. The offerings counted two ways: as an offering to the gods in exchange for ecosystem management, and as payment to temple workers in exchange for enterprise management. This double counting generated an advantage for the temple enterprise that at least partly offsets the inefficiency associated with central control.

A third advantage of temple enterprise is that it solves the free-rider problem for the citizens involved in the enterprises. Rather than asking citizens to contribute some fraction of the output of their private enterprise, the temple simply took the appropriate share for the gods and redistributed the rest. For the remainder of the economy – private enterprise – the temple used sharecropping arrangements to collect contributions to the gods.

3.5.5   The technology of writing

An important part of the economic history of Babylonian cities was the invention and refinement of writing. This development freed people engaging in trade from their reliance on human memory and honesty. Writing was developed by priests, and the immediate effect was probably to strengthen the dependence of the economy on the temple organization. In the long run, however, writing allowed traders to put their trust in permanent and verifiable records, which may have contributed to the increase in private enterprise at the expense of temple enterprises.

The earliest attempts to record transactions, developed in Babylonia in the fourth millennium, employed *bullae*, closed clay containers with counters inside. For example, when a person contributed 10 goats to the temple, the priest would record the transaction with a container holding 10 icons representing the goats, the container being marked with the contributor's unique seal. The bullae were used by temple authorities to record the inputs and outputs of temple enterprises, and to track the contributions of private enterprises. One problem with the bullae system is that to verify the transaction (to tally the goat counters), the container had to be broken. A second problem was that it required each person to have a unique seal for identification purposes, and these personal seals were costly.

Writing developed in Uruk in about 3100 BC. The first writing involved etching symbols (pictograms) into clay tablets, with a unique symbol for each object. For example, the symbol for an ear of corn looks like a cornstalk, while the symbol for an ox is an inverted pyramid with two lines coming out the top. Similarly, each person was assigned a unique personal symbol. Clay tablets recovered from Uruk use pictograms to record the number of oxen received by the temple from different individuals. The symbols were etched into wet clay, which was then baked or left to dry to serve as a permanent record. This simple system allowed information to be retained and conveyed to other people.

The pictogram system was awkward because it required a unique symbol for each object. Archaeologists estimate that the Babylonian pictogram system had about 1,500 symbols. About 100 years after the first object-oriented pictograms, the Babylonians shifted to using symbols to represent sounds (syllables) rather than objects. This allowed objects to be represented by different combinations of a smaller set of symbols. For example, the Sumerian word for "arrow" was pronounced *ti*, and so was the word for "life." Under the phonetic system, the word for life was represented by the symbol for its homophone, the arrow. In general, each word was depicted with a series of symbols, one for each syllable. The phonetic innovation reduced the number of symbols used to about 400. Eventually, most of the pictograms were replaced by symbols that combined straight lines and wedges, known as cuneiform script (*cuneus* is Latin for "wedge").

Writing was invented by temple priests and first used to keep track of temple business. Writing emerged after several hundred years of collecting offerings for the gods and managing temple enterprises. In the Sumerian language, the words for "priest" and "accountant" are used to refer to the same people, suggesting that the priests used their invention to serve as the city's accountants. Writing was used exclusively for commerce between 3100 and 2600 BC. Starting about 2600 BC, writing was used for hymns, prayers, myths, and the relaying of wisdom. This first step toward literature occurred before cuneiform text, so much of the meaning of the texts is obscure.

The timing of the invention and refinement of writing reveals an important feature of innovation. It appears that writing didn't just happen, but instead was a response to the practical problem of how to keep track of transactions in a barter economy. The priests in Uruk had been tracking the transactions of the temple for a long time before they came up with the idea of recording transactions on clay tablets. Over the next several centuries, they perfected the idea of writing, motivated by the challenges of record-keeping.

The development of writing contributed to urban development because it facilitated specialization and trade. Writing decreased transaction costs, so it increased the net gains from trade, allowing a fuller exploitation of underlying comparative advantages. As writing spread beyond Mesopotamia, the opportunities for specialization widened, trade increased, causing the development of trading cities. In the case of Babylonian cities, writing came after the development of cities, so it merely reinforced the growth of cities.

3.5.6   Summary: cities in Babylonia

Why did cities develop in Babylonia about 5,500 years ago? There were many regions with rich and varied ecosystems, and presumably comparative advantages that could have led to widespread specialization and trade. Why did cities develop in Babylonia first? Stated another way, given the high transaction costs in an economy without money and writing, why did cities develop in Babylonia so soon?

The key feature of the Babylonian city was the temple organization. The public-good nature of religion required a central location to both collect offerings to the gods and perform religious rituals. The cluster of purely religious workers may have generated a large town or a small city, but it probably would not have supported the large cities that developed. The population of Uruk was boosted by the many temple enterprises, which required workers to manage the enterprises, collect the output, and distribute the output as payments to managers and rations for workers.

The Babylonian cities also had a large number of workers involved in craft production. The temple's workshops were located in the city, presumably to facilitate management by the temple. In addition, the clustering of workshops would generate the same sort of agglomeration economies that we observe in modern cities. The different workshops could share the suppliers of intermediate inputs, and the cluster would also facilitate innovation and learning.

3.6   CONCLUSION

Our knowledge of the economic life in the world's earliest cities is limited by the evidence from sifting through the rubble of the cities, but we can draw some tentative conclusions about their origins. It appears that Jericho owes its existence to a combination of an accumulated surplus (of unknown nature) and the raiding activities of people in the Jordan Valley. The city of Çatalhöyük developed as a center for the production of craft products (obsidian tools, stoneware, and wood products), and as a trading center. The city's defensive architecture may have promoted urbanization for reasons of defense, but only if local raiders were more easily discouraged than the raiders who tormented Jericho.

Our knowledge of Babylonian cities is vastly superior to our knowledge of Jericho and Çatalhöyük, but is still incomplete. These cities developed before the use of money and writing. Religious organization may have provided a trusted broker in the illiterate barter economy, encouraging specialization and trade beyond the kin group. One advantage of temple enterprise (over private enterprise) was that temple managers were paid from offerings to the gods. A second possible advantage was that direct control by the temple provided a better response to the free-rider problem. Babylonian cities were relatively large because they contained pure religious workers as well as those responsible for managing temple enterprises, collecting the output of temple enterprises, and distributing the output to managers, workers, and other citizens.

Bibliography

Adams, R. M. 1966: *The Evolution of Urban Society: Early Mesopotamia and Prehispanic Mexico.* Chicago: Aldine.

Aharoni, Y. 1982: *The Archaeology of the Land of Israel: From the Prehistoric Beginnings to the End of the First Temple Period.* Philadelphia, PA: Westminster Press.

Bairoch, P. 1988: *Cities and Economic Development.* Chicago: The University of Chicago Press.

Bottéro, J. 1995: *Mesopotamia: Writing, Reasoning, and the Gods*, transl. Z. Bahrani and M. Van De Mieroop. Chicago: The University of Chicago Press.

—— 2001: *Religion in Ancient Mesopotamia*, transl. T. L. Fagan. Chicago: The University of Chicago Press.

Conolly, J. 1999: *The Çatalhöyük Flint and Obsidian Industry: Technology and Typology in Context.* Oxford: Archaeopress.

Ferrill, A. 1997: *The Origins of War: From the Stone Age to Alexander the Great.* Boulder, CO: Westview Press.

Jacobs, J. 1969: *The Economy of Cities.* New York: Random House.

Kenyon, K. M. 1957: *Digging up Jericho.* London: Ernest Benn.

—— 1979: *Archaeology in the Holy Land.* New York: W. W. Norton.

Mellaart, J. 1967: *Çatal Hüyük; A Neolithic Town in Anatolia.* New York: McGraw-Hill.

—— 1975: *The Neolithic of the Near East.* New York: Scribner.

Mumford, L. 1961: *The City in History.* New York: Harcourt.

Oppenheim, A. L. 1964: *Ancient Mesopotamia: Portrait of a Dead Civilization.* Chicago: The University of Chicago Press.

Potts, D. T. 1997: *Mesopotamian Civilization: The Material Foundations.* Ithaca, NY: Cornell University Press.

Todd, I. A. 1976: *Çatal Hüyük in Perspective.* Menlo Park, CA: Cummings.

Van de Mieroop, M. 1997: *The Ancient Mesopotamian City.* New York: Oxford University Press.

CHAPTER FOUR

Cross-Country Patterns of Urban Development

Stephen Malpezzi

4.1 INTRODUCTION

Urban economists love to suggest the following thought experiment to students. Consider a world without cities. More specifically, suppose that the world's population was randomly distributed across space. Omitting some totally uninhabitable places such as Antarctica, there would be, very roughly, about 2 ha of land for each person in the world, some more arable than others. Suppose, in turn, that the capital stock was randomly distributed; there is, *very* roughly, something like $20,000 worth of tangible capital (computers, tools, buildings, furniture, trucks – all the things we use to make other things) per capita. If you were lucky, you might find yourself on somewhat fertile land, well irrigated, in a mild climate, with some tools that might help you gather or grow enough food to stave off starvation. If I were unlucky, I might be in a less favorable location with capital that is now mostly useless. World GDP would fall from something like $40 trillion steeply toward zero. The survivors of this thought experiment would quickly be on the move, banding together and beginning to cluster in more favorable locations. The world's economy would begin to regroup and recover, although it would probably take many decades to rebuild a world in any way recognizable. The thought experiment seems bizarre if not silly, but it does in fact clearly illustrate the importance of *location*.

The thought experiment sounds so weird mainly because it collapses many millennia of migration, capital formation, trading, and technical change – the processes that underlie our long history of economic development – into a very short time frame. Now, anyone who reads newspapers or even watches CNN is aware that the level of economic development varies tremendously between countries such as the United States, France, or Japan, and countries such as India, Ghana, or Mexico. We will discuss some of these differences more rigorously below. But for now we note that these differences across countries provide a sort of natural experiment, or laboratory, for examining some of the relationships between urbanization and economic development.

Other contributions to this volume, especially the other chapters in this part (by Rosenthal and Strange, Duranton, and O'Sullivan) discuss theoretical underpinnings for the relationship between urbanization and development – including a focus on trade, transaction costs, and agglomeration, as well as the "usual" textbook economies of scale. The other contributions also discuss empirical evidence in passing, often from firm or small area-level data. In this chapter we take another empirical, bird's-eye view, largely from the perspective of cross-country comparisons. Other than a motivating paragraph or two, we leave theory to other chapters, and we are not presenting state-of-the-art formal econometric tests; rather, we are presenting basic facts about economic development and urbanization.

The chapter relies heavily on simple analyses of individual country data, most from one of two sources. The World Bank's 2004 *World Development Indicators* database is the source for most of our basic data on population, incomes, and quality of life measures. The United Nations is the source for much of the basic data on the population of individual cities. Other sources are noted as we go. Elaboration of many results summarized in this chapter, including discussion of data issues, can be found in a longer companion publication, Malpezzi (2004). This chapter and a spreadsheet containing the basic data can be found through the author's website, located at www.bus.wisc.edu/realestate.

4.2 PATTERNS OF ECONOMIC DEVELOPMENT AND PATTERNS OF URBANIZATION

Alert readers are already suspicious. "Development" is a multidimensional, not to say slippery, concept. And the common practice of lumping the world's countries into two or three groups, such as "developing" (broadly, low-income countries), "transition" (largely formerly communist countries in Eastern or Central Europe, and the former Soviet Union), and "developed" is crude at best. It is nearly impossible to come up with a simple taxonomy that seems satisfactory.

Let us begin with the consideration of national income, or the closely related concept of gross domestic product (the total value of final goods and services produced within a country's borders in a year). Rich countries, such as the USA, Canada, most of Western Europe, and Japan, have per capita GDPs of the order of $30,000. The poorest countries, such as Angola, Laos, or Burma, have per capita GDPs of around $300. While everyone knows that poor countries contain some very rich individuals and rich countries some poor ones, the fact that national averages differ by about two orders of magnitude is astounding and begs for explanation: see Easterly (2001), Landes (1998), and Maddison (2001), for example.

It is also important to note that GDP per capita is a very useful and widely used measure of the complex and fuzzy notion we have of "development," but like all specific measures it is imperfect. For example, GDP is well known to undervalue nonmarket production, such as housework, and to fail to account fully for many environmental costs. On the other hand, a great many development outcomes – such as literacy, life expectancy, and the cleanliness of the environment – are correlated with income or GDP per capita, albeit imperfectly. Probably the most important development indicator that is largely uncorrelated with GDP per capita is the *distribution* of national income *among* households. But in the end if we have to pick a single measure for initial analysis, GDP per capita is clearly the place to start. To keep our analysis manageable, in this chapter we will focus on relationships between aspects of urbanization and GDP per capita, with a few notes about other measures; Malpezzi (2004) presents some additional detail.

4.2.1 The broad context of urbanization

DENSITIES ACROSS COUNTRIES The simplest way of thinking about urbanization is the existence of *above-average density*. Densities vary both across countries, and within them. We have noted that there are about 2 ha of land for every person in the world. The USA has an above-average endowment of raw land, by world standards: about 3.25 ha per person (or about 0.3 persons per hectare, or pph). But there are some other countries with even larger areas relative to their population. Canada has about 30 ha of raw land per person, Australia 40, Russia a dozen. At the other extreme, examples of higher densities include China's 0.75 ha per person (or about 1.35 pph), while India and Japan have about 3.5 pph, South Korea and the Netherlands about 4.75, Bangladesh 10, and Singapore and Hong Kong about 65 pph.

DENSITIES WITHIN COUNTRIES However, the figures presented in the previous paragraph are extremely gross; within countries, densities vary even more *within* than *across* countries. Within the USA, most of the country's population lives within a few hundred miles of the major coasts (including the Great Lakes); with a few exceptions, such as Denver and Salt Lake City, most of the country is fairly empty from, say, Minneapolis, until one reaches a hundred miles or so of the Pacific Ocean (Rappaport & Sachs 2003). This pattern is not atypical; many countries have some fairly dense areas and some (often large) "empty quarters." For example, almost 90 percent of Canada's population lives within 200 miles of the US border; most of China's population lives within 100 miles of the coast; and very few Australians live very far inland. Figure 4.1, from the Center for International Earth Science Information Network (www.ciesin.org), maps population density around the world. The average densities of US states range from about 4 pph in New Jersey (denser than India or Japan), 3 pph in Rhode Island (denser than Germany), and over 2 pph in Connecticut and Massachusetts to less than

Figure 4.1   World population density.
Source: The Center for International Earth Science Information Network
(CIESIN), Colombia University

0.05 pph in Nevada and New Mexico, and less than 0.2 pph in Alaska. To give
some idea of the statewise differences, if the entire USA *excluding Alaska* was settled
at New Jersey's density, the country would contain well over 3 billion people.

DENSITIES WITHIN CITIES   Within cities, densities vary even more remarkably.
Figure 4.2 presents simple density patterns for half a dozen illustrative locations;
these are taken from Bertaud and Malpezzi (2003), which presents data for a
larger sample of about 50 world cities. Among large cities in the USA, New York
has a central density approaching 200 pph, falling off rapidly to 50 pph or less
about 20 km from midtown Manhattan. But because the central area of the city
comprises a relatively small area, the average density of the New York metropolitan area is only about 40 pph. Chicago and Los Angeles (not shown here)
have central densities of 50–70 pph, and average densities of around 20; the
central density of Chicago is higher, but many readers will be surprised to find
that the average density of Los Angeles, 22 pph, is greater than that of Chicago,
16 pph. At the other extreme, the central density of Atlanta is only 25 pph,
although it exhibits an even faster drop-off with distance from the center, from a
lower base, and an average density of 6 pph.
   It turns out that this pattern, of a high central density, followed by a rapid
initial drop-off, that slows as we move out from the center, is a consequence of a
qualitatively similar pattern in land rents and real estate prices. These, in turn,
are derived from the value of access to a central location; patterns of rents,
property values, and population density are determined by the trade-off between
rent and transport costs between different locations. A very simple analysis of
the process can be found in Alonso (1960); for more details, see Daniel McMillen's
chapter in this volume. This density pattern at least *roughly* corresponds to reality
not only in most US cities, but in fact in most cities in market-oriented economies. It is sometimes referred to as a "negative exponential" pattern, because in a
very idealized form it can be summarized by

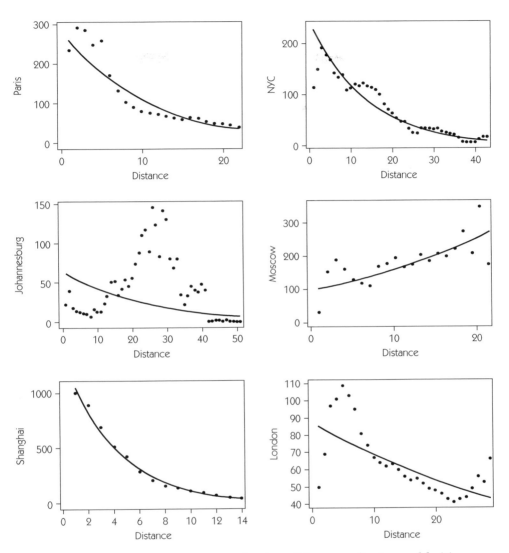

Figure 4.2   Average persons per hectare, 7 km annuli, six world cities.
Source: Bertaud and Malpezzi (2003)

$$y(x) = y_0 e^{-\beta x},$$

where x is the distance from the center, $y(x)$ is the density at any distance x, y_0 is the density at the center, β is a density parameter (often called the "gradient," because it is the rate of change of density as x increases), and "e" is the base of natural logarithms.

Notice that if we take logarithms of both sides, add a disturbance term u, and define $\alpha \equiv \ln(y_o)$, we obtain McMillen's equation (8.2). If β is close to zero, density approaches a flat "pancake"; as β rises in absolute value, density drops off very quickly at first; as β approaches 1 in absolute value, the density pattern starts to approach an L-shape.

Canadian cities tend to be denser than US cities, and European cities denser still. One of the densest large European cities is Paris, with a central density half again as large as that of New York, and an *average* density, 88 pph, greater than the *peak density* of Chicago or Los Angeles. Still, Paris follows the characteristic "negative exponential," even though the government intervenes heavily in land use, compared to US markets. French urban planners work within a market context, and make most of their decisions at least partly with economic feasibility in mind.

Moscow is an unusual city, and a very interesting case. It does not follow the negative exponential, and in fact density *increases* with distance from the center. Why? Until the demise of the Soviet Union, decisions about the size, timing, and location of real estate investments, including housing, were made by central planners. There was no such thing as a land or housing or real estate market; the state allocated "use rights" to enterprises and individuals according to criteria that seem strange to anyone familiar with a market economy. For example, much of the land that was allocated to factories on the then-outskirts of Moscow during the New Economic Program of the 1920s has remained as industrial land ever since, even as the Moscow grew up around it (Bertaud & Renaud 1997). Because no one – not even Soviet industrial enterprises – "owned" land and sales were forbidden, land was rarely redeveloped or densified. Whenever a new round of apartments was required by the plan, Soviet construction *kombinats* built a new ring on the then-outskirts of the city. Over time, as the city grew and building technology changed, the largest apartment structures (of poor construction quality, and even more poorly maintained) were the newest, built farthest out. Huge investments in transportation infrastructure were required to move Muscovites from these large peripheral housing projects to their jobs. Imagine if downtown Chicago had little in the way of high-rise apartment buildings or offices; that a few miles from Chicago's Loop there was a large belt of old rusting factories; and that these were ringed by huge blocks of 50 square meter apartments.

Not all communist cities were or are as strangely formed as Moscow. Broadly, Chinese cities developed in ways much more recognizable to a markets-oriented urban economist, even though they also lacked functioning land markets for many decades. Shanghai has a density of about 1,000 pph at the center and, as Figure 4.2 shows, the density falls off very rapidly with distance from the center. Certainly one reason why large Chinese cities developed very differently from Russian cities was that, especially 20–40 years ago as many of the cities were developing, most commuters walked or bicycled; the distance that one could walk in half an hour or so put a natural bound on housing location relative to jobs in China.

Perhaps today's worst locational pathologies can be found in cities that developed under South Africa's apartheid. Johannesburg has 15–40 pph in the inner, formerly all-white center; but, as Figure 4.2 shows, the density rises to 140 pph in

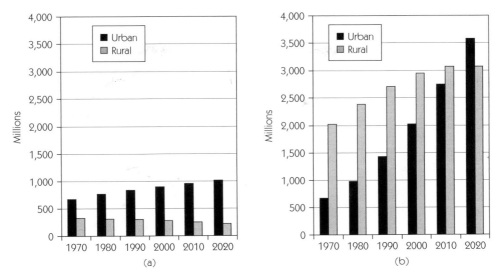

Figure 4.3 Population in (a) developed countries and
(b) developing countries.
Data source: the United Nations

the townships, 20–30 km from the center. Because many black South Africans work in central locations, this pattern implies that blacks incur enormous commuting costs. Johannesburg has peak commuting densities (persons traveling per hour along a given route) about the same as those of Chicago, but without Chicago's transportation infrastructure, greatly increasing the cost and length of commutes (and contributing to a high rate of deaths from traffic accidents).

WORLD URBANIZATION OVER TIME Figure 4.3 shows the growth of rural and urban populations for several recent years, with projections to 2020 from the United Nations (1995). Several important patterns are immediately obvious. Most people – almost 5 billion of the world's 6 billion people – live in "developing countries." Total population in developing countries has been growing at around 1.8 percent per year recently. Most of the inhabitants of developing countries live in rural areas, though that will change sometime in about two decades. Population growth in developing-country rural areas has been increasing at a decreasing rate for at least several decades. Developing-country urban populations have been increasing at an increasing rate, until the past few decades, when the rate of urban population growth has started to slow down as well.

In "developed" countries, Figure 4.3 shows clearly that most of the 1 billion inhabitants live in cities; that urban population has been growing slowly; and that rural population has been declining. In fact, the total population of the developed countries has only been growing at about 0.3 percent per year, and much of this is due to the much higher than average growth of the USA (around 1 percent). When the data for developed and developing countries in Figure 4.3

are added together, a remarkable fact emerges: sometime over the next decade, for the first time in human history, the majority of the world's population will live in cities.

Currently, in developing countries roughly half the growth in urban populations comes from rural to urban migration, and roughly half from internal growth. Growth rates for many cities ranging from 2 to 7 percent per year imply large investments in housing, infrastructure, and social overhead capital. For comparison, the median population growth rate of the 25 largest US cities was less than half a percent per year between 1980 and 1990. The fastest growing of these cities, San Diego, increased at about 2.4 percent per year, which would be considered slow in many developing countries.

But it would be incorrect to leave the impression that such growth is unprecedented. To take just a few examples, during the nineteenth century, London and Glasgow were among large cities in Britain that sustained rates of 2–3 percent per year. New York City grew 3–5 percent per year over much of the nineteenth century (Chandler & Fox 1974). In the mid- to late nineteenth century, Chicago was one of the fastest-growing cities that the world has ever seen. The population of Chicago was 30,000 in 1850, and it had grown to 1.7 million at the turn of the century, yielding an average annual growth rate of 8.4 percent! The *structure* of growth was different, however. During the nineteenth century, the *internal* growth of cities from net births was much slower; most growth came from *migration*. Comparing the cities of today and yesterday, migration was at least as strong during the Industrial Revolution; today's developing countries have added impetus from internal growth.

Two things *are* new about urbanization. The first is the large absolute *number* of people in cities, including the size of the largest cities, which *is* unprecedented. The second is the fact that most really large cities are now in the developing world. The latter is not exactly unprecedented; historically, cities such as Shanghai, Delhi, and Beijing were often among the world's largest. But earlier in this century most of the world's largest cities were in developed countries. By 1950, seven out of the top ten were from the developed world (New York, London, Tokyo, Paris, Shanghai, Moscow, Buenos Aires, Calcutta, Chicago (!) and the Ruhr agglomeration in Germany). [?] Figure 4.4, compiled from UN data, shows that the rapid growth of cities such as Mexico City enabled them to outstrip (comparatively) stagnant cities such as New York and London in just a few decades.

REGIONAL PATTERNS The aggregates in Figure 4.3 mask significant regional variation, among other things. Table 4.1 presents some basic statistics on urbanization and development by region; individual country data, and the regional definitions, are available at the author's website. As Table 4.1 shows, urbanization in Latin America is nearly as high as in Europe and North America, while in Asia and, especially, Africa it is quite low. These rates in turn mask variation even within regions; for example, Asia's low rate of urbanization is driven by low urbanization in China and India (21 and 26 percent, respectively). In East Asia, urbanization is quite high (77 percent in Japan and 67 percent in other East Asian countries – South Korea is more urbanized than the USA).

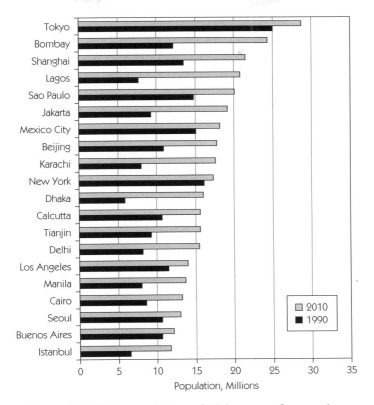

Figure 4.4   The population of 20 large agglomerations.
Data source: the United Nations

There is tremendous variation in most variables in each region; the variation across regions is sometimes surprisingly high. For example, the median or typical GDP per capita in the "developed" region is about $31,000; in most other regions the medians range from about $1,400 to $3,000, or an order of magnitude less. But the "elephant in the room" is the difference between other regions and Africa; African median GDP per capita is an astounding $370, or about two orders of magnitude less than in the richer developed countries.

Regional differences can also be found in each of the other basic statistics in Table 4.1. Consider growth in real GDP per capita. "On average," or when looking at medians, once again Africa stands out; as a region, sub-Saharan Africa has had little measured growth, or actual declines, over most of the past several decades (Collier & Gunning 1999). The transition economies of Eastern Europe and the former Soviet Union have also performed poorly. But it also bears repeating that even in fast-growing regions such as East Asia there are some poor performers; for example, in this period real incomes per capita hardly budged in the Philippines, and countries such as Laos and North Korea have certainly seen incomes declining substantially, although data are lacking. And within

Table 4.1   Basic statistics on urbanization and development, by region

	2000 GDP per capita, constant 1995 dollars	Annual growth in GDP per capita, 1980–2000, constant 1995 dollars	Percent urban, 2000	Annual growth in urban population, 1980–2000	Change in percent urban, 1980–2000
Developed world					
Mean	30,852	2.1%	76.5	0.8%	3.0
Median	31,278	1.9%	82.0	0.7%	2.6
Third quartile	32,924	2.3%	90.2	1.3%	4.8
First quartile	22,981	1.7%	67.4	0.3%	0.7
Maximum	56,206	4.9%	100.0	2.6%	12.6
Minimum	17,067	0.8%	21.4	0.1%	−3.5
Number of countries	22	22	29	24	29
East Asia and Pacific					
Mean	5,575	2.5%	48.0	3.2%	7.6
Median	1,460	1.8%	49.4	3.2%	5.7
Third quartile	5,145	4.0%	65.8	4.3%	11.7
First quartile	744	0.5%	24.1	2.2%	3.3
Maximum	28,462	8.3%	100.0	6.3%	25.0
Minimum	304	−0.5%	16.9	0.7%	−4.7
Number of countries	24	17	31	28	31
East/Central Europe and former Soviet Union					
Mean	3,081	−1.0%	59.5	0.5%	4.7
Median	2,471	0.0%	59.9	0.5%	5.9
Third quartile	4,464	0.6%	68.2	0.9%	7.4
First quartile	1,321	−2.7%	53.3	0.3%	2.4
Maximum	11,653	1.2%	74.5	2.0%	12.9
Minimum	470	−5.2%	41.6	−1.0%	−7.8
Number of countries	19	8	20	19	20
Latin America/Caribbean					
Mean	4,111	1.2%	63.6	2.4%	8.4
Median	3,292	0.7%	62.4	2.5%	7.6
Third quartile	5,314	2.6%	75.2	3.3%	13.4
First quartile	1,730	−0.1%	50.0	1.5%	2.3
Maximum	13,836	4.8%	100.0	5.1%	27.6
Minimum	368	−2.5%	34.1	−0.3%	−1.8
Number of countries	32	32	39	35	39
Middle East/North Africa					
Mean	5,148	1.3%	69.4	3.7%	13.2
Median	2,470	1.0%	67.4	3.7%	13.8
Third quartile	10,302	2.6%	87.2	4.5%	18.2
First quartile	1,365	0.1%	58.6	2.7%	5.1

Table 4.1 *(cont'd)*

	2000 GDP per capita, constant 1995 dollars	Annual growth in GDP per capita, 1980–2000, constant 1995 dollars	Percent urban, 2000	Annual growth in urban population, 1980–2000	Change in percent urban, 1980–2000
Maximum	14,098	4.1%	96.0	8.7%	44.4
Minimum	316	−2.7%	24.7	0.7%	−1.2
Number of countries	21	17	24	24	24
South Asia					
Mean	1,865	3.3%	35.3	2.8%	1.5
Median	497	3.5%	27.6	2.8%	1.5
Third quartile	1,354	3.6%	44.8	4.3%	5.2
First quartile	399	2.6%	22.8	1.3%	−2.3
Maximum	15,242	4.2%	98.8	5.7%	10.1
Minimum	242	2.5%	7.1	0.2%	−6.7
Number of countries	13	5	14	14	14
Sub-Saharan Africa					
Mean	930	−0.3%	37.3	5.0%	12.6
Median	370	−0.1%	34.2	5.1%	11.0
Third quartile	739	0.9%	47.0	5.8%	17.2
First quartile	218	−1.2%	27.5	4.3%	6.1
Maximum	6,557	4.8%	84.0	8.3%	38.7
Minimum	92	−7.1%	6.2	0.9%	−1.1
Number of countries	47	37	47	47	47

For individual country data and region definitions, see the author's website at www.bus.wisc.edu/realestate

sub-Saharan Africa there are isolated countries that have done well, such as Botswana (4.8 percent growth) and Mauritius (4.4 percent); although high levels of HIV infection cloud the outlook for Botswana, which has been one of the world's star economic performers for the past 35 years or so (Acemoglu, Johnson & Robinson 2003).

4.3 URBANIZATION AND DEVELOPMENT

The reasons why urbanization affects economic development were touched on briefly, and largely implicitly, in the thought experiment that opened this chapter. In technical language, we posited a world without trade, and without economies of scale, either internal to firms or external to them. In fact, cities are productive entities largely because of economies of scale, specialization, and trade.

Economies of scale can be subdivided into (1) the "usual kind" (i.e., the kind found in "Principles of Economics" textbooks, giving rise to U-shaped cost curves) that are internal to the firm; and (2) agglomeration economies, or economies of scale external to the firm, that shift cost curves down. Put another way, agglomeration economies are economies of scale from a spatial or locational externality. The return to an investment often depends on where it is made, and on what other investments are made nearby.

Agglomeration economies are commonly attributed to Alfred Marshall (1961 [1890]) and have been discussed by urban economists for many decades. Urban textbooks traditionally discuss two kinds of agglomeration economies: localization economies (external to the firm but internal to the industry) and urbanization economies (external to the firm and external to the industry). In some texts, localization economies are also termed "Marshall–Arrow–Romer" (MAR) externalities, especially if the focus is on dynamics. In a similar vein, urbanization economies are often termed "Jacobs externalities," after the noted urban essayist Jane Jacobs. Whatever terminology is used, in the former, it matters what kind of firms (or other entities) are nearby; it is localization or MAR economies that explain why high tech firms locate in Silicon Valley, or film producers in Los Angeles. On the other hand, urbanization or Jacobs externalities are about diversity, and they are driven primarily by the size of the urban area. Urbanization economies explain why certain specialized legal or financial services can be found in any large metropolitan area, whether it is New York, Chicago, Los Angeles, or some similar city.

The importance of specialization and trade has been a major part of economics since Adam Smith (1976 [1776]) and David Ricardo (1990 [1817]). How much trade takes place as a proportion of economic activity depends a lot on how we draw the boundaries for study. Despite the occasional space probe, or the alien capture of Elvis, there's virtually no trade between the earth as a whole and the rest of the universe. At the other extreme, as individuals most of us trade almost all of what we produce for goods and services produced by others. In the real-world continuum, the smaller the unit of analysis, the more essential trade will be. Small villages and towns will tend to trade a much higher fraction of their output than do large metropolitan areas. An illustrative guesstimate might be that most individuals trade 95 percent or more of their output, whereas a small village might trade something like 80 percent or more of its output, and a large city substantially less. At the US level, about 14 percent of output is exported across the national borders. Trade shares can be much higher for smaller countries, or even for large countries such as Germany that are part of a larger trading area. In any event, cities and urbanization are inherently trade enhancing. They reduce transaction costs and increase specialization and trade within their borders, and across borders.

The three explanations are not mutually exclusive, of course. They are usually all at work together, and they interact. For example, economies of scale, both the "usual kind" and agglomeration, can be thought of as being among the sources of Ricardian comparative advantage and therefore of specialization and trade. Also, many explanations for cities that at first seem "noneconomic" can be

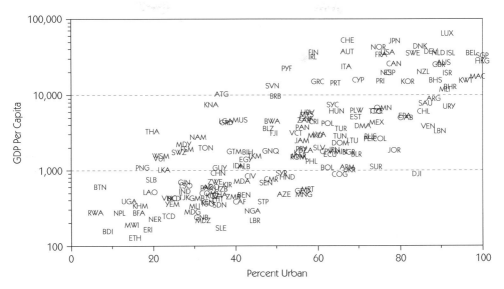

Figure 4.5 GDP per capita and urbanization.
Data source: the World Bank

subsumed within them. For example, early cities arose partly to facilitate defense from (violently) unfriendly neighbors. Economists would note that (at least at that time) there were economies of scale in the production of defense.

In the event, Figure 4.5 presents the familiar correlation between level of urbanization and GDP per capita (logarithmic scale). The finding is unsurprising, because the growth of cities has accompanied urban development for the past 5,000 years. It should surprise no one that the country of Singapore and China's autonomous province of Hong Kong are the most urbanized observations: each is essentially a large city. Among more urbanized countries, Japan, Denmark, and Luxembourg share fairly high incomes, while highly urbanized Lebanon, Djibouti, Venezuela, and Jordan are poorer than their urbanization would suggest. The USA is a little less urbanized than the simple correlation would imply. Among developing countries that are richer than average, given their lower level of urbanization, are some small islands such as St Kitts and Nevis, and Antigua, as well as some larger developing countries such as Thailand and Namibia. Burundi, Ethiopia and Eritrea, Sierra Leone, and Liberia are examples of countries that have low levels of urbanization but even lower incomes, compared to other countries.

This fairly strong correlation between output and urbanization does not, however, imply a simple causal relationship. For example, data presented in Malpezzi (2004) shows that rates of *change* in urbanization and of income over the past 20 years are not correlated. Why are levels correlated while changes are not? After all, today's *levels* are simply the sums of past *changes*. Here are some clues to solving the puzzle. The urbanization rate is bounded (Singapore's population will never be more than 100 percent urbanized) but GDP per capita is not. There is also some evidence that urbanization increases faster at lower levels, and that the growth of urbanization slows down as cities develop. Malpezzi and Lin (2000) study this further using a "panel" of 130 countries over 30 years, and they find that urban growth is a strong predictor of growth in GDP per capita – until a country exceeds an urbanization rate of about 30 percent, after which the contribution of urban growth tails off sharply. While this puzzle is not yet completely solved, in any event it is incontrovertible that *in the long run* economies urbanize as they develop.

4.3.1 Urban primacy

The emergence of a number of large "mega-cities," many in developing countries, was noted in Figure 4.4. Are, in fact, such cities too large? This is the question of primacy, or the size of large cities and their place in the urban structure of the country. Some of the research on this issue, such as that of Henderson (2003), has simply focused on the size of the largest city relative to the rest of the country's population. Other research, such as that of Ades and Glaeser (1995) or Hoselitz (1955), has focused on the types of large cities. The third related body of literature focuses on the emergence of what we usually call "mega-cities," defined variously but something like agglomerations of 10–20 million people.

In fact, a number of papers have argued that countries that are "too primate" or that have some very large cities relative to the size of their total population will find their growth and distribution adversely affected. However, the actual evidence for this is fragmented and somewhat fragile.

Figure 4.6 shows what is probably already obvious: that the degree of primacy, measured by the share of a country's population in its largest city, is strongly related to the size of the country. The largest urban agglomerations in the world are currently of the order of 10–20 million people, depending partly on how one draws the boundaries. But the range of population in countries ranges from well over a billion to under a million. Thus it is no surprise that very large countries such as the USA, India, and China have low values of the primacy index even though they contain some very large cities, such as New York, Shanghai and Beijing, and Calcutta. On the other hand, Singapore and Hong Kong are highly primate because 100 percent of each entity's population lives in one city.

Perhaps surprisingly, not all studies have controlled for the size of the country when looking at the effect of primacy. Malpezzi (2004) shows no obvious relationship between the usual primacy measure and GDP per capita growth rates in the succeeding period. On the other hand, primacy is related to the size of the country, as we have seen, and its region. Cities in Africa tend to be more primate than in Asia or Europe, for example. When we estimate a preliminary regression that controls for other determinants of primacy, including the size of the country and the region, we can then use the residual, or difference, between the actual primacy and that predicted from the regression equation to measure how primate a country is *after controlling for its size and region*. When we use this new variable, we actually find that countries that are more primate than would be expected

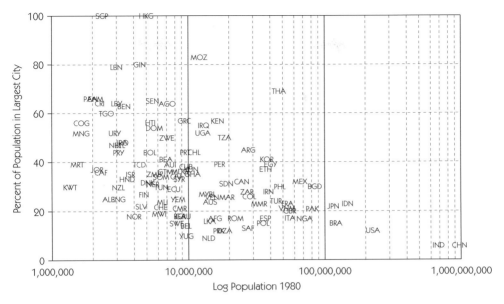

Figure 4.6 Primacy and size of country.
Data source: the World Bank

given their population and region at a baseline date *grow faster* going forward (see Malpezzi 2004). On the other hand, a careful study by Henderson (2003) finds some evidence that there may be an optimal level of primacy, depending on the size of the country and the level of economic development and that departures from the optimal degree of primacy in either direction may slow down growth rates. Clearly, more research is needed on primacy and related issues of the distribution of sizes of cities; with our current state of knowledge, it seems premature to pronounce many countries as "overly primate," as many policy-makers have done (or "underly primate," as less often happens!). Henderson (2003) makes the important related point that it is probably best to think of the optimum size of *a* city, in a particular country and at a particular time, rather than a single optimum size of *the* city that is best for all places and times.

4.4 CONCLUSION

I think my coauthors in this volume would not object too strenuously if I para-phrased Ross Perot during his presidential campaign some years ago to claim that, for all of us, "[we] find this stuff fascinating." If the reader is stimulated to investigate the relationship between urbanization and development further, this chapter has succeeded. In addition to reading the other chapters in this volume, and the literature cited therein, read Henderson (1988), Ingram (1998), and World Bank (1991). Download the raw data from the author's website and see what interesting patterns you can discern. This is an especially exciting time to study urban economics in general, and the distribution of urban population in particular. After millions of years of human history, and some ten millennia of some form of urban settlement, *for the first time in human history we are about to live in a world where more people live in cities than not.* Enjoy!

Acknowledgments

Constructive comments were provided by Kyu Sik Lee and Dan McMillen, and by an anonymous reviewer. However, they are not responsible for remaining shortcomings.

Bibliography

Acemoglu, D., Johnson, S., and Robinson, J. A. 2003: An African success story: Botswana. In D. Rodrik (ed.), *In Search of Prosperity: Analytic Narratives on Economic Growth*. Princeton, NJ: Princeton University Press.

Ades, A. and Glaeser, E. L. 1995: Trade and circuses: explaining urban giants. *Quarterly Journal of Economics*, 110(1), 195–227.

Alonso, W. 1960: A theory of the urban land market. *Papers of the Regional Science Association*, 6, 149–58.

Becker, C. M. and Morrison, A. M. 1999: Urbanization in transforming economies. In P. Cheshire and E. S. Mills (eds.), *Handbook of Regional and Urban Economics*, vol. 3: *Applied Urban Economics*. Amsterdam: North-Holland.

Bertaud, A. and Malpezzi, S. 2003: The spatial distribution of population in 48 world cities: implications for transition economies. ECA Region Working Paper, World Bank.

—— and Renaud, B. 1997: Socialist cities without land markets. *Journal of Urban Economics*, 41, 137–51.

Chandler, T. and Fox, G. 1974: *3000 Years of Urban Growth*. New York: Academic Press.

Collier, P. and Gunning, J. W. 1999: Explaining African economic performance. *Journal of Economic Literature*, 37, 64–111.

Easterly, W. R. 2001: *The Elusive Quest for Growth*. Cambridge, MA: The MIT Press.

Henderson, J. V. 1988: *Urban Development: Theory, Fact, and Illusion*. New York: Oxford University Press.

—— 2003: The urbanization process and economic growth: the so-what question. *Journal of Economic Growth*, 8, 47–71.

Hoselitz, B. F. 1955: Generative and parasitic cities. *Economic Development and Cultural Change*, 3(3), 278–94.

Ingram, G. K. 1998: Patterns of metropolitan development: What have we learned? *Urban Studies*, 35(7), 1,019–35.

Landes, D. S. 1998: *The Wealth and Poverty of Nations: Why Some are so Rich and Some so Poor*. New York: W. W. Norton.

Linden, E. 1996: The exploding cities of the developing world. *Foreign Affairs*, 75(1), 52–65.

Maddison, A. 2001: *The World Economy: A Millennial Perspective*. Paris: OECD.

Malpezzi, S. 2004: Global perspectives on urbanization, and its relationship to economic development. Working Paper, Center for Urban Land Economics Research, University of Wisconsin–Madison.

—— and Lin, S. 2000: Urban transitions and endogenous economic growth. Working Paper, Center for Urban Land Economics Research, University of Wisconsin–Madison.

Marshall, A. 1961 [1890]: *Principles of Economics*, 9th edn. New York: Macmillan.

Rappaport, J. and Sachs, J. 2003: The United States as a coastal nation. *Journal of Economic Growth*, 8, 5–46.

Ricardo, D. 1990 [1817]: *On the Principles of Political Economy and Taxation*, ed. P. Sraffa. Cambridge, UK: Cambridge University Press.

Smith, A. 1976 [1776]: *An Inquiry into the Nature and Causes of the Wealth of Nations*. Oxford: Clarendon Press.

United Nations 1995: *World Urbanization Prospects: The 1994 Revision*. New York, ST/ESA/SER.A/150.

World Bank 1991: *Urban Policy and Economic Development: An Agenda for the 1990s*. Washington, DC: The World Bank.

—— 2003: *World Development Indicators 2003*. CD-ROM database, Washington, DC: The World Bank.

PART II

Urban Land Use

Urban Land Use

Land rents, population densities, building heights, and lot sizes vary dramatically within urban areas. Central business areas may have 60-story office buildings, while small, two- or three-story buildings lie unused and boarded up just a mile or two away. Wealthy people often live near the central businesses areas, even while nearby neighborhoods suffer from extreme levels of poverty, crime, and unemployment. Many offices and other businesses have moved from the central city to suburbs that once were nearly entirely residential. Urban areas continue to expand by acquiring farmland at a rapid rate. The opening essay in this part, "The Spatial Pattern of Land Use in the United States," by Elena Irwin and Nancy Bockstael, documents changes in land-use patterns in the United States over the past several decades. Although 80 percent of the US population lives in urban areas, well under 10 percent of the land area is urbanized.

One of the hallmarks of urban economics is the development of a full general equilibrium model that helps to explain and predict these features of the urban landscape. The *monocentric city model* began as a description of a city that literally has only a single center, a central business district that is the site of all business. In the model, land rents, population densities, and building heights all decline with distance from the city center, because households will pay a premium to avoid costly commutes to their jobs in the central business district. The simplest version of the model produces remarkably accurate descriptions of older cities that are, in fact, dominated by a single center of employment. When distance to the central business district is interpreted as a more general measure of transport accessibility, the basic insights of the model continue to apply to modern "polycentric" cities. The model has been subjected to an extraordinary number of empirical tests, and has been extended to include such features as secondary employment centers, different income groups, durable buildings with costly demolition, traffic congestion, a variety of assumptions regarding the transportation network, a government sector, zoning, and so on.

The monocentric city model is an impressive achievement. It provides a flexible, unifying framework that helps provide a common language for both theoretical and empirical research in urban economics. Marvin Kraus's essay in this part, "Monocentric Cities," provides an excellent, accessible treatment of the theory behind the monocentric city model. In "Space in General Equilibrium," Marcus Berliant and Courtney LaFountain present a novel, primarily diagrammatic treatment of a simple general equilibrium version of the model. Using variants of standard Edgeworth box diagrams, Berliant and LaFountain show that the First and Second Welfare Theorems continue to apply when land is added to a simple exchange economy.

Urban land use and land rents were once a weak link in economic theory. Early models were designed to explain the variation in *agricultural* land rents. David Ricardo developed the earliest model in his book, *Principles of Political Economy and Taxation*, which was published in 1821. In Ricardo's model, land rents vary according to the fertility of the soil. High-fertility soil is less costly to farm than lower-quality land; it requires less fertilizer and less backbreaking work to prepare it for tilling. Thus, farmers will be willing to pay more for high-fertility land. But in the end, competition assures that profits are equal to zero everywhere. This competition for high-fertility land causes land rents to vary over space: land rents will be high where soil fertility is high.

Although this simple version of Ricardo's model is still applicable to rural areas, it does little to explain land rents and land use in urban areas. The land in most cities in the world could conceivably be converted to some type of agricultural use, but clearly the extraordinarily high prices for land – which can amount to millions of dollars for an acre – have nothing to do with the fertility of the soil. Even in rural areas, soil fertility is not the only factor explaining the variation in land rents. The basic concept of "Ricardian rents" generalizes, however. For example, the same sort of competitive bidding process results in differences in such natural amenities as microclimates and a view being capitalized into land values.

The first attempt to incorporate transportation into a model of land rents was a model published in a book by Johann von Thünen in 1826. Von Thünen developed an early model of rural land markets in which land rents vary according to access to a central marketplace. In von Thünen's model, the fertility of the soil is the same everywhere, but farmers must ship their product to a central marketplace in order to sell it. Since shipping is costly, farmers will bid more for land closer to the marketplace. Although it precedes the monocentric model by more than a century, von Thünen's model is the direct predecessor of the monocentric city model. Alonso's (1964) early statement of the monocentric city model extended von Thünen's model to an urban context. In Alonso's version of the model, urban households receive utility from land and a numeraire good. Land does not vary in any way except that sites closer to the central business district offer households lower commuting costs. In an attempt to avoid costly commutes, households are willing to pay a premium for sites closer to the central business district. Working independently, Richard Muth and Edwin Mills extended this model to include a housing production sector. In the Muth–Mills version of the model, households receive utility from housing, which is built by housing producers who combine land and capital to produce the final product. In this version of the model, house prices, land rents, building heights, and population density all decline with distance from the central business district.

Alonso developed one of urban economics' critical analytical tools. The *bid-rent function* shows the maximum amount that a household or a business will pay for a unit of land as a function of distance from the central business area. Land is allocated to the sector that will pay the most for it – the sector with the highest bid-rent function. The boundary between the urban area and the agricultural periphery is the point at which urban bid rents no longer exceed the amount that farmers will pay for land. Population growth and an improved transportation network cause the urban area to expand at the expense of the agricultural hinterland. This view of how land-use decisions are made is in stark contrast to the pejorative catchword, "sprawl." Although the term sprawl is seldom defined precisely, it tends to be associated with low-density suburban developments that can only be checked by restrictive zoning, development taxes, and planning. Urban economists are more likely to view low-density development and the loss of farmland as a direct result of urban population growth, rising incomes, and reduced transportation costs. In other words, "sprawl" is a market outcome that is predicted by urban economic theory rather than a failure of the land market.

The field of urban economics has enjoyed a close cooperation between theory and empirical work. The essay by Daniel McMillen, "Testing for Monocentricity," reviews empirical methods used to test some of the implications of the monocentric city model. Early versions of the monocentric city model were subjected to myriad empirical tests, which generally supported the model and which often led to more realistic extensions of the model. Currently, the same process is under way in developing theoretical and empirical analyses of polycentric cites – urban areas with large areas of employment outside the traditional central business district. Recent empirical work takes advantages of the significant advances that have been made over the past couple of decades in econometrics. However, earlier empirical studies have seldom been revised in light of advances in econometric methods and improvements in data sets. Although it is not a high priority in the field, it would be useful to replicate early tests of the monocentric model using modern econometric methods and expanded data sets. Polycentric cities, though, offer particularly fruitful and challenging opportunities for further theoretical and empirical studies.

Bibliography

Alonso, W. 1964: *Location and Land Use*. Cambridge, MA: Harvard University Press.

CHAPTER FIVE

The Spatial Pattern of Land Use in the United States

Elena G. Irwin and Nancy E. Bockstael

5.1 INTRODUCTION

There is currently great interest in understanding and managing the impacts of land-use changes on individual and social well-being. This interest stems from concerns over fiscal, economic, environmental, and social issues related to changes in the spatial pattern of urban land use, including urban decentralization and the conversion of rural land to low-density urban uses. Understanding the forces that affect land-use change requires first getting the facts right. In this chapter, we attempt to describe changes in land-use patterns in the United States over the past several decades and to a lesser extent link them to economic theories designed to explain these changes. In pursuing this course, we draw on papers that have empirically measured land-use patterns or empirically tested economic theories about those patterns. With regard to some issues, the results are robust. But with regard to others, most notably those related to low-density development, considerable uncertainty remains, uncertainty that can be traced to data problems that continue to plague land-use analysis.

The chapter begins by presenting data on the major land uses of the USA and changes in those land uses in the recent past, especially conversion of rural to urban land. Some basic facts are examined regarding urban land, including its amount, regional variation, and density, and questions are raised about the ability of current data to measure current land-use phenomena accurately. To illustrate the potential problems, we draw on high-resolution land-use data available for the state of Maryland. We then review what we believe to be major trends in urban land-use changes that have received both theoretical and empirical attention in the economics literature. Some thoughts on the current state of knowledge regarding urban land-use trends, the limitations of available information, and the potential biases that may result from these limitations are included in the conclusions.

5.2   Land-Use Patterns and Changes in Patterns

5.2.1   Major land uses

According to a recent report by the Economic Research Service of the US Department of Agriculture (2003), rural land constitutes the vast majority of the 1.9 billion acres comprising the continental USA. As of 1997, rangeland comprised 30.5 percent, forest 29.2 percent, and cropland 24 percent. In comparison, only 3.4 percent was considered to be urban land; that is, any developed land with infrastructure. Recreation and wildlife areas (largely national and state parks, forests, and wilderness areas) accounted for another 5 percent. Substantial regional variations exist in these shares, as described in Figure 5.1.

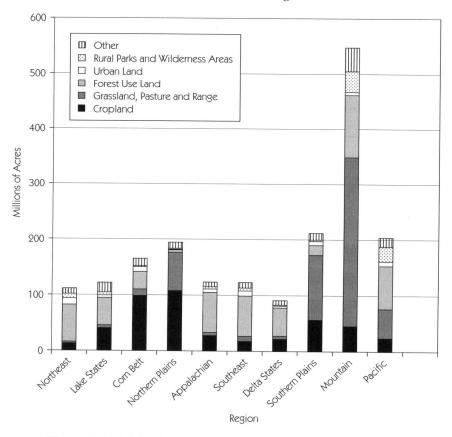

Figure 5.1   Major land uses by region of the USA in 1997.
Source: US Department of Agriculture (2003)

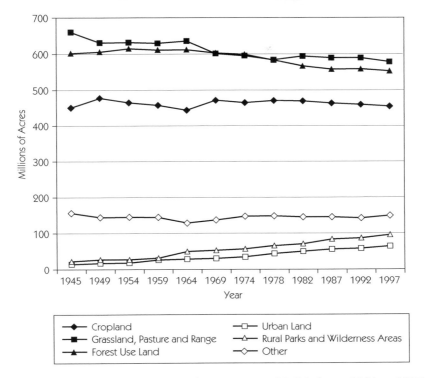

Figure 5.2   Major land uses in the continental USA from 1945 to 1997.
Source: US Department of Agriculture (2003)

We draw on this same report to illustrate trends in major land-use classes over time (Figure 5.2). According to the US Department of Agriculture (USDA), urban, recreational and wilderness lands have expanded steadily since World War II, grazing land and forests have declined, and cropland has remained relatively stable, having varied by no more than 8 percent over the period.

The aggregate statistics conceal considerable movement among land-use categories. Table 5.1, also from the same USDA source, reports that between 1982 and 1992, far more transitions occurred *among* the agricultural/forest categories than from these categories to urban uses. Of the 57.8 million acres of rural land that changed land use, 54 percent (31 million acres) was converted to another rural land use, 11 percent (6.6 million acres) to federally owned land, and 23 percent (13.1 million acres) to an urban land use. Approximately 25 percent of this rural to urban conversion involved "prime farmland" as classified by USDA. However, no significant amount of land is reported to have moved out of the urban land-use category during the period. According to these statistics, urban development appears to be effectively irreversible.

Although 20 percent of the stock of *urban* land in 1992 had been rural as of 1982, these rural land losses represented only about 1 percent of the stock of *rural*

Table 5.1   US land-use transitions, 1982–92 (millions of acres)

		Cropland	Rangeland	1992 Forest	Urban	Federal	Other
	Cropland	526	3.5	11.7	6.1	1.3	4.1
	Rangeland	8.8	391.7	1.5	1.9	3.3	1.4
1982	Forest	4.4	1.1	379.6	5.1	2	1.6
	Urban	0	0	0	51.9	0	0
	Federal	0.7	2	0.7	0	401.1	0.2
	Other	2.4	0.3	1.6	0.2	0.3	74.3

Source: US Department of Agriculture (2003)

land as of 1982. Based on the figures in Table 5.1, annual rates of conversion to urban land were 0.1 percent for all rural land, 0.11 percent for cropland, 0.05 percent for rangeland, and 0.13 percent for forest land. Although some estimates of urban land and conversion rates are higher, as we review below, none of these studies supports the popular notion that rural lands are disappearing at "alarming" rates. Yet, rural lands may be locally, if not globally, scarce – especially in the vicinity of expanding urban areas. This suggests that, from the perspective of the majority of the population, rural land may indeed be disappearing rapidly.

5.2.2   Revisiting estimates of total urban land

In the previous section we relied on US Department of Agriculture (2003) reported figures, compiled from nine federal agencies. But this obscures the remarkable variation that exists among estimates of urban land. Recent estimates of the amount of urban land in the continental USA in the early to mid-1990s have ranged from 1.1 percent to 7.2 percent of the total land area. Estimates of the average annual increase in urban land over the past 20–25 years vary from a low of 0.75 million acres to a high of 2.1 million acres. The disparities are due to differences in spatial resolution and accuracy of data, and to the different methods of data categorization. They are also due to differences in the definition of urban (or developed) land. While defining "what is urban" is relatively clear in the built-up areas of a city, the distinction becomes more difficult as the density of built structures declines. One house on a 100-acre farm is clearly rural land, but what do we call the same land if it is divided into a 5-acre minimum lot subdivision with 20 houses? This is not a trivial question, as the amount of low-density development has been increasing dramatically over the past few decades. USDA estimates that between 1994 and 1997, 10–22 acre lot sizes accounted for 55 percent of the increase in land dedicated to housing in the USA, and lots greater than 1 acre accounted for over 90 percent of this land (Heimlich & Anderson 2001, p. 14).

As of 2000, the US Census counts as urban all land that is located within an Urbanized Area (UA) or Urban Cluster (UC), delineations based on density thresholds and minimum populations. (UCs contain 2,500–50,000 people, and UAs contain at least 50,000 people, with both having cores with a density of at least 1,000 people per square mile.) Although not a direct measure of urban land area, these data are one of the very few sources for nationally consistent estimates of urban areas over time, making them the most commonly used data to track urban land change.

Problems with using the Census definition to measure urban land are well known. Undeveloped land, such as parks and other open space, located within a UC or UA will be counted as developed; developed land outside the UC and UA polygons will be omitted. To examine the possible magnitude of these errors, we compare the 2000 Census data with higher-resolution data on land use in Maryland, produced by the Maryland Department of Planning (MDP). These data are not perfect, but they are superior to anything else we have. They are based on a combination of high-altitude aerial photography and satellite imagery, and are further refined using parcel-level data from a digitized version of the state Division of Taxation and Assessment database. These data are particularly useful because they include several categories of residential land, including low-density development of 0.2 to 2.0 dwelling units per acre. Figure 5.3 illustrates the spatial comparison of Census UA and UC boundaries (designated by the black lines) versus MDP-designated developed areas. The existence of white space within the Census urban boundaries denotes open space categorized by Census as urban and the gray areas outside these boundaries indicate developed land that is missed by the Census definition. The comparison illustrates that in Maryland, where low- and medium-density development at the rural–urban fringe is common, the Census definition misses large tracts of developed land. Statewide, approximately 675,000 acres are common to both the Census and MDP designations of urban land, but approximately 501,000 acres considered undeveloped by the state mapping process fall within an UA or UC, and about 492,000 acres considered developed by MDP fall outside these Census areas.

The seriousness of the two types of errors varies across counties in a systematic way. Table 5.2 shows that the more urbanized a county, the greater is the percentage of undeveloped land that is counted as urban using Census urban designations. Conversely, the less urban a county, the greater is the percentage of developed land that is misclassified as rural. Even in the most urbanized counties, 38 percent of low-density residential land is missed by Census urban designations. This proportion grows to 89 percent in the least urbanized counties.

The magnitude of error is not surprising. Nelson (1992) reports that during the period from 1960 to 1990, population growth in exurban counties (regions outside established urban areas, but within their "commutershed") outpaced suburban and urban population growth. According to Heimlich and Anderson (2001, p. 14), nearly 80 percent of residential land developed between 1994 and 1997 was located outside of metropolitan areas.

In an effort to address the omission of low-density development, US Department of Agriculture (2003) has used the American Housing Survey (AHS) to

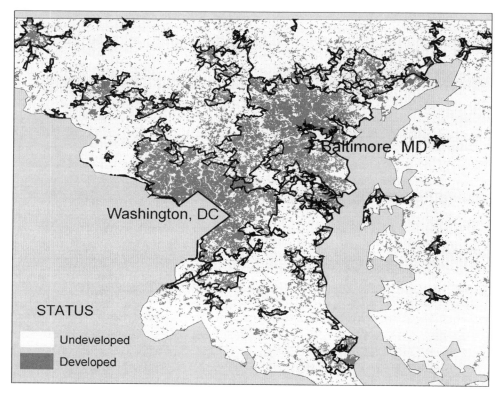

Figure 5.3   A comparison of MDP developed land and US Census Bureau
urban areas, central and eastern Maryland, 2000.
Sources: US Census Bureau, 2000; Maryland Department of Planning (MDP), 2000

estimate rural residential land, defined as nonfarm land consisting of houses and associated lots located outside of urban areas. Using the Census definition of urban areas, alone, urban land was estimated at 64 million acres (3.4 percent of the continental USA) in 1997, and growing by an average of 1.07 million acres per year since 1980. Including the nonfarm rural residential areas identified by the AHS raises the estimate to 137 million acres or 7.2 percent – with an estimated 2.1 million acres of growth in urban land per year.

The National Resources Inventory (NRI), yet another source of land-use data, estimates land cover/use at national and subnational scales based on a longitud- inal sample of about 800,000 sites located on nonfederal US land. Developed land categories include large (greater than 10 acres) and small (0.25 to 10 acres) urban and built-up areas, where the latter term refers to areas of residential, commer- cial, industrial or institutional use, but includes nonurban uses of less than 10 acres completely surrounded by urban land. A third developed category is rural transportation networks. According to these definitions, the total developed land area in the continental USA was 97.6 million acres (5 percent of the total land

Table 5.2 A comparison of US Census Bureau urban areas and Maryland Department of Planning (MDP) developed land by county type, Maryland, 2000

Large urban counties

		MDP						
		Commercial/ high-density residential		Low-density residential		Undeveloped		Total
Census		Acres	Percent	Acres	Percent	Acres	Percent	
Rural	Acres	18,969	6%	25,169	8%	272,493	86%	45%
	Percent	8%		38%		68%		
Urban	Acres	217,946	57%	40,660	11%	125,477	33%	55%
	Percent	92%		62%		32%		
Total		236,915	34%	65,829	9%	397,970	57%	700,714

Large suburban and exurban counties

		MDP						
		Commercial/ high-density residential		Low-density residential		Undeveloped		Total
Census		Acres	Percent	Acres	Percent	Acres	Percent	
Rural	Acres	61,576	4%	148,246	9%	1,366,585	87%	78%
	Percent	21%		68%		92%		
Urban	Acres	238,592	55%	71,087	16%	126,080	29%	22%
	Percent	79%		32%		8%		
Total		300,168	15%	219,333	11%	1,492,665	74%	2,012,166

Small urban and nonmetropolitan counties

		MDP						
		Commercial/ high-density residential		Low-density residential		Undeveloped		Total
Census		Acres	Percent	Acres	Percent	Acres	Percent	
Rural	Acres	48,432	2%	141,064	5%	2,821,980	94%	96%
	Percent	47%		89%		98%		
Urban	Acres	55,071	41%	17,314	13%	60,511	46%	4%
	Percent	53%		11%		2%		
Total		103,503	3%	158,378	5%	2,882,491	92%	3,144,372

Maryland county types: Large urban counties = central counties in metropolitan areas of 1 million or more. Large suburban and exurban counties = all outlying counties in metropolitan areas of 1 million or more. Small urban and nonmetropolitan counties = central counties in metropolitan areas of 250,000 people or less and all nonmetropolitan counties.
Sources: US Census Bureau, 2000; Maryland Department of Planning (MDP), 2000

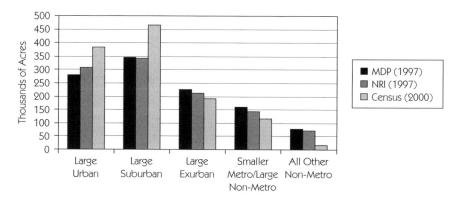

Figure 5.4   A comparison of total urban land estimates for Maryland
by county type.

Maryland county types: Large urban = central counties in metropolitan areas of
1 million population or more. Large suburban = adjacent counties in metropolitan
areas of 1 million population or more. Large exurban = nonadjacent counties in
metropolitan areas of 1 million population or more. Smaller metro/large nonmetro
= counties in metropolitan areas of 250,000 population or less or nonmetropolitan
counties that are adjacent to metropolitan areas with 20,000 urban population
or more. All other nonmetro = nonmetropolitan counties that are adjacent
to metropolitan areas with 2,500 to 20,000 urban population.
Sources: Maryland Department of Planning (MDP), 1997; National Resources
Inventory (NRI), 1997; US Census Bureau, 2000

area) in 1997, with an estimated average increase of 1.65 million acres per year
since 1982. Small sample sizes prevent these data from being reliable estimates
of land use even at the county level. In addition, federal lands, which account
for about 20 percent of the land area of the continental USA, are excluded
and therefore development on federal lands is omitted from these estimates.
But despite its limitations, a comparison of the 1997 NRI estimates (the latest for
which we have regional figures) with 1997 Maryland Department of Planning
(MDP) land-use data yields a surprising correspondence at aggregate levels for
groups of counties. The estimated amount of urban land for the most urban
counties is overestimated by about 9.5 percent and underestimated for the least
urban counties by about 11.6 percent, discrepancies far smaller than that between
Census and MDP data (see Figure 5.4). Whether this correspondence would be
sustained in other geographical areas is difficult to say. In any event, the fact that
NRI data cannot be compared at a resolution less than the multiple county level
prevents its use in analysis of *spatial pattern* at anything but the coarsest level.

The appeal of Census data is its availability in fairly consistent form over time.
Satellite imagery promises to provide another consistent time series of land-use
data. Both the National Land Cover Data (NLCD) and the Multi-Resolution Land
Characteristics (MRLC) Consortium data are based on satellite images from 1992,
and scenes from the new NLCD based on images from 2001 are beginning to be

released. In an attempt to estimate land-use change over time without relying on Census data, Burchfield, Overman, Puga, and Turner (forthcoming) compared 1992 NLCD data with urban land estimates from the Geographic Information Retrieval and Analysis System (GIRAS). The latter, based on aerial photography from 1971 to 1982 (circa 1976), shows approximately 24 million acres in urban land, as compared to the NLCD estimates of about 36 million acres in 1992.

Satellite imagery is an appealing source of land-use data, but it is substantively different from aerial photography or other "on the ground" sources. It relates strictly to land cover that does not always map nicely into land-use categories and is impaired by cloud cover and tree canopy. Translation of images is dependent on classification methods, with the most notable difficulties arising, once again, in the recognition of low-density residential use, where the footprint of the built structure corresponds to a very small percentage of the land parcel (McCauley & Goetz 2004). Figure 5.5 provides a visual representation of this point for two representative areas in Howard County, Maryland, that vary by development density. Areas that are developed (including developed open space and low-, medium- and high-intensity developed) according to NLCD data from 2001 are overlaid with land-parcel boundaries and building footprints, both produced by the Howard County Office of Planning. The results illustrate the ability of the satellite data to record the location of buildings in more densely developed areas, which corresponds reasonably well to the land use of parcels in these areas (Figure 5.5(a)), but the very limited ability of satellite data to capture the presence of buildings and development in less densely developed areas (Figure 5.5(b)).

These images are representative of the ability of satellite data to record higher-versus lower-density development. We compared the NLCD 2001 land-cover data with the Maryland Department of Planning (MDP) 2000 data for a nine-county region in central Maryland that encompasses urban, suburban, and exurban areas of the Washington, DC – Baltimore region. While 24 percent of all land identified by MDP as being in medium- or high-density residential land use is classified as undeveloped by NLCD, 82 percent of all land identified by MDP as low-density residential land is classified as undeveloped by NLCD.

5.2.3   Urban density estimates

Given the popular lament that land is being developed at faster rates than the rate of population growth, we consider the evidence from studies that have measured urban development density and some that have tracked changes in these densities across time. While some studies have defined urban density as the ratio of population to total land area, we consider only those that measure population relative to the amount of urban land, which provides a more accurate measure of the land-use pattern. The evidence supports the notion of declining densities, although results are subject to caveats about how well data sources measure developed land. Using a combination of NRI urban land designations and Census population extrapolations, Fulton, Pendall, Nguyen, and Harrison (2001) estimate a decline in average density from 5.0 to 4.2 people per urbanized acre for 281 metropolitan areas over the period from 1982 to 1997. According to

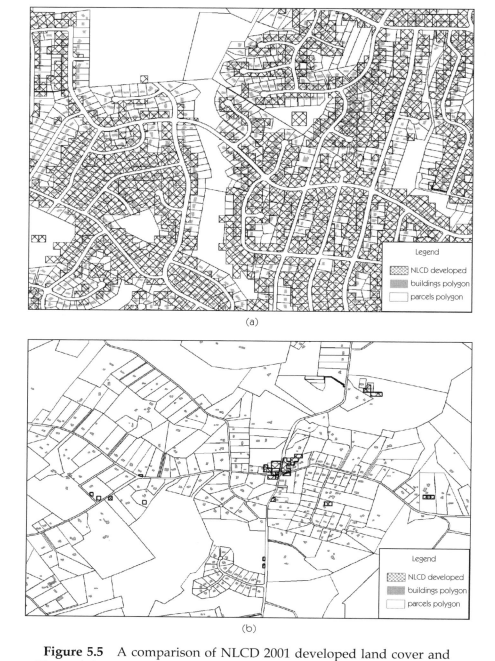

(a)

(b)

Figure 5.5 A comparison of NLCD 2001 developed land cover and Howard County, Maryland, building footprints and parcel boundaries. (a) More densely developed area, eastern Howard County; (b) less densely developed area, western Howard County.

Sources: US Geological Survey, National Land Cover Dataset, 2001; Howard County Office of Planning, 2002

their figures, only 6 percent of these metropolitan areas did not decrease in density during this time period. Outside metropolitan areas, they estimate declines in average density from 4.5 to 3.6 people per urbanized acre. Glaeser and Kahn (2004) suggest similar average density declines from 5.3 to 4.8 people per acre between 1982 and 1995, calculated for 68 select metropolitan areas.

As always, regional trends differ. Fulton, Pendall, Nguyen, and Harrison (2001) find that while the rest of the country grew less dense over time, metropolitan areas in the West became more dense, adding population at approximately three times the density of other regions. High growth in both population and amount of developed land in the South contrasts with low population growth and large increases in developed land in much of the Midwest and Northeast, contradicting the hypothesis that high rates of population growth contribute to low-density development. While many fast-growing areas also grew rapidly in developed land (e.g., Atlanta, Seattle, and Los Angeles), many of the metropolitan areas with large increases in developed land have experienced only modest population growth (e.g., Chicago, Cleveland, Pittsburgh, and St Louis). Comparing the 1976 GIRAS and 1992 NLCD data sets, Burchfield, Overman, Puga, and Turner (forthcoming) determined that no state's aggregate urban areas increased in density, while many states witnessed substantial decreases between the mid-1970s and the early 1990s.

5.3   Theories and Evidence on Trends in Urban Land-Use Patterns

Despite inconsistencies in data, a consensus has emerged on one dominant trend – the decentralization of urban areas. Two longstanding theories of urban location, the monocentric model and the Tiebout model of household location, offer broad explanations of population decentralization. The monocentric model predicts that decentralization occurs as the result of a decrease in transportation costs or rising incomes, both of which have occurred over the past century. The Tiebout model of household location views households as "voting with their feet" by moving to the local jurisdiction providing the bundle of public goods and services that maximizes their utility subject to their budget constraint, where the latter includes the local jurisdictional tax needed to pay for public goods. Under this theory, perceived urban ills (e.g., higher crime rates, lower school quality, more congestion, racial tensions) push households with higher incomes to live in lower-density, suburban communities that offer higher-quality public goods and services and more homogeneous populations. Both the monocentric model and Tiebout hypothesis suggest that the extent of decentralization may differ across cities due to differences in income levels and commuting costs or differing levels of urban services and amenities.

Researchers attempting to empirically test hypotheses about changing decentralization have encountered difficulties in characterizing the spatial representation of density. The most basic representation of density pattern, based on the monocentric model, is a population density gradient that measures the change in population per unit area as distance from the central city increases. Changes in density patterns over time are represented by changes in the slope or curvature of the density gradient. But researchers have found that decentralization can manifest itself in more complex forms that are much harder to represent using a simple density gradient measure, including suburban subcentering, "fractal cities," and fragmented residential development. A consensus does not exist on the prevalence of some of these more complex urban patterns, due in part to differences in the types of data used to measure these patterns and the spatial scale of analysis. The fact that decentralization is dynamic rather than static adds a further challenge. Measurement inherently demands consistent, spatially explicit time series data. These data must be able to detect changes in density (such as infill) in already developed areas and account for the changing spatial extent of the analysis as development emerges in previously rural areas.

5.3.1 Urban density gradients

Urban spatial pattern has often been characterized in terms of a population density gradient – the slope of the relationship between population per unit area and distance to city center (for a comprehensive review, see the chapter by Daniel McMillen in this volume). Studies have typically found these functions to be downward sloping with distance and flattening substantially over time, supporting the notion of increasing decentralization of cities.

McDonald (1989) reviews attempts to explain differences in gradients across cities and identifies a few consistent findings. Some have no obvious connection to either the monocentric or Tiebout models, such as the prevalence of relatively flatter gradients in urban areas with large populations and relatively steeper gradients in older urban areas. But flatter gradients do appear to be associated with higher household incomes, as the monocentric city model suggests, and substandard housing and high ratios of nonwhite households, as the Tiebout theory suggests. Jordan, Ross, and Usowski (1998) find that, for a subset of cities that best matches the monocentric structure, the rate of decentralization in the 1980s was significantly accelerated by the proportion of city residents living in poverty. Anas, Arnott, and Small (1998) estimate a 26 percent decline in the average density gradient for US cities due to changes in transport costs and average income levels between 1950 and 1970, but find that declining transportation costs and increases in income levels do not come close to explaining the full magnitude of the decentralization that has occurred.

Density gradient analysis implicitly assumes continuous development, but in reality a nontrivial amount of vacant land exists in most cities, being more prevalent with distance from the city center. Mieszkowski and Smith (1991) investigate the extent to which declining density gradients are a spurious result due to the spatial pattern of vacant land, and do so using 1980 Census tract data in Houston. By ignoring vacant land, they estimate a density gradient of −0.05, only a fraction of the gross density gradient (−0.148) estimated including vacant land.

Researchers have also come to question the appropriateness of the commonly used negative exponential density function, suggested by monocentric city theory, and have employed more flexible functional forms. Others have suggested that the negative density gradient, if it does provide a good fit to the data, is simply an artifact of history. Urban patterns are seen as the result of a cumulative aggregation of past development, with densities reflecting the economic conditions that prevailed at the time the houses were constructed. In contrast to the monocentric theory, which takes capital as malleable, development may be largely irreversible and changes in densities through redevelopment the exception rather than the rule. Irreversibility implies that densities need not be monotonically decreasing with distance, and if redevelopment does happen, it may produce discontinuities in the density gradient.

5.3.2   Suburban subcenters

Up to this point, we have treated urban spatial pattern as though it were solely a function of residential land use. A fundamental dimension of urban structure and urban decentralization is the spatial pattern of economic activity – often measured in terms of employment. Comparisons of density gradients of employment over time typically support the decentralization hypothesis, but simple density gradients may be even less applicable for employment than for population. Empirical tests across cities of polycentric versus monocentric urban form almost uniformly reject the monocentric assumption. If most urban areas are polycentric in nature, then an important dimension of changing urban spatial pattern is the emergence of subcenters or edge cities – concentrations of employment outside the central business district.

Many theoretical models explain subcentering as the result of a tension between agglomeration economies, providing incentives for firms to cluster together in space, and countervailing dispersive forces, such as rising land rents, competition among firms, congestion externalities, or employee commuting costs. The resulting size, location, and number of clusters depend on the relative strengths of the agglomerative and offsetting forces, and on how rapidly these effects diminish with increasing distances between firms. Other theories of edge city location explain their emergence as the result of strategic actions by large-scale developers (or municipalities) who engineer the relocation of many individual firms and households through coordinated development. Decisions regarding edge city location are modeled as a function of transportation cost/land rent trade-offs, as well as other distance-dependent considerations.

Empirical work on urban subcenters has focused chiefly on questions of measurement: How does one identify a subcenter, so that the number and size of subcenters can be compared over time and over cities and the determinants of subcenters identified? Varying definitions have been proffered in the literature based on different total employment and employment density thresholds. Guiliano and Small's (1991) definition claims to be less arbitrary and more consistently applicable across the USA. They define a subcenter as a zone with employment density of at least 10 workers per acre and total employment of at least 10,000, yielding 28 distinct subcenters in Los Angeles, 15 in Chicago, and 22 in San Francisco as of 1990. By this definition, most large metropolitan areas can be characterized as containing 20 or more subcenters (Anas, Arnott & Small 1998).

By reworking Fujita and Ogawa's (1982) theoretical model of urban spatial structure, McMillen and Smith (2003) show that the number of subcenters should increase as total population and per unit commuting costs increase. Using a locally weighted regression technique to identify subcenters, they estimate a model of the number of subcenters within an urban area and find support for these hypotheses. The model predicts that a city's first subcenter will form at an approximate population level of 2.68 million and the second subcenter at about 6.74 million.

5.3.3 Discontinuous residential development

Residential development is commonly perceived as occurring in a leapfrog or discontinuous pattern, especially in outer suburban and exurban areas. The magnitude of these patterns depends on the spatial scale at which they are analyzed. In describing urban land-use change using the circa 1976 GIRAS and 1992 NLCD data, Burchfield, Overman, Puga, and Turner (forthcoming) determine that 75 percent of observed land conversion to urban use was located within 1.5 km of existing development. This suggests that, if leapfrogging does occur, it occurs at a finer scale. Using parcel- or subdivision-level data, studies such as Irwin and Bockstael (2002), Carrión-Flores and Irwin (2004), and Stanilov (2002) have found pervasive patterns of dispersion, fragmentation, and low-density development, usually in exurban areas. Evidence suggests that these patterns are persistent over time; for example, Carrión-Flores and Irwin find that despite a dramatic increase in the amount of residential land between 1956 and 1996 in their Ohio exurban study region, residential development maintained a dispersed pattern rather than infilling over time. However, because these studies look at parcel- and subdivision-level data, they are necessarily limited in their geographical extent.

Leapfrogging has been traditionally explained within the context of the monocentric model as the result of a dynamically efficient market process in which development is irreversible and future returns to development are expected to increase at a sufficient rate. This prevalent theory of leapfrogging implies that leapfrogging will be temporary at any given location, but that the development "frontier" may always exhibit this pattern. Some have demonstrated that uncertainty and heterogeneity in expectations can lead to "transition zones" that are permanently developed in a discontinuous pattern (Mills 1981; Bar-Ilan & Strange 1996).

Peiser (1989) tests an implication of this theory: that land skipped-over and left vacant is developed later at higher densities than it would have been had leapfrogging not occurred. Limiting his observations to residential developments from three existing suburbs (two in Washington, DC, and one in Dallas, Texas), he finds that more recently built houses are constructed on smaller lots. However, Peiser does not control for the effect of land-use controls, such as zoning, and cautions that the regulatory environment can have a substantial impact on these findings.

Alternative theories of discontinuous or leapfrog development appeal to the existence of spatial externalities among households that can have agglomerative and dispersive effects. Agglomerative forces may consist of the benefits of neighborhoods and the public infrastructure that they provide or the desire to minimize commuting costs to a central location, while dispersive forces include the disutility of congestion and the appeal of open space amenities. Simulations of an agent-based model of household location by Parker and Meretsky (2004) demonstrate that such forces can generate fragmentation in areas that are closer to the urban fringe.

Using a hazard model of land conversion and parcel-level data from Maryland, Irwin and Bockstael (2002) provide empirical evidence of negative externalities associated with surrounding development. Carrión-Flores and Irwin (2004) find that preferences for low-density living and limited agglomeration economies around the central city have increased the dispersion of new residential development, but that positive externalities associated with neighboring residential and commercial development have moderated these effects. However, land heterogeneity and land-use policies, such as urban boundaries, zoning, and preserved open space, have been found to have an effect on fragmentation levels as well (e.g., Irwin, Bell & Geoghegan 2003).

5.3.4   Other dimensions of urban patterns

Up to this point, we have studiously avoided the use of the word "sprawl" despite its popularity in the press and in a growing number of academic articles. While most feel that the term "sprawl" is not a sufficiently definitive concept upon which to base analysis, many see it as synonymous with the multidimensionality of urban land-use patterns. No universal definition of sprawl exists, but most attempts include concepts of low density and a lack of contiguity, compactness, and centrality. Most researchers attempting its measurement agree that sprawl is not a discrete outcome, but rather a matter of degree.

Two recent national studies have attempted to measure multidimensional aspects of land-use pattern. Galster, Hanson, Ratcliffe, Wolman, Coleman, and Freihage (2001) define sprawl as a pattern of land use in an urbanized area that exhibits low levels of some combination of eight distinct dimensions: density, contiguity, concentration, clustering, centrality, nuclearity, mixed uses, and proximity. They measure six of these using 1990 Census data from UAs at the block level aggregated up to 0.5- and 1.0-mile square grid cells for a sample of 13 UAs and compute a composite score for each of these urbanized areas. Using a composite of their measures, Atlanta is ranked as the most, and New York City as the least, sprawling city. But true to the complexity of these concepts, cities tend to be ranked differently depending on the "sprawl" dimension considered. For example, Los Angeles is ranked eighth of 13 in overall severity but first in terms of its lack of clustering.

Ewing, Pendall, and Chen (2002) draw on multiple data sources to measure four dimensions that they say characterize sprawl in 83 US metropolitan areas (with a minimum population of 0.5 million in 2000): low-density development, segregated land uses, lack of significant centers, and poor accessibility. Many of the individual variables used to compute the scores are similar to other studies, but some are more unique; for example, the percentage of residents with "satisfactory" shopping within 1 mile; the percentage of residents with a public elementary school within 1 mile; the degree of "balance" within Census-defined traffic analysis zones (TAZs) between jobs and people; and the percentage of the metropolitan population relating to centers or subcenters within the same metropolitan area. New York City, San Francisco, Boston, and Portland are found to be compact in all dimensions, whereas Atlanta, Raleigh–Durham, North Carolina, and Riverside–San Bernardino, California, are sprawling in all dimensions. But similar to the previous study, rankings for most cities vary considerably over different dimensions. In addition, the direction of change in these measures between 1990 and 2000 is inconsistent for any given city.

Using various definitions of "sprawl," researchers have correlated hypothesized causes or consequences of sprawl. Fulton, Pendall, Nguyen, and Harrison (2001) find that metropolitan areas with a high proportions of black or Hispanic populations and greater political fragmentation of local governments are more sprawling (in terms of the ratio of population to urban land), whereas those with more prime farmland, geographical constraints (e.g., a coastline or international border), and a higher proportion of households serviced by public sewer are less sprawling. Using a similar sprawl measure, Pendall (1999) finds that low-density zoning and building caps are associated with more sprawl, whereas adequate public facility requirements, which require developers to support the cost of public services incurred by the development, are associated with less sprawl. Studying the correlation between sprawl and hypothesized consequences, Kahn (2001) finds evidence that sprawl (as measured by employment decentralization) has made housing more affordable and provided greater equality of housing consumption between black and white households.

A number of other studies, many from geography and some from landscape ecology, have considered other dimensions of urban form that provide evidence of its spatial complexity. For example, by applying a variety of spatial statistics to various urban land data (including Census and remotely sensed data), researchers have found evidence of "fractal" cities (e.g., Batty & Xi 1996) and the changing complexity of form across urban gradients (Luck & Wu 2002).

5.4   Conclusions

A popular perception of land-use change is one of rapid loss of open space, increases in land conversion at rates that far exceed population increases, decentralization of urban areas accompanied by increasingly low-density new development, and substantial fragmentation of the landscape, particularly in urban fringe areas. Is there evidence to support these perceptions? And, equally important, do data exist that make tests of these propositions possible?

Our review of urban land-use trends in the USA suggests that empirical evidence exists to support some of these broad perceptions, but not all. The existing literature suggests the following:

- Urban land comprises a small percentage of the total land area of the continental USA, but estimates from the mid-1990s vary from a low of 1.1 percent to a high of 7.2 percent.
- The amount of urban land has steadily increased over time, but estimates of the increase over the past 20–25 years vary from a low of 0.75 million acres to a high of 2.1 million acres per year.
- Average development densities have declined over time in many, but not all, areas.
- Urban decentralization and subcentering are well-documented trends that have occurred in most, if not all, metropolitan areas of the USA. However, conclusions regarding the extent of decentralization and the number and type of subcenters vary depending on data and methodology.
- Leapfrog or discontinuous development patterns appear to be pervasive at a fine scale (e.g., parcel-level) in some outer suburban and exurban areas, but are not prevalent at coarser scales of analysis. However, the limited geographical extent of these studies and varying spatial scales prohibits conclusions regarding the overall dominance of this trend.
- There is little consensus on the definition and measurement of sprawl. The empirical evidence is highly dependent on the researcher's definition of sprawl and the data used to measure it.
- Exurban development is the least studied of the urban land-use trends and the most difficult to measure. Nonetheless, evidence exists that substantial proportions of recent development activity is of the low-density form and in regions outside established urban areas. Due to the low-density nature of this development, the impact on population redistribution to these areas is far less than the impact on land conversion.

Our review also documents the variability in the evidence depending on data source. In fact, the empirical evidence on urban land-use patterns is subject to several potential sources of bias and must be viewed with these limitations in mind:

- First, all results are dependent on the type and source of the data. For example, an analysis of urban land-use patterns using Census-defined urban areas, satellite imagery, aerial photography, or tax assessment records will employ different definitions of urban land and thus will generate quite different results. Given the undercounting of low-density development by both Census-defined urban areas and land-cover data derived from satellite imagery, many existing national level studies underrepresent this aspect of urban land-use pattern.
- Second, results are highly dependent on the scale of analysis. National-level statistics obscure what can be dramatic regional changes in landscape, which in turn can mask changes at a highly disaggregated scale. In addition, the process of urban pattern change is itself likely to be scale-dependent, implying that the spatial characteristics of patterns are not constant across spatial scales. It is entirely reasonable to find pervasive leapfrog patterns of development

at highly disaggregate levels that disappear at more aggregate scales of analysis.

• Third, analyses of these urban trends are dependent on the spatial extent of the data. The spatial extent of the most commonly used data – urban areas from the US Census – is defined by a minimum threshold for population density and thus does not include outlying areas that are growing and changing, but that are developed at lower densities. Omission of these outer suburban and exurban areas from analysis biases results by suggesting greater centralization, less fragmentation, and a lower proportion of low-density urban land than is actually the case. For these reasons, we suspect that the trends of decentralization, leapfrogging, and low-density exurban development are more pervasive than the current evidence suggests.

Acknowledgments

We thank Dan McMillen, Mathew Turner, and an anonymous reviewer for helpful suggestions. Any remaining errors are our own. This research was supported in part by NASA under Grant #NAG511149 and by the US Environmental Protection Agency under STAR Grant # R-82801201.

Bibliography

Anas, A., Arnott, R., and Small, K. 1998: Urban spatial structure. *Journal of Economic Literature*, 36 (September), 1,426–64.

Bar-Ilan, A. and Strange, W. 1996: Urban development with lags. *Journal of Urban Economics*, 39, 87–113.

Batty, M. and Xie, Y. 1996: Preliminary evidence for a theory of the fractal city. *Environment and Planning A*, 28(10), 1,745–62.

Burchfield, M., Overman, H. G., Puga, D., and Turner, M. A. forthcoming: Sprawl: a portrait from space. *Quarterly Journal of Economics*.

Carrión-Flores, C. and Irwin, E. G. 2004: Determinants of residential land conversion and sprawl at the rural–urban fringe. *American Journal of Agricultural Economics*, 86(4), 889–904.

Ewing, R., Pendall, R., and Chen, D. 2002: Measuring sprawl and its impact. Volume 1. Smart growth America. Retrieved February 2004 from www.smartgrowthamerica.com/sprawlindex/MeasuringSprawlTechnical.pdf

Fujita, M. and Ogawa, H. 1982: Multiple equilibria and structural transition of non-monocentric urban configurations. *Regional Science and Urban Economics*, 12, 161–96.

Fulton, W., Pendall, R., Nguyen, M., and Harrison, A. 2001: Who sprawls the most? How growth patterns differ across the U.S., Brookings Institute, Center on Urban and Metropolitan Policy, Washington, DC.

Galster, G., Hanson, R., Ratcliffe, M. R., Wolman, H. R., Coleman, S., and Freihage, J. 2001: Wrestling sprawl to the ground: defining and measuring an elusive concept. *Housing Policy Debate*, 12(4), 681–717.

Giuliano, G. and Small, K. A. 1991: Subcenters in the Los Angeles region. *Regional Science and Urban Economics*, 21(2), 163–82.

Glaeser, E. L. and Kahn, M. 2004: Sprawl and urban growth. In J. V. Henderson and J.-F. Thisse (eds.), *Handbook of Urban and Regional Economics*, vol. 4: *Cities and Geography*. Amsterdam: Elsevier North-Holland, 2, 481–527.

Heimlich, R. E. and Anderson, W. D. 2001: Development at the urban fringe and beyond: impacts on agriculture and rural land. Agricultural Economic Report 803, Economic Research Service, US Department of Agriculture, Washington, DC.

Howard County Office of Planning (various dates): County Land Parcel Boundary and Building Footprint GIS Database; www.co.ho.md.us/DPZ/DPZ_Homepage.htm

Irwin, E. G. and Bockstael, N. E. 2002: Interacting agents, spatial externalities and the endogenous evolution of land use patterns. *Journal of Economic Geography*, 2(1), 31–54.

Irwin, E. G., Bell, K., and Geoghegan, J. 2003: Modeling and managing urban growth at the rural–urban fringe: a parcel-level model of residential land use change. *Agricultural and Resource Economics Review*, 32(1), 83–102.

Jordon, S., Ross, J., and Usowski, K. 1998: US suburbanization in the 1980s. *Regional Science and Urban Economics*, 28, 611–27.

Kahn, M. 2001: Does sprawl reduce the black/white consumption gap? *Housing Policy Debate*, 12(1), 77–86.

Luck, M. and Wu, J. 2002: A gradient analysis of urban landscape pattern: a case study from the Phoenix Metropolitan Region, Arizona, USA. *Landscape Ecology*, 17, 327–39.

Maryland Department of Planning 1997: Land Use Land Cover Maps. Baltimore, MD; www.mdp.state.md.us

Maryland Department of Planning 2000: MdProperty View. Statewide Property Map and Parcel Database. Baltimore, MD; www.mdp.state.md.us/data.mdview.htm

McCauley, S. and Goetz, S. J. 2004: Mapping residential density patterns using multi-temporal LandSat data and decision-tree classifier. *International Journal of Remote Sensing*, 25(6), 1,077–94.

McDonald, J. 1989: Econometric studies of suburban population density: a survey. *Journal of Urban Economics*, 26(3), 361–85.

McMillen, D. P. and Smith, S. C. 2003: The number of subcenters in large urban areas. *Journal of Urban Economics*, 53, 321–38.

Mieszkowski, P. and Smith, B. 1991: Analyzing urban decentralization: the case of Houston. *Regional Science and Urban Economics*, 21, 183–99.

Mills, D. 1981: Growth, speculation, and sprawl in a monocentric city. *Journal of Urban Economics*, 10, 201–26.

National Resources Inventory (NRI), Natural Resources Conservation Service, US Department of Agriculture (various dates); www.nrcs.usda.gov/technical/land/nri01/nri01lu.html

Nelson, A. C. 1992: Characterizing exurbia. *Journal of Planning Literature*, 6, 350–68.

Parker, D. and Meretsky, V. 2004: Measuring pattern outcomes in an agent-based model of edge-effect externalities using spatial metrics. *Agriculture, Ecosystems, and Environment*, 101(2–3), 233–50.

Peiser, R. B. 1989: Density and urban sprawl. *Land Economics*, 65, 193–204.

Pendall, R. 1999: Do land use controls cause sprawl? *Environment and Planning B*, 26, 555–71.

Stanilov, K. 2002: Postwar trends, land-cover changes, and patterns of suburban development: the case of Greater Seattle. *Environment and Planning B – Planning & Design*, 29(2), 173–95.

US Census Bureau (US Department of Commerce) 2000: TIGER/Line files; www.census.gov/geo/www/tiger/index.html

US Department of Agriculture 2003: *Agricultural Resources and Environmental Indicators*. Ag Handbook No. AH722, Washington, DC.

US Geological Survey (US Department of the Interior) 2001: National Land Cover Dataset; http://landcover.usgs.gov/natllandcover.asp

Monocentric Cities

Marvin Kraus

6.1 INTRODUCTION

Anyone who is even a casual student of cities has noted that, within a particular city, the economic landscape can vary dramatically, especially with proximity to the central business district. The cost of renting an apartment in the city proper can be hundreds of dollars per month higher than for a comparable apartment in an outlying suburb. And the choice might mean a difference between living in a high-rise apartment building (city proper) and a low-rise townhouse development (outlying suburb). The monocentric city model is a descriptive model of resource allocation in a city that was designed to explain precisely such phenomena. Its basic development occurred in the 1960s and 1970s, largely through the work of William Alonso, Richard Muth, and Edwin Mills (Alonso 1964; Muth 1969; Mills 1972). Since that time, cities have become increasingly polycentric, and the monocentric city model, with its assumption of a single concentration of employ-ment, has been criticized on the grounds that the cities it explains are from a different era. My response to this criticism is twofold. First, there are many urban areas for which the assumption of a single employment center serves as a reason-able approximation. But more importantly, the economic forces that arise in monocentric cities are crucial to understanding polycentric cities, and this makes the simpler monocentric city model the natural place to start.

The objective of this essay is to take a monocentric city model that strikes a balance between richness and simplicity and set it out so that it is accessible to a student with no training in economic theory beyond an undergraduate course in micro theory. The chapter relies as much as possible on diagrammatic analysis and makes only minimal use of mathematics. The specific model we set out is taken from Brueckner (1987), to which the reader is referred for a more advanced treatment of the monocentric city model. We are indebted to that paper not only for its model, but also for the insights it provides on the model's operation.

Section 6.2 sets out the model and shows how it can be used to analyze the internal structure of a city. Section 6.3 illustrates how the model can be used to make comparisons across cities. Section 6.4 concludes with a description of some of the interesting ways in which the model has been extended.

6.2   A MODEL OF A CITY

Imagine a circular city in a featureless plain. All employment is in a central business district (CBD), which we take to be a point at the city's center. The city is populated by N identical individuals. Each individual makes one round trip per day to the CBD, where he works a fixed number of hours and receives a daily wage of y. The greater the radial distance from the center at which an individual resides, the greater is the cost of this commute. Specifically, for an individual who lives at radial distance x, daily commuting cost is assumed to be tx, where $t > 0$ is a constant round-trip commuting cost per unit distance. The cost of commuting will be treated as an out-of-pocket cost, rather than a time cost.

An individual has a utility function $v(q,c)$, where q is his consumption of the services of housing, c represents his consumption of a composite of other goods, and both have a positive effect on utility. In actuality, the services that individuals derive from their residences are multidimensional, floor area and yard space being just a couple; here, these various attributes are represented by the scalar variable q, which we will simply refer to as consumption of housing.

An individual who lives at radial distance x faces a rental price (per unit) of housing of $p(x)$. We will refer to this simply as the price of housing.

As for the composite commodity, it can either be produced in the CBD or imported. Its price is assumed to be spatially invariant and is set at unity.

An individual's objective is to maximize $v(q,c)$. In doing so, he is subject to the budget constraint

$$p(x)q + c = y - tx. \tag{6.1}$$

There are two aspects to the problem. One is the individual's location choice, x. The second is the choice of a housing consumption q and other goods consumption c at the chosen location, and is depicted in Figure 6.1 for an individual whose location choice is denoted by x_0. The c-intercept of the budget line is given by $y - tx_0$, which is income net of commuting cost. For convenience, we will refer to this as net income. The slope of the budget line is simply $-p(x_0)$. The label $p(x_0)$ refers to its absolute value. Equilibrium occurs at e_0, a point at which one of the individual's indifference curves (assumed to be strictly convex) is tangent to the budget line. The equilibrium consumption of housing at this location is q_0.

The fact that individuals have a location choice together with the assumption that they are identical means that the same utility level must be realized at all residential locations. The reason is simply that any one individual can replicate the location and consumption decisions of anyone else. The mechanism for satisfying the equal-utility condition is spatial variation in the price of housing. In order to offset the reduction in net income associated with an increase in x (because of higher commuting cost), the price of housing must decrease with x.

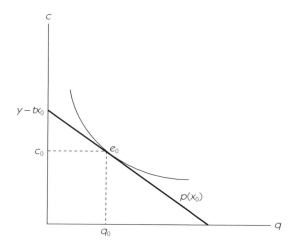

Figure 6.1   Equilibrium housing consumption at a particular location.

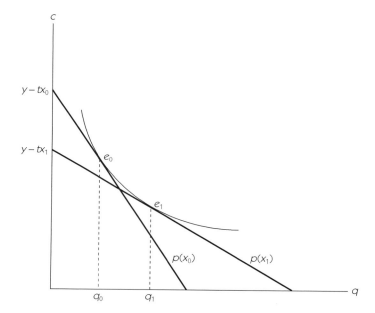

Figure 6.2   The price of housing varies spatially to achieve locational
equilibrium.

This is shown in Figure 6.2, in which the indifference curve drawn is assumed to
correspond to the common utility level in equilibrium, and x_1 and x_0 represent
any two locations such that $x_1 > x_0$. $p(x_0)$ and $p(x_1)$ are such that the equilibrium
utility level is just attainable with budget lines whose respective c-intercepts are

$y - tx_0$ and $y - tx_1$. Net income is lower at x_1 than at x_0, meaning that the budget line there must be flatter. Thus, $p(x_1) < p(x_0)$. We therefore have the following:

Property 1. The rental price of housing decreases with distance from the CBD.

Figure 6.2 can also be used to compare the housing consumption of individuals at different locations. Since the budget line is flatter at x_1 than at x_0, the equilibrium indifference curve is flatter at e_1 than at e_0. With strictly convex indifference curves, this means that the position of e_1 relative to e_0 on the equilibrium indifference curve is to the southeast, or that $q_1 > q_0$. We state this as follows:

Property 2. Individuals who live further from the CBD have higher consumption levels of housing.

To help set the stage for what will come later, we next introduce the notion of a *bid-rent curve*. In Figure 6.2, $p(x_0)$ is the highest price that an individual who lives at x_0 can pay for housing, while still attaining the level of utility associated with the indifference curve in the figure. If the price of housing at x_0 were any higher, the budget line there would be steeper, and the indifference curve in question would be unattainable. $p(x_0)$ is referred to as a bid rent for housing. The preceding discussion of equilibrium housing prices makes clear that for a given level of utility, the bid rent for housing is a decreasing function of x. The bid rent for housing is also affected by a change in the level of utility. This can be seen from Figure 6.3, which compares the bid rent for housing for two different utility levels at the same location. The fact that location is held fixed is reflected in both budget lines having the same c-intercept. The higher indifference curve can only be achieved with a flatter budget line, which is to say that the bid rent for housing must be lower. Denoting the bid rent for housing by $\tilde{p}$ and the level of utility by u, we can write $\tilde{p} = \tilde{p}(x,u)$, where $\tilde{p}$ is a decreasing function of both x and u. The graph of $\tilde{p}$ versus x for a given value of u is called a bid-rent curve for housing. Figure 6.4 shows two members of a family of bid-rent curves. Since $\tilde{p}$ is a decreasing function of u, utility is higher along the lower of the curves. One of the bid-rent curves corresponds to the equilibrium utility level. That bid-rent curve is the graph of equilibrium housing prices.

The quantity of housing demanded by an individual who faces his bid rent is denoted by $\tilde{q}(x,u)$. $\tilde{q}$ is an increasing function of x which, with u set at its equilibrium level, is the equilibrium $q(x)$ function. Under the additional assumption that housing is a normal good (an individual's housing demand positively related to his income), $\tilde{q}$ is also an increasing function of u. In Figure 6.3, the difference between q'' and q' is partly due to an income effect. The normality assumption insures that $q'' > q'$.

For the remainder of the chapter, housing will be assumed to be a normal good. The assumption is weak on prior grounds and is strongly supported empirically.

We now turn to the behavior of housing producers. Housing producers are assumed to be identical and to maximize profit, taking prices as given. An individual housing producer can produce housing at any or all x. Its output of

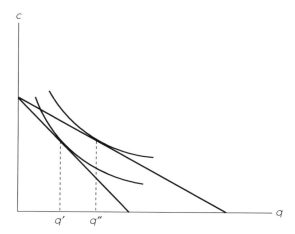

Figure 6.3 A higher level of utility decreases the bid rent for housing.

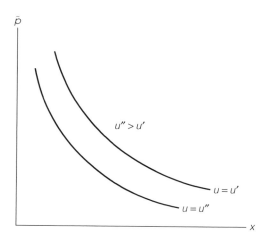

Figure 6.4 A family of bid-rent curves for housing.

housing at a location, $H(x)$, is given by the constant returns to scale (CRS) production function $H(x) = H(L(x),K(x))$, where $K(x)$ is its employment of capital at x and $L(x)$ is its employment of land at x. The rental price of land at x is $r(x)$, while capital has a spatially invariant rental price of i. i is exogenously determined in a national capital market; the rental price of land is endogenous. At a particular location x, a housing producer generates a profit given by $p(x)H(L(x), K(x)) - r(x)L(x) - iK(x)$. The problem it faces is to maximize this with respect to $L(x)$ and $K(x)$ for all x.

To see what the problem entails, we begin by recalling some classic results on constant returns to scale and applying them to our CRS housing producers. The first is that a CRS firm that is a price-taker in factor markets has a long-run average cost that is independent of its output. This means that an individual housing producer has a long-run average cost curve at a location that is horizontal, which we represent by AC in Figure 6.5. Second, under the additional assumption that firms act as price-takers in the product market, the long-run supply curve for an individual firm, and hence for the market as a whole, becomes perfectly elastic at a price equal to the constant level of long-run average cost. In Figure 6.5, AC is therefore the long-run market supply curve for housing at x, meaning that for equilibrium in the housing market at a location, the price of housing and the average cost of housing must be equal. We write this as

$$p(x) = AC(r(x),i),\qquad\qquad(6.2)$$

since in Figure 6.5, an increase in either $r(x)$ or i leads to an upward shift in AC. As x increases, $p(x)$ decreases (Property 1). Together with equation (6.2), this implies that the same must be true of the average cost of housing production. Since the rental price of capital is spatially invariant, this can come about only if $r(x)$ is a decreasing function of x. We state this important property as follows:

Property 3. The rental price of land decreases with distance from the CBD.

In real-world urban areas, the form that housing takes often varies dramatically with distance from the city center. At the closest-in locations, the dominant form of housing might be high-rise apartment buildings or condominiums. In less central areas of the inner city, housing might be predominantly three- to five-story apartment buildings. Out in the suburbs, this might give way to single-family homes, with a general tendency for lot sizes to become progressively larger in the more outlying suburbs. We can summarize this by saying that as distance from the city center increases, there is in general a decrease in the capital–land ratio in housing production. We will now proceed to demonstrate that this is exactly what our model predicts.

The result can be seen in terms of Figure 6.6, in which we have sketched the so-called unit isoquant – those combinations of labor and capital from which an individual housing producer can produce exactly one unit of housing. As shown in the diagram, isoquants are assumed to be strictly convex. To begin with, consider some particular location x_0, and a housing producer that chooses to operate on the unit isoquant there. In order to maximize its profit, the firm must employ the cost-minimizing input combination. This is the point e_0, at which an isocost line that reflects factor prices at x_0 is tangent to the unit isoquant. Factor prices are reflected in the slope of the isocost line, which is $-r(x_0)/i$. Now consider the capital–land ratio at e_0. This is commonly referred to as structural density and is given by the slope of a ray from the origin through e_0. The next thing to see is that all firms that produce housing at x_0 have the same structural density, regardless of the quantity of housing that they produce. This is another

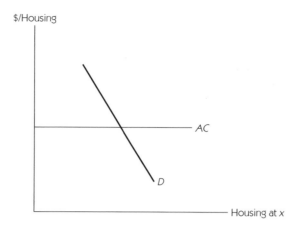

Figure 6.5 Equilibrium in the housing market.

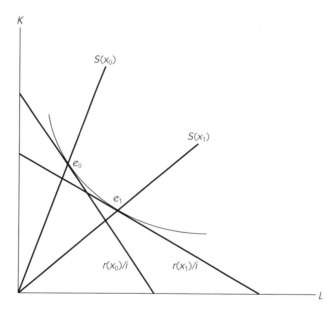

Figure 6.6 Structural density decreases with distance from the CBD.

implication of constant returns to scale. It comes from the fact that for a given ray from the origin in Figure 6.6, the isoquants of a CRS production function are identically sloped at all points along the ray. Thus, if location and hence factor prices are held fixed, all points of tangency between isoquants and isocost lines involve the same structural density. In what follows, the structural density at x is denoted by $S(x)$.

Now consider some second location, $x_1 > x_0$. From Property 3, $r(x_1) < r(x_0)$, meaning that isocost lines are flatter at x_1. Together with strictly convex isoquants, this means that the cost-minimizing point on the unit isoquant, the point e_1, lies on a flatter ray from the origin than does e_0. We therefore have $S(x_1) < S(x_0)$. We state this as follows:

Property 4. Structural density decreases with distance from the CBD.

By way of additional stage-setting, we next consider the notion of a bid-rent curve for land. It has a strong connection to the previously considered notion of a bid-rent curve for housing. Consider some particular location x, and ask "If the price at which a housing producer can sell housing at x is the bid rent for housing $\tilde{p}(x,u)$, then what is the highest price it can pay for land at x, while still satisfying the zero-profit condition (6.2)?" This maximum bid is called a bid rent for land. Denoting it by $\tilde{r}(x,u)$, we have

$$\tilde{p}(x,u) = AC(\tilde{r}(x,u),i). \tag{6.3}$$

We have previously seen that an increase in either x or u decreases $\tilde{p}$. Together with equation (6.3), this implies that an increase in x or u also decreases $\tilde{r}$. The graph of $\tilde{r}$ versus x for a given value of u is called a bid-rent curve for land. One member of the family of bid-rent curves for land corresponds to the equilibrium utility level. That bid-rent curve is the graph of equilibrium land prices.

The structural density chosen by a housing producer that faces its bid rent for land is denoted by $\tilde{S}(x,u)$. $\tilde{S}$ is a decreasing function of x which, with u set at its equilibrium level, is the equilibrium $S(x)$ function. An increase in u also decreases $\tilde{S}$.

Another feature of cities that our model explains is the tendency for net residential density – population per unit of land used for residential purposes – to decline with distance from the CBD. Denoting net residential density at x by $D(x)$, the simplest way to see this is to write $D(x) = h(x)/q(x)$, where $h(x)$ is housing output per unit of land allocated to housing production at x. An increase in x increases $q(x)$ (Property 2), so it is enough to show that $h(x)$ decreases. This is nothing more than the fact that in Figure 6.6, housing output is the same at e_1 as at e_0, but is produced with a greater input of land (given CRS, it is enough to consider a movement along the unit isoquant). We can therefore state the following:

Property 5. Net residential density decreases with distance from the CBD.

To complete our stage-setting, as we have called it, suppose that all economic agents face their bid rents – for housing in the case of individuals and land in the case of housing producers – and consider the resulting net residential density, which we will denote by $\tilde{D}(x,u)$. $\tilde{D}$ is a decreasing function of x which, with u set at its equilibrium level, is the equilibrium $D(x)$ function. An increase in u also decreases $\tilde{D}$.

Through our so-called stage-setting, we have seen how the model gives rise to the functions $\tilde{p}(x,u)$, $\tilde{q}(x,u)$, $\tilde{r}(x,u)$, $\tilde{S}(x,u)$, and $\tilde{D}(x,u)$. If we had a way of determining u, then we could use these functions to determine equilibrium housing and land prices at all locations in the city, as well as other equilibrium spatial profiles. We would also be able to determine the city's equilibrium size. This is illustrated in Figure 6.7, in which $\tilde{x}$ is the city's radius and r_A is a spatially invariant bid rent for land on the part of agriculture. To the left of $\tilde{x}$ in the diagram, the bid rent for land on the part of agriculture is less than for housing production, so that all land up for bid is secured by housing producers. To the right of $\tilde{x}$, it is the agricultural bid rent that is higher, so that only agriculture secures land. Since no housing is produced outside of $\tilde{x}$, that is the city's equilibrium radius.

As shown in Figure 6.7, $\tilde{x}$ occurs where the bid-rent curves for land in its alternative uses in housing and agriculture intersect. We can express this through the equation

$$\tilde{r}(\tilde{x},u) = r_A, \tag{6.4}$$

which can be viewed as an equation for determining $\tilde{x}$ in terms of u.

Exactly where u comes from depends on whether the city is "open" or "closed." In the case of an open city, the value of u is exogenous. It is the prevailing level of utility elsewhere in the economy, and is achieved in the city through costless migration. The city's population, N, is therefore endogenous and is determined as follows. At each radial distance x, assume that a fraction $\theta/2\pi$ of the land at x is available for the endogenous uses housing and agriculture. Then the number of individuals that can be housed in a ring of infinitesimal width dx at radial distance x is $\tilde{D}(x,u)\theta x\, dx$. The city's equilibrium population is the number of individuals that can be housed inside $\tilde{x}$, or

$$N = \int_0^{\tilde{x}} \tilde{D}(x,u)\theta x\, dx. \tag{6.5}$$

In the case of a closed city, the size of the city's population is exogenous, and the equilibrium utility level is endogenous. Equation (6.5) must hold, but now with N given. Like equation (6.4), it involves the endogenous variables $\tilde{x}$ and u. $\tilde{x}$ and u can therefore be determined from equations (6.4) and (6.5). Once this solution is obtained, all equilibrium spatial profiles can be determined.

6.3   COMPARATIVE STATICS

One of the most interesting features of an economic model is its comparative-statics properties. In general, these have to do with how a model's parameters affect its solution. For the model of the preceding section, a very thorough comparative-statics analysis can be found in Brueckner (1987). The objective here is only to demonstrate how the analysis is carried out. For this purpose, we take the closed city variant of the model and work through the effect of an increase in

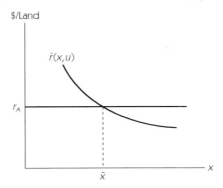

Figure 6.7   Equality of bid rents at the boundary.

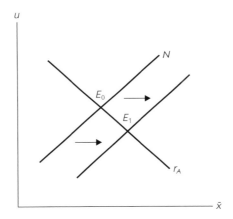

Figure 6.8   Population increase for a closed city.

N. This amounts to asking, "If two cities are identical in all respects except for population, how would they be expected to differ in terms of housing and land prices, geographical size, and so on?"

One of the keys to the analysis is our knowledge of the effect of an increase in u in the functions $\tilde{p}(x,u)$, $\tilde{q}(x,u)$, $\tilde{r}(x,u)$, $\tilde{S}(x,u)$, and $\tilde{D}(x,u)$. Collecting results from the preceding section, we have that $\tilde{p}$, $\tilde{r}$, $\tilde{S}$, and $\tilde{D}$ all decrease with u, while $\tilde{q}$ is increasing.

Given an initial value of N, a solution to equations (6.4) and (6.5) for $\tilde{x}$ and u can be represented by a point such as E_0 in Figure 6.8. The curve labeled r_A represents those combinations of values for $\tilde{x}$ and u for which equation (6.4) holds, while the curve labeled N represents the same for equation (6.5). As shown in the figure, the "r_A-curve" slopes downward, while the "N-curve" slopes upward. First consider the r_A-curve. Its downward slope can be seen from Figure 6.7, which illustrates a solution to equation (6.4). Since $\tilde{r}$ is a decreasing function of

u, an increase in u results in a downward shift in the bid-rent curve for land in housing production, and its intersection with the agricultural bid-rent curve occurs at a lower value of $\bar{x}$. Now consider the N-curve. Since $\tilde{D}$ is a decreasing function of u, an increase in u for which $\bar{x}$ is held fixed decreases the right-hand side of equation (6.5) (a reduction in the number of individuals who are housed). Thus, the only way to house a given number of individuals while providing them with a higher level of utility is to increase $\bar{x}$.

The stage is now set to analyze an increase in N. The first thing to note is that, in the system consisting of equations (6.4) and (6.5), N is a shift parameter of the latter, but not the former. In terms of Figure 6.8, this means that only the N-curve will shift. We can easily work out the direction of the shift. Given an increase in N, the same increase must occur in the right-hand side of equation (6.5) (the number of individuals actually housed). For any given value of u, the only way this can happen is with an increase in $\bar{x}$. Thus, when population increases, the N-curve shifts rightward. The new equilibrium $(\bar{x},u)$ combination is E_1 in Figure 6.8. Thus, an increase in N increases $\bar{x}$, while decreasing u.

Other results can now be easily obtained. The fact that $\tilde{p}$ is a decreasing function of u, together with the decline in the equilibrium utility level, means that there is an increase in $\tilde{p}$ for all x. This implies an increase in the rental price of housing at all locations out to the base city's outer edge. By an essentially identical analysis, the same is true of the rental price of land and both structural and net residential density. At any location x, a resident of the larger city consumes a smaller quantity of housing.

Of the preceding results, the only one that might seem surprising is that individuals who live in the larger city have a lower utility level. This is not necessarily realistic, in part because we have made no account of the possibility that agglomeration economies result in the larger city having a higher wage rate (see, e.g., Henderson 1985). But for what it is, the result can be seen as follows. Since utility is equal at all locations in each city, it is enough to compare the utility of Ms A, a resident of the smaller city who lives at its outer edge, with that of Mr B, who lives at the outer edge of the larger city. Because these individuals live at the outer edges of their respective cities, the price they pay for the housing they consume is the same (the rental price of land at the periphery is the same in both cities and is r_A). Thus, the individual who achieves the higher utility level is the one for whom income net of commuting cost is greater. This is clearly Ms A, since between the two, she has the shorter commute.

If an exogenous change in t or y occurs, things are not as simple. A particular value of each of these parameters is subsumed into the functions $\tilde{p}(x,u)$ and $\tilde{q}(x,u)$, and therefore $\tilde{r}(x,u)$, $\tilde{S}(x,u)$, and $\tilde{D}(x,u)$. As before, the first step is to determine how the parameter change affects the solution to equations (6.4) and (6.5) for $\bar{x}$ and u. But in order to determine the effect on, say, structural density at a location, one has to take into account both the direct effect of the parameter change and the indirect effect of the utility change that it induces. An exogenous change in population size involves only the second of these.

6.4   EXTENSIONS

The monocentric city model has been extended to include a variety of interesting features, each enhancing the model's realism. We conclude by describing some of the interesting directions in which the model has been taken:

- *Different income groups.* A number of authors, including Muth (1969), have generalized the model to allow for different income groups. An interesting new question arises, namely the following: In relation to individuals with low incomes, do individuals with high incomes live closer or farther from the CBD? Although the correct answer to this question is "It depends," usually the answer is "farther." The reason is that, *ceteris paribus*, higher-income individuals consume more housing (all it takes for this is for housing to be a normal good), giving them an added incentive to locate where the rental price of housing is lower, which is further from the CBD. A good source of information for the comparative statics of such a model is Hartwick, Schweizer, and Varaiya (1976).
- *Traffic congestion.* Another way in which the model has been extended is to take into account that commuting entails a very important time cost, and that traffic congestion makes commuting time from a location endogenous (see, e.g., Solow 1972). At any radial distance x, the time it takes to travel a unit distance is assumed to be an increasing function of the number of individuals who live between x and $\bar{x}$, since these outliers of x constitute the traffic at x. This naturally raises questions about how commuting should be priced and how land should be allocated to congestion-reducing road capacity, and has been a primary focus of work in this area.
- *Modal choice and nonradial access costs.* In the model of section 6.2, an individual's commuting cost depends only on the radial distance from his residence to the CBD. In order for this to be plausible, the city's radial road system must be sufficiently dense that circumferential access costs can safely be ignored. Anas and Moses (1979) have analyzed an extension of the monocentric city model in which radial roads are discretely spaced and entail costly circumferential access. Consistent with what is commonly observed in cities, the city will tend to develop along its radial roads, and unlike in the basic monocentric city model, the rural/urban boundary will be noncircular. The Anas and Moses paper is also one of several to have introduced mode choice into the model.
- *The fully closed city.* The model of section 6.2 implicitly assumes that the land employed by housing producers is rented from landowners who are not residents of the city. This follows from the fact that the income of residents is assumed to be exogenous, while aggregate land rents are endogenous. In a variant of the model known as the "fully closed city," aggregate land rents are a source of income to residents. One way to tell the story is that the land employed by housing producers is rented from the city, which in turn rents it

from either the federal government or from farmers, doing so at a rental price equal to the agricultural bid rent r_A. Since the rental price paid by housing producers exceeds r_A, this process generates a surplus for the city, which Arnott and Stiglitz (1981) termed differential land rents. In a fully closed city with identical consumers, each consumer receives an equal share of differential land rents as a transfer from the city. The fact that income is endogenous makes it the most complicated version of the model. For more on the fully closed city model, see Pines and Sadka (1986).

Bibliography

Alonso, W. 1964: *Location and Land Use*. Cambridge, MA: Harvard University Press.

Anas, A. and Moses, L. N. 1979: Mode choice, transport structure and urban land use. *Journal of Urban Economics*, 6, 228–46.

Arnott, R. J. and Stiglitz, J. E. 1981: Aggregate land rents and aggregate transport costs. *Economic Journal*, 91, 331–47.

Brueckner, J. K. 1987: The structure of urban equilibria: a unified treatment of the Muth–Mills model. In E. S. Mills (ed.), *Handbook of Regional and Urban Economics*, vol. 2: *Urban Economics*. Amsterdam: North-Holland, ch. 20.

Hartwick, J., Schweizer, U., and Varaiya, P. 1976: Comparative statics of a residential economy with several classes. *Journal of Economic Theory*, 13, 396–413.

Henderson, J. V. 1985: *Economic Theory and the Cities*, 2nd edn. Orlando, FL: Academic Press.

Mills, E. S. 1972: *Studies in the Structure of the Urban Economy*. Baltimore, MD: Johns Hopkins Press.

Muth, R. F. 1969: *Cities and Housing*. Chicago: The University of Chicago Press.

Pines, D. and Sadka, E. 1986: Comparative statics analysis of a fully closed city. *Journal of Urban Economics*, 20, 1–20.

Solow, R. M. 1972: Congestion, density and the use of land in transportation. *Swedish Journal of Economics*, 74, 161–73.

CHAPTER SEVEN

Space in General Equilibrium

Marcus Berliant and Courtney LaFountain

7.1 INTRODUCTION

How do households distribute themselves in a spatial dimension? Do they distribute themselves efficiently? What determines land-use patterns? Standard intermediate microeconomic theory is ill equipped to answer these questions because households and others using land care about the location, as well as the quantity, of land that they consume. As a result, some of the standard assumptions used in our models lead to predictions that are inconsistent with observed behavior. For example, suppose that households like to consume land and a composite consumption good (a bundle of everything that is not land). A key assumption in standard microeconomic theory is that preferences are strictly convex, which implies under symmetry of preferences that households prefer owning an acre of land and a unit of composite good to owning two acres of land and no composite good, or to owning two units of composite good and no land, all else being equal. However, if households care about the location of the land they consume, then "land in the city" and "land in the suburbs" are essentially two different goods. In this case, convex preferences and symmetry imply that households prefer owning one acre of land in the city and one acre of land in the suburbs to owning two acres of land in the city and none in the suburbs, and to owning two acres of land in the suburbs and none in the city. In general, households will want to diversify their landholdings. This is inconsistent with observed behavior.

To answer the questions we have posed, we turn to the Alonso (1964) model, and rely on Berliant and Fujita (1992) for an analysis of it. This model is a straightforward extension of standard microeconomic theory to urban economics that includes land as a commodity while at the same time incorporating differences between land at different locations in a natural way. In this model, a finite number of identical households live in a long, narrow (one-dimensional) city. They like to consume a composite consumption good and land. In particular, households consume parcels or intervals of land. They simultaneously choose how much composite good and land to consume and the location of their parcel. Households commute from the land they consume to an exogenously determined location, the city center or central business district, in order to receive their endowment of composite good. Commuting is costly, so they care about the location of their parcel of land because the cost of commuting between it and the central business district varies with the distance between the two. The Alonso model is distinguished from other models of urban economics by the following two features: (1) the use of a finite number of households (two in this chapter) instead of a continuum; and (2) the assumption that households like intervals of land in one dimension.

We begin with a brief review of the tools and definitions used in standard microeconomic theory. Next, we introduce the Alonso model. We follow this introduction with an extension of the standard tools and definitions for this model. We then provide a specific example of the model to illustrate how two identical households divide up the available land in a long, narrow city. We conclude with comments on extensions of the basic Alonso model.

7.2 A Brief Review of Intermediate Microeconomic Theory

We begin with an exchange economy populated by two households, A and B, who like to consume two goods, 1 and 2. Household i's consumption of good j is x_j^i. Note that we use superscripts to identify households and subscripts to identify goods. Households' preferences over different consumption bundles, or different combinations of goods 1 and 2, are represented by utility functions. The utility function for household i is $U^i:R_+^2 \rightarrow R$, where $U^i(x_1^i, x_2^i)$ is the level of utility that household i enjoys when it consumes the bundle (x_1^i, x_2^i). Preferences are *convex* if, for all possible consumption bundles (x_1^i, x_2^i) and $(\hat{x}_1^i, \hat{x}_2^i)$, $U^i(x_1^i, x_2^i)$ = $U^i(\hat{x}_1^i, \hat{x}_2^i)$ implies that, for all $\alpha \in (0,1)$, $U^i(\alpha x_1^i + (1 - \alpha)\hat{x}_1^i, \alpha x_2^i + (1 - \alpha)\hat{x}_2^i) \geq U^i(x_1^i, x_2^i)$. In other words, consuming a linear combination of two bundles that both generate the same level of utility does not diminish utility. An *indifference curve* is a collection of consumption bundles that generate the same level of utility for a household. Thus, a household is indifferent between all the consumption bundles that make up an indifference curve. Figure 7.1 illustrates an indifference curve, $IC_{\bar{U}}^i$, where $IC_{\bar{U}}^i = \{(x_1^i, x_2^i) \mid U^i(x_1^i, x_2^i) = \bar{U}\}$ is the set of bundles that generate utility level $\bar{U}$ for household i. Household i's *marginal utility of good* j is $MU_j^i:R^2 \rightarrow R$, where $MU_j^i(x_1^i, x_2^i)$ is the additional utility household i would get if it consumed an additional unit of good j, given that it is consuming the bundle (x_1^i, x_2^i). The marginal utility of good j is the derivative of household i's utility function with respect to good j:

$$MU_j^i(x_1^i, x_2^i) = \frac{\partial U^i(x_1^i, x_2^i)}{\partial x_j^i}.$$

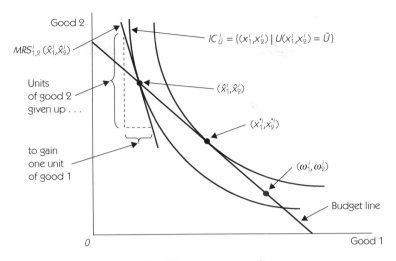

Figure 7.1 The consumer diagram.

Household i's *marginal rate of substitution of good 1 for good 2* is $MRS_{1,2}^i : R_+^2 \to R$, where

$$MRS_{1,2}^i(x_1^i, x_2^i) = \frac{MU_1^i}{MU_2^i}$$

identifies how much of good 2 household i is willing to give up in order to get one more unit of good 1, given that it is consuming the bundle (x_1^i, x_2^i). Figure 7.1 shows that $MRS_{1,2}^i(\hat{x}_1^i, \hat{x}_2^i)$ is the slope of household i's indifference curve at the bundle $(\hat{x}_1^i, \hat{x}_2^i)$. Household i's endowment of good j is ω_j^i. An *allocation* is a list of consumption bundles for each household: $(x_1^A, x_2^A, x_1^B, x_2^B)$. An allocation is *feasible* if there is material balance in both goods: $x_1^A + x_1^B = \omega_1^A + \omega_1^B$ and $x_2^A + x_2^B = \omega_2^A + \omega_2^B$. The set of feasible allocations are those contained in the standard Edgeworth box, illustrated in Figure 7.2. The width of the box is the total quantity of good 1 available in the economy, $\omega_1^A + \omega_1^B$. The height of the box is the total quantity of good 2 available in the economy, $\omega_2^A + \omega_2^B$. Household A's origin is the point $(0,0)$, and household B's origin is the point $(\omega_1^A + \omega_1^B, \omega_2^A + \omega_2^B)$. A feasible allocation is *Pareto optimal*, or is *efficient*, if there is no other feasible allocation that keeps every household at least as well off and makes some household better off. We can use marginal rates of substitution to characterize the set of Pareto-optimal allocations: If the feasible allocation $(x_1^A, x_2^A, x_1^B, x_2^B)$ is Pareto optimal, then $MRS_{1,2}^A(x_1^A, x_2^A) = MRS_{1,2}^B(x_1^B, x_2^B)$, and if preferences are convex, then $MRS_{1,2}^A(x_1^A, x_2^A) = MRS_{1,2}^B(x_1^B, x_2^B)$ implies that $(x_1^A, x_2^A, x_1^B, x_2^B)$ is Pareto optimal, provided that it is feasible. (Note that we are skipping some technical assumptions and details here.) Loosely speaking, the set of Pareto-optimal allocations, or the *contract curve*, is the set of allocations in the Edgeworth box at which households' indifference curves are tangent to

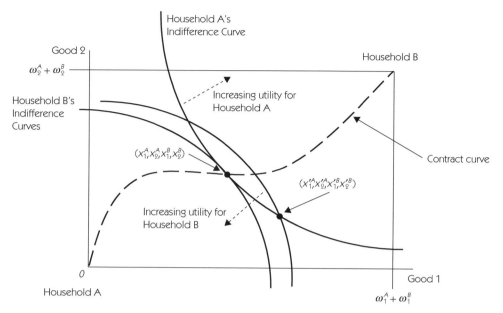

Figure 7.2   The standard Edgeworth box.

each other. The intuition, illustrated in Figure 7.2, is that if the marginal rates of substitution for the two households are unequal at an allocation, such as $(x_1'^A, x_2'^A, x_1'^B, x_2'^B)$, then there are unexhausted gains from trade and the allocation is not efficient. Moreover, if the marginal rates of substitution at an allocation such as $(x_1^A, x_2^A, x_1^B, x_2^B)$ are equal, then the set of allocations that would make one household better off is disjoint from the set of allocations that would make the other household better off, so there is no way to make one household better off without making the other household worse off. Note that finding and characterizing the set of Pareto-optimal allocations – the set of "best" allocations – is a normative exercise that says nothing about the quantities of goods that each household will actually consume.

To find the actual distribution of goods across households, we use the concept of competitive equilibrium, a positive concept. Let good 2 be the numeraire, so that $p_2 = 1$. A *competitive equilibrium* is a feasible allocation $(x_1^{*A}, x_2^{*A}, x_1^{*B}, x_2^{*B})$ and a price p_1^* such that:

(a)   household A maximizes its utility $U^A(x_1^A, x_2^A)$ subject to its budget constraint, $p_1^* x_1^A + x_2^A \leq p_1^* \omega_1^A + \omega_2^A$, and

(b)   household B maximizes its utility $U^B(x_1^B, x_2^B)$ subject to its budget constraint, $p_1^* x_1^B + x_2^B \leq p_1^* \omega_1^B + \omega_2^B$,

at $x_1^A = x_1^{*A}$, $x_2^A = x_2^{*A}$, $x_1^B = x_1^{*B}$, $x_2^B = x_2^{*B}$. An *equilibrium allocation* is an allocation $(x_1^{*A}, x_2^{*A}, x_1^{*B}, x_2^{*B})$ such that there exists a price p_1^* that makes $(x_1^{*A}, x_2^{*A}, x_1^{*B}, x_2^{*B})$ and p_1^*

an equilibrium. Competitive equilibrium is a positive concept that helps us to understand how resources will be allocated using the price mechanism in a decentralized setting with no coordination between the households. Skipping further technicalities and assuming that households exhaust their budgets, the conditions equivalent to equilibrium are that each household's marginal rate of substitution is equal to the price ratio, so for i = A, B,

$$MRS_{1,2}^i(x_1^{*i}, x_2^{*i}) = \frac{p_1^*}{1},$$

and that markets for both goods clear, so for j = 1, 2,

$$x_j^{*A} + x_j^{*B} = \omega_j^A + \omega_j^B.$$

Figure 7.1 shows that if the first condition is not satisfied for some household i, then there exists an affordable consumption bundle that makes that household better off, so that household i is not maximizing its utility subject to its budget. The budget line is the set of bundles (x_1^i, x_2^i) such that $p_1^* x_1^i + x_2^i = p_1^* \omega_1^i + \omega_2^i$. The slope of the budget line is $-p_1^*$. The bundle $(\hat{x}_1^i, \hat{x}_2^i)$ is affordable, but $MRS^i(\hat{x}_1^i, \hat{x}_2^i) \neq p_1^*$. The bundle (x_1^{*i}, x_2^{*i}), for which $MRS_{1,2}^i(x_1^{*i}, x_2^{*i}) = p_1^*$, is also affordable and generates more utility than $(\hat{x}_1^i, \hat{x}_2^i)$.

The welfare theorems provide the connection between equilibrium allocations, a positive idea, and Pareto-optimal allocations, a normative idea, in this simple model. The First Welfare Theorem states that under certain conditions every equilibrium allocation is Pareto optimal. The Second Welfare Theorem states that if preferences are convex and it is possible to redistribute endowments, then under certain technical assumptions every Pareto-optimal allocation is an equilibrium allocation for some set of endowments.

For a more thorough discussion of the topics reviewed in this section, see, for example, Varian (1993).

7.3 THE ALONSO MODEL

The Alonso model adds space to the basic framework we just described. Our two households, A and B, now live in a long, narrow city of length l. The interval from 0 to l describes the length of the city (see Figure 7.3). Households consume a composite good and land. The quantity of composite good consumed by household i is z^i, the location of the driveway or the front of the lot occupied by household i is $x^i \in [0,l)$, and the quantity of land consumed or length of the lot occupied by household i is s^i. Thus, household i owns the interval $[x^i, x^i + s^i)$. There are C units of composite good available in the economy. Households must commute to the city center, located at the origin, in order to pick up their endowment of composite good. In doing so, households incur a cost of t units of composite good per unit distance they travel, measured from the front of their lot. Households A and B have the same utility function, $U(s,z)$, where U is increasing

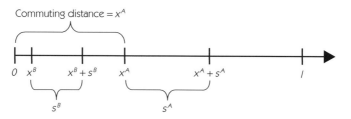

Figure 7.3   The linear city.

in both of its arguments and land is a normal good. Recall that a good is *normal* if households consume more of it when their income increases, all else being equal. Let $U^i = U(s^i, z^i)$. Since both households have the same utility function, we can say how well off one household is relative to the other. An *allocation* is a list specifying quantities of land consumed, quantities of composite good consumed, and driveway locations for both households: $(s^A, s^B, z^A, z^B, x^A, x^B)$. Thus, $s^A, s^B, z^A, z^B > 0$ and $x^A, x^B \in [0, l)$. An allocation is *feasible* if material balance is satisfied for both the composite good and land; namely,

$$z^A + z^B + tx^A + tx^B = C,$$

$$[x^A, x^A + s^A) \cap [x^B, x^B + s^B) = \emptyset,$$

and

$$[x^A, x^A + s^A) \cup [x^B, x^B + s^B) = [0, l).$$

7.4   Pareto-Optimal Allocations and the Contract Curve

A feasible allocation is a *Pareto optimum*, or is *efficient*, if there is no other feasible allocation that keeps every household at least as well off and makes some household better off. What do Pareto optima look like? Consider a feasible allocation, $(s^A, s^B, z^A, z^B, x^A, x^B)$, where $x^A = 0$ and $s^A > s^B$. In this case, household A lives closest to the city center and occupies a lot that is larger than the lot occupied by household B. Household A's commuting cost is zero, household B's commuting cost is $tx^B = ts^A$, and $z^A + z^B + tx^B = C$. This allocation is not a Pareto optimum, because there exists another feasible allocation that makes at least one household better off without making the other household worse off. For example, consider a feasible allocation $(\hat{s}'^A, \hat{s}'^B, \hat{z}'^A, \hat{z}'^B, \hat{x}'^A, \hat{x}'^B)$, where households switch positions but consume the quantity of land given in the original assignment, so that $\hat{s}'^A = s^A$ and $\hat{s}'^B = s^B$. Household B consumes the same quantity of composite good, so that $\hat{z}'^B = z^B$, and household B lives closest to the city center, so that $\hat{x}'^B = 0$ and $\hat{x}^A = s^B$. Figure 7.4 shows how the two allocations are related. Household B's commuting cost is now zero and household A's commuting cost is now $t\hat{x}'^A = ts^B$. Since household

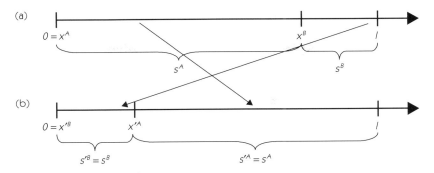

Figure 7.4   A Pareto improvement.

A lives on a larger lot than household B, $t\hat{x}'^A = ts^B < ts^A = tx^B$. This allocation is feasible:

$$\hat{z}'^A = C - t\hat{x}'^A - \hat{z}'^B = C - ts^B - z^B > C - ts^A - z^B.$$

Thus, household B is just as well off as it was with bundle (s^B, z^B), and household A is better off because it is consuming the same amount of land and more composite good. Generalizing this intuition leads to the following proposition:

> PROPOSITION 1 (Berliant & Fujita 1992). *If $(s^{oA}, s^{oB}, z^{oA}, z^{oB}, x^{oA}, x^{oB})$, is a Pareto optimum, then:*

(i) $x^{oA} < x^{oB}$ *exactly when $s^{oA} < s^{oB}$, so household A lives closest to the city center if and only if it occupies a smaller lot;*

(ii) $x^{oA} < x^{oB}$ *implies that $U^A \leq U^B$, so if household A lives closest to the city center, then household B is at least as well off as household A; and*

(iii) $U^A < U^B$ *implies that $x^{oA} < x^{oB}$, so if household B is strictly better off than household A, then household A lives closest to the city center.*

Pareto optima fall into one of two categories: (1) those in which household A lives closest to the city center and (2) those in which household B lives closest to the city center. The contract curve is the union of these two sets of Pareto optima. We can portray the contract curve using an Edgeworth box modified to account for the amount of composite good used up in commuting, where the modification will depend on which household lives closest to the city center.

When household A lives closest to the city center, we modify the box as illustrated in Figure 7.5. Household A's origin is the lower left corner of the box. The bottom of the box is simply the line segment $[0,l]$. The height of the left side of the box is the total amount of composite good available, C. The top of the box is a line that identifies how much composite good remains to be divided between households A and B after household B commutes to the city center. The distance that household B commutes is equal to the length of household A's lot, s^A. Thus,

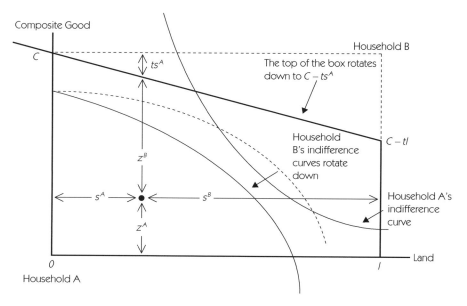

Figure 7.5   The modified Edgeworth box: household A central.

the top of the box is the line $C - ts^A$. Finally, household B's origin is the point $(l, C - tl)$, where $C - tl$ is the amount of composite good that remains if $s^A = l$ and household B commutes the entire length of the city. Since the top of the box has "rotated down" by ts^A, household B's indifference curves must also be "rotated down" the same way. Household A's indifference curves are unchanged. A point in this modified Edgeworth box identifies a feasible allocation in which household A lives closest to the city center, so x^A is at the city center, 0. The quantity of land consumed by household A, s^A, is measured by the horizontal distance from the origin. The driveway of household B, x^B, is at $0 + s^A$. The quantity of land consumed by household B, s^B, is $l - s^A$. The quantity of composite good consumed by household A, z_A, is the vertical distance from the bottom of the box, and the quantity of composite good consumed by household B is the vertical distance from the modified top of the box, $C - ts^A$.

Suppose instead that household B lives closest to the city center. Figure 7.6 illustrates how the required modification of the Edgeworth box is the mirror image of that just described. Household B's origin is now the point (l, C). The top of the box is simply a horizontal line segment of width l. The height of the right side of the box is the total amount of composite good available, C. The bottom of the box is a line that identifies how much composite good remains to be divided between households A and B after household A commutes to the city center. The distance that household A commutes is equal to the length of household B's lot, s^B. Thus, the bottom of the box is the line ts^B. Finally, household A's origin is the point $(0, tl)$, where tl is the amount of composite good that remains if $s^B = l$ and household A commutes the entire length of the city. In this case, the bottom of

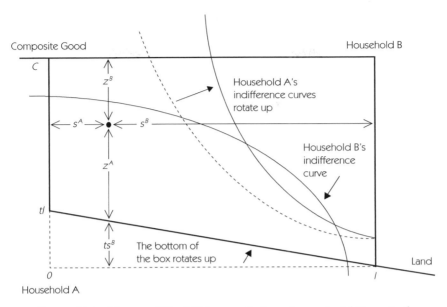

Figure 7.6   The modified Edgeworth box: household B central.

the box has "rotated up" by ts^B, so household A's indifference curves must also be "rotated up" in the same way. Household B's indifference curves are unchanged. A point in this modified Edgeworth box identifies an allocation in which household B lives closest to the city center, and is the same as described in the previous case except that x^B is at the city center and x^A is at $0 + s^B$.

The set of tangencies, or the contract curve, will characterize interior Pareto optima, just as in the standard Edgeworth box. Again, it is useful to characterize the contract curve in terms of marginal rates of substitution. Let $MRS^i : R_+^2 \to R$ be household i's *marginal rate of substitution for land in terms of composite good*, where

$$ MRS^i(s^i, z^i) = \frac{MU_s^i}{MU_z^i} $$

identifies how much composite good household i is willing to give up for an additional piece of land, given that it is already consuming the bundle (s^i, z^i). When household A lives closest to the city center, a feasible allocation $(s^A, s^B, z^A, z^B, x^A, x^B)$ is on the contract curve if $MRS^A(s^A, z^A) = MRS^B(s^B, z^B) + t$ and $s^A < s^B$. We add t to $MRS^B(s^B, z^B)$ because we rotate household B's indifference curves down, just as we rotated the top of the box down to account for composite good used in commuting. Alternatively, when household B lives closest to the city center, a feasible allocation $(s^A, s^B, z^A, z^B, x^A, x^B)$ is on the contract curve if $MRS^B(s^B, z^B) = MRS^A(s^A, z^A) + t$ and $s^B < s^A$. As a result, the contract curve may be disconnected, as in Figure 7.7. Since we know that the household living closest to the city center

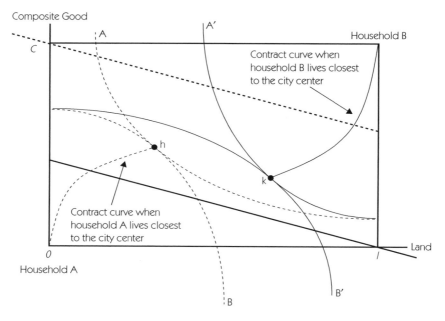

Figure 7.7   The contract curve.

can enjoy a level of utility no higher than the household living farther away from the city center, we know that both households are equally well off at the ends of both pieces of the contract curve and, in fact, enjoy the same level of utility. For example, in Figure 7.7, let h identify the allocation $(s^A, s^B, z^A, z^B, x^A, x^B)$, which is the endpoint of the contract curve when household A lives closest to the city center, and let k identify the allocation $(\hat{s}^A, \hat{s}^B, \hat{z}^A, \hat{z}^B, \hat{x}^A, \hat{x}^B)$, which is the endpoint of the contract curve when household B lives closest to the city center. Then $U^A(s^A, z^A) = U^A(\hat{s}^A, \hat{z}^A) = U^B(\hat{s}^B, \hat{z}^B) = U^B(s^B, z^B)$.

The standard argument from microeconomic theory explaining why the contract curve characterizes Pareto optima applies here. Given a feasible allocation on the curve, there is no alternative allocation in the modified Edgeworth box that makes one household better off without harming the other household. Similarly, with convex preferences, interior Pareto optima occur at tangency points, on the contract curve.

The intuition for these first-order conditions is new. Consider an allocation $(s^A, s^B, z^A, z^B, x^A, x^B)$, where $s^A < s^B$ and $MRS^A(s^A, z^A) > MRS^B(s^B, z^B) + t$. Then we could expand household A's parcel a little, shrink household B's parcel a little to keep the allocation feasible, and transfer some composite good from household A to B, while covering the additional commuting cost. Such an operation could make both households better off, contradicting the optimality of the original allocation. Similarly, if $MRS^A(s^A, z^A) < MRS^B(s^B, z^B) + t$, then we could shrink household A's parcel, expand household B's parcel, save on commuting cost, and transfer composite good to household A, making both households better off. Thus, at any efficient allocation with $s^A < s^B$, $MRS_A(s_A, z_A) = MRS_B(s_B, z_B) + t$.

The final intuition comes from Figure 7.5 and calculus. To account for commuting cost, household B's indifference curves are rotated down by $C - ts^A$. As we have defined marginal rates of substitution to be nonnegative, the condition characterizing tangencies in the figure is actually

$$-MRS^A(s^A, z^A) = -MRS^B(s^B, z^B) - t.$$

The right-hand side follows from the application of calculus to the rotation. The first-order condition follows immediately from this equation.

7.5 EQUILIBRIUM

To explore equilibrium, we need to identify who is endowed with the land and composite good available in the economy. Let ω^i be household i's endowment of composite good. We assume that households are endowed with all the composite good available in the economy, so that $\omega^A + \omega^B = C$. For simplicity, households are not endowed with land. Rather, we introduce an absentee landlord who is endowed with all the land in the economy. The landlord does not like to consume land in the city, but does like to consume the composite good, so $U^L(s^L, z^L) = z^L$.

Adding the landlord to the model necessitates adjusting our definitions of an allocation and of feasibility. Now, an allocation is a list $(s^A, s^B, z^A, z^B, x^A, x^B, z^L)$, which is feasible if

$$z^A + z^B + z^L + tx^A + tx^B = C,$$

$$[x^A, x^A + s^A) \cap [x^B, x^B + s^B) = \emptyset,$$

and

$$[x^A, x^A + s^A) \cup [x^B, x^B + s^B) = [0, l).$$

The definition of a Pareto optimum is the same.

Let the composite consumption good be the numeraire. Let P be the land price function, where $P(V)$ is the price of parcel $V \subset [0, l)$. We would like the price of land to satisfy "no arbitrage," so we would like it to be additive across land parcels. In other words, if V and W are two parcels of land such that $V \cap W = \emptyset$, then $P(V) + P(W) = P(V \cup W)$. Let $p:[0, l) \to R_+$ be a density function. A land price function P such that $P(V) = \int_V p(x)dx$ satisfies this criterion.

If $(s^A, s^B, z^A, z^B, x^A, x^B, z^L)$ is a feasible allocation and p is a price density, then household A pays $\int_{x^A}^{x^A + s^A} p(x)dx$ for parcel $[x^A, x^A + s^A)$ and household B pays $\int_{x^B}^{x^B + s^B} p(x)dx$ for parcel $[x^B, x^B + s^B)$. Since

$$[x^A, x^A + s^A) \cap [x^B, x^B + s^B) = \emptyset$$

and

$$[x^A, x^A + s^A) \cup [x^B, x^B + s^B) = [0, l),$$

the landlord receives

$$\int_{x^A}^{x^A + s^A} p(x) dx + \int_{x^B}^{x^B + s^B} p(x) dx = \int_0^l p(x) dx$$

units of composite good from the sale of land, so $z^L = \int_0^l p(x) dx$.

Now we are ready to define a competitive equilibrium. Composite consumption good is again the numeraire. A *competitive equilibrium* is a feasible allocation $(s^{*A}, s^{*B}, z^{*A}, z^{*B}, x^{*A}, x^{*B}, z^{*L})$ and a price density p^* such that:

(a) (s^{*A}, z^{*A}) maximizes household A's utility subject to its budget constraint,

$$z^A + \int_{x^A}^{x^A + s^A} p^*(x) dx + tx^A \le \omega^A; \text{ and}$$

(b) (s^{*B}, z^{*B}) maximizes household B's utility subject to its budget constraint

$$z^B + \int_{x^B}^{x^B + s^B} p^*(x) dx + tx^B \le \omega^B.$$

Since utility functions are increasing in both arguments, budget constraints will hold with equality. Substituting for z^A and z^B in the respective households' maximization problems, the first-order conditions for maximizing utility over driveway locations and land consumption are, for $i = A, B$,

$$MRS^i(s^i, z^i) = p(x^i + s^i)$$

and

$$p(x^i + s^i) = p(x^i) - t.$$

The intuition for these expressions is as follows. Adding land at the back of a parcel causes no change in commuting costs, so at a household optimum, the willingness to pay for an additional unit of land at the back is equal to its cost. Notice that this condition is analogous to the first-order condition for equilibrium in the standard Edgeworth box. Adding a unit of land at the front of a parcel reduces commuting cost by t, so at a household optimum, adding a unit at the front must cost t more than adding a unit to the back. Otherwise, the household would choose a different parcel at a household optimum.

Since there are three agents in this economy, we cannot illustrate equilibrium allocations using an Edgeworth box. We can, however, illustrate equilibrium price densities. Suppose that $(s^{*A}, s^{*B}, z^{*A}, z^{*B}, x^{*A}, x^{*B}, z^{*L})$ is an equilibrium allocation with household A living closest to the city center. Let $p^A = MRS^A(s^{*A}, z^{*A})$ and let $p^B = MRS^B(s^{*B}, z^{*B})$. We might guess that a price density p, such that

$$p(x) = \begin{cases} p^A, & 0 \leq x < x^{*B}, \\ p^B, & x^{*B} \leq x < l, \end{cases}$$

is an equilibrium price density. See panel (a) of Figure 7.8, where the horizontal axis is location and the vertical axis is price. However, since $MRS^A > MRS^B$, household A will want to expand its lot and consume part of household B's parcel. So, this price density cannot be an equilibrium price density.

What we need to do is to construct a price density so that household A cannot increase its utility by expanding its parcel, so that it has no incentive to do so. Let $\bar{U}^A = U^A(s^{*A}, z^{*A})$ and let $z(\bar{U}^A, s)$ be the amount of composite good that household A must consume to enjoy that same utility level, $\bar{U}^A$, given that it is consuming s units of land, where s may not be equal to s^{*A}. Let $\hat{s}$ be such that $MRS^A(\hat{s}, z(\bar{U}^A, \hat{s})) = p^B$: see panel (b) of Figure 7.8. Then household A will be indifferent between the parcel $[x^{*A}, x^{*A} + s^{*A})$ and a slightly larger parcel if the price density is adjusted so that $p(x) = MRS^A(x, z(\bar{U}^A, x))$ for $s^{*A} \leq x < \hat{s}$. In addition, household B will have no desire to expand its parcel in toward the city center. Thus, p^* such that

$$p^*(x) = \begin{cases} p^A, & 0 \leq x < s^{*A}, \\ MRS^A(x, z(\bar{U}^A, x)), & s^{*A} \leq x \leq \hat{s}, \\ p^B, & \hat{s} \leq x \leq l, \end{cases}$$

is an equilibrium price density. Alternatively, let $\bar{U}^B = U(s^{*B}, z^{*B})$ and let $z(\bar{U}^B, s)$ be the quantity of composite good household B must consume to enjoy utility level $\bar{U}^B$, given that it is consuming s units of land. Let $\tilde{s}$ be such that $MRS^B(\tilde{s}, z(\bar{U}^B, \tilde{s})) = p^A$. Then p^* such that

$$p^*(x) = \begin{cases} p^A, & 0 \leq x < \tilde{s}, \\ MRS^B(x, z(\bar{U}^B, x)), & \tilde{s} \leq x \leq s^{*B}, \\ p^B, & s^{*B} \leq x \leq l, \end{cases}$$

is also an equilibrium price density; see panel (c) of Figure 7.8. Indeed, any price density that "falls between" the two is also an equilibrium price density, so there is a continuum of equilibria. The landlord likes the last one best, since that one generates the highest rent collection.

7.6   WELFARE PROPERTIES OF EQUILIBRIUM ALLOCATIONS

Two features of this model are that equilibrium allocations are Pareto optima, so there is a valid First Welfare Theorem (Berliant & Fujita 1992), and for every Pareto-optimal allocation, there exists a land price density and endowments such that the Pareto-optimal allocation is an equilibrium allocation with respect to that land price density and endowments, so that there is also a valid Second Welfare Theorem (Berliant & Fujita 1992). Intuitively, this can be seen from the first-order

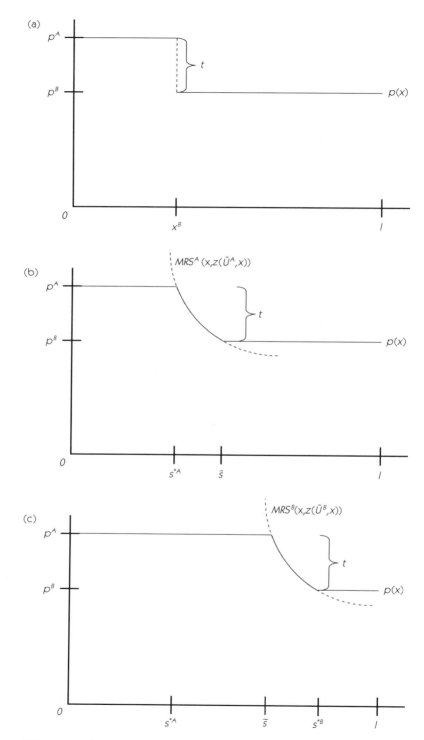

Figure 7.8 A candidate equilibrium price density (a), a low equilibrium price density (b), and a high equilibrium price density (c).

conditions. If household A is located closer to the city center, then the first-order conditions for equilibrium imply

$$MRS^B(s^B,z^B) = p(x^B + s^B) = p(l),$$

$$MRS^A(s^A,z^A) = p(x^A + s^A) = p(s^A) = p(x^B),$$

and

$$p(x^B + s^B) = p(x^B) - t.$$

So, $MRS^B(s^B,z^B) = MRS^A(s^A,z^A) - t$, and this is the first-order condition for Pareto optima. The argument also works in the opposite direction. An important implication is that Proposition 1 applies to any equilibrium allocation, so the predictions stated in Proposition 1 are potentially testable. Moreover, in equilibrium, the consumer with higher income must naturally end up with higher utility. Thus, in equilibrium, the order of households from the city center outward is increasing in income, utility, and parcel size.

7.7   AN EXAMPLE

Consider a linear city of length $l = 8$. Let household A be endowed with 58 units of composite good and let household B be endowed with 154 units of composite good, so that $C = 212$. The transportation cost of commuting per unit of distance is $t = 8$. Suppose that household A's utility function is $U^A(s^A,z^A) = z^A - (16 - s^A)^2$ and that household B's utility function is $U^B(s^B,z^B) = z^B - (16 - s^B)^2$. For household A, the marginal utility of land at a bundle (s^A,z^A) is $2(16 - s^A)$, while the marginal utility of composite good at a bundle (s^A,z^A) is always 1. Similarly, household B's marginal utility of land at a bundle (s^B,z^B) is $2(16 - s^B)$, while the marginal utility of composite good at a bundle (s^B,z^B) is always 1. (For those who know calculus, recall that the marginal utility of land is the derivative of the utility function with respect to land, and similarly for the composite good.) The marginal rate of substitution for land in terms of composite good at a bundle is the ratio of the marginal utilities at that bundle, so for household A, $MRS^A(s^A,z^A) = 2(16 - s^A)$, and for household B, $MRS^B(s^B,z^B) = 2(16 - s^B)$.

What does the set of Pareto optima look like in this model? First, we will identify the part of the contract curve such that household A lives closest to the city center. We can find this part of the curve by setting $MRS^A(s^A,z^A) = MRS^B(s^B,z^B) + t$, which implies that $2(16 - s^A) = 2(16 - s^B) + t$. Since $t = 8$ and $s^B = 8 - s^A$, we can see that $2(16 - s^A) = 2(16 - (8 - s^A)) + 8$. Solving for s^A, we find that $s^{oA} = 2$. It follows that $s^{oB} = 8 - 2 = 6$. When household A lives closest to the city center, its utility level must be less than or equal to household B's utility level, which implies that $z^{oA} - (16 - 2)^2 \le z^{oB} - (16 - 6)^2$. We know that

$$z^{oB} = C - ts^{oA} - z^A = 212 - 8 \times 2 - z^{oA} = 196 - z^{oA}.$$

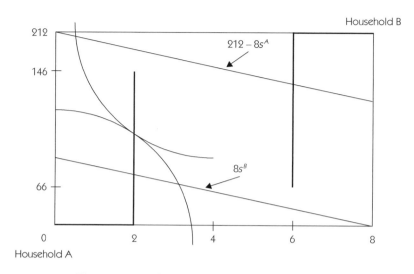

Figure 7.9   The contract curve: an example.

Substituting for z^{oB}, it follows that $z^{oA} \leq 146$. Thus, when household A lives closest to the city center, the set of Pareto optima is the union of the two line segments $[(0,0),(2,0)]$ and $[(2,0),(2,146)]$ (see Figure 7.9). Since the two households have identical utility functions, we know by symmetry that when household B lives closest to the city center $s^{oB} = 2$, $s^{oA} = 6$, and $z^{oA} \leq 146$. When household B lives closest to the city center, the contract curve is the union of the two line segments $[(6,66),(6,212)]$ and $[(6,212),(8,212)]$ (see Figure 7.9).

Next, we will construct an equilibrium price density for this model. Since both the First and Second Welfare Theorems are valid for this model, the only candidates for equilibrium allocations are the Pareto-optimal allocations. Since household A has less endowed wealth than household B, in the end it will have lower utility than household B. It follows from Proposition 1 that household A lives closest to the city center. We want to construct a land price density such that neither household can increase its utility by deviating from an allocation such that $x^{*A} = 0$, $s^{*A} = 2$, $x^{*B} = 2$, and $s^{*B} = 6$. On the margin, the price that household A pays for land should be equal to its marginal willingness to pay for land, which implies that

$$p^*(2) = MRS^A = 2(16 - s^{*A}) = 2(16 - 2) = 28.$$

Similarly, on the margin, the price that household B pays for land should be equal to its marginal willingness to pay for land, so

$$p^*(8) = MRS^B = 2(16 - s^{*B}) = 2(16 - 6) = 20.$$

Note that the difference between the two is equal to the cost of commuting per unit distance. Next, we need to price land at $x > 2$ such that household A cannot

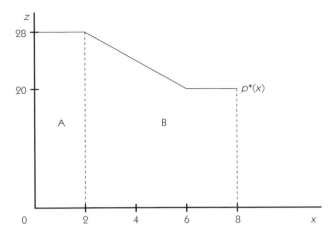

Figure 7.10 Equilibrium price density: an example.

make itself better off by increasing the size of its lot, while keeping its lot front at the origin. In other words, if household A consumes more land, it should have to give up so much composite good that it does not increase its utility. This quantity is revealed by MRS^A, so $p^*(x) \geq 2(16 - x)$. Note that when $x = 6$, $2(16 - x) = 20$, and for $x > 6$, $2(16 - x) < 20$. If we set $p^*(x) = 20$ for $6 < x \leq 8$, then the condition that $p^*(x) \geq 2(16 - x)$ is satisfied, as is the condition that $p^*(8) = 20$. So, an equilibrium price density is p^* such that

$$p^*(x) = \begin{cases} 28, & 0 \leq x < 2, \\ 2(16 - x), & 2 \leq x \leq 6, \\ 20, & 6 \leq x \leq 8. \end{cases}$$

This price density is illustrated in Figure 7.10.

Finally, we will construct the equilibrium allocation associated with this land price density. Since the equilibrium land price density constructed above supports an allocation such that $x^{*A} = 0$, $s^{*A} = 2$, $x^{*B} = 2$, and $s^{*B} = 6$, we just need to figure out how much composite good everyone consumes.

Household A's expenditure on land is

$$\int_{x^{*A}}^{x^{*A}+s^{*A}} p^*(x)dx = \int_0^2 p^*(x)dx = \int_0^2 28dx = 28 \times 2 = 56,$$

which is the area labeled A in Figure 7.10. Household A's utility is increasing in land and composite good, so it exhausts its budget and consumes

$$z^{*A} = \omega^A - tx^{*A} - \int_{x^{*A}}^{x^{*A}+s^{*A}} p^*(x)dx = 58 - 56 = 2.$$

Household B's expenditure on land, the area labeled B in Figure 7.10, is

$$\int_{x^{*B}}^{x^{*B}+s^{*B}} p(x)\mathrm{d}x = \int_{2}^{8} p^*(x)\mathrm{d}x = \int_{2}^{6} 2(16-x)\mathrm{d}x + \int_{6}^{8} 20\mathrm{d}x = 96 + 40 = 136,$$

and its expenditure on commuting is $tx^{*B} = 8 \times 2 = 16$. Since household B also spends all of its income,

$$z^{*B} = \omega^B - tx^{*B} - \int_{x^{*B}}^{x^{*B}+s^{*B}} p^*(x)\mathrm{d}x = 154 - 16 - 136 = 2.$$

Finally, the absentee landlord collects both households' expenditures on land in composite good, so $z^{*L} = 56 + 136 = 192$. So, an equilibrium allocation associated with the price density p^* is $(s^{*A}, s^{*B}, z^{*A}, z^{*B}, x^{*A}, x^{*B}, z^{*L}) = (2,6,2,2,0,2,192)$. Alternative equilibria have the same allocation of land, but the landlord collects more rent from household B.

7.8   CONCLUSION

We have presented in this essay the simplest model of how two households distribute themselves across space and shown that they do so efficiently. Using the welfare theorems and Proposition 1, we can characterize the relationship between household income, the size of the lot the household occupies, and the location of the lot. In equilibrium, the household with the larger endowment of composite commodity will ultimately enjoy a higher level of utility, and so will live further away from the city center and on a larger lot than the household with the smaller endowment of composite commodity. This was, in fact, the outcome of our specific example. The Alonso model can also accommodate n identical households, where n is finite and greater than two. Under certain conditions, Fujita (1989) can be used to show that the model can also accommodate n heterogeneous households.

An important implication of this model is that equilibrium allocations are efficient, so there is no market failure. Thus, under the assumption of perfect competition, the free market yields efficiency, as it does in similar analyses of nonlocational goods.

Acknowledgments

We would like to thank William Alonso and Masa Fujita for divine inspiration. Helpful comments were provided by an anonymous referee and Richard Arnott. The authors retain responsibility for any errors.

Bibliography

Alonso, W. 1964: *Location and Land Use: Toward a General Theory of Land Rent.* Cambridge, MA: Harvard University Press.

Berliant, M. and Fujita, M. 1992: Alonso's discrete population model of land use: efficient allocations and competitive equilibria. *International Economic Review*, 33(3), 535–66.

Fujita, M. 1989: *Urban Economic Theory: Land Use and City Size*. Cambridge, UK: Cambridge University Press.

Varian, H. 1993: *Intermediate Microeconomics: A Modern Approach*. New York: W. W. Norton.

CHAPTER EIGHT

Testing for
Monocentricity

Daniel P. McMillen

8.1   INTRODUCTION

The monocentric city model of Muth (1969) and Mills (1972) is still the dominant model of urban spatial structure. Its central predictions – that population density, land values, and house prices fall with distance from the city center – have been the subject of repeated empirical testing. Indeed, one objective of the model was to explain a set of stylized empirical facts, and extensions of the model were developed in response to empirical testing. This close cooperation between theory and empirical work is one of the hallmarks of the field of urban economics.

A consensus appears to have developed that the monocentric city model is no longer an accurate depiction of urban spatial structure. This view is partly due to the unrealistic nature of the model's assumptions. Clearly not everyone works in the central city, and modern urban areas may be viewed more aptly as polycentric rather than monocentric. The central behavioral assumption of the model, that workers attempt to minimize their commuting cost, is called into question by the literature on "wasteful commuting" (Hamilton 1982). O'Sullivan's (2002) popular textbook perpetuates the notion that the monocentric city model is designed to explain an old-fashioned city by listing as one of the assumptions "horse-drawn wagons," implying that the model does not apply to a modern city with cars.

In this chapter, I review some of the empirical evidence on the monocentric city model's predictions. I contend that the demise of the model is exaggerated. The central city still dominates urban spatial patterns, and the basic insights of the model apply to more complex polycentric cities. Much of the apparent decline in the explanatory power of the monocentric city model is actually a misunderstanding of the empirical evidence. And, importantly, many of the ways in which the model now fails are in fact explained by the comparative-statics predictions of the model itself. Although the model is oversimplified, it remains a useful analytical tool, requiring only modest modifications to be remarkably accurate.

8.2 EMPIRICAL PREDICTIONS

8.2.1 Consumers

In the Muth–Mills version of the monocentric city model, consumers receive utility from housing and other goods. Housing is an abstract commodity in this model. It combines land, square footage, and all other housing characteristics into a single measure. The durability of housing is ignored because the static nature of the model is designed to focus on long-run equilibrium results. Each household has a worker who commutes each day to the central business district (CBD). The simplest version of the model includes neither congestion nor time costs of commuting. Instead, each round trip to the CBD costs $\$t$ per mile. Since consumers have no direct preferences for one location over another, they would all try to live in the CBD in order to minimize their commuting costs unless house prices adjust to keep them indifferent between locations. In equilibrium, the price of housing must fall with distance from the CBD:

$$\frac{\partial P_h(d)}{\partial d} = \frac{-t}{H(d)}, \tag{8.1}$$

where $P_h(d)$ is the price (or rent, since the distinction is irrelevant in a static world) and $H(d)$ is the quantity of housing at a site d miles from the CBD.

Equation (8.1) is simply a formula for the slope of a function depicting the relationship between the price of housing and distance from the CBD. If the quantity of housing does not vary by location, equation (8.1) predicts that the price of housing is a linear function of distance. However, the model predicts that $H(d)$ is lower near the CBD than in more distant locations because consumers substitute away from housing and toward other goods when P_h is high. This substitution implies a particular shape for the house price function: the slope is steep when H is low, meaning that prices rise rapidly when approaching the CBD.

The first major implication of the monocentric model, then, is that, for a group of identical households, house prices decline with distance from the CBD according to a smooth, convex function. Figure 8.1 shows the general form of the function. In a world with different types of households, the general form of the relationship will continue to look much like the function shown in Figure 8.1, because the equilibrium house price function is the upper envelope of the functions for each household type. Since the quantity of housing is low where the price of housing is high, the function for the quantity of housing is upward sloping. Finally, since consumers substitute toward other goods as they consume less housing, the model predicts that Figure 8.1 also represents consumption of the nonhousing good.

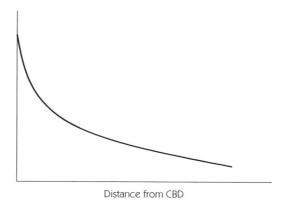

Distance from CBD

Figure 8.1 Functional form prediction.

One critical point to bear in mind is that the monocentric city model makes no direct predictions for the *value* of housing. The value of housing is the product of price times quantity: $V_h(d) = P_h(d)H(d)$. Since price falls with distance and quantity rises, the value of housing can go either way. Once we allow for differences in income among consumers, the model predicts that the value of housing is high where higher-income households choose to live. Again, this relationship between house values and distance from the CBD is ambiguous. Whether house values rise or fall with distance from the CBD has no direct empirical relevance for the monocentric city model. The trick is to isolate the price of a unit of housing from the quantity – a nearly hopeless task, since housing is a complex, multidimensional good that cannot be measured simply.

8.2.2 Producers

Housing producers combine land and capital to produce housing. Producers will pay more for land near the CBD because consumers will pay more for housing there. Figure 8.1 thus can depict the equilibrium relationship between land values and distance from the CBD: land values decline at a decreasing rate with distance. Just as consumers substitute away from housing and toward other goods near the CBD, producers substitute away from land and toward capital where the price of land is high. This result implies that the ratio of capital to land declines with distance from the CBD. Thus, Figure 8.1 also represents the capital–land ratio. Indirectly, we also have a prediction that population density declines with distance, because density must be high where the ratio of capital to land is high.

Lot sizes are easy to measure. But like housing itself, housing capital is a theoretical concept and is not easily measured. Producers substitute capital for land in various ways: building taller buildings, using more floor space, or simply by improving the quality of the nonland inputs. Empirically, building heights and floor areas are easy to observe. The most readily available measure of the capital–land ratio is the "floor-area ratio," which is simply building area divided by lot size. The model predicts that floor-area ratios fall with distance from the CBD, as shown in Figure 8.1.

8.2.3 A summary of empirical predictions for distance from the CBD

The simple version of the monocentric city model produces an impressive number of predictions. The most important of these predictions are that the price of a unit of housing, land values, the capital–land ratio, and population density all decline smoothly with distance from the CBD, as shown in Figure 8.1. The only major alterations to the standard two-good consumer maximization problem are the assumptions that no two households can occupy the same space and that workers must commute to their jobs. A full urban spatial structure follows from these assumptions.

The model has empirical content. Unlike many economic models, we have full functional form predictions. Figure 8.1 implies that distance from the CBD is the primary determinant of urban spatial relationships. For example, we should find that land values decline smoothly at a decreasing rate with distance from the CBD, the function should have no discontinuities, and this basic relationship should hold for different cities at different times.

8.2.4 Comparative-statics results

Although the simple functional form predictions are a powerful test of the model, many different models could produce the same functions. Another commonly used empirical approach is to test the monocentric city model's comparative-statics predictions. The predictions discussed here are based on the "closed-city" version of the model, in which the overall population of the city is an exogenous variable while the utility level of the representative household is endogenous. The model predicts that the function in Figure 8.1 shifts up as population or agricultural land values increase, because either change increases the cost of land throughout an urban area. The increase in land values and house prices leads producers to build homes using higher capital–land ratios, which lead to higher population densities. Decreases in commuting costs make sites farther from the CBD relatively more valuable than closer sites. Thus, a decrease in commuting costs leads to a flatter slope for the functions depicted in Figure 8.1.

The results are ambiguous for the remaining important variable, income. An increase in income increases the demand for housing, which leads consumers to prefer sites farther from the CBD where the price of housing is lower. But it also increases the aversion to time spent commuting, which has an offsetting effect making sites closer to the CBD more valuable. Empirically, it appears that the former effect dominates, as increases in income have generally led to declines in the slopes of the functions in Figure 8.1. However, the empirical trade-off between the housing demand and commuting time cost elasticities has been the subject of very little empirical investigation.

Since the 1800s, most urban areas have enjoyed steadily rising incomes, lower commuting costs, and steady population growth. The path of agricultural land values is less clear; although they may well have declined in real terms, their effect is overwhelmed by the large increase in urban populations. Together, these changes should lead the functions depicted in Figure 8.1 to shift up and have flatter slopes. Thus, one way to test the comparative-statics predictions is to compare estimates for a single city over time. Alternatively, we might compare estimates across cities at a given time if measures are available for income, commuting cost, population, and agricultural land values.

The latter approach – comparing estimates across cities – is far less common because it is more difficult to acquire data for a cross-section of cities than for a single city over time. Excellent examples of the approach include Mills (1972) and Brueckner and Fansler (1983). Mills compares population density estimates for Baltimore, Milwaukee, Philadelphia, and Rochester for 1880–1963. He finds some evidence that intercepts are higher and slopes are flatter when cities have higher populations and incomes and lower commuting costs. However, by far the most important explanatory variable is the lagged dependent variable, indicating that inertia is a critical determinant of the density function coefficients. Brueckner and Fansler compare total land areas across 40 American cities in 1970. As predicted by the model, they find that land areas are lower when population and incomes are lower and when agricultural land values are higher. Evidence on the effect of commuting costs on land area is less clear: their attempts to measure this variable produce the right signs but the coefficients are statistically insignificant. In general, this approach is hampered by the difficulty inherent in measuring variables such as income and commuting costs.

8.3   Empirical Modeling Approaches

8.3.1   Regression-based approaches

The functions shown in Figure 8.1 are estimated easily by ordinary least squares regression procedures. The most commonly used functional form is the simple negative exponential function:

$$\ln y_i = \alpha - \beta x_i + u_i, \tag{8.2}$$

where x_i is the distance from the CBD at location i, u_i is an error term, and α and β are parameters. The dependent variable, y_i, may be the price of a unit of housing, land value, the capital–land ratio, or population density. The negative exponential function generally fits urban spatial relationships well. In this formulation, β is the "gradient" because each additional mile from the CBD causes y to fall by 100β percent. Additional terms can easily be added to the estimating equation. Equation (8.2) imposes the structure implied by the monocentric city model: $\partial y_i / \partial x_i = -\beta y_i < 0$ and $\partial^2 y_i / \partial x_i^2 = \beta^2 y_i > 0$.

Although equation (8.2) is the most commonly used estimating equation, it may not be flexible enough for many urban spatial relationships. The land value gradient, for example, tends to be higher near the city center than in more distant locations. Adding higher-order terms – x^2 or x^2 and x^3 – may improve the fit significantly. One particularly attractive formulation is the cubic spline. In this approach, the distance variable, x, is split into equal intervals and a separate cubic function is applied to each region. The function is constrained to be smooth at the boundaries between regions (which are known as "knots"). For example, in the empirical section of this chapter, I divide distance from the CBD into four intervals. The minimum value is x_0, the boundaries between regions are x_1, x_2, and x_3, and the maximum value is x_4. The distance between each knot is $(x_4 - x_0)/4$. The estimating equation is

$$\ln y_i = \alpha + \beta_1(x_i - x_0) + \beta_2(x_i - x_0)^2 + \beta_3(x_i - x_0)^3 +$$
$$\gamma_1(x_i - x_1)^3 D_1 + \gamma_2(x_i - x_2)^3 D_2 + \gamma_3(x_i - x_3)^3 D_3 + u_i. \qquad (8.3)$$

The D_k terms are dummy variables that equal one when $x_i \geq x_k$. Additional flexibility can be added by defining more regions. Each additional region simply involves a new definition of the knots and an additional interaction term between a dummy variable and a cubic term of the form $(x_i - x_k)^3$.

A good example of the use of spline functions is Anderson (1982). Alternative flexible estimators such as Fourier expansions (Gallant 1982) are also useful. Nonparametric estimators and semiparametric estimators such as that used by McMillen (1996) are popular alternatives. Nonparametric estimators are far more difficult to use and have few advantages when nonlinearity is confined to a single variable. However, interactions between variables may be easier to model using nonparametric techniques.

8.3.2 The two-point method for population density functions

The most widely studied urban spatial relationship is population density. The only necessary data to estimate a population density function are population, land areas, and distance from the CBD for small geographical areas. Such data now are readily available for zip codes, census tracts, and even smaller areas. However, historical data are more apt to be reported only for larger geographical areas, such as municipalities and counties, making it difficult to compare density gradients over a long time.

Mills (1972) proposed a clever method for estimating historical population density gradients using extremely limited data sources. The starting point for his procedure is the simple negative exponential function, equation (8.2), where y is defined as population density. Population density at location d can be written as $P(d)/A(d)$, where $P(d)$ is the number of residents and $A(d)$ is the land area in an infinitesimal ring d miles from the city center. In a circular city, $A(d) = 2\pi d$. Mills generalizes this specification somewhat by assuming that $A(d) = \phi d$. For example, ϕ is approximately equal to π in Chicago or Milwaukee and to the full 2π in Indianapolis. The approach does not work in cities such as San Francisco.

Mills's trick is to integrate the population density function so that only observable variables remain. Given the expression for $A(d)$, we can rewrite equation (8.2) as $P(d) = \phi d e^{\alpha - \beta d}$. Integrating this function by parts from $d = 0$ to $d = d_c$, we have $P_c = (\phi e^{\alpha}/\beta^2)[1 - (1 + \beta d_c)e^{-\beta d_c}]$. If d_c represents the central-city radius, then P_c is the population of the central city. Letting d_c go to infinity, the population of the entire metropolitan area is approximately $P = \phi e^{\alpha}/\beta^2$. The assumption that the metropolitan extends forever simplifies the calculations and causes little bias. Finally, the ratio P_c/P leads to a tractable equation:

$$\frac{P_c}{P} = [1 - (1 + \beta d_c)e^{-\beta d_c}]. \tag{8.4}$$

Given the central city population, the population of the entire metropolitan area, and the radius of the central city, equation (8.4) has only one remaining unknown, β. Thus, this equation can be solved iteratively by choosing a value of β that provides the closest match between the two sides of equation (8.4).

Population data are readily available from the Census Bureau. However, d_c can be difficult to calculate. Although ϕ does not enter equation (8.4) directly, it may be easier to estimate than d_c. The two parameters are related by the identity $A_c = (\phi/2)d_c^2$, where A_c is the land area of the central city. Since data on central-city land areas are available from the Census Bureau and ϕ is usually easy to approximate, the calculations can be simplified by calculating an implicit value for the central-city radius: $d_c = \sqrt{2A_c/\phi}$. Thus, Mills's procedure makes it possible to estimate theoretically appropriate population density gradients with readily available historical data – population of the central city and metropolitan area. Mills (1972) and Macauley (1985) are good examples of the technique.

8.4   Empirical Results – Land Values and Population Density

Figure 8.2 shows the trends in population density and land value gradients since Chicago's founding in the 1830s. McDonald (1997) calculated the density gradients for 1870–1990 using Mills's two-point method, and I used data from 2000 to update the estimates. The land value gradients come from McMillen (1996). For 1836–1928, the estimates are based on data from Hoyt (1933). Hoyt presents maps of average land values for tracts of land with the City of Chicago that typically are about a square mile in area. Mills (1969) was the first to use this classic data source to estimate land value functions. I updated the estimates for 1960–90 using data from *Olcott's Land Values Blue Book of Chicago*. Until recently, *Olcott's* presented land value estimates annually for every block in the city.

The important trend to note in Figure 8.2 is the long-running decline in both land value and population density gradients. Land values decline by more than 60 percent per mile with distance from the CBD in 1836 and 1857. Over the rest of the nineteenth century, the gradient declines to about 50 percent, and it falls to about 20 percent in 1928. By 1960, the land value gradient hovers near zero, but the gradient rises back to 14 percent in 1990. The population density gradient

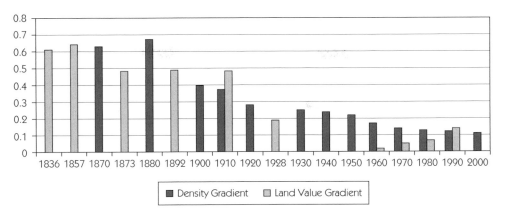

Figure 8.2 Population density and land value gradients in Chicago.

falls from over 60 percent in 1870 and 1880 to 20–30 percent for 1920–50, and to between 10 percent and 20 percent thereafter.

During this long time period, commuting costs fell dramatically, incomes increased, and Chicago grew from a small village of a few thousand people to a city with about 3 million residents and a metropolitan area with a population of about 8 million. The monocentric city model predicts that both the land value and population density functions should shift up and the gradients should decline over time. The data strongly support both predictions. Although the two-point method does not produce standard error estimates, the land value regressions fit the Hoyt data well. The R^2 values indicate that the single explanatory variable, distance from the CBD, explains more than 80 percent of the variation in the natural logarithm of land values in 1836 and 1857, and the R^2 value remains as high as 0.61 in 1910. However, the R^2 value falls to 0.24 in 1928, and is nearly zero in 1960. The R^2 value is 0.10 in 1990. Thus, the evidence is mixed: the model appears to fit well in the 1800s, and the decline in the gradients matches theoretical predictions. But low values of R^2 indicate that the model may have little predictive power now.

The more recent evidence against the model's predictive ability is not as strong as appears at first glance. In a model with a single explanatory variable, the formula for the R^2 value is $b^2 s_x^2 / s_u^2$, where b is the estimated gradient and s_x^2 and s_u^2 are the variances of the explanatory variable and the regression residuals. If the locations for the observations do not change over time and the residual variance stays the same, the R^2 value will decline whenever the gradient declines. Theory has nothing to say about trends in the model error variance. Thus, the model *predicts* that R^2 values should fall over time as commuting costs decline and income increases.

Another commonly overlooked feature of land value and population density gradients is the way in which data sets have changed over time. Data collection has improved greatly in recent years. In the past, data were much more likely to be reported as simple averages for large areas. For example, Hoyt's square-mile tracts are unusually small for historical land value data. *Olcott's* presents much more detailed data: the numbers sometimes vary within a single city block. For population density, Clark's (1951) classic study uses data for square-mile rings around the CBD. A city with a 10-mile radius will only have 10 observations. Modern data sets are much larger. For example, McMillen and Lester (2003) estimate population density gradients using more than 10,000 observations in the Chicago metropolitan area. R^2 values are usually much higher for aggregated data.

Further, in the past researchers usually confined their attention to the central city. Suburban functions are often nearly flat; the R^2 formula implies that the estimated function's predictive power will be low for these observations. Thus, adding suburban data usually drives down the R^2. Finally, the monocentric city model only predicts that the functions should look like those in Figure 8.1; it does not predict that the negative exponential function is the correct one. In McMillen (1996), I find that a more general functional form and the addition of a few explanatory variables – distance from Lake Michigan and distance from O'Hare and Midway Airports – raises the R^2 for the 1990 *Olcott's* land value function from 0.10 to 0.87. Whereas a theory that only accounts for 10 percent of the variation in land values is unimpressive, 87 percent is impressive indeed. No one ever claimed that distance from the CBD was the only variable that matters. If flexible functional forms and a few variables account for nearly 90 percent of the spatial variation in land values across small geographical areas, then the theory is alive and well.

Other evidence does point to important deficiencies of the monocentric city model. The primary problem is the static nature of the model. In fact, age matters. McDonald and Bowman (1979) find that land values increase with distance from the CBD in older areas of Chicago, and McDonald (1979) finds little relationship between land values and population density in these areas. Densities reflect the past, whereas land values reflect expectations about the future. Brueckner (1986) finds evidence in favor of a vintage model of urban spatial structure: population densities increase discretely across distances where building ages are different. To be realistic, the simple model must be altered to take into account the fact that buildings last a long time and are not destroyed whenever economic conditions change. Other changes, such as suburban subcenters and the effect of rivers and lakes on urban spatial form, are more marginal and can be handled by introducing a few additional explanatory variables. Vintage effects are a more fundamental challenge to the monocentric model, requiring significant changes to the theory (e.g., Anas 1978; Wheaton 1982).

8.5 Empirical Results – Floor-Area Ratio

Although floor-area ratios have not been analyzed as extensively as population densities or land values, they are a critical part of the monocentric city model. The model predicts that low commuting costs for sites near the city center lead to

Table 8.1 Floor-area ratio regressions

	Chicago homes	Chicago homes	Cook County Census tracts	Cook County Census tracts
Constant	−0.700	0.782	−0.626	0.268
	(268.518)	(34.604)	(35.829)	(4.465)
x	−0.055		−0.055	
	(205.472)		(39.540)	
$x - x_0$		−0.903		−0.490
		(41.215)		(14.099)
$(x - x_0)^2$		0.151		0.061
		(23.229)		(10.427)
$(x - x_0)^3$		−0.009		−0.003
		(15.332)		(9.534)
$(x - x_1)^3 \times (x \geq x_1)$		0.005		0.004
		(6.814)		(8.776)
$(x - x_2)^3 \times (x \geq x_2)$		0.007		−0.001
		(33.797)		(4.367)
$(x - x_3)^3 \times (x \geq x_3)$		0.007		0.001
		(14.510)		(0.773)
R^2	0.151	0.207	0.556	0.692
Number of observations	237,420	237,420	1,251	1,251

Notes: The dependent variable is the natural logarithm of the floor-area ratio. Absolute *t*-values are in parentheses. The evenly spaced knots for the Chicago spline function begin at $x_0 = 0.780$, with an increment of 4.007 between knots. Comparable values for the Cook County spline function are 0.782 and 8.312.

high land values, which in turn lead to high floor-area ratios. In this section, I present estimates of the relationship between floor-area ratios and distance from the CBD in Cook County, Illinois, which includes Chicago. The data set includes single-family residential homes selling between 1983 and 1999. Data on lot size, floor area, and addresses come from the Cook County Assessor's Office, and the list of sales comes from the Illinois Department of Revenue.

The first two columns of results in Table 8.1 present the results of regressions using the natural logarithm of the floor-area ratio as the dependent variable and distance from the CBD as the explanatory variable. Only data from the City of Chicago are used for these regressions. The first column shows that floor-area ratios decline by 5.5 percent with each additional mile from the Chicago CBD. The R^2 value indicates that only about 15 percent of the variation in this variable is explained by distance. The second column of results is based on a smooth cubic spline with four regions. The R^2 value rises to 0.207, and the coefficients for the additional explanatory variables are all statistically significant. Figure 8.3 shows the estimated functions. The spline function's additional explanatory power

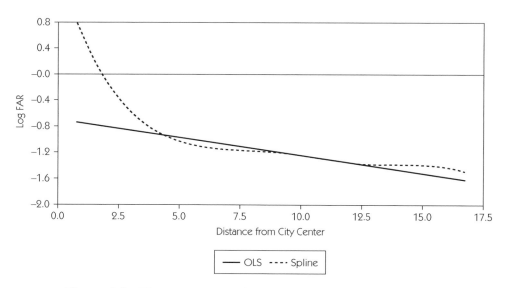

Figure 8.3   Floor-area ratios for individual homes in Chicago.

comes from the sharp rise in estimated floor-area ratios near the CBD. Both functions are consistent with the predictions of the monocentric city model.

The last two columns of results present comparable estimates for all of Cook County. The data for these regressions are averages by census tract. The point of these regressions is to show how dramatically the explanatory power increases when aggregate data are used rather than data for individual homes. The R^2 value for the simple negative exponential function rises to 0.556 even though the estimated gradient does not change at all. The R^2 value for the spline rises to 0.692, indicating that an impressive 69.2 percent of the variation in the logarithm of the floor-area ratio is explained by a single variable, distance from the Chicago CBD. A graph of the estimated function (not shown here) reveals that distance from the CBD no longer has much explanatory power beyond about 18 miles. In fact, the R^2 value is only 0.021 for a spline function with four equally spaced intervals from 15 miles from the CBD to the maximum value of 34 miles. The model works well in the part of the metropolitan area that is still dominated by the CBD; it does not work well in newer suburban areas.

8.6   House "Prices"

Other than population density, the most common test of the monocentric city model is the relationship between house "prices" and distance from the CBD. The word "price" is in quotes because the unit price of housing is not observed in practice. The actual dependent variable for these regressions is the value of housing, which is the product of price and quantity. As we have seen, the model makes no predictions for this variable. The apparent failure of the model is illusory.

How can researchers claim that a regression of house values on distance from the CBD is a test of the monocentric city model? Suppose that the unit price of housing declines with distance from the CBD according to the function $P_h(d) = e^{\mu - \delta d}$. Then the relationship between house values and distance is $\ln V_h(d) = \ln H(d) + \mu - \delta d$. If it were possible to control for all house characteristics (Z), then we would have $\ln V_h(d) = Z\theta + \mu - \delta d$, which is a function that can be estimated easily. A good, careful example of this approach is Coulson (1991), but bad examples are much more abundant.

The problem with this approach is that the full set of housing characteristics is never observed. Suppose we have two houses that have three bedrooms and a garage, are on 1/3-acre lots, and appear to be identical in all measurable ways. House A is 5 miles from CBD and costs $300,000 and house B is 10 miles from the CBD and costs $500,000. There appears to be an upward-sloping house price gradient. Unfortunately, missing variables include school quality, other local public services, and vague concepts such as house quality. If we could control for these variables, we might find a downward-sloping house price function. But the family living in the higher-priced home undoubtedly has a higher income than the family in house A. Thus, what the regression really does is to trace out the places where higher-income families live. As we have seen, the model predicts that the sign of this gradient can go either way.

8.7   CONCLUSION

By definition, a model is a simplification of reality. The monocentric city model uses a very simple idea – that people will pay a premium for sites that lead to lower commuting costs – to generate a complete model of the spatial structure of an entire city. Although the assumptions are not literally accurate, they produce a mathematically tractable model with remarkable predictive power. Even modern urban areas tend to be dominated by the traditional CBD. Land values, population density, and floor-area ratios decline markedly with distance from the CBD. Over time, rates of decline have fallen to the point that the CBD no longer dominates the entire urban area to the same extent as before. But the theory actually predicts the decline in the importance of the CBD: declining commuting costs and increasing incomes lead to significantly lower gradients.

Much criticism of the monocentric city model comes from a misunderstanding of the empirical results. Lower gradients produce lower R^2 values. More disaggregated data sets also lead to lower R^2 values. Suburban data have never been explained well by the monocentric city model, and the low gradients in these areas tend to further reduce the R^2 values. The model makes no predictions regarding the spatial pattern of house values, and empirically it is nearly impossible to measure the theoretically relevant unit price of housing.

Within central cities, the most important deficiency of the monocentric city model is its failure to take into account the longevity of the capital stock. Land values will be low in areas where floor-area ratios are high if existing buildings, which reflect past economic conditions, are costly to demolish. The model's failure is more serious in the suburbs. Modern cities often have large suburban employment centers with marked effects on the spatial structure of the suburbs. Suburban areas have a fragmented system of government. Local variations in zoning practices, tax rates, and the provision of local public goods have significant effects on the spatial patterns of variables such as house prices and population densities. Although distance from the CBD has little predictive power in the suburbs, spatial relationships can often be modeled accurately with a few additional variables such as distance from employment subcenters and access to the transportation system. With a few modifications, the monocentric city model remains a useful tool for understanding urban spatial relationships.

Bibliography

Anas, A. 1978: Dynamics of urban residential growth. *Journal of Urban Economics*, 5, 66–87.

Anderson, J. E. 1982: Cubic-spline urban-density functions. *Journal of Urban Economics*, 12, 155–67.

Brueckner, J. K. 1986: A switching regression analysis of urban population densities. *Journal of Urban Economics*, 19, 174–89.

—— and Fansler, D. A. 1983: The economics of urban sprawl: theory and evidence on the spatial sizes of cities. *Review of Economics and Statistics*, 65, 479–82.

Clark, C. 1951: Urban population densities. *Journal of the Royal Statistical Association Series A*, 114, 490–6.

Coulson, N. E. 1991: Really useful tests of the monocentric city model. *Land Economics*, 67, 299–307.

Gallant, A. R. 1982: On the bias in flexible functional forms and an essentially unbiased form: the Fourier flexible form. *Journal of Econometrics*, 15, 211–45.

Hamilton, B. W. 1982: Wasteful commuting. *Journal of Political Economy*, 90, 1035–51.

Hoyt, H. 1933: *One Hundred Years of Land Values in Chicago*. Chicago: The University of Chicago Press.

Macauley, M. K. 1985: Estimation and recent behavior of urban population and employment density gradients. *Journal of Urban Economics*, 18, 251–60.

McDonald, J. F. 1979: An empirical study of a theory of the urban housing market. *Urban Studies*, 16, 291–7.

—— 1997: *Fundamentals of Urban Economics*. Upper Saddle River, NJ: Prentice-Hall.

—— and Bowman, H. W. 1979: Land value functions: a reevaluation. *Journal of Urban Economics* 6, 25–41.

McMillen, D. P. 1996: One hundred fifty years of land values in Chicago: a nonparametric approach. *Journal of Urban Economics*, 40, 100–24.

—— and Lester, T. W. 2003: Evolving subcenters: employment and population densities in Chicago, 1970–2020. *Journal of Housing Economics*, 12, 60–81.

Mills, E. S. 1969: The value of urban land. In H. Perloff (ed.), *The Quality of the Urban Environment*. Washington, DC: Resources for the Future, Inc.

—— 1972: *Studies in the Structure of the Urban Economy*. Baltimore, MD: Resources for the Future, Inc.

Muth, R. F. 1969: *Cities and Housing*. Chicago: The University of Chicago Press.

O'Sullivan, A. 2002: *Urban Economics*. New York: Irwin/McGraw-Hill.

Wheaton, W. C. 1982: Urban residential growth under perfect foresight. *Journal of Urban Economics*, 12, 1–21.

PART III

Housing and Real Estate

Housing and Real Estate

Whereas the monocentric city model attempts to explain broad spatial patterns in prices and land use within urban areas, the subfields of housing and real estate are generally conducted at more micro levels of analysis. The main difference between the housing and real estate literatures derives from the motives behind the studies. Housing economists are more apt to be interested in public policy, while real estate economics has more of a business perspective. Neither subfield belongs exclusively to urban economics. Housing is also studied by public finance economists, who are particularly interested in the effects of taxes and other government policies on the provision of housing. As the largest component of most households' wealth, housing also plays an important role in macroeconomics and finance. But the study of housing has long been closely associated with urban economics because as by far the largest user of land in urban areas, housing is a critical component of urban models. In addition, the cost and quality of housing is a vital concern of urban households and policy-makers. The study of real estate has traditionally been the domain of business economists, who tend to focus on the institutional features of real estate markets. Urban economists have helped to improve the study of real estate by constructing formal theoretical models that are based on underlying profit- and utility-maximizing behavior on the part of firms and households. Knowledge of the institutional features of real estate markets helps urban economists produce richer and more realistic models of urban areas.

Why is housing singled out for study when it is just one of many goods in the economy? Housing is vitally important to people because we all live in some form of housing, and the cost and quality of our homes greatly influence our quality of life. However, food also meets this criterion, yet it is far less frequently studied. Housing is also important because it is expensive. Although the percentage of household income devoted to housing varies across countries, 30–40 percent is a common figure. Housing is also interesting because it is far from a standardized commodity. At the simplest level, housing consists of a parcel of land and an amount of living space. At a more detailed level, housing includes the number and size of rooms, the presence of a garage, the amorphous concept of "quality," and innumerable features that make it impossible to purchase a house without seeing it in person and inspecting it carefully. Housing is durable and immobile, and it is costly to move or to add on to one's current home. Owner-occupied housing is the primary asset in many households' portfolios, but unlike other assets such as stocks, people also enjoy their home directly as a consumer good. Rental and owner-occupied exist simultaneously, making it necessary to model tenure choice as well as the amount chosen. The theory is reviewed in the essay by Franz Hubert, "The Economic Theory of Housing Tenure Choice." In all countries in the world, governments are actively involved in the housing market either by directly providing homes or through a plethora of taxes, regulations, subsidies, rent controls, and longstanding programs designed to lower the cost and improve the quality of housing. In their essay, "Housing Policy: Low-Income Households in France," Anne Laferrère and David Le Blanc compare government housing policies in France and the United States.

Urban economists formally model housing heterogeneity using the hedonic approach. Under this approach, housing is a combination of a variety of components, such as living area, lot size, and the quality of the structure and neighborhood. Producers combine the different housing characteristics to provide a home that matches the preferences of different households. The home sells or rents for a single price. Theoretically and in econometric practice, sales prices and rents can be decomposed to estimate the implicit contributions of the different housing characteristics. At least in principle, we can calculate what proportion of a home's price is accounted for by structural characteristics and characteristics of the site and neighborhood. By providing monetary measures of the value of school quality, the cost of air pollution, and the like, the hedonic approach has been an important part of many cost–benefit studies.

Households typically have to borrow money to purchase a home. Thus, financial institutions influence how much a household can spend on housing and whether the household owns or rents. At this point, the urban economist's study of housing merges with more traditional real estate studies. Financial institutions vary dramatically across countries. In her essay, "Housing Demand: An International Perspective," Miki Seko discusses the differences between the workings of housing markets in China, Japan, Sweden, and the USA. In "Discrimination in Mortgage Lending," Anthony Yezer analyzes the empirical approaches that have been used to determine whether racial discrimination is a problem in US mortgage markets. The USA relies heavily on private construction of housing and private provision of mortgages. In contrast, some countries have relatively undeveloped mortgage markets, making it more difficult to purchase a home. Although public housing exists in the USA and subsidies help to lower the cost for low-income households, governments in many countries are much more likely to provide housing directly. Owner-occupied housing is more likely to be built at a low density, and governments are typically less responsive than are private firms to market forces. Thus, the size and nature of financial institutions as well as government involvement in the housing market can influence the cost of housing and the spatial layout of urban areas.

Commercial real estate is also a critical part of the urban landscape. In his essay, "Commercial Real Estate," David Geltner presents an overview of the workings of commercial real estate markets. Downtown office buildings sell for millions of dollars and account for a significant percentage of the total value of all real estate in major urban areas. For example, data from the Cook County Assessor's Office show that office buildings in downtown Chicago accounted for more than 22 percent of the total value of all real estate in the city in 2003. The market for office buildings is highly volatile. In his essay, "Housing Price Indexes," Bradford Case shows how real estate economists go about estimating price indexes that allow them to analyze the dynamics of real estate markets. In cities such as Sydney, Tokyo, and London, prices have both risen dramatically and fallen sharply shortly afterward. Construction sometimes continues even in the face of high vacancy rates. With large sums of money at stake, the principles of investment analysis must be used to understand the timing and location of commercial construction. Urban economists have helped to develop models explaining the real estate development decision. They also have developed models explaining the path of prices, construction, and vacancies over time. Interestingly, far less attention has been paid to the industrial sector, despite its importance in many areas. Detailed analyses of real estate markets that combine institutional knowledge with the best features of economics and finance can produce rich, realistic, and useful urban models.

CHAPTER NINE

The Economic Theory of Housing Tenure Choice

Franz Hubert

9.1 INTRODUCTION

Within the theory of housing markets, one may broadly distinguish three approaches, which roughly correspond to the historical development of the discipline. The first retains the assumption of a perfect, frictionless, competitive market mechanism when addressing issues of localization, heterogeneity, durability, housing taxation, and so on. This line of research reached a considerable degree of maturity in the mid-1980s. It has greatly improved our understanding of urban spatial structure, the determinants of housing supply and demand, and the measurement of prices for heterogeneous goods. Given the assumption of a perfect mechanism for the allocation of housing, however, the welfare implications remain humdrum. With the possible exception of neighborhood externalities, housing markets appear efficient, provided that all agents are forward-looking and rational.

The second approach emphasizes imperfect competition and frictions resulting from search cost, mobility cost, and contractual incompleteness. A central question is how markets actually achieve coordination in the absence of a Walrasian auctioneer, given all the particularities of housing. Stimulated by the advances in the theory of imperfect information, incomplete contracts, optimal search, and matching markets, this strand of research "took off" in the 1980s and has made substantial achievements since then. The literature deals with a broad range of issues; for example, the role of real estate agents, the purpose of the various features of rental contracts, vacancy rates, optimal pricing strategies and search behavior, and so on. This approach delivers a more realistic picture of the institutions and mechanisms through which coordination is achieved and adds a cautious note with respect to the welfare properties of the housing market. Due to search and mobility costs, competition is imperfect even with a large number of agents on both sides of the market. Search externalities give rise to vacancy rates that deviate from first-best, and incomplete contracts create subtle turnover externalities. Not surprisingly, the policy implications tend to be more exciting. In principle, efficiency can often be enhanced through appropriate state intervention, though in practice the very same features that prevent the market from achieving first-best efficiency render the desirability of government intervention a moot point.

Building on these achievements, a third strain of literature analyzes the implications of these imperfections for the dynamics of housing markets and their interaction with other sectors, such as financial markets and labor markets. What explains the fluctuations in housing prices? Why does the volume of sales appear to increase and the average waiting time from listing to sale appear to decrease in rising markets as compared to falling markets? Can a downturn in real estate cause a credit crunch through its impact on collateral values? May this in turn aggravate the crisis in the housing market? Recent analysis suggests that imperfections in housing and credit markets may interact and generate fluctuations that are difficult to explain by looking at each market in isolation.

I will not try to provide a comprehensive review of housing market theory here. In particular, this essay does not cover important topics such as models of housing demand, filtering models, and so on, which are well covered in the reviews of Arnott (1987) and Smith, Rosen, and Fallis (1988). Instead, tenure choice has been chosen as the leitmotif of this essay. While many of the alleged particularities of housing markets are, in fact, shared to a considerable extent by other markets, housing appears to be the only commodity for which renting and ownership coexist roughly on equal scales. Since many of the advantages of ownership are the shortcomings of renting and the best reasons for renting are the drawbacks of owning, a thorough understanding of tenure choice will give us a lot of mileage in the analysis of the housing market.

Sometimes the choice of tenure is analyzed narrowly, with an undue focus on the demand side. However, there would be no choice for consumers if all owners would prefer to sell rather than to rent out (or the other way round). Hence, we consider tenure choice as a joint decision on both sides of the market, consumers and suppliers, over the contractual forms of housing exchange. Finally, ownership and renting are fairly complex institutional arrangements, the exact meanings of which differ from country to country due to different regulations and business practices. In this essay, the focus is on principles rather than on the diversity of institutional details.

We start by briefly looking at a perfect, frictionless market for durable housing in which only taxation may affect tenure choice. Then we analyze renting and owning as alternative arrangements for the solution of interrelated problems of asymmetric information, incentives, and contractual incompleteness at the consumption stage. In doing so, we assume that the household has already found the desired house. Next, we ask how landlords and tenants, or sellers and buyers, interact at the allocation stage. What are the implications of heterogeneity and imperfect information for housing search, housing prices, and vacancy rates? Finally, we combine results from the two stages, search and contracting, in order to derive some implications for the dynamics of the housing market.

9.2   DURABLE INVESTMENT AND TAXATION

There is little doubt that the tax system plays an important role for housing investment and tenure choice. As housing investment is of long duration and transaction costs are high, a proper analysis of the impact of taxation requires a look at the whole expected lifetime of the building, including major renovations and perhaps changes of ownership. Important qualitative insights, however, can be gained by analyzing a simple one-period model, abstracting from transaction cost. Let V denote the initial value of the housing unit, δ the appreciation or depreciation factor, reflecting the change in market value over the period, r the interest rate on bonds, and R the rental value (cash flow). In a world without taxes, an investor will be indifferent between investing in housing and investing in bonds if his terminal wealth is the same; hence if $(1 + r)V = R + (1 + \delta)V$. Note that this condition would also make the user indifferent between owning, in which case his end-of-period wealth would be $(1 + \delta)V$, and renting, which yields $(1 + r)V - R$. An alternative representation of the condition states that capital cost has to equal the return on real investment, $r = R/V + \delta$.

When income is taxed at a rate τ, absence of arbitrage requires that after-tax income from financial investment equals after-tax income from real investment: $r(1 - \tau) = R/V + \delta - \Delta$, where the "wedge" Δ summarizes the impact of all the tax rules that apply to the real investment. The theory of income taxation provides two benchmarks to evaluate a tax system. Intersectoral neutrality requires that the tax wedge Δ is the same for every form of real investment; for example, rented and owner-occupied housing. This would insure that marginal gross return on investment is the same for different forms of investment; hence, tenure choice would not be distorted by the tax system. Intertemporal neutrality requires the wedge to be zero. Only in this case can all projects be financed for which gross returns are large enough to compensate the investor for the loss of current consumption.

In reality, taxation of owner-occupied and rented housing is very complex and differs a lot across countries and time. However, as a general rule, income from rented housing is taxed, mortgage interest can be deducted, and the property value is depreciated for tax purposes according to some accrual method. On the tenant's side, rental payments, as any other consumption expenditure, is irrelevant for taxation. In some countries, owner-occupied housing is treated similarly to other ordinary consumption goods, such as cars and so on, with no tax on imputed rent, no deduction of interest, and no depreciation allowances. Other countries allow (limited) interest deduction or depreciation or offer direct subsidies to owner-occupation. On the other hand, there are often additional taxes on housing, land taxes, property taxes, and transaction taxes, which are ignored here. Let V_E and V_D denote the amount of equity and debt, respectively, invested in the project, and let α be the depreciation allowance. The absence of arbitrage requires the after-tax wealth to be equal for financial investment (left-hand side) and rented property (right-hand side):

$$(1 + (1 - \tau)r)V_E = (1 - \tau)R + \tau\alpha V - (1 + (1 - \tau)r)V_D + (1 + \delta)V.$$

If owner-occupation is taxed like a consumption good, we have the corresponding condition for ownership:

$$(1 + (1 - \tau)r)V_E = R - (1 + r)V_D + (1 + \delta)V.$$

Solving these equations for the wedges Δ_r (rented property) and Δ_o (owner-occupation), we obtain

$$\Delta_r = \tau r - \frac{\tau}{1 - \tau}(\alpha + \delta) \quad \text{and} \quad \Delta_o = \tau r(1 - V_E/V).$$

As a rule, these wedges will not be the same. As for rented property, true economic depreciation would require $\alpha = -\delta$, yielding a tax wedge of $\Delta_r = \tau r$, which would conform to the ideal of a comprehensive capital income taxation. However, in many countries depreciation rules are fairly generous, allowing positive depreciation for tax purposes even if property values appreciate. Hence, after-tax capital cost for investment in rented property may be much lower than for other fixed assets such as machinery. The tax burden of owner-occupation, Δ_o, depends on the financial structure V_E/V. The more equity the occupier can provide, the lower is the tax burden on ownership. In the limit, as full equity financing is approached ($V_E = V$), the tax wedge is reduced to zero. This helps to explain (i) why more wealthy people tend to own and (ii) why owners tend to accumulate additional wealth by redeeming their mortgages.

The spirit of this analysis changes little when complexity is added by extending the model to many periods and incorporating more complicated tax schemes. One can ask how different marginal tax rates, inflation, or more durable housing types, as described by a larger δ, influence tenure choice by analyzing their impact on Δ_r compared to Δ_o. For example, Titman (1982) investigates the US tax system which, at that time, allowed owners to deduct nominal interest. He concludes that an anticipated increase of inflation benefits (i) high-income homeowners at the cost of low-income homeowners and (ii) renting at the cost of ownership. However, as a rule, it is difficult to come up with a clear welfare assessment of housing taxation, because optimal intertemporal allocation is achieved only if the tax wedge of all forms of real investment is zero. Hence, a more favorable tax treatment of housing, or a particular form of tenure, while distorting the structure of real investment, may nevertheless help to increase overall investment and economic growth.

Without denying the importance of taxation for the tenure choice, it is clear that other considerations are important as well. For example, there are clear patterns that flats in multistory buildings tend to be rented, whereas single-family houses tend to be owned, and that young households tend to rent and switch to ownership only later. These regularities can be observed for countries with large differences in income levels, tax codes, and even economic systems, suggesting that tenure choice involves other fundamental trade-offs.

9.3 INCOMPLETE CONTRACTS AND INCENTIVES

We will develop the basic problem of contracting over housing from a few simple observations on mobility cost and investment. Most households want to stay in their home for a considerable period of time. The right to stay is valued for a number of reasons. A move to new premises requires time and effort for search, is inconvenient, and is expensive. Moreover, many people tend to develop a psychological attachment to their home and neighborhood, which makes them less willing to move over time. These costs have to be traded off against the possible gains from moving. Apart from the need to relocate, a change of quantity or quality of housing often requires a move due to *ex post* indivisibilities. Hence, a better job offer, changes in income and family composition, and so on often make a move highly desirable. Such events turn moving costs into moving gains. For simplicity, however, we only speak of mobility cost, understanding that moving gains are equivalent to negative mobility cost.

To some extent, mobility cost can be considered as exogenous from the viewpoint of housing market analysis. But there are also elements that are endogenous. Much of the investment in decoration, furniture, and so on is idiosyncratic and lost if the household moves. The more time, effort, and money the householder spends to adjust his home to his particular needs, the less will he be inclined to accept an alternative housing offer – even if it has the same market value as his present accommodation. Both the occupant's investment and many of the exogenous factors determining mobility cost are difficult to observe by third parties and not verifiable in court. Therefore, contracts explicitly depending on mobility cost are generally not feasible. Hence, mobility cost, measured by the difference between the utility in the present home and in the best alternative on the market, (i) is on average positive, (ii) has a stochastic component, (iii) depends on the occupant's investment, and (iv) is noncontractible.

The market value of an accommodation depends on continuous maintenance, care, diligence of utilization, and so on. In apartment blocks, these requirements extend to the common structure. Housing tastes are rather individualistic; therefore, the kind of investment a particular occupant favors most often differs from what would maximize the market value of the premise. Again, many aspects of the occupant's conduct are not contractible – being unobservable by a third party acting as an arbitrator or too vague to be explicitly stipulated. It is also not possible to determine investment in any detail for a longer period in advance.

These observations suggest that, ideally, the occupant should (i) enjoy tenure security, (ii) have the right to decide upon investment, and (iii) be the residual claimant for changes in market value. If the house is a detached bungalow and the household is sufficiently wealthy and risk neutral, this ideal can be achieved through ownership. In all other cases, a compromise has to be found. We will consider rental contracts first and then turn to ownership.

9.4   Rental Contracts

Under a rental arrangement, the landlord is the residual claimant to the property value and retains the right to decide upon major investments, while minor investments are often delegated to the tenant. Perhaps the most important and controversial issue is tenure security. For simplicity, we consider only two types of contracts. These are a short-term contract, which can be terminated at short notice and will be renegotiated many times during the course of a typical tenure, and a long-term contract, which grants the tenant tenure security and predetermined rent. Long-term contracts may have a fixed term or may be for an indefinite duration. In the latter case, they will usually involve clauses for rent reviews and allow the landlord to give notice under special narrowly defined circumstances (demolition of the building, own use, etc.).

Short-term contracts have two advantages. They are easy to write and they create strong incentives on the part of the tenant to keep cost of maintenance and administration low by minimizing wear and tear, avoiding trouble with neighbors, and so on. A landlord who is displeased with his tenant's conduct will give notice to quit or raise the rent to cover these costs.

However, they suffer from an important drawback. Given that most tenants would suffer from a moving cost in case of contract termination, the landlord has an increased bargaining power *ex post* even if the market is competitive *ex ante* when the contracts are negotiated. Tenants will anticipate that their immobility may be exploited at contract renewal and will underinvest in idiosyncratic assets and renovation. This version of the well-known "hold up" problem has been analyzed by Kanemoto (1990). Tenants who have a strong preference for individual investments will, therefore, try to negotiate long-term contracts providing them with tenure security. These contracts protect the tenant against eviction, provided that the landlord has no "just cause" for doing so (e.g., clear-cut breach of contract, rent arrears) and predetermine future rents. Obviously, these contracts will be more complex, and hence costly to write and enforce, and they compromise on the incentives of the tenant.

A number of countries regulate residential leases to insure that all tenants enjoy "tenure security and stable rents." This kind of state intervention has always been controversial. Obviously, the mere fact that tenants appreciate tenure security does not justify that the state imposes it by law. As with any other good, one might expect the market to provide long-term contracts with tenure security if the willingness to pay is large enough to cover the cost of provision. However, this intuition may be misleading if tenants are heterogeneous and information is asymmetric.

Assume that some tenants are more difficult to deal with than others, but that a landlord will not be able to identify them for sure when filling a vacancy. During the course of tenure, he will learn about the true service cost of his tenant.

With a long-term contract, the landlord has to put up with a high service cost until the tenant leaves voluntarily. To the extent that service costs are non-contractible, they will not amount to a clear-cut breach of contract. However, with a short-term contract, the landlord may evict bad tenants or raise their rent. This explains why longstanding tenants tend to pay less than those who entered their contract more recently. By granting a tenure discount, landlords try to reduce the turnover of good; that is, "low-cost" tenants.

With tenure security, all tenants are treated alike, whereas high-cost tenants expect a higher probability of eviction or rent increases than low-cost tenants when entering a short-term contract. Hence, contracts offering tenure security are particularly attractive for high-cost tenants and will, therefore, suffer from adverse selection. Or to put it the other way around, low-cost tenants have an incentive to differentiate themselves from high-cost tenants by foregoing tenure security. By accepting the risk of eviction, they will substantially reduce their rent, because landlords anticipate that only good tenants will do so. However, the rent for high-cost tenants will increase accordingly. This redistribution among tenants is achieved at some cost, the moving cost in case of eviction, but eviction serves no social aim since the evicted tenant rents from another landlord anyway. Due to adverse selection, the private cost of providing tenure security surmounts the true social cost. Hence, in equilibrium, the provision of tenure security is too low (Hubert 1995).

While this claim of market failure is fairly robust, it does not imply that making protection against eviction mandatory for all leases is warranted. If one accounts for the genuine cost of providing tenure security, resulting, for example, from risk aversion on the part of the landlords, impaired incentives to keep service cost low on part of the tenants, and so on, such a drastic intervention may be too strong a therapy, forcing tenants to pay a premium for the insurance that surmounts their valuation of it.

Long-term contracts have to make some provisions for rent reviews. Moving cost and *ex post* indivisibility are features of the housing market that create a strong interest for *ex ante* insurance against *ex post* price uncertainty. Suppose that a tenant selects the optimal size for his new home at current rents. After moving in, he cannot change his housing consumption – except by moving again to a smaller or larger dwelling or by subletting part of his flat, which entails a substantial loss of privacy. Thus, there are discrete and nontrivial costs of adjusting consumption in a response to a change of price in the housing market. In contrast to most other goods, the consumption of which can be adjusted on short notice at little cost, uncertainty over future rents translates into a kind of income risk for immobile households. With housing consumption fixed, an increase of rent automatically decreases net-of-rent income available for other expenditures. In fact, the same holds true with an opposite sign for many landlords.

If landlords and tenants negotiate a long-term contract, they have an interest to protect themselves against the vagaries of market rents for new leases – at least to the extent that these are not related to the cost of provision or the utility derived from consumption. Hence, it is in their interest to fix the real rent in advance, isolating the contract from the development of the market for the duration of the term. In practice, their ability to do so may be limited, because the more rents for new contracts increase or decrease, the stronger the interest of one side becomes to renege on its promise. Hence, if contracts are incomplete, they can only provide partial insurance, for example, limiting the time for which the rent is fixed, or by providing some flexibility through indexing.

Again, one may raise the question of whether decentralized contracting achieves efficiency. Before doing so, it is worthwhile to recall one of the most basic arguments against rent control: those who are lucky to be rationed in, usually the sitting tenants at the time of the introduction of rent control, obtain housing exceptionally cheaply. Those who are unlucky and are rationed out experience greater hardship than necessary, because the protected "sitting birds" have little incentive to economize on space. Hence, the unequal treatment of otherwise equal tenants is not only unfair, but also inefficient.

However, a similar phenomenon will arise in almost any market in which exchange is governed by long-term contracts. In a smaller or greater measure, all forms of tenure inhibit the landlords' (or the tenants') immediate responses to market forces and new opportunities, because that is what they are for. Thus, private contracting will result in a situation similar to the one created by rent control. At a time when the housing market tightens, tenants who have old contracts will be in a favorable position compared to those who have to negotiate new contracts. Their incentive to move will decline and the turnover rate will drop as the market tightens. As the critics of rent control have rightly pointed out, this will exacerbate the crisis and raise market rents for new leases in times of tight markets, by reducing the incentives to economize on space.

How does this compare to what a benevolent social planner would implement as an efficient solution? The socially optimal indexation has to strike a balance between the insurance provided by stable rents within the contracts and the stabilizing effect of a high turnover on future market rents. However, every single landlord–tenant pair is concerned only with individual risk sharing within the contract and ignores the effect of their indexing rule on future equilibrium rents. Privately optimal contracts are generally not efficient, and if tenants are risk averse with respect to market rents for new leases, private contracts provide too much insurance within the contract, resulting in too low a turnover and an excessively volatile market rent (Hubert 1996).

9.5 OWNERSHIP

By granting the occupant tenure security, giving him full control rights and making him residual claimant to the property value, ownership can, in principal, provide first-best incentives with respect to investment, maintenance, and care. However, there are important practical limitations.

First, if several households share a common structure, then it is impossible to align residual control and income rights and give them to the occupant. In an apartment block, decisions regarding structure and site use cannot be separated for different flats. Hence, condominiums either severely curtail the property rights of the individual occupants – for example, allow demolition and site redevelopment by majority voting – or run the risk of costly haggling. With respect to the common structure, the relation between a single occupant and the union of all other occupants shares many problems with the tenant–landlord relation, which diminishes the appeal of ownership. As a result, the ratio between multi-family and single-family houses (which in turn depends on land availability, climate, energy prices, etc.) is a major determinant for ownership rates.

Second, since housing is highly durable, the property value is much larger than the monthly rental value. Less wealthy households will depend on outside financing for purchasing a house that suits their consumption needs. In this, they face two constraints: it is not possible to borrow large amounts against a pledge of future income, and it is not possible to borrow against the full property value of the home. The first constraint requires households to maintain a positive asset balance. The inability to borrow against human capital affects the pattern of life-cycle consumption in general. Young households consume less than they would like, given their expectations of future income growth. This would not cause particular distortions in housing consumption if one could borrow against the full value of the property. However, since ownership grants tenure security and residual control rights, a positive equity margin is required to maintain adequate incentives for investment on part of the occupant. If equity should become negative, it is the financiers who effectively end up as residual claimants on the property value without having control rights, unless the borrower defaults. Obviously, this would create incentive problems as to maintenance and care, which are worse than those in rental contracts. Under ownership, security of tenure implies that the equity position of incumbent homeowners may deteriorate during a decline of house prices. But as long as they service their mortgage, they are entitled to stay. It is only when they decide to move that financiers will require the usual equity margin for the new home. As we will discuss in the last section, this creates similar "lock-in effects" as with long-term rental contracts. The possibility of deteriorating equity positions will be anticipated at the time of the purchase and be taken into account by demanding higher down payments. In a sense, financial contracts are as incomplete as rental contracts – they just present an alternative approach to solve the resulting incentive problems, which is, however, inferior, if not enough wealth can be pledged by the occupant. Limited wealth and constraints on borrowing against the property value will force many households to rent early on in their life cycle to save funds for the down payment (Artle & Varaiya 1978). For poor households, the constraints on consumption may be so severe that they forego the benefits of ownership for the whole of their lives.

Third, ownership may force the occupant to take excessive risk. So far, it has been taken for granted that housing finance is through debt contracts and not through equity participation. While this is true as a matter of fact, it can also be derived from our contracting problem. It is well known, from principal agent models of corporate finance, that debt financing provides higher-powered incentives for value-maximizing behavior than outside equity, while minimizing the agency costs of external financing. However, debt financing puts all the risk on the shoulders of the owner. As a result, the typical asset structure of homeowners is poorly diversified. Henderson and Ioannides (1983) and Fu (1991) provide an analysis of the trade-off between risk taking in ownership and the so-called "rental externality," showing the importance of risk preferences for tenure choice.

Finally, transaction costs play to the disadvantage of owning. Given the large values involved, the documentation of titles to land and property is rather expensive in the case of transfers of ownership. It requires a longer period of staying to make these expenditures worthwhile. Since the benefits of ownership, such as tenure security, the right to adapt the building to particular tastes, and so on, are worth little if the household wants to move soon, while short-term rental contracts can be quite efficient if mobility costs are low, it is not surprising that there is a strong negative correlation between ownership and mobility.

9.6 Heterogeneity, Search, and Trading in Thin Markets

Given that housing is very heterogeneous and locally dispersed, it requires time and effort to become informed over the opportunities to trade. This raises the question of how the two sides of the market meet each other, how they determine the conditions of exchange, and what this implies for the efficiency of average matches and the dynamics of the market. The issues are similar in the rental and the ownership market, but research interest in the former has focused on static efficiency, whereas in the latter, the dynamic implications have attracted more interest.

Arnott and Igarashi (2000) develop the following analysis of the rental market. Upon entering the housing market, tenants collect information about available units. However, easily accessible information is insufficient to make the appropriate decision. Flats differ in too many aspects, which cannot be communicated. Other information is soft and has to be verified. Hence, only a small subset of vacancies is selected and visited, which requires time and effort. When the home-hunter finds a flat that suits his taste, he may accept it even if the price is somewhat higher than for other flats of the same category. The alternative would be to continue the costly search process. If there is plenty of housing on the market, tenants will be able to find a very good "match" with reasonable effort. If only a few units are vacant, the search will be more difficult and tenants will put up with lower match quality.

Since landlords understand that product differentiation, idiosyncratic tastes, and lack of transparency give them market power, they charge a rent above marginal cost. This reduces somewhat the chance to strike a deal within any given period of time. But they do not mind a slight increase in the vacancy spell, because a higher rent in the future will reward them for the lost income. These extra profits trigger market entry, and in the long run equilibrium "excess" capacity will manifest itself in the form of vacant housing, not in the form of higher profits.

However, as usual in models of monopolistic competition, it is not clear on a priori grounds whether capacity is in fact "excessive." A higher vacancy rate also has advantages. It increases the choice for the tenant and makes it easier for home-hunters to find units that suit their tastes; hence, it reduces the search cost and improves the average quality of the matches. The trade-off, therefore, is between low rents and a large variety from which to choose. When deciding upon the rent, every landlord wants to exploit his market power, which suggests that rents and vacancy rates are too high. But on the other hand, with respect to the vacancy spell, he considers only the lost revenues and ignores the fact that a vacant dwelling increases the search efficiency and match quality. This positive externality suggests that vacancy rates and rents may also be too low in equilibrium. Arnott and Igarashi (2000) have developed a formal model in which the first effect dominates the second under fairly general assumptions. This implies that the "natural vacancy" rate and equilibrium rents are too high. A small decrease of rents below their long-run equilibrium would, therefore, be welfare improving.

The basic story is the same for homeowners (Wheaton 1991) – only that most of them are repeat buyers, and hence active on both sides of the market. As sellers, they face the same trade-off as landlords do: by raising the listed price, they decrease the arrival rate of prospective buyers, but increase the chance of selling at a higher price. As buyers, however, they will be cautious to strike a deal unless they have found a buyer for their old house. Owning two houses will put a heavy strain on their financial means. On the other hand, if a particularly good opportunity to buy comes along, then the would-be mover becomes eager to sell and therefore decreases his listing price. Hence, given the intransparencies of the market, we can expect different listing prices for houses of the same intrinsic value.

9.7 THE DYNAMICS OF PRICES, TURNOVER, AND VACANCIES

Housing is one of the most important assets in any economy. Not surprisingly, house price studies have a long history. Initially, the focus of interest was on the explanation of prices from features of the property, such as location, size, amenities, age, and so on. More recently, the dynamics of housing prices have attracted a lot of interest. With immediate adjustment, prices would always reflect all of the currently available information, and price changes could be attributed to the arrival of new information. As in markets for financial securities, "efficiency" would require housing prices to follow some sort of random walk; otherwise, past prices would contain information on future prices that is not incorporated in the current price. At the same time, the price of housing should always equal the capitalized rental income that it generates.

However, empirical studies have found strong evidence that the housing market deviates from this benchmark: there appears to be substantial inertia in price movements; prices fail to fully incorporate predictable movements in real interest rates and deviate systematically from capitalized rent. High transaction costs may explain why the market fails to adjust swiftly to equilibrium, but the empirical evidence is also compatible with rational "bubbles" or irrational formation of expectations. In the fast, flexible, and transparent world of financial securities, significant serial correlation would, in principle, allow highly profitable trading strategies. This is not so in housing markets, where the transaction cost, liquidity constraints, the absence of future markets and short sales, informational asymmetries, and the time it takes to gather and aggregate information and to finally complete a transaction restrict arbitrage.

Of this long list of particularities, liquidity constraints appear to be the most interesting ones. As has been argued above, it is vital to maintain a positive equity margin in order to provide incentives for proper maintenance, care, and so on, if the value of the asset depends on the noncontractible effort of its occupant. Hence, the purchase of a house typically requires a significant down payment, and as a rule, for repeat buyers, proceeds on the sale of the old home contribute a substantial fraction of this expense. Once a substantial part of wealth is tied up in housing, an initial decline in housing prices impairs the ability of some would-be movers to make the down payment on new homes (Stein 1995).

Consider a change of fundamentals leading to a decline of housing prices. There are three possibilities, depending on the size of the outstanding old mortgage. If the old mortgage is small, the impact on liquidity is weak, so that the household's choice of the size of the new house is not distorted. The group of unconstrained movers will increase its housing consumption in response to a decrease in housing prices – the usual effect of price on demand. Households with an intermediate loan-to-value ratio, however, may find their ability to finance their optimal housing consumption impaired by insufficient funds for the down payment. If they decide to move, they will be forced to consume less than they would like were it not for the liquidity constraints. Note that this story depends critically on imperfections in the rental housing market. Otherwise, financially constrained households would switch to renting. They would suffer from a loss of wealth on their investment, but there would be no need to put up the additional burden of distorting housing consumption. If rental housing is only an imperfect substitute for ownership, then the housing demand of constrained movers declines as prices decrease because their financial constraints tighten. This will not only exacerbate the change in price needed to bring about a new equilibrium. If the group is large, aggregate demand may even decline over some range, raising the possibility of multiple equilibria. This may explain why small changes in the fundamentals can lead to dramatic shifts in the equilibrium prices. Finally, highly indebted households will be better off foregoing the gains from moving and staying in their current homes. They will be "locked in" by lack of equity. As prices decline, more households will come into this position, which explains why the volume of sales falls in declining markets.

If we combine the analysis of liquidity constraints with pricing behavior in search markets, the impact on prices will probably be somewhat smaller, while the impact on volumes will be larger. Recall that sellers face a trade-off between selling fast and achieving a high price. Constrained movers and locked-in households have less incentive to sell fast and increased incentives to set high listing prices. In particular, for the latter, "fishing" has little opportunity cost, because they cannot move at all if they do not reach an exceptionally high price. Overall, the theory predicts a positive correlation between listing prices, final selling prices, time to sell, and the loan-to-value ratio: for further intuition and empirical evidence, see Genesove and Mayer (1997). On the aggregate level, the more indebted homeowners are, the more volatile housing prices and sales volume will be. However, the magnitude of the impact depends not only on the average debt level but also on the distribution of debt. A large number of households having moderate loan-to-value ratios may have a stronger impact than a few with extreme ratios, because the latter may be "locked in" in declining markets while the former will move, but demand less due to liquidity constraints.

The theory of housing market dynamics in the presence of borrowing constraints, adjustment cost, and so on is still in its infancy, and many interesting questions are still left for research. For example, I am not aware of a welfare assessment of decentralized mortgage financing. Drawing on the analogy with long-term rental contracts, however, one may suspect that the debt level will be inefficiently high, because individual pairs of homeowners and mortgage lenders do not take into account the impact of their agreements on aggregate house price volatility. It would also be interesting to contrast the turnover dynamics of the ownership market with those of the rental market. If the latter is characterized by long-term arrangements, then an increase of rents decreases the rate of turnover, because sitting tenants have lower incentives to move. In the ownership market, an increase of prices relaxes financial restrictions of repeat buyers, which tends to increases the sales volume. Hence, both dynamics go in opposite directions, but we should observe less change of tenure. Potential first-time buyers who are currently renting will be protected by favorable contracts and, at the same time, miss out on the value increase; hence they will have less incentive and less opportunity to switch to owner-occupation.

Bibliography

Arnott, R. 1987: Economic theory and housing. In E. S. Mills (ed.), *Handbook of Regional and Urban Economics*, vol. 2: *Urban Economics*. Amsterdam: Elsevier, 959–88.

—— and Igarashi, M. 2000: Rent control, mismatch costs and search efficiency. *Regional Science and Urban Economics*, 30, 249–88.

Artle, R. and Varaiya, P. 1978: Life cycle consumption and homeownership. *Journal of Economic Theory*, 18, 38–58.

Fu, Y. 1991: A model of housing tenure choice: comment. *American Economic Review*, 81, 381–3.

Genesove, D. and Mayer, C. 1997: Equity and time to sale in the real estate market. *American Economic Review*, 87(3), 255–69.

Henderson, J. V. and Ioannides, Y. 1983: A model of housing tenure choice. *American Economic Review*, 73, 98–113.

Hubert, F. 1995: Contracting with costly tenants. *Regional Science and Urban Economics*, 25, 631–54.

—— 1996: Rental contracts, endogenous turnover and rent volatility. Discussion Paper, Free University, Berlin.

Kanemoto, Y. 1990: Contract types in the property market. *Regional Science and Urban Economics*, 20, 5–22.

Smith, L. B., Rosen, K. T., and Fallis, G. 1988: Recent developments in economic models of housing markets. *Journal of Economic Literature*, XXVI (March), 29–64.

Stein, J. C. 1995: Prices and trading volume in the housing market: a model with down-payment effects. *Quarterly Journal of Economics*, 110(2), 379–406.

Titman, S. 1982: The effects of anticipated inflation on housing market equilibrium. *Journal of Finance*, 37(3), 827–42.

Wheaton, W. 1991: Vacancy, search and prices in a housing matching model. *Journal of Political Economy*, 98(6), 1,270–92.

CHAPTER TEN

Housing Policy: Low-Income Households in France

Anne Laferrère and David Le Blanc

10.1   INTRODUCTION

Housing consumption and investment remain subsidized even in the most liberal countries. In 2001, the United States spent 1.54 percent of GDP, and France 1.74 percent, on public aid to housing. As in other countries, the French system is a mixture of many interventions, but its three pillars are the construction of public housing, direct rental subsidies to households, and help to low-income owner-occupiers. The goal of this chapter is not to assess the validity of public intervention, whether it stems from the necessity to internalize housing and neighborhood externalities, to dampen the market power of landlords, or to make up for failures of the housing market. Rather, we present in some detail the three main types of French housing subsidies to low-income households, contrasting their setting with their US counterparts. The most acute questions raised by each kind of policy are discussed, with some empirical evidence when available. Evaluating policy measures one apiece and independently of the rest of the welfare package and institutions could be misleading. The hope is that a partial analysis of concrete, yet sufficiently archetypical, situations will shed light on more general mechanisms in housing and welfare policies.

The chapter is organized as follows. Section 10.2 is devoted to an overview of the French housing market and policies, assessing their comparability with the USA. Section 10.3 looks at the public-sector housing. In section 10.4, personal housing subsidies to private-sector renters are discussed. Section 10.5 presents the current policy aimed at facilitating access to homeownership, the PTZ (zero-interest loan). Section 10.6 concludes.

10.2   Comparing French and American Housing Policies

France and the USA differ in terms of tenure modes. As shown in Table 10.1, homeownership is more developed in the USA, where 68 percent of households own their dwellings, versus 56 percent in France. Perhaps more importantly, the proportion of mortgage holders among owners is also much higher in the USA (62 percent) than in France (38 percent). Such differences are not easy to explain. Four possibly related features are the following:

- The higher level of direct transaction costs in France. These include stamp duty and a compulsory notary act. Adding fees to intermediaries, the average costs can be estimated at around 14 percent, compared to 10 percent in the USA.
- The greater fluidity of the primary mortgage market in the USA. In France, early repayment of the loan or refinancing are costly (prepayment entails a penalty, capped by law at 3 percent of the remaining principal); thus, significant changes in inflation or credit rates are needed to see owners renegotiate. Also, defaulting on a loan results in a stigma that prevents future borrowing. In contrast, in the USA, refinancing is common, and defaulting can be a genuine part of the buyers' strategy. Most importantly, loan durations are shorter in France (the standard duration is about 15 years) than in the USA. As a consequence, whereas in the USA the monthly mortgage repayment (for a 100 percent loan-to-value ratio) would only slightly exceed the monthly rent for the same house, in France the difference is huge. This creates a barrier to ownership for low-wealth households (i.e., those needing high loan-to-value ratios). Hence, borrowing constraints may be more important in France than in the USA.
- A greater development of the secondary market for mortgages in the USA.
- US tax policy, which is more favorable to owners, in particular through mortgage interest tax deduction (see below).

The construction-subsidized rental sector (mainly the HLM, *habitation à loyer modéré*) accommodates 17 percent of households in France. Less than 2 percent of US households live in Public Housing and even fewer in privately owned subsidized property. The "market share" of the HLM sector has been steadily increasing over time, both in absolute and relative terms. This is the consequence of both new construction (100,000 units per year between 1954 and 1984, and still 50,000 since), and the crisis of the private rental sector during the 1970s and the 1980s. Nearly half of the renters now live in a HLM.

While the private rental market is liberalized in most of the USA (700,000 units are still rent controlled), it is subject to "tenancy rent control" in France. This type of control allows landlords to set the rent freely when a new tenant moves in, while annual rent changes for sitting tenants are limited by a national index. This chapter does not deal further with rent control. However, it is important to keep in mind that it can affect housing supply and demand, and that it also raises

Table 10.1 Housing tenure modes in France and in the USA

	France, 2001		USA, 2001	
	Number of households (thousands)	%	Number of households (thousands)	%
Owner	*13,796*	*56.3*	*72,265*	*68.0*
Outright owner[a]	8,654	35.3	27,258	25.7
Mortgagers	5,142	21.0	45,007	42.4
Subsidized mortgager[b]	2,168	8.8	9,820	9.2
Other mortgager	2,974	12.1	35,187	33.1
Renter	*10,729*	*43.7*	*33,996*	*32.0*
Public housing[c]	4,231	17.3	1,861	1.8
Rent control[d]	246	1.0	710	0.7
Private-sector renters[e]	5,226	21.3	29,224	27.5
Free dwelling	1,027	4.2	2,201	2.1
All	*24,525*	*100.0*	*106,261*	*100.0*
Number of renters getting direct subsidy (thousands)[f]	4,819		4,448	

[a] France: includes 72,000 farmers. USA: sum of "owned free and clear" and "line of credit, not reported, no regular or lump sum."
[b] France: subsidized low interest rate in France (1,886,000), or direct subsidy (729,000). USA: "state or local program used" (3,791,000) or "federally insured loans" (8,605,000 FHA, VA, and RHS/RD loans), excluding overlap, but excluding the 32,100,000 who deduct their mortgage payments for income tax.
[c] HUD reports only 1.274 million units of public housing: some households misreport themselves in public housing in the American Housing Survey. They are likely to be in the private sector and applying for vouchers.
[d] France: first-generation rent control only.
[e] France: second-generation rent control, and including 396,000 (uncontrolled) furnished or sublet.
[f] France: Comptes du Logement, table 5.3. This table does not include 572,000 renters in institutional units, whose subsidies are included in Table 10.2. USA: American Housing Survey, table 2–8, rent reduction, "Government subsidy" + "Other, income verification," excluding "Subsidy not reported." The subsidies include the rental assistance program and direct loan programs for reduced cost housing. According to Table 15–30 of the Green Book (2000), there were 5.051 million assisted renters in 2000, among which 1.621 million received Section 8 certificates and vouchers.
Sources: Authors' compilation from the INSEE Housing Survey, 2001–2; American Housing Survey, 2001

redistribution issues (see Basu & Emerson 2000). Lastly, tenant protection is higher in France than in the USA: it costs both time and money to get rid of a tenant. Under regular circumstances, the landlord cannot force a tenant out during a lease, unless she wants to occupy the dwelling herself or have a child or a parent occupying it, or if she wants to sell.

We now describe the main features of the French programs of low-income housing subsidies, underlining the differences with their US counterparts.

10.2.1   The construction-subsidized rental sector

The construction of rental housing is subsidized by low-interest loans (a special financial circuit, the so-called *Livret A*, is based on a tax-free savings program) and tax favors (similar to the US Low Income Housing Tax Credit, LIHTC). In the USA, only privately owned new projects are now financed, and there is no more construction of public housing.

The French HLM system is close to US public housing. As a rule, existing units remain in the system forever. They are owned by local companies (Local Housing Authorities in the USA, *Offices Publics d'HLM* in France). In France, these companies are considered as private, in the sense that rents must cover operating costs. In recent years, in both countries, the government has contributed to rehabilitation, maintenance, and sometimes demolition of public housing.

But there are important differences. First, eligibility (based on income and family composition conditions) is such that some 65 percent of households are eligible in France, while public housing is clearly earmarked for the poor in the USA. In both countries, only a small fraction of eligible households are able to enter.

Second, the attribution procedure is not the same. In France, local HLM agencies share the power of allocating the dwellings with the local elected municipality, the local administrator from the central government (the *préfet*), and a body representing firms contributing to the funding of construction by a compulsory tax. Each organization is granted a quota of the vacated or newly built units, and decides who is to occupy them. To enter HLM, households must register at one of the organizations that are granted quotas. The demand then follows a queuing process, which is opaque for the household, since there is no common criterion for admittance. The wait may last for months, and frequently for more than a year (the average wait, for those who succeed, is 10 months in France versus 11 months in the USA). Offers consist of a particular dwelling (the size of which depends on family composition) at a particular rent. The only degree of freedom for the household is to accept the package, or refuse it and go back into the line.

On the exit side, there is no legal possibility of eviction of a HLM tenant who has turned to be noneligible due to increased resources. As a result, the French public sector houses many households who would no longer be eligible for entry. This has been recognized as a problem, and a law has instituted a rent supplement for those whose resources are above the limit. But HLM agencies are faced with the hard choice of keeping "good" (rich) tenants at base rent or making them pay more at the risk of trading them for low-income tenants who might not pay their rent regularly. In practice, rent supplements are levied only on a small fraction of tenants.

The third difference is rent fixation. In both countries, rents are well below the market levels. But while in the USA rents are set as a proportion of the household income adjusted for family composition (generally 30 percent), HLM rents in France are fixed independently of income. HLM companies are free to set the rent below a ceiling value per square meter, set by law according to broad geographical zones and dwelling size, and annual changes are regulated.

10.2.2   Direct rental housing subsidies

Direct rental housing subsidies (called allowances in France, and vouchers or certificates in the USA) are means-tested benefits, covering part of housing expenses of renters who are free to choose where to live. In the USA, the system of Section 8 vouchers is as follows. Expenses above 30 percent of income (adjusted for family composition) up to either a local "fair market rent" or the actual rent, whichever is lower, are met by the voucher. If R is the rent, $\bar{R}$ is the "fair market rent," and Y is the adjusted income, the housing allowance S is generally of the following form:

$$S_{USvoucher} = [\min(R,\bar{R}) - 0.3Y],$$

where $0.3Y < R$. The rent has to be below the fair market rent. In some areas, the fair market rent is so low that as many as one-third of recipients seem unable to find housing, and thus have to do without the subsidy (Department of Housing and Urban Development [HUD] 2001, quoted by DiPasquale et al. 2003).

In France, and in other continental European countries, there is a minimum participation rent (a deductible $R_0(Y)$), increasing with adjusted income, above which part of the rent is met by the allowance, up to a ceiling:

$$S_{France} = k(Y)[\min(R,\bar{R}) - R_0(Y)],$$

with $0 < k(Y) < 0.9$, $k' < 0$ (the lower the income, the higher is the part of the rent covered by the subsidy). The ceiling rent, $\bar{R}$, increases with family size, but is not computed at the MSA level, as in the USA, and varies very little with location (basically there is a ceiling for Paris, and another, lower, ceiling for the rest of France).

Another difference is that housing subsidies are an entitlement in France, whereas only a third of all eligible low-income households receive them in the USA. As many as 45 percent of French renters are helped, versus 13 percent in the USA, and the subsidy covers on average half the rent. Besides, nearly half of the French public housing tenants benefit from a rental subsidy, on top of the low HLM rent.

10.2.3   Help to homeownership

Some 42 percent of French owner-occupiers are helped either by a direct subsidy covering part of the mortgage payment (similar to the rental subsidy described above), or by loans at low rates, or by both (Table 10.1). Also, France has for a long time had a system of contract savings for housing (called *Epargne Logement*). This offers participants the right to obtain a loan at a predetermined rate, after they have completed a compulsory 5-year period of saving. Savings earn interest at a predetermined below-market rate. The amount of the loan depends on the savings in a complicated way. The parameters of the system are such that the loan is generally not sufficient to buy a house and households have to apply for other credits to complement it. In 2002, for those who used it, *Epargne Logement* loans covered, on average, half of the borrowed amount. The importance of *Epargne Logement* has been declining: it now accounts for one-fifth of all housing loans, versus one-third in 1996. For a thorough description of the French system of contract savings and its German counterpart (the *Bausparkassen* system), readers should refer to Lea and Renaud (1995).

Before the mid-1990s, help to low-income homeowners was mainly achieved through government-provided loans, called PAP (*Prêt d'Accession à la Propriété*) and PC (*Prêt Conventionné*). Between 1977 and 1984, nearly 60 percent of the new mortgagers benefited from them and the ownership rate increased markedly. Their success can be attributed to the fact that the high inflation of the period made real interest rates negative. From 1984 on, the situation changed. Inflation fell, but not the interest rates of the PAP and PC. Thus, real interest rates increased sharply. The private credit system was able to propose loans at lower rates than subsidized ones.

The main problem for low-income families was then perceived to be their risk of default, and of borrowing constraints, as private lenders became more restrictive. At the end of 1995, the PAP was replaced by the *Prêt à Taux Zéro* (PTZ). The PTZ is an interest-free loan, granted to first-time buyers to complement their other credits. Eligibility to a PTZ is means-tested. The maximum loan increases with family size, and varies with the geographical zone. It cannot exceed 20 percent of the purchase value and 50 percent of the total credit. For the lowest income brackets, the PTZ can be paid back only after all other loans are totally repaid. Thus, it can be considered as a down payment subsidy. The program has been designed so that mainly households buying a new dwelling can apply, since an existing dwelling has to be renovated for at least 40 percent of its price to be eligible, which rules out most of them. About 600,000 households have benefited from the PTZ between 1996 and 1999, about 35 percent of the flows into ownership over this time period. The average amount of a PTZ was around 15,000 euros.

Direct subsidies to mortgagers are rare in the USA. The federal government encourages homeownership by setting common standardized rules for mortgage requirements, offering insurance on loans for low-income households (FHA loans in particular), and encouraging the development of secondary markets for mortgages through federal agencies such as Fanny Mae and Freddie Mac. There are also state and local programs for low-cost mortgages (Table 10.1). But the main feature is the tax deduction of mortgage interest from taxable income, which benefits three-quarters of American mortgagers. Such deduction is gradually disappearing in France, as it was suppressed for new loans after 1996.

10.2.4 Some macro figures

It should be clear by now that some policies known under similar names in France and the USA differ somewhat in their goals, schedules, and practical implementations. Those differences should be kept in mind when looking at macro figures such as those of Table 10.2, which compares public spending on housing in France and in the USA. Besides, in both countries homeowners are not taxed on rental income from their own home, and this is not counted as a tax advantage in official figures.

- The USA relies more on indirect subsidies (e.g., the interest deductibility provision for homeowners) than on direct subsidies. The reverse is true for France.
- Overall, 36 percent of French households either get rental subsidy, public housing or a subsidized loan, versus only 15 percent in the USA. Due to the importance of the public sector in France, 65 percent of renters benefit either from low rents in HLM dwellings or from personal housing subsidies, or from both. In the USA, the corresponding figure is only 19 percent.
- Direct rental subsidies represent €457 per household per year in France, versus $164 in the USA. However, because the proportion of recipients is far smaller in the USA, average subsidies per recipient are 70 percent higher there than in France.

The rest of the chapter concentrates on the economic effects of specific housing policies.

10.3 THE HLM

Most of the questions raised by the existence of the HLM are standard. But their relative importance may differ from the case of the USA, because of the high share of HLM in the total housing stock. The main issues are the following:

1 Is it more efficient to subsidize construction or to give households personal subsidies? A related question concerns the extent of the crowding out of private construction by public housing.
2 Does the existence of an important public sector affect rents in the private sector? In other words, do private-sector tenants pay higher rents because of HLM?
3 What is the benefit of a below-market rent to a social housing tenant? How does a renter living in public housing change her housing consumption and

Table 10.2   Public spending on housing, France and the USA

	France, 2000		USA, 2001	
Public spending	*€ billions*	*%*	*$ billions*	*%*
Direct (subsidies)[a]	17.68	71.3	34.90	22.4
Including direct allowances to renters[b]	11.20	45.2	17.44	11.2
Indirect (tax expenditure)[c]	7.11	28.7	121.10	77.6
Total	24.79	100.0	156.00	100.0

	France (€)	*USA ($)*
Direct allowance per household	457	164
Direct allowance per beneficiary household	2,324	3,922
Direct allowance per renter	1,044	513

	France	*USA*
Percentage of renters getting direct subsidy	44.9	13.1
Percentage of renters getting direct subsidy or public housing	65.3	18.6
Percentage of households getting direct subsidy, public housing, or subsidized mortgage	36.3	15.2

[a] France: Comptes du Logement (2000), table 5.2. USA: Green Book (2000), table 15–32.
[b] France: *aides personnelles*, including administrative costs (Comptes du Logement 2000, table 312, "*locatif social*" + "*locatif privé*"). USA, from table 15–32 of the Green Book (2000): Section 8 Low-income housing assistance, Section 202/811 Housing for the Elderly and the disabled, Section 236 Rental Housing Assistance, Rent Supplement, Section 235 Homeownership Assistance. This last item should be removed, but the amount is unknown (43,000 households are concerned).
[c] France: the difference between "*aides effectives*" (Comptes du Logement 2000, table 5.2) and "*avantages conférés*" (table 5.1); that is, tax and interest rate advantages. USA: National Low Income Housing Coalition, *Changing Priorities: The Federal Budget and Housing Assistance 1996–2006* (2001).
Sources: Comptes du Logement (2000); Green Book (2000)

her consumption of other goods, as compared to living in the private rental sector?

4   A related question concerns the targeting of the transfers occurring through HLM. Does public social housing benefit the poorest households?

5   Is public housing a mobility trap, with the adverse consequence of spatial mismatch between jobs and housing?
6   What are the consequences of the impossibility of expelling rich tenants from HLM?

Empirical studies on those questions are but a few, especially in France. The answer to question 1 on efficiency in the production of housing services is deferred until section 10.4, on rental subsidies. Let us just mention that, historically, there was an efficiency reason for creating HLM. In a time of acute shortage, when private financing was lacking, HLM companies were supposed to build new housing faster and more efficiently than private developers. Actually, since maintenance costs were to be borne by the HLM companies, they had an incentive to build high-quality housing that would be less costly to maintain, all the more since capital costs were subsidized. No empirical evidence on this topic is available for France. In the USA, there is some evidence that public-sector housing was costly to the taxpayer. Note, however, that because of the trade-off between initial quality and maintenance costs, such results can be misleading if costs are not assessed over the long term.

The fact that the existence of a controlled public rental sector may affect prices in the uncontrolled rental sector (question 2 on price distortion) has been recognized from some time (Fallis & Smith 1984), but empirical evaluations of the impact have been relatively rare (see, e.g., Fallis & Smith 1985). At the micro level in the area of the Paris outskirts, the presence of HLM seems to depress the free sector prices in the same area, through a "bad neighborhood effect," but no evidence exists on the overall effect of the HLM on the private-sector rents at the agglomeration (MSA) level. This lack of empirical results is particularly detrimental in the French case, because the quantitative importance of the public housing sector is likely to induce changes in the aggregate demand for housing and spillovers from the controlled to the uncontrolled sector.

10.3.1   The mobility trap

The huge rent differential between the private and the public sectors, as well as the conditions of admittance into and exit from the HLM sector, are likely to cause "mobility traps" (question 5). Households living in HLM and facing adverse shocks on the labor market will not find it profitable to move away to find a job, because they would have to give up HLM rents and subsidies and face the private-sector rents to relocate (moving to another location means going back to the end of the queue). The problem is exacerbated by the spatial concentration of HLM. In the 1960s and 1970s, some areas were entirely made up of public apartment buildings. Together, those facts could lead to acute spatial mismatch problems. No empirical evaluation of the importance of this mobility trap exists. It would require relating transitions on the labor market to transitions on the housing market. But since such transitions are rare, very large samples would be needed.

10.3.2 Transfers to HLM tenants

To answer questions 3 and 4, on the value of transfers to HLM tenants, we follow Le Blanc and Laferrère (2001), who used the model and estimation strategies of Olsen (1972), studying rent control in New York City. The model is a static, partial equilibrium model, with two goods, housing service and a composite good assimilated to the numeraire, and three markets, the controlled market for housing services (the public sector), the free market sector for housing services, and the market for nonhousing goods. The last two markets are assumed to be perfectly competitive. An important assumption is that the existence of a public sector has no influence on the rents of the private sector (question 2 is assumed away).

Denote by $p_s(p_m)$ the unit price of housing service in the public sector (in the private sector). Suppose (as is empirically true) that $p_s < p_m$. Let $U(c,q)$ represent the preferences of a household over consumption and housing, let $v(p)$ be the associated indirect utility function, and let x be the household's income. If the household lives in the private sector, it consumes a quantity q_m of housing service and a quantity c_m of the composite good. These quantities are the Marshallian demands arising from the maximization of utility under the budget constraint $x = p_m q_m + c_m$, yielding utility level $v(p_m)$. If the household lives in the public sector, it consumes a quantity q_s of housing service, and a quantity c_s of the composite good, with budget constraint $x = p_s q_s + c_s$. It reaches utility level $u_s \equiv U(c_s, q_s)$. Note that q_s is not freely chosen.

The "benefit" of a HLM tenant can be computed as the compensating variation; that is, the maximum amount that she would be willing to pay to avoid moving to the private market sector. This quantity (denoted A) is implicitly defined as follows:

$$U(c_s - A, q_s) = v(p_m). \tag{10.1}$$

Alternatively, one can compute an equivalent variation (denoted B), as the amount a private-sector tenant would need to be as well off as a HLM tenant. If e denotes the expenditure function associated with U, B is defined as follows:

$$B = e(u_s, p_m) - x. \tag{10.2}$$

Inefficiency arises because HLM tenants are not on their demand curves: the only arbitrage for them is to compare their utility levels in the public sector (where the quantity is fixed but the rent is low) and in the market sector, where they are able to adjust the quantity of housing service. Denoting by $S = (p_m - p_s)q_s$ the transfer made to HLM tenants in the form of low rents, the collective surplus loss can be measured by $S - A$ or $S - B$. Figure 10.1 depicts the situation (see also Olsen & Barton 1983).

To estimate the importance of the implicit transfers to HLM renters, two quantities have to be computed for each tenant: the private market rent of his dwelling

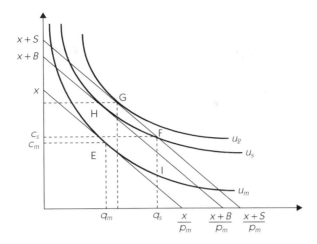

Figure 10.1   The HLM: the household's utility functions and the
Hicksian surplus.

The private-sector renter with income x is located at point **E**. The HLM tenant is located
at point **F** and reaches utility level u_s. For the HLM landlord, the loss resulting from
renting the dwelling below the market price is equal to $S = q_s(p_m - p_s)$. Were he given
this sum in the form of a cash subsidy, the HLM tenant could reach utility $u_2 > u_s$,
locating at point **G**. To reach the utility level u_s in the private sector, the household
would only need the additional income $B < S$; it would then locate at point **H**. B is the
equivalent variation. The welfare loss is then equal to $S - B$. Next, consider the point **I**,
defined by the intersection of the vertical line from point **F** with the indifference
curve u_m. The maximum amount that the HLM tenant would be willing to pay to
stay in the HLM sector, A, is given by the length of segment **IF**.

on one hand – that is, $p_m q_s$ using our notation – and the quantity of housing the
tenant would choose in the private rental sector, $p_m q_m$. The simplest way to achieve
this goal is to estimate two regressions on private-sector dwellings or tenants.
The first relates the market rents to the characteristics of the dwellings, and the
second explains housing expenditures in the private sector as a function of
the renters' characteristics. The parameters of the first regression are used to
compute a free-market rent for each dwelling in the social sector. The parameters
of the second model are used to predict housing consumption for social-sector
tenants.

Empirical estimates from Le Blanc and Laferrère (2001), conducted on a sample
from the 1996 French Housing Survey, indicate that public-sector tenants consume 10 percent more housing services and 11 percent more of other goods than
they would in the private sector. The collective surplus loss due to these transfers
is 8 percent of the transfers. In New York City in the 1960s (Olsen & Barton 1983),
the corresponding figures were 66 percent in housing consumption and 17 percent in nonhousing consumption. Perhaps the closest analogue to New York in

Table 10.3 The gain in housing service and in nonhousing consumption of HLM tenants, by income and location

| Decile of equivalent income | Paris metropolitan area | | Other regions | |
	Gain in housing service (%)	Gain in nonhousing consumption (%)	Gain in housing service (%)	Gain in nonhousing consumption (%)
1	21	49	18	15
2	15	28	12	12
3	17	20	12	9
4	13	18	9	8
5	12	19	9	8
6	11	16	6	7
7	14	14	3	7
8	5	12	0	7
9	2	10	−7	5
10	−7	8	−26	5
Total	10	15	9	9

Source: Le Blanc and Laferrère (2001)

France is the Paris metropolitan area, where the corresponding figures are 10 percent and 15 percent (see Table 10.3). The differences with New York City may stem from different compositions of the public housing populations. In particular, the Parisian HLM residents are not particularly poor: 52 percent have an income above the median income of the whole French population. The relative gains are more important for the poorest households.

10.3.3 Redistribution and horizontal equity

For HLM tenants, the gain in housing services decreases as income increases, to reach zero at the ninth decile. However, the relative gain in nonhousing consumption decreases only slowly with income; it is around 8 percent for the three highest deciles (Table 10.3). For the richest tenants, the only effect of HLM is to allow them to consume more of nonhousing goods (Table 10.3). They live in dwellings equivalent to those that they would choose in the private market sector. This gives them the opportunity to build up a down payment to finance a future home purchase. The collective transfer to households living in HLM, through below-market rents, benefits the lowest income renters more (in relative values). Those in the first income decile gain 17 percent of housing service and 21 percent in consumption of nonhousing goods; up to the fifth decile, the consumption gains are above 10 percent, both for housing and nonhousing consumption. In that sense, the public sector fulfills its role to help low-resource households, allowing them to live in bigger apartments than in the private sector, while consuming more of other goods.

However, the targeting to the poor is quite loose: 45 percent of the public housing surplus goes to households whose income (adjusted for family composition) is above the median. By comparison, direct rental allowances, which in France are also granted to eligible public housing tenants, are better targeted: 95 percent go to the poorest half of the population.

From the point of view of horizontal equity, some low-income households have easier access to the HLM sector than others. Most of the HLM accommodation was built in the 1960s and 1970s for families with children, who constituted the bulk of the low-income households. The existing stock is thus not well suited for part of the new low-income population, which frequently consists of single persons. They have to live in the private sector, where rents are much higher.

10.3.4   Access to and exit from the HLM

The impossibility of expelling rich HLM tenants obviously has adverse consequences on the ability of HLM to house the poor, since fewer dwellings are available. But it also has implications on the spatial concentration of the poorest populations. Indeed, upper-class households, who could afford to live in the private sector, are induced to leave the public sector if their apartment is located in a "bad" neighborhood, whereas they will stay in a well-located apartment. Thus, public-sector apartments that are vacated and offered to new (poor) tenants are mainly located in the worst neighborhoods. This, added to the segregative policies of some HLM companies (which can be seen as a sorting between "good tenants," to be put into the good dwellings, and "bad tenants," to be put into the bad dwellings), makes concentration of the poor a problem in many French cities.

10.4   PERSONAL HOUSING ALLOWANCES: THE EXAMPLE OF THE FRENCH PRIVATE RENTAL SECTOR

Housing allowances were developed at a time when project-oriented policy was criticized for its inefficiency (high maintenance costs), for the fact that it was not targeted to the most needy, and when the main problem was no longer a housing shortage but affordability, and the concentration of low-income households in zones of high public housing density.

As has been shown above, personal allowances are better targeted to low-income households than public housing. We discuss three main questions:

1   Are direct housing allowances more cost-efficient than project-oriented subsidies?
2   How are housing allowances "shared" between low-income households and landlords? Did housing allowances increase rents in the private sector?

3   Do personal housing allowances allow low-income families to consume more housing?

Unfortunately, the empirical evidence on these questions is very scarce in the French context.

10.4.1   Comparing costs

There has never been an assessment of the long-term costs of direct housing allowances compared to project-oriented construction subsidies in France. In the USA, vouchers seem more cost-effective than production programs. DiPasquale, Fricke, and Garcia-Diaz (2003) compare total costs over 30 years of currently active production projects (such as LIHTC) and rental subsidy such as vouchers. The total cost of a voucher is the present discounted value of rents (paid by both the voucher and the assisted household) plus the administrative cost of the program. For production programs, the market rents do not cover total costs, so total cost is the sum of the present discounted value of rents and construction subsidies (below-market interest loan, tax credits). The production program appears to be less efficient. For instance, for two-bedroom units in metropolitan areas, the construction program would cost from 6 percent to 14 percent more, depending on the program.

In France, the focus has been on the huge and expanding cost of personal housing allowances, which was largely unforeseen at the time when the program was created, in 1977. One of the reasons for the drift in costs is the rise in the number of eligible households, which matched the rise in unemployment and in single-parent families. As personal housing subsidies are an entitlement, the number of beneficiaries rose mechanically in response.

10.4.2   Effect on rents

Textbook economics predicts that a direct *ad valorem* subsidy to a consumption good increases demand and pushes up prices. A subsidy reduces the price of housing, compared to other goods. The magnitude of the extra consumption depends on how consumers choose to allocate the extra income between housing and other goods. Another effect of the subsidy is to induce the formation of new households: for instance, children may now choose to live independently from their parents. Note that if they already lived independently but the parents were covering part of the expenses, the latter are the true beneficiaries of the subsidy.

In response to a higher demand, supply reacts. In the short run, it is probably rather rigid, except in areas with high vacancy rates. An increase in demand translates into higher rents, and the only beneficiaries may be the landlords who rent the same dwellings at a higher price. In the longer run, new dwellings are constructed or renovated, and rents settle at a new equilibrium.

The first assessments of the effect of vouchers on prices, following their introduction as an experiment in very limited areas of the USA, did not conclude that there was any effect on rents. However, Susin (2002), using spatial differences in the distribution of vouchers in 90 US metropolitan areas, finds that rents for the poor are 16 percent higher where vouchers were more widely distributed. He attributes this to the very low supply elasticity of low-income housing and the segmentation of housing submarkets. There is no effect of vouchers on rents on the middle- or upper-income submarkets. But the increase in demand following the receipt of a voucher is not matched by an increase in supply at the lower end of the market, where subsidized and nonsubsidized eligible households compete for the same dwellings. Susin concludes that vouchers have been a huge transfer to landlords and a net loss to low-income households, where the recipients benefited and the nonrecipients were worse off.

In France, Laferrère and Le Blanc (2004b), using quarterly panel data on rental dwelling units, prove that landlords charge higher rents to subsidized renters than to nonsubsidized ones. Thus, landlords pocket part of the subsidy. Due to this behavior, when the number of recipients went up from 1.9 million to 3.1 million as the coverage of personal housing subsidies was extended in 1992, the rents of dwellings occupied by subsidy recipients grew at a faster rate than those of units occupied by nonsubsidized tenants. However, the study does not measure the overall impact of personal subsidies on rents.

10.4.3 The effect on housing consumption

Given the effect on prices, do recipients consume more housing services than nonrecipients? Susin (2002) clearly answers in the negative for the USA. It is probable that the adverse effect on poor households found by Susin is less severe in France, for two reasons. First, personal housing subsidies are an entitlement, so all low-income families benefit, and not only those lucky enough to be at the top of the waiting list. The second reason is more hypothetical: there are reasons to believe that housing submarkets are less segmented in France, so that the supply response to housing allowances might be higher. We can only present one casual example: in 1992, personal housing subsidies were extended to students, regardless of their parents' income. The supply response seems to have been fairly high in that case. Between 1988 and 1996, the proportion of students living independently rose dramatically, from 28 percent to 40 percent. Among those living independently, the proportion of those sharing a home decreased from 26 percent to 16 percent. On this topic, see Laferrère and Le Blanc (2004a).

More generally, do subsidies increase total housing consumption? Sinai and Waldfolgel (2005) ask whether markets with more public housing or more vouchers per capita have more total housing units per capita, after accounting for other potential determinants of the number of housing units. As in the case of Murray (1999) before them, they point to an important crowding out of private-sector units by construction-subsidized units: three to four public units are needed to add one net unit, thus crowding out two to three private units. Tenant-based allowances seem more effective than project-based programs at targeting units to people who otherwise would not have their own, the crowding out being much less.

Overall, it would seem that personal housing subsidies are both more efficient and cause less harm to private construction than construction subsidies. But note also that, according to both Murray and Susin, very low income households do not find adequate housing on the market: vouchers are not enough if there are no available affordable houses on the market, and subsidized construction is then needed.

10.5   AN UPFRONT DOWN PAYMENT SUBSIDY
TO OWNERS: THE PTZ

A policy of loan subsidy such as the *Prêt à Taux Zéro*, described in section 10.2.3, raises many questions. It is convenient to start from a stylized demand model of mobility and tenure choice, in which borrowing constraints are explicitly introduced. In such a model, exogenous shocks on family size (divorce, marriage, births) and income make adjustment in the owned or rented housing stock desirable. The only way to adjust is by moving, but moves are costly. The distortion between the current stock of housing capital and the optimal one must be large enough for the family to move. When moving, the households choose between renting and owning. For unconstrained households, the choice relies on the comparison of the rent and the user cost of housing capital. But borrowing constraints can prevent low-wealth households from purchasing the desired type of housing stock, whereas they can choose optimal quantities in the rental sector.

In this framework, it is clear that borrowing constraints not only affect the rental/ownership trade-off, but also have an impact on mobility. The PTZ relaxes the borrowing constraints, shifting up the utility associated with moving and owning and making both alternatives (staying, and moving and renting) less attractive.

The following questions can be asked:

1   What is the impact of the PTZ on the flows into ownership?
2   Where do the "marginal" owners (i.e., the households induced to move-and-own at any period by the PTZ) come from? Would they have stayed in their current dwellings, or would they have moved and owned in the absence of the PTZ?
3   Is the program well targeted? What proportion of households using the PTZ would have moved and owned even without it?
4   What is the impact of the program on the quality of housing construction?
5   Does the program have any long-term effect on the ownership rate, or is it just making the same households own earlier in their life cycles?

Two other important questions would need to be addressed, and would necessitate going beyond a demand model:

6   What is the effect of the PTZ on housing prices?
7   What is the impact of the program in terms of total welfare?

It would require many empirical studies to answer all of the above questions. Oddly enough, it is difficult to find any study of the PTZ on microdata, even though the program started 7 years ago. The first paper to address some of the issues on the basis of a microeconometric study is Gobillon and Le Blanc (2002).

The model allows the simulation of changes on parameters that affect the maximum house value that households can afford, which depends on maximum loan-to-value ratio (LTV), and maximum payment-to-income ratio. The PTZ, which is roughly equivalent to a down payment subsidy, decreases the amount that the household has to borrow and thus benefits mostly households for whom the LTV constraint is binding.

The model predicts that in 4 years, the PTZ would have benefited 533,000 households. Since it does not take into account the restriction of the PTZ to new dwellings (see section 10.2), and since a large proportion of mover-owners choose to buy old dwellings, this number must be a loose upper bound for the real one. From the Ministry of Housing, the real figure for the four years 1996–9 on a comparable field (former HLM renters excluded) is 423,000. Among beneficiaries, the PTZ induced nearly 75,000 households to turn to ownership: 70 percent of these would have been stayers without the PTZ, and only 30 percent would have moved and rented without it. Thus, the PTZ acts as an "ownership accelerator" for renters who otherwise would have waited in their current dwellings, accumulating savings until they could meet the borrowing constraints. However, we are unable to say whether the PTZ just accelerates accession to ownership for households that would become owners in any case, although perhaps later in their life cycles, or whether it induces durable switches to the ownership sector (question 5).

Judging the efficiency of the PTZ only by its effects on the flows into ownership, one would conclude that it suffers from a huge "windfall effect," since 85 percent $(1 - 75/533)$ of the recipients would have chosen to move and own at the same date without it. This figure is in line with other evaluations that have been made by the French Ministry of Housing, using different approaches. However, another goal of the PTZ was also to allow constrained households to buy larger dwellings. Overall, the response of the mean purchase value of "mover-owners" to a loosening of the borrowing constraints is the sum of two effects: on the one hand, households that would have moved and owned in the benchmark case continue to turn toward ownership, but buy more expensive dwellings. On the other hand, some households that would not have chosen ownership now decide to move and own. These marginal owners are less wealthy than supramarginal ones, and buy cheaper dwellings. Which effect dominates is an empirical matter. Gobillon and Le Blanc (2002) find that implementing the PTZ leads to a *decrease* in the average purchase value.

Considering that the PTZ is used only for new dwellings, one possible interpretation of this last result is that the PTZ might have led to the building of cheaper (i.e., lower-quality) dwellings than would have been the case without the policy. Another interpretation is in terms of location: as the price gradient declines with the distance to city centers, lower values could signal construction in the outermost suburbs. This is in line with factual observations of entire neighborhoods of "PTZ homes" being built by developers in newly urbanized areas far from the centers. Strictly speaking, however, the model does not allow a choice between these two interpretations, because neither quality nor space is explicitly modeled. Qualifying those potential explanations could have important consequences. One might fear that new construction farther from city centers would increase the risk of spatial mismatch. This is especially relevant because the PTZ beneficiaries are among the less wealthy of owners, and thus are more exposed to shocks on income.

At this point, we have some answers to questions 1, 2, 3, and 4. No empirical result is known concerning the impact of the PTZ on housing prices (questions 6 and 7). However, it is commonly believed that this impact was sizeable. One reason is the segmentation of the housing market. Only relatively poor households use the PTZ, so that "PTZ homes" are a separate product aimed at the lower end of the market. The PTZ then becomes a rent, of which developers get some part, reflected in higher housing prices. When the above model is used to simulate a uniform extra rise of 5 percent of housing prices (which seems modest for a 4-year period), the effects of the PTZ on the flows of owners are halved. A 12 percent rise totally annihilates the extensive effect of the PTZ on flows to ownership. Therefore, the results presented above must be taken as an upper bound for the effects of the PTZ.

10.6 Conclusion

We have examined the main French housing subsidy programs and looked at their targeting to low-income households. We have argued that personal housing subsidies are better targeted than public housing. However, they push rents up, so that their overall effect on welfare is not clear. Concerning help to homeownership, the PTZ program has sizeable effects, but generates huge windfall gains. As emphasized in the Introduction, it would be important to go beyond the analysis of particular housing policies and consider their interactions with the whole welfare system. A good example is labor supply. Presumably, as argued above, the low rents in HLM constitute a poverty trap. The same could be said of personal housing subsidies: since they decrease with income, they constitute an implicit taxation of the household's work and thus tend to reduce labor supply. But these programs interact with others that are directly linked to the job market, so that examining, say, the effect of the sole HLM on labor supply makes little sense.

Space permitting, it would have been worthwhile to look at the other side of the coin; that is, to start from low-income households and assess how well (or how badly) housing policies perform. Perhaps the main preoccupation of recent housing policy both in France and in the USA is the effect of neighborhood externalities on outcomes. There is an increasing awareness that a dwelling is not only a place to live, but comes with a package of public goods, such as schools, peers, and community life. In France, a rather extreme way to achieve "social diversity" was a law passed in 2000, which prescribes a standard of 20 percent of public housing for every community. Communities not meeting this threshold must pay taxes that are redistributed among the communities of the same MSA that have the highest shares of public housing. Interestingly, many rich communities prefer to pay the tax than build any public housing units. This has happened in a context in which hardly anything is known of the effects of the presence of low-income households in a neighborhood.

In the USA, experiments such as the Moving to Opportunity program, which consisted in giving housing vouchers to randomly selected public housing families to allow them to relocate, have given rise to a growing body of literature. No clear-cut conclusions seem to emerge. In Boston, Katz, Kling, and Liebman (2001) found that some outcomes are definitely better for relocated households (improved health, increased safety, reduction in male children behavior problems), but others are unaffected (employment, earnings, welfare receipt). Looking at public housing demolition in Chicago, Jacob (2003) shows that children who left after a demolition do no better nor worse than peers who did not move out. In fact, many families moved to very similar neighborhoods, and children did not end up in significantly better schools. Clearly, large-scale and long-term random experiments remain to be done, but are hard and costly to implement.

Acknowledgments

We thank Laurent Gobillon, Guy Laroque, and an anonymous referee. Errors are ours alone.

Bibliography

Basu, K. and Emerson, P. M. 2000: The economics of tenancy rent control. *The Economic Journal*, 110, 939–62.

Comptes du Logement, Ministère de l'Equipement, des Transports et du Logement 2000; www.statistiques.equipement.gouv.fr/ (Construction-Logement, Données d'ensemble).

DiPasquale, D., Fricke, D., and Garcia-Diaz, D. 2003: Comparing the costs of the Federal Housing Assistance Program. *Federal Reserve Bank of New York Economic Policy Review*; based on *Federal Housing Assistance: Comparing the Characteristics and Costs of Federal Programs*, US General Accounting Office no. 02-76, 2002.

Fallis, G. and Smith, L. B. 1984: Uncontrolled prices in a controlled market: the case of rent controls. *American Economic Review*, 74(1), 193–200.

—— and —— 1985: Price effects of rent control on controlled and uncontrolled rental housing in Toronto: a hedonic index approach. *Canadian Journal of Economics*, 18(3), 652–9.

Gobillon, L. and Le Blanc, D. 2002: The impact of borrowing constraints on mobility and tenure choice. CREST working paper 2002–28; www.crest.fr/doctravail/liste.htm

Green Book 2000: US House of Representatives, Ways and Means Committee; www.access.gpo.gov/congress/wm001.html

Jacob, B. A. 2003: Public housing, housing vouchers and student achievement: evidence from public housing demolitions in Chicago. NBER Working Paper 9652.

Katz, L. F., Kling, J. R., and Liebman, J. B. 2001: Moving to opportunity in Boston: early results of a randomized mobility experiment. *Quarterly Journal of Economics*, 116(2), 607–54.

Laferrère, A. and Le Blanc, D. 2004a: Gone with the windfall: the effect of rental subsidies on student co-residence in France. *CESifo Economic Studies*, 50(3), 451–77.

—— and —— 2004b: How do housing allowances affect rents: an empirical analysis of the French case. *Journal of Housing Economics*, 13, 36–67.

Le Blanc, D. and Laferrère, A. 2001: The effects of the existence of public social housing on households' consumption in France. *Journal of Housing Economics*, 10, 429–55.

Lea, M. and Renaud, B. 1995: Contractual savings for housing: How suitable are they for transitional economies? World Bank Policy Research Working Paper 1516.

Murray, M. P. 1999: Subsidized and unsubsidized housing stock 1935 to 1987: crowding out and cointegration. *Journal of Real Estate Finance and Economics*, 18(1), 107–24.

Olsen, E. O. 1972: An econometric analysis of rent control. *Journal of Political Economy*, 80, 1,081–100.

—— and Barton, D. M. 1983: The benefits and costs of public housing in New York City. *Journal of Public Economics*, 20, 299–332.

Sinai, T. and Waldfogel, J. 2005: Do low-income housing subsidies increase housing consumption? *Journal of Public Economics*, 89, 3137–64.

Susin, S. 2002: Rent vouchers and the price of low-income housing. *Journal of Public Economics*, 83, 109–52.

CHAPTER ELEVEN

Housing Demand: An International Perspective

Miki Seko

11.1 INTRODUCTION

Housing markets reflect distinctive national and regional policies and practices. It is important to increase understanding of housing markets and, in particular, of housing demand behavior, to cope with various housing problems and develop better housing policies. At present, the vast majority of empirical studies have been conducted in North America and the United Kingdom. However, housing markets can differ significantly among different countries because of housing tenure arrangements, housing finance arrangements, and the form and extent of government intervention. We must therefore take into consideration relevant national and regional differences when we conduct empirical studies about housing demand behavior in each country. The goal of this essay is to compare Asian and non-Asian empirical housing demand studies outside North America and the UK, to highlight the importance of national and regional differences that affect housing policies. In addition, this essay also examines more general mechanisms in housing demand behavior, housing markets and housing policies in comparative perspective.

In the following, we focus on the demand for housing services. In section 11.3, we compare simultaneous decisions of housing tenure choice and housing demand studies from Japan and Sweden. The comparison sheds light on how various differences require different econometric specifications for analyzing the countries' housing markets. In section 11.4, we discuss studies concerning the demand for floor space in Japan and China. Given differences in political systems and geographical conditions, what are the key factors in determining floor space size and how can we account for these in our econometric analysis? In section 11.2, we first briefly overview and compare several relevant characteristics of Japan, Sweden, and China. This allows us to better understand how to incorporate evident differences in specifying econometric models used in subsequent sections.

11.2 A REVIEW OF THE HOUSING MARKETS IN JAPAN, SWEDEN, AND MAINLAND CHINA

In this section, we survey the characteristics of housing markets in Japan, Sweden, and Mainland China. For reference, several housing and related indicators for four countries (Japan, Mainland China, Sweden, and the United States) are summarized in Table 11.1.

11.2.1 Japan

In Japan, housing prices are relatively high, due in large part to the much higher price of land compared to almost all other countries. The purchase price of housing is approximately 5.6 times (1999) the average worker's pre-tax income. Over the past two decades, Japan has experienced a dramatic rise and fall in land values and this phenomenon has forced Japan, *inter alia*, to significantly transform its housing finance arrangements. The population density is also high. The proportion of owner-occupied housing in Japan stands at roughly 60 percent, while private rental tenure accounts for roughly 26 percent of the overall housing market. In general, Japan has maintained a very high level of housing construction since World War II. The size and quality of Japanese housing has also rapidly improved, though the differences in the size and quality of owned houses and rented houses remain large. For example, in 1998, the average total floor space per owned dwelling was 122.7 m^2, while that per rented dwelling was only 44.6 m^2. For a variety of reasons, the market for used houses is small in Japan. Significantly, intergenerational transfers relating to housing are more common than in other countries. This occurs because for real estate, as opposed to financial securities, the inheritance tax is reduced, since the assessed value used to calculate the inheritance tax is usually considerably less than the market value. In addition, mobility rates are low. It is also important to note that in Japan, land and the dwelling structure are considered to be separate real assets and are assessed separately.

Japan's housing finance system involves an unusual combination of private- and public-sector lending. Government-subsidized lending has played an important role in the Japanese housing finance system. The government-run Japan Housing Loan Corporation (JHLC) is the largest single mortgage lender in the world and accounts for some 25–35 percent of housing loans in Japan. The JHLC was established in 1950 as a special public corporation that provides long-term capital at a low rate of interest for the construction and purchase of housing. However, it is now phasing out its lending operations and will be terminated in

Table 11.1 Several housing and related indicators of four countries

	Japan	Sweden	Mainland China	USA
Population density	337 (1997)	20 (1997)	130 (1997)	29 (1997)
Floor space per person (m²)	15.8 (1990)	40.0 (1990)	9.3 (1990)	68.7 (1990)
Persons per room	0.8 (1990)	0.6 (1990)	1.5 (1990)	0.4 (1990)
Total floor space per dwelling (m²)	92.4 (1998) 122.7 (owned) 44.58 (rented)	79.5 (1998)	75.6 (1996)	181.3 (1998)
Homeownership rate (%)	60.3 (1998)	45 (1993)	8 (1993)	65.8 (1997)
Median house price ($)	441,719 (1990)	187,780 (1990)	15,945 (1990) (1 US$ = 4.8 RMB yuan)	194,150 (1990)
Raw land price ($ per m²)	1,488.1 (1990)	17.5 (1990)	n.a.	36.0 (1990)
Construction cost ($ per m²)	2,604 (1990)	1,527 (1990)	90 (1990)	500 (1990)
Land-value ratio	0.6 (1980s)			0.75 (1981)
Housing price – income ratio	11.6 (1990)	4.6 (1990)	14.8 (1990)	3.9 (1990)
Tenure types (%)	(1998) Owned: 60.3	(1990) Owned: 40	(1989) State-owned: 84.5	(1997) Owned: 66
	Rented (private): 26 Rented (public subsidized): 6.8 Employer-provided: 5.0	Rented (private): 20 Rented (public): 25 Cooperative shares: 15	Own-built: 6.5	Rented (private): 28 Rented (subsidized): 6.0

Sources: Angel (2000), Green and Malpezzi (2003), Seko (2001), Turner (1997), and Zax (1997)

2006 as a result of Japan's dire fiscal situation. Unlike other advanced industrial nations, Japan has no major private-sector institutions that specialize in housing finance, like the savings-and-loan associations in the USA and the building societies in the UK. Moreover, there is no active secondary mortgage market, although in recent years mortgages have been bundled together and securitized. There are several housing-related subsidies in Japan. Housing loans offered by the JHLC are provided at subsidized rates. About 6.8 percent of Japanese households live in subsidized public rental housing for low- and middle-income households, while 5 percent of households live in employer-provided housing that is either free or offered to employees at nominal, subsidized rents, irrespective of their income (see Seko 2001).

Since the early 1990s, the land price bubble that emerged in the late 1980s in Japan has collapsed, and land prices as of 2003 have fallen by about two-thirds from their 1989 peak. The bubble is usually attributed to a combination of government miscues, poor oversight, lax lending procedures, and inadequate risk assessment by banks. Land served as the collateral for much of the lending and as prices fell and the economy swooned, borrowers could not repay their loans and the banks were left holding collateral that was worth considerably less than the value of the loan. The rising level of nonperforming loans that resulted in the 1990s has cut a swathe through corporate Japan, and left the enfeebled banking sector on government-sponsored life-support measures. In addition, buyers of housing during the bubble who took on large mortgages to finance their purchases are now saddled with negative equity in what often constitutes their largest investment.

11.2.2   Mainland China

Land in China has been nationalized and owned by the state since the founding of the People's Republic of China in 1949. Until recently, state-owned enterprises (SOEs) have routinely provided housing for their workers as a form of compensation. In general, housing has been viewed as an amenity guaranteed by the state and as a responsibility of employers. SOEs were required to provide their employees with housing units, some of which have become privately owned units through employee purchases. Employers in nonstate-owned enterprises may purchase housing units and house employees in those units. Another option is to purchase the units on behalf of their employees, who then can gain ownership of the unit if they remain with the firm for a specified period of time. Eighty-five percent of all employees in China were in the SOE sector as of 1996. Due to the large scale of SOEs, and the general practice of providing housing for employees, the public housing market accounts for the majority of housing units. The size of the private housing market is influenced strongly by the common practice of granting long-term employees ownership of the housing that originally was provided to them as a form of compensation.

As China has adopted a series of market-oriented economic reforms since the late 1970s, significant changes have occurred in the housing market. The introduction of joint ventures and foreign firms means that the employment practices of nonstate-owned enterprises are becoming more prevalent. In general, they have followed local custom and taken responsibility for housing employees by providing housing allowances or residential units. The 1980s were marked by the emergence of privately owned residential units (also called "commodity houses"), which formed the basis for the private residential property market. This "commodity housing" is the newly built private housing constructed by private developers. Chinese citizens can acquire legal rights to occupy the land and building for a specific period, and can transfer the title and rights to a unit to another party. Although the pace of change has been rapid in some of the larger coastal urban areas such as Shanghai, the overall market for privately owned houses remains small. However, it does seem clear that government policy aims to stimulate private ownership. The troubled finances of SOEs have given considerable impetus to this shift in policy.

This is a period of sweeping transition and rapid, ongoing change. The shift from state to private ownership is under way and will vastly alter the housing market in years to come. Chinese housing policy underwent a series of changes in the 1990s. Since 1992, the government has urged its citizens to purchase their place of residence. This is a cost-cutting move by cash-strapped local governments and SOEs, since maintenance costs are now shifted to residents. The resident-owners now have a greater incentive to contribute toward the maintenance of their housing complexes and common facilities, because this is reflected in the market value of their residences. In order to facilitate this shift toward private ownership, housing funds were established at the local government level to provide subsidized financing for workers. These housing funds helped stimulate the growth of a residential property financing market and a market for private housing.

A new housing policy was announced at the general Assembly of the People's Congress in March 1998. The new policy eliminates the practice of SOEs providing housing units for their employees and replaces this with a cash allowance that is now included in the total compensation of workers. Thus what had been a guaranteed employee benefit has been monetized as part of employees' wages and the responsibility for securing housing is now also theirs. This policy change is speeding up the privatization of residential housing and as a result is also stimulating developments in the home financing market. In 1992, Housing Funds were established at the city government level to fund the purchase of residential units by workers. SOE employees contribute a fixed percentage of their income to the fund, and their employers put in a matching contribution. The Fund thus represents a pool of funds for financing home purchases with subsidized interest rates. While land is ultimately owned by the state, existing laws in China permit Chinese citizens to gain title (meaning usufruct rights) to land and buildings. The law also defines and protects property rights for housing units. In addition, property rights (titles) can be transferred from one party to another. As China sheds ideologically driven property policies and practices, and proceeds in the transition toward more market-oriented policies, the housing market will experience considerably more change (B. Y. Chan, pers. comm., 1999).

Housing prices vary significantly among the major cities of China. In 1995, for example, the average price of commodity housing was \$192 per m^2, whereas the price in Shenzhen was \$652 per m^2, while that in Chongqing was \$121 per m^2 (1 US\$ = 8.4 RMB yuan in 1995). The average housing price to income ratio was 6.52, while that in Beijing was 9.16 (Liu 1998).

11.2.3   Sweden

In Sweden, population density is low and timber resources are abundant, so that the cost of land and construction materials is low. As a result, the ratio of housing price to income is also relatively low, at 4.6 in 1990.

Single-family housing in Sweden is generally owner-occupied by families and mostly constructed by private builders. Multi-family cooperative dwellings are individual flats in multi-family buildings, and are tenant owned. Owners have the same rights as single-family dwelling owners in purchasing and selling these units, except that they are subject to some control by the cooperative association in the areas of repair and renovation. Also, the maintenance of common facilities in these buildings is financed by means of an assessment levied on the tenants by the association. This form of tenure is very similar to condominium ownership in North America. The Swedish cooperative market is dominated by large national cooperative associations.

A large part of the housing stock in Sweden consists of rental flats in multi-family buildings. Approximately half of these buildings are owned and managed by private landlords. However, since World War II, the bulk of multi-family buildings has been built by nonprofit housing companies. These companies generally retain ownership of the buildings and provide managerial services. Each municipality owns at least one nonprofit housing corporation. These nonprofit housing corporations are accorded the most favorable terms with regard to state-subsidized loans.

The public sector (nonprofit corporations, municipalities, etc.) and the cooperative sector increased their share of the multi-family housing market in the 1970s and 1980s (Harsman & Quigley 1991, pp. 37–9). This trend is consistent with the welfare state model that prevails in Sweden.

The housing finance market in Sweden is dominated by government, and semigovernmental and private, housing finance institutions. Some of these institutions are controlled by commercial and savings banks. Funds are raised through bond issues. The government provides subsidies that cover the difference between market interest rates and the lower interest rates set by the government for housing loans. Generally, the system is among the most regulated in industrialized countries (Boleat 1985).

Sweden has an extremely high rate of personal income taxation. The state income tax is progressive for individuals. The total income tax rate for the average industrial worker is about 40 percent, and the marginal income tax rate is about 60 percent. The treatment of housing within the Swedish income tax system relies on assessed (or taxation) value. In Sweden, buildings are assessed every 5 years, and the assessed value is defined as 75 percent of the estimated fair market value. Housing is an asset from which income is imputed. Nonprofit companies and cooperative associations impute a flat 3 percent of assessed value. Owners of single-family homes must impute as income a percentage that increases with assessed value. This percentage starts at 2 percent and increases to a maximum of 8 percent (1988). From the imputed income, the owner subtracts mortgage interest payments. Independent of imputed income calculations, all housing owners pay a flat-rate national property tax of 1.5 percent of the assessed value (Harsman & Quigley 1991, pp. 57–9).

During much of the post World War II era, Sweden has had a housing policy that emphasizes: interest rate subsidies for investment; neutrality between tenures; generous overall benefits to housing both in the form of general subsidies and income-related benefits; and low risks to financiers, investors, and households alike.

However, Sweden has reduced and restricted housing subsidies since the early 1990s and has begun a process of deregulation. In 1990, all new building was being heavily subsidized, tax benefits were significant, and social-sector rents were related to historic costs. That is to say, a rent control system based on a negotiated "fair-rent" system prevailed. In contrast, by 1998, general subsidies had been slashed, as had the tax benefits for owner-occupiers. In addition, rent controls on public housing have been relaxed to some degree and are meant to better reflect actual market conditions. Interest rate subsidies on new construction have been phased out as a result of the 1991 tax reform and the 1993 housing finance reform. The 1991 tax reform decreased the marginal tax rate from 47 percent to 30 percent for most income earners, leading to a large fiscal deficit. The fiscal deficit has led to a slashing of interest rate subsidies for rental and cooperative housing and an increase in indirect taxes. A tax reform in 1991/2 broadened the tax base, introducing, *inter alia*, a value-added tax on housing maintenance. As a consequence of these various reforms and increased taxation on real estate companies, real housing rents have increased. Demand for new housing has decreased, particularly in areas where the economic recession has hit hardest. Vacancies have increased especially in the municipal housing companies. Swedish housing policy is changing toward fewer subsidies, reduced tax benefits, and more targeted and limited assistance directed at lower-income households and depressed areas. Thus, the overall social character of the local municipal housing policy is being challenged by a shift in political sentiments away from welfare state policies that is reinforced by depressed market conditions. This trend is compelling drastic changes in housing policies to an extent that is without precedent (Turner 1997, p. 4; Turner & Whitehead 2002, pp. 201, 205, 207–8).

11.3   A COMPARISON OF STUDIES OF SIMULTANEOUS DECISIONS OF HOUSING TENURE CHOICE AND DEMAND FOR HOUSING IN JAPAN AND SWEDEN

In this section, we compare simultaneous decisions of housing tenure choice and tenure-specific housing demand studies in Japan (Horioka 1988) and Sweden (Hansson-Brusewitz 1997).

A household's choice of tenure and its demand for housing services are a joint decision. A household solves for the maximum utility conditional on owning and the maximum utility conditional on renting. It then chooses owning over renting if the maximized utility conditional on owning exceeds the maximized utility conditional on renting. It is assumed that owning and renting housing are mutually exclusive activities. Both owner-occupied and rental units yield housing services composed of all housing attributes, but they are distinct goods because their characteristics differ (Rosen 1979, pp. 6–7). In general, the quantity of housing demanded by households depends on its price, on household income, and also on demographic characteristics such as the household's age, sex, and size. In Western studies, tenure is largely determined by economic variables such as income and price differences, and demographic variables related to stages in the life cycle. Typically, tenure constraints are financial and to some extent reflect investment risks (Henderson & Ioannides 1983).

11.3.1   Japan

Horioka (1988) analyzed tenure choice and tenure-specific housing demand based on Japanese household-level data from 1981. He estimated the parameters of tenure choice and tenure-specific housing demand equations simultaneously using the maximum likelihood method and the two-stage procedure. His uncompensated price elasticity estimate, −0.8, is comparable to those found for Western countries, but the permanent income elasticity estimate, 1.4, is significantly higher than in the USA (around 1.0). The user cost of capital for owner-occupied housing in Japan is independent of the marginal tax rate, because at that time neither mortgage interest payments nor local property taxes were tax-deductible and most income from nonhousing assets was tax exempt. Currently, mortgage payment deductions are permitted on a temporary basis. In Japan, the tenure choice and housing demand decisions are apparently not made simultaneously. This may be because in Japan, the owner-occupied housing sector is clearly larger and of higher quality than the rented housing sector and thus vastly more preferable. Therefore, households may not care about other housing attributes when deciding which tenure to choose. The income and age variables are positive and highly significant for homeowning in Japan. Housing demand was apparently price-inelastic and elastic with respect to permanent income when there was no public policy toward homeownership, such as tax deduction for mortgage interest payments and property taxes. This was especially true when other investments such as interest income on housing-related and other types of savings were tax exempt.

11.3.2   Sweden

Hansson-Brusewitz (1997) analyzed tenure choice and tenure-specific housing demand based on Swedish household-level data from 1980. He estimated the parameters of the reduced-form tenure choice equation and the tenure-specific structural form housing demand equations jointly, taking the nonlinearity of budget constraints and the sample selection problem into proper consideration. The nonlinearity of the budget constraint arises from the fact that taxpayers were permitted to deduct interest payments on home mortgages under the progressive income tax system while including a tax-assessed rental value of the home in their taxable income. For example, in housing tenure choice analysis, sample selection problems may arise when the data used in the estimation have been generated by households that are exclusively homeowners, thus ignoring the renters sample. The model permits a correlation between random terms representing unobserved heterogeneity of preferences in the demand function and the tenure choice equation. The estimated model resembles the Tobit model in that these random terms are perfectly correlated. Hansson-Brusewitz's average uncompensated price elasticity estimate is −0.98, and the income elasticity estimate is 0.98. Those elasticities are evaluated at the observed point of each owner in the sample and are valid for budget constraints linearized at this point.

11.3.3   A Comparison of Japan and Sweden

In both models, each year the household is assumed to solve the following utility maximization problem, if it chooses to own its home:

$$\underset{c,h}{Max}\ U(c,h) \tag{11.1}$$

$$s.t.\ c + ucc \times P \times h = y, \tag{11.2}$$

where consumers obtain utility from housing services h and other goods c. $ucc \times P$ is the user cost of capital for owner-occupied housing. P is the unit price of owner-occupied housing. y is after-tax permanent income, consisting both of labor income and nonlabor income. Equation (11.1) is the utility function. Equation (11.2) is a budget constraint, where the composite of other goods is a numeraire commodity.

The user cost of capital for owner-occupied housing in Japan is in the following form:

$$(ucc \times P)^{JPh} = (i - \pi + k_s d + t_p)P, \tag{11.3}$$

where i is the nominal interest rate (which is assumed to equal the rate of return on other assets), π is the expected rate of increase in housing prices, k_s is the ratio of the value of the structure to the total value of the investment, d is the rate of depreciation and maintenance, and t_p is the property tax rate. This form of user cost in Japan reflects the fact that neither mortgage interest payments nor local property taxes are tax-deductible and most income from nonhousing assets is tax exempt. That is, neither i nor t_p are multiplied by $(1 - t_y)$ where t_y is the marginal income tax rate. It also reflects the fact that capital gains on owner-occupied housing are not taxed if certain conditions are met. That is, π is not multiplied by $(1 - t_y)$. Moreover, $k_s d$ is also not multiplied by $(1 - t_y)$, because depreciation expenses on owner-occupied housing are not tax-deductible. The resulting linear budget constraint is shown in Figure 11.1.

For reference, the user cost of capital for owner-occupied housing in the USA is in the following form:

$$(ucc \times P)^{US} = \{(1 - t_y)i - \pi + k_s d + (1 - t_y)t_p P\}, \tag{11.4}$$

because mortgage interest payments and local property taxes are tax-deductible.

In Sweden, budget constraint (11.2) becomes

$$c + (i - \pi + k_s d)Ph = y - T\{y - iPh + \theta(Ph)\}, \tag{11.2'}$$

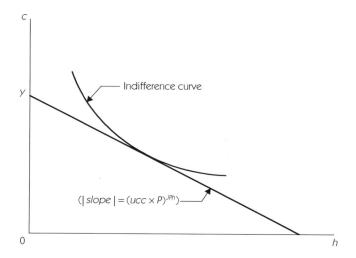

Figure 11.1   Linear budget constraints in Japan: (c,h) space.
Notation: c, other goods; h, housing services; y, income; P, unit price of owner-occupied housing; $(ucc \times P)^{JPh}$, user cost of capital for owner-occupied housing. Budget constraints from equation (11.2): $c + (ucc \times P)^{JPh} \times h = y$ [for the definition of $(ucc \times P)^{JPh}$, see equation (11.3)].

where $T\{\cdot\}$ is the nonlinear income tax function. The taxable income is calculated as y minus payments on home mortgages and the opportunity cost of equity, iPh, plus the imputed rental value of the home, $\theta(Ph)$. When we define the marginal imputed rent θ' as the increase in rental income imputed for tax purposes for an extra dollar of house price, the (marginal) user cost of capital for owner-occupied housing in Sweden becomes:

$$(ucc \times P)^{SW} = \{i - \pi - (i - \theta')t_y + k_s d\}P. \tag{11.5}$$

The marginal price of equation (11.5) changes at a kink point, where either the assessed income passes into another income tax bracket or the assessed value of the house passes into another bracket of the imputed rent function. This occurs as taxpayers are allowed to deduct interest payments on home mortgages and must include a tax-assessed rental value of the home in their taxable income under the progressive income tax system. In 1980, the imputed rental value of the home was a piecewise linear function of the tax-assessed value of the house, with marginal imputed rents rising stepwise as the tax-assessed value moved into higher brackets. Since this type of tax system makes the tax rate endogenous, it requires special econometric methods (see, e.g., Olsen 1987; Hansson-Brusewitz 1997; Seko 2002).

As for after-tax permanent income, Horioka (1988) calculated the after-tax permanent income of each household by first estimating an auxiliary regression of current income related to various demographic and occupational variables and taking the weighted average of current income and the fitted value from this regression. He then subtracted his estimates of taxes and social security contributions from this pre-tax permanent income and finally added the imputed rent on owner-occupied housing. In Japan, imputed rent is not taxed, which is different from the situation in Sweden. Hansson-Brusewitz (1997) calculated the pre-tax permanent income consisting of labor and nonlabor income (which includes the imputed rental value of the home) and government interest subsidies. Then he calculated the income tax and assessed income, and subtracted them from the pre-tax income based on equation (11.5). The derived budget constraint is nonlinear (piecewise linear) with kink points.

Assuming that the household chooses to own its home, the general model, equations (11.1) and (11.2) shown above, is applicable in both countries. The user cost of capital for owner-occupied housing sharply differs between Japan and Sweden because government policy, especially the income tax system, differs between these countries. In Japan, income tax does not affect the demand for housing services and tenure choice much, but in Sweden, income tax greatly affects both decisions. To analyze housing demand, we have to take into consideration each country's unique government policy. Of course, appropriate econometric specification becomes different when institutional systems such as the tax system differ. In Sweden, we have to explicitly take into consideration the piecewise linear budget constraint arising from its progressive income tax system and adopt the econometric estimation method to deal with it. In Japan, the progressive income tax system does not influence housing demand decisions and/or tenure choice decisions much. For example, the marginal income tax rate for the average worker in Sweden is about 60 percent, while that in Japan is about 15 percent or less.

11.4 A COMPARISON OF STUDIES ON THE DEMAND FOR FLOOR SPACE IN JAPAN AND MAINLAND CHINA

In this section, we draw on studies concerning the decision about total floor space in Japan and Mainland China, and the factors that influence floor space demand in the context of significantly different political and governmental systems. These differences are key in accurately specifying econometric models for housing demand in each country.

11.4.1 Mainland China

Zax (1997) analyzes tenure-specific dwelling size demand and tenure choice based on 1989 microdata from urban China using a switching regression model with endogenous switching. This is a model in which the behavior of the agents is described by two regression equations corresponding to regimes 1 and 2. There is also a criterion function that determines which of these two equations is applicable, and random terms of the criterion function are correlated with those of two regression equations. It is assumed that sample separation is available and only contemporaneous correlation between the random terms is allowed (see Maddala 1983). Horioka (1988) has also used the type of model explained in section 11.3 to analyze simultaneous decisions of tenure-specific housing demand and tenure choice in Japan. In Zax's paper, two modes of tenure, own-built housing and state-owned housing, are considered. The average own-built dwelling is approximately 73–75 percent larger than the average state-owned dwelling. Most state-owned housing is in multi-unit apartment blocks. Most own-built housing is constructed in structures with only one or two dwelling units. Families residing in state-owned housing are likely to have more privileges in the Chinese economic system than families living in own-built housing. However, families in own-built housing generally have more nonlabor income.

The behavioral mechanisms that determine dwelling size differ by tenure. The choice of dwelling size for own-built housing reflects family demand for housing services. This is derived from an implicit utility maximization, constrained by incomes and other substantial resource limitations that exist in the urban economy in China. The empirical relationship between own-built dwelling size and family characteristics represents an approximation of the underlying relationship between dwelling size and family preference functions. In contrast, the relationship between state-owned dwelling size and family characteristics is determined bureaucratically. The empirical relationship thus becomes a reduced-form estimate of the interaction between the supply of dwellings to the work unit or municipality and that organization's allocation system.

The opportunity to choose state-owned housing is not equally available to all families. The subsamples of families in own-built and state-owned housing are not randomly drawn from the population of urban families in China. Families in state-owned housing probably anticipated that their work unit or municipality would offer them housing of reasonable quality. Because of negligible rents in this sector, they would have no incentive to build their own dwellings. Families in own-built housing endured these costs and difficulties because they must have expected that their work unit or municipality would have offered them undesirable accommodation or none at all.

Tenure assignment is thus endogenous and the choice of own-built or state-owned housing is related to the dwelling size. These are the reasons why a switching regression model with endogenous switching was adopted. Let

$$F_{ij} = X_{ij}\gamma_j + u_{ij} \tag{11.6}$$

denote the population relationship between dwelling size F_{ij} and family characteristics X_{ij} for family i under tenure choice j, where $j = 1$ refers to own-built housing and $j = 2$ refers to state-owned housing. γ_j is the parameter column vector measuring the effects of the row vector X_{ij} on F_{ij}. u_{ij} is the unobserved random term of dwelling size for family i under tenure choice j. The propensity to choose own-built rather than state-owned housing is given by

$$I^* = Z_i\beta + \varepsilon_i, \tag{11.7}$$

where Z_i represents the row vector of characteristics for family i that determine the propensity to choose own-built housing, β is the parameter column vector measuring the effects of Z_i on I^*, and ε_i is the random term of this propensity. The data only report whether the family actually chooses state-owned or own-built housing. It is assumed that the family chooses own-built housing if $I^* > 0$, or $\varepsilon_i > -Z_i\beta$. Then, in a single-equation setting, β can be estimated as a probit, where the dependent variable is $I = 1$ if $I^* > 0$, and $I = 0$ otherwise. The presumption that the choice of state-owned or own-built housing is related to the dwelling size is the assumption that ε_i is correlated with u_{i1} and u_{i2} (Zax 1997, p. 389).

The result shows that families with a lesser claim on or expectation of government assistance are more likely to reside in own-built housing. The relationships between family characteristics and sizes of dwelling in the own-built and state-owned sectors differ dramatically. However, unobserved characteristics, probably including *guanxi* (social status, such as parental background and personal connections), play crucial roles in housing tenure choices and dwelling size decisions. Depending on these characteristics, families in state-owned dwellings might have two-thirds more living space were they to choose own-built dwellings based on the estimation results.

11.4.2 Japan

As in the rest of Asia, overcrowded housing in Japan is a serious problem (see Table 11.1). There are some housing policy measures that are particularly related to the floor space of the house. In Japan, government-subsidized lending plays an important role in the housing finance system (see section 11.2). In financing housing purchases, Japanese consumers typically self-finance about 40 percent of the purchase price, of which about 25–30 percent is from personal savings, and about 40 percent is financed through government-subsidized loans. The loans mainly come from the government-run JHLC, although its lending operations will be phased out by 2006. The JHLC places limits on the amount and cost of its loans. The size of a JHLC loan is specified according to the floor space of the house. The interest rate is also calculated according to the size of the house.

The household is assumed to solve the following utility-maximization problem:

$$\underset{c,F,Q}{Max} \ U(c,h(F,Q)) \tag{11.1'}$$

$$s.t. \ c + ucc \times P(Q) \times F = y, \tag{11.2''}$$

where F is the total floor space of housing and Q is all other attributes of housing, which is called the quality. The unit price of owner-occupied housing is assumed to depend on quality, Q. Utility function (11.1') and budget constraint (11.2") are variants of equations (11.1) and (11.2), because the main focus of this chapter is the policy-induced distortions related to the total floor space, F.

The user cost of capital for floor space for a household that borrows from both government and private institutions is in the following form:

$$(ucc \times P(Q))^{JPF,Gov \, \& \, pri} = \left[i_{pri} + k_s d + t_P - \frac{\{0.8(i_{pri} - i_{gov})P(\bar{Q})\}}{P(Q)} \right] P(Q), \quad (11.8)$$

where i_{pri} is the mortgage rate of private financial institutions and i_{gov} is that of government lending agencies (for the derivation of equation (11.8), see Seko 2002, Appendix A). $P(\bar{Q})$ is the standard construction cost. In Japan, the maximum amount that people can borrow from government-run JHLC is $0.8 \times$ (some standard construction cost per m²) × (total floor space of the house). The rate of interest on JHLC loans varies with home size. If someone with less than a 10 million yen income demands floor space between 50 and 110 m², and wants to borrow from JHLC, the borrowing rate is 5.5 percent. However, if the floor space is between 135 and 165 m², the borrowing rate becomes 7.2 percent for the entire space (as of 1985). JHLC loans are only available to households that have already obtained their own land. The user cost for floor space for a household that takes out a housing loan covering the entire amount needed from a private institution is similar to equation (11.3), as follows:

$$(ucc \times P(Q))^{JPF,pri} = (i_{pri} + k_s d + t_p)P(Q). \quad (11.9)$$

In this chapter, for simplicity, the expected rate of increase in housing prices, π, is assumed to be zero. The resulting budget constraint becomes nonlinear (piecewise linear) as shown in Figure 11.2 because of the space-linked interest rates of the JHLC.

Seko (2002) estimated the floor space demand model using the maximum likelihood estimation by explicitly considering those policy-induced kinked budget constraints arising from the JHLC policy of space-linked subsidized interest rates. The advantages of the structural form piecewise linear approach compared to the simple reduced-form estimation for demand functions are numerous. First, ignoring observations at kink points probably leads to selection bias. Second, the simple reduced-form estimation is an unsatisfactory approach because the OLS estimates are inconsistent. The error term in the floor demand equation will be correlated with right-hand-side variables such as income and price variables, because they are partly selected by the individual through choice of each segment, as represented in Figure 11.2. That is to say, individuals having higher income (a right-hand side variable) may choose larger floor space (a left-hand-side variable). Third, we need to know a household's preferences or, equivalently, its utility function for the comparative statics. The comparative statics of consumer demand in the usual sense holds up in the presence of kinked budget sets only within segments. Therefore, it is necessary to estimate statistically with proper consideration the kink points in the demand schedule and nonlinearities in the response, along with the parameters of the demand function when budget constraints are nonlinear.

The estimation results indicate that if the JHLC loan system operated like a private lending institution (that is to say, if households faced linear budget constraints rather than nonlinear kinked budget constraints), it would eliminate the current excess burden per household arising from policy-induced, space-linked

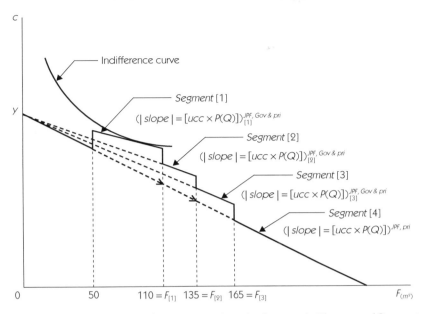

Figure 11.2   Nonlinear budget constraints in Japan: (c,F) space (Q constant where $h = h(F,Q)$).
Notation: F, floor space; c, other goods; Q, quality; y, income; $[ucc \times P(Q)]_{[k]}^{JPF,Gov \& pri}$, user cost of capital for floor space of the kth segment for a household borrowing from both government and private institutions (*Segments* [1]–[3]); $[ucc \times P(Q)]^{JPF,pri}$, user cost of capital for floor space for a household borrowing only from private institutions (*Segment* [4]); h, housing services (space-linked JHLC interest rates, $i_{gov} = 0.055$ for $50 \leq F \leq 110$ (*Segment* [1]), 0.065 for $110 < F \leq 135$ (*Segment* [2]), 0.072 for $135 < F \leq 165$ (m²) (*Segment* [3]); budget constraints, $c + [ucc \times P(Q)]^{JPF} \times F = y$ (11.2"); P, unit price of owner-occupied housing).
Source: Seko (2002)

subsidized interest rates. This burden is approximately 9 percent of the amount of the average JHLC credit subsidy for a home, or about \$2,167 per household.

11.4.3   A Comparison of Mainland China and Japan

In urban China, demand for total floor space is related to tenure choice. This reflects China's transition from a socialist economy to a market-oriented economy. That is to say, demand for floor space depends on the political system and/or the form of government intervention, because the choice between own-built and state-owned houses is not based on people's preferences. Rather, it depends to a large degree on informal mechanisms and human networks. Thus, the size of the dwelling is related to type of housing (own-built or state-provided), which is determined by nonmarket mechanisms. In contrast, in Japan where a more market-oriented economy prevails, demand for floor space for owned houses depends on the distinctive nature of space-linked subsidized housing loan policies. Because Japan's housing policies have been focused on coping with overcrowding linked to the high cost of land, interest rate subsidies have focused only on one attribute of housing – that is, the size of the house – while ignoring other attributes of housing. Thus, quality or cost of housing is not considered in evaluating loan applications.

11.5   CONCLUSION

In Japan, income tax does not affect the demand for housing services and tenure choice much; but in Sweden, income tax greatly affects both decisions. The comparison in section 11.3 has shown that to analyze housing demand we have to take into consideration each country's unique government policy. Of course, appropriate econometric specification becomes different when institutional systems such as the tax system differ.

The comparison in section 11.4 has shown that even if we focus on one attribute of housing, dwelling size, its major determinant differs greatly if the political system, scarcity of natural resources, and other economic conditions differ. In Japan, high land prices are the main problem affecting owner-occupied housing demand. To influence floor space demand, space-linked interest rate subsidies were devised that created both maximum and minimum sizes favored with the lowest interest rates. As a result, loan applicants adjusted their floor space demand to minimize the interest rate on their loans. It appears that this policy induced households to overconsume space, because the number of lenders who built houses larger than they wanted to meet the minimum criteria exceeded the number of lenders who reduced the size of their housing to meet the maximum size criteria. In Japan, floor space demand is thus distorted by the housing finance policy. In China, demand for floor space greatly depends on social status and whether this leads one to rely on state-provided housing or own-built housing; floor space for the latter group is higher, suggesting that state intervention in supplying housing depresses average floor space.

Although I have only focused on studies of the demand for housing services in the three countries in this essay, it is clear that it is important to carefully take into consideration each country's different institutional and cultural backgrounds as well as economic systems and conditions when we empirically analyze housing demand. For example, the relationship between demographic factors and housing demand should be explicitly considered in the analysis, especially in Asia. In China, the one-child policy and residence restrictions have had a significant impact on the housing market. The colossal influx of rural migrants to China's burgeoning cities in recent years will clearly shape the emerging housing market; there is pent-up demand for low-cost housing in urban areas to accommodate the migrants. Local governments have also been active in displacing low-income urban dwellers living in older, low-density neighborhoods in central districts to free up land for large-scale real estate developments. The displaced families are typically relocated to apartment blocks far from the city center. The implications for floor space demand are uncertain in a housing market that is going through major convulsions driven by commercial interests and by powerful government officials who have considerable discretionary authority. In Japan, low birth rates and an increasing ratio of elderly people may also have an impact on space demand, tenure choice, and other aspects of housing demand. The separation of land and structure property as in Japan creates several different tenure types other than simple owned versus rented houses. For example, we now see owned houses on leased land. This is a rational response to high land prices and tax structures influencing the use and sale of land. When we analyze the tenure choice decision in Japan, we should distinguish this type of tenure from the usual owned houses: Seko (unpublished work, 2004) analyzes tenure varieties, including owned houses with fixed leased land. In Sweden, the high cost of the welfare state is a controversial political issue and a growing economic burden; the diminished role of the state in the housing market is having significant consequences. In addition, Sweden's demographic time bomb may also generate consequences similar to those in Japan. Developments linked to the European Union – for example, allowing citizens of EU states to purchase land in other EU states – could also have major implications.

It is desirable to further expand housing demand studies internationally. These various models of housing demand in Asian and non-Asian countries indicate the complexities of the challenge.

Bibliography

Angel, S. 2000: *Housing Policy Matters: A Global Analysis*. New York: Oxford University Press.

Boleat, M. 1985: *National Housing Finance Systems*. London: Croom Helm.

Green, R. K. and Malpezzi, S. 2003: *A Primer on U.S. Housing Markets and Housing Policy*. Washington, DC: The Urban Institute Press.

Hansson-Brusewitz, U. 1997: Self-selectivity and kinked budget constraints: the demand for housing in Sweden. *Journal of Housing Economics*, 7, 243–73.

Harsman, B. and Quigley, J. M. 1991: *Housing Markets and Housing Institutions: An International Comparison*. Boston: Kluwer.

Henderson, J. V. and Ioannides, Y. M. 1983: A model of housing tenure choice. *American Economic Review*, 73(1), 98–113.

Horioka, C. Y. 1988: Tenure choice and demand for housing in Japan. *Journal of Urban Economics*, 24(3), 289–309.

Huang, Y. and Clark, W. A. V. 2002: Housing tenure choice in transitional urban China: a multilevel analysis. *Urban Studies*, 39(1), 7–32.

Liu, H. 1998: Government intervention and the performance of the housing sector in urban China. *Journal of the Asian Real Estate Society*, 1(1), 127–49.

Maddala, G. S. 1983: *Limited-Dependent and Qualitative Variables in Econometrics*. Cambridge, UK: Cambridge University Press.

Olsen, E. O. 1987: The demand and supply of housing service: a critical survey of the empirical literature. In E. S. Mills (ed.), *Handbook of Regional and Urban Economics*, vol. 2: *Urban Economics*. Amsterdam: Elsevier, 989–1,022.

Rosen, H. S. 1979: Housing decisions and the U.S. income tax. *Journal of Public Economics*, 11, 1–23.

Seko, M. 2001: Housing and land in Japan: policies and markets. In *Proceedings of Asian Real Estate Society Sixth Annual Conference in Japan*, CD-ROM (available from the author upon request).

—— 2002: Nonlinear budget constraints and estimation: effects of subsidized home loans on floor space decisions in Japan. *Journal of Housing Economics*, 11(3), 280–99.

Turner, B. 1997: Municipal housing companies in Sweden: on or off the market? *Housing Studies*, 12, 477–88.

—— and Whitehead, C. 2002: Reducing housing subsidy: Swedish housing policy in an international context. *Urban Studies*, 39(2), 201–17.

Zax, J. S. 1997: Latent demand for urban housing in the People's Republic of China. *Journal of Urban Economics*, 42, 377–401.

Discrimination in Mortgage Lending

Anthony M. Yezer

12.1   Introduction

Mortgage market discrimination has been categorized as *blatant treatment*, *differential treatment*, and *adverse impact*. Blatant treatment involves explicit refusal to lend or explicit lending policies that consider prohibited demographic characteristics, race, sex, and ethnicity. Differential treatment discrimination arises when lending criteria are applied differently based on prohibited characteristics, even though there is no explicit policy of discrimination. Such differential treatment, because it is implicit, is inferred by statistical analysis of lending outcomes. Adverse impact discrimination arises when lenders use lending criteria that are significantly correlated with prohibited characteristics when alternative criteria could be used. Of course, demographic characteristics are correlated with many economic characteristics, such as income and wealth, which are good predictors of creditworthiness. Lenders are only allowed to use these factors if they can show that alternative economic indicators, not correlated with minority status, are not sufficient to predict credit risk in mortgage lending. The concept of *statistical discrimination* is closely related to adverse impact. Statistical discrimination arises when lenders use readily available characteristics that are correlated with minority status in the underwriting process rather than using alternative information that might be more costly to collect.

Mortgage markets have several distinctive characteristics that must be understood before considering the possibility that there is discrimination against any particular category of mortgage applicant. The first task of this essay will be to review these distinct features. Armed with an understanding of the process of application, loan taking, underwriting, loan approval, closing, repackaging, and sale to the ultimate investor, we will be equipped to consider how discrimination might arise and, more importantly, how to test for its existence. Thus far, concern with discrimination in mortgage lending, both as the object of academic inquiry and public policy action, has been concentrated in the United States. However, concern with equal access to credit is spreading to other countries, particularly in Europe and lessons learned in the USA may be valuable elsewhere.

The next section of this essay reviews important institutional characteristics of mortgage lending and mortgage markets that must be understood before modeling the lending process or testing for discrimination. Then the relation between this institutional structure and possibilities for discrimination is traced. Subsequently, alternative procedures that have been used to test for discrimination are presented and evaluated. For an excellent review article that covers the subject of this essay, see LaCour-Little (1999).

12.2   THE INSTITUTIONAL CHARACTERISTICS OF THE MORTGAGE MARKET

The mortgage lending process involves several agents, whose characteristics are essential to any discussion of discrimination in mortgage lending. Naturally, we begin with an *applicant*, a person seeking a mortgage in order to *purchase* or *refinance* residential real estate. In the case of a new purchase, the applicant is often guided by a *realtor*, who identifies properties in a price range appropriate for the applicant and frequently intervenes in the mortgage application process. Applicants interact directly with *loan originators*, who take information supplied by the applicant and provide advice regarding alternative mortgage products, pricing, and underwriting policy. Loan originators often work on a commission basis and have a strong incentive to direct applicants toward mortgage products for which they are qualified. The originator works with the applicant to make sure that the information in the loan file meets standards set by the lender. One important decision is whether to apply for a *government guaranteed* loan – that is, FHA, VA, or Farmer's Home – or a conventional mortgage, which will require private mortgage insurance (*PMI*) if the loan-to-value (*LTV*) ratio exceeds 0.8. A higher LTV increases credit risk in mortgage lending for two reasons. First, it makes default more likely, as borrowers have less equity at risk. Second, it increases expected loss in case of default, because owner's equity helps to protect the lender against large losses.

In most cases, loan originators pass the partially completed application on to a *loan processor*, who assembles private information on the applicant's financial and employment history that is obtained with the applicant's formal permission. This private information includes bank and employment references, documentation for other sources of income and debt service, and *credit history*, including the *credit score*. Under the Fair Credit Reporting Act, the USA has an elaborate system in which information on how promptly and completely individuals pay debts and any legal actions taken against them is collected in a uniform fashion for people living across the country. Concerns with privacy have made credit reporting a controversial issue in many countries. Credit history includes detailed information on credit outstanding and payment history, as well as past debt problems such as write-offs and even bankruptcy. The loan processor also secures an estimate of the market value of the house. This is usually done by an *appraiser*, although increasingly automated appraisal techniques using statistical models of local house prices are used. The loan processor verifies the accuracy of information taken by the loan originator.

Once the loan processor has completed the application, an *underwriter* makes the decision to accept or reject, relaying that information back to the loan processor and originator. If the loan is initially rejected, the applicant, often with the assistance of the loan originator, may request that the loan be reconsidered based on extra information provided or modified loan terms. *Cosigners* may be added to the loan at this point. Applications that were initially rejected may be accepted by the underwriter upon reconsideration. The underwriter's decision is based on credit risk associated with the application, including applicant income, assets, liabilities, and credit history; the appraisal; and provisions of the loan, particularly the LTV ratio and the presence of cosigners.

Underwriters generally do not consider the interest rate, discount points, and fees associated with the transaction, except insofar as these factors change the monthly payment to income or loan-to-value ratios used in underwriting. The total price of the mortgage includes *discount points*, *fees*, and *interest rate*. All those applications judged qualified by a given underwriter pay a similar price for credit except those with LTV > 0.8, who will usually pay mortgage insurance. Thus within the group of accepted applicants, credit risk may vary considerably although the applicants pay the same price for credit. This *price discrimination* in mortgage lending, in which the lowest-risk borrowers pay the same price as higher-risk borrowers, should not be confused with discrimination based on race or ethnicity.

The division of labor into loan originators paid commissions based on approved loans and loan processors and underwriters whose compensation is not tied to the approval decision solves an incentive problem for the lender. It is important to have loan originators directing applicants to appropriate loan products, but it is equally important that those with final responsibility for verifying information and underwriting do not have a financial incentive to approve unqualified applicants. Commissions paid to loan originators sometimes include a bonus payment, called an *overage*, based on the difference between the price paid by an applicant and a minimum acceptable price posted by the lender. Loan processors and underwriters are salaried employees, whose compensation is not based on the fraction of loans approved.

Rejected applicants whose loans are not approved, even upon reconsideration, are generally not offered alternative mortgage credit at higher rates. Instead, they must apply to other lenders, or sometimes to subsidiaries of the same lender. Thus *nonprice rationing* of mortgage credit has resulted in a market divided into *prime* and *subprime* lenders. Prime, or A and A−, mortgage lending dominates the market. However, subprime lending is a significant activity and applicants rejected by prime lenders may turn to subprime lenders, where the cost of credit is higher but underwriting criteria, particularly tolerance for a blemished credit history, are more lenient. The subprime market is not well understood or documented. It includes many small lenders about whom little is known. Subprime lending is more commonly refinancing, as opposed to new-purchase mortgages, and lending for specialized types of housing, particularly manufactured housing.

Although information on subprime lending is limited to selected samples of loans, it appears that credit scores are lower, the cost of credit higher, and rejection rates higher in subprime lending. While the first two points may appear consistent with expectations, the higher rejection rate for subprime lenders is, at first, curious. If these lenders take greater credit risk, why do they reject more applicants? In fact, the answer is quite logical. Applicants are aware of differences in lending criteria and the higher-risk applicants self-select into the subprime market. Typically, application costs are higher at prime than subprime lenders. High-risk applicants avoid lenders where the combination of high application cost and likely rejection outweigh the possibility of getting lower-cost credit. This self-selection by applicants is very important in the cost structure of mortgage lenders, because application fees cover only a fraction of the cost of underwriting and prime lenders cannot afford to have high rejection rates.

Thus far, this institutional description has given the impression that mortgage lending involves a single firm or organization. In practice, several different types of firms are involved in mortgage lending. First, the lender discussed is seldom the ultimate holder of the debt. Even before the mortgage is endorsed, lenders often secure commitments to purchase from the secondary market. Much of the credit risk associated with the mortgage passes on with this sale. Second, it is quite common for loan originators, either alone or with loan processors, to operate as independent mortgage brokers and to sell processed loans to lenders. The relation between loan originator and lender ranges from one in which the originator only brings applicants to the lender for processing and underwriting to one in which processing and underwriting are delegated to the originator by the lender, who then purchases the loan, perhaps after doing secondary underwriting. In this case, the lender will generally record the loan as *purchased* or wholesale rather than originated or retail. The image of applicants interacting with loan originators, processors, and underwriters all employed and controlled by a single lender is simply not correct.

In the USA, government-insured mortgages are important to understanding mortgage supply. The primary program serving low-income applicants is FHA Section 203b mortgage insurance. Although all aspects of FHA loan originations, ranging from the loan originator through the underwriter and including the appraiser, were once performed inside FHA, today most FHA mortgage insurance is based on direct endorsement by private lenders under the supervision of the Department of Housing and Urban Development (HUD). FHA mortgage insurance allows higher loan-to-value and monthly-payment-to-income ratios than private mortgage insurance, making it particularly attractive for young, first-time homeowners. Today, it is generally assumed that FHA mortgage applicants are not subject to discrimination, but that was initially not the case. Indeed, the term *redlining*, which is used to indicate the practice of limiting mortgage lending in high-minority or low-income communities, originated at a time, in the 1960s, when red lines were literally found on maps in FHA area offices. FHA appraisals required an assessment of general neighborhood condition and the red lines indicated "less desirable" areas. Needless to say, both the red lines and the practice of assessing neighborhood condition when appraising individual properties were quickly dropped!

A final institutional aspect of mortgage lending is the rise of electronic loan application, whether by telephone or Internet, during the 1990s. Electronic lending eliminates the need for personal contact between the applicant and the loan originator and, in most cases, between the loan processor and the applicant. None of the standard information used in underwriting, including credit reports, tax records, payroll reports, and so on, contains information on the race or ethnicity of the applicant. Of course, names may reveal some information, particularly regarding the sex and marital status of applicants, but the only regular source of information on applicant characteristics in the completed loan file is the required HUD disclosure form, and applicants may decline to respond to this request for information by the government. Thus electronic application is essentially racially and ethnically blind.

12.3 THE INSTITUTIONAL CHARACTERISTICS OF THE MORTGAGE MARKET AND LENDING DISCRIMINATION

The discussion of the institutional characteristics of the mortgage market leaves us with two apparently contradictory views of the potential for discrimination, at least as manifest in the USA. First, the origins of the term "redlining" are based on a form of blatant discrimination in government-guaranteed mortgage insurance. Clearly, discrimination has existed in mortgage lending. Second, the rise and rapid growth of electronic application indicates that a significant segment of the mortgage market cannot be engaging in blatant or differential treatment discrimination, because credit decisions are made without observing the demographic characteristics of applicants. Furthermore, the possibility of adverse impact discrimination in electronic lending can be easily assessed as the underwriting criteria are apparent – indeed, underwriting is often automated.

These contradictory views of discrimination in mortgage lending are easily resolved. FHA redlining existed in the late 1960s. By the 1970s, FHA policies had been reversed and FHA underwriting criteria became more lenient in formerly redlined areas. The structure of the mortgage lending industry in the USA changed with the problems of the thrift industry, beginning in the late 1970s, and the increase in government attention to equal credit opportunity in mortgage lending. Mortgage lending was transformed from local lending by depository institutions, using funds collected locally, into a national enterprise, with large mortgage banking firms originating mortgages across the country, for sale packaged together in mortgage-backed securities. Similar changes are occurring in countries around the world. The connection between local banking services and mortgage lending has been broken. The rise of electronic lending and statistical underwriting was simply a product of the competitive pressures that arose when mortgage lending was transformed from a local to a national enterprise. Lenders did not move to the current remote, electronic system because it virtually eliminated the possibility for discrimination in mortgage lending. Instead, market forces produced the transformation to lower-cost electronic systems. Elimination of direct contact between applicant and agents of the lender was a byproduct of the changing technology. It is paradoxical that the only way in which demographic information can enter the loan file is if the HUD declaration form is filled out accurately by the applicant.

In spite of these changes in mortgage lending, the possibility for discrimination still exists, but it is concentrated in segments of the market where there is significant personal contact between the loan originator and the applicant. Applicants fail to take advantage of electronic application techniques for a variety of reasons. Some may be uncomfortable with the impersonal nature of the transaction or may lack information on application procedures. Others have special credit problems, including lack of a credit history or difficulty in verification of income, that require extensive contact with the loan originator. In such cases, the loan originator may serve as financial advisor to the applicant, providing credit counseling services. Individuals whose use of credit in the past has been insufficient to generate a credit score or those with a history of repayment problems may work with loan originators for months to produce an application that has a chance of passing the scrutiny of an underwriter. For expositional purposes, such individuals will be termed *at-risk applicants*, because for them the opportunity for discrimination is certainly real and there is little prospect that electronic lending will be able to serve these individuals in the near future. Note that most of the subprime market should be considered to be at risk.

12.4 Testing for Discrimination by Mortgage Lenders

Various techniques have been proposed to test for discrimination in mortgage lending, ranging from tests applied to individual lenders or metropolitan areas. The purpose of this review is to present the rationale for each test, give examples of the types of results obtained, and discuss problems in interpreting the results. Initially, the mortgage lending discrimination literature proceeded as though mortgage application was analogous to employment application. Tests that had been successful in detecting employment discrimination were adapted to the case of lending discrimination. Unfortunately, the mortgage application process is quite complex and differs substantially from employment transactions. Finding adequate tests for lending discrimination has proved to be a very difficult task, and the analogy with employment discrimination has led to some unfortunate testing mistakes.

Most of the discussion of discrimination in mortgage lending concerns discrimination against individuals based on their minority status. However, it is also possible to argue that there is discrimination against geographical areas, based on minority composition of the neighborhood. For minority groups whose housing is highly segregated, the hypothesis of individual discrimination can become confused with geographical discrimination. However, for dispersed groups it is possible to argue that there might be discrimination against minorities living in minority neighborhoods, but not for minorities living in white neighborhoods. Testing for geographical discrimination is analogous to testing for individual discrimination. In order to economize on space, the discussion concentrates on testing for individual discrimination.

12.4.1 Tests based on segregation of applicants or loans

A classic result in the economics of discrimination is that discrimination tends to produce market segregation. In the case of mortgage markets, if minorities are charged higher prices and/or rejected more often at some lenders than others, they will tend to apply to the lenders who are offering more favorable terms. In labor markets, discrimination resulted in segregation of the workforce, a classic example being the rise of minority sports leagues in the presence of discrimination by existing major leagues.

To implement the segregation test in mortgage markets, it is necessary to first identify a nondiscriminating sector. Based on the experience of the 1970s, when there was a sharp reversal in policy, the FHA has been used as the nondiscriminating sector. The test for discrimination through segregation then involves estimating an FHA participation equation. To test for discrimination by prime conventional mortgage lenders, the dependent variable would be binary, equal to zero if the household has a conventional mortgage and equal to unity if the household has an FHA mortgage. To implement such a test, a sample of households from a given geographical area is needed. The financial characteristics of the households that might explain the choice of conventional versus FHA financing are necessary in addition to information on the minority status of the households. The market segregation test then rests on the estimated coefficients of dummy variables that indicate minority status. If these variables are positive, this indicates that minorities are concentrated in FHA rather than conventional mortgages in a fashion not accounted for by differences in their financial condition. When such tests have been implemented, the general finding is that, holding financial condition and even credit score constant, African-American households are more likely to have FHA mortgages than white households.

The best publicized tests for discrimination in mortgage lending were a series of articles by Dedman (1988), entitled "The Color of Money," which resulted in subsequent television programs. These articles documented the relative lack of conventional lending by depository institutions in African-American neighborhoods. Differences for other minority households were generally not significant and were even reversed in the case of Asian households. Taken at face value, such tests seem consistent with the hypothesis of discrimination against African-American households.

There are two obvious problems with the type of test used in "The Color of Money." First, the Home Mortgage Disclosure Act (HMDA) data used in the test lack information on borrower creditworthiness and loan terms used in underwriting. These omissions render HMDA data inadequate to test for discrimination in lending. Second, HMDA data, at this time, did not cover mortgage bankers, who made most use of the FHA loans. Given that African-American households tend to be differentially concentrated in the FHA sector, where required down payments are lower, it is not surprising that depository institutions in Atlanta were making relatively few loans to African-American households. Overall, "The Color of Money" is a very poor example of testing for discrimination in mortgage lending based on market segregation.

Unfortunately, the simplistic segregation test for discrimination produces even more misleading results when it is extended to choice of other types of mortgage products. If a mortgage choice equation is estimated for conventional prime versus subprime mortgages, the finding is that African-American households are, other factors held constant, more likely to choose subprime loans. Using the segregation test, this would imply that, relative to prime lenders, subprime lenders are less likely to discriminate against minorities. Such a result seems highly improbable in itself and calls into question the general validity of tests based on segregation.

12.4.2   Tests based on performance

An important result in the economics of discrimination, noted by Ferguson and Peters (1995), is that if members of a particular group are subject to higher performance standards, the marginal members of that group will perform better than the marginal members of other groups. When this test is applied to discrimination against minority athletes by professional sports teams, it compares the performance of the weakest member of a minority group to make a team with the performance of the weakest nonminority athlete. If equal standards of team membership are applied regardless of demographic considerations, then there should be no association between demographic characteristics and the ability of the last player to make the team.

When this argument is applied to mortgage lending, it generally takes the form of tests based on loan performance. Using loans endorsed by a particular lender or group of lenders, a single-equation statistical model of serious delinquency, default, or foreclosure is estimated. The simplest form of such models has a binary dependent variable equal to unity if the loan defaulted and equal to zero if it was paid off normally. The default model is estimated using information available to the lender at the time of endorsement, including all factors used in the underwriting process. In addition to variables reflecting the underwriting decision, demographic variables are added to reflect the protected status of the borrower.

The test for discrimination based on loan performance is that the partial effect of minority status on default or foreclosure is negative; that is, if lending criteria are applied more rigidly to minorities, they should be, at the margin, less likely to be default. Estimates of loan performance models by Berkovec, Canner, Gabriel, and Hannan (1994) and by Martin and Hill (2000) show that default and foreclosure loss is lower for white borrowers. This indicates discrimination in favor of African-American borrowers. Recall from the previous section that market segregation tests implemented for FHA-insured mortgages tend to find African-American applicants concentrated in FHA-insured mortgages, indicating potential discrimination. Thus the results of loan performance tests tend to indicate discrimination in just the opposite direction to that found in market segregation tests! This contradiction in test results is even more remarkable because the segregation test indicates that African-American applicants appear segregated in FHA programs and the loan performance studies have generally been performed using FHA-insured mortgages.

How can we resolve the contradiction between the segregation and loan performance tests? One possibility is that there are *omitted variables* – that is, variables not observed in the loan file – which predict default and foreclosure and that these variables are correlated with race. The problem with an appeal to omitted variables is that such an argument can be used to invalidate any statistical test, because there are always omitted variables that are correlated with demographic characteristics.

An alternative view of the loan performance test is that it should consider more than credit risk. Another aspect of loan performance is prepayment risk. If borrowers refinance aggressively when interest rates fall, then mortgage lending is less profitable. The empirical evidence is that groups that have higher credit risk tend to have lower rates of prepayment, and that the gain in profitability from lower refinancing rates approximately offsets higher default and foreclosure losses. Given the way in which mortgages are packaged and sold in securitized form, it is not clear that differences in prepayment risk on individual mortgages are always priced. Nevertheless, the implications of moving from credit risk to loan profitability, including prepayment, as the basis for loan performance testing are worth examining. If loan profitability is the basis for loan performance testing, then the tests may show no relation between minority status and profitability of the marginal loan.

12.4.3   Tests based on differential rejection rates

Tests for discrimination in mortgage lending based on the partial association between applicant rejection rates and minority status have received widespread attention. Bank regulators have used these tests to examine lenders for discrimination against minority applicants and neighborhoods, as discussed in Tootell (1996). They are also used by plaintiffs in fair lending cases.

Differential rejection rate tests require data on mortgage applications to a given lender or group of lenders. Black, Schweitzer, and Mandell (1978) were the first to suggest a test based on a single-equation model of mortgage rejection. The dependent variable is equal to unity if the application is rejected and to zero if accepted. The regressors include variables affecting the underwriting decision as noted above. Demographic variables reflecting minority status are added to the equation to determine whether there is any partial effect of prohibited factors on the probability of rejection holding creditworthiness constant, as reflected in the variables used in the underwriting process.

Initial rejection rate tests were plagued by lack of information on applicant characteristics. Home Mortgage Disclosure Act (HMDA) data provided information on the acceptances and rejections, but credit history, loan-to-value ratio, and other factors important in underwriting were omitted. Rejection rate tests using only HMDA data affirmed the hypothesis of discrimination, but were heavily criticized because omitted variables used in underwriting were likely correlated with applicant demographics.

To remedy these charges of omitted variable bias, the Federal Reserve Bank of Boston (the *Boston Fed*) secured the cooperation of Boston-area banks in providing access to individual loan files. To the extent possible, information in the loan files provided to underwriters was coded into a data set. Single-equation estimates of a rejection equation indicated that the demographic characteristics of the applicant had a partial influence on rejection, even after a good faith effort to consider all of the information in the loan file. Subsequent studies have found similar results and, in particular, estimated coefficients for African-American applicants tend to be positive and significant, indicating that race plays a role in rejection. These single-equation models have been used by bank regulators and by plaintiffs' experts in mortgage lending discrimination cases.

Unfortunately, as noted in the discussion of the institutional characteristics of the mortgage market, applicants frequently work with realtors, and particularly with loan originators, to avoid rejection. In the Boston Fed study this was called "coaching" and it was suggested that coaching was applied differently based on race: "Similarly, if white applicants are more likely than minority applicants to be 'coached' when filling out the application, they will have stronger applications than similarly situated minorities. In this case, the ratios and other financial information in the *final* application, which is the focus of this analysis, may find themselves to be the product of differential treatment. This study does not explore the extent to which coaching occurs . . ." (Munnell, Tootell, Browne & McEneaney 1992, p. 43; emphasis present in the original).

The problem with tests based on differential rejection rates is that these single-equation tests assume that applicants are not coached by loan officers and that they choose loan terms without regard to the likelihood of rejection. Horne (1994) has noted that 20 percent of the applications in the Boston Fed study were reviewed more than three times and that applicants clearly adjusted loan terms. If the applicants, particularly using information from the loan originator, choose loan terms to meet underwriting criteria, then the estimated coefficients of a single-equation model of rejection are biased and inconsistent. Furthermore, Yezer, Phillips, and Trost (1994) have shown that the direction of bias will tend to show discrimination against less affluent minority groups even when no differential treatment exists. Put another way, the bias is in the rejection equation test, not at the banks.

One possible solution to the bias in rejection equation tests suggested by Maddala and Trost (1982) and by Barth, Cordes, and Yezer (1980) is to formulate a simultaneous equations model in which the probability of rejection and the loan terms that applicants manipulate to avoid rejection are jointly determined by economic and demographic factors. There are two problems with a simultaneous equations model. First, applicants adjust several loan terms, including loan-to-value ratio, monthly-payment-to-income ratio, term to maturity, and the presence of a cosigner. In some cases, applicants remedy problems in their credit history, by paying off or closing outstanding credit lines or removing incorrect information. Modeling so many jointly determined variables is not feasible (see Munnell, Tootell, Browne, and McEneaney 1996). Second, information used in the rejection equation comes from the credit files assembled by the loan processor. It is not easy to find the exogenous information, variables collected by lenders but not considered in the underwriting decision, that would be needed to identify the rejection equation.

Although tests based on differential rejection rates tend to produce false indications of differential treatment discrimination when none exists, they are still used. Typically, single-equation models find that single females have significantly lower rejection rates than single males. Does this indicate that lenders are discriminating against single males or that the test for discrimination is biased? One legitimate use of a biased test is as an initial screening device to show nondiscrimination. Any lender whose rejection rates are not associated with the minority status of the applicant is clearly not discriminating against minorities. Unfortunately, it is common to see studies that use any positive association between rejection rates and minority status as an indication of discrimination, rather than as an indication of bias in tests based on differential rejection rates.

12.4.4   Tests based on differential pricing

Given the difficulty of testing for discrimination based on differential rejection rates, the next logical step is to test for differences in actual pricing of mortgages. Once again, the hypothesis of discrimination would be based on an association between the minority status of the borrower and the mortgage price. A first problem with this approach is that prices are only observed for mortgages that are endorsed, and pricing to rejected applicants cannot be considered. The second problem is the complex nature of mortgage pricing. Even restricting the discussion to a single type of mortgage product, borrowers trade off discount points for an interest rate based on their expected prepayment strategy. Third, borrowers routinely try to time the market during the period between application and final endorsement of the mortgage by "floating" or reserving the option of adjusting the price downward if interest rates fall. The fourth problem arises from the institutional structure of the mortgage market. Loan originators may collect fees independent of the lender. Thus the mortgage price paid by the borrower may include a specific component of compensation for the loan originator. Fifth, the use of single-equation models of mortgage pricing is not appropriate because applicants adjust loan terms to manipulate the price that they will pay – that is, all the difficulties associated with the analysis of differential rejection rates also apply to mortgage pricing.

Because of the complexity of mortgage pricing and the lack of generally available data on pricing, few tests of discrimination in pricing have been performed. Some researchers have attempted to find a shortcut to discrimination based on pricing by using the concept of overages in the mortgage transaction. As noted in the institutional discussion, loan originators are often paid a commission. One basis of that commission is the difference between the price paid and a *daily rate sheet* supplied by the lender giving the minimum acceptable prices. Any surplus in price over the daily rate sheet is termed an overage and may determine the loan officer's commission. One possible test for discrimination in loan pricing that appears to cut through much of the complexity is to examine the statistical relation between borrower characteristics and the amount of overages.

While it is tempting to regard the overage as a pure price premium paid by the borrower, this view is false. Loan originators use overages as compensation for extra effort needed to qualify marginal applicants. Without overages, loan originators would have no incentive to work with such applicants. Also, overages are determined by the behavior of borrowers who try to time the market by preserving the option to lock in an interest rate during the period between application and endorsement. There is every reason to suspect that differences in floating behavior may be associated with borrower demographic characteristics in ways that have nothing to do with discrimination. The final overage paid by the borrower is, in effect, determined by the loan originator, the lender, and the borrower through their behavior during the period when the option to lock in a final loan price is being exercised.

Given the complexity of mortgage loan pricing, it is not surprising that it has been largely neglected as a basis for testing for discrimination in mortgage lending.

12.5 The Paradox of Adverse Impact Discrimination

While it has proved most difficult to find unbiased and unambiguous tests for differential treatment discrimination, the attempt to regulate adverse impact discrimination in mortgage lending has proved to be even more frustrating. Recall that adverse impact discrimination arises because minority status is naturally correlated with many economic characteristics that can be used in the lending decision. Lenders are required to choose, from among the economic variables, those that are least associated with minority status, provided that they predict default and foreclosure loss as well as other variables. For example, assume that two variables, "number of bank accounts" and "average bank balance in all accounts," are close substitutes in predicting creditworthiness, but that number of accounts is negatively associated with minority status, while average balance is not. Adverse impact discrimination would occur if lenders used number of accounts in underwriting rather than average balance, if both variables could be readily observed. Lenders, under pressure from regulators to increase minority lending, have an incentive to eliminate adverse impact discrimination.

The paradox of adverse impact discrimination arises because government inaction and regulation have, thus far, impeded two possible approaches to the problem. One approach would involve a major government-sponsored research effort to identify the variables that could be used to identify creditworthiness with the least adverse impact on minorities. The problem with relying on private lenders to develop this information is that credit-scoring schemes must be held as a trade secret in order to be valuable. Therefore, research on these schemes is generally not publicly available and it is difficult for lenders to determine what variables minimize adverse impact. Another approach would be to allow lenders to estimate separate credit-scoring equations for different demographic groups. This approach allows for the possibility that the relation between economic variables and credit risk for minority groups is different; that is, it introduces an element of diversity into the credit-scoring scheme. While either of these approaches would likely increase lending to minority borrowers and lower the problem of adverse impact discrimination, to the average person they appear to be discriminatory. Thus the problem of dealing with adverse impact discrimination may be largely political. Separate credit-scoring schemes for minority groups appear unequal to the public. Paradoxically, it may be that equality of access to credit is furthered when underwriting is based on specially fitted credit risk equations.

Two other approaches to adverse impact discrimination that are not solutions at all have been proposed. One approach would require that lenders include demographic characteristics in their credit-scoring equations. Then credit score would be computed ignoring demographic characteristics. To the extent that an economic variable had an effect on credit risk but was strongly associated with minority status, this procedure would insure that the effect was not translated into the final credit score. The problem with this approach is that it biases the estimated coefficients of the credit-scoring equation and results in denial of credit to the creditworthy and granting of credit to higher-risk applicants.

A second proposed approach would reveal information on the details of the credit-scoring scheme to the applicant. This has been advanced as a fairness issue that potentially lessens adverse impact. Unfortunately, credit-scoring models presume that applicants do not know the model used to evaluate their application. If applicants are sufficiently coached in the details of underwriting, they will behave in ways that invalidate the initial credit-scoring scheme. The argument here is directly analogous to giving out test questions before an examination. If students know the questions before the examination, they will modify their study accordingly and grading of the examination must be changed to recognize the additional student information.

12.6 CONCLUSIONS

Mortgage lending is a very complex process that presents a challenge for economic analysis. Discrimination in mortgage markets cannot be detected using techniques that have succeeded in labor markets. While there is evidence of past discrimination, it appears that regulators and lenders have taken steps to insure against future discrimination. The government program charged directly with insuring mortgage lending for low-income and minority homebuyers, FHA mortgage insurance, has certainly remedied past failures and now lends aggressively to needy borrowers. Electronic lending virtually eliminates any possibility for discrimination. Thus research on discrimination should focus on the applicant groups that have the least affinity with electronic commerce and on high-risk applicants for whom underwriting requires personal contact.

One promising frontier for research is adverse impact discrimination. Building efficient credit-scoring schemes that are appropriate for minority groups remains a challenge both for researchers and the political system. There is a common perception that separate credit-scoring systems are inherently unequal. But, para-doxically, it is likely that separate underwriting schemes for minority groups may be needed to provide equal opportunity access to mortgage credit.

Research and regulatory experience with discrimination in mortgage lending has thus far been concentrated in the USA. However, across the world, mortgage markets are changing in ways that often mimic the evolution of the industry in the USA, including the rise of mortgage securitization and electronic lending. It may be that the lessons reviewed in this essay about the complexity of mortgage lending and the effects of regulation may be valuable and applicable to many countries in the near future.

Bibliography

Barth, J. R., Cordes, J. J., and Yezer, A. M. J. 1980: Financial institution regulations, redlining, and mortgage markets. In *The Regulation of Financial Institutions*. Conference Volume 21. Boston: Federal Reserve Bank of Boston, 101–43.

Berkovec, J. A., Canner, G. B., Gabriel, S. A., and Hannan, T. H. 1994: Race, redlining, and residential mortgage loan performance. *Journal of Real Estate Finance and Economics*, 9(3), 263–94.

Black, H., Schweitzer, R. L., and Mandell, L. 1978: Discrimination in mortgage lending. *American Economic Review*, 68(2), 186–91.

Dedman, W. 1988: The color of money. *Atlanta Journal Constitution* (published in four installments, May 1–4).

Ferguson, M. F. and Peters, S. R. 1995: What constitutes evidence of discrimination in lending? *Journal of Finance*, 50(2), 739–48.

Horne, D. K. 1994: Evaluating the role of race in mortgage lending. *FDIC Banking Review*, 7(2), 1–15.

LaCour-Little, M. 1999: Discrimination in mortgage lending: a critical review of the litera-ture. *Journal of Real Estate Literature*, 7(1), 15–49.

Maddala, G. S. and Trost, R. P. 1982: On measuring discrimination in loan markets. *Hous-ing Finance Review*, 1(3), 245–66.

Martin, R. E. and Hill, C. 2000: Loan performance and race. *Economic Inquiry*, 38(1), 136–50.

Munnell, A. H., Tootell, G. M. B., Browne, L. E., and McEneaney, J. 1992: Mortgage lend-ing in Boston: interpreting HMDA data. Federal Reserve Bank of Boston, Working Paper #92-7.

——, ——, ——, and —— 1996: Mortgage lending in Boston: interpreting HMDA data. *American Economic Review*, 86(1), 25–53.

Tootell, G. M. B. 1996: Redlining in Boston: Do mortgage lenders discriminate against neighborhoods? *Quarterly Journal of Economics*, 111(4), 1,049–79.

Yezer, A. M. J., Phillips, R. F., and Trost, R. P. 1994: Bias in estimates of discrimination and default in mortgage lending: effects of simultaneity and self-selection. *Journal of Real Estate Finance and Economics*, 9(3), 197–216.

CHAPTER THIRTEEN

Commercial Real Estate

David Geltner

13.1   INTRODUCTION

Imagine a city with nothing but houses, public institutions, and parks. It might be serene, but what a dull place it would be – not really a city at all. Commercial real estate is what gives a city much of its life and character. Commercial buildings largely occupy the most central sites in the city, the most accessible places. They define the skylines of the downtowns and edge cities. They give visual image and focus, a sense of place, even to neighborhood centers. They provide the vital nodes in the system of manufacturing production and distribution. Alas, they fill the linear "strips" of the suburban sprawl that characterizes too much of the modern metropolis. But commercial buildings are the economic heart of the city, where people and capital and resources come together to add value, to create, and to recreate. Commercial buildings are *where the action is*.

No treatment of urban economics would be complete without considering the economics of commercial real estate. The aim of this chapter is to provide an introduction to this topic. We will do this by focusing on the commercial real estate development investment decision, the decision that causes the creation of new built space, the fabric of the city. As commercial real estate consists of income-producing assets, it represents a major component of the capital market, the market for income-producing assets. Commercial development results from investment decisions, and these decisions are themselves underpinned by the economics of the "space market," the market for the usage of commercial space. This chapter will take you through a brief introductory tour of how these markets and decisions come together to create the commercial heart of the city.

13.2   An Illustrative Example at the Micro Level

Perhaps the best way to gain an understanding of the economics of commercial real estate development is to examine a specific real-world example project. The project we will look at is called Montrose Technology Park. It is a proposal for a pension fund (a type of financial institution that controls a lot of capital) to invest in the development of a new "office/R&D" complex in Milpitas, a town in the "Silicon Valley" area of northern California, in December 1999, at the height of the "Technology Boom." The project would consist of four two-story buildings totaling 228,000 rentable square feet ("SF" in what follows), on a 12.4 acre site at the intersection of an Interstate highway and a major arterial highway.

For this development to make sense from an economic and business perspective, the proposed type of building must represent the "**highest and best use**" (HBU) of the site, given its location and the relevant zoning constraints. This means that if the vacant site of the proposed development were put up for auction, the proposed development must be able to outbid other possible alternative uses for the land (and still offer sufficient profit for its developer and investors).

Office/R&D buildings are a relatively new class of commercial real estate, a type of property designed to serve the needs of the high-technology industry that burgeoned in the last decades of the twentieth century, especially in places demonstrating agglomeration economies for such industry, like Silicon Valley. Office/R&D buildings combine some characteristics of more traditional industrial warehouse or light manufacturing facilities, with some of the characteristics of low-frills suburban office space. The need is for facilities that support small entrepreneurial firms or similar nonhierarchical-style branches of larger technology firms, where research, development, and light manufacturing or engineering occur in the same premises with the management functions of the firm or operation. Rents per SF are higher than warehouse rents, but usually lower than those of retail space or upscale ("Class A") office space.

In addition to the attraction of location within a geographical agglomeration of related technology firms, office/R&D properties often need locations with good truck and air-freight access. Our 12-acre site at the intersection of an Interstate and a major arterial highway in a town at the growing edge of Silicon Valley would seem to be ideal for this type of space in 1999, provided that the land cost is not too high. As noted, the land cost will reflect the highest and best use of the site, what the most productive use of the site could "bid" for the land.

The economic and business viability of the Montrose Technology Park project depends fundamentally on the nature and current state of the "space market" in the Milpitas area, the market for the usage of built space of specific types. The land value (and hence opportunity cost) of the site reflects the space market, dictating what type of development is feasible. For example, if the land cost is too high to support office/R&D development, this would suggest that a more intensive land use would be the highest and best use of the site, such as retail or Class A office space, or perhaps multi-family housing.

On the other hand, if office/R&D is the most productive use for the site, but the market for this type of building is currently saturated to the point that new buildings are not likely to be sufficiently valuable to support the land acquisition cost (i.e., there is currently excess supply of such building stock making rental of new space problematic), then current development on our site would have a negative "net present value" (NPV) when examined from an investment perspective. That is, it would cost more to develop the site (including land cost) than the site would be worth upon completion. This would suggest that it is optimal to hold the land at our site vacant temporarily as a speculative investment, waiting for a turn in the market that will make development viable. This could occur either by a reduction in land value (hence land cost) to allow a less intensive or lower-value building to be profitable, or by an increase in office/R&D usage demand that lifts the prospects and likely values of such buildings so as to make current office/R&D development profitable at the given land cost. Thus, the first step in our analysis of Montrose Technology Park is to consider the space market for office/R&D space in Silicon Valley and particularly in Milpitas at the time of the proposed development, 1999.

13.3 THE MARKET FOR COMMERCIAL SPACE

Montrose and its Milpitas office/R&D market is a specific example of a general phenomenon that urban economists refer to as the **space market**, or the market for built space usage. Panel (a) in Figure 13.1 depicts the short-run supply and demand in a typical commercial real estate space market. The demand function slopes downward, reflecting some price elasticity, the ability of space users to occupy and use more or less space (Q on the horizontal axis) in response to the rental price (R on the vertical axis). While firms often have less flexibility to alter their space usage than they do to alter other factors of production, they nevertheless have some such flexibility through the use of arrangements such as short-term leases and various types of expansion and cancellation options.

On the other hand, the ability to alter the stock of space supply in the market is usually perceived to be much more constrained in the short run (meaning less than a year or two). Expansion of space supply requires real estate development projects that have a long lead time for planning, permitting, financing, and construction. Contraction of space supply requires demolition or conversion of space, which normally either does not make economic sense in response to short-run movements in the space market or also requires long lead times to address legal, political, and construction obstacles.

With supply quite inelastic in the short run, an increase in demand could result in a sharp run-up in rents on new leases. (Recall that an "*increase in demand*" refers to the demand function moving out and up to the right in the supply and demand diagram, potential space users wanting to use more space at a given price, such as from the D_0 schedule to the D_1 schedule in panel (a).) For example, rent might rise from $R_0 = \$16/SF/year$, to $R_1 = \$20/SF/year$.

Now suppose that it is actually profitable to develop new space at the original R_0 level of rent. In this case, the R_0 rent level of \$16 would be called the

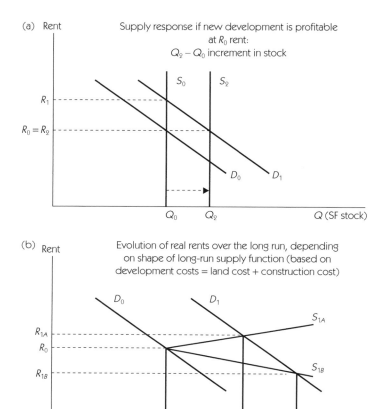

Figure 13.1 Space market supply and demand: (a) short-run supply and demand in a typical commercial property space market; (b) real rents in the long run.

"**replacement cost rent**" in this market. For example, suppose that construction costs are $150/SF, and land costs $50/SF of building rentable area (where both of these costs reflect sufficient profit for the parties involved in the project). Thus, total development costs are $200/SF of rentable space. Now suppose that in the capital market the current income yield required on commercial real estate investments is 8 percent. (This yield is referred to as the "**cap rate**" in the real estate asset market.) This means that for every $100 of capital invested, the investor must be able to expect to receive $8 per year in income. This implies that an expected net rent of $R_0 = \$16/SF/year$ will be sufficient to trigger new development. At the 8 percent current yield, a building producing net rent of $16/SF will be worth $200/SF, the price that – as we stated – is sufficient to cover costs and provide developers with the profit they need to undertake development projects.

Thus it would be profitable (hence, feasible) to "replace" the existing building stock as long as the space market will support annual rents of \$16/SF.

Of course, new development projects may take 2–3 years to complete. But they will eventually expand the stock of space supply in the market, and competition among landlords will then drive equilibrium rents back down to the R_0 level of \$16/SF if they have spiked temporarily above that level. The new short-run equilibrium is indicated in panel (a) of Figure 13.1 by the D_1 and S_2 demand and supply functions, and the Q_2 and R_2 quantity of space usage and rent price level.

A longer-run perspective is portrayed in panel (b) of Figure 13.1. The demand function in panel (b) may have greater elasticity (a shallower slope) than that in the short-run diagram in panel (a). But the biggest difference is in the supply function, which now appears kinked at the current equilibrium stock of space and the replacement cost rent. Contractions in demand below the current level (i.e., movements of the demand function down and to the left) will leave the supply of space pretty much constant, at least for several years, as indicated by the vertical part of the long-run supply function at the current quantity of Q_0. This inelasticity of supply will result in a sharp reduction in the equilibrium rent. On the other hand, asymmetrically, growth in demand above the current level (movements of the demand function up and to the right in the diagram) will stimulate new development at the replacement cost rent, leading after what is usually a fairly short lag to additional quantity of supply in the market at a long-run equilibrium rent level equal to the replacement cost rent (at least when rent is measured in real terms, net of inflation).

The kinked supply function reflects the fact that buildings are very long-lived products, and in most space markets in the United States new built space supply can be added more easily and quickly than old supply can be removed. This is particularly true where land is plentiful and the legal, political, and financial environment is conducive to commercial development, and where the market for alternative uses for existing structures is limited or the legal and political environment constrains such conversion.

It is not always the case that new development requires the same R_0 level of rent as the previous development in order to be profitable, within a given space market. The long-run supply function in the space market traces out the marginal cost of development in the market, including both construction cost and land cost. In most markets, construction costs tend to be fairly constant over the long run, at least in real terms after controlling for inflation and quality of product, though costs may tend to cycle around a long-run average, reflecting the cyclical nature of construction demand. However, the other main component of development costs, land, may follow a long-run trend in real terms.

In any given location, the quantity of land is fixed, and thus its scarcity value will rise or fall with the demand for that location. Development site acquisition costs also reflect the existence of preexisting structures on the site. Even if an old structure no longer reflects the HBU of the site, such a structure will normally still have a value that is part of the opportunity cost of site acquisition for a new structure. On the other hand, while any given location is unique, most locations have potential substitutes, similar sites either nearby or in places of comparable accessibility and appeal elsewhere in the metropolitan area. Central locations in particular, where much commercial development tends to locate, are susceptible to loss in location premium value as improvements in transportation and information technology and telecommunications flatten out the rent gradients across the metropolitan area, reducing the need for businesses to locate in central points. The result is that land costs may either rise or fall over time, in real terms (net of inflation), especially in central areas.

This has important implications for the long-run equilibrium rent in the space market. The general possibilities are represented in the alternative shapes of the long-run supply function depicted in panel (b) of Figure 13.1. If development costs rise in a given location over the long run (probably due to rising location premia in land values), then the replacement cost rent rises, and the long-run equilibrium real rent level in that space market tends to rise to the extent that demand for space usage in that market grows, as indicated by the S_{1A} supply function. The opposite situation is indicated by the S_{1B} function, which shows a market in which real development costs decrease over time (again, probably due to declining location premia in the land values), resulting in decreasing equilibrium real rents in the market even in the face of growing demand for space in that market. In fact, there is evidence that commercial property space markets in the USA exhibit a variety of trends, with some markets exhibiting real growth in rents over time, and others exhibiting real declines.

13.4   SPACE MARKET ANALYSIS

When real estate developers and investors examine a space market to consider specific projects in those markets, such as our proposed Montrose Technology Park development, they need to ascertain and understand the nature of the relevant space market. What are the current conditions in the market, and where is it is headed, within the framework that we discussed in the previous section? To perform such analysis, decision-makers typically focus on several quantifiable indicators of rental market supply and demand:

- vacancy
- rent
- construction
- absorption.

Each of these indicators will be briefly discussed below.

The **vacancy rate** refers to the percentage of the stock of built space in the market that is not currently occupied. To compute the vacancy rate, it is obvious that one must know two more fundamental quantities: the total **stock** (or "inventory") of space in the market, and the amount of space that is currently vacant. To be most meaningful, the vacancy rate should include all space that is currently unoccupied and available for occupancy, including space that may be currently under lease but available via subleasing. The vacancy rate is one indicator that reflects the current balance between supply and demand in the market (the other is the current market rent level). Vacancy is thus an equilibrium indicator rather than an indicator of either the supply side or the demand side alone.

It is important to keep in mind that in a typical real estate market it is normal for some vacancy to exist. Both landlords and tenants suffer costs when tenants move (including, for landlords, lost rent due to vacancy and/or a need for expenditure on new tenant finishes, and for the tenant, moving expenses including work flow disruption). This makes it rational for parties to commit to long-term leases in commercial structures. But long-term leasing makes it worthwhile for both parties to spend some time and expense to search for a good rental deal. The leasing process contains *optionality*; that is, rights without obligation to make irreversible decisions. Vacant space gives the landlord the option to lease the space at any time (at the then-prevailing market rent). Optionality provides valuable flexibility, but only until the option is exercised. Option theory and rational search theory suggest that it is optimal for some space to be held vacant – "waiting," in effect, for better deals to show up.

Vacancy is also caused by the "lumpy" nature of real estate development. Supply is not added to the stock in infinitesimal units, but in structures that have sufficient scale to be economical to build. And as noted, once added to the supply side of the market, stock is difficult to remove. Yet rental space demand grows more incrementally and variably, sometimes shrinking temporarily. It takes time to build, and construction decisions must be made in the absence of perfect information about the future balance of supply and demand in the market at the time when the building will be completed. The result is that some excess space will inevitably be provided in the typical real estate market from time to time. This growth-based source of vacancy tends to be more important in markets where demand is growing faster, and with more "volatility," or "ups and downs," in the growth rate.

For all of these reasons, each real estate market is characterized by a "**natural vacancy rate**," the vacancy rate that tends to prevail on average over the long run in the market, and which indicates that the market is approximately in balance between supply and demand. The idea of a natural vacancy rate is that, when vacancy is falling below the natural rate, rents will tend to be driven up, and when vacancy is rising above the natural rate rents will tend to be driven down. The natural vacancy rate tends to be higher in faster-growing, more volatile, space markets, and also in markets where there are fewer regulatory or geographical constraints on new development.

A second important indicator of the condition of the space market, which is often tracked, is the current **market rent**, which refers to the level of rents being charged on typical new leases currently being signed in the market. In principle, rents are the most important indicator of the balance between supply and demand in the space market. In practice, however, it is more difficult to accurately and reliably quantify changes and trends in rents than in vacancy rates. In part, this is because one must control for differences in the specific sites and spaces being rented, and for the terms of the lease. Also, merely surveying the "*asking rents*" that are reported by landlords does not generally reflect what may be happening with the "**effective rents**" that tenants actually pay (including the effect of concessions and rent abatements which are often part of the lease deal). Furthermore, in order to use rental changes to gauge actual changes in the space market balance between supply and demand, one must control for general inflation, to examine the changes in "**real rent**," net of inflation.

The quantity of new **construction** started and/or completed is the third important indicator of real estate markets. Construction represents the addition of new supply into the stock of space available in the market. As construction takes time, there is a lag between construction starts and completions, representing the "pipeline" of new space that will be coming on line. It may also be important to consider demolition or conversion of old structures to arrive at the net addition of supply in the market.

The fourth general market indicator that is widely used is space **absorption**. This refers to the amount of additional space that is occupied per year. Just as construction is the indicator of change on the supply side of the market, "**net absorption**" is the indicator of change on the demand side of the market. Net absorption differs from "**gross absorption**" (sometimes referred to as "leasing velocity"), which measures the total amount of space for which leases were signed during the year, regardless of where the tenants came from. Gross absorption measures the volume of rental transaction activity, which is relevant for indicating how much business leasing brokers are doing. But tenants moving from one site to another in the same market do not indicate an increase in overall demand within that market.

Comparing net construction completed to net absorption indicates whether or not demand and supply are growing at the same rate. When net absorption exceeds net construction completions, vacancy declines in the market, as indicated by the following equation:

$$(Vacant\ Space)_t = (Vacant\ Space)_{t-1} + (Construction)_t - (Net\ Absorption)_t.$$

The three physical quantitative indicators of the space market described above can be examined together to provide a summary measure of the condition of the market, referred to as the "**months supply**" (*MS*) measure. The formula is as follows:

$$MS = \frac{Vacant\ Space\ SF + Construction\ SF}{(Net\ Absorption\ SF)/12},$$

assuming that the construction and absorption are measured in annual rates.

The months supply is an indicator of how long it will take (in months) until all of the vacant space in the market is absorbed, considering only what is in the current construction pipeline. The months supply can be compared to the length of time that it takes to complete the typical construction project. If the months supply is less than the construction time, then this indicates that the market can support additional new construction. If it is not practical for the market to go all the way down to zero vacancy (as we suggested earlier), or if there is likely to be demolition or abandonment of existing occupied space in the market, then the market can handle additional new construction even when the months supply is somewhat greater than the average construction project duration.

13.5 BACK TO MONTROSE . . .

Let's return now and examine our Montrose Technology Park proposal in its space market context. In 1999, the Silicon Valley area south of San Francisco in Santa Clara and southern Alameda counties was home to over 5,000 high tech companies, employing over 250,000 people. The region represented the greatest concentration of venture capital investment in the world, including one-third of all US venture capital spending. The 1999 office/R&D market in the Silicon Valley consisted of 135 million SF of existing stock, with a vacancy rate of 5.6 percent, well below what was considered to be the natural vacancy rate of around 10 percent in the market. There was strong upward pressure on rents, as the demand side of the market was recovering from the 1998 Asian debt crisis and absorption was heating up to peak rates of over 10 million SF per year, while new construction had recently been curtailed as a result of the financial shocks of 1998, bringing the months supply measure of space availability down to less than 1 year, arguably less than the time required to develop new buildings.

In these circumstances, it seemed prudent to predict that the Montrose Technology Park would be able to lock in long-term leases at net rents estimated at around $19/SF/year (including step-up provisions for later years in the leases). Such a projected rent level was supported by rents being charged on new leases written earlier in 1999 in buildings and locations similar to Montrose. It even seemed prudent to commence the development project without pre-leasing the space, to build on a speculative basis. A joint venture partnership was formed between a local entrepreneurial developer specializing in warehouse and office/R&D projects and an out-of-state pension fund that would provide the equity capital. The land was purchased at a price of $15,124,000, or $66.33/SF of rentable space in the to-be-completed project. The project was quickly scoped out, with development costs specified including $16,510,000 of hard construction costs, and another $4,895,000 of so-called "soft costs" associated with design, permitting, marketing, and financing, including over $1 million in expected interest cost on a loan to finance the construction. Thus, the total development cost was projected to be $36,529,000, or $160.21/SF of rentable space, of which the land cost represented over 40 percent.

The projected cash flows for the planned temporal staging of the project are shown in the operating budget in Table 13.1, from the land purchase at the beginning of "Year 1" through to projected fully stabilized operation in "Year 3." Note that there is zero net cash flow to or from the developer and equity investor during Year 1, a year during which the project will be under construction and the cash outlays will be covered by the construction loan. Those construction costs are reflected in the $21,405,000 projected balance due on the construction loan, including accrued interest, at the end of Year 2.

Table 13.1   The Montrose Technology Park development project cash flow
projection

For the years ending	Year 0	Year 1 2000	Year 2 2001	Year 3 2002
POTENTIAL GROSS REVENUE				
Base rental revenue		$222,735	$3,410,017	$4,349,783
Absorption and turnover vacancy		$0	$0	$0
Scheduled base rental revenue		$222,735	$3,410,017	$4,349,763
Expense reimbursement revenue				
Operating expenses		$36,196	$565,778	$725,706
Total reimbursement revenue		$36,196	$565,778	$725,706
TOTAL POTENTIAL GROSS REVENUE		$268,931	$3,975,795	$5,075,489
General vacancy		−$10,357	−$159,032	−$203,020
Collection loss		−$5,179	−$79,516	−$101,510
EFFECTIVE GROSS REVENUE		$243,395	$3,737,247	$4,770,959
OPERATING EXPENSES				
Operating expenses		$243,395	$704,520	$725,656
TOTAL OPERATING EXPENSES		$243,395	$704,520	$725,656
NET OPERATING INCOME		$0	$3,032,727	$4,045,303
LEASING AND CAPITAL COSTS				
Tenant improvements		$0	$0	$0
Leasing commissions		$0	$0	$0
Capital reserves		$0	$35,226	$36,283
Construction costs (pay off construction loan)		$0	$21,405,000	$0
TOTAL LEASING AND CAPITAL COSTS	$0	$0	$21,440,226	$36,283
LAND	$15,124,000			
CASH FLOW BEFORE DEBT SERVICE AND INCOME TAX	−$15,124,000	$0	−$18,407,499	$4,009,020

Before we can know whether these development costs are warranted by the projected rents that we have estimated based on our analysis of the space market, we need to evaluate the proposed Montrose development project as an investment. To do this, we need to understand the capital market and the basics of investment analysis.

13.6   THE REAL ESTATE CAPITAL MARKET

Physical capital is driven by financial capital. Whether or not developments get built depends on whether investors are willing to put their money into the projects. Large sums of money for investment are referred to as "capital," and capital is traded in the **capital market** (or financial market). The investment industry is the industry that serves this market and its participants. The branch of that market and industry that deals in the ownership of real estate assets is called the **real estate investment industry** and the **real estate asset market** (or property market). Investment in relatively large commercial projects such as our Montrose complex is dominated by large financial and investment institutions.

Figure 13.2 summarizes the institutional real estate investment industry, showing the major sources of capital for commercial real estate investment. The figure shows that this investment comes in two major forms, "equity" and "debt." **Equity** investors generally come first in time in a development project, but last in priority for getting their money back or any profits out of the project. Equity investors essentially "own" the project, either in perpetuity until they sell their share, or until they default on any debt they owe, which would enable the lender to take over ownership control. In our Montrose example, the developer and their pension fund partner are providing the equity capital. Although equity capital typically plays the lead and more entrepreneurial role in project development and control, note in Figure 13.2 that most real estate financial capital is in the form of debt investment, or loans.

Debt investors have priority over equity investors in getting their investment back and making a profit. Debt investment also differs from equity in that it is based on contractually fixed returns (e.g., the "interest" on a mortgage), and in that it is typically finite-lived. Because debt is less risky than equity investment, it also on average provides a lower return than equity investment (over the long run).

Figure 13.2 provides a breakdown of the financial capital structure and sources of institutional capital available specifically to the type of large-scale commercial real estate assets that have the biggest impact on the character and form of the city, including developments such as our Montrose complex. These assets totaled some $2.7 trillion in value in the USA as of 2002, consisting of over $1.8 trillion of debt (mortgages) loaned on those properties and some $0.9 trillion of equity value residing with the owners of the properties. (All income-producing commercial real estate in the USA, including owner-occupied and smaller "mom & pop" properties, totaled over $5 trillion in value in the early 2000s; Figure 13.2 only covers larger investment properties.) The different types of equity and debt

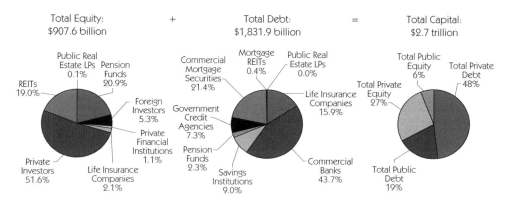

Figure 13.2   Investable real estate capital structure.
Source: Roulac Group (Investment Property Report, 12/11/02) and PPR Inc.

investors are enumerated in the left-hand side of the figure. The right-hand side pie chart summarizes the overall "**capital structure**" (the share of equity and debt), including a breakout of the proportion of capital that is sourced (and traded) in the **public capital markets** (the stock and bond markets of "Wall Street"), as distinguished from the older **private capital markets** that have traditionally supplied real estate finance ("Main Street").

The most important types of commercial property owners (sources of equity capital) for these relatively large-scale properties include wealthy private individuals, pension funds, and REITs, while the most important types of debt-holders (sources of debt capital) for these properties include commercial banks (especially for construction loans used to finance new development), CMBS investors, and life insurance companies. The term "**REITs**" refers to "real estate investment trusts," commercial real estate investment firms whose equity shares are traded in the public stock exchanges, while "**CMBS**" refers to "commercial mortgage backed securities," commercial real estate debt-based securities often traded in the public bond markets.

Anyone interested in the nature, evolution, and development of the physical stock of commercial real estate in the city needs to understand the investment objectives and constraints, and the investment decision-making procedures, of the sources of commercial real estate financial capital enumerated in Figure 13.2. It is important to understand, for example, that a life insurance company or pension fund needs to invest in assets that provide a safe and stable source of long-term income flow in order to balance and service their liabilities (which consist of long-lived term life, whole life, and annuity policies). In contrast, a REIT, which needs to satisfy stock market investors seeking higher returns, would typically be willing to make riskier investments in mortgaged properties or development opportunities that provide higher expected returns and greater growth prospects. Even a conservative institution such as a pension fund, however, will often earmark a small part of their well-diversified portfolio for more risky, potentially higher-return investments, which is how our Montrose project would be considered by its pension fund equity partner. (Often, such a link between the pension fund source of capital and the development project investment is made through an investment vehicle such as a professionally managed fund.)

13.7   REAL ESTATE INVESTMENT ANALYSIS

To understand how a development project such as Montrose Technology Park would be analyzed at the micro level as an investment by the types of institutions described above, we must consider some of the basics of real estate investment analysis. What are the types of things that investors look for at the level of individual real estate projects? This lies at the heart of the process by which decisions are made and commercial real estate assets are developed in the real world.

While investors are a heterogeneous population, they are all driven fundamentally by the objective of earning "**returns**" on their investments. The investment return is the way in which we quantify the profit that matters to investors. At a very simple level, the return on an investment can be thought of as what the investor gets, minus what she puts in, as a fraction of what she puts in. Returns come in two forms: income that is periodically given out over time to the investor by the investment, and growth over time in the remaining value of the investment asset held by the investor. The return that the investor is looking for in considering whether to invest in a given proposed project is a forward-looking expectation, or *ex ante* return. The return that is actually achieved historically by a given investment is a backward-looking *ex post* (or "realized") return.

When analyzing investments and their returns, it is vital to keep in mind the fundamental relationship between the *ex ante* return and the risk in the investment. Investors are risk averse. Other things being equal, they prefer less risky investments to more risky ones. Hence, in equilibrium in the capital markets, the prices or values of different investment opportunities must be such that more risky investments offer investors higher *ex ante* returns, proportionately to the amount of risk in the investment (as perceived and evaluated by the capital market). Other things being equal, asset prices are inversely related to the *ex ante* returns offered by those assets. The lower the price I pay today for a given asset, the greater is my expected return on my investment in that asset, and vice versa. Thus, investors will not pay as much for more risky assets, because those assets need to offer higher *ex ante* returns.

The *ex ante* return required by the capital market for a given investment represents the "**opportunity cost of capital**" (*OCC*) for that investment. Investors can expect to earn the *OCC* as the return on alternative investments of similar risk. Thus, they incur an "opportunity cost" of foregoing earning that return if they invest in something else of similar risk. The *OCC* for more risky investments is greater than that for less risky investments. But the *OCC* is positive even for a (hypothetical) investment that contains no risk. This is because investors want to be compensated for the "**time value of money**," the fact that during the time when their money is invested, being used by someone else, they can't use it themselves for consumption. Thus, the *OCC* consists of two components, a risk-free interest rate that compensates investors for the time value of money, and a **"risk premium"** that compensates them for the risk in the investment.

The essence of investment analysis at the micro level of consideration of individual proposed "deals" or investment projects is to consider whether the *ex ante* return presented by the proposed investment at least equals its *OCC*. If so, then the investment can usually be justified. This type of analysis is normally performed best by examining the "**net present value**" (*NPV*) of the proposed project. The *NPV* equals the value of the benefit to be obtained from the investment minus the cost of obtaining it, both measured in present certainty-equivalent dollars (i.e., controlling for differences in time and risk of the dollars of costs and benefits). The basic normative investment rule is as follows:

"THE *NPV* INVESTMENT DECISION RULE":

(1) MAXIMIZE THE *NPV* ACROSS ALL MUTUALLY EXCLUSIVE ALTERNATIVES; AND

(2) NEVER CHOOSE AN ALTERNATIVE THAT HAS: *NPV* < 0.

Real estate investments typically span multiple periods of time. Therefore, the measure that is usually used to quantify investment returns is the "**internal rate of return**" (*IRR*). The *IRR* is defined as the rate that discounts all of the investment's net cash flows (including the price paid for the investment) to an *NPV* of zero, where net cash flows are measured each period as the difference between cash received by the investor from the investment (positive cash flow, either from income or sale of the asset) minus cash paid out from the investor to the investment (for purchase of the asset, operating expenses, or capital improvement expenditures). Mathematically, the *IRR* is defined by the following equation:

$$0 = CF_0 + \frac{CF_1}{(1 + IRR)} + \frac{CF_2}{(1 + IRR)^2} + \ldots + \frac{CF_N}{(1 + IRR)^N}, \tag{13.1}$$

where CF_t refers to the net cash flow in period t. CF_0 would normally be negative from the investor's perspective, reflecting the cash outflow required to purchase or develop the investment asset in period 0. CF_N would normally be positive from the investor's perspective, including the value of the asset at the end of the projected investment in period N. For commercial real estate investments, the intermediate cash flows between period 1 and period N typically reflect the net cash from property operations – essentially, rental revenue minus the operating expenses of the property. The *IRR* value that solves this equation represents the "return" presented to the investor as of period 0 from the future net cash flows during periods 1, 2, . . . , N, given the price paid for the investment as reflected in the CF_0 amount.

If CF_0 in equation (13.1) reflects the market value of the investment asset as of period 0, and the remaining CF_t values in the equation are realistic (unbiased) projections as of period 0 of the future expected net cash flows presented by the investment, then the *IRR* value that solves the equation will represent the *OCC* of the investment. This is because the market value of the investment is defined as the asset price that presents investors with an *ex ante* return equal to the investment's *OCC*.

Now suppose that an investment asset can be obtained for a price of *P*, which may or may not equal its market value. Then the *NPV* of the investment is defined as follows, where *MV* represents the market value of the asset:

$$NPV = -P + MV$$

$$= -P + \frac{CF_1}{(1 + OCC)} + \frac{CF_2}{(1 + OCC)^2} + \ldots + \frac{CF_N}{(1 + OCC)^N}. \qquad (13.2)$$

13.8   BACK AGAIN TO MONTROSE . . .

We are now in a position to make a complete economic and business investment analysis of the proposed Montrose Technology Park commercial development project, combining our space market analysis with our knowledge of real estate investment analysis principles. In essence, we must compare the values of the benefits and costs of the project within the *NPV* framework. In this evaluation, we must account for both the time value of money and for risk.

The first step is to estimate what the stabilized (fully operational) building will be worth upon completion of the development project at the end of Year 2. At that point, the construction project will have produced a building complex that is expected to generate net operating income (*NOI*) at a rate of $4,045,303 per year, as seen in Table 13.1. This information, combined with knowledge about "cap rates" prevailing in the property asset market, enables an estimate of the projected completed property value. In 1999, cap rates on office/R&D properties in the Silicon Valley averaged 9.35 percent in sales of properties similar to the subject project. In the absence of any reason to expect cap rates to trend one way or the other during the time of construction, the implication is that at the end of Year 2 the completed property will be worth approximately $43,265,000:

$$Value = \frac{NOI}{Cap\ Rate} = \frac{\$4,045,303}{0.0935} = \$43,265,273.$$

The next step is to estimate the opportunity cost of capital (*OCC*) for the development phase of the investment; namely, the up-front investment of the land. As noted, the *OCC* is the expected return required in the capital market for investments of similar risk to this development project. As development projects are rather unique, it is often difficult to observe directly in the capital market the required *OCC* for the development phase of the investment. However, we can take advantage of knowledge about typical expected returns in other related markets to derive what is the OCC for the development investment. In particular, there are two types of capital asset markets relevant to the Montrose development project, in which the expected returns are relatively well known.

The market for stabilized real estate investment assets of the kind that the completed Montrose property will be at the end of Year 2 deals with assets whose risk is similar to that of the Montrose completed building. In 1999, such leased-up fully operational buildings were widely perceived as providing expected investment returns ("going-in IRRs") of around 10 percent per year. (As US Treasury Bills were yielding about 6 percent at this time, this suggests that the risk premium in the completed building OCC was about 4 percent.) Thus 10 percent would be the OCC that would be relevant for discounting back to present both the $43,265,000 projected property value as of the end of Year 2 and the $2,998,000 projected net cash flow from the operation of the partially completed property during Year 2. (Both of these cash flows have the risk characteristic of operational real estate assets.) Thus, the total value of the "benefit" expected from the project as of the end of the development phase at the end of Year 2 is estimated to be $46,263,000 = $43,265,000 + $2,998,000.

The construction cost represented by the loan balance of $21,405,000 has a very different risk characteristic, presenting very low risk. The magnitude of the construction cost cash outflow will be determined by engineering and contractual factors that allow for very little unexpected variance over time, and with any such variance likely to be uncorrelated with broader economic and financial factors (which allows such risk to be diversified away in the capital markets). Given the yields in the bond market in 1999, an OCC of about 6.5 percent was appropriate as a discount rate for the construction costs to reflect the risk in these costs.

Thus, the investment NPV of a commitment to the proposed Montrose development project in late 1999 was as follows:

$$NPV = -Land\ Cost - PV[Construction\ Cost] + PV[Completed\ Building]$$

$$= -\$15,124,000 - \frac{\$21,405,000}{(1 + 0.065)^2} + \frac{\$46,263,000}{(1 + 0.10)^2}$$

$$= -\$15,124,000 - \$18,872,000 + \$38,234,000$$

$$= +\$4,238,000.$$

As this is a positive NPV (and presumably superior to any other legal alternatives on that site), it made sense to commit to the project at that time.

Notice that this calculus implies an OCC of the development investment *per se* as given by the following equation:

$$\frac{\$46,263,000 - \$21,405,000}{(1 + OCC)^2} = \frac{\$46,263,000}{(1 + 0.10)^2} - \frac{\$21,405,000}{(1 + 0.065)^2},$$

which implies OCC = 13.3 percent. The development actually presented a going-in IRR expectation of 28.2 percent, computed as follows:

$$\$15,124,000 = \frac{\$46,263,000 - \$21,405,000}{(1 + IRR)^2}.$$

This is another way of seeing that the development project made economic sense as an investment in 1999, as the project presented an expected return (28.2 percent) in excess of its cost of capital (13.3 percent). The difference between the development investment OCC of 13.3 percent and the stabilized property investment OCC of 10 percent indicates how much more risky is the development investment compared to investment in a stabilized operating property. If the risk-free OCC was 6 percent at that time, this suggests the development project required a risk premium of 7.3 percent, almost twice as large as the 4 percent risk premium in investments in already completed stabilized properties, as implied by the 10 percent OCC for those investments.

With the advantage of hindsight, we can see clearly the high stakes involved in this kind of investment. Within a year of the decision to invest in Montrose, the Silicon Valley office/R&D market went into a near frenzy of leasing as the infamous "Dot.Com Bubble" drew to its peak, and technology firms competed against each other to lease scarce space. By late 2000, it was possible for landlords to rent out space in buildings such as Montrose for rents more than twice the $19/SF projected in the plans for the project. However, the bursting of the bubble in the following year resulted in a crash in the office/R&D market in Silicon Valley. By 2002, there was nearly 30 percent vacancy in the market and landlords were lucky to sign leases at $10.00/SF. The timing and leasing effectiveness of the Montrose development team would be crucial to determining whether the project would be a tremendous success or a disastrous failure, from an investment perspective.

13.9   CONCLUSION

We have covered a lot of ground in this chapter. We have presented the basics of commercial property space markets and asset markets, including real estate investment analysis. We have attempted to make the discussion concrete, and to show how it relates to the development of the city, by focusing on a specific real-world commercial development project as an example. While this chapter has presented a lot of material, it has only been an introduction to the exciting world of commercial real estate and its vital role in the modern city.

CHAPTER FOURTEEN

Housing Price Indexes

Bradford Case

14.1 Introduction: Why are Accurate Housing Price Indexes Important?

The value of owner-occupied housing accounts for upwards of one-third of total household net wealth in the United States. The most recent economic recession appears to have been moderated by growth in house prices, which supported consumer spending; conversely, the recession of the early 1990s may have been exacerbated by real declines in house prices.

Single-family mortgages account for around one-fifth of the total assets held by US financial institutions. Losses on mortgages are typically quite small, but the possibility that sharp declines in house prices could cause mortgage losses to surge prompts banks to develop sophisticated risk management models in which house price fluctuations play a leading role.

For most individuals, the value of a residence represents their greatest asset. Not only are consumption decisions based in part on housing wealth: job changes, retirement timing, savings, portfolio allocation, home purchase, and even household formation decisions may be affected by movements in housing values.

For lower-income households, governments at the federal, state, and local levels offer housing assistance such as Section 8 vouchers, direct rent subsidies, or home purchase subsidies. Government officials designing and administering such programs need accurate information not only on the price of owner-occupied properties but also on prices paid in the rental market.

In short, a huge number of decisions at all levels stand to be improved by a greater understanding of the path of housing prices and rents. In this chapter, we introduce house price indexes by focusing on a foundation – the hedonic price model – that is quite straightforward. We also describe extensions from the hedonic techniques that are more sophisticated but still easy to understand and implement.

14.2 HOUSE PRICE INDEX METHODOLOGIES

Several empirical methods can be used to estimate housing price indexes, and selecting the most appropriate method depends on the function to be served as well as on the data available. For most purposes, however, the hedonic price model provides at least the essential foundation for a good housing price index. We briefly review two alternatives that are commonly published but that are inadequate for most purposes, and then focus on the hedonic model as well as on repeat-sales and hybrid models, both of which are derived from the hedonic.

Before discussing the methods, however, we should note what a "price" index represents. The *price* in a housing transaction is reached through negotiation amongst the seller and prospective buyers, each of whom has a different notion of the underlying *value* of the house. Similarly, the *price* in a rental transaction is an agreement on the regular rental payment based on the landlord's and tenant's views of the *value* of the right to live in the house. The purpose of an index is generally to track movements in *value* – of a given property (as an asset or simply as a rental unit), a portfolio, or the entire housing stock. Transaction prices are not the only measures of value: other measures include, for example, contract rents, tax-assessed values, appraisals, asking prices, or owner-assessments. Transaction prices are often preferred because, in aggregate, they are probably the best measure of the underlying market value of the asset, but the other measures have all been used to construct "value" indexes. For convenience, however, the discussion in this chapter is couched in terms of transaction prices.

14.2.1 Indexes of average or median prices

The most straightforward method for constructing housing price indexes is simply to compute the *average* or *median price* of properties that transacted during each time period. The distribution of prices is sharply skewed (in fact, it is approximately log-normal), which means that the average price (the *expected* value at which a randomly chosen property would have transacted) exceeds the median price (the *most likely* value at which it would have transacted). It also means that fluctuations in sales volume among expensive properties have a strong effect on average price but a muted effect on median price. For these reasons, the median price is generally preferred; for some applications, however, the average might be preferable. The data requirements for this method are minimal: simply the prices at which all (or a representative sample of) properties transacted during the time period.

The major problem with this method, however, is quite substantial: it fails to control at all for changes in the quality or mix of properties whose prices were observed in each period. Quality tends to improve over time as new properties are constructed, older properties are demolished, and existing properties are renovated; because of this, an average- or median-price index tends to overstate the increase in price for a constant-quality property, or for any existing (and depreciating) property. Empirical estimates suggest, for example, that a comparable constant-quality index increases at less than half the average rate of the most widely cited median-price index, published by the National Association of Realtors. (In the other direction, this method also fails to control for age-related depreciation in the quality of existing properties that are not renovated, but during most periods this seems to be outweighed by quality improvement.) Moreover, the mix of transacting properties is not constant over time, so an average- or median-price index tends to overstate price increases, for example, when all that is happening is that relatively expensive properties are overrepresented among transactions.

14.2.2 The representative-property method

A second straightforward method is to define a *representative property* and then record the price of that property in each time period. The only data item that is actually collected is the price of the representative property in each period; in order to implement this method, however, all of the defining characteristics must be observed to identify one conforming to the definition.

One problem with this method is that data points may not be comparable across markets or over time, because data collectors may differ in subjectively interpreting and applying the definition of the representative property. A second is unmeasured quality change: for example, if a property is defined with respect to location, lot size, and number of rooms but not major amenities, then any increase in the prevalence of those amenities will show up as an increase in the price index. Finally, because the method focuses on the price of only one property, it does not make use of information from other properties; in fact, it may misrepresent movements in the general price level if the representative property's price does not move in the same way.

14.2.3 The hedonic price model

In order to avoid the problems inherent in the average/median-price and representative-property methods, economists most often estimate price indexes using *hedonic price* models. These models postulate that the transaction price of any given property is a function of the *implicit market values* of the property's hedonic characteristics – that is, the physical features of the house, and the features of its location and neighborhood, that are bundled together and embodied in that particular house, multiplied by the *implicit market price* per unit for each of those hedonic characteristics. Prices also fluctuate in response to changes in the supply of and demand for housing, and these changes – the price index – are represented by a series of dummy variables ("intercept shifters") indicating the time period during which the property transacted.

For example, house prices observed annually over 10 years might be represented in the following hedonic price model:

$$\ln P_i = \alpha + \beta_1 \ln X_{1i} + \beta_2 X_{2i} + \sum_{t=2}^{10} \gamma_t T_{ti}. \tag{14.1}$$

Here, P_i is the price of property i, and is expressed in logarithmic form because transaction prices are log-normally distributed. The coefficients β_1 and β_2 are the implicit market prices of the hedonic characteristics (two of them, in this example), and α is an intercept that can be interpreted simply as the (average) portion of every property's value that is not reflected in the implicit market values of its specified hedonic characteristics. X_1 represents any continuously measured characteristic (e.g., lot size) and X_2 represents any discretely measured hedonic characteristic (e.g., number of bathrooms, presence of garage). In this semilogarithmic specification, the coefficient β_1 can be interpreted as the estimated elasticity of the market price of housing with respect to a marginal change in the quantity of the continuously measured characteristic. β_2 yields the percentage difference in transaction price between otherwise-identical properties with a one-unit increase in the discretely measured hedonic characteristic: if $\beta_2 > 0$, then the percentage increase is $e^{\beta_2} - 1$, and if $\beta_2 < 0$, then the percentage decline is $1 - e^{\beta_2}$.

The intercept shifters T_{ti} take the value 1 if property i transacted during period t and 0 if it did not transact during that period; notice that one time period (typically the first) is excluded, because otherwise the series of time dummies would be perfectly collinear. The coefficients on this series of dummy variables, γ_t, represent the price index for housing, with a reference value of 0 for the excluded time period. Note that after the price index coefficients γ_t are re-transformed, the reference value for the excluded time period is $e^0 = 1$ or 100 percent, making interpretation of the price index easy.

Differences in transaction prices between any two houses are explained explicitly with reference to differences in hedonic characteristics; similarly, if the hedonic characteristics of a given property are modified over time, then the difference in transaction prices is explained by the differences in the characteristics of that property before and after the change.

Equation (14.1) reflects two implicit assumptions: first, that the implicit price on each specified hedonic characteristic remains constant across time periods; and, second, that the statistical properties of the disturbance term are likewise constant across time periods. To relax these assumptions is quite straightforward (assuming that the data are available), and two flexible alternatives are commonly used. First, the set of time-interval dummy variables can be interacted with each (or any) hedonic characteristic:

$$\ln P_{it} = \alpha + \sum_{t=1}^{\tau} \beta_{1t} T_{ti} \ln X_{1it} + \sum_{t=1}^{\tau} \beta_{2t} T_{ti} X_{2it} + \sum_{t=2}^{\tau} \gamma_t T_{ti}, \tag{14.2}$$

where τ is the number of time periods. This approach permits the implicit marginal prices to vary in time, but restricts the statistical properties of the disturbance term to be identical across time periods. The index for each hedonic characteristic is represented by its own series of coefficients, while the estimated coefficients on the time-interval dummy variables can be interpreted as the price index for "housing in general."

The alternative to this "explicit time-variable" approach is sometimes called the "strictly cross-sectional" model: equation (14.1) can be estimated separately for each time interval using data for the subset of properties that transacted during that time period. This method permits the implicit marginal prices to vary in time, and also permits the statistical properties of the disturbance term to vary as well. A price index can then be constructed by "chaining" together the intercepts (or any set of estimated implicit prices) using any of several methods, such as the Paasche, Laspeyres, or Fisher Ideal formulas.

It is important to discuss what is widely considered the primary disadvantage of the hedonic price model: its data requirements. In order to estimate the model, a researcher must collect data not just on the price and date at which each property transacted, but also on all of its hedonic characteristics – that is, on all of the property, locational, and neighborhood characteristics that are relevant in determining the market price of that property. To the extent that data on some relevant characteristics (and there could be hundreds of them!) are not collected, the parameter estimates of the hedonic price model (including the price index parameters) will suffer from omitted-variable bias. In practice, though, the hedonic price model is surprisingly robust, in the sense that a hedonic price model estimated using data on the most important characteristics – lot size, number of rooms (or unit square feet), and minimal additional variables such as major amenities, dwelling age, or major aspects of location – generally produces a price index that is adequate for nearly all purposes.

14.2.4   The repeat-sales model

The hedonic price model is extremely powerful, but it fails to make full use of data specifically on those properties that have sold twice (or more frequently) during any study period. Two observations on the same property are treated exactly the same as two observations on different properties that have the same *measured* hedonic characteristics, but when there are two observations on the same property we know that the *unmeasured* characteristics are also the same between transactions. This means that, in principle, the observed change in prices over the time period between transactions can be attributed solely to changes in the price index, as opposed to differences in unmeasured characteristics.

The possibility of making better use of data has given rise to the *repeat-sales model*, an analogue of fixed-effects models that uses repeat observations on the price of a given property (whose hedonic characteristics remained the same between transactions) to estimate the price index. The repeat-sales model is derived explicitly from the hedonic price model by expressing the ratio of two transaction prices for the same property as the ratio of the hedonic functions shown in equation (14.1):

$$\ln \frac{P_{it}}{P'_{it}} = \beta_1 \ln \frac{X_{1i}}{X'_{1i}} + \beta_2(X_{2i} - X'_{2i}) + \sum_{t=2}^{\tau} \gamma_t(T_{it} - T'_{it}), \tag{14.3}$$

where P', X'_1, and X'_2 are the values of price, a continuously measured hedonic characteristic, and a discretely measured characteristic at the time of the earlier transaction, and T' indicates the time period of the earlier transaction. If the hedonic characteristics remain unchanged between transactions, then $X_1 = X_1'$ and $X_2 = X_2'$ and this simplifies to

$$\ln \frac{P_{it}}{P_{it}'} = \sum_{t=2}^{\tau} \gamma_t(T_{it} - T_{it}'), \tag{14.4}$$

which is the standard form of the repeat-sales model. The right-hand side consists only of a series of price index dummy variables taking the value −1 during the time period of the earlier transaction, +1 during the time period of the later transaction, and 0 in every other time period.

Shiller (1993) showed that the repeat-sales model, like the hedonic price model, can be used to estimate not just an overall price index for housing but also a price index for individual hedonic characteristics. Take the ratio of equation (14.2) for two transactions of the same house:

$$\ln \frac{P_{it}}{P_{it}'} = \sum_{t=1}^{\tau} \beta_1(T_{it}X_{1i} - T_{it}'X_{1i}') + \sum_{t=1}^{\tau} \beta_2(T_{it}\ln X_{2i} - T_{it}'\ln X_2') + \sum_{t=2}^{\tau} \gamma_t(T_{it} - T_{it}'). \tag{14.5}$$

Note that in Shiller's formulation the right-hand side variables include a set of price index variables for each hedonic characteristic (along with the original set of price index dummies for the intercept). For each characteristic, the variable takes the value −X′ during the time period of the first transaction, +X during the time period of the second transaction, and 0 in every other time period. Note also that this formulation does not restrict the analysis to properties that did not change at all between transactions.

If it is known that no hedonic characteristics changed between transactions, then the data requirements of the repeat-sales model are minimal: only the time period in which each house transacted, the price, and some information (e.g., address or tax identification number) that ties together observations on the same property. The value of this "advantage," however, has been wildly overstated. In truth, the data requirements of the repeat-sales model are exactly the same as those of the hedonic price model, because only by observing data on all relevant characteristics can the analyst know whether any have changed between transactions. In practice, analysts generally simply assume that characteristics have not changed between transactions: see, for example, the widely cited indexes published by both Freddie Mac and the Office of Federal Housing Enterprise Oversight (OFHEO). To the extent that this assumption is invalid, the failure to take into account changes in hedonic characteristics – that is, the use of the incorrect equation (14.4) in place of the correct equations (14.3) or (14.5) – will result in omitted-variable bias affecting estimates of the price index. And it is easy to see that the data requirements of the correct repeat-sales model given in equations (14.3) or (14.5) are identical to those of the hedonic price model.

The primary disadvantage of the repeat-sales model relative to the hedonic price model is that it can be estimated only on pairs of transactions of properties that sell at least twice during the study period. Depending on the length of the study period, this may restrict the analysis to a small fraction of the total number of observations on housing transactions. Moreover, the sample of properties that transact repeatedly during any finite study period is probably not representative of the entire housing stock.

14.2.5   Hybrid models

The repeat-sales model makes full use of the added information that is contained in repeated observations on the same property, but at great cost because it uses only the small subsample of properties that have transacted at least twice during the study period. In principle, however, the hedonic and repeat-sales models can be combined into a hybrid model that makes full use of the information contained in both repeat-transacting *and* once-transacting properties. In the original formulation of the hybrid model by Case and Quigley (1991), equations (14.1), (14.3), and (14.4) are simply "stacked" and estimated jointly with the coefficients constrained to be equal across all three equations:

$$\ln P_i = \alpha + \beta_1 \ln X_{1i} + \beta_2 X_{2i} + \sum_{t=2}^{\tau} \gamma_t T_{ti},$$

$$\ln \frac{P_{it}}{P'_{it}} = \beta_1 \ln \frac{X_{1t}}{X'_{1i}} + \beta_2 (X_{2i} - X'_{2i}) + \sum_{t=2}^{\tau} \gamma_t (T_{it} - T'_{it}), \qquad (14.6)$$

$$\ln \frac{P_{it}}{P'_{it}} = \sum_{t=2}^{\tau} \gamma_t (T_{it} - T'_{it}).$$

Hybrid models are occasionally dismissed on two grounds: first, that they are difficult to estimate; and, second, that – like the hedonic model – they have onerous data requirements compared to repeat-sales models. In truth, however, the data requirements of the repeat-sales model are no less onerous than those of the hedonic or hybrid models, because hedonic characteristics must be observed in order either to identify properties that remained unchanged between transactions or to estimate the correct (Shiller) form of the model. And the leading formulations of the hybrid model – those developed by Quigley (1995) and by Englund, Quigley, and Redfearn (1998) – are actually not very difficult to implement using generalized least squares.

14.3   AN EMPIRICAL EXAMPLE

An example using real-world data illustrates the differences among the house price index methods described above. The TReND multiple listing service (MLS) maintains proprietary data sets recording, for transacting properties in the Philadelphia metropolitan area, transaction dates and prices along with contemporaneous values of hedonic characteristics including: structure age; lot and unit square feet; numbers of bedrooms, full baths, and half baths; presence of air conditioning, a garage, or any fireplaces; and an indicator of whether it is in "fix-up" condition. After slight data cleaning, we have complete records on 36,458

Table 14.1 Summary statistics

Characteristic	Mean	Std Dev	Minimum	Maximum
Transacting properties				
(n = 36,458)				
Transaction price	$232,330	$124,469	$50,000	$1,000,000
Land area	18,994 ft^2	15,005 ft^2	2,000 ft^2	87,120 ft^2
Living area	2,150 ft^2	792 ft^2	800 ft^2	5,000 ft^2
Bedrooms	3.59	0.72	2	6
Full baths	1.81	0.65	1	4
Half baths	0.75	0.52	0	3
Structure age	35.0 years	23.6 years	0	99
Central air conditioning	63.6%	48.1%	0	1
Garage	80.2%	39.8%	0	1
Any fireplaces	71.2%	45.3%	0	1
Fix-up condition	3.6%	18.6%	0	1
Transaction date	December 2000	2 years 4 months	January 1996	July 2004
Repeat transactions				
(n = 3,696)				
Most recent transaction price	$266,818	$128,598	$50,000	$955,000
Previous transaction price	$209,064	$105,656	$50,000	$850,000
Price ratio	1.31	0.30	0.43	4.0
Most recent transaction date	March 2002	1.93 years	January 1996	July 2004
Previous transaction date	April 1999	1.91 years	January 1996	June 2004
Time between transactions	2.94 years	1.94 years	0 years	8.32 years

single-family detached properties that transacted during 1996–2004, including 3,696 properties that transacted twice. Table 14.1 shows summary statistics for the sample.

Table 14.2 shows the coefficients of two versions of a hedonic price model and two versions of a repeat-sales model estimated on these data. The constant-age hedonic is the standard form of this model. For this group of properties, the data show essentially no age-related depreciation, so there is virtually no difference between the constant-age and varying-age hedonic models. This is hardly the usual result, though: generally if structure age is not included then the effect of

Table 14.2 Estimated regression coefficients

Year	Constant-age hedonic	Varying-age hedonic	Repeat-sales (standard)	Repeat-sales (Shiller)[a]
Intercept	6.43[b]	6.34[b]	–	–
Bedrooms	−0.005	−0.004	–	–
Full baths	0.114[b]	0.113[b]	–	–
Half baths	0.073[b]	0.072[b]	–	–
Age × 10^{-3}	−1.69[b]	–	–	a
Age^2 × 10^{-5}	2.19[b]	–	–	a
LnUnitSqFt	0.550[b]	0.565[b]	–	–
LnLandSqFt	0.107[b]	0.102[b]	–	–
Central A/C	0.115[b]	0.113[b]	–	–
Garage	0.052[b]	0.053[b]	–	–
Any fireplaces	0.066[b]	0.066[b]	–	–
Fix-up	−0.211[b]	−0.210[b]	–	–
1997	0.011	0.011	0.008	−0.001
1998	0.037[b]	0.037[b]	0.033[b]	0.030[b]
1999	0.085[b]	0.086[b]	0.082[b]	0.082[b]
2000	0.141[b]	0.141[b]	0.138[b]	0.144[b]
2001	0.210[b]	0.210[b]	0.225[b]	0.223[b]
2002	0.335[b]	0.334[b]	0.339[b]	0.333[b]
2003	0.447[b]	0.446[b]	0.457[b]	0.446[b]
2004	0.535[b]	0.534[b]	0.574[b]	0.542[b]

[a] The table shows the sum of year and age effects.
[b] Significantly different from zero at the 99 percent level of confidence.

age-related depreciation is confounded with the price index (as it is in the standard form of the repeat-sales model) and the estimated price index appreciates less rapidly. The Shiller form of the repeat-sales model, however, controls for the effect of age-related depreciation, and so is more comparable to the constant-age hedonic.

Table 14.3 shows the number of properties transacting in each year, the median and average transaction prices, and the price of a representative property. It also shows the price indexes implied by the coefficients estimated for the hedonic and repeat-sales models, where the value of the price index is the antilog of the parameter estimate.

The six estimates of the price index are shown in Figure 14.1. The representative-property method suggests wild annual price fluctuations, as can be expected with even a careful application of this method. The other five methods, though, all yield similar estimates of annual housing price growth rates; the median-price method deviates noticeably but not sharply from the other methods.

Table 14.3   Estimated price indices

Year	N	Median ($)	Average ($)	Representative property ($)	Hedonic (constant age)	Hedonic (varying age)	Repeat (standard)	Repeat (Shiller)
1996	2,147	160,000	183,356	149,900	1	1	1	1
1997	3,192	164,500	189,903	192,500	1.0107	1.0111	1.0076	0.9989
1998	3,906	166,000	194,283	158,000	1.0376	1.0381	1.0337	1.0308
1999	4,501	170,000	203,076	170,000	1.0890	1.0895	1.0854	1.0852
2000	4,256	180,000	213,549	220,000	1.1510	1.1514	1.1485	1.1551
2001	4,264	190,000	227,580	205,000	1.2341	1.2336	1.2519	1.2494
2002	5,462	219,900	252,864	265,000	1.3979	1.3971	1.4042	1.3946
2003	5,704	245,000	278,552	264,500	1.5633	1.5616	1.5796	1.5617
2004	3,209	266,000	304,778	295,000	1.7066	1.7057	1.7758	1.7190

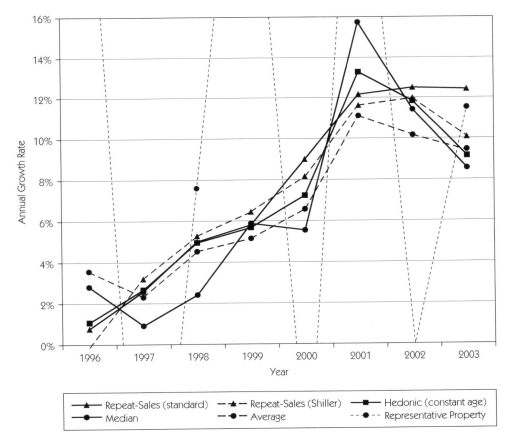

Figure 14.1   Alternative estimates of annual price changes.

In most applications, the repeat-sales model is used because no data on hedonic characteristics are available, and the analyst must simply assume that no properties were improved between transactions. This means that the increase in property values that would otherwise be attributable to improvements is instead confounded with the price index, so that the price index estimated from the standard repeat-sales model generally shows the most rapid rate of increase. Our application illustrates this upward bias: on average, the standard repeat-sales model shows the largest annual price increases. In contrast, the constant-age hedonic price model and the Shiller repeat-sales model control for improvements, and therefore yield the best estimates of price increases of a constant-quality property. Of course, these models cannot be estimated without contemporaneous observations on hedonic characteristics. For many purposes, though, the added accuracy of a price index estimated using the full set of hedonic data will be important.

14.4   DATA SOURCES

As noted, transaction prices provide the most reliable information about underlying market values, but they are not necessarily easy to obtain. Moreover, there are typically few transactions in any given market over any limited study period, even in the USA where properties transact relatively frequently. Fortunately, the near-universal application of real property taxes and deed transfer/recording fees in the USA gives local governments an incentive to keep relatively good records on both transactions and hedonic characteristics. Although the standard practice – as in the empirical example – is to retain data for only the most recent transaction (or two) of each property, and for only the latest set of hedonic characteristics, declining data storage costs suggest that saving older data will gradually become the norm.

Several other sources of data on estimated market values of properties are also available. Property tax assessment records, of course, show the assessed value of each property, and have been used to estimate price indexes; moreover, these databases include information on nontransacting properties – which is essential for correcting sample selectivity bias.

The robust US mortgage market means that appraisals are conducted for most properties not just at purchase but also for relatively frequent refinancings; for purchases, transaction prices are recorded as well. Unfortunately, these mortgage transaction databases, which form the basis for the OFHEO and Freddie Mac repeat-sales price indexes, do not record hedonic characteristics and are not public.

Real estate agents in the USA maintain multiple listing service (MLS) databases of properties offered for sale (and sometimes for rent), typically including extensive information on hedonic characteristics as well as transaction date and price. These data represent a probably nonrandom sample of all transactions, and may possibly include errors of exaggeration in their property descriptors, but may be adequate for price index estimation.

Finally, the US federal government conducts the biennial American Housing Survey, recording information on an extremely rich set of hedonic characteristics as well as demographic and other household characteristics. Each homeowner is asked to assess the value of the property, although these owner-assessments may be biased. Similarly, each renter is asked to report rent paid, although it can be difficult to adjust fully for utilities and other services that may be included in the contract rent. Transaction prices and dates are recorded for recently transacting properties, but the small sample size in each metropolitan area makes it difficult to use AHS data to estimate price indexes.

14.5 CONCLUSION

The uses to which high-quality housing price indexes can be put are myriad. Government stabilization policy may depend on estimates of growth in household wealth, of which the largest component is housing equity. Risk management of mortgage portfolios depends on accurate modeling of default and prepayment behavior, in which price movements are of first-order importance. Property development and business expansion decisions may be driven by projections of local market strength, in which housing prices are a primary indicator. Household formation and migration decisions are affected by the level and rate of increase of house prices. Government rental assistance programs are designed using information on typical rents for local units of a given quality. And both academic and policy-oriented researchers require good estimates of housing price indexes to study these and other issues, from the effectiveness of housing-assistance programs to the adequacy of retirement savings.

The purpose of this chapter has been to introduce housing price index estimation in a way that reveals its essential accessibility. The basic hedonic price model is highly intuitive, and repeat-sales and hybrid models are fairly straightforward extensions of it. Most of the varied econometric issues that arise are fairly easy to address. Moreover, in truth the estimation of a price index using the hedonic price model, or any of its extensions, is fairly robust to econometric and data problems, in the sense that even a fairly rudimentary application of these models will yield a price index that is "good enough" for most purposes.

Bibliography

Case, B. and Quigley, J. M. 1991: The dynamics of real estate prices. *Review of Economics and Statistics*, 83, 50–8.

Englund, P., Quigley, J. M., and Redfearn, C. L. 1998: Improved price indexes for real estate: measuring the course of Swedish housing prices. *Journal of Urban Economics*, 44, 171–96.

Quigley, J. M. 1995: A simple hybrid model for estimating real estate price indexes. *Journal of Housing Economics*, 4, 1–12.

Shiller, R. J. 1993: Measuring asset values for cash settlement in derivative markets: hedonic repeated measures indices and perpetual futures. *The Journal of Finance*, 48, 911–31.

PART IV

Urban Transportation

Urban Transportation

Transportation economics is a well-defined field of economics. Its subfields can be categorized along three dimensions: transport mode, passenger/freight, and supply/demand/policy; maritime freight supply is therefore a subfield according to this categorization. Supply deals with both technology and industrial organization, and policy subsumes regulation.

Urban transportation economics by definition deals with transportation in cities. But, as with urban economics, its core material has been determined by the intellectual history of the subject. Two bodies of urban transport economic theory, the theory of congestion and applied discrete choice theory, are especially important. Both have been extensively adapted to problems in other areas of economics, and the principal developer of each is a Nobel Prize winner – William Vickrey and Daniel McFadden, respectively.

The theory of marginal cost pricing has a long and distinguished history. The basic idea is that individuals will make socially efficient decisions if they face the social cost of their decisions and enjoy the social benefits from them. When they do not, there is an *uninternalized externality*. Arthur Pigou proposed taxation as a way to internalize externalities. The best-known example is that of pollution. When a firm emits pollution that it does not pay for, the marginal social cost of its production exceeds the marginal private cost. Since the firm does not face the full cost of its production, it overproduces. This externality can be corrected by imposing a tax on the firm for each unit it produces, equal to the difference between its marginal social and marginal private costs. Imposition of such a tax will cause the firm to face the full marginal social cost of its production, and hence to make efficient output decisions. William Vickrey was among the first to recognize that this argument applies to congestion in transportation, since an individual's travels impose a cost on others, by slowing them down, and the individual is not charged for this cost. Pigouvian pricing of the externality in this context is called *congestion pricing*. Vickrey championed congestion pricing of transportation throughout his life, and most urban transport economists have followed his lead.

The economic theory of congestion has three principal components. The *pricing* of congestible facilities is one. The choice of the capacity or size of congestible facilities is another. The optimal choice of capacity is in principle simple: capacity should be expanded to the point at which the marginal social benefit from increasing capacity equals the marginal social cost. Combining efficient pricing and efficient capacity yields the "self-financing result" that when a congestible facility exhibits constant long-run average costs, the revenue from the optimal congestion toll just covers the cost of constructing optimal capacity. More generally, the efficient subsidy rate is simply related to the degree of returns to scale of the facility. The current wisdom is that freeway travel exhibits more or less constant long-run average cost, while mass transit exhibits decreasing long-run average cost due to economies of density and service frequency. The economic theory of congestion therefore provides a rationale for mass transit receiving a limited subsidy from the public coffers, but not freeway travel. These are *first-best* principles that apply when full efficiency can be achieved. The third principal component of the economic theory of congestion deals with how these principles need to be modified when full efficiency cannot be achieved. A sample question asked in the second-best theory of congestible facilities is how capacity should be chosen when congestion tolls cannot be applied. Yoshitsugu Kanemoto's essay, "Urban Transport Economic Theory," provides an exposition of this body of theory.

In the early 1970s, Daniel McFadden was asked to forecast the demand for a proposed subway line in San Francisco, which at that time had no subway. Note that modal choice is a *discrete* or *qualitative* choice, a choice of *which* rather than how much. How to proceed? He could have studied the modal split in other cities that had subways, and attempted to apply what that revealed about the demand for subway travel to San Francisco. But he adopted a much more ingenious approach. He reasoned that, on a particular journey, individuals choose the mode that gives them the highest utility, and base their choices on the attributes of each potential mode – travel time, schedule frequency, accessibility, comfort, and so on. He posited that the utility an individual obtains from a mode on a journey is the sum of two components, a systematic component, which is common across individuals in a particular income-demographic group, and an idiosyncratic component capturing unobserved individual attributes and personal tastes. Positing too that the systematic component of utility for individuals in a particular group for a particular journey on a particular mode is a linear function of that mode's attributes for that journey, and treating the idiosyncratic component as an error term, on the basis of microdata that he had on individuals' modal choices in the San Francisco Bay area, he was able to estimate the parameters of the systematic component of utility for the various groups in the population. Then, knowing what the characteristics of the subway would be for the various journeys, he was able to estimate the systematic component of utility for subway travel for individuals in a particular group on a particular journey. Then, applying the principle that each individual chooses the mode that provides the highest utility, he was able to forecast the proportion of individuals in each group on each journey who would choose to switch from their current mode to the subway.

The procedure that McFadden developed forms the conceptual basis for all sophisticated travel demand forecasting done today. The details of McFadden's procedure and how it has been adapted to forecast the effects of alternative congestion pricing schemes, in one study on a private toll road in Orange County and in another on the San Francisco Bay bridges, is the topic of "Urban Passenger Travel Demand," by André de Palma, Robin Lindsey, and Nathalie Picard.

It was mentioned in the Preface that one of the major developments that led to the creation of urban economics as a field was the transportation and land-use studies of the 1950s and 1960s. Interest in the relationship between urban transportation and land use has continued unabated. Transportation availability strongly affects land use, but land use also strongly affects transportation demand. Forecasting land use is the weakest link in urban traffic demand forecasting, and has been made more difficult by the suburbanization of employment and the increased importance of noncommuting trips. John McDonald's essay, "Urban Transportation and Land Use," examines how economists go about forecasting the effects of urban transportation improvements on land use.

Urban transport policy generates heated debate. One reason is that it so directly affects people's lives, another that winners and losers are usually clearly identifiable, and yet another that professional cultures collide. Economists favor market-based, pricing solutions; planners, bureaucrats, and regulators instinctively want to regulate; and engineers incline toward technology- and infrastructure-based solutions. In "Urban Transport Policies: The Dutch Struggle with Market Failures and Policy Failures," Piet Rietveld surveys the landscape of urban transport policy in the Netherlands, which has the highest density of population among developed countries.

Scarcity is central to economics. We – economists and students of economics – need to continually remind ourselves that a situation that is unpleasant or even morally offensive may, because of scarcity, nonetheless be efficient or even socially optimal. Traffic congestion is an example. The spatial concentration of economic activity that is the defining characteristic of cities generates agglomeration benefits but also traffic congestion. While our instincts may tell us that long delays in traffic are "outrageous," as economists we should aim not to eliminate traffic congestion but to insure that its level is socially optimal.

CHAPTER FIFTEEN

Urban Transport Economic Theory

Yoshitsugu Kanemoto

15.1 INTRODUCTION

Although the transportation sector constitutes a small share of total production (about 3 percent of GDP in the United States), transportation costs play a critical role in the formation and workings of cities. For example, the introduction of urban transit such as trolley lines and subways in the nineteenth century was the key to the emergence of giant cities such as New York (Mills & Hamilton 1989). In the twentieth century, the internal combustion engine caused another revolution in urban structure, leading to more decentralized metropolitan areas. The striking difference in urban form between Tokyo and Los Angeles is clear evidence of the importance of transportation. Tokyo is a mass-transit-based city and the population density of the metropolitan area is about 3,424 per km^2. Los Angeles, an automobile-based city, has a much lower density: the population density of Los Angeles – Riverside – Orange County CMSA is 188 per km^2 and even for the core area (Los Angeles – Long Beach PMSA) the density is 916 per km^2.

Urban transportation is associated with a variety of externalities, and for technological and political reasons it is difficult to "price" them properly. Most important among them, quantitatively, is traffic congestion. Traffic jams during morning and evening rush hours are common in most cities in the world. The magnitude of congestion externalities varies enormously depending on location and time. The Federal Highway Administration in the USA estimates the average congestion cost for passenger cars to be 7.7 cents per mile for urban interstate highways, compared with 0.78 cents for their rural counterparts (Federal Highway Administration 2000). According to Newbery (1990), "Urban central areas at the peak have an average congestion cost of 10 times the average over all roads, and more than 100 times that of the average motorway or rural road." Economists have advocated the adoption of congestion tolls for road transportation for a long time, but – except for a very small number of places, such as Singapore – they have not been instituted. Even where congestion tolls have been introduced, they are rather crude and do not fully reflect wide variations over time and space.

Environmental pollution and accident externalities also involve substantial social costs. The Federal Highway Administration estimates the air pollution costs of passenger cars to be 1.33 cents per mile for urban interstate highways (Federal Highway Administration 2000). Their estimate of crash costs is 1.19 cents per mile. Although these figures are lower than the congestion cost estimates, they are still quite substantial.

Mass transit is not immune from significant externalities either. When demand is low relative to capacity, positive externalities between passengers exist because an increase in demand enables more frequent services. When demand is high, the externalities turn negative, as observed on commuter railways in Tokyo. According to Yamazaki and Asada, optimal congestion tolls can be close to three times as large as the current fares (Yamazaki & Asada 1999).

This chapter examines pricing and investment decisions in the presence of these urban externalities. In particular, we focus on second-best problems under the constraint that many of the externalities are improperly priced.

15.2 Pricing and Investment Decisions: The Basics

15.2.1 Private and social costs

The cost structure of urban transportation is complicated for two reasons. First, because of the high density of activities and interactions in a city, urban transportation causes a variety of externalities such as traffic congestion, air pollution, noise, and that part of accident costs not borne by drivers. Second, consumers incur many different types of user costs in addition to user fees (tolls and fares). For example, automobile users incur motor vehicle running costs (the cost of fuel, tires, engine oil, maintenance, and the value of vehicle wear-and-tear), the opportunity cost of travel time, and traffic accident costs. Users must also pay taxes. Taxes on gasoline are especially heavy in Europe and Japan, where more than half of the retail price is tax. Even in the USA, where the tax rate is much lower, it was about 35 percent of the retail price in 2003. Because taxes are transfers of wealth and do not represent social resource costs, we treat them separately from other cost categories.

We denote the *user cost* per trip by p. This user cost corresponds to the "price" in standard textbook microeconomics. The user cost contains *user fees* such as fuel tax, tolls, and fares. The rest of the user cost is the resource cost, such as *vehicle running costs* and the *value of travel time*. The suppliers of transport services, such as highway authorities and mass transit operators, incur *production costs* of these services. These costs are at least partly covered by user fees. *External costs*, such as air pollution costs, constitute part of the social cost. The social cost does not, however, include user fees because these are simply transfers of income.

Among external costs of transportation, congestion costs have special characteristics because they are externalities imposed by users on users. Each user is simultaneously causing and suffering the congestion externality. Other externalities, such as air pollution, are externalities imposed by the transportation sector on others. Let us briefly explain the congestion externality by taking an example of automobile users. Vehicle running costs depend critically on the speed of traffic. Time and fuel costs are clear examples, but other costs such as tires and maintenance costs also increase when the speed becomes slower. With a small number of vehicles on a road, an increase in traffic does not significantly affect traffic speed. As more and more vehicles enter the road, the speed gets slower, which raises the user costs of all drivers on the same road at that time. The externality arises because an additional vehicle raises the costs of other vehicles.

Let $TSC(Q,K)$ denote total social cost when transport demand is Q and capacity is K. The total social cost is divided into the variable-cost component, $C(Q,K)$, with $C(0,K) = 0$, and the fixed-cost component, $F(K)$. *Marginal social cost (MSC)* is the increase in the total social cost caused by a small increase in transport demand. Mathematically, it can be written as follows:

$$MSC(Q) = \partial TSC(Q,K)/\partial Q = \partial C(Q,K)/\partial Q. \tag{15.1}$$

Since fixed cost does not depend on demand, the marginal social cost equals the marginal social variable cost. Noting that integrating a derivative brings us back the original function, we have

$$C(Q,K) = \int_0^Q MSC(q,K)dq. \tag{15.2}$$

Average social cost (ASC) is $ASC(Q,K) = TSC(Q,K)/Q$ and the *average variable social cost (AVSC)* is $c(Q,K) = C(Q,K)/Q$. The relationship between the total, average, and marginal cost curves is shown in Figure 15.1, where the total variable social cost equals the area below the marginal social cost curve – that is, the hatched area $IHQO$ – as well as the average variable cost times transport demand; that is, rectangle $cGQO$ with thick borders. In the rest of this chapter, we shall repeatedly use the fact that these two areas are equal.

15.2.2   The consumer's surplus

Because of fuel and other taxes, a consumer is faced with a "price" that is different from the resource cost. If the price is denoted by p, the demand curve can be written as $Q = D(p)$. The *consumer's surplus (CS)* is the triangle between the demand curve and the price; that is, the hatched area in Figure 15.2. The *social benefit (SB)* is defined as the area below the demand curve (trapezoid $EGQO$), which includes the expenditure on transportation in addition to the consumer's

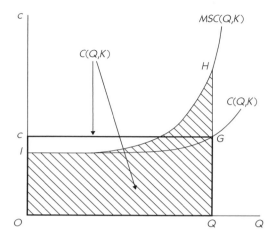

Figure 15.1   The total, marginal, and average cost curves.

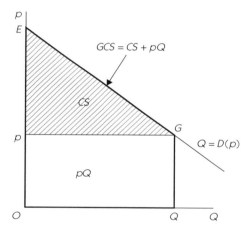

Figure 15.2   The demand curve and the consumer's surplus.

surplus. In Figure 15.2, the hatched area is the consumer's surplus and the rectangle $pGQO$ shows the revenue.

15.2.3   A mass transit example

Let us take an example of a hypothetical mass transit line in a city where heavy subsidies are necessary for it to compete with automobile transportation. Most American and European cities fit this category. The largest Japanese cities, such as Tokyo and Osaka, are in a very different situation where many of the commuter railways are financially self-sufficient and congestion externalities are significant. The analyses of those cases are left to the reader.

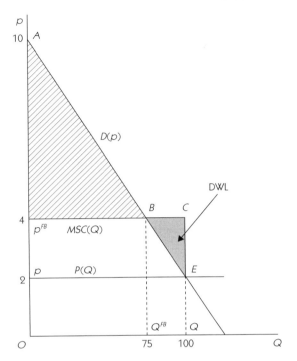

Figure 15.3   The net surplus and the deadweight loss: a mass transit example.

The marginal social cost of the transit system is $4 per trip, where the average trip length is 10 miles. We examine a subsidy to lower the fare to $2 per trip. For simplicity, we assume that the MSC curve is horizontal. The $AVSC$ then equals the MSC. The number of trips is 100,000 per day.

Figure 15.3 shows the net social surplus for this example. With the subsidized fare of $2, the equilibrium is point $E = (p,Q) = (2,100)$, and the SB is trapezoid $AEQO$. Since the area below the MSC curve (area $p^{FB}CQO$) gives the total variable cost, the net surplus is area ABp^{FB} minus area BCE. Raising the price to the level of the MSC increases the net surplus by area BCE. By checking whether any other point along the demand curve has a smaller surplus, one can see that the net surplus is maximized at this point. The optimal solution therefore requires that the price equal the MSC:

$$p^{FB} = MSC(Q,K),\qquad\qquad (15.3)$$

where the superscript FB denotes the first-best solution. The difference in net surplus from the first best is called the *deadweight loss*, which is indicated by DWL in Figure 15.3.

Figure 15.3 assumes that lowering the fare from $4 to $2 increases demand by 25,000 (from 75,000 to 100,000). In this case, the revenue of the transit operator decreases by $100,000 per day (from $300,000 to $200,000), and the deadweight loss is $25,000. If transit demand is more responsive to the fare, the revenue decrease becomes smaller and the deadweight loss larger. For example, if halving the fare increases demand by 75,000, then the revenue remains the same and the deadweight loss is $75,000.

15.2.4   Optimal pricing and capacity investment

The net surplus maximization can be reformulated as social welfare maximization with an aggregate utility function. Let us represent the welfare of society by a quasi-linear utility function, $U(z,Q) = z + u(Q)$, where z is a composite consumer good. This functional form is restrictive, but we can extend our results to a general utility function if we choose an appropriate welfare measure (Kanemoto & Mera 1985).

The budget constraint for the consumer is $Y = z + pQ + T$, where Y is income and T is the lump-sum tax to finance the transportation sector deficit. Maximization of the utility function subject to the budget constraint yields the first-order condition that marginal utility (MU) equals price, $u'(Q) = p$. This condition gives the inverse demand function: the height of the demand curve equals marginal utility. The usual demand function, $Q = D(p)$, is the inverse of the marginal utility function.

Now, without loss of generality, we can normalize the utility function so that $u(0) = 0$. Then, we can show that the transportation component of the utility function coincides with the social benefit: $u(Q) = SB$. SB is the area below the demand curve and the integration of the marginal utility function from 0 to Q yields the SB; that is,

$$u(Q) = \int_0^Q u'(q)dq = SB. \tag{15.4}$$

Substituting into the budget constraint the tax to finance the transportation-sector deficit, $T = -[pQ - C(Q,K) - F(K)]$, we can rewrite the utility function as

$$SW = u(Q) - C(Q,K) - F(K) + Y. \tag{15.5}$$

We call this *social welfare*. Maximization of this social welfare with respect to Q yields the first-order condition that marginal utility equals the MSC: $u'(Q) = \partial C/\partial Q$. Since the consumer's utility maximization requires that marginal utility equal price, we obtain the same optimality condition as before: $p^{FB} = MSC$, as in equation (15.3).

Maximizing social welfare with respect to capacity yields $-\partial C/\partial K = F(K)$. The left-hand side is the reduction in the total variable social cost by a marginal increase in capacity. We call this the *marginal direct benefit of capacity expansion* (MBK). The right-hand side is the *marginal cost of capacity expansion* (MCK), and optimality requires that they be equal (MBK = MCK).

15.3   PRICING AND INVESTMENT WITH DISTORTION
IN OTHER SECTORS

So far, we have implicitly assumed that there is no price distortion in other sectors of the economy. This is simply not true in the real world, where taxes, monopoly power, and improper congestion pricing make market prices diverge from corresponding marginal social costs. For example, it is almost impossible to raise tax revenue in a nondistortionary fashion, and the deadweight loss associated with tax distortion needs to be considered in evaluating any public policy. We take a simple example of mass transit that competes with a highway whose pricing is distorted. The same framework can be applied to other situations, such as two competing highway routes, off-peak pricing with underpriced peak hours, and transportation investment under the presence of urban agglomeration economies.

We use similar notation as in the preceding section and indicate mass transit by subscript 1 and the highway by subscript 2. For example, the prices of mass transit and the highway are p_1 and p_2, respectively. We suppress the capacity of the highway, K_2, because it is taken as exogenous.

In order to represent distortion in highway pricing, we assume a general pricing rule: $p_2 = P_2(Q_2)$. This formulation includes, as its special cases, those with a zero congestion toll and optimal congestion pricing.

We continue to assume a quasi-linear form for the aggregate utility function, $U(z,Q_1,Q_2) = z + u(Q_1,Q_2)$, which now includes two transportation modes. The consumer's utility maximization yields the first-order condition that marginal utilities equal prices: that is, $\partial u(Q_1,Q_2)/\partial Q_1 = p_1$ and $\partial u(Q_1,Q_2)/\partial Q_2 = p_2$. By solving these two equations for Q_1 and Q_2, we obtain demand functions for mass transit and the highway: $Q_1 = D_1(p_1,p_2)$ and $Q_2 = D_2(p_2,p_1)$. Because of the quasi-linear form, the demand functions do not depend on the income of the consumer.

15.3.1   General equilibrium demand functions

Let us now examine the effect of changing the mass transit price, p_1. A change in the transit price changes the demand for the highway and causes a change in its price. This in turn affects demand for the transit system. We obtain the effect of a transit price change on each of these two modes, taking into account the repercussions on the other mode.

Note that the pricing rule, $p_2 = P_2(Q_2)$, and the highway demand function, $Q_2 = D_2(p_2,p_1)$, have only three variables including the transit price. Given the transit price, p_1, therefore, these two equations determine the remaining two variables, Q_2 and p_2. In particular, the highway price is determined as a function of the transit price, which we write as $p_2 = p_2^*(p_1)$. By substituting this relationship into the demand function for mass transit, we obtain the demand for mass transit as a function of its price only:

$$Q_1 = D_1(p_1,p_2^*(p_1)) \equiv d_1(p_1). \tag{15.6}$$

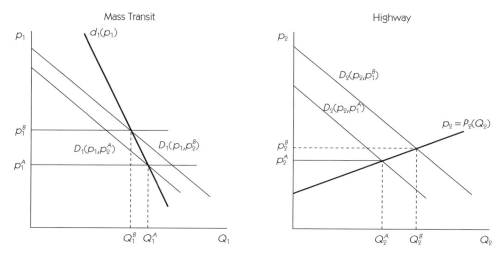

Figure 15.4 Partial and general equilibrium demand curves.

We call $Q_1 = d_1(p_1)$ the *general equilibrium demand function* for mass transit, since it depicts the relationship between its price and demand, taking into account general equilibrium repercussions on other sectors of the economy.

Figure 15.4 illustrates the derivation of the general equilibrium demand function. Let us start with the transit price, p_1^B. Given this price level, we can draw the (partial equilibrium) demand curve for the highway sector, $Q_2 = D_2(p_2, p_1^B)$. The intersection of this demand curve with the pricing rule curve, $p_2 = P_2(Q_2)$, gives the equilibrium highway price, p_2^B. Coming back to the mass transit sector, this highway price, coupled with the transit price that we set earlier, determines demand for mass transit, $Q_1^B = D_1(p_1^B, p_2^B)$. If the transit price falls to p_1^A, then some of the highway users shift to the transit system, and the highway demand curve moves down to $Q_2 = D_2(p_2, p_1^A)$. This lowers the highway price to p_2^A, which in turn shifts down the demand curve for mass transit. Demand for mass transit is then $Q_1^A = D_1(p_1^A, p_2^A)$. Connecting points such as (Q_1^B, p_1^B) and (Q_1^A, p_1^A), we obtain the general equilibrium demand curve, $Q_1 = d_1(p_1)$.

The general equilibrium demand function for the highway is defined by

$$Q_2 = D_2[p_2^*(p_1), p_1] \equiv d_2(p_1). \tag{15.7}$$

This demand function gives demand for the highway as a function of the transit price. We can change the argument of the demand function to the highway price, p_2, using the relationship between the two prices, $p_2 = p_2^*(p_1)$, obtained above. Note however that, since the pricing rule uniquely determines the relationship between Q_2 and p_2, this demand function must coincide with the pricing rule.

15.3.2   The consumer's surplus with general equilibrium demand functions

Next, let us examine how to measure the consumer's surplus in our multi-market situation. The difficulty we face is that the consumer's utility, $U(z,Q_1,Q_2) = z + u(Q_1,Q_2)$, is not separable between the two markets. We have to find a way to divide the utility between the two markets. The trick is to evaluate small changes and sum them to obtain a welfare measure for a large change.

In the single-market case, we have seen that the SB coincides with the transportation component of the utility function, $u(Q)$, if the utility function is normalized so that $u(0) = 0$. Here, we also assume that $u(0,0) = 0$. Figure 15.5 shows the effect of lowering the transit price from p_1^B to p_1^A. This change increases demand for transit from Q_1^B to Q_1^A and reduces demand for the highway from Q_2^B to Q_2^A. We divide these changes into small changes and evaluate them separately.

A small change in the mass transit price, Δp_1, changes demands for mass transit and the highway by $\Delta Q_1 = d_1'(p_1)\Delta p_1$ and $\Delta Q_2 = d_2'(p_1)\Delta p_1$. The induced change in utility is obtained by multiplying these demand changes by marginal utilities of the transportation services: $\Delta u = (\partial u/\partial Q_1)\Delta Q_1 + (\partial u/\partial Q_2)\Delta Q_2$. Since the consumer's utility maximization insures that marginal utility equal price, this utility change can be rewritten as $\Delta u = p_1\Delta Q_1 + p_2\Delta Q_2$. We can therefore obtain a change in utility by multiplying a change in quantity demanded by the price. In Figure 15.5, these are represented by narrow hatched rectangles in the transit market and shaded ones in the highway market. The sum of these areas yields the utility change. By reducing the size of Δp_1 to zero, we obtain the exact estimates. Thus, the area under a general equilibrium demand curve gives the social benefit.

The general equilibrium demand curve in the highway market coincides with the pricing rule. The pricing rule is typically based on supply-side conditions. For example, in the case of road transportation, it is determined mainly by time costs, operating costs, and fuel taxes. The reader may have difficulty in understanding why this supply-side relationship determines the consumer's surplus. We can offer the following intuitive explanation. The height of the partial equilibrium demand curve shows the consumer's willingness to pay, but the demand curve shifts when the mass transit price changes. For example, p_2^B in Figures 15.4 and 15.5 gives willingness to pay at quantity Q_2^B when the transit price is p_1^B. If the transit price becomes lower, the partial equilibrium demand curve shifts leftward and demand for the highway decreases. Since the new equilibrium point must be on the pricing rule curve, the highway price falls to a level such as p_2'. Willingness to pay at this new point given by the new partial equilibrium demand curve is p_2'. Since the equilibrium point moves along the pricing rule curve, the area below the curve gives the SB.

15.3.3   A mass transit example: a fare subsidy

We now extend the earlier numerical example in Figure 15.3 to allow for price distortion in the highway market. Recall that we examined the effects of lowering

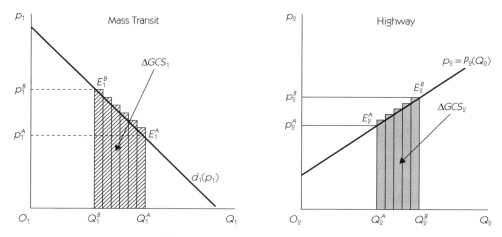

Figure 15.5   The social benefit.

the fare from the *MSC* of $4 per trip to the subsidized fare of $2. Mass transit demand is 75,000 per day if the fare is $4, and becomes 100,000 if it is lowered to $2. On the highway side, we assume that demand is 225,000 trips in the $4 case and 200,000 in the $2 case. Total demand is then the same at 300,000 in both cases. We assume moderate congestion on the highway so that traffic congestion there is slightly mitigated if the transit fare is reduced to $2. The user cost per trip is $3.20 if the fare is $4, and it becomes $3 if the fare is lowered to $2. These user costs include time costs, operating costs, and fuel taxes. In order to obtain the social cost, we have to subtract the fuel tax and add external costs such as air pollution costs. The fuel tax is assumed to be $0.20 and external costs to be $0.50 per trip in both cases. The social costs are then $3.30 and $3.50. Note that these costs are not marginal costs, but average costs. The external costs of $0.30 do not include the congestion externality, because this is implicit in the increase in user cost from $3 to $3.20. Average costs per trip are summarized in Table 15.1.

Table 15.1   Average costs per trip

	$4 fare case		$2 fare case	
	Mass transit	*Highway*	*Mass transit*	*Highway*
Traffic (1,000 trips)	75	225	100	200
User cost	$4.00	$3.20	$2.00	$3.00
Fuel tax or fare	$4.00	$0.20	$2.00	$0.20
Supplier cost	$4.00	$0.00	$2.00	$0.00
External costs	$0.00	$0.50	$0.00	$0.50

Note: External costs in the last row do not include a congestion externality.

Panel (a) in Figure 15.6 shows changes in the SBs caused by lowering the fare from \$4 to \$2. The hatched area on the left shows the increase in the SB in the mass transit market and the shaded area on the right is the decrease in the SB in the highway market. Henceforth, we adopt the convention that a hatched area indicates an increase in benefits (or a decrease in costs) and a shaded area a decrease in benefits. The increase in the SB in the mass transit market is \$75,000 and the decrease in the highway is \$77,500. In order to obtain the benefit of the price change, we have to subtract the increase in total social cost from the increase in the SB. As shown in panel (b) of Figure 15.6, the increase in demand for mass transit raises the social cost by \$100,000 per day, which is indicated by the shaded area. The induced decrease in highway traffic from 225,000 to 200,000 lowers the social cost by \$127,500. By subtracting these from the changes in the SB, we can see that the social surplus decreases by \$25,000 in the mass transit market and increases by \$50,000 in the highway market. The net benefit is then \$25,000. Even though we assume fairly mild congestion on the highway, subsidizing mass transit to reduce its fare is socially beneficial.

15.3.4 The second-best price and capacity for mass transit

Next, we derive the condition for the second-best optimum when the highway price is distorted. The budget constraint for the consumer is $z + p_1 Q_1 + p_2 Q_2 = Y - T$, where, as before, T is the tax to finance the deficit of the transportation sector and satisfies

$$T = -[p_1 Q_1 - C_1(Q_1, K_1) - F_1(K_1)] - [p_2 Q_2 - C_2(Q_2) - F_2]. \tag{15.8}$$

Substituting the budget constraint and the general equilibrium demand functions into the utility function yields

$$U^*(p_1, K_1) = u[d_1(p_1), d_2(p_1)] - C_1[d_1(p_1), K_1] - F_1(K_1) - C_2[D_2(p_1)] - F_2 + Y. \tag{15.9}$$

The first-order conditions for optimal price, p_1, and capacity, K_1, are as follows:

$$\frac{\partial U^*}{\partial p_1} = \left[\frac{\partial U}{\partial Q_1} - MSC_1\right] d_1'(p_1) + \left[\frac{\partial U}{\partial Q_2} - MSC_2\right] d_2'(p_1) - 0, \tag{15.10}$$

$$\frac{\partial U^*}{\partial K_1} = -\frac{\partial C_1}{\partial K_1} - F_1'(K_1) = 0. \tag{15.11}$$

As seen before, utility maximization of the consumer yields $p_i = MU_i$ for both sectors. Substituting these relationships into equation (15.10) and rearranging terms, we obtain

$$p_1 - MSC_1 = -\frac{d_2'(p_1)}{d_1'(p_1)}[P_2(Q_2) - MSC_2]. \tag{15.12}$$

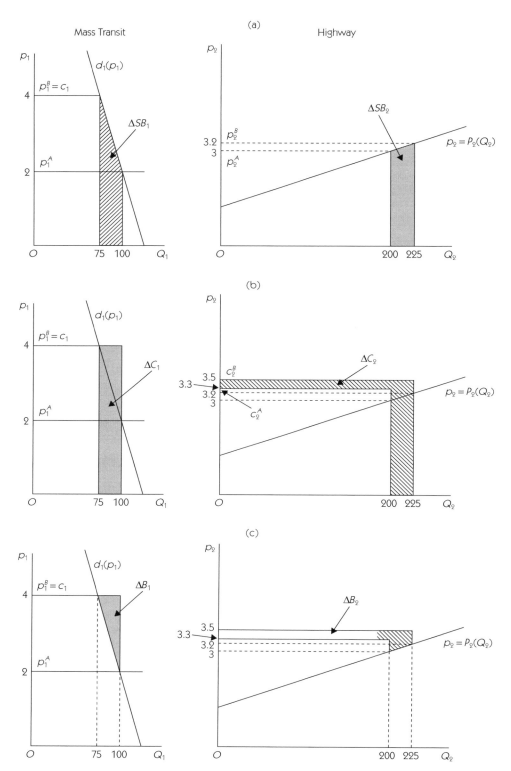

Figure 15.6 The effects of a reduction in transit price: (a) the social benefit; (b) the total social costs; (c) the social surplus.

It is usually the case that general equilibrium demand for mass transit is downward sloping: $d_1'(p_1) < 0$. If there is sufficient substitutability between mass transit and the highway, a rise in the price of mass transit will increase demand for the highway: $d_2'(p_1) > 0$. In such a case, when the highway is underpriced – that is, $p_2 < MSC_2(Q_2)$ – the mass transit price must also be lower than the MSC.

In a special case where the total demand for the two modes is fixed, we have $d_1(p_1) + d_2(p_1) = \text{const}$. In this case, the decrease in demand for mass transit equals the increase in demand for the highway – that is, $d_1'(p_1) = -d_2'(p_1)$ – and we obtain

$$p_1 - MSC_1 = P_2(Q_2) - MSC_2; \qquad (15.13)$$

that is, the price–MSC margins for the two modes must be equal. Arnott and Kraus (2003) offer more general and detailed discussions on this special case.

Linear demand and pricing rule functions consistent with our numerical example are as follows:

$$d_1(p_1) = -12.5p_1 + 125, \qquad (15.14)$$

$$d_2(p_2) = 12.5p_1 + 175, \qquad (15.15)$$

$$P_2(Q_2) = \frac{1}{125}Q_2 + 1.4, \qquad (15.16)$$

and the marginal social costs are

$$MSC_1 = 4, \qquad (15.17)$$

$$MSC_2 = 0.2p_1 + 4.5. \qquad (15.18)$$

Since the sum of the demands in the two markets is constant, the differences between the prices (user costs) and the $MSCs$ are equal in the two markets, as in equation (15.13). Substituting equations (15.14)–(15.18) into equation (15.13), we obtain the second-best prices, $p_1^{SB} = 23/11 \cong 2.0909$ and $p_2^{SB} \cong 3.0909$. In this example, a heavy subsidy to make the transit fare almost a half of the MSC is second-best optimal.

We have examined an example with mild congestion on a highway. In large metropolitan areas such as Tokyo and New York City, with more acute congestion, the price–MSC margin in road transportation is much larger. In downtown Tokyo, it is estimated to be about 27 yen per km per vehicle. Mass transit fares per person are somewhere around 12–20 yen per km. If the two modes are substitutes and the total demand for the two modes is inelastic, the second-best optimal transit fares could be significantly negative. In Tokyo, however, congestion in mass transit is also severe in peak hours. Furthermore, most of the commuters are already using mass transit and it is not clear how much traffic will shift from automobiles to mass transit. Rigorous empirical studies are necessary to determine the optimal subsidies to mass transit. Unfortunately, in many countries substantial subsidies are given to mass transit without rigorous economic analysis to justify them.

The condition for optimal capacity given in equation (15.11) is the same as the single-market case: the marginal direct benefit of capacity expansion, $MBK_1 = -\partial C_1/\partial K_1$, must equal its marginal cost, $MCK_1 = F_1'(K_1)$. Note that this condition is obtained because the price of mass transit is chosen (second-best) optimally. Otherwise, a change in the price caused by capacity investment induces a change in the deadweight loss.

15.3.5   Cost–benefit analysis of transportation investment

The framework that we have used in analyzing a fare subsidy can be applied to transportation investment. The only addition is the effect of the investment on the social cost. Let us take the example in Figure 15.6 and examine the investment in mass transit to reduce its operating costs from \$4 per trip to \$2. In the fare subsidy case, the same reduction in the mass transit price was not accompanied by a decrease in the social cost. We now have to add this element. The effects on the SB are the same as in Figure 15.6. Because of the cost reduction in mass transit, the effects on total social costs are different from those of Figure 15.6. In panel (a) of Figure 15.7, the hatched area on the mass transit side shows the reduction in social costs due to the operating cost reduction. The shaded area represents the increase in costs due to the demand increase. Adding Figure 15.6 and panel (a) of Figure 15.7, we obtain the benefit of investment shown in panel (b) of Figure 15.7.

Although the figures look somewhat complicated, the calculation of the benefit is quite simple. First, based on demand forecasts, we estimate the general equilibrium demand functions. In practice, demand curves are assumed to be straight lines connecting equilibrium points with and without the investment project. Second, we compute the areas below the demand curves to obtain SBs. Third, given the demand forecasts, we estimate the changes in total social costs. Finally, we subtract the sum of the latter from that of the former to yield the benefit of the project. This process is the same as cost–benefit analysis in a first-best world. So long as we use the right prices and costs, no change is necessary even in a second-best world with distorted prices.

If we make the usual assumption that the demand curves are straight lines, we have a simple cost–benefit formula. If demand changes from Q_i^B to Q_i^A in market i, and if prices and total social costs change from p_i^B and C_i^B to p_i^A and C_i^A, respectively, the increase in the SB is as follows:

$$\Delta SB_i = \frac{1}{2}(p_i^A + p_i^B)(Q_i^A - Q_i^B), \tag{15.19}$$

and the increase in social costs is

$$\Delta C_i = C_i^A - C_i^B \tag{15.20}$$

in market i. Summing the difference between these two over all markets yields the social surplus of investment:

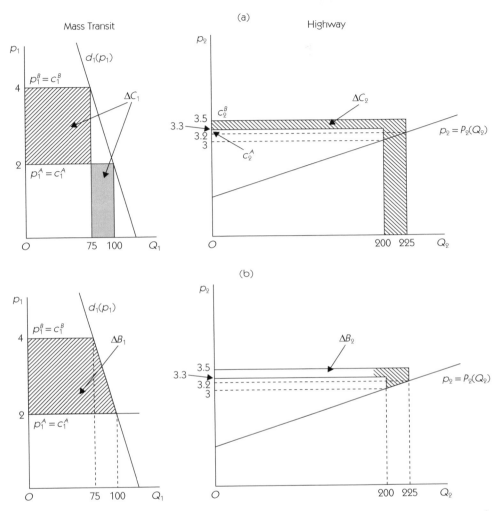

Figure 15.7 The effects of investment in mass transit on total social costs and the social surplus: (a) the total social costs; (b) the benefits.

$$\Delta B = \sum_i \left\{ \frac{1}{2}(p_i^A + p_i^B)(Q_i^A - Q_i^B) - (C_i^A - C_i^B) \right\}. \tag{15.21}$$

In cost–benefit analysis, we compare this benefit with the cost of the investment.

15.4 CONCLUSION

We have seen how to analyze the welfare impact of pricing and investment policies in urban transportation. The fact that cities inevitably have many externalities that are not properly priced makes the analysis somewhat complicated. Furthermore, tax revenue to finance a public project is almost always raised in a distortionary fashion, and the deadweight loss associated with this needs to be taken into account. What you have to do in evaluating real-world problems, however, is quite simple, as long as you assume convenient functional forms such as linear demand functions.

It would be a rewarding exercise to pick an example in the city in which you live and conduct a cost–benefit analysis of a change of some aspect of transportation policies. What you have to obtain, or estimate, are prices, costs, and quantities demanded in the cases with and without the proposed change. With these numbers, you should be able to apply the methodologies explained in this chapter to calculate the benefits of the proposal. For detailed explanations of techniques used in cost–benefit analysis, we refer readers to Boardman, Greenberg, Vining, and Weimer (2001).

Acknowledgments

I would like to thank Richard Arnott, Yukihiro Kidokoro, and an anonymous referee for valuable comments. Support from the Research Institute of Economy, Trade, and Industry is gratefully acknowledged.

Bibliography

Arnott, R. and Kraus, M. 2003: Principles of transport economics. In R. W. Hall (ed.), *Handbook of Transportation Science*, 2nd edn. Norwell, MA: Kluwer, 689–726.

Boardman, A. E., Greenberg, D. H., Vining, A. R., and Weimer, D. L. 2001: *Cost–Benefit Analysis: Concepts and Practice*, 2nd edn. Upper Saddle River, NJ: Prentice Hall.

Federal Highway Administration 2000: *Addendum to the 1997 Federal Highway Cost Allocation Study Final Report*. Washington, DC: US Department of Transportation, Federal Highway Administration.

Kanemoto, Y. and Mera, K. 1985: General equilibrium analysis of the benefits of large transportation improvements. *Regional Science and Urban Economics*, 15(3), 343–63.

Mills, E. S. and Hamilton, B. W. 1989: *Urban Economics*, 4th edn. Glenview, IL: Scott, Foresman.

Mohring, H. 1976: *Transportation Economics*. Cambridge, MA: Ballinger.

Newbery, D. M. 1990: Pricing and congestion: economic principles relevant to pricing roads. *Oxford Review of Economic Policy*, 6(2), 22–38.

Yamazaki, F. and Asada, Y. 1999: The estimation of social costs of railway congestion and optimal fares. *The Quarterly Journal of Housing and Land Economics (Jutaku Tochi Keizai)*, 34, 4–11 (in Japanese).

CHAPTER SIXTEEN

Urban Passenger Travel Demand

*André de Palma, Robin Lindsey,
and Nathalie Picard*

16.1 INTRODUCTION

The idea of tolling roads to reduce traffic congestion was suggested back in 1920. For several decades, road pricing was largely dismissed as impractical and publicly unacceptable, and early attempts to introduce tolls on urban roads foundered because of poor marketing strategies and political opposition. But a number of road-pricing projects are now in operation or planned around the world, and in the 1990s the US federal government introduced a Value Pricing program to fund innovative road and parking pricing schemes.

This essay reviews two econometric studies of road pricing in the United States. One, by Lam and Small (2001), concerns a toll-lanes project on State Route 91 in Orange County, California, which was the first Value Pricing project to be implemented. Lam and Small use data obtained from users of the freeway to estimate individual choice models of whether to drive on the toll lanes and related travel decisions. The second study, by Bhat and Castelar (2002), investigates the effects of hypothetical congestion-pricing initiatives in the San Francisco Bay Area. Their study illustrates how traveler responses to policies that have yet to be implemented can be estimated.

The two studies focus on the role of road pricing to alleviate traffic congestion, which is a rising scourge in large urban areas. In part, support for road pricing derives from the basic economic principle of efficient pricing that motorists should pay the full marginal costs of driving – including congestion, air pollution, and other external costs. Support for road pricing also stems from the fact that more traditional policies to improve personal mobility have not been particularly successful. One policy, which was emphasized in the United Kingdom until the 1980s, was to forecast traffic demand and then to add enough road capacity to accommodate it. This "predict and provide" approach was undermined by the tendency – known as induced or latent demand – for new roads or lanes to fill up with traffic generated by new trips or diverted from other routes or times of day. And by encouraging auto travel, "predict and provide" exacerbated auto-related externalities such as emissions and noise. Another policy, which was popular in the USA during the 1960s and 1970s, was to spend heavily on mass transit systems. The systems were generally very expensive, and some attracted far fewer riders than proponents claimed they would. Moreover, some of the riders were drawn away from buses rather than from their cars, so that reductions in auto traffic were even less than ridership statistics would have suggested.

The sobering experiences from building roads and transit systems highlight the importance of developing a sound conceptual understanding of urban passenger travel demand, and the need for methods to predict modal choice and other personal travel decisions with acceptable accuracy. Careful analysis is also required when planning road-pricing systems that involve large and potentially sunk costs in technology and infrastructure. And because of longstanding opposition to road pricing, it is important to estimate not only its aggregate benefits and costs, but also distributional impacts on potentially disadvantaged groups such as poor families and city-center businesses and residents.

Although the number of established road-pricing projects is still limited, there have been several surprises. For example, when Singapore introduced an area-licensing scheme in 1975, the volume of automobile traffic entering the center during the morning charge period fell by much more than had been forecast, whereas evening traffic fell surprisingly little. Likewise, London's congestion charging scheme, introduced in February 2003, has reduced traffic in the center more than expected while yielding correspondingly lower toll revenues.

The State Route 91 toll-lanes project, featured in the study by Lam and Small (2001) study, also did not develop as envisaged. SR91 was launched in 1995 as a Build–Operate–Transfer (BOT) project, with ownership reverting to the State of California in 2030. The private firm was granted a "noncompete" clause that banned capacity improvements to the freeway. But rapid population growth in the SR91 corridor led to mounting congestion on the toll-free lanes, and in January 2003 the freeway was taken over by a public authority.

The history of the SR91 project illustrates not only difficulties in travel forecasting, but also challenges in harnessing private-sector involvement in urban transportation projects. Various other road-pricing initiatives are under consideration in Europe, the USA, and elsewhere. To avoid further surprises, it will be necessary to develop accurate forecasts of travel demand that account for travel mode, departure time, and other dimensions of behavior. Section 16.2 presents a schema for studying these travel choices, and discusses alternative modeling approaches. Section 16.3 provides a mathematical review of the discrete-choice econometric methods used by Lam and Small (2001) and Bhat and Castelar (2002). The two studies are covered in section 16.4, and conclusions are drawn in section 16.5.

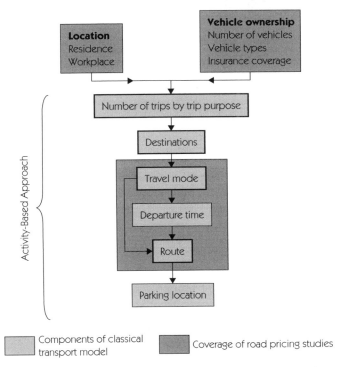

Figure 16.1   Dimensions of urban travel demand.

16.2   TRAVEL AND TRAVEL-RELATED CHOICES

Travel demand is determined by a number of interdependent decisions. Figure 16.1 presents a list of travel or travel-related choices in approximate order from long run to short run. At the top are location and vehicle ownership decisions, and at the bottom is choice of parking location – which is often made on the spur of the moment while cruising for a free parking spot. The three choices to be considered in the two road-pricing studies, travel mode, departure time, and route, are typically intermediate in their time frame. The scheme in Figure 16.1 is not set in stone. Other decisions can be added, such as whether to purchase a transit pass, whether to chain trips, driving speed, and so on. And the time frame for decisions varies by type of trip and person. For example, the parking location decision of a commuter with employer-provided free parking is effectively determined when the job is taken.

Analyzing the full range of travel-related decisions in Figure 16.1 would appear to be a daunting task because of the number of decisions and the range of alternatives available for each one. Indeed, the number of combinations of destinations, modes, departure times, routes, and so on is typically so large that individuals cannot possibly identify the best one via an exhaustive evaluation. And even with today's computing power it is infeasible to model every choice combination even for one person – let alone everyone in an urban area.

It would simplify matters greatly if travel decisions could be modeled as if they were made sequentially, rather than simultaneously. However, for a sequential approach to be valid the choices must be linked consistently in both "forward" and "backward" directions; that is, from top to bottom and from bottom to top in Figure 16.1. Consistency in the forward direction matters because choices made at one level impose constraints on lower levels. For example, a man who decides not to own a car cannot take a trip by driving alone unless he borrows or rents (or steals) one. And a woman who opts for the bus is constrained in her choice of departure time and route by the timetables and routes of bus lines in service. Consistency in the backward direction also matters because choices made at one level should affect the utility of choices made at earlier levels. Choice of route, for example, may affect travel time and therefore the attractiveness of driving rather than taking another mode.

There are several modeling approaches for studying travel demand that differ with respect to their inclusiveness of choice dimensions and their forward and backward consistency. Urban transportation planners have traditionally used the so-called classical (four-step) model, which incorporates the four choice boxes with heavy borders in Figure 16.1. The classical model has been applied with some success to analyze major infrastructure investments. But it is not well suited for evaluating policies such as road pricing that are designed to modify travel behavior in a substantial and/or comprehensive way. For one, the classical model excludes the other choice boxes in Figure 16.1. More fundamentally, the classical model lacks backward consistency because it does not incorporate complete or adequate feedback between the choice levels.

The Activity-Based Approach (ABA) provides another methodology for travel-demand analysis. The ABA seeks to derive travel behavior from the underlying demand to engage in work, shopping, recreation, and other activities. It incorporates feedback between choice dimensions and, as indicated on the left-hand side of Figure 16.1, it encompasses the full range of short- and medium-run travel choices. However, despite rapid progress in recent years, a general ABA theory has yet to be developed, and applications continue to face difficulties with limited data availability.

Discrete-choice models offer a third approach for studying travel demand. They have been applied in numerous travel-demand studies, including the two studies reviewed here. And forward consistency and backward consistency are intrinsic to the structure of discrete-choice models, as the review in the following section points out.

16.3   Discrete-Choice Models of Travel Demand

16.3.1   The model specification

Discrete-choice models became a standard tool for studying travel demand in the 1980s (Ben-Akiva & Bierlaire 1999; Small & Winston 1999). They are used to predict what choices an individual will make from a discrete set of alternatives such as combinations of destination, travel mode, departure time, and so on. Because of differences in their preferences, individuals who are faced with the same set of alternatives may make different choices. Each individual is assumed to know his or her utility from each alternative, and to select the one with the highest utility. But the analyst/econometrician does not know the individual's utilities with certainty because of four potential sources of randomness:

- Unobserved attributes of the alternatives; for example, cleanliness of buses or the attractiveness of a shopping center.
- Unobserved socioeconomic or psychological factors; for example, family-related trip-scheduling constraints.
- Errors in measurement of alternative attributes (e.g., travel time) or socio-economic characteristics (e.g., income).
- The use of instrumental or proxy variables in lieu of the attributes of direct interest; for example, family size as a proxy for availability of a car to commute.

To reflect these uncertainties, and to insure that the theory is consistent with the econometrics, utility is modeled as a random variable. Formally, the utility from alternative i is written as follows:

$$U_i = V_i + \varepsilon_i. \tag{16.1}$$

Term V_i in equation (16.1) is the deterministic part of the utility. It is a function of observable variables and taste parameters, and is referred to as *measured utility* or *systematic utility*. Term ε_i is a *random term* that measures the influence of unobservable individual-specific factors on utility. The model in equation (16.1) is referred to as a Linear Random Utility Model (LRUM), because ε_i enters the utility additively. The simplest case with a *binary* choice will be considered first, followed by the *multinomial* case with three or more alternatives.

16.3.2   The binary choice model

Suppose that there are two alternatives, 0 and 1. The probability that an individual selects alternative 1 is equal to the probability that U_1 is larger than U_0:

$$P_1 = \Pr(V_1 + \varepsilon_1 > V_0 + \varepsilon_0) = \Pr(\varepsilon_0 - \varepsilon_1 < V_1 - V_0) = \Pr\left(\frac{\varepsilon_0 - \varepsilon_1}{\mu} < \frac{V_1 - V_0}{\mu}\right), \tag{16.2}$$

where μ ($\mu > 0$) is a *scale parameter* with a value chosen so that $(\varepsilon_0 - \varepsilon_1)/\mu$ has a standard (normalized) probability distribution. If $F(\cdot)$ is the cumulative distribution function of this distribution, then in equation (16.2), $P_1 = F[(V_1 - V_0)/\mu]$: the choice probability of alternative 1 is an increasing function of the difference between its measured utility (V_1) and the measured utility of the competing alternative (V_0).

The choice probabilities depend *a priori* on the probability distribution assumed for ε_0 and ε_1. The two most common choices are the Gumbel (also called double exponential) distribution and the normal distribution, which lead to the logit and probit models, respectively. While the two distributions have very similar shapes, only the logit model yields closed-form expressions for choice probabilities. Since logit models are featured in the two road-pricing studies, only the Gumbel distribution is considered henceforth.

The Gumbel distribution has a cumulative distribution function $F(\varepsilon) = \exp[-e^{-\varepsilon}]$. If ε_0 and ε_1 are identically and independently distributed (i.i.d.) Gumbel variables, then their difference, $\varepsilon_0 - \varepsilon_1$, has a logistic distribution and the probability of choosing alternative 1 in equation (16.2) is given by the *binary logit* formula:

$$P_1 = \frac{\exp\left(\dfrac{V_1}{\mu}\right)}{\exp\left(\dfrac{V_1}{\mu}\right) + \exp\left(\dfrac{V_0}{\mu}\right)} = \frac{1}{1 + \exp\left(-\dfrac{V_1 - V_0}{\mu}\right)} = \frac{1}{1 + \exp\left(-\dfrac{\Delta V}{\mu}\right)}, \quad (16.3)$$

where $\Delta V \equiv V_1 - V_0$. P_1 is an increasing S-shaped function of ΔV, and is equal to 0.5 if $\Delta V = 0$. If μ is small, the model is nearly deterministic, and the choice probabilities are close to zero or one when ΔV differs much from zero. But if μ is large, P_1 remains close to 0.5 even for large absolute values of ΔV. This means that the model is limited in its ability to forecast travelers' choices. When there are many travelers in a sample who have the same values of ΔV, then P_1 can be interpreted as the proportion of these travelers who choose alternative 1.

16.3.3 The multinomial model

In a multinomial model the number of alternatives in the universal choice set, A, exceeds two. The probability that alternative $i \in A$ is chosen, P_i, is given by the extension of equation (16.2):

$$P_i = \Pr(V_i + \varepsilon_i > V_j + \varepsilon_j, \forall j \neq i, j \in A) = \Pr\left(\frac{\varepsilon_j - \varepsilon_i}{\mu} < \frac{V_i - V_j}{\mu}, \forall j \neq i, j \in A\right). \quad (16.4)$$

If the error terms for all alternatives are i.i.d. Gumbel distributed, the *multinomial logit* (MNL) model results, and the choice probabilities are given by a generalized version of equation (16.3):

$$P_i = \frac{\exp\left(\dfrac{V_i}{\mu}\right)}{\sum_{j \in A} \exp\left(\dfrac{V_j}{\mu}\right)}, \quad i \in A. \quad (16.5)$$

For evaluating the welfare impact of a change in the travel environment such as a new toll, a measure of consumer's or traveler's surplus is required. A measure of surplus is also needed to extend the MNL model to the nested logit model considered below. Traveler's surplus is defined to be the expected value of the maximum utility and, similar to conventional consumer's surplus, it corresponds to the area under the demand curve. For the MNL model, traveler's surplus is given (up to an additive constant) by the expression

$$CS = E\left(\max_{j \in A} U_j\right) = \mu \ln \sum_{j \in A} \exp\left(\frac{V_j}{\mu}\right). \tag{16.6}$$

This term is variously called the *logsum*, *inclusive value*, or *accessibility*. Surplus is an increasing function of the systematic utility of each alternative, with a derivative $\partial CS / \partial V_i = P_i$, $i \in A$ equal to the corresponding choice probability. Note that in a degenerate choice situation where 0 is the only alternative, equation (16.6) reduces to $CS = V_0$.

THE INDEPENDENCE OF IRRELEVANT ALTERNATIVES (IIA) PROPERTY The closed-form expression for the MNL choice probabilities in equation (16.5) helps to reduce computation time for econometric estimation. But the MNL model has a property known as *Independence of Irrelevant Alternatives* (IIA) that is unrealistic in certain choice contexts. The IIA property can be stated in two equivalent ways (Ben-Akiva & Bierlaire 1999, p. 11): (i) "The ratio of the probabilities of any two alternatives is independent of the choice set," or (ii) "The ratio of the choice probabilities of any two alternatives is unaffected by the systematic utilities of any other alternatives."

To illustrate IIA, assume that a trip can be made either by auto or bus. If the two modes are equally attractive in terms of systematic utility, then $V_0 = V_1 \equiv V$, and by equation (16.3) each mode is chosen with probability 1/2. Suppose that the bus company now paints half of its buses red, and leaves the other half blue. Unless travelers care about color, red buses and blue buses will provide the same utility. But if the two types are treated as separate modes, there are now three alternatives and by equation (16.5) each will be chosen with probability 1/3. According to the MNL model, merely repainting the buses has increased bus ridership from 1/2 to 2/3. Furthermore, the ratio of the choice probabilities for auto and blue buses is unchanged (at unity) by introduction of the new red buses. And according to equation (16.6), surplus increases from $V + \mu \ln(2)$ to $V + \mu \ln(3)$, which erroneously suggests that painting buses with different colors is beneficial to travelers.

These implications of the MNL model are clearly unrealistic. One would expect patronage of the red buses to come (almost) exclusively at the expense of blue buses, so that the aggregate bus share of trips remains about 1/2, while the ratio of auto to blue bus travel rises to about 2.

Independence of Irrelevant Alternatives can be avoided by altering the structure of the decision tree. To continue with the mode choice example: instead of a

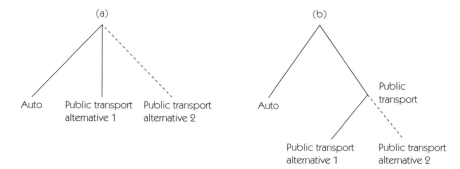

Figure 16.2   Decision trees for the (a) multinomial and (b) nested choice models.

single multinomial choice level, as shown in panel (a) of Figure 16.2, the choice can be decomposed into two nested stages, as shown in panel (b). In the first or outer stage, the traveler chooses between auto and public transport. If public transport is selected in the first stage, then a choice between public transport alternatives is made in the second or inner stage. If the two alternatives are essentially identical, as they are for red buses and blue buses, then the traveler effectively faces a binary choice between auto and homogeneous public transport, and the nested choice model collapses to the multinomial model with two alternatives. And if the two public transport modes are as dissimilar from each other as they are dissimilar from the auto, then the nested model again simplifies to the multinomial model, but now with three alternatives rather than two.

In most circumstances, public transport alternatives will be differentiated, but they will not be as distinct as public transport is from auto. If alternative 1 is bus, and alternative 2 is introduced as a new light rail system, rail can be expected to draw proportionally more travelers from buses so that the modal share of buses will fall by a larger percentage than the share for auto. This is consistent with the experience of US urban light rail systems, as mentioned in the Introduction. It should be noted that the IIA property does not hold in the aggregate if individuals have different systematic utilities, because their choice probabilities differ. However, the IIA property is still restrictive, and this motivates consideration of the nested logit model.

THE NESTED LOGIT MODEL   The nested logit model is obtained by nesting the choices of a MNL model as just described. Let the universal choice set A be partitioned into M subsets or nests, A_m, where $U_{m=1,\ldots,M}A_m = A$. The individual first selects one of the nests, and then chooses an alternative from it. An example with $M = 3$ is $A_1 = \{drive\ alone, carpool\}$, $A_2 = \{bus, subway, tram\}$, $A_3 = \{bicycle, walk\}$. The two auto alternatives are included in one nest because of their reasonable similarity, and likewise for the three public transportation modes and the two "slow" modes.

In the nested logit model, the error term for an alternative is assumed to include one component that is specific to the alternative (ε_i), and one that is specific to the nest (η_m). For an alternative i in nest m, utility can be written as a variant of equation (16.1):

$$U_i = V_i + \eta_m + \varepsilon_i, \quad i \in A_m. \tag{16.7}$$

Error terms (ε_i) for alternatives within nest m are assumed to be i.i.d. Gumbel distributed with scale parameter μ_m (which may depend on m). The conditional choice of alternative $i \in A_m$ is therefore described by a MNL model (see equation (16.5)):

$$P_{i|A_m} = \frac{\exp\left(\dfrac{V_i}{\mu_m}\right)}{\sum\limits_{j \in A_m} \exp\left(\dfrac{V_j}{\mu_m}\right)}, \quad i \in A_m. \tag{16.8}$$

According to equation (16.6), the (random) surplus from choosing the best alternative from subset A_m is $\mu_m \ln \sum_{j \in A_m} \exp[(V_j + \eta_m)/\mu_m] = CS_m + \eta_m$ with $CS_m = \mu_m \ln \sum_{j \in A_m} \exp(V_j/\mu_m)$. At the outer choice level, the nest-specific error terms (η_m) are assumed to be i.i.d. Gumbel distributed with a common scale parameter μ. The probability of choosing subset A_m is therefore as follows:

$$P_m = \frac{\exp\left(\dfrac{CS_m}{\mu}\right)}{\sum\limits_{l=1,\ldots,M} \exp\left(\dfrac{CS_l}{\mu}\right)}, \quad A_m \subset A. \tag{16.9}$$

Finally, the unconditional probability of choosing alternative $i \in A_m$ is

$$P_i = P_m \cdot P_{i|Am}. \tag{16.10}$$

It can be shown that the correlation coefficient for the utilities of two alternatives, i and j, within nest m is $Corr(U_i, U_j) = 1 - \mu_m^2/\mu^2$. Since the correlation coefficient is assumed to be nonnegative, and by definition cannot exceed unity, it follows that $\mu_m/\mu \in [0,1]$. If the estimated value of μ_m/μ lies outside this interval, it is evidence that the nested logit model is mis-specified. In the limiting case where $\mu_m = \mu$, $m = 1, \ldots, M$, the nested logit model reduces to the MNL model.

THE MIXED LOGIT MODEL   In the LRUM specification of equation (16.1) it is assumed that unobserved heterogeneity is fully captured by the additive random terms, ε_i. This implies that all differences between individuals in systematic utility are due to the observed characteristics included in V_i. This hypothesis is relaxed in the *mixed logit model*, where it is assumed that V_i also depends on unobserved characteristics that are modeled as random parameters γ distributed in the population according to a density function $g(\gamma)$, $\gamma \in \Gamma$. Given a function $V_i(\gamma)$, the logit choice probability for alternative i conditional on γ, $P_i(\gamma)$, is as follows:

$$P_i(\gamma) = \frac{\exp\left(\dfrac{V_i(\gamma)}{\mu}\right)}{\displaystyle\sum_{j \in A} \exp\left(\dfrac{V_j(\gamma)}{\mu}\right)}, \quad i \in A.$$

The unconditional choice probabilities are obtained by integrating over the distribution of γ, and equation (16.5) is replaced by the mixed logit probability:

$$P_i = \int_\Gamma P_i(\gamma)g(\gamma)\mathrm{d}\gamma, \quad i \in A. \tag{16.11}$$

The mixed logit model is very flexible in the sense that any random utility model can be approximated by it. The main drawback of the model relative to the logit model is that because more parameters are included, a larger sample size is required to obtain accurate parameter estimates.

16.3.4   Summary

Discrete-choice models have several merits for studying travel demand (Small & Winston 1999). They are firmly grounded in individual utility-maximizing behavior. The models are flexible in terms of inclusion of explanatory variables, functional form, and the degree of individual heterogeneity that is considered. Because individual rather than average values are used, better use can be made of information, and when large samples or panels of individuals are available the number of independent observations is also large. Discrete-choice models allow precise estimation of demand functions, and consequently also the benefits from transport improvements. And the models can be run "off the shelf," using a number of user-friendly software packages.

A final advantage is that discrete-choice models provide an integrated and consistent treatment of choice situations with multiple dimensions. To see this, reconsider panel (b) of Figure 16.2 and note that the choices at the lower level, labeled public transport alternatives 1 and 2, could correspond to different departure times or different routes as per the general schema in Figure 16.1. The (prospective) utilities derived from choices made at each branch of the lower level are accounted for through the inclusive values. And the probability of each combined choice is specified by an expression of the form given in equation (16.10). Choices that in practice may be made simultaneously by individuals are thus treated as if they were sequential – thereby circumventing the difficulty of dealing with large numbers of choice combinations.

16.4   Studies of Behavioral Responses to Road Pricing

The discrete-choice modeling framework reviewed in section 16.3 is used by Lam and Small (2001) and Bhat and Castelar (2002) in their studies of road pricing in the USA. Lam and Small employ data from an existing toll road, whereas Bhat and Castelar consider a hypothetical application of congestion pricing. Both studies examine behavioral responses to tolls, although the settings are quite different. Lam and Small's analysis is described in some detail to demonstrate the importance of model specification and the ways in which travel-demand preference parameters can be estimated.

16.4.1 Time-of day congestion pricing in Orange County, California

As noted in the Introduction, State Route 91 (SR91) was the first Value Pricing project. In 1995, two toll lanes were added to the median separating the five general-purpose free lanes that run in each direction. Tolls vary by time of day in each direction, and vehicles with three or more occupants (HOV3+) are charged half the published toll during certain congested hours and nothing the rest of the time. To study drivers' propensity to use the toll lanes, Lam and Small (2001) obtained data for about 400 individuals from a 1998 mail survey and a one-week trip diary. Travel times on the toll lanes and free lanes were calculated with loop-detector data. These data were used to estimate discrete-choice models of travel mode, departure time, and route. Route choice is a choice between the toll lanes and the free lanes, which Lam and Small refer to as a choice of lane. Travel mode, departure time, and lane choices can be estimated individually or jointly. Joint estimation is preferable because of potential endogeneity bias from individual choice estimation if related choices are treated as fixed. (An example of endogeneity bias is given below.) But following Lam and Small, it is instructive to consider both estimation procedures in order to examine the robustness of the estimates. Attention is focused here on their model of choice of lane, and their model of joint choice of departure time and lane.

CHOICE OF LANE ALONE In the lane-choice model, both travel mode and departure time are treated as fixed, and travel time and cost are assumed to be exogenous. Drivers therefore face a binary choice between the free lanes ($i = 0$) and the toll lanes ($i = 1$). A binary logit model is used for estimation. The main explanatory variables are expected travel time (t), variability of travel time (r), and travel cost (c). Since individuals typically dislike each of these attributes, the estimated coefficients on each are expected to be negative. The measured values of t, r, and c vary by time of day. The loop-detector data show that free-flow conditions prevail on the toll lanes almost all the time. Travel time on the free lanes has a larger expected value and a larger variability.

Since the values of the choice attributes, and possibly also the behavioral parameters, differ across individuals, individuals will now be distinguished by an index n. The utility of choice i for individual n, given generically by equation (16.1), is written

$$U_{in} = V_i(t_{in}, r_{in}, c_{in}; x_n) + \varepsilon_{in}, \quad i = 0,1, \tag{16.12}$$

where x_n is a vector of individual socioeconomic characteristics such as age and income. The explanatory variables, t_{in}, r_{in}, and c_{in}, $i = 0,1$, are evaluated at the time when individual n travels. Expected travel time, t_{in}, is measured by the median travel time on lane i, and travel time variability, r_{in}, by the difference between the 90th and the 50th percentiles of the travel time. (These two measures provided a better fit than did the mean and standard deviation.)

The third explanatory variable, c_{in}, is the toll cost on lane i. Whereas t_{in} and r_{in} are the same for all individuals who use lane i in the same 30-minute time period, c_{in} depends on n through vehicle occupancy in two ways: first, because the toll cost is assumed to be shared evenly between occupants; and, second, because vehicles with three or more occupants pay either half the published toll or nothing. The simplest version of equation (16.12) to be estimated is linear in the attributes:

$$U_{in} = \gamma_{in0} + \gamma_{nt}t_{in} + \gamma_{nr}r_{in} + \gamma_{nc}c_{in} + \varepsilon_{in}, \quad i = 0,1. \tag{16.13}$$

Because the free lanes and toll lanes are on the same highway, the attributes t_{in}, r_{in} and c_{in} are assumed to be valued equally, so that the corresponding coefficients γ_{nt}, γ_{nr} and γ_{nc} do not depend on i. (In other choice situations, the coefficients could differ; for example, the disutility of travel time may be less on scenic routes.) However, the coefficients are allowed to vary by individual. For purpose of normalization, the constant term for the free lanes, γ_{0n0}, is set to 0, and the scale parameter of the MNL is set to unity ($\mu = 1$). The difference between the systematic utilities of the toll lanes and free lanes, $\Delta V = V_{1n} - V_{0n}$ in equation (16.3), is therefore

$$\Delta V = \gamma_{1n0} + \gamma_{nt}(t_{1n} - t_{0n}) + \gamma_{nr}(r_{1n} - r_{0n}) + \gamma_{nc}c_{1n}. \tag{16.14}$$

The relative disutility from travel time is referred to in the transportation literature as the *Value of Time* (VOT). Formally, the VOT is defined to be the marginal rate of substitution between travel time and money. From equation (16.13), this is given by

$$VOT_n = \frac{\partial V_{in}/\partial t_{in}}{\partial V_{in}/\partial c_{in}} = \frac{\gamma_{nt}}{\gamma_{nc}}. \tag{16.15}$$

By analogy with the VOT, the *Value of Reliability* (VOR) is defined to be the marginal rate of substitution between travel time variability and money:

$$VOR_n = \frac{\partial V_{in}/\partial r_{in}}{\partial V_{in}/\partial c_{in}} = \frac{\gamma_{nr}}{\gamma_{nc}}. \tag{16.16}$$

Finally, the ratio of VOR and VOT serves as a measure of risk aversion to variability in travel time:

$$RA_n = \frac{VOR_n}{VOT_n} = \frac{\partial V_{in}/\partial r_{in}}{\partial V_{in}/\partial t_{in}} = \frac{\gamma_{nr}}{\gamma_{nt}}. \tag{16.17}$$

Column 3 of Table 16.1 presents the estimation results for the best-fitting variant of the lane-choice model. The dependent variable is the choice of lane. All variables are measured in minutes and dollars except for income, which is measured in thousands of dollars. In the lower half of Table 16.1, N denotes the sample size. The log-likelihood statistic in the next row is the maximum value of the likelihood function achieved in the maximum likelihood estimation procedure; it can be used to compare similar models in terms of goodness-of-fit. (Note that the models corresponding to columns 3 and 4 are not similar, since the second one includes additional variables that appear in column 6.) Finally, the *Pseudo-R²* statistic is given by $1 - \mathcal{L}/\mathcal{L}^0$, where $\mathcal{L}$ is the log-likelihood of the model, and $\mathcal{L}^0$ is the log-likelihood of a restricted model that includes only constant terms. Since $\mathcal{L}^0 \leq \mathcal{L} \leq 0$, the *Pseudo-R²* lies in the interval [0,1].

Estimates for the three main explanatory variables are reported in the middle rows of Table 16.1. The standard errors of the estimates can be obtained from the point estimates and the asymptotic t-statistics (in parentheses). For example, the standard error for the lane dummy, γ_{n0}, is $-2.811/-2.884 = 0.9747$. The coefficients γ_{nt} and γ_{nc} are assumed to be independent of individual-specific characteristics. Both have the expected negative sign. Expressed in terms of equation (16.14), the probability of choosing the toll lanes is a decreasing function of the difference between the toll and free lanes in expected travel time and also a decreasing function of the toll. Using equation (16.15), the point estimate of VOT is as follows:

$$VOT = \frac{\gamma_{nt}}{\gamma_{nc}} = \frac{-0.176\left[\text{min}^{-1}\right]}{-0.401\left[\$^{-1}\right]} \times 60\left[\text{min hr}^{-1}\right] \times \frac{1}{1.37} = 19.22\left[\$\text{ hr}^{-1}\right].$$

(The factor of 1.37 is added to correct for missing loop-detector data; see Lam and Small (2001, p. 234).)

To allow for differences between the sexes in the cost of travel-time variability, an interaction term is included between r and a dummy variable *male*, set equal to 1 for males and 0 for females. The coefficient on this variable is positive, which indicates that men are less sensitive to travel-time variability. Indeed, the estimated coefficient for men of $-0.263 + 0.154 = -0.109$ is less than half in magnitude the estimated value of -0.263 for women. The point estimates of VOR for men and women are derived in the same way as for VOT. Given the assumption of equal VOT, the risk aversion estimates (0.62 and 1.49) are correspondingly much higher for women. This finding – which is supported by other recent research – may be due to the tighter time constraints that women face as they juggle work demands with a lion's share of family responsibilities.

Estimates for the lane constant, which includes several interaction terms, are reported at the top of Table 16.1. The toll lanes are favored by individuals with high incomes, who speak English at home (lang = 0), and who have greater work-hour flexibility (*flex* corresponds to the width of the acceptable work-arrival-time

Table 16.1 Estimates for lane choice and combined lane and time-of-day choice on SR91 (asymptotic t-statistics in parentheses)

1	2 Variables	3 Coefficients Lane-choice model	4 Coefficients Lane and departure-time choice model	5	6 Variables	7 Coefficients Lane and departure-time choice model
γ_{ln0}	lane	−2.811 (−2.884)	−1.563 (−1.907)	Time of day γ_{nh}	$D_{4:30-5:00}$	0.815 (0.706)
	income*lane	0.0197 (3.905)	0.0172 (3.630)		$D_{5:00-5:30}$	2.312 (2.185)
	lang*lane	−1.129 (−2.737)	−1.00542 (−2.535)		$D_{5:30-6:00}$	3.0343 (2.858)
	flex*lane	0.00518 (1.958)	0.00456 (1.831)		$D_{6:00-6:30}$	3.507 (3.197)
	distance*lane	0.0481 (1.700)	0.0548 (1.984)		$D_{6:30-7:00}$	4.470 (3.985)
	distance²*lane	−4.76 × 10⁻⁴ (−1.721)	−6.05 × 10⁻⁴ (−2.192)		$D_{7:00-7:30}$	4.782 (4.251)
γ_{ht}	median travel time (t) [min]	−0.176 (−2.208)	−0.0463 (−2.059)		$D_{7:30-8:00}$	5.395 (4.658)
γ_{hr}	time variability (r) [min]	−0.263 (−3.983)	−0.0725 (−2.959)		$D_{8:00-8:30}$	5.182 (4.311)
	r*male	0.154 (2.631)	0.0166 (0.821)		$D_{8:30-9:00}$	5.006 (4.464)
γ_{nc}	cost (c_{ni}) [$]	−0.401 (−2.790)	−0.428 (−3.236)		$D_{9:00-9:30}$	4.494 (4.142)
					$D_{9:30-10:00}$	3.432 (3.186)
				γ_{ne}	SDE	−0.0285 (−7.213)
					male*SDE	0.0126 (2.633)
					(age−41)*SDE	5.42 × 10⁻⁴ (2.345)
	N	341	341	γ_{nl}	SDL	−0.0465 (−3.988)
	Log-likelihood	−203.902	−760.0746		flex*SDL	1.70 × 10⁻⁴ (1.965)
	Pseudo-R²	0.1373	0.2986	γ_{nd}	Dlate	−1.0784 (−2.341)
	VOT [$/hr]	19.22	4.74			
	VOR [$/hr] men	11.90	5.72			
	VOR [$/hr] women	28.72	7.42			
	RA men	0.62	1.21			
	RA women	1.49	1.57			

Source: Lam and Small (2001), tables 5 (Model 1g) and 8 (Model 2d)

interval). A possible explanation for the counter-intuitive positive effect of flexibility is that people with flexible hours may have more opportunity than do workers with rigid hours to advance their careers by spending time at the office and/or being punctual when they have appointments. Finally, the variable *distance*, which refers to total trip distance in miles, is interacted quadratically with the lane dummy. The estimates indicate that up to a distance of about 50 miles (which covers about three-quarters of the sample), people who make longer trips favor the toll lanes, possibly because they face tighter daily time constraints than do people with short trips and therefore value more highly savings in time.

CHOICE OF LANE AND DEPARTURE TIME   Departure time is treated as given in the lane-choice model. This is a dubious specification because departure time affects all three of the explanatory variables: expected travel time, variability in travel time, and toll. Because there may be unobserved factors that influence both departure time choice and lane choice, the explanatory variables and the error terms in equation (16.13) may be correlated, which invalidates the binary logit model.

To correct for this type of endogeneity bias, lane choice and time-of-day choice must be modeled as a joint decision. Time-of-day choice was modeled as a choice between 12 half-hour arrival-time intervals from 4:00 to 10:00. Trip-timing preferences were included by adding four terms to the systematic utility function:

- Constants for each arrival time interval.
- SDE: Schedule Delay Early, equal to $Max[0,T]$, where T is the difference between official work time and the lower limit of the half-hour time interval.
- SDL: Schedule Delay Late, equal to $Max[0,-T]$.
- Dlate: A dummy variable equal to 1 if $T < 0$, and 0 otherwise.

Variable SDE measures the extent to which individuals arrive at work earlier than desired. SDL is defined analogously for late arrival. Dlate is a discrete variable that captures any fixed costs of arriving late, such as disapproval from the employer. With the inclusion of these variables, the estimating equation becomes, in place of equation (16.13),

$$U_{ihn} = \gamma_{in0} + \gamma_{nt}t_{ihn} + \gamma_{nr}r_{ihn} + \gamma_{nc}c_{ihn} + \gamma_{nh}D_h + \gamma_{ne}SDE_{ihn}$$
$$+ \gamma_{nl}SDL_{ihn} + \gamma_{nd}Dlate_{ihn} + \varepsilon_{ihn}, \qquad (16.18)$$

where γ_{nh} is the coefficient for arrival time interval h, D_h is a dummy variable for work arrival during this interval, and index h indicates that variables now also depend on the time interval.

A complication in estimating equation (16.18) is that data for travel times on roads other than SR91 were unavailable. This did not matter for the lane-choice model, because lane choice only affects travel time on SR91, but it does matter for the joint model, because travel times elsewhere are likely to vary systematically by time of day. To address this complication, the 50th and 90th percentile travel times per mile on the free lanes of SR91 were assumed to be applicable to other roads as well, except for a 5-mile segment that was assumed to be congestion free.

With two decisions, lane and time of day, it is natural to consider a nested logit model for estimation. Since it is not obvious whether lane choice or time-of-day choice belongs at the upper branch of the decision tree, both specifications were tested. However, both produced estimates of the scale parameter ratio, μ_m/μ, outside the admissible [0,1] interval. Therefore, a MNL model was used instead.

The MNL estimates for variables that also appear in the lane-choice model are presented in column 4 of Table 16.1. Estimates for the lane constant and interaction terms do not differ greatly from those of the lane-choice model, and the coefficient on cost, γ_{nc}, is also similar. However, the coefficients on expected travel time and variability, γ_{nt} and γ_{nr}, are much smaller. One possible reason is that the assumption about travel times outside SR91 is inaccurate. But an alternative specification in which outside travel times were ignored also yielded relatively low estimates for these parameters. This suggests that the differences in results are driven by severe endogeneity bias in the lane-choice model from treating departure time choice as given. Such a bias could be tested formally using a Hausman specification test. The large differences between the coefficient estimates in the two models would undoubtedly lead to rejection of the null hypothesis that departure times are exogenous. (Lam and Small also estimated MNL and nested logit models for joint lane and mode choice decisions. The estimates for VOT and VOR were broadly similar to those for the lane-choice model, which indicates that any endogeneity bias from disregarding mode choice is less severe.)

The estimates for VOT and VOR will be biased upward if there are unobserved factors that incline people to choose the toll lanes at peak times, because median travel time and variability are higher during the peak. For example, an individual with a job that starts at a popular time and requires punctuality will prefer to travel at the height of the rush hour and to use the toll lanes to reduce the chance of delay. If so, the unobserved factor, type of job, induces a positive correlation between departure time at the peak and use of the toll lanes. In any case, the relatively low estimated coefficients in the joint model for expected travel time and variability translate to low values for VOT and VOR as reported at the bottom of column 4. The risk aversion coefficient remains larger for women than for men, although this difference is no longer statistically significant.

Column 7 of Table 16.1 reports estimates for variables related to departure-time choice. The reference alternative for time of day is the earliest time interval, 4:00–4:30. Time-of-day coefficients, γ_{nh}, for the remaining 11 time intervals exhibit a hump-shaped pattern, with a maximum at 7:30–8:00. Predictably enough, this implies an aversion to traveling either very early or very late in the morning. All three schedule-delay cost coefficients are negative as expected. The positive interaction term coefficients for *SDE* indicate that males and older workers are less averse to arriving early – perhaps because they have fewer family obligations. Using the coefficient estimates, it is possible to compute various marginal rates of substitution. For example, to avoid arriving late an individual would be willing to pay a price of $\widehat{\gamma_{nd}}/\widehat{\gamma_{nc}} = (-1.0784)/(-0.428) = \$2.52$. In order to avoid arriving a minute earlier, a 31-year-old female would be willing to incur an extra travel time of $[-0.0285 + (31 - 41) \times (5.42 \times 10^{-4})]/(-0.0463) = 0.73$ minutes. These estimates are representative of those obtained from various trip-timing studies over the past 20 years.

16.4.2   Congestion pricing in the San Francisco Bay Area

For their study of SR91, Lam and Small (2001) were able to use *Revealed Preference* (RP) data; that is, data on travel choices that people actually made. But sufficient RP data are sometimes lacking. This was the case for Bhat and Castelar's (2002) study of congestion pricing in the San Francisco Bay Area. Several congestion-pricing schemes have been proposed for the Bay Area over the past 30 years, but none have been implemented. And although the Golden Gate and several other bridges are tolled, the tolls are constant throughout the day. RP data on responses to time-of-day toll differentials were therefore not available.

To overcome this deficiency, Bhat and Castelar drew on a survey of people who reported crossing one of the Bay Bridges at least once a week during the morning peak. Those surveyed were asked to make choices from a set of hypothetical alternatives, discussed below. Their responses comprise what is called *Stated Preference* (SP) data. Bhat and Castelar combined this SP data with RP data from the 1996 San Francisco Bay Area Travel Study.

To accommodate unobserved heterogeneity in individual preferences, Bhat and Castelar adopt a mixed MNL model (see equation (16.11)). This model also allows them to test for behavior known as *state dependence*. State dependence occurs in a combined RP/SP context when a respondent's revealed choice influences his or her stated choices. Habit persistence or risk aversion will tend to create positive state dependence, whereas variety-seeking or frustration with the alternative currently chosen will induce negative state dependence. Both the sign and the intensity of the state-dependence effect can vary across individuals, and the mixed MNL model can accommodate this type of heterogeneity.

The SP data used in Bhat and Castelar's study were generated for each survey respondent by taking his or her reported trip as a reference, and developing SP scenarios that involve alternative combinations of mode and time of day. The modes include driving alone, carpooling, and two forms of public transportation. Peak and off-peak periods were also defined for the drive-alone auto mode, giving a total of five alternatives. Two congestion-pricing scenarios were constructed by assuming a $2 or $4 increase in the cost of the "drive alone – peak" alternative (an increase of 44 percent or 87 percent in mean travel cost). Discussion is limited here to the $4 scenario and to the two most diverse model specifications considered: an MNL model that uses cross-sectional data, and a general model that uses panel data and includes both unobserved heterogeneity and state-dependence effects. The results are reported in Table 16.2.

Both the MNL model and the general model predict reductions in the "drive alone – peak" modal share, and increases in shares for each of the other four alternatives. But the magnitudes differ. Compared to the general model, the MNL model slightly overpredicts the reduction in driving alone. Due to the IIA

Table 16.2 Simulated percentage changes in alternative choice shares in response to a $4 increase in the "drive alone – peak" travel cost, San Francisco Bay Area

Choice alternative	Multinomial logit model	General model
Drive alone – peak	−19.16	−18.44
Drive alone – off-peak	36.40	26.39
Carpool (peak and off-peak)	31.82	39.98
Alameda County Transit (ACT)	31.53	36.91
Bay Area Rapid Transit (BART)	28.65	28.66

Source: Bhat and Castelar (2002), table 6

property, the MNL model predicts similar percentage increases in shares of the other alternatives. (The increases are not identical because the sample of individuals is heterogeneous and, as noted in Section 16.3, aggregate MNL choice shares do not obey IIA.) The general model predicts a substantially smaller percentage increase in driving alone off-peak, and a substantially larger percentage increase in carpooling. In terms of congestion relief, the MNL therefore slightly overpredicts the benefits that would accrue from reduced peak driving by solo drivers, but underpredicts the potential increase in congestion from more carpooling during the peak.

Bhat and Castelar also report estimates of VOT, which they assume to be homogeneous in the population. When the RP data are used, their MNL model yields an estimate of about $20 per hour. But when the SP data are used either alone or in combination with the RP data, the estimated VOT falls to about $11 per hour. Though not as drastic as the differences in estimated VOT in Table 16.1, the discrepancy is still appreciable. In part, it may be due to lack of adequate variation of monetary costs and travel times in the RP data. One advantage of using SP data is that the degree of variation can be controlled through the design of the hypothetical alternatives. The discrepancy is also consistent with a well-documented tendency of SP survey respondents to overstate their propensity to change behavior. This would mean that changes in travel time induced by the $4 charge would be inflated, with corresponding reductions in the implied VOT.

16.5 CONCLUSION

The modeling approach and the road-pricing studies reviewed in this essay offer several lessons for studying urban passenger travel demand. One lesson is that it is important to include all relevant dimensions of travel behavior in the analysis. For example, because road-pricing schemes are often designed to reduce peak-period congestion, it is essential to account for changes in the timing of trips. This is evident in Lam and Small's study of SR91 from the fact that their combined lane and departure-time choice model yields very different estimates of VOT and VOR than does their lane-choice model.

A second lesson is that model specification can influence results materially. For instance, Bhat and Castelar's general model predicts different responses to a toll than does their more restrictive multinomial logit model, which suffers from the Independence of Irrelevant Alternatives property. It is also important to include the appropriate explanatory variables in the regression equations. For example, several road-pricing studies have found that motorists dislike travel time under congested conditions much more than under free-flow conditions, and it is therefore crucial to distinguish the two variables when predicting travel behavior.

A third lesson is that people differ widely in their travel behavior. Some are wedded to their cars and have rigid daily schedules, while others are more adaptable and will shift mode, travel time, or route in response to tolls. Opportunities to save travel time are the main attraction of using toll roads, and estimates of the value that people place on time savings and enhanced reliability vary with income, sex, trip purpose, and other socioeconomic characteristics. Not surprisingly, high-income individuals are more inclined to use toll lanes, and this might suggest that road pricing favors the rich. However, studies of SR91 and other toll-lanes projects show that usage is actually quite varied. Few people take the toll lanes consistently, and even lower-income people use them occasionally when they are especially pressed for time.

The benefits and welfare-distributional effects from road pricing naturally depend on the design of the scheme and the setting. There is a big difference between the toll-lanes projects that have been introduced in the USA and the much larger area-based systems in place or planned for Europe. One should not expect the findings derived from a facility such as SR91 – which has toll-free lanes running in parallel with the toll lanes – to be transferable to a much larger and more complex scheme such as in London, where payment is difficult to avoid.

In the long run, the impacts of road pricing will extend beyond the relatively short-term choice dimensions considered in the two studies reviewed here to encompass other dimensions of behavior shown in Figure 16.1, such as residential and workplace locations and vehicle ownership. Both the practice of road pricing and an understanding of its impacts are developing rapidly, and many of the details in this essay will soon be obsolete. Nevertheless, it is hoped that readers, with the advantage of hindsight, can still benefit from the relatively early perspective on road pricing and urban passenger travel demand offered here.

Acknowledgments

The authors are most grateful to Richard Arnott for helpful editorial comments and to Ken Small for answering questions. Lindsey would also like to thank the Social Sciences and Humanities Research Council of Canada for financial support.

Bibliography

Travel demand

Bates, J. 2000: History of demand modeling. In D. A. Hensher and K. J. Button (eds.), *Handbook of Transport Modelling*, vol. 1. Oxford: Elsevier Science, 11–33.

Small, K. A. and Winston, C. 1999: The demand for transportation: models and applications. In J. A. Gómez-Ibáñez, W. B. Tye, and C. Winston (eds.), *Essays in Transportation Economics and Policy: A Handbook in Honor of John R. Meyer*. Washington, DC: Brookings Institution Press, 11–55.

Discrete-choice models

Ben-Akiva, M. and Bierlaire, M. 1999: Discrete choice methods and their applications to short term travel decisions. In R. W. Hall (ed.), *Handbook of Transportation Science*. Boston: Kluwer, 5–33.

Studies of road pricing

Bhat, C. R. and Castelar, S. 2002: A unified mixed logit framework for modelling revealed and stated preferences: formulation and application to congestion pricing in the San Francisco Bay area. *Transportation Research B*, 36B, 593–616.

Brownstone, D., Ghosh, A., Golob, T. F., Kazimi, C., and Van Amelsfort, D. 2003: Drivers' willingness-to pay to reduce travel time: evidence from the San Diego I-15 congestion pricing project. *Transportation Research A*, 37A, 373–87.

Burris, M. W. and Pendyala, R. M. 2002: Discrete choice models of traveler participation in differential time of day pricing programs. *Transport Policy*, 9, 241–51.

Erhardt, G. D., Koppelman, F. S., Freedman, J., Davidson, W. A., and Mullins, A. 2003: Modeling the choice to use toll and high-occupancy vehicle facilities. *Transportation Research Record* 1854, 135–43.

Lam, T. C. and Small, K. A. 2001: The value of time and reliability: measurement from a value pricing experiment. *Transportation Research E*, 37, 231–51.

Urban Transportation and Land Use

John F. McDonald

17.1   INTRODUCTION

This chapter is an introduction to the economics of the connection between urban transportation and land use. The nature of the transportation system strongly influences the patterns of land use in an urban area. Indeed, the long-run histories of urban areas sometimes are identified with the dominant mode of transportation of the time; the age of rail, the age of the automobile, and so on. Suppose that we wish to investigate the effect of an improvement in the urban transportation system on the urban land-use pattern. How does one go about studying this question? The purpose of this essay is to discuss the methods that are employed in this area of applied research.

This essay largely concentrates on this influence – the direction of causation from transportation system to land-use pattern. However, it is also true that the pattern of land use influences both the performance of an existing transportation system in the short run and the investments in transportation that are made in the long run. This direction of causation – from land-use patterns to transportation system performance and investment analysis – has been emphasized in the related field of urban transportation planning, but is discussed only briefly here.

The analysis of the effect of transportation on land use involves the fundamental concept in urban economics that was introduced by Alonso (1964) – bid rent. The economic reason for the existence of cities is to bring people and economic activities into proximate locations. Higher accessibility (lower transportation costs) of an urban site to desirable destinations increases the rent that is offered for that site. The urban economy is made up of different "sectors" such as households (of various types), businesses in the various industries, and governmental entities. Bid rent is defined as the maximum amount that a household or firm is willing to offer for a unit of land, given a level of utility (for a household) or profits (for a firm). All have their own hypothetical bid rent for each urban site. If the land market is permitted to function so that the highest bidder occupies the site, then both the allocation of the land to a particular use (e.g., housing, retail trade, and so on) and the intensity of that use (e.g., the ratio of floor space to land) are determined by the market. In this essay, land use is defined as both type and intensity of land use. Population density is the measure of land-use intensity that is used most often.

The essay is organized as follows. The next section is a brief discussion of the regulation of land use that is employed in nearly all of the urban areas in the United States, and a short introduction to urban transportation planning. This is followed by a discussion of the economics of the effects of transportation improvements on urban land use. The essay concludes with a brief review of empirical studies and suggestions for further research.

17.2   Zoning and Urban Transportation Planning

As noted above, the use of urban land has two distinct components; the allocation of land to particular uses and the intensity of that use. With the exception of the City of Houston (which does not have zoning), both components are regulated in detail by local zoning ordinances in all major metropolitan areas in the USA. Zoning became widespread in the 1920s, and most local zoning ordinances now specify the type of land use to which a parcel of land has been exclusively allocated. The US Supreme Court ruled in 1926 that zoning is a legitimate exercise of the police power granted to local governments by the state government. Early zoning ordinances specified a hierarchy of land uses (e.g., single-family residential, apartment buildings, commercial, industrial), and permitted "higher" uses in areas zoned for "lower" uses. In effect, single-family houses could be constructed anywhere. Such a hierarchy was based on the idea that the amount of negative externalities produced by land uses followed this ranking (in reverse order). However, these hierarchical ordinances were replaced by exclusive zoning over time. For example, the original zoning ordinance of the City of Chicago from 1923 was hierarchical, and this ordinance was replaced by exclusive zoning in 1957. Land uses that did not "conform" to the new zoning ordinance were required to be eliminated within a certain time period (although this was not enforced completely).

Many zoning ordinances also regulate the intensity of land use. For example, the 1957 Chicago zoning ordinance specifies that land allocated to residential use must adhere to a particular "floor-area ratio" (the ratio of floor space to land area). Eight floor-area ratios are used, ranging from 0.5 to 10.0. If the floor-area ratio is limited to 0.5, a two-story house can cover 25 percent of the lot. If the floor-area ratio is 10, then an apartment building that covers 25 percent of the lot can be 40 stories tall. Commercial and industrial floor-area ratios vary from 1.2 to 7.0, except in the central business area, where the top ratio is 16.0.

Courts have ruled consistently that, provided that the zoning ordinance covers the entire jurisdiction, local governments (usually the municipal government) have the power to specify both the type and intensity of land use for every land parcel. As such, the urban land market would appear to be the most regulated market in which private property is bought and sold. However, an important issue that is unresolved is whether the zoning ordinance "follows the market" in some sense and produces a pattern of land use that comes close to replicating the pattern that an unregulated market would produce.

The other area of local government activity that is of immediate relevance to this essay is urban transportation planning. A series of federal laws were enacted that, since 1965, have required every metropolitan area in the USA to have a Metropolitan Planning Organization (MPO), with duties that include the preparation of a transportation plan for the entire metropolitan area. This plan must include a long-range component on the order of 20 years, be updated annually, cover all modes of transportation, and include short-range plans for improvements in transportation systems management and programs and projects for the upcoming year. The staff members of the MPO are engaged daily in the study of the urban area – its growth, its changing spatial patterns, and its transportation problems. These people are valuable resources for urban economists.

The basic urban transportation planning (UTP) process can be outlined as follows:

1   Forecast metropolitan population and employment for the target year.
2   Allocate population and employment to small analysis zones according to land availability, zoning, and other factors.
3   Specify alternative transportation programs given steps 1 and 2 (including the null alternative). Determine the cost of each alternative.
4   Use demand forecasting models to predict travel flows for the target year for each alternative program (including the null alternative). This step involves the use of models to predict trip generation from origin zones and trip distribution to destination zones, as well as the choice of mode and route.
5   Estimate user benefits and compare costs and benefits for each alternative project or program.

All metropolitan areas in the USA must undertake studies that follow these basic steps, if for no other reason than to qualify for the federal transportation funds to which they are entitled. Note that there is a close connection between land use and transportation in these types of studies, but that this connection normally runs from projections of land-use patterns (population and employment by zone) to trip generation to transportation flows and transportation system performance (e.g., congestion levels). Future travel demand is predicted from forecasts of land uses, and most of the studies have made little or no effort to make land-use forecasts sensitive to transportation system performance; there is no "feedback." As Kain (1998) noted, the models of land use employed by transportation planners were insensitive to transportation system performance, so it made little sense to require full consistency between the land use and the transportation system forecasts. Literally dozens of models and systems of models have been developed for the UTP process, and these models have been reviewed – sometimes critically – by urban economists such as Lowry (1972), Anas (1987), and Kain (1998).

17.3   Effects of Transportation Improvements on Urban Land Use

Suppose that a major transportation improvement is planned. The project could be a new link in the urban highway system or a new mass transit facility. What impacts will the completed project have on land use? What economic models are employed to conduct the study?

An issue that must be resolved first is the geographical scope of the study. Will the effects of the transportation project be only nearby in some sense, or will the effects be broader – possibly affecting the entire urban area? For example, will the transportation project attract households and firms to its immediate area and cause reductions in other locations? On the other hand, can we safely assume that the negative impacts on other locations are negligible? In essence, must we specify a general equilibrium model of the urban land market, or can we work with a partial equilibrium model in which these "other" locations are ignored? There is no general answer to the question, but each case must be examined on its own. The construction of an entire modern highway system in a metropolitan area, such as those completed in the 1960s in the USA, would clearly call for a model of the land market of the whole urban area. On the other hand, a study of the construction of a single mass transit line in a large urban area might only require a partial equilibrium model. This discussion shall proceed under the assumption that a partial equilibrium model is sufficient to capture the effects of the transportation project. Other chapters in this book provide general equilibrium models of the urban land market.

The impacts of a transportation project on urban land use can be broken down into four stages:

- impacts on bid rent for the different types of land use;
- impacts of changes in bid rent on market values for land;
- effects of changes in market values on the allocation of land to the various uses; and
- effects of changes in market values on the intensity of land use.

Each category is discussed in turn.

A pattern of land use (both land allocation and intensity of use) already exists in the vicinity of the proposed transportation project. Once the project is completed, households and firms will change their bid rents for locations proximate to the new transportation facility. For the most part, we expect that annual bid rents will increase to match the annual savings in transportation costs experienced by the households or firms, but it may be that some sites near the new facility are affected negatively by noise or congestion. We leave open the possibility that negative effects can occur.

We hypothesize that changes in bid rent will occur only once the transportation facility is ready for use, but that market values for land will change prior to "opening day." Most studies have examined market values rather than annual rents. Assume that the transportation project is announced at some point in time, and it is completed at a later date. The change in land value for a given land use at a time prior to opening is

$$\Delta V_a = \Delta V_t/(1 + r)^{t-a} = \Delta R_t/r(1 + r)^{t-a}, \qquad (17.1)$$

where t is the year in which the transportation project opens, a is the year under study, r is the real discount rate, and ΔR is the permanent change in land rent from time t forward – assume that it is a positive amount in this example. The facts about the transportation project are known with certainty prior to time a; the date of completion is known to be t, and the features of the project are known (e.g., travel time savings, fares, and so on). Equation (17.1) simply says that the addition to land value at time t is discounted back to time a. Rents do not rise before opening day, but land values do rise in anticipation of the increase in rents. Land value jumps when the project is announced, and rises at rate r up to opening day.

The empirical estimation of the effect of a transportation improvement on land values requires a statistical model that controls for other possible influences on land values. A simple before-and-after comparison will likely yield biased results. Furthermore, cross-section analysis of only the "after" period will also likely generate biased estimates. A better method might be called a generalized before-and-after method.

Suppose that land values in a particular use (e.g., residential) are determined in the "before" period prior to the announcement that the transportation project will be built according to

$$\ln V_b = \beta_0 + \beta_1 X_{1b} + \ldots + \beta_n X_{nb} + \delta_b D + e_b, \qquad (17.2)$$

where V_b is the land value at a location (with the subscript for location omitted), X_{1b} through X_{nb} are various variables that influence land value, β_0 through β_n are coefficients, D is the proximity of the site to the future transportation facility, δ_b is a coefficient, and e_b is a normally distributed error term with zero mean and constant variance. Note that the X variables take on values that are specific to the "before" period, but some of these variables (such as distance to the central business district) have the same numerical values in the "before" and "after" periods. And note that the model assumes that $\ln V_b$ might be related to proximity to the transportation facility in the "before" period. Coefficient δ_b might be different from zero. Obviously, in the "before" period land values cannot be related to proximity to the future transportation facility for the reason that transportation costs are lower, because such information is not available. But there might be other factors, such as proximity to employment or shopping or other local factors, that generate a relationship between $\ln V_b$ and D. This possibility should not be ruled out beforehand.

The equation for land value after the nature of the transportation project is fully known is assumed to be

$$\ln V_a = \alpha_0 + \alpha_1 X_{1a} + \ldots + \alpha_n X_{na} + \delta_a D + e_a, \tag{17.3}$$

where the subscript a attached to the variables refers to the values of the variables in the "after the project is known" period, α_0 through α_n are coefficients in the "after" period, and δ_a is the coefficient of proximity to the transportation project. The statistical model represented by equations (17.1) and (17.2) permits all variables to have different effects on land values in the two periods. The effect of the transportation improvement in partial equilibrium in percentage terms is measured as $\delta_a - \delta_b$, the change in the effect of proximity to the transportation project. Following equations (17.1), (17.2), and (17.3), the percentage change in land value at time a attributable to the transportation improvement can be written as follows:

$$\Delta V_a / V_a = \delta_a - \delta_b = \Delta V_t / V_a (1 + r)^{t-a}, \tag{17.4}$$

where $t - a$ is the number of years prior to the opening of the transportation facility.

Several restrictive assumptions can be made that will make the simple before-and-after comparison yield unbiased results. Suppose that proximity to the transportation project is measured simply as a dummy variable ($D = 1$ for proximate, 0 otherwise). Also assume that $\beta_1 = \alpha_1, \ldots, \beta_n = \alpha_n$ and that none of the X variables changes from "before" to "after." Given these restrictive assumptions, we can write

$$\ln V_a - \ln V_b = (\alpha_0 - \beta_0) + (\delta_a - \delta_b) + e_a - e_b. \tag{17.5}$$

The percentage change in land value simply consists of a general inflation factor and the added change associated with proximity to the transportation facility. (Note that this simple before-and-after method can be used provided that a control group of locations has been selected to provide an estimate of the general inflation in land values.) In general, the problem with the simple before-and-after method is one of specification error through the omission of variables. The omission of relevant variables leads to bias of unknown direction and magnitude in the estimated coefficients of the included variables.

The cross-section estimation of equation (17.2) will yield an estimate of δ_a, which is an unbiased estimate of the partial equilibrium effect of the transportation facility if $\delta_b = 0$; that is, if there is no pre-project effect of proximity to the facility on land values.

Does economic theory predict the magnitude of the change in land value shown in equation (17.5), and the expected change in the intensity of land use as well? The answer is yes, and as we shall see, the change in land value will depend upon whether the intensity of land use is permitted to increase with the value of land. Consider a numerical example involving a block of single-family houses located near a transit station on a new mass transit line. Suppose that each house is worth $120,000, and that the value of the lot on which each house rests is $24,000 of that value (i.e., 20 percent of the property value, which is fairly typical). The cost of building the house is $96,000. Assume that the new transit line will save each household 30 minutes per workday in travel time. This translates into 120 hours per year (for 240 work days) and, if travel-time savings are valued at $12.50 per hour, into $1,500 per year. Competition in the housing market means that annual rent for houses on the block will go up by this amount. The value of each house on the block will go up by $1,500 divided by the real interest rate. If the real interest rate is 5 percent, then the value of a house will go up by $30,000 – from $120,000 to $150,000. If no change in land-use intensity is permitted by the zoning officials, this is the end of the story. House values rise by the value of the travel-time savings. The (imputed) value of the land underneath each house has gone up from $24,000 to $54,000.

Given the transportation improvement, the demand for housing on the block has increased. Households are now willing to pay $150,000 for a housing unit on the block of quality equal to the existing units. This represents a 25 percent shift upward in the demand curve, from $120,000 to $150,000. The demand curve for housing on an individual block is perfectly elastic at the demand price because an individual block contains only a small fraction of housing supply. Housing suppliers have an incentive to respond to this increase in demand by supplying more housing units on the block. It is known that the long-run supply elasticity for housing units on a fixed land area is about 4.0; that is, a 25 percent increase in the demand price will call forth a 100 percent increase in housing units supplied (a doubling of units). Figure 17.1 depicts this demand shift and supply response.

Therefore, suppose that there is no zoning constraint, and the intensity of land use is increased by building a second house on each lot, tearing houses down to be replaced by duplex units, and so on. Because each house now occupies only 50 percent of a lot, in order to make each new house equal in value in the market to the older houses, somewhat nicer or larger interior space must be created. In particular, suppose that the construction cost of a new house is $120,000. Each house is worth $150,000, but now each lot contains two houses worth a total of $300,000. Since each house, excluding the land value, costs $120,000 to build, this means that the value of the lot is now $300,000 minus $240,000, which equals $60,000.

In the end, the transportation improvement has increased the value of land from $24,000 to $60,000 per lot. This total increase consists of two parts – the increase at a given intensity of land use to $54,000, and a further increase to $60,000 that is a result of the doubling of land-use intensity. Note that the value of the land has increased by 150 percent, and that the amount of capital has increased from $96,000 to $240,000 – an increase of 150 percent. The outcome that land value and the amount of housing capital per unit of land increase by equal percentages is consistent with available empirical evidence from the housing market. Also note that the value of the land remains at 20 percent of the total value of the property.

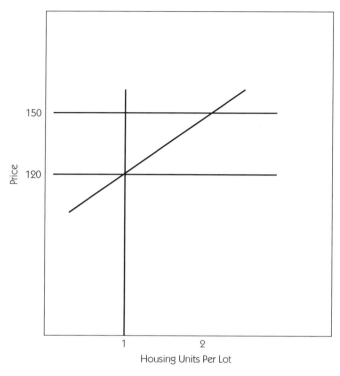

Figure 17.1 Supply and demand for housing units on a lot.

   The effects of changes in land values on land use doubtless take years to materialize, if ever. As noted above, there can be a change in the allocation of land to alternative uses as well as changes in the intensity of use within a land-use category. Changes in the allocation of land to alternative uses operate through the zoning process, so an empirical study of this effect is a description of the behavior of the zoning officials in response to requests for zoning changes. One would presume that land-use zoning would be responsive to land-value increases that are larger for one type of land use compared to others. However, this pro-cess may be very slow and incomplete. Also, the effect of an increase in land values in a given land-use type may take many years. An increase in land value creates an incentive to increase land-use intensity, of course, but such a change often will require demolition and new construction. The market incentive to demolish exists if the market value of the raw land (less demolition costs) exceeds the market value of the old property – including both the structure and the land. Large increases in land values are often needed to satisfy this condition.

17.4   Empirical Studies

There are many empirical studies of the effect of a new transportation facility on property values or land values. The study by McDonald and Osuji (1995) was the

first to use the "before-and-after" method described above, and also found that
residential land values had anticipated the opening of a mass transit line in
Chicago. A study by Gatzlaff and Smith (1993) examined the time pattern of the
response of housing value to the new Metrorail in Miami. McMillen and McDonald
(2004) studied the time pattern of response to the new Midway Line in Chicago,
starting 10 years before the opening of the line in 1993 and extending to 1999,
6 years after the line opened.

There are very few studies of the effect of transportation on the allocation of
land to various uses. As noted above, one difficulty is that zoning ordinances
intervene and potentially alter the allocation of land away from the market-
determined outcome. It is reasonable to suppose that zoning follows the market
in some aggregate sense, but it is unclear whether zoning follows the market in
detail, or whether zoning acts to alter land-use patterns (in pursuit of some
planning objective, for example). One approach to this question is to compare
land-use allocations with and without zoning, a strategy that has been followed
by McMillen and McDonald in a series of studies for Chicago. The study of land
use in 1921 (prior to the 1923 zoning ordinance) by McDonald and McMillen
(1998) shows that the detailed allocation of land to residential, commercial,
and manufacturing use was strongly influenced by proximity to transportation
facilities and distance to the CBD. For example, residential use was negatively
related, and commercial and manufacturing uses were positively related, to proximity to an elevated train line, a main street, a river or canal, a commuter rail
station, and a rail line. Another study of land use in 1921 (McMillen & McDonald
1999), however, found numerous instances of manufacturing and commercial
use mixed with residential use, especially in older areas of the city and along
major streets and near public transportation. Other studies of land use as determined by zoning, such as McMillen and McDonald (1990, 1991) for suburban
Chicago in 1960, show that land use with zoning displays strong similarities
to the results of the study of land use for 1921. However, there is less mixing of
land uses with zoning than without. The strong influence of the transportation
variables is clear in 1960. More detailed empirical studies of actual land-use
patterns are needed.

Studies of the effect of transportation facilities on the intensity of land use
include McMillen and McDonald (1998a,b). These are studies of gross population
density and gross employment density, respectively, in the suburban areas of
metropolitan Chicago. They show that both are positively influenced by proximity to transportation facilities such as a commuter rail station, a highway inter-
change, and O'Hare Airport.

The effects of new mass transit stations on changes in land use have been
studied recently, most effectively by Bollinger and Ihlanfeldt (1997, 2003). The
first study examines employment and population change in the Census tracts in
the Atlanta metropolitan area from 1980 to 1990 as a function of close proximity
to the stations of the new transit system, most of which opened between 1979
and 1982. The study concludes that location near a station had no discernable
impact on either total population or employment change, but that government
employment did increase near the stations targeted for high-intensity land use.
The later study shows that the share of metropolitan employment located in a

Census tract did not increase near the transit stations, but that expenditures on highway improvements did lead to a higher employment share in the Census tract. Neither study employed standard measures of land-use intensity such as employment or population density.

17.5 Conclusion

This essay shall conclude with suggestions for further empirical research on urban land use. The first suggestion pertains to data. Researchers should improve the measures of land use and land-use intensity that are used, so that data and theoretical concepts match. Gross population density and gross employment density are useful measures, but other measures that might be considered include:

- net population density
- net employment density
- gross and net employment density by industry sector
- residential floor-area ratio
- floor-area ratio for employment sectors.

The effect of zoning on land use, and whether zoning follows the market, are unresolved questions. Indeed, there is no agreed-upon standard to judge whether zoning follows (or does not follow) the market.

The basic bid-rent model concludes that greater access to transportation leads to higher bid rent for one or more sectors of the urban economy, which in turn changes land use and increases land-use intensity. There are many empirical studies of the effect of transportation access on prices (real estate values, land values, and so on), and a sizable number of studies that examine the effect of transportation on land use directly – some of which are reviewed in this essay. But there are very few studies that examine both steps – the effect on prices and the effect of prices on land use. One reason for this lack of studies is the fact that effects on prices can, most probably, be seen rather quickly. The effects on land use, if any, probably take several years to emerge. This timing issue is discussed by Bollinger and Ihlanfeldt (1997), but not resolved. McMillen and McDonald (2004) have studied the timing of the effects of a new rapid transit line in Chicago on single-family house prices. The time pattern is shown to be complex, and includes price increases in anticipation of the opening of the transit line as well as additional adjustments after the line opened in 1993. The implications of these results for changes in land use have not been explored.

Recent research has concentrated on the effects of new mass transit facilities on land use. More work is needed on the effects of access to highways and highway interchanges. Research is also needed on the impacts of airports on land use. Airports do not provide transportation within the urban area, of course, but they are central points for interurban transportation that have largely replaced the railroad stations of an earlier era.

Bibliography

Alonso, W. 1964: *Location and Land Use*. Cambridge, MA: Harvard University Press.

Anas, A. 1987: *Modeling in Urban and Regional Economics*. Chur, Switzerland: Harwood.

Bollinger, C. R. and Ihlanfeldt, K. R. 1997: The impact of rapid rail transit on economic development: the case of Atlanta's MARTA. *Journal of Urban Economics*, 42(2), 179–204.

—— and —— 2003: The intraurban spatial distribution of employment: Which government interventions make a difference? *Journal of Urban Economics*, 53(3), 396–412.

Gatzlaff, D. and Smith, M. 1993: The impact of the Miami Metrorail on the value of residences near station locations. *Land Economics*, 69(1), 54–66.

Kain, J. F. 1998: Computer simulation models of urban location. In E. S. Mills (ed.), *Handbook of Regional and Urban Economics*, vol. 2: *Urban Economics*. Amsterdam: North Holland, 847–75.

Lowry, I. 1972: Seven models of urban development: a structural comparison. In M. Edel and J. Rothenberg (eds.), *Readings in Urban Economics*. New York: Macmillan, 151–74.

McDonald, J. F. and McMillen, D. P. 1998: Land values, land use, and the first Chicago zoning ordinance. *Journal of Real Estate Finance and Economics*, 16(2), 135–50.

—— and Osuji, C. 1995: The effect of anticipated transportation improvement on residential land values. *Regional Science and Urban Economics*, 25, 261–78.

McMillen, D. P. and McDonald, J. F. 1990: A two-limit Tobit model of suburban land-use zoning. *Land Economics*, 66(3), 272–82.

—— and —— 1991: A simultaneous equations model of zoning and land values. *Regional Science and Urban Economics*, 21(1), 55–72.

—— and —— 1998a: Population density in suburban Chicago: a bid-rent approach. *Urban Studies*, 35(7), 1,119–30.

—— and —— 1998b: Suburban subcenters and employment density in metropolitan Chicago. *Journal of Urban Economics*, 43(2), 157–80.

—— and —— 1999: Land use before zoning: the case of 1920s Chicago. *Regional Science and Urban Economics*, 29(4), 473–89.

—— and —— 2004: Reaction of house prices to a new rapid transit line: Chicago's Midway Line, 1983–1999. *Real Estate Economics*, 32(3), 463–86.

CHAPTER EIGHTEEN

Urban Transport Policies: The Dutch Struggle with Market Failures and Policy Failures

Piet Rietveld

18.1 INTRODUCTION

Transport is characterized by various market failures that are of particular importance in urban settings. A basic market failure concerns environmental externalities, such as pollution and noise, that are of special relevance in densely populated areas. Traffic safety is also germane in this context. Other externalities relate to congestion on expressways leading into the cities, and on the underlying urban transport networks. Regarding the supply of infrastructure, cities have to deal with the public character of roads: it is so difficult and costly to charge city road users for their use of roads that a private supplier would never supply them. Another failure is the criminality, which affects travelers and transport companies and adds to the cost of urban transport, as it calls for expensive preventive actions from the side of private and public actors. Still another example of market failure is that suppliers of transport services in monopolistic markets may supply poor and expensive services. Related failures occur due to lack of information on, for example, the availability of unoccupied parking places, the supply of taxi services, and public transport services. This failure leads to constrained efficiency.

In the light of these examples, it is inevitable that in many countries the public sector is heavily involved in urban transport policies. However, it is well known that public-sector involvement to foster social welfare considerations may well have unintended side-effects of considerable magnitude. For instance, the introduction of paid parking in cities to stimulate efficient use of parking places will probably lead to shorter parking durations, more car movements, and hence more nuisance by cars in cities. And subsidies to public transport with the aim of reducing car use and its environmental effects may well have adverse effects on the environment when the substitution between car and public transport is limited.

I will use the Netherlands as a special case here, because it is a highly urbanized country that has considerable experience, not only of successful policies but also of policies that have failed, that is relevant for other countries. Insiders claim that the reputation of the Netherlands for its well-developed transport policy is mainly based on the visionary policy memoranda and that the actual implementation is much less impressive. But the policy failures may also contain interesting lessons, as I will demonstrate below. The main focus in this essay is on the private car (car use and parking, discussed in sections 18.2 and 18.3). Since parking is of special relevance in urban areas, I will treat this subject in more detail. Public transport and nonmotorized transport (in particular, the bicycle) are dealt with briefly in sections 18.4 and 18.5. Section 18.6 concludes.

18.2   Curtailing Car Use in Cities

Externalities in car use in the form of emissions, noise, accidents, and congestion have been a dominant policy concern in the Netherlands during the past 15 years. The Netherlands is a small country, smaller than almost all the states in the United States. It is no surprise, therefore, that the national government plays a large role in the formulation of transport policies. A major aim has been to slow down the growth of car use. Congestion has gradually become the major concern, since it has increased strongly during this period. It is concentrated in the western part of the country known as the "Randstad," situated below sea level, where the four major cities (Amsterdam, Rotterdam, The Hague, and Utrecht) are located in an urban ring. These metropolitan areas have populations ranging from 500,000 to 1 million. With distances of 30–70 km between the centers of these four cities, these metropolitan areas are very close to each other. However, in contrast to many gridlocked city centers in the rest of the world, in the Randstad most congestion problems occur on expressways at distances of 10–25 km from each of the main city centers.

During the 1970s and 1980s, transport policy was mainly supply oriented, by the building of expressways. Since then, road construction has continued, but at a more moderate pace, mainly in the form of adding lanes to existing links. A new development was that, on certain expressways, extra road capacity was built to create *dedicated lanes for freight traffic*. Another initiative was an experiment with dedicated lanes for high-occupancy vehicles (a driver plus two or more passengers). This pilot scheme failed because of public acceptability problems: most car drivers seem to be more prepared to accept travel-time losses in the long term with the hope that new roads will finally be built in the future, instead of accepting demand management principles in the present.

In the 1980s, taxes on petrol were already relatively high in the Netherlands. They were further increased to €0.8 per liter, but this did nothing to prevent the emergence of the congestion problems. This is no surprise, given the rather low price elasticities of demand, in particular during the peak. A fuel tax does not divert traffic from the peak to other times of the day and, to make matters even worse, the demand of commuters (who are the major road users during the morning peak) has a low fuel price elasticity compared with other trip purposes. Therefore, as a promising alternative, road pricing differentiated according to time and place has been prominent in policy proposals during the past 15 years. Indeed, from an economic perspective, road pricing should be an indispensable element of policy-making to address congestion. Policy initiatives have come mainly from the central government and, given the polynuclear structure of the Dutch city system, these proposals had to be involved and implemented in more than one city. The first proposal, launched at the end of the 1980s, involved a fee to be paid by electronic means for passing two cordons around the Randstad cities during peak hours. This proposal led to lengthy debates on the technical feasibility of the system, the problem of rat running (traffic diverted to the underlying road network in order to avoid the payment of fees), and the problem of privacy. The proposal met with heavy criticism and was replaced by a much more modest proposal in the form of conventional tolls.

In 1995, a new government returned to the high tech proposal; it involved the introduction of electronic tolls around the four major Dutch cities in the year 2001. Again a cordon system was proposed (with one or two cordons). The system was only envisioned for the morning peak hours between 7.00 and 9.00 a.m., with a flat fee of about €2.50 for those who paid electronically and €3.50 for those who paid otherwise. The proposed system resembled the ERP (electronic road pricing scheme) implemented in Singapore in 1998.

A constant feature of the various proposals has been that the cordons are at some distance from city centers. In most cases, the proposed distance is about 7.5–20 km away from the center. Given the fairly small size of the Dutch cities under consideration, this means that the toll points would all be located outside the cities. This scenario implies a spatial setting that is different from that of Singapore or from the Norwegian toll rings, where the cordon is much closer to the center, and also from the system introduced in Central London in 2003. An important consequence is that in the Netherlands modal shift would be more difficult, because at these greater distances there would be no fine-meshed urban transport system as an alternative for car users. Hence, the major behavioral effect of road pricing that one might expect in this case would be a change in departure time to avoid the toll.

Given the social and political resistance to congestion pricing, in 2000 the national government finally decided to drop the congestion pricing proposal and replace it with a kilometer charge similar to the model introduced in Switzerland for freight traffic in 2001. This was intended to become a flat charge per kilometer that would be differentiated according to car type, but not according to location and time of day. As a consequence, its contribution to the solution of congestion problems could only be minor. After another election in 2002, the new Dutch government decided to drop the whole idea of congestion and kilometer charges.

This led to the interesting situation whereby the Netherlands, which was the forerunner in congestion charge proposals at the end of the 1980s, gradually became part of the rearguard. Price-related measures in terms of tolls or congestion charges were unacceptable to the public, and therefore their introduction nationwide in the short run is improbable. The policy discussion of road pricing appears to be much more sensitive to issues related to equity than to efficiency; and policy-makers largely ignore the voices of economists who argue that congestion pricing can have both attractive efficiency and equity effects; that is, when the receipts flowing to the government are redistributed in a proper way (Rietveld & Verhoef 1998). A possible alternative scenario would be the gradual introduction of road pricing schemes on newly opened expressways, as observed in the USA (see, e.g., Richardson & Bae 1998; Small & Gomez-Ibanez 1998). The 2003 London congestion charging program is another example of how regional or local authorities may in the end be more successful than the national government. This is indeed a striking result obtained by considering the development of parking policies in the Netherlands, which is the topic of the next section.

18.3   PARKING PROBLEMS

To date, parking has received relatively little attention in the transportation research literature (Young 2000). This is rather surprising, since parking is a major policy issue in many cities. One may also note that the average duration per day for which a car is actually used is only about 1 hour, which leaves 23 hours when it is just parked, making the parking theme even more pertinent. So, whereas the car is parked for about 96 percent of the time, it seems that parking attracts less than 4 percent of the time of the researchers in the field. As a small step in the correction of this lack of balance, I shall pay extra attention to the theme of parking in this chapter. The market for parking space is characterized by various distortions. Examples of distortions are externalities, lack of information, the monopoly power of the owner of private parking places, and high transaction costs. We will discuss some of these in more detail below.

18.3.1   Parking and market distortions

Parking is an activity that may easily give rise to *externalities*. A well-known example is that of a lorry parked on a city-center street to be loaded or unloaded, thus blocking the way for other road users. Also, road capacity that is used for parking cannot be used for traffic, which implies a reduction in capacity that may reduce driving speeds. Another example is the effect that parking a car in a parking place may have on extending the time that other road users have to spend trying to find a parking place. Non-road users may also be affected by parked cars, as parked cars reduce the scenic quality of city centers for both visitors and residents, and they reduce the opportunity to use the road for other purposes; for example, as a playground for children. Note also that cars parked on sidewalks hinder pedestrians. Indirectly, parking is also related to the externalities of car traffic, such as noise, emissions, accident risks, and so on. Another problem with parking is the *lack of information* on demand and supply, which leads to constrained efficiency. This may cause car drivers to look for a parking place, implying search and waiting costs that could have been avoided had adequate information been available. The *monopoly pricing* issue is relevant because parking facilities usually serve a very local market, and within many cities there are clear barriers to entry for new entrants in the parking area market. *Transaction costs* relate to the costs of letting car users pay for the use of parking places (for example, by introducing metering for on-street parking). These costs may be so high that the authority responsible for the parking places may decide to offer them free. This is an example of the *nonexcludability* property of infrastructure, meaning that it is impossible, or very costly, to exclude people who do not want to pay for its use.

I will distinguish four important submarkets in the analysis of policy efforts to address these market failures:

- parking in residential areas – new city neighborhoods versus existing areas;
- parking at workplaces – new versus existing.

As will become clear, capacity planning and parking regulations play an important role in the case of new areas, whereas prices are more important for existing areas. The background is that, at the land-use design stage in a new area, it is quite inexpensive to take into account the parking needs of the car users in a quantitative sense. But when land use is already fixed, the expansion of parking space becomes very expensive, so here capacities are assumed as given and price measures become pertinent. However, as we will show below, there are some striking exceptions to this rule that the price instrument will do the job.

18.3.2   Parking in new residential areas

Housing plots in the Netherlands tend to be rather small. The share of single-standing or semidetached houses is limited, especially in urban areas, and also the share of dwellings with a private garage or a parking place is low. Hence, residents of most dwellings park their car on the public road. This leads to the question of how many parking places should be allowed on public roads. In the Netherlands, about 60 percent of households own one car and about 20 percent own two or more cars. This brings the average number of cars per dwelling close to 1.0 per dwelling. Most municipalities apply a parking standard of about 1.5 parking places (including places on private land) per dwelling in new residential areas (Dijken 2002). This seems sufficient, but in reality there may soon be capacity problems at the very local level where some multiple car households are neighbors, and when parking by visitors and of freight vehicles is taken into account. In addition, new neighborhoods often attract households with an above-average numbers of cars.

Some municipalities use parking regulations as a policy measure to reduce car ownership and use by applying low parking standards, slightly above 1.0 per dwelling, in certain neighborhoods. However, this policy is problematic. It easily leads to competition between municipalities in terms of parking standards, so that developers in municipalities with lax parking standards are more successful in attracting new residents. Municipalities that apply strict parking standards will receive less for the land that they sell to developers.

18.3.3   Parking in existing residential areas

In older residential areas, the demand for parking places at zero price level is usually higher than the available capacity. In the large cities, this lack of capacity is substantial. Most medium-sized and large municipalities have introduced paid parking on the public roads during the past decade. Paid parking usually starts in centrally located neighborhoods near shopping areas and then spreads to a much wider area. An interesting question is that of who has to pay the bill: residents or visitors (e.g., commuters). Since the municipality introduces the system, it is not surprising that it tries to shift the tax burden to visitors. The local residents receive preferential treatment: they usually get a parking pass at a low price that gives them the right to park throughout the year. Even in large cities, the price does not exceed €200 per year. So, naturally, especially in the centers of large cities, there is still a large excess demand for parking places. This leads to a system of rationing, which means that many households who would like to have a parking pass have to wait many years before they actually get one.

One possibility that has not been implemented thus far is a combination of rationing and pricing in the form of tradable parking permits. For example, in a certain area with 50 parking places and 100 dwellings, a limited number of parking permits may be distributed among the households such that each household receives, say, a 0.5 permit. Then trading will lead to a situation in which the half of the households who have a low willingness to pay for the permits will sell their permits to the other half, who have a higher willingness to pay. This insures that total parking remains within capacity, so that unnecessary search costs are avoided. Households for whom parking space is most important are guaranteed a place. The advantage for the other households is that they get an additional source of income. The differences with the current situation are as follows: parking places are distributed according to willingness to pay; total receipts are higher, and these receipts do not accrue to the municipality, but to the residents.

An interesting case is where the public sector supplies not only on-street parking space but also off-street parking in garages. There are a good number of examples where the prices charged for renting the garages are lower than those for on-street parking. From a cost perspective, one would expect the reverse, because the provision of parking places in garages tends to be much more expensive (about 40 times, according to Dijken 2002). The reason behind this pricing policy is that on-street parking is perceived to have a negative effect on the attractiveness of residential areas.

Quite a substantial number of urban authorities have even taken further steps to enhance the environment by turning part of the city center into car-free pedestrian areas. Parking facilities have been created on the fringe of the pedestrian areas, and sometimes also underground. Where there is no space for this, parking places have been created at greater distances, with public transport connections linking these places to the central cities. The general result is that the shops in these pedestrian areas have benefited in terms of extra trade. However, much depends on the precise demarcation and size of the pedestrian areas.

As already mentioned above, economists usually prefer the use of prices to correct for externalities, but in the present case of pedestrian areas, economic theory can be used to defend the policy of imposing constraints instead of pricing. Figure 18.1 sketches what the marginal external costs will look like in the case of attractive historical city centers. The striking point is that as the number of parked cars increases, the marginal costs involved decrease: when a street is already almost completely lined on both sides with parked cars, the additional negative effect on the attractiveness of the street will be very small. This has some interesting implications for the use of parking charges to arrive at the optimal balance between the benefits and costs of parking. As Figure 18.1 demonstrates, there may be two or more points of intersection between the curves related to the marginal costs and benefits of parking: the analysis below bears some resemblance to that of Rouwendal, Verhoef, Rietveld, and Zwart (2002), although the context is different.

Case B in Figure 18.1 implies that the optimum is found near full use of the parking space. In this case, the marginal costs are low. On the other hand, in case A, the volume of parked cars is low, and here the marginal costs and benefits are both high. However, this cannot be an optimum, since moving away from A to

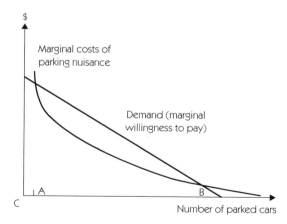

Figure 18.1   Pricing policies addressing the negative effect
on historical cities of parked cars.

the left will lead to an allocation where the benefits will decrease less than the gain in environmental quality. A move to the right will also be favorable, which means that point A relates to minimum instead of maximum net benefits.

A third policy option would be the extreme zero parking solution C. Whether C is more attractive than B depends on the exact form and location of the curves. This leads to an interesting conclusion. If one wanted to correct for this type of parking externality by means of prices, the charge will be either very small (case B) or very high (case C). This means that prices are probably not a good means of solving this type of parking externality. If case C were to be the optimum, a much more straightforward solution would be to impose the physical constraint that parking is forbidden. This is in fact what many cities do: they introduce a car-free zone, or the construction of underground parking space so that parking does not spoil the historical center of the city. If, on the other hand, case B were to be optimal, it would most probably be better not to impose a parking charge, since the welfare gain from a very low charge would most probably be smaller than the transaction costs of collecting the money. This example is a nice illustration of the fact that prices do not deal well with nonconvexities.

18.3.4   Parking at new work locations

During the 1990s, the national government implemented a rather stringent siting policy with respect to firms at new locations. This was known as the "ABC policy" and its aim was to stimulate modal shift away from the car to public transport by getting "the right firm in the right place." This policy attracted wide attention and contributed to the view expressed by Hall (1998): "In The Netherlands, the government has taken some kind of world-wide lead in trying to integrate land use and transport planning, within an environmental strategy, at the national level." The policy was based on a differentiation of locations: *A locations* are places that are easily accessible by public transport and not by car (for example, locations close to inter-city railway stations in city centers); *B locations* are easily accessible via both public transport and car; and the *C location* category includes the remaining locations. The parking standards associated with these locations are given in Table 18.1.

The rationale behind these parking standards is that firms that attract many workers or customers (e.g., business services) are only allowed at A locations. At the other extreme, firms with small numbers of workers per m^2, and that rely on freight transport, are only allowed at C locations. At B locations, firms are welcome that have an intermediate position in terms of the traveler flows that they generate.

The ABC location policy was a rather stringent one, and it generated a number of tensions that appeared so problematic that the fixed parking standards were finally abolished in 2001. One area of tension related to the level of government: the policy was formulated by the national government, but implemented by municipalities. Many of the municipalities with A or B locations had a tendency to give priority to employment growth, and were afraid that the strict parking standards would discourage potential users and developers. Therefore, these

Table 18.1 Maximum parking standards for firms according to type of
location

Type of location	Number of parking places per 100 workers	One parking place per m^2 gross sales area
A locations in the Randstad and large cities outside the Randstad	10	250
A locations elsewhere	20	125
B locations in the Randstad and large cities outside the Randstad	20	125
B locations elsewhere	40	65
C locations	No constraints	No constraints

municipalities tried to be as flexible as possible in issues such as interpreting
whether a location is an A or B location, and what types of firm would qualify for
a B or C location. Another source of tension arising from the ABC policy concerned the competitive position of new locations with restricted parking versus
existing ones where parking standards are less strict. This led to a distortion of
competition that discouraged the development of new sites.

One of the features of the ABC policy is that it was imposed at the level of
individual firms. But some firms may find it much easier than others to live with
strict parking standards. Therefore, an alternative would be to impose a constraint
on the collective of employers in a certain zone. However, such refinements have
no chance: although the ABC location policy was implemented during the 1990s,
for the reasons mentioned above, the use of fixed parking standards was discon-
tinued in 2001.

18.3.5   Parking at existing workplaces

The gradual introduction of paid parking in public parking space in many
municipalities has made firms become more active in terms of parking policies.
In the short run, the parking space in their areas is fixed, so that they face the
problem of distributing parking places among their own personnel.

When there are capacity problems, employers sometimes distribute parking
permits according to certain hierarchy rules. However, the distribution of tradable
parking permits among employees would be an interesting and more efficient
and equitable alternative to insure that the scarce parking places are used only by
those with the highest willingness to pay. As indicated by Gomez-Ibanez (1997),
the case of free parking is an example of bundling a trip and the related activity,
such as work or shopping, with the supply of a parking place. The consequence
of bundling is that employees are not encouraged to look for other transport

modes. The cashing-out of parking subsidies (meaning that those who do not use the parking place get compensation for this) would change the situation: employees would be stimulated to use carpooling or public transport as alternatives (see, e.g., Shoup 1997). A similar result is found when people are obliged to pay for the parking place. Whether cashing-out really leads to a change in modal choice depends on the amount of money involved, and on the availability of travel alternatives. It is clear that in the case of jobs in the centers of large metropolitan areas, both factors are more favorable for inducing such a change compared with other locations.

An interesting question is whether counting the value of a free parking place provided by an employer as part of taxable income would have noticeable effects on commuting behavior. It appears that in high-density areas, the value of a parking space is indeed substantial. If we assume that the cost of providing an underground parking place would be about €30,000, the addition to annual income might be about €3,000, which would mean that, with a marginal income tax of about 50 percent, net income would decrease by about €1,500 per year, which is significant. However, for the large majority of commuters one would find much lower values of parking space, so that counting the value as income would have negligible effects on travel behavior. Given the very local-specific aspects of valuing parking places, one can understand why the national Ministry of Finance has to date been reluctant to bring free parking space under the umbrella of income tax.

The pricing of parking is sometimes advocated as a *second-best policy for road pricing*. If for some reason the direct solution of road pricing is not possible, one may charge road users in an indirect way via parking. However, this is only a rather crude pricing measure, since a parking charge does not differentiate according to the origin of the trip: it may be charged to car drivers who did not contribute to congestion. Additional problems are that a parking charge does not address through traffic (Glazer & Niskanen 1992), and that some of the cars that are involved in congestion will park in private parking places. Hence, the pricing of parking places is in general a rather ineffective way of addressing congestion problems.

It can be concluded that, in the Netherlands, the introduction of pricing has proceeded further with parking than with driving. This is probably due to the fact that parking charges can easily be implemented in a gradual way so that citizens get used to them, whereas road-charging programs were conceived as large-scale high tech initiatives that cannot easily be tested at a smaller scale. The low tech character of parking charges and the availability of alternatives (parking facilities somewhat further away) will also have made their acceptance easier.

18.4   PUBLIC TRANSPORT: A PLUS FOR THE ENVIRONMENT?

The share of public transport is rather low in the Netherlands – about 12 percent of the total distance traveled, about half of which is on the national railways. One important reason for the low share of public transport is that cycling is a very popular and viable alternative (see also section 18.5). Urban public transport receives substantial subsidies from the public sector: the share of subsidies in total receipts varies between 40 percent and 65 percent. There are several good reasons why the government should support public transport in urban areas. First, given average occupancy rates, public transport is more environmentally friendly than private transport. Second, public transport helps to mitigate congestion on the road, so that cities remain accessible. And, further, it may help to reduce social exclusion of handicapped and elderly residents. A final reason concerns the argument that extra travelers in public transport justify the provision of a greater service frequency, which lowers expected waiting times as well as the costs of early and late arrival for all travelers. This is the well-known Mohring effect, as it is an example of a positive externality that can be used to argue in favor of public transport subsidies (Mohring 1976).

From an economic perspective, however, some of these reasons for subsidizing public transport are not entirely convincing. First, consider the environmental argument. A public transport subsidy is essentially a second-best approach to a first-best policy that explicitly addresses the negative externalities of the private car. Such a first-best policy would not only discourage car use in general, and at places with high nuisance levels in particular, but it would also stimulate road users to choose cars with a favorable environmental performance. With a second-best subsidy approach, the favorable effect on technology choice is lost. Concerning the level of car use, a second-best approach is only attractive when (1) there is a high degree of substitutability between car use and public transport and (2) low public transport fares do not attract many new travelers or alternatives from other modes. However, in the case of the Netherlands, these conditions are not met. It appears that demand for public transport has a rather high elasticity with respect to fares, but that this is not primarily because of a modal shift between car and public transport. Cheaper public transport induces many current users to use it more extensively by making more and longer trips, but the modal change between car and public transport is limited. Thus, public transport subsidies are a rather inefficient way of reducing the environmental externalities of car use.

An example of the substitution between car and train is provided in Van Wee and Rietveld (2003). Given estimates of own and cross-price elasticities, it appears that cheaper train tickets that reduce car use by one car passenger–kilometer will induce an increase of no less than five train passenger–kilometers. Even from the perspective of environmental effects, this is not favorable since, on the basis of average emissions per passenger, the reduction in car emission is more than offset by an increase in train emissions.

An extreme example of subsidized transport can be observed in the city of Hasselt, just across the border in Belgium. Here, the municipality decided to introduce free public transport for its bus services. The effect is indeed as may be expected according to the above arguments (Veeneman 2002): car use has declined only marginally and bus use has more than doubled.

Given these results, one may wonder why policies are so strongly oriented toward the stimulation of public transport. A first reason is that the environmental performance of public transport seems to be overrated. Given the rather low occupancy rates in public transport, the emissions per passenger are higher than is technically feasible. Second, there is a clear misperception among policy-makers and the general public concerning the degree of substitutability between car and public transport. Third, while equity issues may be a correct reason for government subsidies, the question remains as to whether the present subsidy system is the best way to address it. More focused income support, or user-side subsidies, might well be considered for this purpose.

18.5   CYCLING BELOW SEA LEVEL

An essay on urban transport policy in the Netherlands cannot be complete without a discussion of the bicycle, which – after the tulips, the windmills, and the wooden shoes – has become one of the major symbols of the country, and with good reason. The bicycle has been a surprisingly robust transport mode in the Netherlands over the past century. While many European cities had high bicycle shares during the first part of the twentieth century, these shares later dropped to low levels (less than 5 percent of all trips) in most countries, whereas in the Netherlands bicycle use has remained at a high level of about 35 percent of all trips within a range of 7.5 km. There are medium-sized municipalities with bicycle shares close to 50 percent of all trips within this distance range. The average number of bicycle trips per person per day is very close to 1.0, implying that, on average, half of the population of the country makes a return cycle trip per day.

Obvious factors that stimulate cycling in the Netherlands are the country's physical conditions, such as a mild climate and a flat surface. But in many cities in other countries with similar conditions, this has not led to similar patterns of cycling, and in Dutch cities that happen to be hilly (found in the southeastern part of the country), the share of cycling is still about 15 percent. Thus, there must be other factors at play, including cultural ones: migrants from foreign countries and their children tend to cycle much less than native Dutch residents. But it is not culture alone that matters. Little can be achieved without the long-run commitment of municipalities to develop and maintain adequate bicycle networks and facilities (see Rietveld & Daniel 2004).

Although, from an international perspective, the infrastructure is adequate for Dutch cyclists, there appear to be substantial differences between municipalities in their policies with respect to cyclists. These differences concern, among other things, the maintenance of cycling lanes, priority rules at crossings, and the detours that cyclists have to make. An interesting example is the municipality of Houten, a new town with about 40,000 inhabitants, with a bicycle share of about 45 percent. Here, cyclists and pedestrians have their own direct routes to the city center, while cars have to make considerable detours. In addition, parking charges appear to impact on bicycle use. There is a clear tendency for the bicycle share to be lower in large cities than elsewhere. For example, in the four largest cities it is about 25 percent. Some factors that may explain this lower figure are the high service levels of public transport in these cities, the high share of residents of foreign origin who have no cultural experience of cycling, and the high risk of theft of bicycles in the large cities. It may well be that the risk of bicycle theft and the perception of lack of public safety in cities are the main reasons why local residents do not to use the bicycle as much as in more rural areas. This would also imply that measures to counter these types of "minor crimes" may be more effective in stimulating cycling than policies in the transport domain itself.

18.6   CONCLUSIONS

Given the high population density in the Netherlands, market failures are important, and it is therefore no surprise that the public sector has been heavily involved in urban transport. The success of this involvement to address the market failure is mixed. In some cases, such as the use of road pricing to mitigate congestion externalities, government intentions have been good, but their plans have never been implemented. And in other cases, such as the subsidization of public transport to avoid problems of social exclusion, the costs for the taxpayer are substantial. But particularly in the field of parking provision, substantial progress has been made during the past decade.

This development runs parallel to a general shift from national to municipality initiatives. In terms of both effectiveness and social and political acceptability, the municipal policies definitely score better. Of special importance in urban areas is the position of nonmotorized transport modes (pedestrians and cyclists). Given the vulnerability of these transport modes, they cannot function adequately without government intervention. Cycling has been a surprisingly vital element in Dutch urban transport. This is the result not only of the country's favorable physical conditions, but also of the municipalities' consistent and long-run commitment to develop bicycle-friendly road infrastructures.

Bibliography

Dijken, K. van 2002: *Parkeren in Nederland.* Zoetermeer/Rotterdam: IOO/AVV.

Glazer, A. and Niskanen, E. 1992: Parking fees and congestion. *Regional Science and Urban Economics*, 22, 123–32.

Gomez-Ibanez, J. A. 1997: Estimating whether transport users pay their way. In D. L. Green, D. W. Jones, and M. A. Delucchi (eds.), *The Full Costs and Benefits of Transportation.* Berlin: Springer-Verlag, 149–72.

Hall, P. 1998: *Cities in Civilization: Culture, Innovation and Urban Order.* London: Weidenfeld and Nicolson.

Mohring, H. 1976: *Transportation Economics.* Cambridge, MA: Ballinger.

Richardson, H. W. and Bae, C. C. 1998: The equity impacts of road congestion pricing. In K. Button and E. Verhoef (eds.), *Road Pricing, Traffic Congestion and the Environment.* Cheltenham, UK: Edward Elgar, 247–62.

Rietveld, P. and Daniel, V. 2004: Bicycle use in the Netherlands: Do municipal policies matter? *Transportation Research A*, 38, 531–50.

—— and Verhoef, E. 1998: Social feasibility of policies to reduce externalities in transport. In K. Button and E. Verhoef (eds.), *Road Pricing, Traffic Congestion and the Environment.* Cheltenham, UK: Edward Elgar, 285–308.

Rouwendal, J., Verhoef, E., Rietveld, P., and Zwart, B. 2002: A stochastic model of congestion caused by speed differences. *Journal of Transport Economics and Policy*, 36, 283–301.

Shoup, D. 1997: Evaluating the effects of cashing out employer paid parking: eight case studies. *Transport Policy*, 4, 201–16.

Small, K. A. and Gomez-Ibanez, J. A. 1998: Road pricing for congestion management. In K. Button and E. Verhoef (eds.), *Road Pricing, Traffic Congestion and the Environment*. Cheltenham, UK: Edward Elgar, 213–46.

Veeneman, W. 2002: Mind the gap; bridging theories and practice for the organisation of metropolitan transport. PhD dissertation, TUD, Delft.

Wee, B. van and Rietveld, P. 2003: Openbaar vervoer en milieu: mythen en feiten. *Milieutijdschrift ArenA*, 9(5), 74–8.

Young, W. 2000: Modeling parking. In D. A. Henscher and K. J. Button (eds.), *Handbook of Transport Modeling*. Oxford: Pergamon Press, pp. 409–20.

PART V

Urban Public Economics

Urban Public Economics

The central issues in public economics – the form of government, the method of taxation, and decision-making on public projects – have been at the center of public debate at least since the dawn of history (the earliest forms of taxes were labor duties and payment of crops). It should therefore come as no surprise that public economics has a long and distinguished intellectual history. Modern urban public economics, however, did not emerge as a well-defined field until the early 1970s, and even now remains somewhat amorphous. Because local government institutions differ so strongly between countries, the field is even more American than the rest of urban economics, though the issues it has taken up will receive increasing attention in other countries.

To understand the scope of urban public economics, it is therefore necessary to understand the broad characteristics of local government in the United States. Like many other countries, the USA has three principal levels of government – central (or federal), state, and local. In many countries, authority essentially rests with the central government, which it delegates to the state governments, which in turn delegate it to local governments. In other countries with a federalist system, the central and state governments operate on a more equal footing, each having its own set of taxes and expenditure responsibilities, as defined in the constitution. But local governments in most of these countries are subservient to state governments. In the USA, in contrast, there is essentially a double layer of federalism, with the federal constitution describing the balance of powers between the federal and state governments, and state constitutions describing the balance of powers between state and local governments. Local governments therefore enjoy a considerably greater degree of autonomy and discretion than they do in most other countries. Another important feature of local government in many metropolitan areas in the USA is *jurisdictional fragmentation* – many small jurisdictions, each with its own local government, surrounding a compact central city, the historical core; the Boston CMSA, for example, has some 200 local governments.

The literature on urban public economics has a number of intertwined strands: fiscal federalism, local taxation, the Tiebout hypothesis, strategic interaction between local governments, and urban political economy.

The central work in fiscal federalism is Oates (1972). The book asks how tax and spending powers *should* be allocated across the three levels of government to achieve efficiency and various measures of equity. Central government provision exploits economies of scale and reduces the problems of interjurisdictional spillovers and fleeing tax bases, but local government permits local control and greater choice. The book, and the literature that has evolved from it, had a major impact on the constitutional debate in Canada, and subsequently on debates concerning the allocation of powers between the European Union central government and the member states.

Historically, the dominant revenue source for local governments in the USA is the property tax. Intergovernmental grants and user fees have become increasingly important sources of revenue to finance local government expenditures, but academic interest in the property tax remains undiminished. Property taxation has taken many forms, but today is predominantly a tax on the market value of real estate, with different effective tax rates applied to different classes of property, the lowest on undeveloped land, followed by single-family housing, multi-unit housing, and commercial property, with industrial property somewhere in the middle. The tax is essentially an equal-rate *ad valorem* tax on land and structures. The immobility of real estate makes it an especially attractive tax base for local government. There is broad agreement that the land component of the property tax is close to neutral and is backward shifted to landowners, but considerable disagreement remains concerning the effects of the structure component of the tax. At least a vocal minority of urban public economists favor replacing the property tax with a tax on land value alone. "Property and Land Taxation," by John Wilson, provides a thorough treatment of the debates.

Paul Samuelson (1954, 1955) argued that there is no effective mechanism by which individuals can register their demand for pure public goods. In reply, Charles Tiebout (1956) argued that individuals register their demand for *local* public goods through their choice of community. This mechanism has come to be termed "voting with the feet." The effectiveness of this mechanism has been the subject of a voluminous literature. One issue is how large a menu of tax/public service packages a household has to choose from; the mechanism may be effective in large, but not medium-sized, cities.

There are unquestionable advantages from having an extensive choice of tax/public service packages, each offered by a separate local government. Diverse tastes for public services are on average better accommodated. Also, keenly aware that local government policies have a strong impact on their property values, homeowners have a strong incentive to be civically active. But there are strong disadvantages too. Whether *voluntary* segregation by political taste is desirable is moot. But Tiebout sorting encourages *exclusion*. The higher classes have an incentive to exclude the lower classes, since "undesirable" neighbors lower property values. And the rich have an incentive to exclude the poor since, under property taxation, owners of more expensive homes subsidize other residents' public services. The most common form of exclusion is zoning; less expensive homes are zoned out by imposing minimum lot sizes (of as much as two acres) and multi-family housing by density restrictions. "Racial steering" by real estate agents is another form of exclusion, but is less common today than it was. "A Theory of

Municipal Governance with an Application to Land-Use Regulation," by William Fischel, looks at this nexus of issues from a governance perspective.

Adam Smith argued that one of the virtues of markets is that by pursuing their self-interest individuals are promoting the social good. That may be true of markets, but it is certainly not true of the collective effects of exclusionary zoning practices by a metropolitan area's suburban jurisdictions. First, imposing myriad restrictions on development drives up housing prices, hurting metropolitan economic development. Second, exclusion spatially concentrates the poor, resulting in the inner-city ghettoes that are so familiar from US cop shows and movies. And, third, gaming between local governments can lead to Nash equilibria that are Pareto inferior in many respects. That last is the topic of Jan Brueckner's essay, "Strategic Interaction among Governments."

In this environment, many central cities face a vicious circle. Their past ills have caused a mass exodus of the middle class to suburban jurisdictions. The resultant decline in property values downtown has caused erosion of the property tax base. In response, the central-city governments have raised tax rates and lowered the quality of already inadequate public schools and other public services. The central city has the added disadvantages that its disproportionate share of institutional property is tax exempt, that state legislatures are dominated by suburban jurisdictions, that many of its residents have "special needs," and that its transportation system is clogged by suburban residents on their journeys to work downtown. Offsetting these disadvantages, as historically the major employment center it can impose taxes on nonresidents who work downtown. But this may just speed up the already rapid suburbanization of jobs. Robert Inman's essay, "Financing Cities," is written against this background.

In discussions of local government reform in the EU, "devolution" seems to be the watchword. The thought of no longer having to navigate an insensitive, impersonal, and Byzantine central government bureaucracy on local issues, having greater choice in local public services, and having direct input into local governance is indeed most appealing. Furthermore, land and property offer promising undertapped tax bases to fund this new-found freedom. But look before you leap, choosing your institutions to avoid the problems that have plagued the US urban public economy.

Bibliography

Oates, W. 1972: *Fiscal Federalism*. New York: Harcourt Brace.

Samuelson, P. A. 1954: The pure theory of public expenditure. *Review of Economics and Statistics*, 36, 387–9.

—— 1955: Diagrammatic exposition of a theory of public expenditure. *Review of Economics and Statistics*, 37, 350–6.

Tiebout, C. M. 1956: A pure theory of local expenditures. *Journal of Political Economy*, 64, 416–24.

CHAPTER NINETEEN

Financing Cities

Robert P. Inman

19.1 INTRODUCTION

In 1904, St Louis, Missouri hosted the World's Fair. The seven-month fair included exhibits from 62 countries and had an attendance of over 2 million visitors. At the time of the Fair, St Louis itself had a legitimate claim to being one of the premiere cities in the USA. It was the country's fourth largest city behind New York, Philadelphia, and Chicago, and it had an average worker's wage that was 20 percent higher than the nation's per capita income. The city's population had grown at an annual rate of 4 percent over the previous 20 years, roughly twice as fast the nation's overall population growth. St Louis had become the gateway to the West. At the time of the 1904 World's Fair, the song "Meet Me in St Louis" promised a good job, a good home, and a good time.

Today, few willingly accept that invitation. The city population has been in a steady decline since its peak at 856,796 residents in 1950. At the time of the most recent US Census (2000), the average city income was $16,000 per person, 26 percent below the national average. The city's unemployment rate was 6.6 percent, compared to a national average rate of 4 percent. The rate of poverty for St Louis residents was 25.7 percent, roughly twice the national average. It is true that economic trends have been moving against older industrial cities, but even against 11 sister cities of the Northeast and Midwest, St Louis offers a poor comparison. She ranks 12th of 12 in current rates of population growth (*negative* and actually last of *all* large cities in the USA), third highest in the percentage of residents living in poverty, third highest in the rate of city unemployment, highest in the rate of crime, and 10th in the rate of real appreciation in median city home values. In 1952, St Louis had 51 percent of the region's employment within its borders. Today, only 12 percent of area jobs are in the city. Over the past 50 years, the suburbs have been gaining jobs at the rate of 2.7 percent per year, while the city has been losing jobs at the rate of 1.7 percent per year.

What happened? St Louis's decline was, to an important degree, a product of its own doing. City public spending per resident in St Louis rose at an annual real rate of 3.4 percent over the period from 1955 to 2000, compared to a national average annual rate of growth of 2 percent for all large US cities, including her 11 Northeast and Midwest comparison cities. The causes of high city spending were high growth rates in public employee compensation and a rising ratio of public employees to city residents. Growing city poverty played a role too. Facing a potentially significant gap between taxes paid and services received, it is not difficult to see why the middle class and businesses stopped "meeting in St Louis."

On January 13, 1999, The Governor of the central bank of Brazil resigned and the country devalued the national currency, the *real*, by 8 percent. The Brazilian stock market fell by 10 percent over the next month and the yield on Brazil's dollar bonds rose by 400 basis points relative to US Treasuries. As two of Brazil's leading trading partners, the prices of Argentinian and Mexican bonds fell as well. Shares in US banks with significant Latin American exposure fell sharply too. While the Brazilian financial markets have now stabilized, there was a significant temporary interruption in the flow of capital into the economy and a slowing of national growth.

What happened? For much of the previous two decades, Brazilian budgetary policies had been determined "from the bottom up." Local politicians in the nation's largest cities controlled local service provision and, as a consequence, local votes. Local votes determined state election outcomes, and state elections for senators and governors drove national policy. The best political strategy for those wanting to hold national office was to provide nationally collected tax revenues to the nation's largest cities. Having broken the connection between revenues collected and services provided, the mayors of Rio de Janeiro, São Paulo, and other large cities were never held responsible for the management of their local budgets. Rather than raise local taxes, mayors lobbied for more grants. When grants slowed, mayors borrowed money from state and national banks. When the local debt was not repaid by the cities, the banks demanded, and received, a deficit bailout from the central government. To pay for the bailouts, the central government itself chose to borrow money. In the end, local fiscal excesses became national debts. When national debt repayment was postponed in 1999 and the currency devalued, Brazil fell into a financial crisis. Once again, mismanaged city finances damaged the private economy – this time the economy of an entire country.

This essay outlines what might be done to avoid the damaging fiscal histories of a St Louis or of the entire Brazilian local sector, for their stories are not exceptional.

19.2   CITIES AND VALUE

Cities exist because of the economic and social advantages of closeness. Today, a city's role is to serve as the economy's idea centers, the place where product innovation occurs, new deals are done, and the creative arts can flourish. Philadelphia and Boston (health care), Tel Aviv, Bangalore, and San Francisco (hardware/software), London, Tokyo, and New York (finance and the arts), Nashville and Paris (music), Bombay and Los Angeles (entertainment), Milan,

Paris, and New York (fashion) are all examples of cities that successfully encourage idea exchange, innovation, and new product development. Today's productive cities support valued creativity through the provision of efficient telecommunication networks, safe and walkable streets, and an educated workforce; these are the essential city services in today's successful cities.

What has always made cities work as economic centers – from Manchester, England, in the 1700s to New York City, London, and Tokyo today – are agglomeration economies, the gain in efficiency that comes from having many firms and workers in close proximity to one another. A growing body of empirical research demonstrates the importance of city agglomeration for today's economy. Ciccone and Hall (1996) find that doubling aggregate employment density in a US county increases the productivity of all county workers by an average of 6 percent; Ciccone (2002) found similar gains in worker efficiency from agglomeration for European regions. Beardsell and Henderson (1999) find that doubling high tech employment density raises the overall factor productivity of high tech firms by 6 percent after 1 year, and perhaps by as much as 17 percent after 4 years. Rosenthal and Strange (2003) provide strong evidence that these economies are greatest within 1 mile of the center of current firm concentration and are typically exhausted within 5 miles. Efficiencies from firm and worker agglomeration are economically important and, particularly important for our story, the benefits are localized to the agglomerating city's economy. The people who benefit from an efficiently organized city are the workers who work there, the homeowners who live there, and the entrepreneurs who have invested in the city's land and structures (see Rauch 1993). Both theoretically and empirically, cities with more spatially concentrated economic activities are more economically valued cities.

19.3   CITIES AND FINANCES

Yet for any city to realize its full economic potential, the efficient provision of city-specific infrastructure and public services is essential. City firms need roads, bridges, and telecommunication networks and city residents need education, safe streets, and clean and healthy environments. These are the tasks of city government. Efficient city finances will require, first, an appropriate assignment of spending and taxing powers and then, second, a structure of city political institutions and rules of governance to insure that these assigned powers are used to maximize resident welfare and firm profitability. Even with appropriate assignment and governance, however, there may be instances in which state or national government assistance in the form in intergovernmental grants-in-aid will be needed to help city governments maximize city economic value. Here I outline what it takes for city finances to be efficient. Table 19.1 summarizes the analysis.

19.3.1   City services

What public services should the efficient city government provide? Successful cities require public services and infrastructure that complement private capital

Table 19.1 Financing cities efficiently

Local service	Financed by:	Organized as:	Governed by:	Assisted by:
Residential services K-12 education	Neighborhood residential property or income taxation *or* resident user fees	Neighborhood council	Majority rule in a neighborhood council elected by "one person, one vote" from neighborhood residents	City-wide or state-wide *matching* equalization aid
Residential services Police/fire patrols	Neighborhood residential property or income taxation	Neighborhood council	Majority rule in a neighborhood council elected by "one person, one vote" from neighborhood residents	–
Residential services Trash collection Parks and recreation Libraries	Neighborhood residential property or income taxation *or* resident user fees	Neighborhood council with an *option to contract* to a private firm	Majority rule in a neighborhood council elected by "one person, one vote" from neighborhood residents	–
Residential services K-12 equalization aid Courts and prisons	City surcharge on residential property or income taxation	City mayor	Strong city mayor elected by "one person, one vote" of city residents	–
Residential services Higher education Water/electricity Public health	City surcharge on residential property or income taxation *plus* user fees	City mayor with an *option to contract* to a private firm	Strong city mayor elected by "one person, one vote" of city residents	–
Residential infrastructure Research library/museums Concert hall/sports stadiums	City-wide debt paid for by city surcharge on residential property or income taxation *plus* user fees	City mayor with an *option to contract* to a private firm	Strong city mayor elected by "one person, one vote" of city residents	–
Business services Police/fire patrols	Business district land taxes or business user fees	Business district/neighborhood council	Majority rule in a business district council elected by voting in proportion to assessed business land values	–
Business services Trash collection Open-space maintenance	Business district land taxes or business user fees	Business district with an *option to contract* to a private firm	Majority rule in a business district council elected by voting in proportion to assessed business land values	–
Shared infrastructure Roadways and parking Water, sewer, electricity Telecommunications Airports and ports	City-wide debt paid for by city surcharge on residential and business taxation *plus* user fees	City mayor with an *option to contract* to a private firm	Strong city mayor elected by "one person, one vote" of city residents in consultation with business district representatives	State-wide or multi-state *matching* aid for environmental spillovers and transit/communications interdependencies

and labor in production and create physical and social environments valued by the cities' residents. Among these services, city governments should be limited to financing those with spatially confined spillovers or congestible sharing technologies. Services with significant spatial spillovers should be financed by higher levels of government, as should government services such as national security with significant economies of scale ("publicness") in production. Candidate city services will include access and neighborhood roads, communication networks, airports and public transit, sewer and water infrastructure, parks and recreation, public health, libraries and cultural centers, police and fire services, courts and prisons, and K-12 education. What city governments should *not* do, at least from their own tax resources, is redistribute incomes. Mobile upper-income households and businesses will simply leave the city, and in the process undermine city agglomeration economies and then finally city economic efficiency (see Haughwout & Inman 2001, 2002). Poverty services should be financed at least at the level of the metropolitan area, and more ideally by state or national governments (see Brown & Oates 1987; Inman 2003a). Table 19.1 lists the public services that the efficient city should provide.

19.3.2   City financing

Current-period services should be financed by current-period taxes and user fees; future-period services should be financed by future-period taxes and user fees facilitated through the issuance of public debt.

TAXES   Economists identify two forms of taxation: *source-based taxation* that taxes factors of production where they are employed, and that taxes goods and services where they are purchased; and *resident-based taxation* that taxes factors of production by owners' residences, and that taxes goods and services by consumers' residences. To the extent that a city resident is both a producer and a consumer of a city good or service, then any city tax on that good or service will be, by definition, both a source-based and a resident-based tax. The taxation of resident-owned city housing is the important example.

But most taxes are either source-based or resident-based. Prominent source-based city taxes include: (1) taxes on city employees' wages regardless of residence (e.g., a commuter tax); (2) taxes on city firms' capital or profits (e.g., commercial–industrial property taxes); (3) taxes on local retail sales; and (4) taxes on city firms' total sales (e.g., a gross receipts tax or turnover tax). Prominent resident-based city taxes include: (1) taxes on residents' wages or more generally all income, and as mentioned, (2) a tax on resident-owned properties. Efficient city financing should pick that mix of taxes that maximizes the profitability of city firms and the welfare of city residents.

Most cities use source-based taxation, for two quite understandable reasons. These taxes are easy to administer, as the collecting agent is typically a firm or business located within the city, and at least initially, a significant share of the burden of such taxes may fall upon nonvoting taxpayers residing outside the city. Unfortunately, source-based taxation often has large negative effects on the overall economic performance of the city's private economy. (It is true that such taxes will collect revenues from outsiders using city services, but there are more efficient ways to charge those visitors; for example, user fees and excise taxes targeted to the outsiders' access to (parking, rail, airport, roadway fees) and stays within (hotel taxes) the city.) Commercial–industrial property taxes, taxation of commuter workers, and the taxation of firm output or sales all reduce firm profitability at the taxing location. Unless the resulting reduction in firm profits is matched by at least a fully compensating profit increase from added city services, the firm, constrained to earn the competitive rate of return, must leave the city. From the perspective of economic efficiency, there is little to recommend source-based taxation.

How cities should finance their local public services is through user fees and resident-based taxation for residential services and user fees and business-based land value taxes for business services. The resident tax might be a tax on residential property or resident wage or income, the latter administered as a locally decided additional tax rate (called "piggybacking") applied to all, or perhaps just a locally decided portion, of the state or federal income tax bases. Business should be charged a combination of user fees for the use of city services (e.g., water, trash, and parking fees) and then a tax on the value of business land when the administration of user fees is not possible (e.g., police and fire services and general infrastructure maintenance). Pittsburgh (USA) and Queensland (Australia) have both successfully administered a business land tax (see Oates & Schwab 1997). Table 19.1 lists an appropriate means for financing each city service.

BORROWING   For the financing of the construction and maintenance costs of city infrastructure – schools, public transit, water works, airports, communication networks, major access roads, prisons and courts, waste treatment facilities – economic theory is clear: Tax payments should be smoothed over the productive life of the government asset through the use of long-term borrowing (see Barro 1979; see also Table 19.1). Ideally, taxes on the resulting improvement in the value of city land should then be used to repay the debt's principal and interest and all ongoing costs of maintenance. The now common use of "tax increment financing" (TIFs) for city capital projects illustrates the feasibility of this approach (see Brueckner 2001). However, if such assessments prove difficult – What is the "reach" of economic benefits from the new sports stadium or museum? – then city-wide taxes on residential incomes or property should be used to fund borrowing for residential projects and, similarly, city-wide taxes on business land should be used to fund business-related projects. Debt for projects that benefit both residents and businesses as such should be repaid by city-wide taxation on both resident and business tax bases.

What should not be allowed is the use of city long-term debt to finance an annual shortfall between current spending (labor, materials, and interest costs) and current revenues (taxes, fees, and grants) by borrowing "off-the-books" through special project accounts, reclassifying current-period expenditures such as janitor salaries as "capital outlays" (once a New York City favorite), or underfunding of defined-benefit public employee pensions, or by just "rolling-over" last year's deficit into this year's budget. Enron's chief accountant and financial officer did nothing that their public-sector counterparts hadn't tried long before; for details, see Inman (1983).

There are two potentially important consequences for economic efficiency of undetected deficit financing. First, if repaid by city taxpayers, as was the case for New York City and Philadelphia deficits, city property values then fall by the discounted present value of all required taxes. Hidden city deficits therefore create uncertainty for new investors, uncertainty that will discourage future investment in an otherwise productive city's economy. Second, if not repaid by city residents – a "bailout" as in the cases of Rio de Janeiro and São Paulo – then the deficit acts as an implicit subsidy to current accounts spending. As a consequence, city spending will be inefficiently too large; see Inman (2003b). To control the first inefficiency, city deficits should be actively monitored by reputable accountants using "generally accepted accounting practices" (GAAP) and the city's surplus or deficit position made known to all potential investors in city properties. Investors will then be able to discount ("capitalize") future taxes into the price they pay for city assets. Lacking reputable monitoring, however, deficit regulation through balanced budget rules may be needed (see Bohn & Inman 1996). To control the second inefficiency, the national government must adopt a credible position against city government bailouts, much like President Ford's response when New York City requested federal assistance following its 1974 fiscal crisis: "Ford to City: Drop Dead." (*New York Daily News*, October 29, 1975; see Inman 2003b). City borrowing is an important tool for efficient city financing, but it must be watched, publicized, and if necessary, regulated.

19.3.3 Fiscal organization

In organizing the responsibility for city finances, the objective is to insure that each dollar raised in taxes is matched by at least a compensating dollar of economic benefits from the provision of city services. The fiscal performance of competitive US suburbs provides compelling evidence in favor of a decentralized system of public financing for city services as a way to insure that marginal benefits exceed, or are at least equal to, marginal costs in the provision of city services. Mobile and informed households and firms, coupled with resident-based taxation for residents, as noted by Hamilton (1975), coupled with business land taxes and user fees for firms, as noted by Fischel (1975), will lead to such an efficient matching of benefits and costs in local budgets. Families and firms that want more or less public services move to locations that provide what they require and, through targeted resident and business taxes and user fees, pay the marginal costs of the extra services they consume. This sorting of firms and households into locations by their favored service/tax packages has become known as "Tiebout shopping," after Charles Tiebout (1956), who first described the logic of such a marketplace. The empirical evidence strongly supports the efficacy of such a system of fiscal governance (see Brueckner 1982; Rubinfeld 1987).

Can the same combination of resident and business-based taxation coupled with firm and household sorting also work to improve fiscal performance in large cities? It's certainly possible, but first a significant reconfiguration of governing responsibilities for city services will be needed. Service responsibility should be based on a simple principle: neighborhood services should be financed and managed by neighborhood governments, and city-wide services should be financed and managed by city government. The key distinction between neighborhood and city-wide services is the geographical or population size of the community needed to provide the service efficiently, allowing for congestion in resident and business use and service spillovers across locations. For most residential city services, economies of scale in population are exhausted with about 20,000 residents and spillovers are rare between communities. For example, education, police and fire protection, trash collection, parks and recreation, and libraries can be well financed and managed by relatively small, neighborhood governments. Where economies of scale or service spillovers are more significant – for example, water and electrical services, telecommunications, trash and waste disposal (but not collection), public health, public transportation, museums and stadiums, and courts and prisons – then city-wide fiscal governance will be appropriate (see Table 19.1).

Whether managed at the neighborhood or city level, residents should retain the legal right to contract with private suppliers for service provision. The option to "contract out" is particularly appropriate when households are not mobile but suppliers are. The bidding process for the right to provide public services gives immobile residents, often the city's lower-income households, the same competitive edge that mobile middle-income families now enjoy from Tiebout shopping. But the contracting process must be done with care. It works best when private suppliers' expertise and capital are easily reproduced and entry barriers are low (Williamson 1976), and when the important dimensions of service output, particularly service quality, are relatively easy to monitor from outside the firm (Hart, Shleifer & Vishny 1997). If service quality from the contractor can only be assured by watching the daily performance of the supplier, then there is little to distinguish managing a contractor from managing one's own public employees; you may as well just call the provider "government." Finally, when contracting out, it is essential that the neighborhood or city government retain ownership of any unique assets essential for service provision. Public ownership prevents contractor "hold-up" and monopoly pricing. Services that might be provided successfully through contracting out include running and maintaining public transit and communication networks, water and sewer services, roadway and park maintenance, libraries, cultural centers, and trash collection. Services likely to be best provided directly by local government, for reasons of assuring quality control, include police and fire services, public health, courts and prisons, and (though many might disagree) K-12 education (see Table 19.1). If contracting out is the chosen option, then currently unionized city workers should be allowed to bid (experience counts), and one supplier might service several contiguous neighborhoods as production or purchasing economies require (see Donahue 1989).

Just as city resident services are best managed by an efficient combination of neighborhood and city governments, so too will be business services, where neighborhood business services might include police and fire, trash collection, and open-space maintenance. The decision by many US cities to allow geographically concentrated firms to create "business improvement districts" (BIDs), with supplemental taxing and spending powers for district-specific services, illustrates both the administrative feasibility and the potential economic attractiveness of the "neighborhood" approach for governing local business services (see Briffault 1999). Here too, when economically appropriate, the business improvement district should be allowed to contract out to private firms for the provision of neighborhood services. Again, see Table 19.1.

There is no reason to think that the families and firms that choose to live and work within the city are any less informed about the quality of their local public goods than their suburban counterparts. Just as we organize local service provision to give choice to suburban residents, so too should we organize the provision of city services. Choice and competition, whether through neighborhood governments or through contracting out, go a long way toward ensuring more efficient city finances and, in the end, maximal firm productivity and household welfare; Rouse (1998), Hoxby (2000), and Holmes, deSimone, and Rupp (2003) provide initial evidence on the point for K-12 education, one of the most important city services.

19.3.4 Fiscal governance

Once the appropriate financing and organizational structures are in place, the task remains to actually choose the level of city, or neighborhood, spending and taxes. Again, we seek to align service marginal benefits with the marginal costs of taxation. Costs are usually known, but how are benefits to be revealed? It is here that we need political institutions and rules for governance.

RESIDENTIAL SERVICES   Citizens reveal their preferences for city services by voting for city spending, either directly through a referendum or indirectly through the election of a local representative. Although there are many alternative ways to aggregate votes, majority rule has much to recommend it. Specifically, it finds a compromise or median position when one exists (see Young 1997).

While there is no guarantee that the median chosen position will be efficient in the economic sense, it can come close. As long as (1) the efficient residential tax structure applies, (2) all citizens vote, (3) citizen preferences for services are separable in the sense that the chosen level of one service (e.g., education) does not influence the preferred level for another good (e.g., police protection), and (4) the distribution of preferences for any public service is not too "badly skewed," then the majority rule outcome for each public service will approximately satisfy efficiency's requirement that social marginal benefits equal social marginal costs (see Bowen 1943; Bergstrom 1979). It does not matter if the budget is set by a referendum for each public service or by a "mayor" or "council" elected at large. In both cases, budget outcomes converge toward the overall median allocation (see Shepsle 1979).

When preferences are not separable, however, then the ordering of the referenda can affect the chosen allocation. In this case, the agenda matters and the agenda-setter can become a dictator. It is essential, therefore, that the agenda-setter be elected by the citizens. Now city and neighborhood budgets are best decided not by issue-by-issue referenda but, rather, by elected city or neighborhood representative government. Representative city government can take either of two forms: legislative-only or *council government*, or executive-only or *strong mayor government*.

Council governance has a problem, however: policy gridlock. Three or more legislators who differ on how best to spend city money may never be able to reach a majoritarian agreement. A majority of the legislators can always team up to disadvantage a minority, but the excluded minority then has a strong incentive to offer a slightly better deal to one of the majority members, to form a new majority. But that budget is then threatened by another deal and a new majority. So it goes on, with the risk that no budget gets approved at all. One way to escape gridlock is through legislative log-rolling, allowing each legislator to submit his or her most favored project for inclusion in the budget. To avoid gridlock and the risk of no new spending, legislators now vote to include *all* new initiatives. Such budgeting is likely to be very inefficient, however, much like what happens when a group of friends agree to share the dinner check. Why order salad when you share the costs of everyone else's steak and lobster? At the end of the evening, the dinner bill is very expensive and, for the same reasons, so too will be the city's budget.

Further, the more legislators around the city council's "dinner table," the larger will be the *per resident* or *per legislator* budget. Baqir's (2002) study of city budgeting finds that, all else being equal, doubling the size of a typical city council, say, from the study's sample mean of seven to 14 members, leads to a 20 percent increase in city spending per resident. Inman's (1995) case study of Philadelphia provides more direct but consistent evidence on the point. In 1979, the leadership of Philadelphia's then nearly all white (there was one black councilman) city council got caught seeking bribes in the federal government's Abscam sting operation. Six of 17 council members were either convicted or forced to resign, all just before the city's November election. As a result, six new black and Hispanic members were elected to city council. It is fair to think of this result as a 33 percent increase in effective council membership, as the majority of Philadelphia's minority neighborhoods received effective representation for the first time. The budgetary consequence of this "natural experiment" was a one-time 25 percent increase in city-wide spending on neighborhood services and a 5 percent increase in overall city spending.

Fortunately, city government is destined neither to gridlock nor to log-roll. The strong executive form of governance – a neighborhood or city-wide elected executive granted broad agenda-setting powers and a line-item veto – provides a middle ground. Projects whose neighborhood-wide (for neighborhood services) and city-wide (for city services) benefits do not exceed their costs will never appear on the agenda – or if they do, they will be vetoed. Strong executives, perhaps supported by strong local political parties, will typically be able to sustain those vetoes through their control over the votes of the legislature's party members (see Fitts & Inman 1992). Budgets in strong-mayor cities are typically less expensive, and arguably more efficient, than the "something for everyone" budgets normally found in council-only cities (see Baqir 2002).

BUSINESS SERVICES   Owners of businesses within the city, unless they are residents as well, are not allowed to participate directly in the setting of city fiscal policies. The exception to this rule is in setting policies for "business improvement districts," or BIDs, which are business associations created by state law, and granted supplemental taxing, borrowing, and spending authority for district-specific services and capital improvements that benefit business (see Briffault 1999). However, little careful thought has been given to how BIDs might best decide their assigned fiscal policies. Here, the new literature on shareholders' rights and corporate governance may be instructive. In its fundamental form, a BID is a much like a corporation, with business property owners within the BID acting as stockholders, whose "share" holdings are proportional to the value of their of business property. Like the corporation, the sole objective of the BID is to maximize the value of business (stockholder) property wealth. Much as the rule of "one share, one vote" is the efficient voting rule for corporate control (Harris & Raviv 1988), wealth-based voting – votes proportional to the market value of property held within the BID – will typically be the efficient means for deciding the BID's public goods spending. Such a rule will allocate greater voting power to the largest property owners in the BID, creating appropriate incentives to collect information on the effects of BID-wide services on value and to insure efficient monitoring of the BID's management staff (see Shleifer & Vishny 1997). Small shareholders must not be ignored, however, particularly if district projects have differential effects on the value of types of properties. Wealth-based voting insures that all property owners will have a say.

SHARED INFRASTRUCTURE   The primary beneficiaries of city-wide infrastructure investments that benefit both residents and businesses will be the residential and business property owners within the city (see Haughwout & Inman 2001). Shared city-wide infrastructure includes access roads and boulevards, telecommunication networks, subways and buses, courts and prisons, airports, parking garages, and sewerage and water systems. Such investments should be debt financed with principal and interest paid using land taxation. Since the ultimate beneficiaries of such investments are property owners, city-wide referenda for approval of debt issuance using wealth-based voting designed to include owners of residential *and* business property is likely to be efficient. It seems appropriate to allow the residentially elected city mayor to set the agenda for city-wide infrastructure referenda, perhaps in consultation with BID representatives.

19.3.5   Fiscal assistance

As a general rule, city residents and firms should be solely responsible for the financing and management of the city services listed in Table 19.1, but there are two instances when outside fiscal assistance may be appropriate. The first arises when the city provides a public service that qualifies as a national or state constitutionally protected "merit good" demanding equal provision to all residents. K-12 education is the prominent US example, with protection provided by state constitutions (see Inman & Rubinfeld 1979; Murray, Evans & Schwab 1998). Protection comes either as guaranteed equal access to tax resources for the financing of education – called "tax base equalization" – or as equal access to a court-defined minimal level of school spending for all children. Even when such protections are not constitutionally required by the state, city residents might wish to offer their own protections for all city children.

To achieve either standard, matching aid is the efficient policy response (see Inman 1999). To insure that all neighborhoods finance local education from a common tax base, local council own tax revenues should be matched at the rate $m_n = (B^*/B_n - 1)$, where B^* is the target common tax base per child and B_n is the neighborhood's tax base per child. Wealthy neighborhoods where $B^* < B_n$ contribute revenue into the aid program ($m_n < 0$), while poorer neighborhoods where $B^* > B_n$ receive equalization aid ($m_n > 0$). Equalization aid received equals $m_n(\tau_n B_n)$. Total neighborhood revenues will now equal own tax revenues ($\tau_n B_n$) plus equalization aid, or: revenues $= \tau_n B_n + m_n(\tau_n B_n) = \tau_n B_n(1 + m_n) = \tau_n B_n(B^*/B_n) = \tau_n B^*$. Each locally chosen tax rate raises revenues from a common tax base, just as required for tax base equalization.

To insure that all children receive a minimal level of school spending, the efficient matching grant should stimulate spending in low-performing neighborhoods while leaving spending unaffected in high-spending neighborhoods. Own-neighborhood spending is often well described by a log-linear relationship between spending (g_n), neighborhood average income (I_n, or other pro-education attributes), and the net cost of a dollar spent $(1 - m_n)$: $g_n = I_n^\alpha (1 - m_n)^{-\beta}$, where α is the income elasticity of demand for spending and β is the (absolute value of) the price elasticity of demand for school spending (see Rubinfeld 1987). To insure minimal standards for all children, neighborhoods predicted to spend $g_n < g^*$ should receive a matching grant at the rate $m_n = 1 - (I^{\alpha/\beta}/g^{*1/\beta})$. With such aid, $g_n = g^*$. Neighborhoods predicted to spend $g_n \geq g^*$ already achieve the minimal standard and therefore receive no aid: $m_n \equiv 0$. The minimal standard matching rate falls toward zero as neighborhoods value education more highly (i.e., as I rises) and rises as the minimum standard increases.

The second case for fiscal assistance to the city budget occurs when the city provides a service with significant positive economic spillovers to nonresidents. Plausible examples include city infrastructure spending for inter-city transit connections, water and air quality, and telecommunication networks. Residents and city firms may fail to fully internalize the full social benefits of such services when deciding city investment – that is, city-only marginal benefits (CMB_c) may be less than social marginal benefits (SMB_c): $\varphi_c \times CMB_c = SMB_c$, where $\varphi_c > 1$. Again, a matching grant for city own spending on the relevant service is appropriate, now specified as $m_c = [1 - (1/\varphi_c)]$ (see Inman 1999). Larger marginal spillovers (φ_c increases) require larger matching grants. Such grants should be funded by the largest political jurisdiction affected by city spillovers, generally the city's immediate state or adjacent states (see Table 19.1).

19.3.6 Are we asking too much?

The fiscal and political institutions of city financing proposed here require city residents and firms to monitor the provision of 10 or so local services and three local tax rates, and to vote three times – for a mayor, for a neighborhood or BID representative or manager, and for infrastructure spending. Might this be institutional overload?

An important lesson learned from California's financing of city services gives us reason to pause in our desire to create new local governments. During its population explosion of the 1970s, California responded with a new local government for each local service, and each new government was given its own property tax rate. This structure – designed to match marginal benefits to marginal costs as well – would have been fine with stable tax rates, but in California's booming housing market and with court-required property reassessments, constant fine-tuning of property tax rates became a necessity. When local tax rates were not adjusted downward, the many local governments received large, and largely unintended, increases in homeowner tax revenues. To check this explosion in tax payments, California residents had to complain to as many as 10 separate local governments. Citizen control collapsed under the weight of too many local governments. In the end, the only answer was a state-wide cap on total local property taxation at 1 percent of assessed value, a law known as Proposition 13 (see Oakland 1979). The loss of local control over local taxation led to a decline in overall spending on local services, and on local schools in particular, and a fall in the overall quality of city services (see Sonstelie, Brunner & Ardon 2000).

The proposals here for city financing are not so extreme. The lines for service and tax responsibilities are clearly drawn between the proposed layers of city government, and each resident or firm must decide at most three local tax rates and monitor at most two local governments. This is the current institutional oversight now expected of most suburban residents and firms. There is no reason to believe that city residents and firms are not up to these tasks as well.

19.4 CITY FINANCES AND CITY VALUE

The economic contribution of city finances to the welfare and profitability of city residents and firms is best measured by what those outside the city are willing to pay to live and work within the city. As long as the benefits from city services exceed the costs paid through taxes or user fees to consume those services, then households and firms now outside the city will find moving into the city an attractive option. To consume city services, however, new entrants will need to buy an "admission ticket" into the city. This ticket is a parcel of city land. The price of land will rise until it fully reflects the net gain from city services – benefits minus costs – to firms and households now in, or planning to locate in, the city. Efficient city finances maximize service benefits minus service costs, and as a consequence, city land values as well (see Brueckner 1983). A footprint of more efficient city finances is therefore rising city land prices. There is growing evidence that adopting the service and tax assignments and the institutions of governance recommended in Table 19.1 will do just that.

19.4.1 Service assignment and value

Among city services, the most important *mis*-assignment, at least for US cities, is the required shared fiscal responsibility for poverty services to low-income city residents, services such as public housing, public medical care, child foster care, income transfers, and administration. Currently, mandated poverty expenditures impose a tax burden on city middle-class families and city firms averaging from $400 (Philadelphia) to as much as $600 (New York City) per taxpaying family, or about 1 percent of median family income. Not surprisingly, middle-class families will be discouraged from locating in such cities, and to the extent that city businesses share in this fiscal burden, so too will firms. City land values will decline. Haughwout and Inman (2002), for example, estimate econometrically that, over the decades 1970 to 1990, a 10 percent increase in the rate of city poverty – say, from 0.20 to 0.22 – reduced median city home values in US cities by between 8 percent in small cities (MSAs with less than 250,000 residents) and 15 percent in large cities (MSAs with more than 250,000 residents), even after controlling for fiscal assignment and other city fixed effects.

There are three possible effects at work here. The first is simply redistributive; the second and third have important consequences for city economic efficiency. The redistributive effect arises from the fact that the city budget takes tax money from middle-class families living in the median value home and gives those resources to low-income families. For example, a $400 transfer from city taxpayers to low-income residents reduces the value of taxpaying properties by approximately $10,000 if there is full market capitalization at a 4 percent real market interest rate (−$10,000 = −$400/0.04), roughly a 16 percent fall in a large US city's median home value of $60,000 in 2000. By this reasoning, a 10 percent increase in the city's share of families in poverty (or, equivalently, in city poverty spending) will reduce middle-income home values by an additional $1,000, or 1.6 percent. While significant to be sure, such fiscal redistributions alone do not account for the 8–15 percent effect of poverty on city land values as estimated by Haughwout and Inman (2002). Something more must be going on.

Haughwout and Inman (2002) suggest that part of the larger effect may be due to poverty spending's adverse effect on city agglomeration economies, as middle-class families and firms leave the city as their taxes rise or services decline. The resulting fall in city productive efficiency leads to a further decline in city attractiveness and thus land values. Haughwout and Inman provide an estimate of this second, indirect, effect of poverty spending using a general equilibrium model of an open city economy with agglomeration. Calibrated to match the Philadelphia metropolitan economy and the best recent evidence on the economic advantages of city agglomeration, they find that a 10 percent increase in city poverty leads to a 10 percent decline in city land values. By the model's specification, this 10 percent decline in value includes both the direct redistribution effect of having more poor families, leading to the direct 1.6 percent fall in value, plus the indirect fiscal effect of lost city agglomeration economies, accounting for the remaining 8.4 percent fall in value. This 8.4 percent fall in land values is an estimate of the adverse efficiency effect of mandated poverty spending on the city's private economy. Still, there remains, at least by Haughwout and Inman's estimates for large cities, an additional 5 percent adverse effect of poverty on city land values that is not yet explained. What else is going on? A third adverse effect, now a spillover from city poverty to the cost of providing public services to city residents is one possible answer. K-12 education (Dunscombe & Yinger 1997) and police services (see the chapter by Stephen Raphael and Melissa Sills in this volume) are likely to be the most affected city services.

The solution to the mis-assignment of poverty spending to cities is to remove the associated unfunded mandates from the city's budget, either directly through state or federal provision or equivalently through state or federal funding of the mandates. Further, if city poverty imposes added production costs for the provision of city services, then matching aid to cover these added costs will be appropriate (see Dunscombe & Yinger 1997). The effects will be exactly what one would expect – a more efficient city economy and rising city land values (Inman 2003a).

19.4.2   Tax assignment and value

Among city taxes, the most important *mis*-assignment, again prominent in US cities, is to allow the use of business taxes to finance residential services. The resulting fiscal redistribution from firms to households discourages firm location within the city, reduces city agglomeration economies and productive efficiency, and thereby depresses city land values. The available empirical evidence strongly suggests that city business taxes drive business from the city (see Bartik 1991). Haughwout, Inman, Craig, and Luce (2004) provide a detailed look at the effects of city sales and labor taxes on the city economies of New York City and Philadelphia over the decades from 1970 to 2000. Given the mobility of shoppers across city boundaries, sales taxes (New York City) and gross receipts taxes (Philadelphia) will be largely borne by city firms. City sales decline and firms leave the city to avoid the tax. Haughwout et al.'s estimates of the elasticity of city sales with respect to the two taxes are large and statistically significant: −0.5 for New York City and −0.3 for Philadelphia. City wage or income taxes have much the same effect. While nominally levied on city residents – though both New York City and Philadelphia also taxed commuters directly during the period of the study – the tax can be avoided by choosing to live, and mostly likely then work, outside the city. This requires city firms to raise city wages by an amount equal to the burden of tax so as to attract workers to the firm. Again, a portion of the tax is borne by city firms, and firms leave the city. Haughwout et al.'s estimates of the elasticities of city jobs with respect to city income taxes are also significant: −0.2 for New York City and −0.4 for Philadelphia. The larger effect for Philadelphia likely reflects the relatively larger tax rate on commuters in this city, a tax whose direct burden is more nearly fully borne by city firms.

While business taxes drive firms from cities, it is not obvious that city land values fall. Residents still benefit from the fiscal redistribution. Land values may rise if the residents' demands for city locations more than offsets lost business demand. This does not appear to be the case, however, when agglomeration economies are present. A general equilibrium analysis of the Philadelphia city economy finds that, even with modest agglomeration, the elasticity of city land values with respect to business taxation can be sizeable: −1.3 with respect to a tax on business capital (Haughwout and Inman 2002) and −0.2 with respect to a wage or commuter tax on labor (Inman 2003a). Voith's (2003) recent econometric study of the effects of the Philadelphia commuter wage tax on city property values finds comparable elasticities.

As recommended by Table 19.1, the solution here is to substitute business land taxation and business user fees for direct taxes on business sales, capital, and labor. Pittsburgh did just this in 1979 as part of an overall economic development reform. The city significantly increased the rate of land taxation, offered exemptions from taxation on new business structures, and held the line on city wage taxation. The tax reforms appear to have made a significant difference for the Pittsburgh economy. Oates and Schwab (1997) compared the trend in the value of new building permits (a correlate with city land values) in 15 cities in the industrial Midwest over the decades from 1960 to 1989. Until 1979, the trend is either flat or downward in all cities, including Pittsburgh; cities were either stagnant or in decline. After the 1979 tax reforms, however, Pittsburgh breaks away from the group and shows a significant upward jump in the value of new construction, by an amount nearly sufficient to offset in 10 years the previous 20 years of declines. Oates and Schwab are careful to note that such business tax reforms alone will not save a declining city, but if residents and firms want to live and work in a particular location – and Pittsburgh in the 1980s was such a city – then an efficient tax structure allows the city to reach its full economic potential.

19.4.3 Governance and value

Although the appropriate assignments of spending responsibilities and financing instruments are necessary for efficient city finances, they are not sufficient. City politicians who implement those assignments must have an incentive to do so in ways that maximize the economic net fiscal benefits to city residents and firms. The institutions of city governance must align the political interests of elected city officials to the economic interests of those who live and work within the city. Table 19.1 suggests that fiscal competition between local neighborhood governments for services that can be efficiently provided to small communities of, say, 10,000–20,000 families coupled with a strong mayor form of governance for city-wide services and infrastructure might be such a governance structure. What's the evidence?

There is little doubt that citizens are willing to pay for good local public services offered at low tax rates and that they do so through the purchase of land in communities or neighborhoods that offer a favored fiscal package (see Rubinfeld

1987). When the service and tax package is efficiently provided, then local land values will be maximized (see Brueckner 1983). Communities that over- or underspend relative to resident preferences will see their land values decline. Barrow and Rouse (2004) use this observation to econometrically test for the efficiency in the provision of K-12 education across 9,000 local school districts in the USA; overspending districts will see their property values decline as spending increases. This is indeed what Barrow and Rouse find. Most relevant for the arguments here, their results strongly support the proposition that fiscal competition encourages fiscal efficiency. Efficient school districts are more likely to be found in counties with many school districts, and all else being equal, central-city school districts are less efficient than small and median-sized school districts. Further, it appears to be fiscal choice by residents that provides the discipline. Brueckner's (1982) study of Massachusetts communities in fiscal year 1976 reached much the same conclusions as Barrow and Rouse, but then in November 1980, Massachusetts passed Proposition 2½, limiting local taxation to 2.5 percent of local property values. Those communities not in compliance with the law were required to reduce revenues and spending until the constraint was met. Examining local property values in 1992, Lang and Jian (2004) found that all communities facing a binding spending limitation suffered significant declines in local property values. Choice plus competition appear to promote local government fiscal efficiency. Still, large cities seem immune to these disciplinary pressures.

One possible explanation for overspending in large US cities is the control over service provision given to public employee unions where state law requires an "explicit-duty-to-bargain." Residents in these cities cannot set wages, benefits, and employment levels (e.g., class size for education) without an agreement with the union. "Contracting out" also must be negotiated. If the net effect of such strong unionization is fiscal inefficiency, then residents and firms who can leave the city will choose to do so. City land values should decline. This is just what Haughwout and Inman (2002) find in their study of large city finances, where cities with strong unions depress city land values by an average of 12 percent. The fact that suburban land values also decline in the MSAs with strong union cities – by an average of 7 percent – suggests these fiscal inefficiencies lead to private-sector inefficiencies as well, presumably through lost agglomeration economies as firms and middle-income households leave the city (see Haughwout & Inman 2002). Fiscal competition provided by neighborhood governments with neighborhood-negotiated labor contracts or contracting out generally could serve to check these union-induced fiscal inefficiencies (see Hoxby 1996).

A second explanation for large city fiscal inefficiencies is the need for political log-rolls between locally elected city legislators when deciding the city's budget. The evidence is clear that such deal-making leads to higher spending – about $450 more per city family when council size is doubled – and that a strong mayor with a veto can fully neutralize the increases (see Baqir 2002). But is this extra spending inefficient? The evidence from Haughwout and Inman (2002) is again suggestive on the point. Property values in large cities with a council-only form of governance are 4 percent lower than in cities with strong mayor governance, a loss in value of about $2,100 per central-city home. So too in the suburbs, as this apparent fiscal inefficiency induces a less efficient private economy with lost agglomeration economies; in MSAs whose cities have council-only governance, suburban property values are 5 percent lower, which implies a loss of about $2,800 per suburban home.

We should also ask: How inefficient is this extra spending? Combining the Baqir spending estimates with the Haughwout and Inman capitalization estimates – both studies sample all large US cities in the 1990s – suggests, with a bit of creative accounting, that each extra dollar of council-only spending generates perhaps only $0.33 in net economic benefits. From Haughwout and Inman, the total loss in MSA property values because of council-only governance is $7,700 per city family (= $2,100 per city family + [$2,800 per suburban family] × 2 suburban families per city family) or $300 per city family in lost economic value per year assuming a real interest rate of 4 percent (= 0.04 × $7,700). From Baqir, council-only governance adds about $450 per year in city spending. Thus, the net economic gain from council-induced spending is only $150 per city family (= $450 per city family – $300 per city family), or about $0.33 per marginal dollar spent. While only an example, these calculations make a quite general point. The institutions of fiscal governance, like those of fiscal assignment, matter for ensuring an efficient city.

19.5 Conclusion

All economies do two things: first create and then divide an economic surplus. City economies are no different. What makes city economies unique, and therefore not easily reproducible, is their natural location advantages and their, perhaps historically dictated, agglomeration economies. Once in place, city productive assets should be employed as efficiently as possible. To that end, a well-run city government is essential, providing those goods and services that best complement the city's private economy. Public infrastructure investments in access, local roads, and public transit, in waste disposal, in telecommunications, in electrical generation and distribution, and in ongoing service provision for K-12 education, public safety, environmental quality, public health, and the cultural life of residents are all part of the efficient city's service portfolio. The appropriate financial instruments to fund these services are income and/or property taxes on city residents and land taxes and user fees on city firms. To insure that each dollar of revenues raised provides at least a compensating dollar of benefit in services provided, city governance must allow for competition and choice when the efficient scale of city services is relatively small and strong, but for democratically elected, mayoral leadership when the efficient scale of services is city-wide. The evidence suggests that such a structure of fiscal assignment and governance goes a long way toward ensuring an economically efficient, surplus-maximizing, city.

It is in dividing the city's surplus that fiscal inefficiencies might then arise. Requiring cities to fund a significant share of poverty services for low-income households, allowing residents to tax business assets to pay for residential services, granting public employee unions monopoly control over the provision of public services, and adopting a system of fiscal governance that encourages a "something-for-everyone" budget all lead to a less efficient public sector and, in the end, a less efficient private sector too.

The central lesson of this essay is clear. Efficient city finances facilitate efficient private economies, but we must leave to city finances those tasks it can do well; namely, the provision of public services that facilitate the city's competitive position in the wider private market economy.

Bibliography

Baqir, R. 2002: Districting and government overspending. *Journal of Political Economy*, 110, 1,318–54.

Barro, R. 1979: On the determination of government debt. *Journal of Political Economy*, 87, 940–71.

Barrow, L. and Rouse, C. 2004: Using market valuations to assess public school spending. *Journal of Public Economics*, 88, 1,747–70.

Bartik, T. 1991: *Who Benefits from State and Local Economic Development Policies?* Kalamazoo, MI: W. E. Upjohn Institute for Employment Research.

Beardsell, M. and Henderson, V. 1999: Spatial evolution of the computer industry in the USA. *European Economic Review*, 43, 431–56.

Bergstrom, T. 1979: When does majority rule supply public goods efficiently? *Scandinavian Journal of Economics*, 81(2), 216–26.

Bohn, H. and Inman, R. 1996: Balanced budget rules and public deficits: evidence from the U.S. states. *Carnegie–Rochester Conference Series on Public Policy*, vol. 45 (December) 13–76.

Bowen, H. 1943: The interpretation of voting in the allocation of economic resources. *Quarterly Journal of Economics*, 58, 27–48.

Briffault, R. 1999: A government for our time? Business improvement districts and urban governance. *Columbia Law Review*, 99, 365–476.

Brown, C. and Oates, W. 1987: Assistance to the poor in a federal system. *Journal of Public Economics*, 32, 307–30.

Brueckner, J. 1982: A test for allocative efficiency in the local public sector. *Journal of Public Economics*, 19, 311–31.

—— 1983: Property value maximization and public sector efficiency. *Journal of Urban Economics*, 14, 1–15.

—— 2001: Tax increment financing: a theoretical inquiry. *Journal of Public Economics*, 81, 321–43.

Ciccone, A. 2002: Agglomeration effects in Europe. *European Economic Review*, 46, 213–27.

—— and Hall, R. 1996: Productivity and the density of economic activity. *American Economic Review*, 86, 54–70.

Donahue, J. 1989: *The Privatization Decision: Public Ends, Private Means*. New York: Basic Books.

Dunscombe, W. and Yinger, J. 1997: Why is it so hard to help central city schools? *Journal of Policy Analysis and Management*, 16 (Winter), 85–113.

Fischel, W. 1975: Fiscal and environmental considerations in the location of firms in suburban communities. In E. S. Mills and W. E. Oates (eds.), *Fiscal Zoning and Land Use*. Lexington, MA: D. C. Heath.

Fitts, M. and Inman, R. 1992: Controlling congress: presidential influence in domestic fiscal policy. *Georgetown Law Journal*, 80, 1,737–85.

Hamilton, W. 1975: Zoning and property taxation in a system of local governments. *Urban Studies*, 12, 205–11.

Harris, M. and Raviv, A. 1988: Corporate governance: voting rights and majority rule. *Journal of Financial Economics*, 20, 203–35.

Hart, O., Shleifer, A., and Vishny, R. 1997: The proper scope of government: theory and an application to prisons. *Quarterly Journal of Economics*, 112, 1,127–63.

Haughwout, A. and Inman, R. 2001: Fiscal policies in open cities with firms and households. *Regional Science and Urban Economics*, 31, 147–80.

—— and —— 2002: Should suburbs help their central city? *Brookings–Wharton Papers on Urban Affairs*, 2002, 45–88.

——, ——, Craig, S., and Luce, T. 2004: Local revenue hills: evidence from four U.S. cities. *Review of Economics and Statistics*, 86, 570–85.

Holmes, G., DeSimone, J., and Rupp, N. 2003: Does school choice increase school quality? NBER Working Paper 9683, May.

Hoxby, C. 1996: How teachers' unions affect education production. *The Quarterly Journal of Economics*, 111, 671–718.

—— 2000: Does competition among public schools benefit students and taxpayers? *American Economic Review*, 90, 1,209–38.

Inman, R. 1983: Anatomy of a fiscal crisis. *Business Review: Federal Reserve Bank of Philadelphia*, June, 15–22.

—— 1995: How to have a fiscal crisis: lessons from Philadelphia. *American Economic Review*, 85, 378–83.

—— 1999: On designing intergovernmental transfers with an application in the new South Africa. In A. Panagariya, P. Portney, and R. Schwab (eds.), *Environmental and Public Economics: Essays in Honor of Wallace Oates*. Northampton, MA: Edward Elgar, 222–52.

—— 2003a: Should Philadelphia's suburbs help their central city? *Business Review: Federal Reserve Bank of Philadelphia*, June, 24–36.

—— 2003b: Transfers and bailouts: enforcing local fiscal discipline with lessons from U.S. federalism. In J. Rodden, G. Eskeland, and J. Litvack (eds.), *Fiscal Decentralization and the Challenge of Hard Budget Constraints*. Cambridge, MA: The MIT Press, 35–83.

—— and Rubinfeld, D. 1979: The judicial pursuit of local fiscal equity. *Harvard Law Review*, 92, 1,662–750.

Lang, K. and Jian, T. 2004: Property taxes and property values: evidence from Proposition 2$^{1}/_{2}$. *Journal of Urban Economics*, 55, 439–57.

Murray, S., Evans, W., and Schwab, R. 1998: Education finance reform and the distribution of education resources. *American Economic Review*, 88, 789–812.

Oakland, W. 1979: Proposition 13: genesis and consequences. *National Tax Journal*, 32 (June, Supplement), 387–409.

Oates, W. and Schwab, R. 1997: The impact of urban land taxation: the Pittsburgh experience. *National Tax Journal*, 50, 1–21.

Rauch, J. 1993: Productivity gains from geographic concentration of human capital: evidence from cities. *Journal of Urban Economics*, 34, 380–400.

Rosenthal, S. and Strange, W. 2003: Geography, industrial organization, and agglomeration. *Review of Economics and Statistics*, 85, 377–94.

Rouse, C. 1998: Private school vouchers and student achievement: an evaluation of the Milwaukee Parental Choice Program. *Quarterly Journal of Economics*, 113, 553–602.

Rubinfeld, D. 1987: The economics of the local public sector. In A. Auerbach and M. Feldstein (eds.), *Handbook of Public Economics*, vol. 2. New York: North-Holland.

Shepsle, K. 1979: Institutional arrangements and equilibrium in multidimensional voting models. *American Journal of Political Science*, 23, 27–59.

Shleifer, A. and Vishny, R. 1997: A survey of corporate governance. *Journal of Finance*, 52, 737–83.

Sonstelie, J., Brunner, E., and Ardon, K. 2000: *For Better or for Worse: School Finance Reform in California*. San Francisco: Public Policy Institute of California.

Tiebout, C. 1956: A pure theory of local government expenditures. *Journal of Political Economy*, 60, 415–24.

Voith, R. 2003: Philadelphia city tax structure and the metropolitan economy. Mimeo., May.

Williamson, O. 1976: Franchise bidding for natural monopolies – in general and with respect to CATV. *The Bell Journal of Economics*, 7 (Spring), 73–105.

Young, P. 1997: Group choice and individual judgements. In D. Mueller (ed.), *Perspectives on Public Choice: A Handbook*. New York: Cambridge University Press.

Strategic Interaction among Governments

Jan K. Brueckner

20.1 Introduction

Strategic interaction among governments has recently become a major focus of theoretical and empirical work in public economics. One branch of the literature analyzes strategic interaction due to various kinds of "spillovers." For example, in a model with pollution spillovers, the preferred level of abatement in one jurisdiction depends on policies chosen elsewhere (for a survey, see Wilson 1996). While other types of spillovers also lead to interaction, a different mechanism is at work in tax competition models, where governments levy taxes on a mobile tax base. Recognizing that their tax bases shrink as tax rates rise, large jurisdictions choose their rates in strategic fashion, with an eye on choices made elsewhere (for a survey, see Wilson 1999). A related body of literature focuses on "welfare competition," analyzing income redistribution by state governments when the poor migrate in response to differentials in welfare benefits. In such models, states choose benefit levels in strategic fashion taking account of the mobility of the poor and the choices of other jurisdictions (for a survey, see Brueckner 2000).

Spurred in part by these theoretical developments, strategic interaction among governments is now the focus of a growing empirical literature. Most studies in this literature test for strategic interaction by estimating reaction functions, which show how a jurisdiction responds to the choices of neighboring jurisdictions in setting the level of its own decision variable. If the estimated reaction function shows interdependence among policy choices, the presence of strategic interaction is confirmed.

The purpose of this chapter is to provide an overview of conceptual issues in the theoretical and empirical literatures on strategic interaction. The discussion begins by showing how most theoretical models of interaction fall into one of two main categories: spillover models such as the pollution model discussed above, and "resource-flow" models, a category that embraces both tax- and welfare-competition models. The discussion in section 20.2 provides a general characterization of each type of model, while sections 20.3 and 20.4 provide detailed analysis of particular examples. To illustrate the spillover model, section 20.3 analyzes a model of strategic interaction in the choice of pollution abatement levels. To illustrate the resource-flow model, section 20.4 provides a detailed analysis of the welfare-competition model.

Section 20.5 explains the main econometric issues that arise in testing for strategic interaction. A fundamental problem in estimating jurisdictional reaction functions is the endogeneity of key covariates. In particular, the decision variables of other jurisdictions, which appear on the right-hand side of the regression, are jointly determined along with dependent variable in a Nash equilibrium. As a result, ordinary least squares estimates of the reaction-function coefficients are inconsistent, so that a different estimation method must be used. Another problem concerns the potential for the emergence of false evidence of strategic interaction. When unobservable determinants of policy choices are correlated across jurisdictions, this correlation can generate a spurious association between policy choices that may be mistaken for strategic interaction. The discussion outlines methods for dealing with this problem, which is known as spatial error dependence.

20.2   A Typology of Models with Strategic Interaction

Models of strategic interaction among governments can be classified into two broad types: the "spillover" model and the "resource-flow" model. Despite their different structures, these models ultimately generate a same kind of behavioral relationship, a jurisdictional reaction function, which can be estimated empirically. The subsequent discussion provides a general characterization of the spillover and resource-flow models, and sections 20.3 and 20.4 provide concrete examples.

20.2.1   The spillover model

In the spillover model, each jurisdiction i chooses the level of a decision variable z_i. However, the jurisdiction is also directly affected by the z's chosen elsewhere, indicating the presence of spillovers. Thus, jurisdiction i's objective function is written

$$V(z_i, z_{-i}; X_i), \tag{20.1}$$

where z_{-i} is the vector of z's for the $n-1$ other jurisdictions and X_i is a vector of characteristics of i, which help determine preferences.

Under Nash behavior, jurisdiction i chooses z_i to maximize equation (20.1), taking z_{-i} as parametric. The resulting first-order condition is $\partial V/\partial z_i \equiv V_{z_i}(z_i, z_{-i}; X_i) = 0$, and solving this equation for the optimal z_i yields a solution that depends on z_{-i} and X_i. Thus, the optimal value of jurisdiction i's decision variable depends on choices elsewhere and on i's characteristics. The solution can be written

$$z_i = R(z_{-i}; X_i). \qquad (20.2)$$

The function R represents a *reaction function*, which gives jurisdiction i's best response to the choices of other jurisdictions. Note that the position of the reaction function depends on jurisdiction i's characteristics.

Empirical work on strategic interaction focuses on estimating the slope of the reaction function, as explained in detail below. In the spillover model, this slope depends on the nature of preferences. Differentiation of the above first-order condition shows that $\partial z_i / \partial z_j \equiv R_{z_j} = -V_{z_i z_j} / V_{z_i z_i}$, $j \neq i$, where z_j is one of the elements of z_{-i} and the latter expressions are the second partial derivatives of V. Although $V_{z_i z_i}$ must be negative for the second-order condition to be satisfied, $V_{z_i z_j}$ can take either sign, depending on the nature of preferences. If an increase in jurisdiction j's z value raises the marginal utility of z_i, then $V_{z_i z_j}$ is positive, and the reaction function is an upward-sloping function of z_j. Conversely, if an increase in z_j decreases the marginal utility of z_i, then the reaction function is downward sloping in z_j.

The reaction function's slope could also be zero, an outcome that arises when preferences are additively separable in z_i and z_j, implying $V_{z_i z_j} \equiv 0$. As a result, a zero estimated slope for an empirical reaction function does not necessarily imply the absence of strategic behavior among jurisdictions. However, since a zero slope is theoretically "unlikely," such an empirical finding is probably best viewed as disconfirmation of the underlying model, indicating either that spillovers are absent or that jurisdictions do not take them into account in their decisions.

The Nash equilibrium in the spillover model is determined by the intersection of the jurisdictional reaction functions, which corresponds to the solution of the equation system consisting of (20.2) for $i = 1,...,n$. If jurisdictions are symmetric, with $X_i = X$ for all i, then the equilibrium is also symmetric, with a common z value across all jurisdictions. This value is determined by the single equation $V_z(z,z;X) = 0$, where the partial derivative is understood to refer to V's first argument, and where the second argument represents an $n - 1$ vector with each element equal to z. Equivalently, using the reaction function, the equilibrium satisfies $z = R(z;X)$, where the z on the right-hand side is again an $n - 1$ vector.

In the spillover model, Nash equilibria are inefficient, failing to maximize social welfare. This conclusion is most easily seen in the symmetric case, where the common socially optimal level of z maximizes $V(z,z;X)$, satisfying $V_{z_i} + \sum_{j \neq i} V_{z_j} = 0$. At the Nash equilibrium, the first term in this expression is zero, while the summation is positive, assuming positive spillovers. As a result, the entire expression is positive at the Nash equilibrium, indicating that social welfare is still increasing in z and that equilibrium value is too low relative to the social optimum. The problem, of course, is that each jurisdiction does not take into account the external benefits that result from an increase in its z value. The conclusion is reversed if spillovers are negative, with the equilibrium z too large.

20.2.2 The resource-flow model

In the "resource-flow" model, a jurisdiction is not directly affected by the z levels in other jurisdictions. But the jurisdiction cares about the amount of a particular "resource" that resides within its borders. Because the distribution of this resource among jurisdictions depends on the z choices of all, jurisdiction i is then indirectly affected by z_{-i}.

Jurisdiction i's objective function in the resource-flow model is written

$$\tilde{V}(z_i, s_i; X_i), \qquad (20.3)$$

where s_i is the resource level enjoyed by i. The distribution of resources depends on the entire z vector as well as on jurisdiction characteristics, with the resources available to i given by

$$s_i = H(z_i, z_{-i}; X_i), \qquad (20.4)$$

Note that since X_i can be measured relative to the average characteristics of all jurisdictions, X_{-i} need not appear in equation (20.4).

To derive the reduced form of the resource-flow model, equation (20.4) is substituted into equation (20.3), yielding

$$\tilde{V}(z_i, H(z_i, z_{-i}; X_i); X_i) \equiv V(z_i, z_{-i}; X_i). \qquad (20.5)$$

Thus, even though the underlying model is different, this objective function has the same form as equation (20.1), with z_i, z_{-i}, and X_i appearing as arguments. As a result, maximizing equation (20.5) by choice of z_i yields a reaction function like equation (20.2).

The slope of the reaction function, which is again ambiguous in sign, now depends jointly on the derivatives of the H and $\tilde{V}$ functions. Since this greater complexity means that the slope can be zero only under unusual conditions, a zero slope for an empirical reaction function is strong evidence against the underlying model.

As in the spillover model, the Nash equilibrium in the resource-flow model is inefficient. However, because of the greater complexity of the model, it is not possible to state simple, primitive conditions (e.g., spillovers positive versus negative) that determine the direction of the inefficiency. Whether the decision variables are set at too high or too low a level depends on the details of the model's structure.

20.3 A SPILLOVER EXAMPLE: POLLUTION ABATEMENT

20.3.1 Model

To illustrate the spillover model, consider the case of pollution abatement, following Murdoch, Sandler, and Sargent (1997) and Fredriksson and Millimet (2002).

Let preferences for jurisdiction i be given by $U(c_i, P)$, where c_i is consumption and P is the level of air pollution, which is assumed to be uniform across all jurisdictions. Suppose that pollution depends on the total abatement expenditures of all jurisdictions, with $P = P(\sum_j a_j)$, where a_j is abatement expenditure in jurisdiction j and $P' < 0$. Letting y_i denote income in i, it follows that $c_i = y_i - a_i$, assuming for simplicity that each jurisdiction has a single resident.

Substituting in U, preferences can be written

$$U(y_i - a_i, P(\sum_j a_j)) \equiv V(a_i, a_{-i}; y_i). \tag{20.6}$$

The first-order condition for choice of a_i is $V_{a_i} \equiv -U_{c_i} + U_p P' = 0$. Assuming for simplicity that the P function can be written in the linear form $\tau - \gamma \sum_j a_j$, so that $P' = -\gamma < 0$, the previous condition can be rewritten as

$$-\frac{\gamma U_p}{U_{c_i}} = 1. \tag{20.7}$$

This equation says that the marginal benefit from pollution abatement within jurisdiction i equals the unitary marginal cost (note that $U_p < 0$). Since a_i and a_{-i} are arguments of both U_p and U_{c_i}, equation (20.7) implicitly defines jurisdiction i's reaction function, as in equation (20.2) (the a's replace the z's).

To analyze the social optimum, consider the symmetric case, where income takes a common value y for all jurisdictions. Optimal abatement levels are then uniform, and the optimal value maximizes $U(y - a, \tau - \gamma na)$. The first-order condition is

$$-\frac{n\gamma U_p}{U_{c_i}} = 1. \tag{20.8}$$

The factor of n, which is not present in equation (20.7), captures the benefits arising in all jurisdictions when any one jurisdiction's abatement level is increased. Since this spillover effect is not considered in individual decisions, the Nash equilibrium abatement level is smaller than the socially optimal level.

20.3.2 Reaction functions

To analyze reaction functions for this model, suppose that U takes the Cobb–Douglas form $c_i^\rho P^\lambda$, where $\rho > 0$ and $\lambda < 0$. Then, after substituting as above, differentiation with respect to a_i yields the relevant form of equation (20.7), which can be solved for a_i to give

$$a_i = \Gamma_i - \frac{\rho}{\rho + \lambda} \sum_{j \neq i} a_j, \tag{20.9}$$

where Γ_i is a constant that depends on y_i. Given that $\rho + \lambda < 0$ must hold for the jurisdiction's second-order condition to be satisfied, it follows that the reaction function in equation (20.9) is an upward-sloping function of the a_j's. Since it can be verified that $V_{a_i a_i} > 0$ holds in the Cobb–Douglas case as long as $\rho \gamma > 0$, this positive slope is consistent with the general analysis above. Note that the abatement level in the symmetric Nash equilibrium is found by replacing the a's in equation (20.9) with a common value and solving (Γ loses its i subscript under symmetry).

20.3.3 Other spillover models

Other spillover models involve more general public expenditure spillovers across jurisdictions. In such models, residents of one jurisdiction effectively consume the public goods provided by other jurisdictions along with those provided by their own governments. The best-known study of this type is that of Case, Rosen, and Hines (1993), who focus on interstate expenditure spillovers. A number of other studies consider spillovers across local jurisdictions. Examples of expenditure spillovers might include the benefits from using highways in an adjacent state, or the benefits from visiting a municipal museum in a nearby city.

Models of "yardstick competition," exemplified by the work of Besley and Case (1995), involve *information* spillovers across jurisdictions. In their model, voters look at public services and taxes in other jurisdictions to help judge whether their government is wasting resources (through inefficiency or rent-seeking) and deserves to be voted out of office. Knowing that voters make such comparisons, government officials take other jurisdictions' choices into account in making their own decisions, leading to strategic interaction.

20.4 A RESOURCE-FLOW EXAMPLE:
INTERSTATE WELFARE COMPETITION

20.4.1 Model

To illustrate the resource-flow model, consider a model of welfare competition between the states, following Wildasin (1991) and Brueckner (2000). For simplicity, let the economy contain just two jurisdictions (states), denoted 1 and 2. Each state contains M nonpoor, immobile consumers, referred to as the "rich." The economy contains $2\bar{N}$ poor consumers, who work at low-paying jobs as well as receiving welfare benefits from the state where they reside. The poor are assumed to be mobile across states, with N_1 and $N_2 = 2\bar{N} - N_1$ giving the poor populations in states 1 and 2 respectively. The poor populations correspond to the "resource" that appears in the resource-flow model, although in the present case, this resource turns out to be a "bad" rather than a good.

State output $f(N)$ depends on the amount N of unskilled labor along with other fixed factors. The unskilled wage, earned by the state's poor residents, is then given by $w(N) \equiv f'(N)$, where f' is the marginal product. Since f is concave, the wage falls as the unskilled labor pool grows, with $w'(N) \equiv f''(N) < 0$. Wages in states 1 and 2 are thus $w_1 = w(N_1)$ and $w_2 = w(N_2)$, and letting T_1 and T_2 denote the welfare benefits paid to the poor, the total income of a poor resident equals $w(N_1) + T_1$ in state 1 and $w(N_2) + T_2$ in state 2.

Assuming that migration costs are zero, migration equilibrium is achieved when poor income is equalized between the two states. The equilibrium condition is then $w_1 + T_1 = w_2 + T_2$, or

$$w(N_1) + T_1 = w(2\bar{N} - N_1) + T_2. \tag{20.10}$$

This condition, which shows how the poor-population resource distributes itself conditional on the levels of the decision values T_1 and T_2, is analogous to equation (20.4) in the general discussion of the resource-flow model.

By making state 1 more attractive, an increase in T_1 causes welfare migrants to flow from state 2 to state 1, raising N_1. Differentiating (20.10),

$$\frac{\partial N_1}{\partial T_1} = -\frac{1}{w'(N_1) + w'(2\bar{N} - N_1)} > 0, \quad \frac{\partial N_1}{\partial T_2} = -\frac{\partial N_1}{\partial T_1} < 0, \tag{20.11}$$

where $w' < 0$ is used. Note that wage adjustment is the force that equilibrates migration flows. The wage falls in state 1 and rises in state 2 as the poor population relocates, eventually restoring the equality of gross incomes.

The level of each state's welfare benefit is chosen by its rich residents, who care about the well-being of the local poor. The rich in both states have the same quasi-linear utility function, which is written $c_i + U(w_i + T_i)$, $i = 1,2$, where c_i gives consumption expenditure for the rich in state i, and where $U' > 0$ and $U'' < 0$. Note that the rich care about the total income of a representative poor resident, $w_i + T_i$, which depends on wage income as well as the welfare benefit. Letting y_i denote the rich income in state i, the budget constraint of a rich resident in state 1 is then given by $c_1 + N_1T_1/M = y_1$, with an analogous constraint applying in state 2. Note that the welfare cost for each rich resident equals the total outlay, N_1T_1, divided by the number of rich, M.

20.4.2   Benefit choices

The rich in state 1 choose T_1 to maximize utility subject to the budget constraint. To analyze this problem, suppose first that the poor were immobile and evenly divided between states, with $N_1 = \bar{N}$. Under this assumption, the first-order condition for the utility-maximization problem is

$$MU'(w_1 + T_1) = \bar{N}. \tag{20.12}$$

where $w_1 = w(\bar{N})$. This equation says that the sum across the rich population of the gains from increasing the income of the poor by a dollar should equal the cost, equal to $\bar{N}$. Equation (20.12) characterizes the socially optimal level of welfare benefits, conditional on an equal division of the poor across the states.

Now consider the case in which the poor are mobile. In this case, the rich in state 1 choose the welfare benefit taking account of the fact that an increase in T_1 raises N_1 through migration. The first-order condition for this problem is

$$MU'(w_1 + T_1) = \frac{N_1 + \dfrac{\partial N_1}{\partial T_1}T_1}{1 + w'(N_1)\dfrac{\partial N_1}{\partial T_1}}, \qquad (20.13)$$

where $w_1 = w(N_1)$. Recognizing that N_1 and hence w_1 depend on both T_1 and T_2 via equation (20.10), equation (20.13) has the form of the condition $V_{z_i}(z_i, z_{-i}; X_i) = 0$ from the general discussion, with the T's replacing the z's. Thus, equation (20.13) implicitly defines state 1's reaction function, as discussed further below.

Although the left-hand side of equation (20.13) again equals the sum of the marginal gains from an increase in the income of the poor, the right-hand side differs from equation (20.11) because of the effects of migration. The numerator of this expression gives the increase in total welfare outlays from an increase in T_1. While the N_1 term again captures the effect of the higher benefit per recipient, the additional $(\partial N_1/\partial T_1)T_1$ term (which is positive from equation (20.11)) captures the effect of a larger poor population.

To understand the denominator of equation (20.13), note that in the immobility case, increasing the welfare benefit by a dollar raises the income of the poor by a dollar. However, with migration, the wage falls as additional poor move into state 1, offsetting the effect of the higher T_1, and this effect is captured by the denominator of equation (20.13). Using equation (20.11) and $w'(N_1) < 0$, it can be seen that the denominator is less than one but greater than zero, which implies that a dollar increase in T_1 raises $w_1 + T_1$ but does so by less than a dollar. Migration of the poor thus reduces the "productivity" of welfare benefits in raising poor incomes.

The combination of the above effects reduces the welfare benefit below the socially optimal level. To see this conclusion, note first that since the Nash equilibrium will be symmetric, the wage levels on the left-hand side of equation (20.13) will equal $w_1(\bar{N})$, the same value as in equation (20.12). Next, observe that the right-hand side of equation (20.13), which is evaluated with $N_1 = \bar{N}$, takes on a value greater than $\bar{N}$, given the extra positive term in the numerator and the fact that denominator is less than unity. For equation (20.13) to be satisfied, the equilibrium T_1 value must then be smaller than the one in equation (20.12) (recall that $U'' < 0$). Thus, equilibrium welfare benefits are inefficiently low. Because the perceived cost of redistribution is raised by welfare migration, the rich naturally choose to limit their generosity.

20.4.3 Reaction functions

As noted above, state 1's reaction function is implicitly defined by the first-order condition (20.13). Since N_1 and thus w_1 depend on both T_1 and T_2 via equation (20.10), both sides of equation (20.13) depend on both benefit levels. In principle, equation (20.13) can then be rewritten to give T_1 as a function of T_2, yielding state 1's reaction function.

To derive the reaction for a special case, assume that the production function f is quadratic, so that $f'(N_1)$ and hence $w(N_1)$ is given by the linear function

$\alpha - \mu N_1$, where $\alpha, \mu > 0$. Assume that the U portion of the utility function is also quadratic, so that $U'(w_1 + T_1) = \eta - \delta(w_1 + T_1)$, where $\eta, \delta > 0$. Substituting the linear f in equation (20.10) and solving for N_1 yields $N_1 = \bar{N} + (T_1 - T_2)/2\mu$. This equation shows that state 1's poor population is increasing in T_1 and decreasing in T_2, as noted in equation (20.11). Using this equation to substitute for N_1 and $\partial N_1/\partial T_1$ in equation (20.13), and substituting the above expression for U', equation (20.13) can be rewritten as

$$T_1 = \Phi + \frac{2 - \mu\delta M}{4 + \eta\delta M} T_2, \qquad\qquad (20.14)$$

where Φ is a constant. Equation (20.14) gives state 1's reaction function, and state 2's function is gotten by interchanging T_1 and T_2. The intersection of these two reaction functions yields the common equilibrium value of T_1 and T_2, which is inefficiently low. This value is found by setting $T_1 = T_2 = T$ in equation (20.14) and solving for T.

The reaction function in equation (20.14) is linear, and it may slope up or down depending on parameter values. The function is upward sloping if $2/\mu > \delta M$, with state 1 raising T_1 in response to an increase in T_2. For this condition to hold, the μ parameter from the production function must be small relative to the δ parameter from the utility function. Conversely, the function is downward sloping if $2/\mu < \delta M$, with state 1 reducing its welfare benefit in response to an increase in T_2. The slope is zero only in the unlikely knife-edge case in which $2/\mu = \delta M$.

20.4.4   Other resource-flow models

The public economics literature contains other models of strategic interaction based on a resource-flow framework. The tax competition literature, surveyed by Wilson (1999), offers the largest set of examples. In such models, local governments finance public spending with a tax on mobile capital, which plays the role of the resource (now a "good" rather than a "bad"). When a jurisdiction raises its tax rate, the net-of-tax return is driven below the level prevailing elsewhere in the economy, and capital relocates until net returns are once again equalized. This capital flight reduces a jurisdiction's incentive to raise its tax rate, leading to underprovision of public goods.

When jurisdictions are large, this tax-setting behavior involves strategic interaction, with tax rates elsewhere affecting a given jurisdiction's decision. As in the welfare-competition model, reaction functions under tax competition can slope up or down, with the direction depending on the parameterization of preferences and production.

20.5   Testing for Strategic Interaction

As seen above, both the spillover and resource-flow models of strategic interaction generate reaction functions, which relate each jurisdiction's chosen z to its own characteristics and to the choices of other jurisdictions. The goal of empirical work is to test for strategic interaction by estimating such functions.

The previous discussion showed that, when strategic interaction occurs, the reaction function slope is nonzero except in unlikely cases. As a result, a proper test for interaction involves a simple significance test on the slope coefficient. If the null hypothesis of a zero reaction-function slope can be rejected, then the evidence points to the existence of strategic interaction among jurisdictions.

Assuming linearity of the reaction function, and following equation (20.2), an appropriate estimating equation can be written

$$z_i = \beta \sum_{j \neq i} \omega_{ij} z_j + X_i \theta + \varepsilon_i, \tag{20.15}$$

where β and θ are unknown parameters (the latter a vector), ε_i is an error term, and the ω_{ij} represent nonnegative weights, which are specified *a priori*. These weights indicate the relevance of other jurisdictions j in the process of interaction, and they can be viewed as part of jurisdiction i's characteristics. The weights typically capture the location of i relative to other jurisdictions, and a scheme that assigns weights based on contiguity is commonly used. Under such a scheme, $\omega_{ij} = 1$ for jurisdictions j that share a border with i and $\omega_{ij} = 0$ for noncontiguous jurisdictions. Thus, for example, in Saavedra's (2000) study of welfare competition, nonzero weights are given to states adjacent to a given state, while nonbordering states receive a weight of zero. Generally, the weights are normalized so that their sum equals unity for each i. Thus, in Saavedra's study, if a state has four states adjacent to it, each receives a weight of $1/4$.

As explained above, X_i in equation (20.15) is a vector of characteristics for jurisdiction i. In Saavedra's paper, X_i includes the per capita income of the given state, the African-American proportion of its population, its female unemployment rate, a measure of the political makeup of the state's legislature, and other variables. The dependent variable z_i in her study is the dollar welfare payment for a family of size three.

While choice of the weights in equation (20.15) is based on prior judgment about the pattern of interaction, the parameter β, which reflects the strength of interaction among jurisdictions, is estimated from the data. Note that equation (20.15) implies that the direction of i's interaction with all other jurisdictions is the same, with its sign determined by the sign of β. The magnitude of the effect, however, depends on the relevant weight, with $\partial z_i / \partial z_j = \beta \omega_{ij}$.

As is well known from the literature on spatial econometrics (see Anselin 1988), two main econometric issues must be confronted in estimating equation (20.15). These are endogeneity of the z_j's and possible spatial error dependence. These issues are considered in turn in the following discussion.

20.5.1 Endogeneity of the z_j's

Because of strategic interaction, the z values in different jurisdictions are jointly determined. As a result, the linear combination of the z_j's appearing on the right-hand side of equation (20.15) is endogenous and correlated with the error term ε_i. To see this point formally, the first step is to rewrite equation (20.15) in matrix form, which yields

$$z = \beta W z + X\theta + \varepsilon, \tag{20.16}$$

where z is the vector of the z_j's, X is the characteristics matrix, and W is the weight matrix, with representative element ω_{ij} (note that $\omega_{ii} = 0$ for all i). Then, equation (20.16) can be used to solve for the equilibrium values of the z_i's, which yields

$$z = (I - \beta W)^{-1} X\theta + (I - \beta W)^{-1}\varepsilon. \tag{20.17}$$

The key implication of equation (20.17) is that the random component of z_k is equal to the inner product of the kth row of the matrix $(I - \beta W)^{-1}$ and the error vector ε. Each element of z thus depends on *all the* ε's. As a result, each of the z_j's on the right-hand side of equation (20.15) depends on ε_i, the equation's error term. The resulting correlation means that OLS estimates of the parameters of equation (20.15) are inconsistent, requiring use of an alternate estimation method.

To understand the correlation between the z_j's and ε_i on a more intuitive level, consider the case of just two jurisdictions, 1 and 2. In this case, only one z_j appears on the right-hand side of the reaction function in equation (20.15), and the matrix equation (20.16) consists of just two reaction functions, one for each jurisdiction. The solution in equation (20.17) then corresponds to the intersection of these reaction functions in two-dimensional space. It is clear that the z_1 value at this intersection point depends on the magnitudes of the intercepts of both reaction functions, as does the value of z_2. But observe that the reaction-function intercept itself depends on the magnitude of the jurisdiction's error term. When ε_1 increases, jurisdiction 1's reaction function shifts up in a parallel fashion, and an increase in ε_2 has an analogous effect. The upshot is that *the value of z_1 at the intersection point depends on both ε_1 and ε_2*, as does the value of z_2. Thus, z_2 on the right-hand side of jurisdiction 1's reaction function depends on ε_1, the function's error term, and z_1 on the right-hand side of jurisdiction 2's function depends on ε_2. Exactly the same conclusion holds with a larger number of jurisdictions, establishing that the z_j's on the right-hand side of equation (20.15) are correlated with the error term.

In the literature, two methods are used to address this econometric problem. Under the first method, the reduced-form equation given by equation (20.17) is estimated using maximum-likelihood (ML) methods. Note that since the key parameter β enters nonlinearly in this equation, a nonlinear optimization routine must be used to estimate it.

The second method is an instrumental variables (IV) approach. Under this approach, the offending z_j's on the right-hand side of equation (20.15) are replaced by fitted values from a first-stage regression. Since these fitted values are asymptotically uncorrelated with the error term, OLS then yields consistent estimates of the reaction-function parameters. A typical IV procedure is to regress

Wz on X and WX, and to use the fitted values $\hat{W}z$ as instruments for Wz. Note that this procedure involves regressing the weighted linear combination of the z_j's from the right-hand side of equation (20.15) on X_i and on the same linear combination of the X_j's.

20.5.2 Spatial error dependence

The presence of spatial dependence in the errors also complicates the estimation of equation (20.15). When spatial error dependence is present, the error vector ε satisfies the relationship

$$\varepsilon = \phi S\varepsilon + v, \tag{20.18}$$

where S is a weight matrix, which is often assumed to be the same as W in equation (20.16), v is a well-behaved error vector, and ϕ is an unknown parameter. Solving equation (20.18) yields

$$\varepsilon = (I - \phi S)^{-1}v, \tag{20.19}$$

which shows that each element of ε is a linear combination of the elements of v, implying that ε_i is correlated with ε_j for $i \neq j$.

Such spatial error dependence arises when ε includes omitted jurisdiction characteristics that are themselves spatially dependent. For example, suppose that z measures the park acreage in a community, and suppose that such acreage is inversely related to a community's innate topographical amenities, which may affect its willingness to invest in parks. For example, if a community lies on the ocean or has attractive mountains nearby, then it may be less willing to invest public funds in park acreage than a community without such natural amenities. Since topographical amenities may be unobservable in the data, the amenity level may thus be part of the error term ε_i in equation (20.15). Assuming that ε is an inverse measure of amenities, it follows that z and ε are positively related.

The source of trouble in this setup is that topographical amenities, and hence the error terms in ε, are likely to be spatially correlated. In other words, a high amenity level in one community may imply a high level in nearby communities, with low amenities also associated with low amenities nearby. For example, if one community has a nearby beach or mountains, then its neighbors will probably enjoy the same amenities. If one community lacks amenities, its neighbors are likely to lack them as well. Such a pattern implies spatial error dependence.

When this spatial dependence is ignored, estimation of equation (20.15) can provide false evidence of strategic interaction. To understand this outcome, suppose that $\beta = 0$, so that strategic interaction in the choice of park acreage is actually absent. Then, note from above that ε (and hence z) will be low in communities with high natural amenities, while ε and z will be high in communities with poor amenities. But since communities of each type will tend to be near one another because of spatial dependence in the errors, estimation of equation (20.15) will indicate a positive association between the z levels in nearby communities, yielding a positive estimate of β. This result, however, reflects spatial error dependence and not strategic interaction.

To deal with this problem, one approach is to use maximum likelihood to estimate equation (20.15), taking account of the error structure in equation (20.18). This approach, however, is computationally challenging. In addition, the similar roles played by the parameters β and ϕ in the model may lead to difficulties in identifying their individual magnitudes (see Anselin 1988).

An easier remedy is to rely on the IV estimation method discussed above. Kelejian and Prucha (1998) show that this method generates a consistent estimate of β even in the presence of spatial error dependence. To see how the IV approach achieves consistency, eliminating false evidence of strategic interaction, the following discussion is useful. First, observe that, if the true β equals zero, indicating no strategic interaction, then the z's are not jointly determined, and this source of correlation between the z_j's and the error term in equation (20.15) is eliminated. However, with spatial error dependence, a new source of correlation emerges. The problem is that, while a particular z_k on the right-hand side of equation (20.15) is affected only by its own error term ε_k, that error term is correlated with ε_i as result of spatial error dependence. Thus, z_k is correlated with ε_i, so that estimation of equation (20.15) yields inconsistent parameter estimates. By using a fitted value of z_k, the IV method purges this correlation and generates consistent estimates.

A third approach is to estimate equation (20.15) by ML under the assumption that spatial error dependence is absent, relying on hypothesis tests to verify this absence. Because a test based on the ML results themselves is invalid if spatial dependence is actually present, the robust tests of Anselin, Bera, Florax, and Yoon (1996) can be employed instead. These tests are based on OLS estimates of equation (20.15), and they are not contaminated by uncorrected spatial error dependence.

20.5.3 Empirical studies

A growing empirical literature is directed toward testing for strategic interaction among governments. Most studies estimate an equation such as (20.15), usually taking account of the econometric issues discussed above. Among studies based on the spillover model, Murdoch, Sandler, and Sargent (1997) and Fredriksson and Millimet (2002) test for interaction in the choice of pollution abatement levels. Case, Rosen, and Hines (1993), Murdoch, Rahmatian, and Thayer (1993), and Kelejian and Robertson (1993) test for interaction using other expenditure spillover models to motivate the exercise. The yardstick-competition model motivates the tests for interaction carried out by Besley and Case (1995), Bivand and Syzmanski (1997, 2000), Revelli (2001, 2002, 2003), and Bordignon, Cerniglia, and Revelli (2003).

Among studies based on the resource-flow model, Figlio, Kolpin, and Reid (1999) and Saavedra (2000) test for strategic interaction in the choice of state welfare benefit levels. Tests based on the tax competition model or its variants are carried out by Ladd (1992), Brueckner (1998), Heyndels and Vuchelen (1998),

Brett and Pinkse (2000), Buettner (2001), Brueckner and Saavedra (2001), Esteller-Moré and Solé-Ollé (2001), and Hayashi and Boadway (2001).

20.6 CONCLUSION

This chapter has provided an overview of conceptual issues in the literature on strategic interaction among governments, focusing on both the theoretical and empirical sides of the literature. The discussion has argued that most theoretical models can be classified as either spillover or resource-flow models, and the structure of a representative model of each type has been explained in detail. In addition, the chapter has discussed the main econometric issues that arise in testing for strategic interaction and outlined the methods for dealing with them.

While the path from a theoretical model to an empirical reaction function may be clear, as seen in the above discussion, it is important to recognize that the reverse path may involve ambiguity. To understand this point, suppose that empirical results provide evidence of strategic interaction among jurisdictions in the choice of a particular policy variable. The question then is: What underlying jurisdictional behavior is likely to have generated the observed interaction? This issue can be seen most clearly in the choice of tax rates. Strategic interaction in choosing tax rates could arise through the tax competition model, with jurisdictions concerned about the loss of tax base to neighboring jurisdictions. But interaction could also arise through the yardstick-competition model, with government officials looking at neighboring jurisdictions to avoid setting tax rates at levels that will displease the voters.

Several papers in the literature address this ambiguity by providing auxiliary evidence to uncover the source of observed strategic interaction. For example, to substantiate the comparative behavior underlying the yardstick-competition model, Besley and Case (1995) estimate an auxiliary equation that relates voter approval of an incumbent to taxes in neighboring jurisdictions (expecting a positive coefficient). Similarly, to support their view that tax competition behavior underlies interaction in the choice of tax rates, Brett and Pinkse (2000) estimate an equation relating a jurisdiction's tax base to its tax rate (expecting a negative coefficient). By illuminating the source of the interaction, such auxiliary evidence lends credibility to claims, based on reaction-function estimates, that governments engage in strategic behavior.

Bibliography

Anselin, L. 1988: *Spatial Econometrics*. Dordrecht: Kluwer.
——, Bera, A. K., Florax, R., and Yoon, M. J. 1996: Simple diagnostic tests for spatial dependence. *Regional Science and Urban Economics*, 26(1), 77–104.
Besley, T. J. and Case, A. C. 1995: Incumbent behavior: vote seeking, tax setting and yardstick competition. *American Economic Review*, 85(1), 25–45.
Bivand, R. and Szymanski, S. 1997: Spatial dependence through local yardstick competition: theory and testing. *Economics Letters*, 55(2), 257–65.

—— and —— 2000: Modeling the spatial impact of the introduction of compulsory competitive tendering. *Regional Science and Urban Economics*, 30(2), 203–19.

Bordignon, M., Cerniglia, F., and Revelli, F. 2003: In search of yardstick competition: property tax rates and electoral behavior in Italian cities. *Journal of Urban Economics*, 54(2), 199–217.

Brett, C. and Pinkse, J. 2000: The determinants of municipal tax rates in British Columbia. *Canadian Journal of Economics*, 33(3), 695–714.

Brueckner, J. K. 1998: Testing for strategic interaction among local governments: the case of growth controls. *Journal of Urban Economics*, 44(3), 438–67.

—— 2000: Welfare reform and the race to the bottom: theory and evidence. *Southern Economic Journal*, 66(1), 505–25.

—— and Saavedra, L. A. 2001: Do local governments engage in strategic property-tax competition? *National Tax Journal*, 54(2), 203–29.

Buettner, T. 2001: Local business taxation and competition for capital: the choice of the tax rate. *Regional Science and Urban Economics*, 31(2–3), 215–45.

Case, A. C., Rosen, H. S., and Hines, J. C. 1993: Budget spillovers and fiscal policy interdependence: evidence from the States. *Journal of Public Economics*, 52(3), 285–307.

Esteller-Moré, Á. and Solé-Ollé, A. 2001: Vertical income tax externalities and fiscal interdependence: evidence from the U.S. *Regional Science and Urban Economics*, 31(2–3), 247–72.

Figlio, D. N., Kolpin, V. W., and Reid, W. E. 1999: Do states play welfare games? *Journal of Urban Economics*, 46(3), 437–54.

Fredriksson, P. G. and Millimet, D. L. 2002: Strategic interaction and the determinants of environmental policy across US states. *Journal of Urban Economics*, 51(1), 101–22.

Hayashi, M. and Boadway, R. 2001: An empirical analysis of intergovernmental tax interaction: the case of business income taxes in Canada. *Canadian Journal of Economics*, 34(2), 481–503.

Heyndels, B. and Vuchelen, J. 1998: Tax mimicking among Belgian municipalities. *National Tax Journal*, 51(1), 89–101.

Kelejian, H. H. and Prucha, I. R. 1998: A generalized spatial two-stage least squares procedure for estimating a spatial autoregressive model with autoregressive disturbances. *Journal of Real Estate Finance and Economics*, 17(1), 99–121.

—— and Robinson, D. 1993: A suggested method of estimation for spatial interdependent models with autocorrelated errors, and an application to a county expenditure model. *Papers in Regional Science*, 72(3), 297–312.

Ladd, H. F. 1992: Mimicking of local tax burdens among neighboring counties. *Public Finance Quarterly*, 20(4), 450–67.

Murdoch, J. C., Rahmatian, M., and Thayer, M. 1993: A spatially autoregressive median voter model of recreation expenditures. *Public Finance Quarterly*, 21(3), 334–50.

——, Sandler, T., and Sargent, K. 1997: A tale of two collectives: sulphur versus nitrogen oxide emission reduction in Europe. *Economica*, 64(2), 281–301.

Revelli, F. 2001: Spatial patterns in local taxation: tax mimicking or error mimicking? *Applied Economics*, 33(9), 1,101–7.

—— 2002: Testing the tax mimicking vs. expenditure spill-over hypothesis using English data. *Applied Economics*, 34(14), 1,723–36.

—— 2003: Reaction or interaction: spatial process identification in multi-tiered governmental structures. *Journal of Urban Economics*, 53(1), 29–53.

Saavedra, L. A. 2000: A model of welfare competition with evidence from AFDC. *Journal of Urban Economics*, 47(2), 248–79.

Wildasin, D. E. 1991: Income redistribution in a common labor market. *American Economic Review*, 81(4), 757–74.

Wilson, J. D. 1996: Capital mobility and environmental standards: Is there a theoretical basis for the race to the bottom? In J. Bhagwati and R. Hundee (eds.), *Fair Trade and Harmonization: Prerequisites for Free Trade?* Vol. 1: *Economic Analysis*. Cambridge, MA: The MIT Press.

—— 1999: Theories of tax competition. *National Tax Journal*, 52(2), 269–304.

CHAPTER TWENTY-ONE

Property and Land Taxation

John Douglas Wilson

21.1 INTRODUCTION

Local governments in the United States and elsewhere rely heavily on property taxation to finance their expenditures. This state of affairs is not surprising, because the property tax enjoys several advantages over other taxes. The tax base is relatively easy to calculate, since it lies within the jurisdiction imposing the tax. Although the infrequent sales of some properties make them difficult to value, information obtained from property inspections can be employed to compute the tax base. In contrast, collecting an income tax from residents often requires information on income earned outside the jurisdiction, and sales taxes are similarly disadvantaged. As a local tax base, property may also be less sensitive than income to taxation, due to the durability of a jurisdiction's housing stock (see Nechyba 1997).

Property taxes rank relatively low as a percentage of a country's total tax revenue, rarely rising above 10 percent in OECD countries. This value is slightly above 10 percent in the USA, which is significantly higher than the 5.4 percent unweighted average from OECD countries and the 4.7 percent unweighted average for the European Union (OECD 2001). The property tax is more important at the local level in most of these countries, although there are wide variations. Local governments in the USA raise about three-fourths of their tax revenue from the property tax, but this value is less than 10 percent in Nordic countries, while rising above 90 percent in New Zealand, the United Kingdom, Australia, and Ireland (Söderström 1998). The theoretical models in the present chapter identify important cases in which independent local governments choose to give property taxes a prominent role, but many central governments strongly control or influence the expenditure and revenue-raising activities of their local governments.

This chapter emphasizes the potential efficiencies that can be gained by allowing local governments to independently choose their levels of property taxation, but nevertheless it will conclude that complete independence is a bad idea.

The property tax is widely viewed as satisfying to two traditional principles of taxation: the ability-to-pay approach and the benefit approach. "Ability to pay" has long been a controversial topic, in part because reasonable measures of this ability should be based at least partially on attributes of households that are unobservable (e.g., the cardinal properties of their utility functions). But the value of a resident's house would seem to have some advantages as a proxy for this ability, at least relative to a tax on annual income. The latter tax suffers from the potential failure of annual income to reflect the household's lifetime income, as measured by a discounted sum of annual incomes. On the other hand, lifetime income might not measure ability to pay at any point in time if households cannot freely borrow and save. The purchase of housing reflects both current income and lifetime income, with their relative importance depending on borrowing constraints. Consequently, a household's property might serve as a rough "compromise" between annual income and lifetime income as a measure of ability to pay. However, heterogeneity in consumer preferences for housing reduces the usefulness of this measure. Moreover, the taxes collected on business property cannot be justified by an ability-to-pay approach, since the owners of a given piece of property may have widely varying incomes and wealth levels. If these owners reside elsewhere, then there is also the problem of their facing taxes imposed by multiple governments in an uncoordinated fashion (the "double taxation" problem), which would surely violate ability-to-pay principles. Finally, the whole ability-to-pay approach is not well grounded in the principles of modern welfare economics, including the rules for an efficient allocation of goods and resources, which are the basis for the analysis in the current chapter. For example, the ability-to-pay approach includes the principle, "equal treatment of equals," also known as "horizontal equity," but Kaplow (2000) argues that "there is no normative basis for deeming it [horizontal equity] to be important and, in fact, it conflicts with the basic foundations of welfare economics."

The benefit approach to tax policy is based on the idea that tax burdens should be related to the benefits that taxpayers receive from their consumption of the goods and services provided by governments. While this approach was at one time related to notions of fairness, it too has been faulted for not being based on the principles of modern welfare economics, under which efficiency considerations play a central role. But there does exist an efficiency argument for the use of the property tax as a benefit tax. According to the Tiebout hypothesis, as originally formulated by Tiebout (1956), households "vote with their feet" by choosing to reside in those jurisdictions with their most preferred package of taxes and public goods and services. In this case, local taxes represent payments, or "user fees," for these goods and services. Tiebout's original theory largely ignored the types of taxes typically levied by local governments, assuming instead that governments can directly collect head taxes from residents. But subsequent research has developed a view of the property tax, known as the "benefit view," which explains how property taxes serve the role of efficient user fees. In other words, if a household moves to a jurisdiction, then the property taxes that it pays (either directly as a homeowner or indirectly through higher rents) represent payments for the benefits it receives from the public goods there.

The benefit view remains quite controversial. According to a major competing view, a country's property tax system is largely a tax on the land and capital that compose the tax base. The debate about which of these two views most accurately describes the property tax is one of the most interesting and important debates in the field of public economics, not only because the arguments on both sides make use of a lot of interesting economics, but also because any resolution of the debate would have profound implications for some of the most important policy controversies in public economics, including the desirability of land-use controls. This chapter will therefore highlight this debate.

As a preliminary, the next two sections discuss how the property tax is typically levied, including distinctions made between different forms of property and the rates at which they are taxed. Taxes on land are distinguished from taxes on other types of property in this chapter, and the term "property tax" refers to a tax that includes improvements to land in the tax base. These improvements are referred to as "capital" throughout the chapter, and the property tax treats both land and capital identically, unless otherwise noted. Sections 21.4 and 21.5 discuss the incidence of land and property taxation, respectively, emphasizing some considerations that do not normally appear in the textbook treatment of this issue. The incidence of a tax describes the distribution of real tax burdens across groups of individuals, accounting for how the tax affects equilibrium product and factor prices. We shall see that it can be difficult to separate incidence issues from efficiency considerations, and so sections 21.4 and 21.5 also address the latter. Section 21.6 presents an efficiency case for land taxation and asks whether there is any tendency for a system of independent jurisdictions to implement tax and expenditure policies that are efficient from the viewpoint of the entire system of jurisdictions. The efficiency role of a residential property tax is then examined in section 21.7. This role is the basis for the benefit view of property taxation. Section 21.8 provides some conclusions and extensions, including a brief discussion of how the benefit view of a residential property tax can be extended to include business property.

21.2 WHAT IS TAXED?

The property tax is actually a combination of two taxes, a tax on the value of land and a tax on the value of improvements to land, most notably structures. With few exceptions (see the discussion of Pittsburgh below), the two are taxed at the same rate in the USA. But some countries use some form of land taxation, also known as site value taxation. For examples of land taxation, see the discussion on Kenya, New Zealand, Jamaica, and South Africa in McCluskey (1999).

A common argument in favor of taxing land alone is that doing so leaves unchanged decisions to invest in improvements. But we shall see that such an argument is inconsistent with the benefit view of the property tax, which typically justifies some taxation of structures (though maybe at a different rate from land). Even if land taxation were socially optimal, it would be quite difficult to fully implement. Vacant land is relatively easy to tax, but once a structure occupies the land, it becomes difficult to disentangle the value of land from the value of the structure. The way to tax land in a neutral way – that is, in a way that does not change incentives concerning when to develop the land and how densely to develop it – would be to tax "raw site value." In the case of developed land, raw site value would equal the value of land if there were no building on the site (see Tideman 1982). But raw site value is difficult to estimate for land that has long been developed, since we are dealing with a counterfactual. An alternative way to tax land would be to levy a tax on "residual site value," equal to the excess of the value of the property over the value of the structure on the property. The problem here is that an owner of undeveloped land will benefit from increasing the size of a structure on a piece of land only if residual site value rises, but then the owner's tax payments will rise. For this reason, Arnott (2002) shows that a residual site tax reduces the density of development. Comparing raw site taxation with residual site taxation, it appears then that there is a trade-off between the administrative simplicity of the system and the degree to which it distorts decisions. A property tax that does not attempt to distinguish between land and improvements is the simplest of them all, but it has the potential to be the most distortionary (though Arnott shows that this is not always the case).

21.3   A CACOPHONY OF TAX RATES

Although the US property tax treats land and improvements equally, little else is given equal treatment. Tax rates often vary across commercial, industrial, and residential property, a system known as a "classified property tax," and some studies therefore focus on the taxation of residential or business property alone. These two taxes have distinct features that I discuss below.

The tax treatment of property in the same class also varies widely, in a manner that often seems capricious. It is important to distinguish between the effective and statutory tax rates on property. The statutory tax rate for a particular property is actually calculated on the taxable value of property, which is typically substantially lower than the market value. If, for example, property is valued at half its market value, then the statutory rate will be twice the effective rate, measured by dividing annual tax payments by the market value of property. Unless noted otherwise, the rates referred to in this chapter are effective rates, since statutory rates have no economic significance by themselves.

Compared with income taxation, both statutory and effective rates may look quite low (typically about 2 or 3 percent of market value), but only because the property tax is a form of wealth taxation. Wealth represents claims on future income, and therefore the value of property equals the present value of all future income generated from it. For owner-occupied housing, this income is the imputed value of the consumption services that housing provides to its inhabitants. Imputed income would, of course, be quite difficult to measure directly, but the purchase price of a house should reflect the present value of its current and future imputed rents, net of taxes and maintenance costs.

The variation of property tax rates within the same class of property is both an intended outcome of public policies and a product of the difficulties associated with collecting the property tax. To encourage economic growth, jurisdictions often give tax breaks to new investment, and one way to do so is to effectively tax new property less heavily than old property. For business property, granting tax holidays, whereby little or no tax is collected for an initial time period, may serve this purpose. For residential property, however, newly purchased homes are often taxed more heavily than homes that have not sold recently. One way this is done is through statewide caps on how much a given homeowner's property tax payments can rise each year. Thus, new homeowners may be taxed according to the full assessed value of their homes, whereas the taxable value of homes with long-time inhabitants may lie substantially below the assessed value. In areas where the market values of homes have risen substantially, such as coastal California, long-time inhabitants may face extremely low effective tax rates. Such outcomes reflect the politics of property taxation. If tax policies are designed to maximize the well-being of existing homeowners, then taxes on new owners should be set in a way that takes advantage of any market power that the tax authority is able to exert. To the extent that coastal land is a scarce resource, new owners should therefore face relatively high tax burdens.

On the other hand, if interstate competition for business investment is fierce – that is, market power is low, as measured by the relevant price elasticities – then it makes sense to tax new business investment relatively lightly. Once a firm's buildings and equipment have been installed, however, it becomes difficult to quickly relocate them; that is, they become substantially less elastic. To the extent that existing homeowners possess more political power than business owners, we might therefore expect "old" business property to be taxed relatively heavily. One problem with this argument is that potential investors will attempt to anticipate future tax burdens and plan their investments accordingly. State and local governments therefore have an incentive to commit to not increasing future tax rates. Such commitments are difficult to maintain, however, particularly since government decision-makers change over time. Tax holidays for new investment may be viewed as a method of offsetting high future taxes on old investment.

With politics and market-power considerations motivating the differential taxation of property according to its type and age, the resulting system of property taxes can be expected to exhibit both inefficiencies and inequities from the viewpoint of the nation as a whole. For example, variations in taxes on business property over time are inefficient, because they encourage inefficiently high levels of firm entry and exit in a region, whereby old firms attempt to escape high taxes by moving to new regions (Wilson 1997). In contrast, taxing existing homeowners more lightly than new homeowners is inefficient because there is not enough household turnover; to avoid higher property taxes, existing homeowners have an incentive to remain in their houses for inefficiently long periods of time.

The incentives created by Proposition 13 in California provide a good example of this inefficient "lock-in effect." Passed in 1978, Proposition 13 capped property tax rates throughout California at the purchase price of the property plus a maximum inflation adjustment of 2 percent per year. However, Proposition 60 modified Proposition 13 in 1986 in a way that effectively allowed 55-year or older households to carry their frozen property taxes to a new home in the same county, and some inter-county transfers were later allowed. Taking advantage of the different treatment of 55- and 54-year-old households, a study by Ferreira (2004) estimates that the probability of moving is 5.2 percent for a 55 year old, but only 4 percent for a 54 year old. This difference of approximately 25 percent in mobility rates indicates a sizable lock-in effect.

In the model of Tiebout competition introduced later in this chapter, inefficient politics do not arise, because a central assumption of the model is that there is no market power. Rather, all jurisdictions are price-takers on the market for business investment, and they are utility-takers on the market for residents. In other words, they can obtain any number of households of a given type by effectively offering them the "equilibrium" utility level, which equates the demand and supply for these households, summed across jurisdictions.

Finally, property tax rates may vary across similar property because of difficulties involved in valuing illiquid assets; that is, assets that are not often bought and sold. One way to value a house would be to use the sale prices of similar houses that have recently sold. But no two houses are exactly the same, if only because their locations differ. Even houses initially built to the same specifications will differ over time, due to different home improvements and maintenance. Various remedies have been offered for more accurately measuring house values. For example, Plassmann and Tideman (2003) suggest that homeowners should be required to self-report their house values but then be required to sell them to anyone willing to pay the reported price! But this procedure might create an upward bias in reported house values, as homeowners attempt to reduce the risk of being forced to move out of their houses. Measuring house values remains to a sizable extent an art, rather than a science.

21.4 THE INCIDENCE OF A LAND TAX

To the extent that a land tax does not vary with the use of the land, it may be viewed as a tax on a fixed factor. Consequently, the land tax does not distort consumer or producer decisions, and is fully borne by the owners of land – or at least this is the conclusion from the partial equilibrium treatment of a tax on a fixed factor that dominates undergraduate textbooks. But even here, this statement needs to be interpreted with care. At the time a land tax is levied, it can be expected to reduce the value of land by the present value of future tax payments, but only if the tax was not previously anticipated. Anticipated taxes will reduce the value of land before they are levied. In either case, future landowners will bear none of the burden of the tax, because they have already reduced the amount they are willing to pay for the land by the present value of their future tax payments. This distinction between current and future landowners does not arise in static models typically used in textbooks and later in this chapter.

Moving from partial equilibrium to general equilibrium, where the equilibrium for multiple markets is determined, the incidence of a tax cannot be described without first specifying the use of the tax revenue. It makes little sense to ignore this use; we would then be ignoring the need to adjust some other tax or public expenditure to keep the government budget balanced following the imposition of the land tax. Textbooks often distinguish between "differential tax incidence" and "balanced-budget incidence." The former assumes that another tax is altered to keep the government budget balanced, whereas the latter assumes that an expenditure program changes.

Oates and Schwab (1997) argue that the property tax reforms implemented by Pittsburgh in 1979–80 essentially represented a rise in the tax on land and fall in another tax, as would occur in an exercise in differential tax incidence. The tax rate on land was raised to a level more than five times the rate on structures, and this rise was offset with a reduction in the effective tax rates on structures, brought about mainly through the use of tax abatements on new commercial and residential construction. The empirical analysis presented by Oates and Schwab shows that the shift toward land taxation helped produce a dramatic increase in building activity in the 1980s, and this conclusion survives in a regression analysis that controls for the high occupancy rates for office buildings during that time. Nonetheless, their results are consistent with the traditional view that the land tax is neutral. The increase in building activity may be interpreted as partially the result of a move away from a tax that provides disincentives to invest toward one that does not affect investment decisions; that is, the land tax. In the next section, I discuss further how taxing structures affects investment incentives.

To isolate the effects of the tax in question from other taxes or expenditures, a balanced-budget exercise is often employed by assuming that the government spends the tax revenue in the same way that the private sector would spend it. An equivalent exercise is to return the tax revenue to consumers in a lump-sum manner, allowing them to directly spend it. This second exercise may be interpreted as differential tax incidence, because the revenue from the tax is being returned to consumers by reducing an existing lump-sum tax or providing a lump-sum subsidy (viewing subsidies as negative taxes). Both exercises affect product and factor prices in the same manner, implying the same distribution of tax burdens. In the case of a land tax, we are then essentially imposing one lump-sum tax and offsetting it with a lump-sum subsidy of identical magnitude. This tax/subsidy scheme will have no impact on the demand for land, implying no shifting of the tax burden away from the initial landowners, unless it effectively redistributes income across households in a way that alters the demand for land.

Using a dynamic model with overlapping generations, Feldstein (1977) provides an interesting example where these demand effects become central to the analysis. Each generation lives for two periods, working only in the first and consuming in both. To save for retirement consumption, a young individual purchases assets, which then provide future income. There are two assets, capital and land, which are used with labor to produce output. Whereas land and labor are fixed in supply, the economy's capital stock is determined by the saving behavior of the young and the investment demands of firms. Feldstein considers a tax on land alone, with the proceeds distributed to the young. Since the tax is imposed on the return to land received by old workers, income is being redistributed from the current old to the current young in each time period. This redistribution destroys the neutrality of a land tax; that is, its burden is now shifted. As Feldstein explains, the tax reduces the value of land assets, and individuals try to stem the decline in savings by increasing their capital assets. The resulting rise in the long-run (steady-state) level of capital increases the marginal productivity of land. As a result, some of the burden of the land tax of the tax is shifted to capital. Calvo, Kotlikoff, and Rodriguez (1979) clarify Feldstein's results and demonstrate that introducing intergenerational bequests restores the neutrality of the land tax. Fane (1984) provides additional clarification.

Traditional tax incidence exercises attempt to separate income distribution issues from efficiency issues. But in cases in which a particular tax plays an important efficiency role in the economy, this separation is misleading at best. According to the benefit view of the property tax, for example, an efficient Tiebout equilibrium is supported by a system of local property taxes, but not by lump-sum taxes. The benefit view is discussed in section 21.6. But first I consider some competing views.

21.5 THE INCIDENCE AND EFFICIENCY EFFECTS OF THE PROPERTY TAX

As noted previously, the property tax is a combination of a land tax and a tax on improvements to land. The land-tax component was discussed in the previous section, so this section focuses mainly on the tax on improvements. In the models discussed below, this tax is levied by local governments on the value of capital located within their jurisdictions. Recognizing that the value of an asset equals the present value of the future income that it generates, this tax may be also be described as a source-based tax on capital income. In contrast, a residence-based tax would be collected on the worldwide capital income of residents, regardless of where they earn it. This latter tax would leave unchanged the relative attractiveness of different regions for investment, but it would affect saving incentives.

Consider first a property tax that is collected at a uniform rate on capital in all uses within a single jurisdiction's borders. Investors will be willing to supply their capital to this jurisdiction only if they receive at least the after-tax return to capital that is available elsewhere. This return adjusts to bring the nation's (or world's) capital market into equilibrium. But if the jurisdiction is small, then the tax will have a negligible affect on this equilibrium return. Consequently, capital bears none of the burden. Instead, the property tax reduces the amount of capital invested in the jurisdiction, increasing the marginal productivity of the remaining capital. This higher productivity compensates firms for the tax, allowing them to pay investors the required after-tax return. As an example of the investment disincentives created by the property tax, recall Oates and Schwab's analysis of Pittsburgh's shift away from taxing structures and toward land taxation. With mobile capital able to escape the tax, the burden falls on those factors that are immobile, including land.

In addition to affecting overall investment incentives, property taxes can be expected to have an impact on the spatial structure of a city, including the important issue of whether property taxation encourages or discourages urban sprawl. Simulation studies by Arnott and MacKinnon (1977), and more recently by Brueckner and Kim (2003), explore this issue using a monocentric city model. In this model, the jurisdiction that imposes the property tax is modeled as a city with a fixed population of households, each of which engages in costly commuting to a central business district (CBD) and is therefore willing to pay more for housing to live closer to the CBD. In their models, housing consists of bundles of structures and land, and the value of this housing is taxed at a uniform rate. Arnott and MacKinnon (1977) find that the property tax reduces the equilibrium city size, whereas Brueckner and Kim (2003) generalize their model in a way that allows for the possibility that city size increases.

This ambiguity is the product of two conflicting effects of the property tax. On the one hand, the property tax decreases the cost of land relative to structures, because landowners bear a significant portion of the property tax burden. As a result, housing producers substitute land for structures, which by itself leads to lower population densities and therefore more urban sprawl, measured by the distance of the city boundary from the CBD. On the other hand, the property tax also increases the price of housing, causing households to demand less housing. This second effect increases population densities and therefore leads to less urban sprawl. Moreover, it more than offsets the first effect if the substitution elasticity between housing and other goods in household consumption exceeds one, as in Arnott and MacKinnon. But urban sprawl may result when the substitution elasticity is less than one. Brueckner and Kim (2003) note that empirical evidence points toward low values of the substitution elasticity, suggesting that the property tax does cause urban sprawl. In either case, the behavioral changes create excess burdens, and Arnott and MacKinnon calculate marginal excess burdens of the property tax equal to about 18 percent of additional tax revenue.

Who bears the total burden of the property tax in these models? Land is obviously a major recipient of the burden, although in one version of Arnott and Mackinnon's model, landowners bear a somewhat lower percentage of the burden than their share of income, reflecting the burden-shifting possibilities inherent in a city without a fixed land area. The remainder is borne by the immobile households, in the form of higher land rents. More generally, immobile households might suffer from lower wages or higher prices of goods that are produced using taxed property and are not easily transportable across different cities. Once again, capital avoids being burdened by the tax if it is highly mobile across jurisdictions.

There is an important qualification to this claim that a jurisdiction's property tax does not burden capital. As described above, the basic idea behind this result is that capital is reallocated to other jurisdictions until the after-tax return is no lower than before. Assuming that the taxing jurisdiction is small, the other jurisdictions are able to absorb the additional capital without an appreciable fall in the marginal productivity of their capital. As a result, capital owners throughout the nation experience only a negligibly small decline in the after-tax return on capital. The problem with this argument is that this small decline is multiplied by the nation's entire stock of capital, creating a total decline in capital income that is not small relative to the size of the single jurisdiction that has implemented the tax. For a detailed discussion of this issue, see Wildasin (1988).

One response to this argument is that the incidence of a property tax levied by a single jurisdiction is mainly of interest to that jurisdiction, not the nation as a whole. The jurisdiction should care mainly about how the tax affects the incomes of its resident capital owners, not those who live throughout the entire rest of the country. On the other hand, households should care not only about their own jurisdiction's property tax, but also about the property taxes levied throughout the country, because the entire system of property taxes does have a significant impact on the equilibrium after-tax return on capital.

This last observation forms the basis for the "new view" of the property tax (only now it is over 30 years old!). As developed by Mieszkowski (1971), this view analyzes the incidence of a country's property tax system under the assumption that capital is mobile across jurisdictions (or regions), but fixed in supply for the country as a whole. Under this assumption, a uniform tax on all capital income throughout the nation would be borne entirely by capital (assuming a "neutral" use of the revenue, as previously discussed). But with the property tax imposed locally, its rate may differ across different jurisdictions. Mieszkowski concludes that the property tax system lowers the return on capital by approximately the average rate of taxation, but differences in property tax rates create "excise tax effects," whereby the prices of goods sold in high-tax jurisdictions rise relative to the prices of goods in low-tax jurisdictions. Courant (1977) qualifies the result, showing that the average tax rate may poorly approx- imate the drop in the after-tax return to capital because tax rate differences cause capital to be inefficiently allocated across regions, producing excess burdens. The claim about excise tax effects can hold only for goods that are not freely traded across jurisdictions (e.g., housing), since free trade equalizes the prices of traded goods. Moreover, Mieszkowski recognizes that the excise tax effects may also consist of low wages and returns on land in high-tax jurisdictions, compared with low-tax jurisdictions. Wilson (1984) investigates these possibilities further in a model with a nontraded good and shows how the migration of households between jurisdictions can lead to the elimination of differences in nontraded good prices.

As already discussed, property tax rates vary not only across jurisdictions, but also across property within a single jurisdiction. Such differences appear to represent an additional source of excess burdens. Under a federal system, how- ever, the inefficiencies associated with local tax systems cannot be fully assessed without also considering the policies of higher levels of government. For example, corporate income is taxed in the USA at both the state and federal levels. Such taxes act like taxes on capital at least to some extent, although how much they raise the cost of capital is an extremely complex issue. In contrast, the federal government has pursued tax policies that effectively grant tax-favored status to homeowners, most notably the mortgage interest deduction. Such policies may offset the heavy use of residential property taxes by local governments. Hoyt

(2001) suggests that such an offset is part of a more general phenomenon: tax policies pursued by one level of government may look quite inefficient, but they may merely be offsetting inefficient-looking policies pursued by another level of government. The interaction of different levels of government falls within the area of fiscal federalism, an important topic but one that is largely beyond the scope of this chapter.

Let us revisit the assumption that the country's capital stock is fixed. This assumption has been traditionally justified by the failure to empirically demonstrate a positive relation between savings and the after-tax return to savings. But in a world economy with an increasingly integrated capital market, the property tax may cause a sizable outflow of capital from the country under consideration. In this case, the property tax system acts like the property tax for a single jurisdiction within the country, albeit a large one. Capital outflows allow capital to escape a portion of the tax burden. Note also that a large capital-importing country can export part of the burden to nonresidents, because the tax drives down the return paid to foreign investors. In contrast, the tax would cause a capital-exporting country to export more capital, thereby driving down the return foreign investors are willing to pay.

In any case, capital can be expected to be more mobile between jurisdictions within a country than between countries, in part because of the informational difficulties that investors encounter when investing abroad. (Multinational corporations have arisen in part to deal with these difficulties.) Thus, capital's ability to escape a single region's property tax gives a misleading view of the ability of capital to escape an entire country's system of property taxes.

The discussion so far has treated property tax rates as exogenous to the model. In contrast, a theme of the tax competition literature is that competition for scarce business capital leads to inefficiently low tax rates and local public expenditures from the viewpoint of the entire country. Wilson (1999) provides an extensive review of this literature. Although tax competition models endogenize the level of capital taxation, they have been criticized for placing exogenous restrictions on the availability of more efficient tax instruments. The next section describes a model in which local governments face no such restrictions.

21.6 Efficient and Equilibrium Land Taxation

This section describes a model in which local governments compete for labor in a manner that is efficient from the viewpoint of the entire system of jurisdictions. The results suggest a central role for land taxation. In fact, I identify a benchmark case where only land taxation is needed to finance the optimal supplies of local public goods. Some qualifications to this central role are provided at the end of this section.

Intergovernmental competition may be modeled by treating governments in the same way as profit-maximizing firms. Thus, suppose that there is a "market" for developing plots of land into residential communities (again referred to as "jurisdictions"), and assume that there is an unlimited supply of identical plots, an assumption that corresponds to free entry in the textbook model of a competitive industry. For concreteness, assume that the development process consists of purchasing undeveloped land at its opportunity cost, hiring firms to construct housing by combining this land with "housing capital," and then choosing public good supplies and the tax system used to finance them. Given the efficiency properties of competitive private markets, the developer may be viewed as giving private firms free rein over how to employ land in the production of housing. Households purchase the jurisdiction's housing, and they may also be viewed as setting up their own government once they move into the jurisdiction. But in this static framework, they have no reason to alter the public policies initially chosen by the developer. This analysis, based on Stiglitz (1983), ignores the internal spatial features of a jurisdiction, in order to concentrate on competition among jurisdictions for these households.

Now consider developer behavior in more detail. Corresponding to profit-maximization in competitive markets, the objective of a single developer is to maximize the value of the jurisdiction's land, which in this static context corresponds to the rent obtained per period, minus any land taxes. The assumption of land value maximization has a long tradition in local public economics, not only because there are powerful incentives for property owners to make sure their governments behave in this manner, but also because it produces an equilibrium with desirable efficiency properties (as we shall shortly see). The developer's choice variables are the levels of public good provision and the taxes used to finance them, consisting of the land tax and a uniform head tax collected from each resident. No other taxes are needed.

To model perfect competition, assume that the number of developed jurisdictions is large, and that there is free entry into the development business. Any single jurisdiction faces an infinitely elastic supply of households of any given type, meaning that it can attract any desired number of households of a particular type by offering the utility available to them elsewhere. In general, this utility will depend on a household's employment opportunities, public good levels, taxes, and the prices of private goods and services. But to eliminate unessential clutter from the model, let us treat household income as exogenous and assume that there is a single public good, which is distributed uniformly across residents. Here and elsewhere, this public good benefits only the jurisdiction's residents; interjurisdictional spillovers of these benefits would represent a positive externality, thereby resulting in underprovision of the public good. Finally, assume that the price of housing is the one market price that is important for residential location decisions.

Each developer faces a trade-off in choosing the optimal population size of a jurisdiction. To the extent that there are scale economies in public good provision, additional residents will lower the effective per capita cost of public good provision, enabling the developer to reduce taxes. But to accommodate more households without reducing per capita housing consumption, more housing must be built on each acre of land. Housing producers will supply this additional housing only if they receive higher prices. To continue to attract residents in the face of higher housing prices, the developer must either provide more of the costly public good or lower head taxes, both of which require higher land taxes to balance the budget. To conclude, the optimal population size for a developer resolves the trade-off between the benefits of additional scale economies in public good provision and the costs associated with increasing the housing stock.

In this model, the developer uses the head tax to control the number of households who choose to reside in the jurisdiction. The general rule followed by the competitive developer is that the head tax should equal the "marginal congestion cost" from public good provision; that is, the increase in the total cost of public good provision created by the entry of a new resident into the jurisdiction. If marginal congestion costs differ across residents, then they should pay different head taxes. But we should expect different types of households to sort themselves across different jurisdictions until a Tiebout equilibrium is established, with public good levels tailored to differences in household incomes and preferences.

To analyze the tax on land, start with the observation that free entry into the development business implies that jurisdictions are developed until the value of land is driven down to land's opportunity cost; that is, its value in an undeveloped state (e.g., farming). This means that the "residual value" of a jurisdiction's land, given by the excess of gross land rents over land's opportunity cost, is fully taxed away in equilibrium. Otherwise, there would be an incentive to develop more jurisdictions.

Having modeled jurisdiction formation and the design of taxes and public good supplies as the outcome of competitive behavior, it should be expected that the efficiency properties of perfect competition carry over to the current setting. This is indeed the case: the equilibrium is socially optimal from the entire system of jurisdictions.

A notable feature of the model is that land taxation plays a potentially sizable role in financing public good provision. In fact, only land taxation will be used in a benchmark case. If there are no congestion costs, as defined above, then developers will choose not to use the head tax, and so we obtain an equilibrium where the residual land rents are exactly sufficient to finance the optimal public good supplies in a system of optimally sized cities. This conclusion is known as the Henry George Theorem, in honor of the nineteenth-century economist who championed the use of land taxation.

There are two important components to the Henry George Theorem. First, all land rents in excess of the opportunity cost of land should be taxed away. Second, no other taxes should be used. As noted above, adding congestion costs to the model eliminates the second component but keeps the first. The result is a "modified" Henry George Theorem, which Wellisch (2000) states as follows: "The socially optimal population of a jurisdiction is achieved if the aggregate land rent [our residual land rent] plus any user charges for internalizing marginal congestion costs of the local public good are equal to total costs of providing the local public goods." This extension is important because congestion costs are sizable for important public goods provided locally. Indeed, some goods that the local government provides would more accurately be called "publicly provided private goods" (although I stick with the term "public goods"), because there are minimal scale economies in production or consumption, and residents could be excluded from consuming them. Public schools are one example, although excludability is not practiced. Gramlich and Rubinfeld (1982) provide empirical support for assuming that scale economies are small in local public good provision.

In practice, land rents are not fully taxed and jurisdictions do not employ head taxes. The presence of untaxed land rents may be explained by restrictions on the number of available jurisdictions, which leads to excess land rents. The lack of head taxes reflects the difficulties involved in levying a system of "fair" head taxes in jurisdictions with heterogeneous populations. Note too that head taxes would not alone control the optimal usage of public goods if residents within a jurisdiction could choose the frequency with which they use a public good. Rather, user fees based on frequency of use would also be needed.

Despite these difficulties, head taxes appear to be a necessary ingredient of an efficient system of taxes. The heavy use of local property taxation therefore raises the question of whether property taxes may serve as a useful substitute for head taxes. The benefit view of property taxation answers in the affirmative.

21.7 THE BENEFIT VIEW OF THE PROPERTY TAX

In a set of highly influential papers on the property tax, Hamilton (1975, 1976) develops the benefit view of the property tax by abandoning the use of differential tax incidence. As we have seen, this methodology typically assumes that revenue from the tax in question is returned to consumers in a "neutral way," as a lump-sum transfer. But because the property tax is a local tax, it finances benefits that are primarily available to those households residing where it is levied. To replace these benefits with a lump-sum subsidy, provided independently of the household's location decision, would therefore ignore the local nature of the property tax. In other words, it would be rather odd to assume that the household's property tax payments do depend on its location, but not the benefits financed by these payments.

This strong connection between benefits and tax payments suggests a form of balanced-budget incidence, involving the use of property tax revenue to finance local public expenditures. However, the efficiency properties of the system of tax rates and expenditures would depend on exactly how the rates are chosen. Rather than fix the rates arbitrarily, Hamilton focuses on rates that finance the efficient levels of local public expenditures in a system of jurisdictions. In other words, the question is: Can a system of local property taxes support an efficient Tiebout equilibrium?

Our modified Henry George Theorem has already described the efficient tax system as consisting of head and land taxes. But the latter tax is needed only because there exist scale economies in public good provision. If we follow Hamilton by assuming constant returns, then marginal congestion costs equal average congestion costs in public good provision, and the efficient head tax alone balances the government budget. But then we must assume a fixed number of jurisdictions, because the absence of scale economies means that there are no longer any benefits from an increase in jurisdiction size. To provide each resident with more housing, developers would set up increasingly smaller jurisdictions in terms of population, and no equilibrium would exist.

Now the property tax as modeled here would seem to behave more like an inefficient excise tax, causing households to consume too little of the taxed good, housing. Hamilton's insight is that a jurisdiction can design a system of zoning restrictions that prevents households from responding in this way. With no opportunity to lower property tax payments by consuming less housing, they are effectively paying a head tax. By appropriately designing its zoning require- ments, the government should then be able to insure that the housing market remains efficient while the tax-inclusive price of housing rises by an amount that corresponds to an efficient head tax, equal to marginal congestion costs. In this respect, the property tax is a benefit tax for public good provision. Moreover, it should not matter whether a household rents or owns. In either case, the house- hold is effectively paying a "user fee" for public good provision.

Although Tiebout's theory is widely recognized as containing a grain of truth, households clearly do not perfectly sort themselves into homogeneous jurisdic- tions. One of the many reasons for heterogeneous populations is that housing is a durable good; that is, it deteriorates slowly. Hamilton (1976) captures this aspect of housing by considering a short-run model of a jurisdiction with fixed amounts of two types of housing. Although the owners of different types of houses will generally pay different property taxes, Hamilton demonstrates that the benefits from local public good provision will be capitalized into the house prices in a way that effectively offsets such property tax differentials. For example, if a household wishes to move to a jurisdiction with better schools, but desires to continue to live in the same type of modest dwelling, then the household will have to pay more for the dwelling. The combination of the price differential and any property tax differential replicates an efficient difference in head tax payments. Since the numbers and sizes of dwellings are fixed in this short-run model, the need for complex zoning policies does not arise.

Much of the controversy surrounding the benefit view revolves around the assumption of efficient zoning. This assumption looks rather innocuous in Hamilton (1975), where housing is measured by a single variable – quantity – and jurisdictions contain homogeneous populations. In Hamilton (1976), the need for complex zoning policies is not an issue, because the numbers and sizes of dwellings are fixed in his short-run model. But even in the simple model developed in the previous section, an efficient zoning policy would require not only restric- tions on the value of housing, but also a separate constraint on the capital–land ratio in housing. Otherwise, a jurisdiction's property tax would lead to less investment in housing capital on a given plot of land.

Thus, it seems useful to investigate models that encompass important features of both the new view and benefit view, without relying on the assumption of efficient zoning. Zodrow and Mieszkowski (1986a) provide a "reformulated new view" with these properties. Their model generates new-view incidence results with the benefit-view assumption that jurisdictions use their property tax revenue to finance local public goods. But they maintain the new view's focus on capital mobility by treating as exogenous the number and type of households in each jurisdiction.

More recently, I have developed a model (Wilson 2003) with both household mobility and capital mobility. Following Mieszkowski (1971), capital is mobile across jurisdictions but fixed in supply for the entire system of jurisdictions. To retain Hamilton's focus on the residential property tax, this capital is combined with land to produce housing. But zoning restrictions are not available, implying that the property tax can no longer serve as an efficient user fee for public good consumption. Nevertheless, the results suggest that the property tax retains benefit-view elements, as might be expected from this "hybrid model."

To demonstrate this claim, I analyze how local governments behave with and without access to a tax on housing. In other words, I endogenize government behavior, but I consider exogenous restrictions on the available tax systems. The analysis is conducted by first allowing jurisdictions to tax only land. In this case, additional public good provision attracts new residents into the jurisdiction, but existing residents are not compensated for the cost of providing these new residents with the public good. As a result, the public good is underprovided. If jurisdictions are now allowed to impose a property tax on housing, they respond by raising their public good supplies to levels closer to first-best value. The basic idea is that the increase in the property tax used to finance a higher public good supply retards the entry of new households into the jurisdiction, because it discourages the production of new housing. With fewer households entering, additional public good provision generates less in the way of congestion costs. For this reason, the effective marginal cost of the public good is lower than when the property tax is absent.

Thus, the property tax tends to partially control population flows, as a user fee should, leading to more efficient public good provision. But this user fee is imperfect: allowing jurisdictions to use head taxes causes equilibrium public good provision to rise further, until the efficient level is reached. Moreover, this substitution of a head tax for the property tax raises the returns on capital and land throughout the economy, in accordance with the new-view incidence results. Thus, the hybrid model gives hybrid results: some "benefit view" in terms of desirable effects of the property tax on public good supplies, but a lot of "new view" in terms of the remaining inefficiencies in public good provision and how the property tax affects factor rewards.

Income differences between households have new and important implications in this hybrid model. Although Wilson (2003) initially abstracts from such differences, they take center stage in the latter part of the paper. As before, the property tax serves the role of an imperfect user fee, but an equilibrium may no longer exist. Instead, we may encounter the "musical suburbs problem," where the "poor" chase the "rich" in hopes of obtaining public goods that are subsidized by the high taxes paid by rich residents (for a focus on this issue, see Wilson 1998). This problem does not arise when housing is perfectly zoned, because the poor are then unable to purchase small houses as a means of avoiding high property tax payments in rich jurisdictions. The next section discusses further the problems that a system of property taxes presents for interactions among households with different incomes.

21.8   CONCLUSIONS AND EXTENSIONS

This chapter began by describing how the property tax is levied, including the apparently inefficient ways in which effective tax rates vary across and within different classes of property. I then discussed the incidence of both property and land taxes. In particular, I described the "new view," which treats the property tax as a tax on capital, with "excise-tax effects" created by interjurisdictional differences in tax rates. For the remainder of the chapter, a model was developed and refined to show how the independent decision-making by local governments could lead to a system of efficient local taxes and public expenditures. For the property tax to be part of this efficient system, as claimed by the "benefit view," local zoning ordinances must be used to prevent the tax from distorting decisions in the housing market. With such distortions absent, the property tax becomes an efficient head tax, or user fee, for public goods. A separate land tax is also needed to support the efficient equilibrium, but it becomes relatively unimportant if there do not exist sizable scale economies in public good provision. Finally, I presented a "hybrid model," which contains elements of both the new view and benefit view, but not the assumption of zoning. Here, property taxation leads to better government policies (but not the best), because it limits the entry of new residents in response to improved public good provision, thereby controlling congestion.

A major difference among the modeling approaches reviewed here is whether government policies are determined outside the model or as part of the model. Table 21.1 describes the various models of property taxation discussed in this chapter (including extensions discussed below), making this distinction between exogenous and endogenous policy determination. This distinction is critical, because it would be small comfort to know that local governments could employ property taxation in a socially useful manner, if in fact they lacked the incentives to do so. There are two issues here: Do local governments face incentives to act in the best interests of their residents? And are such actions desirable from the viewpoint of all jurisdictions?

To answer the first question, the benefit view relies on the capitalization mechanism, under which desirable public policies are capitalized into higher house and land prices. This mechanism gives property owners a strong incentive to participate in the political process to insure that their interests are well represented. If renters are free to move among jurisdictions, their incentives are weak: if they object to particular government policies, they can choose another jurisdiction more to their liking. By representing the interests of property owners, local governments implement policies that are efficient from the viewpoint of all jurisdictions, in the same way that competitive firms behave efficiently by acting in the interests of their shareholders. Note, too, that these results do not break down if jurisdictions contain business property. In this case, the property tax would be

Table 21.1 Property taxation models

Model	What is taxed?	How are tax rates determined?	Who bears the burden?	Inefficiencies?
Traditional view	A single jurisdiction's fixed land supply and mobile capital ("land improvements"), taxed at a common rate	Exogenous	Land tax portion: landowners (assuming "neutral" uses of the revenue). Capital tax portion: the jurisdiction's fixed factors	The land tax is efficient, but the capital tax discourages investment in the jurisdiction
Spatial modification of the traditional view	Residential property, consisting of land and capital, within a single city	Exogenous	Housing occupants (treated as immobile) and landowners, with the division affected by the variability of city land	Housing demands are reduced, and the land intensity of housing is increased, resulting in an outflow of capital. "Urban sprawl" occurs in important cases
New view	Mobile capital in an exogenous number of jurisdictions (a land tax would obey the traditional view)	Exogenous	Capital throughout the system of jurisdictions, with residents in high (low) tax jurisdictions burdened (helped) by excise tax effects	Tax differences misallocate capital across jurisdictions
Models of horizontal tax competition	Mobile capital in an exogenous number of jurisdictions	Chosen by local governments	Capital throughout the system of jurisdictions	Competition for capital leads to inefficiently low tax rates and public expenditure levels

Table 21.1 *(cont'd)*

Model	What is taxed?	How are tax rates determined?	Who bears the burden?	Inefficiencies?
Henry George models	Land and mobile households (head taxes) in an endogenous number of jurisdictions. Extension: taxes on mobile firms	Efficiently chosen by a central government or by local governments	The residual value of land is reduced to zero (Henry George Theorem)	An efficient equilibrium is supported by the land tax, combined with taxes on households and firms to efficiently price congestion
Benefit view	Residential property in an exogenous number of jurisdictions. Extensions: industrial property, endogenous number of jurisdictions with land tax	Exogenous or chosen by local governments	The property tax is paid by consumers of public goods, as an efficient "user fee"	An efficient equilibrium is supported by the property tax
Hybrid model	Land and residential property (consisting of land and capital) in an endogenous number of jurisdictions	Chosen by local governments	Similar to the new view because zoning is absent	Supplementing the land tax with the property tax improves government decision-making

a payment for public services provided to firms (e.g., "infrastructure"). Fischel (1975) and White (1975) provide the classic analysis of this extension of the Tiebout model to firm mobility. Extended to include both capital and labor mobility, the theory is consistent with the classified property tax system mentioned in section 21.3, with business and residential property taxed at rates reflecting the different costs involved in providing public goods and services to businesses and households.

But the capitalization mechanism in benefit-view models relies on some controversial assumptions. First, households must be mobile. It is the movement of households into a jurisdiction that increases housing demand and thereby bids up housing prices in response to a desirable policy changes. Moreover, mobility is also needed to justify land-value maximization as the government's objective. I have already discussed the case of renters. For homeowners, perfect mobility insures that personal preferences for taxes and public expenditures do not matter. For example, a homeowner may not directly benefit from good neighborhood schools, but he or she will be willing to vote for the taxes needed to finance them if doing so raises property values, since he or she can then sell the house and move to a jurisdiction with lower taxes. The situation is similar to that of an investor who is seeking capital gains in the stock market. The investor cares about maximizing the value of the firm, not whether the firm is producing a particular mix of goods that the investor personally finds appealing. With household immobility, not only will policy changes fail to be quickly and fully capitalized into higher property values, but a homeowner's personal tastes for local public goods will also become important, leading to objectives other than land-value maximization. For an analysis of local decision-making in this case, see Brueckner (1991). For taxes on business property, the mobility of firms and capital is similarly important.

An objection to the view that household mobility leads to efficient government behavior is that the political process may not give owners of land or other fixed factors sufficient influence to rein in the wasteful behavior of self-interested government officials. But Wilson and Gordon (2003) describe how household mobility does reduce this wasteful behavior under a property tax system. The basic idea is that officials benefit from the extra revenue that can be obtained by expanding the property tax base, and one way to achieve this expansion is to attract more households to the jurisdiction by providing those goods and services that they value. Wilson (2005) analyzes a similar mechanism for the case of capital mobility.

In addition to household mobility, the capitalization mechanism applied to residential property also requires that this property not be infinitely elastic in supply. If the supply elasticity were infinite, then increased housing demand would result only in the construction of new housing, not a rise in its price. The model of the benefit view discussed in the present chapter has assumed a finite elasticity, created by the assumption of a fixed amount of developable land in each jurisdiction. Alternatively, we could assume that particular parcels of land possess different accessibility characteristics, such as their closeness to jobs. In a dynamic setting, a distinction would be made between short- and long-run supply elasticities, with capitalization occurring in the short run because of the durable nature of housing. Even if land is not scarce, thereby allowing housing to be produced at constant cost (as in Hamilton 1975), the capitalization mechanism can be kept in force through residential land-use controls that place restrictions on the land available for housing. Competition among jurisdictions would insure that such restrictions do not inefficiently inflate housing prices in equilibrium, in the same way that competition among competitive firms eliminates economic profits.

The capitalization mechanism works best when there are a large number of competitive jurisdictions, allowing for Tiebout sorting. In practice, however, there exist important constraints on the formation of new jurisdictions, caused by the scarcity of undeveloped land in metropolitan areas and institutional restrictions on the flexibility of municipal boundaries (Epple & Romer 1989). Such constraints lead to jurisdictions with heterogeneous populations living in diverse types of housing. We should then not be surprised to find conflicts between different groups of landowners. In particular, some of the existing homeowners may find that they can drive up their house prices by using zoning controls to restrict new development in the jurisdiction. As previously noted, the large diversity in the rates imposed on different, and similar, types of property within a given jurisdiction suggests that such market-power motivations are not unimportant.

Note too that there are efficiency justifications for departing from the Tiebout world of jurisdictions with homogeneous populations. One is the desirability of having workers with complementary labor skills reside in the same jurisdiction, to be near a common workplace. Another is the potential benefits arising from interactions among dissimilar households. Such interactions create desirable "peer-group effects," where some households benefit from being close to others, either through classroom interactions in a school setting or through interactions in neighborhoods. The existence and strength of neighborhood effects has been the subject of extensive research. In a recent study, Kling and Liebman (2004) find that moving female children to low-poverty neighborhoods results in improvements in education and mental health, along with the reduction of "risky behaviors," but they do not find similar effects for male children.

It is a simple matter to extend Tiebout's theory to cases in which such mixing of different household types is efficient (see Stiglitz 1983). But such models stretch the reasonableness of the zoning arrangements needed to make the property tax equivalent to a system of efficient user fees. Moreover, I have already noted that actual property tax systems often seem to reflect the exploitation of market power by individual jurisdictions, combined with imperfect politics.

The extent to which zoning is used in a way envisioned by the benefit view has been the subject of intense debate. For recent contributions to each side of the debate, see Zodrow (2001) and Fischel (2001). One problem in interpreting the evidence is that zoning as actually practiced is never going to fully satisfy the requirements for fully efficient zoning, and it is not clear how "imperfect" zoning rules can be recognized and evaluated. Suppose, for example, that each jurisdiction uses zoning to achieve a homogeneous housing stock that is optimal for a particular type of household. Then all residents of a jurisdiction will pay the same property tax. Suppose also that it is socially desirable to mix low- and high-income households in the same jurisdiction, due to peer-group effects in public schools. In particular, low-income students benefit from being in the classroom with high-income students. Due to restrictions on the tax system, no such mixing will occur, however. An equilibrium, if it exists, will consist of high- and low-income jurisdictions and no mixed jurisdictions. Yet this equilibrium might appear to be an efficient Tiebout equilibrium, because each household is paying taxes equal to the marginal congestion cost, as required for efficiency, although this is only possible because households are not efficiently mixed. The problem here is that high-income households have no incentive to occupy jurisdictions containing low-income households, because they would incur the costs associated with mixing with low-income households but would not be compensated for the benefits they confer on low-income households, at least indirectly in the form of lower housing costs. An efficient property tax and zoning system for local governments would effectively provide such compensation, with the central government using its tax and welfare system to correct any deficiencies in the distribution of income.

To conclude, the benefit view of property taxation is most convincing in cases in which the objective is to achieve a Tiebout equilibrium, with perfect sorting of households across jurisdictions according to their incomes and preferences for public good provision. But there is cause for concern about a system that leads to the segregation of particular socioeconomic groups in their own communities, particularly if the central government does not step in to undertake policies designed to mitigate the adverse consequences of this segregation, including unequal schooling. One potential social cost of property taxation may be that its use encourages the enactment of zoning policies that are overly exclusionary. Although the benefit view contains an important grain of truth, central-government intervention is needed to reduce the inefficiencies and inequities that are likely to result from unfettered competition among local governments.

Acknowledgments

I thank Richard Arnott, a referee, and Patricia Wilson for helpful comments.

Bibliography

Arnott, R. J. 2002: The property tax as a tax on value: deadweight loss. Unpublished manuscript, Boston College.

—— and MacKinnon, J. G. 1977: The effects of the property tax: a general equilibrium simulation. *Journal of Urban Economics*, 4, 389–407.

Brueckner, J. K. 1991: Voting with capitalization. *Regional Science and Urban Economics*, 21, 453–67.

—— and Kim, H.-A. 2003: Urban sprawl and the property tax. *International Tax and Public Finance*, 10, 5–23.

Calvo, G. A., Kotlikoff, L. J., and Rodriquez, C. A. 1979: The incidence of a tax on pure rent: a new reason for an old answer. *Journal of Political Economy*, 87, 869–74.

Courant, P. 1977: A general equilibrium model of heterogeneous local property taxes. *Journal of Public Economics*, 8, 313–27.

Epple, D. and Romer, R. 1989: On the flexibility of municipal boundaries. *Journal of Urban Economics*, 26, 307–19.

Fane, G. 1984: The incidence of a tax on pure rent: the old reason for the old answer. *Journal of Political Economy*, 92, 329–33.

Feldstein, M. 1977: The surprising incidence of a tax on pure rent: a new answer to an old question. *Journal of Political Economy*, 85, 349–60.

Ferreira, F. V. 2004: You can take it with you: transferability of Proposition 13 tax benefits, residential mobility, and willingness to pay for housing amenities. Center for Labor Economics, University of California, Berkeley, Working Paper No. 72.

Fischel, W. A. 1975: Fiscal and environmental considerations in the location of firms in suburban communities. In E. S. Mills and W. E. Oates (eds.), *Fiscal Zoning and Land Use Controls: The Economic Issues*. Lexington, MA: D. C. Heath.

—— 2001: Municipal corporations, homeowners, and the benefit view of the property tax. In W. E. Oates (ed.), *Property Taxation and Local Public Finance*. Cambridge, MA: Lincoln Institute for Land Policy.

Gramlich, E. and Rubinfeld, D. 1982: Micro estimates of public spending demand functions and tests of the Tiebout and median-voter hypotheses. *Journal of Political Economy*, 90, 536–60.

Hamilton, B. W. 1975: Zoning and property taxation in a system of local governments. *Urban Studies*, 12, 205–11.

—— 1976: Capitalization of intrajurisdictional differences in local tax prices. *American Economic Review*, 66, 743–53.

Hoyt, W. H. 2001: Tax policy coordination, vertical externalities, and optimal taxation in a system of hierarchical governments. *Journal of Urban Economics*, 3, 491–516.

Kaplow, L. 2000: Horizontal equity: new measures, unclear principles. NBER Working Paper No. 7649.

Kling, J. R. and Liebman, J. B. 2004: Experimental analysis of neighborhood effects on youth. Working Paper, Princeton University.

McCluskey, W. (ed.) 1999: *Property Tax: An International Comparative Review*. Aldershot, UK: Ashgate.

Mieszkowski, P. 1971: The property tax: An excise tax or a profits tax? *Journal of Public Economics*, 1, 73–96.

Nechyba, T. J. 1997: Local property and state income taxes: the role of interjurisdictional competition and collusion. *Journal of Political Economy*, 105, 351–84.

Oates, W. E. and Schwab, R. M. 1997: The impact of urban land taxation: the Pittsburgh experience. *National Tax Journal*, 50, 1–21.

OECD 2001: Tax and the economy: a comparative assessment of OECD countries. *OECD Tax Policy Studies*, 6.

Plassmann, F. and Tideman, T. N. 2003: Accurate valuation in the absence of markets. SUNY Binghamton Working Paper WP0101.

Söderström, L. 1998: Fiscal federalism: the Nordic way. In J. Rattsø (ed.), *Fiscal Federalism and State-Local Finance*. Cheltenham, UK: Edward Elgar.

Stiglitz, J. E. 1983: Public goods in open economies with heterogeneous individuals. In J.-F. Thisse and H. G. Zoller (eds.), *Locational Analysis of Public Facilities*. Amsterdam: North-Holland.

Tideman, T. N. 1982: A tax on land value is neutral. *National Tax Journal*, 35, 109–11.

Tiebout, C. M. 1956: A pure theory of local expenditures. *Journal of Political Economy*, 64, 416–24.

Wellisch, D. 2000: *Theory of Public Finance in a Federal State*. Cambridge, UK: Cambridge University Press.

White, M. J. 1975: Firm location in a zoned metropolitan area. In E. S. Mills and W. E. Oates (eds.), *Fiscal Zoning and Land Use Controls: The Economic Issues*. Lexington, MA: D. C. Heath.

Wildasin, D. E. 1988: Indirect distributional effects in benefit–cost analysis of small projects. *Economic Journal*, 98, 801–7.

Wilson, J. D. 1984: The excise tax effects of the property tax. *Journal of Public Economics*, 24, 309–29.

—— 1997: The tax treatment of imperfectly mobile firms: rent-seeking, rent-protection, and rent destruction. In R. Feenstra, G. Grossman, and D. Irwin (eds.), *The Political Economy of Trade Policy: Essays in Honor of Jagdish Bhagwati*. Cambridge, MA: The MIT Press.

—— 1998: Imperfect solutions to the musical-suburbs problem. In D. Pines, E. Sadka, and I. Zilcha (eds.), *Topics in Public Economics*. Cambridge, UK: Cambridge University Press.

—— 1999: Theories of tax competition. *National Tax Journal*, 52, 269–304.

—— 2003: The property tax: competing views and a hybrid theory. In S. Cnossen and H.-W. Sinn (eds.), *Public Finances and Public Policy in the New Millennium: A Conference on the Occasion of Richard Musgrave's 90th and CES's 10th Birthdays*. Cambridge, MA: The MIT Press.

—— 2005: Welfare-improving competition for mobile capital. *Journal of Urban Economics*, 57, 1–18.

—— and Gordon, R. H. 2003: Expenditure competition. *Journal of Public Economic Theory*, 5, 399–417.

Zodrow, G. R. 2001: Reflections on the new view and the benefit view of the property tax. In W. E. Oates (ed.), *Property Taxation and Local Government Finance*. Cambridge, MA: Lincoln Institute of Land Policy.

—— and Mieszkowski, P. 1986a: The new view of the property tax: a reformulation. *Regional Science and Urban Economics*, 16, 309–27.

—— and Mieszkowski, P. 1986b: Pigou, Tiebout, property taxation, and the underprovision of local public goods. *Journal of Urban Economics*, 19, 356–70.

CHAPTER TWENTY-TWO

A Theory of Municipal Corporate Governance with an Application to Land-Use Regulation

William A. Fischel

22.1 Introduction: Political Schizophrenia

In the United States, neither the political left nor the political right have much use for the thousands of local governments that employ more than half of America's government workforce. The left does not like local government because it is local. Localism connotes parochialism, a narrow view of the world, and a shortsighted agenda, one that precludes redistributive taxation. The right usually sees local government as just another layer of government, one given to personal feuds among cigar-chomping political bosses. The paradigmatic failure of local governance is the so-called "race to the bottom," in which localities sell their environmental patrimony for a mess of pottage or, worse, engage in "beggar thy neighbor" policies by putting fiscally profitable but environmentally problematic land uses on their borders, downwind and out of sight of their own residents.

To be fair, there is an element of the left that sees localism as the embodiment of communitarian values, the place most likely to inculcate participatory democracy (Frug 1980). And an important element of the right sees local government as superior to national government in that residents can "vote with their feet"

(Tiebout 1956) to avoid adverse consequences of inefficient government policies. But neither side has much admiration for local governance as it currently exists. The communitarians would cast off legal doctrines that inhibit local redistribution of wealth. Most "vote with your feet" theorists regard local governance structure as inherently uninteresting. Why care about voting at the ballot box if the important vote is selecting residence in one of the scores of municipalities than exist in most American metropolitan areas?

Political disdain for the subject may explain why there has been so little attempt to construct an economic model of local governance. This is in distinct contrast to theories about the governance of the modern business corporation. Economists and legal scholars have developed behavioral models of the connections between shareholders, boards of directors, and chief executive officers and other managers (Easterbrook & Fischel 1991). In this essay, I will borrow from the economic literature on business corporate governance to sketch the elements of a theory of how localities are governed. At the core of this structure are homeowners, who are the dominant shareholders of most American municipal corporations. Their inability to diversify their primary – often their only – financial asset leads them to be overly risk averse with respect to land-use changes in their community.

22.2 A Very Short Review of Corporate Governance

An academic course on "corporations" at the end of the nineteenth century would examine both business corporations and municipal corporations. Both would be covered under the same section of most state constitutions. Both were (and are) "creatures of the state" in the sense that the granting of a corporate charter would be an act of the state (and not the federal) government. Municipal and business corporations are also "legal persons." They can make contracts and be liable for their breach; they can own property and transfer it; and they can institute civil suits against other people and other corporations and are themselves liable for torts. Both business and municipal corporations are "immortal" in the sense that their continued existence does not depend upon any particular set of human members. Stockholders and residents and managers and mayors can come and go, but General Electric and the City of Cleveland will live on.

There were always differences between municipal and business corporations, of course. Municipalities were more closely tied to the state's business. In some respects, they acted as administrative units of the state government. One should not, however, confuse municipalities with counties, which were originally only administrative units to implement state laws. Municipalities have long had the ability to adopt laws on their own, without the prodding of the state.

Around 1900, the business corporation was subject to what we now call the managerial revolution. Instead of having owners who participated fairly closely in the management of the corporation, the modern corporation (which had actually arisen much earlier in the railroad industry) developed a tripartite structure that is outlined in Figure 22.1. The shareholders do not participate in management or even in selecting managers. Instead, they elect a board of directors, who

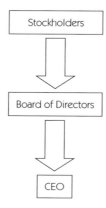

Figure 22.1 The business governance template.

in turn select the CEO and other top managers. The CEO runs the company as the agent of the stockholders.

The civic reformers of the early twentieth century were aware of the managerial revolution in business corporations, and they saw in it a new paradigm for municipal corporations, as well. The most influential of these reformers was Richard Childs (East 1965). He left his mark in the business world by promoting a product that did not leave marks: Bon Ami cleanser, whose famous logo was a newly hatched chicken and the words "hasn't scratched yet."

Childs left the business world to promote the adoption of what we now call the "council-manager" form of local government. Before 1900, most cities elected legislative councils by subdistricts called wards. The independently elected mayor served as chief executive. But in reality the council members intervened frequently in executive affairs in order to promote the interests of their neighborhoods. Moreover, executive ability was not especially widespread among elected mayors.

Childs's council-manager paradigm sought to reduce the influence of city councils in everyday affairs and to make the chief executive into a nonpolitical professional. Voters would select a council – preferably by city-wide votes rather than wards – and the council would then hire a manager, just as in the business corporation. The paradigm of control is illustrated in Figure 22.2.

Neither of these paradigms turned out to work in the way they are illustrated in Figures 22.1 and 22.2. They went divergent ways not because one is "economic" and the other "political." Nor is their essential difference the result of differences in their voting rules, with the business corporation (usually) voting by share and the municipality (always) by person. (There is more on voting rules in the last section.) The essential difference is in the ability of shareholders to diversify.

Shareholders in business corporations could diversify their assets after stock markets became liquid enough to allow it. Successful diversification, however, came with a price. It made most business stockholders inattentive to the operation of any particular business. With only a small fraction of his or her wealth in a

Figure 22.2   The municipal council-manager paradigm.

given corporation, there is little incentive for any stockholder to make much effort to understand how well it is run. If managers of a particular business seem about to make poor decisions, most stockholders just sell the stock and add a different one to the portfolio. Indeed, it is usually hardly worth paying any attention to any single company if it forms only a small fraction of one's wealth. Rational ignorance is the order of the day for the well-diversified stockholder.

Inattention by shareholders meant that the business corporation's board of directors got little feedback, positive or negative, from those they were supposed to represent. The party that had a much more intensive interest in the corporation was the CEO and his allies. With the rise of the powerful CEO, directors became rubber stamps for whatever the full time CEO wanted to do (Berle & Means 1932; Roe 1994). This state of affairs is summarized in Figure 22.3. Shareholders are not

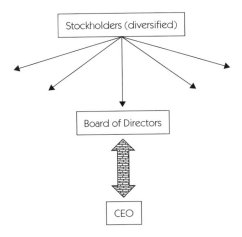

Figure 22.3   Business corporate reality (Berle & Means 1932).

indifferent to the operation of their corporation, but their interest is too diffuse to give it much attention. (The multiple arrows in Figure 22.3 are to suggest owner-ship of many different stocks.) Thus the board of directors and the CEO are part of a team that provides reciprocal benefits to one another, as the double-headed arrow in Figure 22.3 is intended to suggest.

I hasten to point out that there are other methods of making the CEO respon-sive to the interests of the shareholders. The corporate takeover is one such method (Manne 1965). Managers and directors who get too comfortable at the shareholders' expense are at risk of having their shareholders sell their shares to a takeover team, who can oust the former team and set up their own.

22.3   MOST MUNICIPAL CORPORATIONS
RESPOND TO "HOMEVOTERS"

The "shareholders" of municipal corporations are those whose permanent residence is located within the boundaries of the local government. In the vast majority of American local governments, homeowners are the dominant group. Two-thirds of Americans live in a home for which they are the residual claim-ants. If the municipal government makes a mess of things, homeowners will pay for it. Higher taxes, worse schools, and unmaintained streets depreciate the value of almost all homes, regardless of whether their current occupants have children in schools or drive cars on the streets. They know that prospective buyers of their property are likely to care.

Mismanagement of municipal corporations cannot be corrected by corporate takeovers, at least not of the usual kind. This is not because the ownership shares in municipalities have no market. Homes are bought and sold all the time; the real estate side of the capital market is as big as the market for business corporations. The problem with residential real estate is that it cannot easily be diversified (Caplin, Chan, Freeman & Tracy 1997). One cannot own a fraction of a home in Binghamton and fractions of homes in Sausalito, Abeline, Jacksonville, and St Paul. Insurance for depreciation in land value is not available. The market discipline is thus too severe for homeowners to leave it to takeover specialists to fix poor governance.

For the vast majority of homeowners, their home is by far the largest financial asset they have. Many homeowners actually have no other financial asset of any significance. Thus they take a much stronger interest in their local government than they would if they could diversify their holdings. The concentration of assets in one place makes homeowners behave like Mark Twain's speaker in *Pudd'nhead Wilson*:

> Behold, the fool saith, "Put not all thine eggs in the one basket" – which is but a
> manner of saying, "Scatter your money and your attention"; but the wise man saith,
> "Put all your eggs in the one basket *and – watch that basket!*"

Undiversified homeowners thus became what I have characterized as "home-voters" (Fischel 2001a). Their voting in local elections is far more influenced by their

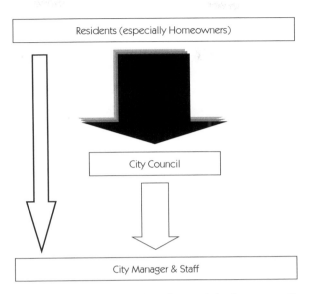

Figure 22.4   Homevoters and municipal corporations.

home values than by political ideology or employment considerations. My characterization of how this affects municipal corporate governance is presented in Figure 22.4. Homevoters actively influence governance both through participation in local politics and by direct monitoring of city managers and city employees. Residents actually consume most of the services provided by the city, so they are in a far better position to monitor employee performance than are the stockholders of most business corporations. The larger and darker arrows in Figure 22.4 are to suggest that this interest is far stronger than in business corporations because of the home's importance (relative to other assets) and the lack of diversification of the typical homeowners.

One objection to this model immediately surfaces every time I present it. Average participation rates in local elections are notoriously low, lower even than in most state and national elections. If homeownership is the key to voter attention, why should voter turnout not be higher at the local level than it is?

One reason for low participation is sorting of the type proposed by Charles Tiebout (1956). Because there are many local governments in most metropolitan areas, households tend to sort themselves in communities with other people whose demand for local public goods is similar. In such a setting, it is rational for voters not to participate in most local elections, since those who do participate will be reasonably representative of those who abstain. Tiebout sorting also makes it easier for city councils and managers to determine what people actually want, so that they are less likely to require the discipline of the ballot box as often as state and national officials.

A second reason is that balloting is only one means of expressing preferences at the local level. City hall is not as distant as the state capital or Washington, DC.

Most city councils are large enough that the odds are strong that any given resident knows someone who knows a council member who can then be button-holed about a problem. This is especially true in the smaller (less than 100,000 population) municipalities in which the majority of urban Americans actually live. Homeowners can also affect local outcomes by participation in meetings and hearings, a process that is dominated by paid lobbyists at the state and national level. Finally, average electoral participation rates obscure the fact that at the local level, variance can be very high. When a controversial issue arises, voter turnout in local elections can vary by factors of two or three above the mean, while similar variation in voter turnout at state and national elections is almost unheard of.

Thus the low average turnout in local elections is not much of a barrier to my theory. And there are a good number of studies that indicate that homeownership by itself seems to promote better citizenship (DiPasquale & Glaeser 1999). There's nothing especially moral about homeownership. "Good citizenship" is for the most part consistent with watching over a large and vulnerable asset.

22.4   HOMEVOTERS AND LAND USE

The homevoter approach to municipal governance helps explain why land-use issues are of paramount concern for most local governments. At the neighborhood level, land-use decisions are critical because of their immediate impact on home values. A zoning board considering a variance to permit a commercial use or a large apartment house in a single-family neighborhood will in most cases incite a very strong reaction. Turnout at the hearing will be large, and homeowners will not be reluctant to express their opposition if the proposed use has even the slightest chance of having any adverse effect nearby property values.

Opposition to land-use change is often derided by the acronym applied to the homeowning opponents, NIMBY ("not in my back yard"). Once one understands the financial nature of homeownership, however, NIMBYs do not seem quite so irrational. Lacking any insurance for their biggest asset, homeowners regard zoning as the closest substitute (Fischel 2001b). Changes in zoning are for them like having an insurer unilaterally change the terms the policy.

Economists have sometimes found that the supposedly undesirable non-conforming uses in reality have little impact on nearby home values (Crecine, Davis & Jackson 1967). What such studies overlook is that zoning has been around for a long time in most places, so that the usual sample of nonconforming uses has been subject to considerable public oversight. The city planners may have made the nonconforming use behave in ways that internalize its neighborhood effects. Most urban neighborhoods are an exquisitely censored sample produced by a long history of public oversight.

The structure of zoning law also reflects the riskiness of homeownership and the use of zoning as an alternative to home value insurance. Most states have adopted similar zoning enabling acts and still bear the stamp of the original Model Standard State Zoning Enabling Act of 1922. The workings of this act involve a startling amount of public participation when compared to many other municipal functions, such as infrastructure maintenance and budgeting (Fischel 1985, ch. 2). The making and amending of land-use laws involves many mandatory public hearings. Even minor exceptions to zoning laws are usually made only after a public hearing. Notice of such hearings must be extensively disseminated, and nearby property owners are usually sent notices of the hearings by registered mail. While the officials who conduct the hearings are ostensibly mere fact finders, the "fact" of public opposition to (or, more rarely, support for) the proposed project is often most decisive in their deliberations.

Laws adopted under the standard zoning act almost always assume a hierarchy of land uses. At the top of the zoning "pyramid," to use a once-popular visual metaphor, is the single-family home. It is presumed to require the most protection, and other uses are deemed subsidiary to it. This idea is so pervasive that we seldom stop to think that it is an odd normative preference. Apartment dwellers are no less citizens than homeowners. Owners of businesses are as much affected by who their neighbors are as homeowners. Opportunities for employment and production are, in the larger scheme of things, as important to society as homeownership. Yet the latter uses are all presumed to require less protection than homes.

This hierarchy makes sense, though, when the ability to spread risks is considered. Commercial establishments, multi-family housing, and industrial properties are usually owned by business corporations, multiple partners, or Real Estate Investment Trusts. Business owners' location risks can often be diversified by having multiple locations. Even if they have but one plant or store, the stockholders of the corporation usually own shares in other assets, so that a land-use insult to one location is hardly catastrophic.

The primacy of homeowners and their aversion to the risk of devaluation can also explain the scarcity of real examples of the "race to the bottom." Far from being eager to trade away environmental quality for jobs or fiscal benefits, homevoters are among the most reluctant of traders. Environmental degradation usually lowers nearby home values. Even if the net fiscal benefits of an environmentally problematical project are positive for the community as a whole, the determined opposition of a faction of nearby homeowners can slow and significantly modify the transaction if it does not stop it entirely.

22.5 Private Covenants are Complements to Zoning, not Substitutes

The history of the adoption of zoning in the USA is also consistent with the view of zoning as an alternative to insurance. My survey of secondary works on zoning history strongly indicates that zoning arose with near simultaneity in American cities and suburbs because of risk considerations (Fischel 2004). The first cause was the invention of the motor vehicle. It was not the automobile that brought about a demand for zoning. It was the motor truck and the motor bus. The truck enabled large industrial and commercial uses to choose low-cost locations away from docks and railroads. The motorized bus allowed builders of larger multi-family apartments to locate away from interurban trolley lines. The truck and the bus could follow the developer rather than vice versa.

The newly footloose industrial and apartment developers overwhelmed the previous mix of forces that had protected single-family residential districts from incursions. Informal agreements, *ad hoc* laws against specific threats, and legal covenants were all used in the pre-zoning era. These proved to be insufficient in the face of rapidly declining costs for moving freight and masses of people over residential arteries and streets. Aside from the difficulty of enforcing private covenants, few were able to cover a sufficiently large territory to afford the protection that homebuyers sought.

Large-scale developers in California complained of "curbstoners," small-scale developers who would place incompatible uses on the edges of the larger, covenanted subdivisions. The larger residential developers found that they could not market their product successfully without public controls. Developers were actually among the most active lobbyists of state legislatures to adopt zoning laws (Weiss 1987). California developers were influential in persuading the US Commerce Department, headed by native son Herbert Hoover, to draft and promulgate the original Standard State Zoning Enabling Act.

Covenants and their modern successors, residential community associations, have existed side by side with zoning since zoning was first established. Almost all privately planned communities of the twentieth century have been subject to the zoning rules of the municipalities or counties in which they were located. Most sizable private community associations are active watchdogs, if not actually participants in the zoning process of the larger community. Far from displacing zoning and other public controls, community associations have strengthened it. Covenants, community associations, and zoning reflect a "belt and suspenders" strategy for protecting the value of the single family's home. If anything, the modern community association has made zoning more entrenched than ever.

22.6 CONCLUSION

This essay has sought to persuade the reader that urban land-use issues can be usefully thought of through the lenses of corporate governance and asset management. I will conclude by limning two research projects in which this view might profitably be applied.

22.6.1 Voting rights

Land-use regulations are among the most crucial political decisions made by local governments. Voting procedures are thus very important to most homeowners. It is possible that homevoters exert an influence on several aspects of voting rights.

An important difference between municipal and business corporations is how voting rights are allocated. For most business corporations, voting about corporate affairs is by number of shares; the rule is one dollar, one vote. This allocation is normally thought to promote efficiency (Grossman & Hart 1988). Municipal corporations have always allocated votes on the per capita basis. In the distant past, many residents were excluded from voting (women, slaves, tenants, religious minorities), but the critical fact is that no municipality in the USA ever allocated votes by wealth. One may have needed a minimum amount of property to obtain the franchise, but double or triple that minimum did not get one more than a single vote. The municipal rule has long been "no more than one vote per person."

This rule can be the source of considerable mischief in land-use regulation. In large-scale private developments, the owner of the undeveloped tracts typically holds a majority of votes in the new homeowner association so that new residents cannot collectively block completion of the project (Reichman 1976; Henderson 1980). Owners of developable land cannot do that in a municipality. Thus the typical scenario in a developing suburb is for the first few landowners to develop at profitable densities. The new residents then become influential in local politics and attempt, figuratively, to pull up the drawbridge behind them, adopting increasingly restrictive land-use regulations. Thus the "one person, one vote" rule often ends up promoting a highly inegalitarian policy of exclusionary zoning.

Suggestions for dealing with this problem have ranged from an energized legal protection for landowners (Fischel 1995, ch. 9) to proposals to allow owners of undeveloped land to withdraw from the municipality (Nelson 1999). Only a few have suggested a rearranged voting pattern. Robert Ellickson (1982) has gingerly suggested that votes on some issues should be allocated by acreage or land value. This is legally less improbable than it might seem. While the US Supreme Court has held that municipalities are subject to the "one person, one vote" standard, it has allowed local governments some exceptions for specific, and sometimes very important, government functions (Briffault 1993).

It might, then, be worth asking whether the longstanding municipal practice of allocating no more than one vote per person has a sensible economic basis. I have suggested, using historical analogies, that existing municipal voting rules could be a rational response to risk aversion by owners of smaller properties (Fischel 2001a, ch. 2). This was the concern of the original *business* corporate shareholders in the early 1800s, before the advent of efficient stock markets in which they could diversify risks. The numerous owners of small shares in a business worried that owners of many shares might adopt oppressive or self-dealing policies. In order to attract their capital, then, early business charters often put a cap on the number of votes that large shareholders could exercise (Dunlavy 2004). Only after stock markets became liquid enough to enable shareholders to protect themselves by diversification did voting by share become the norm.

An important theoretical question might be the conditions under which the existing municipal voting rule, which protects smallholders from political risks, are worth the costs. The costs include the potential for oppression of the few owners of large amounts of developable land. This disregard for landowners' rights in turn raises housing costs and promotes segregation by income class in metropolitan areas. In other words, do the benefits of the "one person, one vote" rule exceed the costs that such rules impose on the rest of society? A related, more practical, research area could be the design of a hybrid voting rule that would incorporate features of both the existing allocation of votes with some variation on business corporations' voting rules.

22.6.2 Home value insurance

I have emphasized in this essay that scholars of land use need to think about the riskiness of homeownership. The discussion has simply assumed that home value insurance is unavailable. A potentially fruitful area for research is to investigate the barriers to formation of this type of insurance. If they can be overcome by a modest application of public policy, home value insurance might remove many of the apparent inefficiencies of the market for development permits. Developers would give more than verbal assurance to NIMBYs that oppose their projects. They could put their money where their mouths are and offer to compensate neighbors in the event that the project does devalue their homes.

The reasons why developers do not do this are legion. One is that their projects really do reduce nearby home values, and expected payouts would make their projects unprofitable. In that case, of course, the insurance requirement has done the right thing, since that outcome would normally be a signal that the project was socially undesirable. (This may have been why a prominent, large-scale apartment developer scoffed at this idea when I presented it at a developers' forum.) Since preventing a project can already be accomplished by the active intervention of NIMBYs, it does not warrant the creation of an insurance market. But often it does seem likely that potential gains from trade between developers and neighborhoods are inhibited by uncertainty of how things will turn out rather than their expected value. In this case, a viable home value insurance market would make a difference.

The one large experiment in home value insurance has been controversial though apparently successful. Faced with the possibility that its mostly white residents would sell their homes in a panic as their neighborhoods became racially integrated, Oak Park, Illinois (adjacent to Chicago), adopted home value insurance as part of a larger plan to promote orderly integration of its housing (Goodwin 1979). It offered to pay homeowners who subscribed to the plan (by getting an appraisal) 80 percent of the appraised value if the home was later sold for less than its appraised value. This helped keep residents from selling in a panic. It seems to have been successful in that racial transition has been uncontroversial and the insurance fund, financed by local property taxes, has not had to make any payouts.

Oak Park's plan has since been adopted by other cities in Illinois and Missouri. Its adoption remains controversial because it appears to classify blacks as a potential neighborhood nuisance. Other places have had payouts, and I have heard stories that developers have used it to persuade potential NIMBYs not to oppose their plans.

The barriers to private creation of this insurance for risks other than panic selling thus do not seem insuperable. Shiller and Weiss (1994, 1998) address the issue for a larger-scale home value insurance scheme for metropolitan housing prices, but the same authors caution that there are more than the usual moral hazard problems in developing such a market. For example, if a homeowner was fully insured against devaluations and was expecting to move soon, she might shirk from some otherwise necessary political activity in defense of her neighborhood. A proposed land-use change on the lot next door might devalue her property, and the only way that land-use authorities have of knowing this is that the neighbors tell them so. If the party in the best position to relay this information is fully insured against adverse outcomes, authorities may end up allowing some projects whose net effects are negative. In other words, sometimes it is desirable to have a NIMBY response to a project (Fischel 2001b).

Another problem with home-value insurance for local land-use changes is that it is more difficult to create a baseline price from which home values are to be insured. Homes in a neighborhood may be devalued by events over which the developer of a new project has no control. A builder of apartments in a single-family neighborhood might want to ease opposition by providing neighbors with home value insurance. If a new freeway is developed nearby at the same time, home values may decline because of freeway noise over which the developer has no control, but he (or his insurer) could still be stuck with a bill if his insurance contract was not carefully written. Despite such problems, there does seem to be room for creative thinking about home-value insurance to mitigate some of the problems of local zoning. Creative thinking about an important urban regulatory problem might best come from minds that are well versed in the seemingly unrelated fields of finance and corporate governance.

Bibliography

Berle, A. A. and Means, G. C. 1932: *The Modern Corporation and Private Property*. New York: Macmillan.

Briffault, R. 1993: Who rules at home? One person/one vote and local governments. *University of Chicago Law Review*, 60, 339–424.

Caplin, A., Chan, S., Freeman, C., and Tracy, J. 1997: *Housing Partnerships: A New Approach to a Market at a Crossroads*. Cambridge, MA: The MIT Press.

Crecine, J. P., Davis, O. A., and Jackson, J. E. 1967: Urban property markets: some empirical results and their implications for municipal zoning. *Journal of Law and Economics*, 10, 79–100.

DiPasquale, D. and Glaeser, E. L. 1999: Incentives and social capital: are homeowners better citizens? *Journal of Urban Economics*, 45, 354–84.

Dunlavy, C. A. 2004: *Shareholder Democracy: The Forgotten History*. Cambridge, MA: Harvard University Press.

East, J. P. 1965: *Council-Manager Government: The Political Thought of Its Founder, Richard S. Childs*. Chapel Hill, NC: University of North Carolina Press.

Easterbrook, F. H. and Fischel, D. R. 1991: *The Economic Structure of Corporate Law*. Cambridge, MA: Harvard University Press.

Ellickson, R. C. 1982: Cities and homeowners associations. *University of Pennsylvania Law Review*, 130, 1,519–80.

Fischel, W. A. 1985: *The Economics of Zoning Laws: A Property Rights Approach to American Land Use Controls*. Baltimore, MD: Johns Hopkins University Press.

—— 1995: *Regulatory Takings: Law, Economics, and Politics*. Cambridge, MA: Harvard University Press.

—— 2001a: *The Homevoter Hypothesis: How Home Values Influence Local Government Taxation, School Finance, and Land-Use Policies*. Cambridge, MA: Harvard University Press.

—— 2001b: Why are there NIMBYs? *Land Economics*, 77, 144–52.

—— 2004: An economic history of zoning and a cure for its exclusionary effects. *Urban Studies*, 41, 317–40.

Frug, G. 1980: The city as a legal concept. *Harvard Law Review*, 93, 1,057–154.

Goodwin, C. 1979: *The Oak Park Strategy: Community Control of Racial Change*. Chicago: The University of Chicago Press.

Grossman, S. J. and Hart, O. D. 1988: One share – one vote and the market for corporate control. *Journal of Financial Economics*, 20, 203–35.

Henderson, J. V. 1980: Community development: the effects of growth and uncertainty. *American Economic Review*, 70, 894–910.

Manne, H. G. 1965: Mergers and the market for corporate control. *Journal of Political Economy*, 73, 110–20.

Nelson, R. H. 1999: Privatizing the neighborhood: a proposal to replace zoning with private collective property rights to existing neighborhoods. *George Mason Law Review*, 7, 827–80.

Reichman, U. 1976: Residential private governments: an introductory survey. *University of Chicago Law Review*, 43, 253–306.

Roe, M. J. 1994: *Strong Managers, Weak Owners: The Political Roots of American Corporate Finance*. Princeton, NJ: Princeton University Press.

Shiller, R. J. and Weiss, A. N. 1994: Home equity insurance. NBER Working Paper 4830.

—— and Weiss, A. N. 1998: Moral hazard in home equity conversion. NBER Working Paper 6552.

Tiebout, C. M. 1956: A pure theory of local expenditures. *Journal of Political Economy*, 64, 416–24.

Weiss, M. A. 1987: *The Rise of the Community Builders: The American Real Estate Industry and Urban Land Planning*. New York: Columbia University Press.

PART VI

Urban Labor Markets and Macroeconomics

Urban Labor Markets and Macroeconomics

Urban economists have a longstanding interest in the workings of urban labor markets in general and in the problem of unemployment in particular. Unemployment is far from an urban problem; indeed, in many countries unemployment rates are far higher in rural areas than within cities. However, the problem is often more noticeable in cities because high unemployment rates tend to be spatially concentrated. Neighborhoods with high rates of unemployment and poverty are often in close proximity to areas of great wealth. It is human nature to be more concerned about nearby than distant problems. In addition, high poverty rates can increase the tax burden for the employed, raise crime rates, and affect school quality. Both for selfish and unselfish reasons, the spatial concentration of unemployment and poverty make the workings of urban labor markets a vital concern of urban residents.

Labor economists and macroeconomists traditionally do not incorporate space directly into their studies. Although well-known studies of local labor markets have used US states as their unit of analysis, few believe that Los Angeles and San Francisco are in the same labor market, let alone the agricultural areas of the San Joaquin Valley. Indeed, the San Francisco labor market may be more similar and more closely tied to labor markets in Boston and Seattle than to rural areas in northern California. More significantly, space affects the workings of the labor market directly. People tend to look close to home when searching for jobs. The typical metropolitan area has neighborhoods with few jobs and high unemployment even as other areas are growing rapidly, with available jobs going unfilled. Searching for a new job is costly, commuting is costly, and changing residential locations is costly. All of these factors mean that high unemployment rates can stay in place for a long time despite sincere and well thought out attempts to combat them. In their essay "Urban Labor Markets," Timothy Bartik and Randall Eberts discuss what constitutes an urban labor market and provide the framework to model the residential and workplace location decisions. They also review empirical evidence on how changes in labor demand and supply affect labor-market outcomes.

Problems of unemployment and poverty can be exacerbated by changes in economic structure. Urban areas in developed countries that once were dominated by low-skill but high-paying jobs in the manufacturing sector have come to be dominated by high-skill service-sectors jobs. The new jobs are often in distant locations and they require a different set of skills than the ones held by residents of high-unemployment areas. A recent body of literature emphasizes the role of networks in obtaining jobs – family and friends who recommend a person to an employer. The fact that networks tend to be local makes it harder for a resident of a high-unemployment area to find a job in a distant location. Even the nature of the transportation network may work against the residents of high-unemployment areas, who are more likely than high-income people to rely on mass transit. Transportation networks are typically designed to bring workers into the center of a city. It is far harder to commute to remote locations, even if these areas are the ones experiencing job growth.

In the United States, this mismatch between the locations of job growth and low-skilled potential workers has come to be known as the *spatial mismatch hypothesis*. In his essay "A Primer on Spatial Mismatch within Urban Labor Markets," Keith Ihlanfeldt discusses the causes and consequences of spatial mismatch, and shows how empirical studies attempt to test the theory. The idea, which goes back to a classic study by Kain (1968), has been the subject of a massive amount of empirical study. Theoretical analyses have lagged behind. In the USA, the spatial mismatch hypothesis has a decidedly racial dimension. African-American residents of urban areas tend to be concentrated in inner-city areas that have high rates of unemployment and poverty. They tend to have less education and lower incomes than other ethnic groups. The neighborhoods in which African-Americans live are often far from areas of employment growth. These are all readily documented empirical facts. The question is why blacks have not moved to suburban locations – the sites with new jobs – in sufficient numbers to lower the high rates of unemployment and poverty. The answer to this question is usually asserted rather than documented: African-Americans stay in the inner city because exclusionary zoning and white discrimination prevent them from moving to the suburbs. This step in the analysis is harder to prove conclusively because it is not at all clear that zoning is highly restrictive in American suburbs, discrimination is illegal, and it is possible that African-Americans prefer living in nonwhite areas. However, while proof is elusive, most researchers believe that discrimination and prejudice help to increase unemployment rates among African-Americans.

The spatial mismatch hypothesis is not exclusively an American phenomenon. In his essay "Urban Labor Economic Theory," Yves Zenou outlines a theoretical model that is capable of dealing with spatial mismatch in both an American and a European context. In Europe, unemployment rates are often much higher in suburban areas. Jobs are more apt to be located in the central city or in distant suburban locations. Costly commuting increases the probability that a worker will remain unemployed. Nor is racism an entirely American phenomenon. Discrimination against nonwhites and immigrants is not unknown in Europe and Asia. Immigrants often are concentrated in ethnic enclaves with few local job prospects.

While urban economists have a longstanding interest in labor economics, only recently has macroeconomics had a strong impact on the urban economics literature. In part, this lack of attention to macroeconomics is due to the inability to do anything about macro problems: monetary and fiscal policy is not the domain of local governments. Urban researchers have a stronger training in micro- than macroeconomics. The formation of the European Union changed this emphasis somewhat. With significantly different industrial structures, each European country can be expected to respond different to monetary policy and macroeconomic shocks. A new body of literature uses macroeconomic tools to analyze the response of regional economies to macroeconomic conditions. In the USA, the same approach is used to conduct macroeconomic analyses of traditional regions – the Northeast, the South, and so on. Two essays in this part of the volume deal with urban and regional macroeconomics. Gerald Carlino and Robert DeFina's essay, "Macroeconomic Analysis Using Regional Data: An Application to Monetary Policy," shows how subnational data are helpful in understanding the effects of national monetary policy actions on incomes in different regions with the USA. Edward Coulson's essay, "Measuring and Analyzing Urban Employment Fluctuations," reviews the techniques used to study fluctuations in employment across urban areas.

Although less attention has been paid directly to urban areas, we can expect macroeconomic shocks to have different effects in rural and urban areas. Responses may differ across cities as well, and within a single metropolitan area. Some areas concentrate heavily in service-sectors jobs, while others concentrate heavily in manufacturing. A macroeconomic shock that has its most pronounced impact on manufacturing will most directly affect regions that specialize in industrial jobs, whether those regions are European nations, US regions, or individual cities. Regional macro studies require a thorough knowledge of time series econometrics. Vector autoregressions, impulse responses, and cointegration are tools well known to macroeconomists – Robert Engle and Clive Granger shared the 2003 Nobel Prize for developing time series methods – but they are still not used routinely in urban economics. But space still does play a prominent role in macro- and labor economics. As long as labor markets and macroeconomists have a spatial component, urban economists can make important contributions to the fields.

Bibliography

Kain, J. 1968: Housing segregation, negro employment, and metropolitan decentralization. *Quarterly Journal of Economics*, 82, 175–97.

CHAPTER TWENTY-THREE

Urban Labor Markets

Timothy J. Bartik and Randall W. Eberts

23.1 INTRODUCTION

Why should we care about urban labor markets? To some this might seem like a rhetorical question, since it is difficult not to include urban areas when studying labor markets. Over 80 percent of the US population lives in metropolitan areas. In this respect, most labor-market analysis is "urban" labor-market analysis. Yet, the focus on the "urban" aspect of labor markets is much more profound than simply tallying up the number of people who live in urban areas. The fact that people work and live in a specific location and that markets respond to the attributes of their location is what makes studying urban labor markets so important. Adding the "urban" to labor-market analysis, therefore, is to add the spatial proximity of place of residence with place of work. Thus, one needs to understand the interaction between the location of households and businesses and the institutions and site-specific characteristics that affect the choice of location in order to gain a fuller understanding of the factors that affect wages, employment rates, and earnings not only in urban markets but also in national ones. Moreover, since the effectiveness of many government policies depends upon the circumstances at specific sites, accounting for urban attributes also enhances our understanding of policy outcomes.

This chapter focuses on key features of the urban spatial landscape that influence labor-market outcomes. In particular, we look at what constitutes an urban labor market, provide the framework to model the simultaneous decisions of residential and workplace location, identify the key features determining the interaction of demand and supply in urban labor markets, and review the evidence on how shifts in labor demand or supply, occurring "naturally" or due to policy, affect labor-market outcomes.

23.2   WHAT CONSTITUTES URBAN LABOR MARKETS?

The urban labor market is best thought of as a metropolitan area that encompasses most commuting flows. The stereotypic configuration of an urban area is a monocentric urban center in which jobs are concentrated in the urban core and a sufficient number of workers commute from outside the core to work in the central city. Chicago is a classic example of a monocentric city. At the beginning of the twentieth century, the City of Chicago accounted for 82 percent of the population within the six-county area that today defines the Chicago metropolitan area (McMillen & Smith 2003). Since then, there has been a steady decentralization of residents and firms to the suburbs, as transportation has improved and a rise in income has increased the demand for more land and larger houses. Yet today, the City of Chicago still accounts for 36 percent of the residents of the metropolis. Even with a strong urban core, many subcenters of employment have sprung up within the Chicago area, particularly along interstate highways. McMillen and Smith (2003) estimated 32 subcenters in the Chicago area in 2000. The same polycentric configuration has evolved in other urban areas. McMillen and Smith estimated that all but 14 of the 62 largest US metropolitan areas have subcenters, with Los Angeles (46) and New York (38) claiming the most. Nonetheless, for all of these metropolitan areas, employment density is still the highest in the traditional city center.

With employment concentrated in the urban core or in subcenters and a disproportionate share of households located outside of these employment clusters, metropolitan areas are marked by considerable mobility. Nearly everyone works outside the home (96.7 percent), and most are employed outside their residential neighborhood. With the vast majority (89 percent) commuting by car and averaging more than 25 minutes per trip, the average distance between work and home is at least a dozen miles (US Census Bureau 2003a). Such long commutes typically cut across several cities within metropolitan areas and in many cases workers are employed in a different city from which they live.

23.3   INTRAURBAN WAGE GRADIENTS

The standard urban land-use model predicts that both per unit housing prices and nominal wages will decline with distance from the central business district (CBD). Equilibrium for workers within an urban labor market requires that utility is the same at all locations (Rosen 1979; Roback 1982). Equilibrium for firms requires that unit costs of production are equal across all locations. Since both a worker's utility function and a firm's cost function are functions of wages, land rents, and distance from the CBD, wages and rents are determined by the interaction of the equilibrium conditions for suppliers (workers) and demanders (firms) of labor. A declining housing price gradient implies that wages must also decline with distance from the CBD. Workers who work closer to the CBD demand higher wages to compensate them for the higher housing prices found closer to the CBD or for the higher transportation costs (both out-of-pocket and opportunity costs) associated with the longer commute for workers living farther from the CBD.

Studies have shown that wages decline about 1 percent for each additional mile the job is located from the CBD, for distances of 10 miles or less from the CBD. Wage gradients appear to be flatter for workers living farther out. As a result, wages vary up to 15 percent within metropolitan areas, simply due to location (Eberts 1981; Timothy & Wheaton 2001). Thus, even though an urban area is considered a single labor market, the principle of one wage for identical workers does not prevail. Wages of identical workers differ according to the distance at which the employer is located from the urban core and from those subcenters that have a sufficiently high concentration of employment relative to households. However, we still consider the urban area to be one labor market, as the wages of workers at different locations are strongly linked, with all wages responding and relative wage differentials being maintained when the overall urban area is subject to a shock (which we define and discuss later) to overall labor demand or supply.

The location of firms and households within a metropolitan area can be affected by changes in factors that influence equilibrium conditions. For instance, the steady process of decentralization of jobs and residents away from the urban core is a result of improvements in transportation, which in turn give workers and firms access to low-cost land in the outlying areas. Such changes in location are evident in the relatively high intraurban mobility rates. The 2000 Census records that one-fifth or more of all workers switch jobs each year, and 9 percent of all householders over 15 years of age move to a different house (US Census Bureau 2003b). Martin (2001) examined the effect of employment shifts within metropolitan areas from central counties to ring counties on the location decisions of residents. He found that the total population responded to this shift in employment, and that the population movement from central counties to the ring counties more than compensated for the employment shift, reducing the overall spatial mismatch between place of work and place of residence.

However, not everyone has equal access to information about new job opportunities; nor do they have the networks, formal or informal, or the skills, to access new jobs. Low-income groups and racial minorities, in particular, may be constrained in their residential and commuting choices. These impediments lead to situations in which there is a mismatch in the access of certain groups of workers to jobs. In his chapter in this volume on spatial mismatch, Keith Ihlanfeldt critiques the evidence of the importance of these impediments in explaining economic disparities between races. He presents convincing evidence that these impediments to mobility help to explain racial disparities for youth in terms of employment rates, school dropout rates, and criminal activity. Evidence for adults is not as convincing, however, because reliable tests of the mismatch hypothesis are difficult to perform. Nonetheless, results from various studies suggest that workers are impeded from fully responding to economic incentives. For example, Martin (2001) found that the black population in these same metropolitan areas, as discussed above, did not respond as fully to employment shifts as the total population. The shift in the black population offset approximately 57 percent of the effects of the employment shift away from the metropolitan core. Those who did not respond to the shift presumably incurred longer commuting times and perhaps were unable to follow their jobs or find alternative jobs closer to their place of residence. The combined impact of employment and population shifts increased the disparity between the spatial distribution of place of work and residence for blacks by more than 20 percent.

23.4   INTERURBAN WAGE DIFFERENTIALS

With sufficient mobility of labor and/or capital across metropolitan areas, the simple model of labor markets predicts that in long-run equilibrium, wages across all metropolitan areas would be equal, except perhaps for a small differential reflecting the cost of moving. Estimation of wage differentials across metropolitan areas does not comport with this model, however. On the contrary, Beeson and Eberts (1989) show that wages of observationally equivalent workers vary by as much as 22 percent between the highest and lowest wage metropolitan area (out of the 35 largest US metropolitan areas). And the wage differential persists over long periods of time. Eberts and Stone (1992) show that the rank ordering of metropolitan areas by wages does not change appreciably over time. The correlation between any two adjacent years is 0.90 and for 10-year intervals is 0.70.

One reason for the persistence in wage differentials could be the lack of labor mobility across metropolitan areas. Granted, mobility is much lower across metropolitan areas than within metropolitan areas, particularly for lower wage groups. Only 4 percent of the population typically switches metropolitan areas each year (US Census Bureau 2003b). Shifts in labor supply or demand across metropolitan areas or other local labor-market areas are apparently sufficiently weak that labor-market outcomes are less affected by national economic conditions than they are by local economic conditions, at least in the short run. For example, metropolitan job growth significantly affects average family incomes, but after controlling for metropolitan job growth, average family income is unaffected by national job growth (Bartik 1994). A state's wage rates are better predicted by the state's unemployment rate than by the national unemployment rate (Blanchflower & Oswald 1994).

However, Marston (1985) argues that movement toward equilibrium merely requires that a small part of the labor force be mobile. He calculates that only 0.8 percent of the labor force for his sample of metropolitan areas need to move in order to achieve equilibrium, which is about a quarter of the size of the population that actually moves. Consistent with this notion is the fact that other urban labor-market outcomes, such as unemployment rates, are much more volatile across markets. Although the consecutive-year correlations of unemployment rates across metropolitan areas are similar to the wage correlations described above, the correlations for unemployment rates quickly decay for longer time spans, with a correlation of 0.40 for a span of 5 years and zero for a span of 10 years. Another explanation of the persistence of wage differentials is the inherent rigidity of wages due to institutional constraints such as explicit or implicit labor contracts. Hyclak and Johnes (1992), in a study of wage flexibility across states, find that wages are less flexible in regional labor markets in which firms are more likely to use efficiency wage mechanisms, workers are more heavily unionized, and labor markets are located in right-to-work states. We will consider further below how long-run equilibrium wage rates and employment rates respond to labor demand or supply shocks.

The persistence in interurban nominal wage differentials in the presence of factor mobility suggests that wage differentials should be viewed as an equilibrium phenomenon related in part to differences in site characteristics across metropolitan areas. Thus, the same general equilibrium model of household and firm location that explains *intra*urban wage differentials can also explain in part the persistence of *inter*urban wage differentials. Site characteristics are valued by both households and firms. Households value certain amenities, such as proximity to transportation, lakefront property, and parks; firms similarly value site-specific features that increase productivity, such as proximity to major highways, proximity to suppliers, and adequate public infrastructure. Households are willing to pay higher rent and accept lower wages to live in an area with an abundance of amenities that they value, and firms are willing to pay higher wages and pay higher rent to locate in an area that offers site-specific characteristics that increase their productivity.

Thus, one can think of long-run nominal wage differentials as being largely composed of two components: a supply-shift portion and a demand shift portion. Beeson and Eberts (1989) find that productivity differences (demand shift) explain 60 percent of the wage differential between metropolitan areas and the amenity component (supply shift) accounts for the remaining 40 percent. However, the relative importance of these factors varies from one metropolitan area to another. In some areas, relatively low wages are found to be primarily the result of high amenities, which increases the supply of labor in the area. The below-average wages in Miami, for example, reflect the high amenity value of its climate to households. In other areas, such as New York, high wages are found to be primarily the result of the high-productivity enhancing site characteristics, which increase the demand for labor.

23.5   WAGE DIFFERENTIALS ACROSS INDUSTRIES OR FIRMS

Wage rates within urban areas differ widely across industries and firms. Much of these wage differentials persists even after researchers control for all human capital characteristics of workers and amenity characteristics of jobs that researchers are able to measure. The remaining "wage premia" are large. Katz and Summers (1989), for example, found that across industries, typical wage differentials for similar workers are 15–20 percent. Groshen (1991) found that across firms in the same industry, typical wage differentials for similar workers are 10–15 percent.

One interpretation of these wage differentials is that they reflect genuine differences in the well-being for otherwise identical workers, which can be explained by efficiency wage theory. This theory postulates that firms and industries differ in their ease of monitoring worker performance, and their costs of worker turnover, hiring, and training, and that these differences lead to differences in the wage that would maximize profits. Empirical studies suggest that higher industry premia are strongly positively correlated with higher industry profitability, which may reflect the fact that higher industry profits increase workers' norms for what is considered a "fair wage" (Akerlof 1982; Dickens & Katz 1987; Katz & Summers 1989).

Another interpretation is that these observed wage premia differentials may reflect unobserved worker or job characteristics. Higher-wage premia industries or firms would be industries or firms in which unobserved worker skills were higher, or the unobserved amenities of the jobs were less pleasant. The wage differentials would be "compensating differentials" that compensate workers for their higher skills or willingness to endure unpleasant jobs.

Empirically, we observe that a shift in a metropolitan area toward higher-wage premium industries actually has "multiplier" effects that tend to raise average area earnings per worker at least twice as much as one would predict based on the shift in industry mix (Bartik 1993a, 1996). The available estimates are not precise enough to determine whether this extra increase in earnings is due to wages increasing beyond what one would expect, or employment rates and work hours increasing. Under efficiency wage theory, an extra increase in wage rates could reflect shifts in an area's norms about fair wages, whereas greater employment or work hours could be a labor supply response to higher real wages. Under compensating differential theory, this multiplier effect may reflect shifts in unobserved worker or job characteristics in the local area.

Employment growth and increases in a metropolitan area's average wage premia are positively correlated with each other (Bartik 1993a). Metropolitan areas that grow faster tend to shift toward higher-wage premia industries. This may occur because faster metropolitan growth increases wages, which may disproportionately discourage low-wage industries from locating in the metropolitan area. Conversely, metropolitan areas that shift toward higher-wage premia industries tend to grow faster. This may reflect the effects of higher wages in increasing local demand for retail goods and services.

Under either interpretation of wage premia, knowledge about changes in a local area's industry or firm mix with respect to wage premia would be important. Under the efficiency wage interpretation, an area's shift toward higher-wage industries or firms would increase a given worker's well-being by increasing wage opportunities. Under the compensating differential interpretation, an area's shift toward higher-wage industries or firms would make measured wage rates more misleading as a guide to a given worker's well-being, since the higher wage compensates a worker for characteristics within the metropolitan area that are less desirable.

23.6   Labor-Market Adjustments

Urban labor markets are continuously bombarded by shocks that alter the current equilibrium position of the market. Shocks may originate from market forces or interventions, and these may happen inside or outside the market. Examples of external shocks include sudden swings in oil prices, increases in foreign competition, broad improvements in technology, immigration, and changes in government programs. Internal shocks may come from new technology developed and implemented specifically within an urban area, increased worker quality gained through worker training initiatives, improvement in labor–management relations, or enhancement of a region's amenities, such as public infrastructure investment. Conceptually, market forces and local labor-market interventions can affect local labor-market outcomes in three ways: by shocking some type of labor demand, by shocking some type of labor supply, or by affecting how demand and supply interact.

23.6.1   Demand shocks

There is much more extensive and convincing evidence of the effects of local labor demand shocks than there is of the effects of local labor supply shocks. Empirical studies of the effects of these shocks typically relate changes in some measure of local labor-market outcomes, such as changes in unemployment, labor force participation, or wage rates, to an indicator of the shock such as local employment or population growth, either overall growth or growth of some sector of employment or of the labor force. The empirical problem is that growth in either employment or population could be due to both demand and supply shocks, yet we want to distinguish between the potentially quite different effects of the shock. This section follows the methodology used by Bartik (1991), Bradbury, Downs, and Small (1982), and Houseman and Abraham (1993) to distinguish empirically between growth due to demand shocks versus growth due to supply shocks. To illustrate this approach, however, we report Bartik's specification and findings.

These three studies use an "instrumental variables" approach to distinguish between supply and demand effects. Policy or natural variables that directly shock only one side of the market, which is either demand or supply, can act as instrumental variables. For demand shocks, it is easy to find one very powerful and convincing instrument for demand shocks, specifically the change in demand for the area's labor due to predicted growth of the area if all area industries grew at each industry's national average. This predicted growth is referred to as the "share effect" (from industry share) prediction of growth. It can be shown that this predicted growth corresponds to the growth expected due to national demand for the area's industries that export to the national market. In practice, this share-effect prediction is usually a highly significant predictor of year-to-year growth in an area's employment. In contrast, it is harder to find a supply-side variable that is a convincing instrument for shocks to labor supply that will cause significant variation in labor supply on a year-to-year basis.

A related empirical finding is that estimated effects of employment growth using the share effect "demand shock" instrument are very similar to estimated effects of employment growth when no instruments are used. This suggests that most of the year-to-year fluctuations in local employment growth are due to labor demand shocks, not labor supply shocks. This makes sense because it is easy to see how labor demand in an area might quickly shift in large ways due to shifts in the national fortunes of markets for an area's specialized industries. In contrast, labor force participation and migration seem to have more persistent trends that shift less frequently in an area from year to year.

It is less clear whether, in the long run, most growth at the local level is due to labor demand or labor supply shocks; that is, whether it is due to factors shifting the labor supply or labor demand in an area. Some regional economists believe that over time the influence of labor supply on long-run growth of local areas has increased. Over time, industries have become more footloose due to declining transportation costs for both inputs and outputs, and therefore less dependent on being close to national resources, intermediate imports, or customers. Industries, therefore, have become more sensitive to the cost and quality of labor supply, which increases the influence of changes in household amenities, household taxes, and household public services on long-run area growth.

What are the results from the empirical literature on the estimated effects of labor demand shocks? First, consider the effects of overall labor demand shocks on labor-market quantities such as unemployment rates, labor force participation rates, and population before considering effects on wages. Mathematically, the percentage growth in employment in an area can be divided into the sum of the percentage growth in the local employment to labor force ratio (one minus the unemployment rate), the percentage growth in the local labor force participation rate (labor force divided by population), and the percentage growth in local population. In the short run (1–2 years after the shock), the empirical literature suggests that for employment growth induced by a demand shock, 30–50 percent of the net new jobs in the area are absorbed by changes in net migration to the local area, either through increased in-migration or reduced out-migration. Of the remaining 50–70 percent of the net new jobs, about three-fifths cause reductions in the local unemployment rate and the other two-fifths cause increases in the local labor force participation rate.

In the long run, say 8 years or more after the shock, a one-time demand shock to local employment growth appears to result in 60–90 percent of the new jobs being absorbed by increased in-migration or reduced out-migration. Effects on unemployment rates in the long run drop to close to zero, so the remaining 10–40 percent result in permanent (or at least very persistent) increases in the local labor force participation rate.

There is one very prominent and widely cited paper that disagrees with this conclusion about the long-run effects of a once-and-for-all shock to the employment demand level. Blanchard and Katz (1992) conclude that 100 percent of a demand shock to employment levels in US states is absorbed by migration changes within 9 years. However, reestimation using Blanchard and Katz's data and similar data suggests that their results are biased by measurement error (Bartik 1993b). Their model in part estimates the speed at which state labor force participation rates return to their pre-shock level by looking at how current state labor force participation rates are related to several lags in labor force participation, and how errors in measuring the lagged participation rates will tend to bias estimates of how strongly state labor force participation needs to persist.

A 1 percent demand shock to overall local employment tends to increase local nominal wage rates by 0.4–0.6 percent, and local prices by 0.2 percent, so that "real" wages increase by 0.2–0.4 percent. A substantial part or even all of this real wage increase may take place through persons with a given level of education and other credentials moving up to a better-paying occupation, rather than for the wage for a particular occupation going up. These real wage effects and price increase effects appear to be very persistent.

The short-run and medium-run effects of demand shocks on growth are reasonably consistent with what one would expect from the underlying labor supply and demand elasticities. In general, the effects of a labor demand shock on labor-market outcomes will depend on the elasticities of both labor demand and labor supply with respect to wages, where labor demand and supply responses include responses of migrants as well as the urban area's current residents and employers. In a model with unemployment, the effects of a labor demand shock on labor-market outcomes will also depend on the elasticities of both labor demand and supply with respect to unemployment, and the response of local wages to unemployment (the wage curve that is thoroughly explored in Blanchflower & Oswald 1994). For an example of simulation studies of demand or supply shock effects, using assumed or estimated elasticities of the underlying demand and supply relationships, see Appendices 1 and 2 of Bartik (2001).

The long-run effects of overall local labor demand are consistent with theories of labor-market hysteresis, which posits that temporary shocks may lead to a persistent change from the previous equilibrium level (Phelps 1972). In the short run, because in-migration does not absorb all new jobs from a demand shock, some of the new jobs provide local residents with additional work experience. This additional work experience increases the job skills, credentials, and self-confidence of these persons in the long run, which increases their participation in the labor force and the wage levels of the occupations they are able to attain (Bartik 1991, 2001).

What about differential effects of the type of labor demand? Thus far, there have been few attempts to look at this issue, and it has been difficult to find effects. In general, it is hard to find relative wage or employment effects across groups of labor demand shocks with respect to the mix of employment demand for different groups in the local area. For example, shifts in a metropolitan's labor demand mix toward industries with more highly educated workers does not appear to be associated with large shifts in relative wages or earnings across different education groups. One exception is that studies of the Summer Youth Employment Program suggest that one half to two-thirds of the jobs provided by the program increase the employment rates of the disadvantaged youth targeted by the program (Ellwood & Crane 1984).

Shifts in the mix of local labor demand toward manufacturing or other high wage premia industries do tend to significantly raise earnings for local residents. This increase in earnings occurs both due to higher wages and due to increases in local labor force participation.

23.6.2 Supply shocks

It is harder to find convincing evidence of the effects on urban labor markets of labor supply shocks than labor demand shocks, largely because it is difficult to find "natural experiments" in the form of instrumental variables that will exogenously shock local labor supply. Most of the literature that looks at urban labor markets and labor supply shocks examines the effects of immigration from other countries on wages and employment rates of native workers in local labor markets. The overall consensus of most of this literature is that immigration has but modest effects on native workers' wages and employment rates (Smith & Edmonston 1997).

Some research has also examined how internal migration affects local employment. This body of literature finds surprisingly high effects of increased population in a local area on local employment. For example, two studies find that a 1 percent increase in local population due to an increase in migration will increase local employment by about 1 percent, even in the short run (Muth 1971; Greenwood & Hunt 1984). As a result, and contrary to our expectations, increased native migration to an area has little negative effects on local employment rates.

Two alternative hypotheses could explain these findings. One hypothesis is that these studies of immigration and native migration are not adequately separating out the effects of supply shocks from demand shocks. Positive demand shocks to an urban labor market will attract additional labor supply. Perhaps the estimated effects of increased foreign immigration or native migration to an area represent a combination of the true effects of these supply shocks with the effects of positive demand shocks that will attract immigration or migration. A second hypothesis is that immigration and native migration may inherently produce demand effects beyond those allowed for by reducing wage rates and adding to unemployment rates. For example, perhaps such supply shocks to the local population add household assets and nonlabor income that boost labor demand. Alternatively, perhaps there are agglomeration economies that cause productivity to increase with local population, which will cause positive shocks to the local population to increase labor supply.

The likelihood of migration varies across types of households. Yet, even fewer studies have looked at the effects on local labor markets of shocks to the labor supply of current residents. Bartik (2002) examines the effects of increases in the labor force participation of single mothers, due to welfare reform, on the wages and employment rates of various groups. This study identifies the separate effects of the welfare reform supply shock by using instrumental variable "supply shifters," various measures of welfare reform policy, and pre-welfare reform levels of welfare caseloads. Bartik finds that welfare-reform induced increases in the labor supply of single mothers may reduce the wage rates and employment rates of male high school dropouts. Fortin (2003) examines the effects of increased numbers of college graduates in a state on the return to a college education. This study identifies the separate effects of a supply shock to the number of college graduates by using as a "supply shifter" past state expenditures on higher education. This study finds that increases in college labor supply may significantly reduce the relative wages of a state's college-educated versus high-school-educated workers.

Of these factors, age has consistently been shown to be the single most important factor in determining who migrates. The peak mobility years are ages 20–29, when 13 percent move across county lines (US Census Bureau 2003b). Education – more specifically, a college education – is the single best predictor of who will move within an age group.

Most migration studies find that older and less-skilled workers are the least mobile. Flaim and Sehgal (1985) report that less than 2 percent of displaced workers leave the area in which they lost their jobs. Consequently, workers who are left behind may bear the largest cost of negative employment shocks in local labor markets. In times of economic prosperity for a region, these same immobile workers may not reap the full benefit of the upturn because workers from other areas, who are presumably more qualified, quickly move into the region and claim the newly created jobs.

23.6.3 Other local labor-market interventions

In addition to shocking local labor demand and supply, policy-makers can intervene by trying to affect how demand and supply interact. This interaction is quite imperfect, particularly for certain groups of workers, because employers have poor information about prospective workers and vice versa. Employer information about worker productivity is imperfect in part because of the importance of soft skills. Soft skills refer to skills dealing with people, such as coworkers, supervisors, or customers, or skills in organizing one's life to regularly attend work in a timely fashion and ready to work. In contrast, hard skills refer to skills related to numbers or written material, or technical know-how skills. Soft skills are hard to assess before the worker is actually observed on the job. Even hard skills are difficult to measure, particularly since employers are reluctant to test prospective employees for fear that the tests may lead to charges of violating equal opportunity laws. Therefore, an efficient labor market requires the ability to match workers with jobs effectively.

The longest-standing government-sponsored labor-market intermediary program is the US Employment Service (ES), started during the Great Depression and run by state governments under federal rules and guidelines. The main service provided by the Employment Service is "labor exchange." Job seekers register with the ES, employers voluntarily may choose to list job openings with the ES, and the ES tries to refer job seekers to suitable job openings. The ES has a poor public image, in part because many of the jobs listed with the ES are for low-wage positions, and many of the job seekers registering with the ES have relatively low skill levels. However, empirical studies suggest that the ES services are cost-effective, lowering the average length of time that job seekers are unemployed and raising their short-run earnings (Balducchi, Eberts & O'Leary 2004).

In recent years, a variety of groups concerned with poverty issues have tried to set up labor-market intermediaries that might be more effective than the ES in helping low-income persons access somewhat better-quality jobs. The Minneapolis Neighborhood Employment Network, sponsored by the City of Minneapolis, is one example in which city job developers aggressively solicit voluntary listings of job openings from local employers, and the different neighborhood groups in the city then seek to find local residents who would be good matches for these openings. As yet, there are no rigorous evaluations of these alternative labor-market intermediaries.

There is some evidence that training programs that target labor supply can be more effective if the program is also designed to fit with the information needs of employers. For example, among the most effective training programs, according to rigorous experimental evidence, is the Center for Employment Training (CET), started in San Jose. CET trains for particular industries in high demand, uses advisory boards of industry employees to help design its training curricula, employs ex-industry employees as instructors, requires students to meet minimum standards appropriate for that industry before graduation, and aggressively markets its trainee graduates to the target industry.

Demand-side programs that subsidize wages also seem to be more effective if they are sensitive to employers' problems in getting accurate information on a new hire's productivity. As mentioned before, there is much evidence that taking some disadvantaged group, such as welfare recipients, giving them all a voucher entitling an employer hiring them to a wage subsidy, and sending these vouchered individuals out to look for jobs does not work. However, wage subsidy programs that use job developers to work with employers to identify disadvantaged job seekers who may be suitable for employment seem to be more successful (Bartik 2001).

Some interventions can affect both demand and supply. As stated earlier, intraurban transportation enhances the mobility of workers, and improvements in transportation modes grease the interaction of the markets. Eberts and Stone (1992) show that public infrastructure investment in metropolitan areas, of which transportation is a large component, is important in the location decisions of firms and households. An increase in public infrastructure, holding wages constant, increases labor demand. This suggests that areas with larger-than-average infrastructure development are able to attract firms, presumably because infrastructure enhances a firm's productivity. Similarly, areas with higher-than-average infrastructure investment, holding taxes constant, are able to attract households in the area. This subsequently increases labor supply and lowers wages.

23.7 CONCLUSION

As this chapter has tried to show, we care about urban labor markets because they have many characteristics that affect the level and distribution of economic well-being. Urban labor markets have an internal spatial structure, with regular relationships between wages at different locations. The relative wages and prices in one urban labor market are predictably linked in the long run to wages and prices in other labor markets, due to both household and firm migration, with relative wages and prices depending on an area's relative amenities affecting households and firms (supply and demand shifters). Yet urban labor markets also have a definite unity and integrity, with wages and other labor-market outcomes responding over time to shocks to labor demand and supply.

What are the most critical areas for urban labor-market research? First, we would like to know much more about how urban labor markets respond to supply shocks, to catch up with our growing knowledge of the effects of demand shocks. Understanding supply shocks has considerable policy importance, given that public policy has important effects on such supply shocks as immigration, welfare reform, and the share of college-educated labor.

In addition, understanding effects of changes in the structure of labor demand, not just aggregate labor demand, is of increasing importance. The structure of labor demand is rapidly changing in the United States due to technological change and globalization. Urban labor-market analysis provides a useful way to better understand the effects of these important phenomena.

Finally, it is important to better understand how specific policy interventions and institutional changes in urban labor markets can affect labor-market outcomes. For example, we need to understand more fully how changes in transportation infrastructure affect the internal spatial structure of urban labor markets, and how changes in labor-market intermediaries may affect urban labor markets. Such policy interventions are complex and may affect both the demand and supply side of the labor market. However, in many cases such policy intervention may offer a cost-effective way of achieving desired policy goals.

Over 200 years ago, Adam Smith wrote in *The Wealth of Nations* that "a man is of all sorts of luggage the most difficult to be transported" (Smith 1937 [1776], p. 75). We might add to this "difficult, but not impossible." It is this partial mobility of persons within and across urban labor markets that ultimately makes urban labor-market analysis complex, fascinating, and important for public policy.

Bibliography

Akerlof, G. A. 1982: Labor contracts as partial gift exchange. *Quarterly Journal of Economics*, 97, 543–69.

Balducchi, D., Eberts, R. W., and O'Leary, C. J. 2004: Experience and prospects for labor exchange policy. In D. Balducchi, R. W. Eberts, and C. J. O'Leary (eds.), *Labor Exchange Policy in the United States*. Kalamazoo, MI: W. E. Upjohn Institute for Employment Research, ch. 8.

Bartik, T. J. 1991: *Who Benefits From State and Local Economic Development Policies?* Kalamazoo, MI: W. E. Upjohn Institute for Employment Research.

—— 1993a: Economic development and black economic success. W. E. Upjohn Institute for Employment Research, Technical Report 93-001.

—— 1993b: Who benefits from local job growth, migrants or the original residents? *Regional Studies*, 27(4), 297–311.

—— 1994: The effects of metropolitan job growth on the size distribution of family income. *Journal of Regional Science*, 34(4), 483–502.

—— 1996: The distributional effects of local labor demand and industrial mix: estimates using individual panel data. *Journal of Urban Economics*, 40, 150–78.

——— 2001: *Jobs for the Poor: Can Labor Demand Policies Help?* New York: Russell Sage Foundation.

——— 2002: Spillover effects of welfare reforms in state labor markets. *Journal of Regional Science*, 42(4), 667–701.

Beeson, P. E. and Eberts, R. W. 1989: Identifying productivity and amenity effects in interurban wage differentials. *Review of Economics and Statistics*, 71(3), 443–52.

Blanchard, O. and Katz, L. F. 1992: Regional evolutions. *Brookings Papers on Economic Activity*, 1, 1–75.

Blanchflower, D. G. and Oswald, A. J. 1994: *The Wage Curve.* Cambridge, MA: The MIT Press.

Bradbury, K., Downs, A., and Small, K. 1982: *Urban Decline and the Future of American Cities.* Washington, DC: The Brookings Institution.

Dickens, W. T. and Katz, L. F. 1987: Inter-industry wage differences and industry characteristics. In K. Lang and J. S. Leonard (eds.), *Unemployment and the Structure of Labor Markets.* Malden, MA: Blackwell.

Eberts, R. W. 1981: An empirical investigation of intraurban wage gradients. *Journal of Urban Economics*, 10(1), 50–60.

——— and Stone, J. A. 1992: *Wage and Employment Adjustment in Local Labor Markets.* Kalamazoo, MI: W. E. Upjohn Institute for Employment Research.

Ellwood, D. T. and Crane, J. 1984: Summer Youth Employment Program: private job supplement or substitute. Report prepared for US Department of Health and Human Services, Washington, DC.

Flaim, P. O. and Sehgal, E. 1985: Displaced workers of 1979–1983: How well have they fared? *Monthly Labor Review*, 108, 3–16.

Fortin, N. M. 2003: Higher education policies and decelerating wage inequality: cross-state evidence from the 1990s. University of British Columbia Centre for Labour and Empirical Economic Research Working Paper 001.

Greenwood, M. J. and Hunt, G. L. 1984: Migration and interregional employment redistribution in the United States. *American Economic Review*, 74(5), 957–69.

Groshen, E. L. 1991: Five reasons why wages vary among employers. *Industrial Relations*, 30(3), 350–81.

Houseman, S. N. and Abraham, K. G. 1993: Labor adjustment under different institutional structures: a case study of Germany and the United States. NBER Working Paper No. W4548, October.

Hyclak, T. and Johnes, G. 1992: *Wage Flexibility and Unemployment Dynamics in Regional Labor Markets.* Kalamazoo, MI: W. E. Upjohn Institute for Employment Research.

Katz, L. F. and Summers, L. H. 1989: Industry rents: evidence and implications. *Brookings Papers on Economic Activity. Microeconomics*, Special Issue 1989, 209–90.

Marston, S. T. 1985: Two views of the geographic distribution of unemployment. *Quarterly Journal of Economics*, 100(1), 57–79.

Martin, R. W. 2001: The adjustment of black residents to metropolitan employment shifts: How persistent is spatial mismatch? *Journal of Urban Economics*, 50(1), 52–76.

McMillen, D. P. and Smith, S. C. 2003: The number of subcenters in large urban areas. *Journal of Urban Economics*, 53, 321–38.

Muth, R. F. 1971: Migration: chicken or egg? *Southern Economic Journal*, 37(1), 295–306.

Phelps, E. 1972: *Inflation Policy and Unemployment Theory.* New York: W. W. Norton/London: Macmillan.

Roback, J. 1982: Wages, rents, and quality of life. *Journal of Political Economy*, 90(6), 1,257–78.

Rosen, S. 1979: Wage-based indexes of urban quality of life. In P. Mieszkowski and M. Straszheim (eds.), *Current Issues in Urban Economics*. Baltimore, MD: Johns Hopkins University Press, 74–104.

Smith, A. 1937 [1776]: *The Wealth of Nations*. New York: The Modern Library.

Smith, J. P. and Edmonston, B. (eds.) 1997: *The New Americans: Economic, Demographic, and Fiscal Effects of Immigration*. Washington, DC: National Academy Press.

Timothy, D. and Wheaton, W. C. 2001: Intra-urban wage variation, employment location and commuting times. *Journal of Urban Economics*, 50(2), 338–66.

US Census Bureau 2003a: *Statistical Abstract of the United States, 2003*, tables 1090, 1093. December.

—— 2003b: Geographic Mobility: March 2000 to March 2001, Detailed Tables, March.

CHAPTER TWENTY-FOUR

A Primer on Spatial Mismatch within Urban Labor Markets

Keith R. Ihlanfeldt

24.1 INTRODUCTION

There are three features that almost all metropolitan areas in the United States have in common: (1) job growth is occurring predominately in the suburbs, (2) the black population is concentrated within the central city, and (3) employment and earnings are low for blacks in comparison to whites. Taken together, these features raise the obvious question of whether the relatively poor labor-market outcomes of blacks are related to the distances that exist between their homes in the central city and new jobs in the suburbs. This question has been formalized within the urban economics literature as the "spatial mismatch hypothesis" (SMH), which maintains that the employment opportunities of blacks have been eroded by their inability to follow jobs from the central city to the suburbs as job suburbanization accelerated after World War II. The SMH is one of the most researched issues in urban economics, as evidenced by the fact that more than 100 journal articles have been written on the SMH in the past 30 years (for reviews of early and more recent studies of the SMH, see, respectively, Kain 1992; Ihlanfeldt & Sjoquist 1998). Despite all of this research, urban economists are still highly divided in their opinions on the importance that spatial mismatch plays in explaining economic disparities between the races. The reason for this is that, while the question posed by the SMH may be obvious, reliable empirical tests of the SMH are notoriously difficult to conduct. Because the importance of spatial mismatch remains an unresolved issue, it will continue to be high on urban economists' research agendas for the foreseeable future. This is even more true today than in the past, due to recent reforms in the US welfare system that require welfare recipients to find a job. Will people on welfare, who are disproportionately black and concentrated within America's central cities, be able to overcome spatial mismatch in the labor market for lower-skilled workers in searching for and obtaining a successful job match?

First discussed in this essay are the causes and consequences of spatial mismatch. This will set the stage for addressing the question that is the central focus of the essay: How have social scientists tested for spatial mismatch and what econometric problems arise in conducting these tests? This essay also (1) highlights gaps in our knowledge of spatial mismatch in order to set an agenda for future research, and (2) provides an overview of policy options for dealing with spatial mismatch.

24.2 THE CAUSES OF SPATIAL MISMATCH

John Kain, while an urban economist at Harvard University during the 1960s, was the first social scientist to write about the SMH (Kain 1968). He developed and tested the SMH using data for Chicago and Detroit. Kain emphasized that blacks are unable to move to the suburbs in response to job decentralization due to the discrimination that they encounter in the housing market. This discrimination can take many forms, from suburban apartment managers refusing to rent to blacks to realtors not showing blacks houses that are available for purchase within white suburban neighborhoods. Also, blacks may unfairly be denied a loan to purchase a home, which forces them to keep renting within the central city. In addition to discrimination, other urban economists writing on the SMH have emphasized that exclusionary zoning and other exclusionary land-use regulations, such as stringent building codes, make it difficult for lower-skilled black workers to find affordable housing in those suburban areas where jobs are growing. For example, many suburban political jurisdictions require homes to be built on large lots, and either ban or severely limit the construction of apartments. This has been labeled "snob zoning" by its opponents, who allege that it reflects prejudice against lower-income households.

Land-use regulations make it difficult for all lower-skilled workers, regardless of their race or ethnicity, to find affordable housing near suburban jobs. Hence, spatial mismatch should perhaps be thought of as a lower-skilled worker problem, rather than a black or minority problem. However, blacks are disproportionately impacted by spatial mismatch, because their residential locations are more severely constrained than those of lower-skilled whites due to racial discrimination in housing and mortgage markets. In addition, blacks are more likely to hold lower-skilled jobs, which have decentralized to a greater extent than have higher-skilled jobs.

As an illustration of the residential immobility of blacks, consider the case of Atlanta, Georgia. Within the Atlanta metropolitan area, blacks are highly concentrated within the central city. According to the 2000 Census, blacks comprise 28.4 percent of the metropolitan area population, but account for 61.4 percent of the population within the City of Atlanta. Fair housing audits that have been done in Atlanta have consistently shown that blacks encounter far greater housing discrimination in the suburbs than within the central city. (These audits involve sending both a black and white to the same apartment complex or realtor's office, having them inquire about the same type of housing, and comparing how they are treated.) In addition, the absence of affordable housing has long been a major concern within Atlanta's suburbs, especially on the north side of the region, which contain a number of America's fastest-growing counties in terms of jobs. The residents of the northern suburbs are affluent and white, and they have fought fierce battles to keep low-income housing out of their neighborhoods. Hence, in the case of Atlanta, low-skilled black workers are largely excluded from living near new suburban jobs.

Constraints on the residential locations of blacks, and low-skilled workers generally, are only one of three conditions that must obtain for spatial mismatch to emerge within an urban labor market. In addition, firms must face higher costs (setup/production costs) in areas where lower-skilled workers are constrained to live, and the search or commuting costs of these workers must be nontrivial. If the first condition is not satisfied and firms can easily locate within the central city, then we would expect that employers would locate there in order to capitalize on the excess labor supply. In the long run, the in-migration of firms would expand the demand for lower-skilled labor within the central city and eliminate spatial mismatch. If the second condition is not satisfied and central-city workers can easily commute to jobs in the suburbs, this would also serve to eliminate a mismatch problem in the long run.

Available evidence confirms that firms do indeed encounter high costs if they locate within the central city. These include the difficulty of land assembly, high crime, high property taxes, and the high cost of hiring skilled workers who prefer not to work within the central city because they would rather not have to commute from their homes in the suburbs. Among these factors, crime has been found to be a particularly strong employment repellent (Bollinger & Ihlanfeldt 2003). Crime increases firms' costs by raising their insurance premiums, increasing their self-protection measures, and requiring them to pay their workers a premium for working in unsafe areas. Despite the higher costs associated with locating within the central city, many firms find that agglomeration economies (especially those related to the convenience for face-to-face interaction) make them attractive locations. This attraction, however, is generally not a strong locational pull for manufacturing and other types of firms that hire significant numbers of lower-skilled workers.

The cost of searching for jobs in the suburbs or commuting to these jobs may be high for central-city blacks for three reasons. First, lower-skilled black workers have little knowledge of suburban job openings, because they rely on informal rather formal methods of job search. Consulting with friends and neighbors and making direct applications without referrals are used often, while methods that would better inform blacks of suburban jobs, such as responding to classified advertisements in local newspapers or registering with a local employment agency, are seldom employed. Second, these workers rely heavily on public transit to make the journey to work and this mode of travel does a poor job in meeting the needs of reverse-commuters. The basic problem is that suburban jobs are highly dispersed and most are not located within walking distance of a suburban transit stop. Finally, the search costs of blacks are increased because they encounter greater labor-market discrimination in the suburbs. The prejudices of white employers, white employees, and white customers all act to decrease the hiring rates of blacks in the suburbs, forcing them to make more applications for each of the job offers that they receive.

Again, Atlanta can be used to illustrate these issues. Based on a recent survey, only 19.9 percent of the blacks in Atlanta identified the northern suburbs as having the most job opportunities for people without college degrees, despite the phenomenal job growth that has occurred on the north side of the region (Ihlanfeldt 1997). Commuting to the northern suburbs by public transit from the central city is constrained not only by the dispersal of jobs but also because most of the northern suburbs offer either little or no public transit. Finally, housing discrimination against blacks in the northern suburbs has been documented and is a commonly held perception among Atlanta's blacks. For example, in the same survey that revealed blacks' poor information on the whereabouts of jobs, they were asked whether they thought employers would discriminate against them in the northern suburb of Roswell-Alpharetta, where among all of Atlanta's suburban areas the greatest growth has occurred in lower-skilled jobs. Fifty percent of the queried blacks stated that they would not take a job in Roswell-Alpharetta because they feared that employers would discriminate against them (Sjoquist 2000).

24.3 THE CONSEQUENCES OF SPATIAL MISMATCH

If low-skilled jobs move to the suburbs and blacks seeking these jobs cannot shift their labor supply to the suburbs by either moving their home to the suburbs or reverse-commuting, there will be a surplus of low-skill workers relative to the number of low-skill jobs available within the central city. The supply and demand model indicates that if wage rates are flexible in a downward direction, the labor surplus will cause wages to fall to a new lower equilibrium level. Hence, one expected consequence of spatial mismatch is that wage rates for low-skilled workers will be lower in the central city than within the suburbs. The supply and demand model also shows that employment levels will be lower within the central city in the new equilibrium. Of course, if wages are downwardly inflexible because of minimum wage laws or other factors, then spatial mismatch will cause higher unemployment among black workers. Joblessness may push significant numbers of black workers to take suburban jobs, despite the protracted commutes and discrimination that may be associated with these jobs. Hence, another possible consequence of spatial mismatch is that it may increase the commuting costs of the average black worker.

In addition to the impacts that spatial mismatch may have on blacks' earnings, employment, and commuting costs, there are three other possibly important consequences: staffing problems experienced by suburban employers, greater crime within central-city neighborhoods, and higher school dropping out among black teenagers.

If blacks, and low-skilled workers generally, have difficulty shifting their labor supply to the suburbs in response to job decentralization, suburban employers may find it hard to staff their low-skill positions. Jobs may remain vacant longer and employers may eventually have to raise wages and benefits to alleviate worker shortages. The welfare of suburban consumers will be directly impacted by these events as they see higher labor costs passed on to them in the form of higher prices and/or they experience poorer customer service. Hence, the exclusion of lower-skilled workers from suburban neighborhoods is not without a potential price that must be paid by suburban residents.

It is well known that crime is a problem within many of America's central-city neighborhoods. A number of reasons suggest that spatial mismatch may lie at the heart of this problem. First, crimes in problem neighborhoods are disproportionately committed by young males between the ages of 16 and 24. Second, these young criminals are known to commit the vast majority of their crimes within or near their home neighborhood. Third, a growing amount of evidence suggests that the young male's decision to engage in crime is strongly affected by his employment opportunities within the legitimate labor market. As these opportunities improve so does the opportunity cost of crime, which we know from the economic model of crime will cause the rate of return from crime to decline relative to the return obtained from legitimate work. Finally, spatial mismatch is expected to impact youth to a greater extent than adults, because the geographical extent of youths' job search areas is frequently reduced by a variety of factors. These include the absence of an automobile, commuting time constraints resulting from school attendance, unfamiliarity with distant places, and a reliance on informal sources of job-market information that result in this information declining with distance. Taken together, these reasons point to spatial mismatch as a cause of the crime problem within central-city neighborhoods. For example, in a recent paper I have reported findings for Atlanta that show that 21 percent of the difference in property crime between black and white neighborhoods can be attributed to the relatively poor job accessibility of black youth (Ihlanfeldt 2002).

While poor job accessibility may reduce the opportunity cost of crime, it may also reduce the opportunity cost of staying in school. Hence, one positive effect of spatial mismatch may be that it keeps black youths in school who otherwise may have dropped out to take a nearby job. On the other hand, spatial mismatch may prevent youths who are desirous of present earnings to both stay in school and work part-time. Without part-time opportunities located nearby, these youths may drop out of school, either to search for full-time employment or to engage in illicit income-producing activities. There is therefore the possibility that the spatial mismatch and school dropout problems are interconnected (for evidence that supports this interconnection, see Ihlanfeldt 1992).

24.4   TESTING THE SPATIAL MISMATCH HYPOTHESIS

Tests of the spatial mismatch hypothesis have involved compiling evidence on the three possible consequences of spatial mismatch: lower earnings, higher unemployment (or lower employment), and longer commutes for black workers. Social scientists from many different disciplines have used a wide variety of alternative empirical approaches and data to investigate these consequences. However, the most popular approach has been to estimate employment and earnings (and to a lesser extent commuting time) equations that include one or more variables that measure the individual worker's neighborhood job opportunity. The latter can be defined as the number of job vacancies per job seeker within the maximum commuting area of the worker residing within a particular neighborhood. The commuting and locational constraints identified in the previous section imply that the commuting area of the black worker is smaller than the entire metropolitan area and that job opportunity is worse in central city than in suburban neighborhoods.

The approach that is most frequently used to measure neighborhood job opportunity is to estimate a gravity model that discounts more distant job opportunities using a distance-decay function:

$$J_i = \sum_{j=1}^{J} JOBS_j * \exp(-\gamma d_{ij}), \tag{24.1}$$

where i represents the home neighborhood (typically defined as the Census tract), JOBS is the number of jobs within each neighborhood that are suitable for lower-skilled workers, d_{ij} is the distance in miles (or travel time) between neighborhoods i and j, and γ is the "distance-decay" function. The weighting of opportunities by distance is based on the assumptions that information on jobs decline with distance and that workers base their employment decisions on offer wages net of commuting costs. To capture the competition among workers for available jobs, J_i should be computed on a jobs per worker basis or a separate gravity variable for competing labor supply should be included in estimated equations.

To illustrate the basic spatial mismatch equation along with the difficulties it presents, consider using ordinary least squares to regress hourly wages (E) on neighborhood job opportunity (J) and a standard set of human capital variables (X) (e.g., education and experience):

$$E = \alpha J + \beta X + \varepsilon. \tag{24.2}$$

If α is positive and statistically significant and if blacks have lower J than whites, then part of the E difference between the races can be attributed to spatial mismatch. The same independent variables can be used to estimate the probability of unemployment or having a job using a logit or probit model.

The chief econometric problem with the basic model is that residential location (and thereby J) is not exogenous. One reason for this is that residential locations are self-selected. People are not randomly assigned a residential location but, instead, choose their location subject to constraints to maximize their utility. If more productive workers happen to choose neighborhoods with lower or higher values of J, then the estimate of α may be biased. Bias would be avoided only in the unlikely event that X fully captures differences in productivity among workers. The biggest concern among spatial mismatch researchers has been that blacks who are able to overcome the difficulties encountered in moving to white suburbs where jobs can be found are also likely to possess unmeasured productivity characteristics (such as motivation or perseverance) that increase their earnings. The estimate of α will then be upwardly biased, reflecting both the tighter labor market found within these areas and the greater productivity of blacks that choose to live in white suburban neighborhoods.

The second reason that residential location may not be exogenous is that there may exist reverse causality running from E to J. Both the standard theory of residential location (Alonso 1964) and evidence on work trips show that commuting distance rises with income. As income increases, people trade off job accessibility for other housing and neighborhood attributes that are more important to them that can be consumed less expensively farther from where they work. This will tend to result in a downwardly biased estimate of α, since E will tend to be higher where J is lower.

Much of the evidence on the spatial mismatch hypothesis, especially that coming from the early studies, can be questioned because researchers did not adequately deal with the possibility that residential location is not exogenous. However, there are a number of recent studies that have tried to handle this problem. The most popular approach has been to focus the analysis on youths still living at home, based on the assumption that for them residential location is exogenously determined by their parents or guardians. Three conclusions have been reached by these studies: (1) job access has a strong effect on the employment of youths; (2) black and Hispanic youths have worse access to jobs than white youths; and (3) racial differences in job access make an important contribution to racial differences in youth employment, explaining between one-third to one-half of these differences.

While these results are interesting and important, they have their limitations. First, they should not be generalized to adults. As noted above, youths are probably less able than adults to overcome the distance to jobs barrier; hence, spatial mismatch may have a relatively stronger effect on youth. Second, while a focus on youths still living at home may eliminate the possibility of reverse causation, it is unclear whether the self-selection problem is solved by this approach. If children share behavioral characteristics with their parents (either due to nature or nurture), the omitted productivity characteristics in equations estimated for youths may still be correlated with measures of neighborhood job opportunity.

There is no greater need in future research on spatial mismatch than to focus on lower-skilled adult workers using a research design that effectively handles the endogeneity of residential selection. Two different methodologies can be used in an attempt to provide unbiased estimates of the effects of spatial mismatch on adults. One approach is to simultaneously model both employment and residential location. However, this requires that variables be identified that affect residential location but that do not affect employment. It is difficult but not impossible to think of variables that would satisfy this condition. For example, because suburban living offers a distinctive lifestyle, some studies have included variables that measure the preference for this lifestyle in the residential location equation but have excluded these variables from the employment equation. A drawback of this approach is that measures of residential preferences are rarely provided in available databases.

The second approach that could be used to handle the residential selection problem in a study of the SMH for adults is to conduct a social experiment. This would involve randomly assigning low-skilled central-city workers to neighborhoods providing different degrees of job accessibility (and also observing whether those who obtain jobs in the assigned neighborhood subsequently move to neighborhoods where jobs are less accessible). Through random assignment, any excluded X variable should be uncorrelated with J (the measure of job opportunity), resulting in an unbiased estimate of the effect of job access on employment.

Currently, the US Department of Housing and Urban Development is conducting a social experiment called "Moving to Opportunity" (MTO). MTO randomly assigns housing subsidy recipients to three groups: a treatment group who receive a housing voucher that is only usable in a low poverty neighborhood, a comparison group who receive a voucher that can be used anywhere within the region, and an in-place control group, who receive their current project-based housing assistance. The goal of the experiment is to determine whether the lives of low-income households are improved by moving into a higher-quality neighborhood. Of course, one mechanism whereby a better neighborhood may improve an individual poor person's welfare is by providing improved access to jobs. But there are other mechanisms at work, including positive peer group effects and less concern for one's personal safety in going back and forth to work. MTO may therefore be unable to isolate the effect of job access. Early results indicate that heads of households who moved into low-poverty neighborhoods experienced no difference in their employment or earnings in comparison to the comparison or control group (Katz, Kling & Liebman 2001). However, many low-poverty neighborhoods do not offer improved job opportunity for lower-skilled workers. One way to isolate the effect of job access would be to require the treatment group to move into neighborhoods that are otherwise similar but offer different degrees of job accessibility. If done right, this could provide a definitive test of the SMH as it applies to adult workers.

24.5 FUTURE RESEARCH ON SPATIAL MISMATCH

In addition to dealing with the endogeneity of residential location, there are a number of omissions in the present literature that point to a need for future research. Studies investigating the spatial mismatch hypothesis have largely focused on individual large metropolitan areas. This makes it hard to generalize findings to other areas, especially those that are smaller in size. We know a fair amount about spatial mismatch (at least for youth) in places such as Atlanta, Los Angeles, and Chicago, but virtually nothing about the problem in places such as Birmingham or Indianapolis. Given their limited and more centralized geographies, it may even be the case that spatial mismatch does not even exist within these smaller urban areas.

Other limitations of the empirical literature on the SMH include: (1) comparatively little analysis of spatial mismatch as it applies to females and Hispanics; (2) no analysis of how the problem of spatial mismatch varies with the business cycle; and (3) the existence of only a couple of studies that have focused on the factors that act to perpetuate spatial mismatch in the long run.

Lower-skilled women living in the central city may be impacted differently than their male counterparts by job decentralization. While blue-collar jobs and jobs in service occupations are heavily suburbanized, this is less true for clerical jobs due to the continued strong presence of firms in finance, insurance, and real estate within the central business district of the central city. Because clerical jobs are disproportionately filled by women, their job accessibility may be better than that of men. Possibly offsetting this advantage, however, is the fact that distance to jobs is a greater barrier for women to overcome in finding a job, given their greater childcare and home responsibilities. Studies have shown that, due to these responsibilities, women place a higher value on their travel time than men. The question of whether spatial mismatch is more or less relevant to the labor-market problems of central-city lower-skilled women is therefore complicated and can only be answered by conducting comparative empirical analyses of men and women. Another reason for studying the job access of lower-skilled women living in central cities is that this is the primary population served by the welfare system within the USA. The success of welfare reform may depend on how severely spatial mismatch limits the work opportunities of these women. Will there be sufficient numbers of jobs near to where they reside such that they can succeed in their capacities as both workers and mothers?

According to the 2000 Census, Hispanics now outnumber blacks in 30 of 67 cities with populations of 250,000 people or more. Fair housing audits consistently show that Hispanics encounter racial discrimination in the housing market about as frequently as blacks. Like blacks, the earnings and employment of Hispanics are low in comparison to those of whites. What role does spatial mismatch play in explaining these differences?

Improvements in macroeconomic conditions tighten the labor market within both the central city and the suburbs, and the degree of tightening may be different between these two areas. There is therefore the possibility that the surplus of low-skilled workers within the central city that results from spatial mismatch varies in magnitude over the course of the business cycle. Research is needed that would investigate how national and regional macroeconomic conditions affect the magnitude of the spatial mismatch problem. Does spatial mismatch exist only when the economy is in a recession? What role could macroeconomic policy play in solving spatial mismatch?

Finally, I have identified the following list of factors that work toward perpetuating the spatial mismatch problem within urban areas: the high cost of commuting from central city to the suburbs, poor information of suburban job openings, racial discrimination in suburban housing and labor markets, exclusionary land-use regulations within many suburban political jurisdictions, and the high cost of firm location within central cities. While each of these factors has been studied and in isolation is found to matter, research is needed on the relative importance that these factors have in sustaining spatial mismatch. Without knowledge of what matters most, it is difficult to determine what policies would work best in eradicating the spatial mismatch problem.

24.6 POLICY OPTIONS

Spatial mismatch implies that low-skilled central-city workers reside too far away from available jobs in the suburbs. So what can we do to bring workers and jobs closer together? There are three options: place-based initiatives, residential mobility strategies, and personal mobility programs. Place-based initiatives attempt to bring jobs back into those central-city neighborhoods where low-skilled workers reside. Residential mobility strategies seek to open up housing opportunities in those suburban areas where jobs are growing. Personal mobility programs are different than the first two options; instead of trying to reduce the distance between workers and jobs, the goal is to make distance less of a barrier. Recall that long distances to suburban jobs impinge on the employment opportunities of central-city workers in two ways. First, a long distance translates into a difficult commute, especially if the job is not within walking distance of a suburban transit stop. Second, the more distant the jobs, the less information central-city workers are going to have of their existence. Therefore, to make distance less of a barrier a two-pronged attack is needed: we must improve the low-skilled central-city worker's knowledge of suburban job openings and provide these workers with an affordable means of transportation to these jobs. The strengths and limitations of place-based, residential mobility, and personal mobility policies are considered below.

24.6.1 Place-based initiatives

A number of strategies fall into the category of place-based initiatives, but the one that has received the most attention and most use has been the urban enterprise zone (UEZ). As originally conceived, the zone would encompass an economically distressed area in the central city in which taxes and government regulations would be reduced or eliminated in order to stimulate the origination of small, new enterprises. In practice, the urban enterprise zones established by state and local governments have offered businesses tax and other financial incentives along with technical assistance.

There is wide disagreement among scholars and policy-makers regarding the desirability of urban enterprise zones as a policy instrument. The critics of UEZs have made three arguments:

- The benefits accruing to individual firms from locating in an urban enterprise zone are inefficient to overcome the high costs of locating and producing in the central city. These costs were discussed earlier in this essay.
- Growth in jobs may occur as the result of zone inducements, but it will not result from the origination of new firms. Instead, growth will occur if existing

firms or new firms that would have started up even without the zone choose to locate in the enterprise area. Hence, the zone's employment gain is offset by a loss of jobs elsewhere.

- Regardless of the source of the job growth that occurs in enterprise zones, the expansion in jobs will not help indigent residents, because they do not possess the skills necessary for employers to hire them.

Evidence relevant to the first criticism has been highly mixed. However, the lion's share of this evidence should be disregarded, since it has been compiled using impressionistic or descriptive rather than analytical methods. Just because some employers locate within UEZs does not mean that the incentives made the difference. Other factors have to be controlled for. One approach to doing this is to estimate an econometric model. In fact, a few models have been estimated. But the results of these models have also been mixed regarding the effectiveness of UEZs. It appears to be the case that UEZs exert little impact on where a firm chooses to locate within a state, but they can affect the neighborhood that a firm chooses once it has decided on a particular metropolitan area. This is not surprising, since different locations within a metropolitan area are better substitutes for one another than locations in different metropolitan areas. Once a firm selects a city, because of its access to markets, raw materials, or labor supply, UEZ inducements can make a difference at the margin in affecting the intra-area location decision (for some evidence that supports this conclusion, see Bollinger & Ihlanfeldt 2003).

The evidence on the second criticism of UEZs confirms that the incentives offered to firms do not create jobs but, instead, cause a diversion of activity that would otherwise have occurred elsewhere. UEZs are therefore "locational" rather than "generative." This, however, is not altogether bad. It all depends on where the jobs that settle within UEZs would have otherwise located. If they come from other central-city neighborhoods, there may be little effect on the job accessibility of lower-skilled central-city workers. But if they come from the suburbs, mismatch could be alleviated.

The evidence on the third criticism – that new jobs do not go to residents of the zone – is really too thin to reach any kind of a conclusion regarding its validity. But this criticism does serve a useful purpose by underscoring the importance of taking a multi-faceted approach to the employment problems of low-skill central-city workers. The mismatch problem should not be addressed in isolation. Many workers, especially those that are more aptly described as unskilled rather than low-skilled, will require training for the jobs that are available. Useful training may involve not only teaching work skills but also providing so called "soft skills," such as helping inexperienced workers understand the world of work and employers' expectations.

24.6.2   Residential mobility strategies

As discussed earlier in this essay, two forces work to keep central-city less-skilled workers from moving into suburban neighborhoods: regulatory barriers that artificially inflate the cost of housing, and racial discrimination in housing and mortgage markets. In the light of these forces, what can be done to open up housing opportunities for lower-skilled central-city workers in suburban neighborhoods?

Excluding the poor is in the economic self-interest of suburban residents. Because they consume less housing than the average suburban resident, the poor pay less in property taxes. However, the costs of providing them with local public services is no less and may even be more (for example, children from poor families are more likely to have learning disabilities that require additional services from local schools). Poor people therefore do not pay their "fair share" of the costs of local government and impose a financial burden on suburban residents. It is therefore not surprising that suburban jurisdictions practice exclusion.

Given that the home rule powers of local jurisdictions make it nearly impossible for states or courts to restrict exclusionary practices, reducing the exclusion of the poor from the suburbs has not been easy. One approach would be to create financial incentives for suburban jurisdictions to accept more lower-income households. These incentives, which would be offered by the state or federal government, would have to be sufficiently large to offset the fiscal burden suffered by suburban residents from having low-income neighbors. Thus far, there has been little commitment on the part of higher levels of government to provide these incentives. However, this may change if political coalitions are formed among groups that have a common interest in expanding affordable housing in the suburbs. These groups could include churches and other advocates for the poor, suburban employers facing shortages of lower-skilled workers, and developers who want to build low-cost housing in the suburbs. Another approach would be to encourage suburban jurisdictions to adopt impact fees. Impact fees are set to cover the costs of the additional public infrastructure (e.g., roads, sewers, and schools) needed by new development. As a result, new development is more apt to pay its own way, which would lessen the fiscal motive for exclusion.

What about policies to combat discrimination within the suburban housing market and the mortgage market? There is wide agreement among urban economists that random audit-based testing of apartment managers, realtors, and lenders, combined with stiff penalties for guilty parties, can play a major role in reducing discrimination. After the testing is initiated and used for some time, potential discriminators will alter their behavior out of the fear that the minority applicant they are currently dealing with may be a tester.

Unfortunately, even if the above policies succeed in opening up more suburban neighborhoods to lower-skilled workers, the mismatch problem may only be temporarily alleviated. The reason for this is that suburban residents may respond to the infiltration of their neighborhoods, especially by lower-skilled blacks, by moving to more decentralized and isolated locations. As they move, many of the lower-skilled jobs would follow, because they are in retail and consumer-service establishments, dependent on the consumption demands of higher-income households. Spatial mismatch may then emerge between the inner and outer suburbs of the metropolitan area.

Is there anything that can stem white flight from suburban neighborhoods in the event that blacks and lower-income households are able to infiltrate these neighborhoods? One idea that has received some attention is to impose an urban growth boundary around the metropolitan area. These boundaries, which are a type of land-use regulation that confines development to only the area that falls within the boundary, have been proposed as a solution to urban sprawl and are currently used in a growing number of states for this purpose. But they may also contribute to integrated neighborhoods by constraining the further decentralization of affluent whites in response to the infiltration of their neighborhoods.

24.6.3 Personal mobility programs

As mentioned above, the objectives of these programs are twofold: (1) to inform central-city low-skill workers of suburban job openings; and (2) to provide them with a cost-effective means of commuting to these jobs. One approach toward achieving the first objective would be to set up a computerized job-matching service. This would work like a computerized dating service, but instead of identifying compatible couples it would match workers and jobs throughout the metropolitan area based on workers' qualifications and employers' skill needs. How to achieve the second objective is not as apparent. The basic problem is that suburban jobs are highly dispersed and public transit lines in the suburbs are not within walking distance of the vast majority of jobs. One option that is sometimes advocated is to have the government subsidize the central-city worker's purchase or leasing of an automobile. While this would provide the greatest possible personal mobility, it is probably not politically feasible. Worsening automobile congestion and air pollution within American cities work against any program that would add still more cars to the roads. A more promising approach would be to negotiate with local transit authorities to give up their current status as monopoly suppliers of public transit. In recent years, this idea has been promoted as a solution to the chronic deficits experienced by mass transit authorities, and as an approach to decreasing the reliance on the private car for the journey to work. The idea is that the private sector would provide new transit options that the public would find more attractive and more competitive with the private car than traditional public transit. In addition, in a deregulated environment, creative entrepreneurships providing reverse-commuting services would have an opportunity to develop. Although their completely free entry onto the transportation scene may not be in the offing, reverse-commuting services that would complement rather than compete against existing public transit are a real possibility. For example, an attractive option for getting central-city lower-skilled workers to suburban jobs would be jitneys, which would operate like the shared-ride limousines that take people from airports to downtown hotels. The jitneys would pick up workers at transit stops along major cross-suburban routes and drop them off near their places of employment.

24.7 CONCLUSION

Spatial mismatch in the labor market for lower-skilled workers living in urban areas merits the continued attention of urban economists. Because of spatial mismatch, the job accessibility of central-city youth is generally inferior to that of suburban youth, which helps explain racial disparities in youth employment rates, school dropout rates, and criminal activity. More research is needed on whether spatial mismatch also limits the labor-market opportunities of adult lower-skilled workers. We would especially like to know how important spatial mismatch is relative to other factors that impinge on the labor-market performance of minority workers, such as their limited human capital and the discrimination they encounter. Hopefully, this essay has accomplished its dual goals of conveying the complexity of the spatial mismatch issue and inspiring young urban economists to research the issue.

Bibliography

Alonso, W. 1964: *Location and Land Use*. Cambridge, MA: Harvard University Press.

Bollinger, C. R. and Ihlanfeldt, K. R. 2003: The intraurban spatial distribution of employment: Which government interventions make a difference? *Journal of Urban Economics*, 53(3), 396–412.

Ihlanfeldt, K. R. 1992: *Job Accessibility and the Employment and School Enrollment of Teenagers*. Kalamazoo, MI: W. E. Upjohn Institute for Employment Research.

—— 1997: Information on the spatial distribution of job opportunities within metropolitan areas. *Journal of Urban Economics*, 41, 218–42.

—— 2002: Spatial mismatch in the labor market and racial differences in neighborhood crime. *Economic Letters*, 76(1), 73–6.

—— and Sjoquist, D. L. 1998: The spatial mismatch hypothesis: a review of recent studies and their implications for welfare reform. *Housing Policy Debate*, 9(4), 849–92.

Kain, J. 1968: Housing segregation, negro employment, and metropolitan decentralization. *Quarterly Journal of Economics*, 82, 175–97.

—— 1992: The spatial mismatch hypothesis: three decades later. *Housing Policy Debate*, 3(2), 371–460.

Katz, L. F., Kling, J. R., and Liebman, J. B. 2001: Moving to opportunity in Boston: early results of a randomized mobility experiment. *Quarterly Journal of Economics*, CXVI, 607–54.

Sjoquist, D. L. 2000: *The Atlanta Paradox*. New York: Russell Sage Foundation.

CHAPTER TWENTY-FIVE

Urban Labor Economic Theory

Yves Zenou

25.1 INTRODUCTION

In the United States, it is generally observed that unemployment is unevenly distributed both within and between metropolitan areas. In particular, in most cities, the unemployment rate is nearly twice as high downtown as in the suburbs (see Table 25.1), mainly because of the concentration of blacks in these areas (see Table 25.1), who are mainly unskilled (see Table 25.2). Indeed, because of massive migration of blacks from the rural south to the urban north after the two world wars, and because of discrimination in the housing market, blacks had no choice but to live in the central-city ghettoes. While there has been substantial suburbanization of blacks in some cities, the legacy of that period remains in the form of inner-city ghettoes. During the same period, there has been massive suburbanization of jobs (see Table 25.3). To what extent does this history explain the higher rates of unemployment among blacks than whites?

Since the seminal work of Kain (1968), many economists contend that the spatial fragmentation of cities can entail adverse social and economic outcomes. These adverse effects typically include the poor labor-market outcomes of ghetto dwellers (such as high unemployment and low income) and a fair amount of social ills (such as low educational attainment and high local criminality). Even though there is no general theory of ghetto formation, there has been a series of theoretical and empirical contributions, each giving a particular insight into some of the mechanisms at stake.

An interesting line of research revolves around the "spatial mismatch hypothesis," which states that, because minorities are physically distant from job opportunities, they are more likely to be unemployed and to obtain low net incomes. Table 25.4 documents these features by using the Raphael and Stoll (2002)

Table 25.1 Unemployment rates and the percentage of blacks per MSA in 2000

	Unemployment rates (%)		Percentage of blacks (%)	
	Central city	Suburbs	Central city	Suburbs
Los Angeles – Long Beach	5.9	4.9	11	8
New York	5.7	3.0	24	12
Chicago	5.5	3.4	33	8
Boston	2.7	2.1	11	2
Philadelphia	6.4	3.1	43	9
Washington	4.3	2.0	44	22
Detroit	6.1	2.5	70	6
Houston	5.0	3.2	24	10
Atlanta	4.7	2.6	61	25
Dallas	3.8	2.5	23	9
Ten largest MSAs	5.4	3.0	27	11

Source: Calculated by Gobillon, Selod, and Zenou (2003) from the Current Labor Force Survey

Table 25.2 The distribution of jobs and people in 1994 (in percent): pooled sample of MSAs

	Central city			Suburbs			
	Total central city	Black central city	White central city	Total suburbs	Black suburbs	Integrated suburbs	White suburbs
All jobs	25.2	7.6	6.2	74.8	3.0	7.0	64.8
Low-skill jobs[a]	20.4	10.2	2.7	79.6	2.7	7.5	69.4
People 25 years and older							
All people	27.2	10.1	6.9	72.8	2.5	11.2	59.1
Black	65.3	57.1	5.3	34.8	10.4	6.6	17.8
White	13.1	2.5	6.3	86.9	1.8	8.7	76.4
High school dropouts							
Black	76.3	67.5	5.0	23.6	7.1	4.2	12.3
White	22.2	4.4	10.0	77.9	2.1	10.2	65.6
Total	44.8	15.6	7.7	55.2	2.1	12.5	40.6

[a] No high school diploma, no experience of training, no reading, writing, or math.
The black (white) central city is defined as that area within the central area with contiguous Census tracts of blacks (whites) representing 50 percent or more of the population. The black (white) suburbs are defined as that area within the suburbs with contiguous Census tracts of blacks (whites) representing 30 (80) percent or more of the population. The remaining suburban Census tracts are defined as integrated suburban areas.
Source: Stoll, Holzer, and Ihlanfeldt (2000)

Table 25.3 The percentage of jobs in the central city and the average annual growth rates of jobs by workplace, 1980–90

	Percentage of jobs (central city)		Growth rates, 1980–90	
	1980	1990	Central city	Suburbs
Los Angeles – Long Beach	51	51	1.9	2.1
New York	91	89	1.1	3.3
Chicago	50	44	–0.2	2.3
Boston	46	41	0.6	2.4
Philadelphia	41	35	–0.0	2.4
Washington	46	38	1.4	4.5
Detroit	38	28	–2.1	2.5
Houston	78	72	1.0	3.9
Atlanta	35	25	0.9	5.6
Dallas	69	60	1.4	5.6
Ten largest MSAs	57	51	0.8	3.0

Source: Calculated by Gobillon, Selod, and Zenou (2003) from the US Census

measure of spatial mismatch. The authors measure the spatial imbalance between jobs and residential locations using an index of dissimilarity, which ranges from 0 to 100, with higher values indicating a greater geographical mismatch between populations and jobs within a given metropolitan area. For instance, a dissimilarity index of 50 for blacks means that 50 percent of all blacks residing in the metropolitan area would have had to relocate to different neighborhoods within the metropolitan area in order to be spatially distributed in perfect proportion with jobs. Table 25.4 shows that, in the largest metropolitan areas in the USA, the access to jobs for blacks is quite bad (especially in Detroit and New York).

Surprisingly, the numerous empirical works that have tried to test the existence of a causal link between spatial mismatch and the bad labor-market outcomes of minorities (see, e.g., the survey by Ihlanfeldt & Sjoquist 1998) are not based on any theory. The typical approach is to look for a relationship between job accessibility and labor-market outcomes for blacks, using various levels of aggregation of the data: individual level, neighborhood level, and metropolitan level. Most papers have shown that bad job accessibility worsens labor-market outcomes, confirming the spatial mismatch hypothesis. However, following three decades of empirical tests, it was only in the late 1990s that theoretical models of spatial mismatch began to emerge. This is why most theoretical models have not yet inspired specific empirical tests (Gobillon, Selod & Zenou 2005).

Table 25.4   The US MSAs with the worse spatial mismatch for blacks in 2000

	Blacks			Whites			Total population
	% Pop	SM	% Un	% Pop	SM	% Un	
Atlanta, GA, MSA	29	54	8.98	63	40	3.09	4,112,198
Baltimore, MD, PMSA	27	52	11.69	67	37	3.05	2,552,994
Chicago, IL, PMSA	19	69	17.27	66	34	4.18	8,272,768
Cleveland–Lorain–Elyria, OH, PMSA	19	62	14.09	77	31	4.17	2,250,871
Detroit, MI, PMSA	23	71	14.89	71	36	4.27	4,441,551
Houston, TX, PMSA	17	57	10.85	61	40	4.46	4,117,646
Los Angeles – Long Beach, CA, PMSA	10	62	15.57	49	37	6.64	9,519,338
Miami, FL, PMSA	20	65	13.44	66	36	6.23	2,253,362
New York, NY, PMSA	25	70	14.63	49	44	5.61	9,314,235
Newark, NJ, PMSA	22	65	13.90	66	34	3.96	2,032,989
Oakland, CA, PMSA	13	55	12.08	55	37	3.95	2,392,557
Philadelphia, PA–NJ, PMSA	20	64	13.93	72	34	4.47	5,100,931
St Louis, MO–IL, MSA	18	63	14.21	78	38	4.11	2,603,607
Washington, DC–MD–VA–WV, PMSA	26	56	8.64	60	42	2.63	4,923,153

% Pop, the percentage of (black or white) individuals in the population in the MSA or PMSA; SM, a measure of the spatial mismatch (for black or white) between people and jobs using the Raphael and Stoll (2002) dissimilarity index; % Un, the percentage of (black or white) male unemployed in the MSA or PMSA.
Source: Raphael and Stoll (2002) and the US Census Bureau

How can we go about constructing a model consistent with the empirical regularities? One needs to develop theoretical models of urban labor markets in which unemployment is endogenous. The aim of this chapter is precisely to use urban labor theory to better understand these empirical features and to propose different policies aimed at fighting against high unemployment rates among black workers.

One popular model in labor economics is the efficiency wage model, initially developed by Shapiro and Stiglitz (1984). In this framework, because shirking is very costly, firms set a (high) wage in such a way that the cost of being caught while shirking is so high that workers are induced to work hard. This (efficiency) wage is lower the higher the unemployment rate, because the cost of shirking increases with unemployment. The efficiency wage model has strong empirical support. The traditional attempts to test efficiency wage theory showed that there are large wage differences between sectors for identical workers due to differences in supervision/monitoring rates (see, e.g., Kruger & Summers 1988; Neal 1993). So identical individuals working in different sectors can experience different unemployment rates because of inter-industry wage differences.

We first develop a simple urban efficiency wage model in which housing prices and workers' location (the land market), as well as wages and unemployment (the labor market) are determined in equilibrium. In this model, in which workers' relocation is costless, firms set efficiency wages to prevent shirking and to compensate workers for commuting. The interaction between these two markets is here explicit, since both wages and unemployment depend on commuting costs, and housing prices as well as location are in turn based on workers' wages.

We then adapt this model to the US spatial mismatch in order to provide two different mechanisms. First, by assuming that workers' effort negatively depends on distance to jobs, we show that, in equilibrium, firms draw a red line beyond which they will not hire workers. This is because, depending on their residential location, workers do not contribute to the same level of production, even though the wage cost is location independent. As a result, the per-worker profit decreases with distance to jobs and firms stop recruiting workers who reside too far away; that is, when the per-worker profit becomes negative. This model offers an explanation of the spatial mismatch of black workers by focusing on the point of view of firms. If housing discrimination against blacks forces them to live far away from jobs, then, even though firms have no prejudices, they are reluctant to hire black workers because they have relatively lower productivity than whites.

Second, we introduce two employment centers and high relocation costs so that workers do not change residence as soon as they change employment status. We show that housing discrimination, by skewing black workers toward the city center, increases the number of applications for central jobs and decreases it for suburban jobs. As a result, blacks living in the central part of the city but working in the suburbs experience lower unemployment rates and earn higher wages than blacks living and working in the central part of the city.

25.2 THE BASIC URBAN LABOR ECONOMIC MODEL

We here develop a simple model of an urban labor market based on Zenou and Smith (1995). This model was constructed with the European situation in mind, where the unemployment rate is higher in the suburbs (as, for example, in Paris or London), and is introduced primarily to set out the method of construction of models in urban labor economic theory. This model will obviously have to be adapted to deal with the US spatial mismatch. This will be done in sections 25.3 and 25.4 below.

There are N identical workers and M identical firms. Among the N workers, L are employed and U unemployed, so that $N = L + U$. Each individual is identified with one unit of labor and can decide either to work hard or to shirk (Shapiro & Stiglitz 1984). In the former case, the worker provides full effort, $e > 0$, and contributes to e units of production, while in the latter, no effort is exerted on the job ($e = 0$) and the contribution to production is nil.

For the ease of exposition, we will first present the urban equilibrium and then the labor-market equilibrium. The city is a line whose origin, $x_0 \equiv 0$, consists of the central business district (CBD hereafter) where all firms are located and whose end point is the city-fringe, denoted by x_f. Workers are uniformly distributed along this line and decide where to locate between $x = 0$ and $x = x_f$. The city is closed so that there is no relation with the outside world, which implies that the population is fixed. Absentee landlords own all land. There are no relocation costs, either in terms of time or money.

Each employed worker goes to the CBD to work and incurs a fixed commuting cost t per unit of distance. When living at a distance x from the CBD, he or she also pays a land rent $R(x)$, consumes one unit of land and earns a wage w. We adopt the following notations. The subscript L refers to the employed, whereas the subscript U refers to the unemployed. Among the employed workers, the superscripts NS and S refer, respectively, to nonshirkers and shirkers. In this context, the instantaneous (indirect) utilities of an employed nonshirker and shirker residing at a distance x from the CBD are, respectively, given by:

$$V_L^{NS} = w - e - tx - R(x), \tag{25.1}$$

$$V_L^S = w - tx - R(x), \tag{25.2}$$

Concerning the unemployed, they commute less often to the CBD, since they mainly go there to search for jobs. So, we assume that they incur a commuting cost st per unit of distance, with $0 < s < 1$. For example, $s = 1/2$ implies that the unemployed make only half as many CBD-trips as the employed workers. Each unemployed worker earns a fixed weekly unemployment benefit $b > 0$, pays a land rent $R(x)$, and consumes one unit of land. In this context, the instantaneous (indirect) utility of an unemployed worker is equal to:

$$V_U = b - stx - R(x). \tag{25.3}$$

We have first to determine where workers reside and the price of land at each location x in the city. In equilibrium (this will become clear below), none of the employed workers will shirk, so that we only need to analyze the urban land-use equilibrium for nonshirkers and unemployed workers. Since there are no relocation costs, the urban equilibrium is such that all the employed enjoy the same level of utility $V_L^{NS} \equiv V_L$, while all the unemployed obtain V_U. Indeed, any utility differential within the city would lead to the relocation of some workers up to the point at which all differences in utility disappear. We are now able to derive the bid rent, which is a standard concept in urban economics. It indicates the maximum land rent that a worker located at a distance x from the CBD is ready to pay in order to achieve a utility level. The bid rents of (nonshirking) employed and unemployed workers are given, respectively, by

$$\Psi_L(x, V_L) = w - e - tx - V_L, \tag{25.4}$$

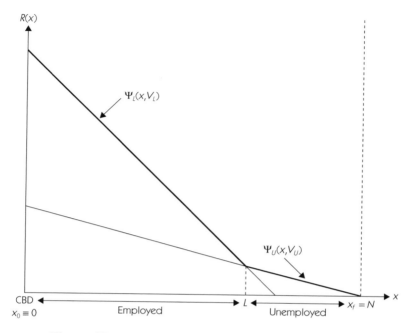

Figure 25.1 Urban equilibrium in the basic model.

$$\Psi_U(x,V_U) = b - stx - V_U. \tag{25.5}$$

It is easy to see that the bid rent of the employed is steeper than that of the unemployed, and thus the employed will occupy the core of the city. This is because the employed do commute more often to the CBD than the unemployed and thus value more highly the accessibility to the center.

As a result, since each worker consumes one unit of land, the employed reside between $x = 0$ and $x = L$, whereas the unemployed reside between $x = L$ and $x = N$ (see Figure 25.1). Let us determine the urban equilibrium. It is such that the bid rents of employed and unemployed workers intersect at location L and that, at the city fringe N, the bid rent of the unemployed is equal to the land rent outside the city (which is normalized to zero for simplicity). Formally,

$$\Psi_L(L,V_L) = w - e - tL - V_L = \Psi_U(L,V_U) = b - stL - V_U,$$
$$\Psi_U(N,V_U) = b - stN - V_U = 0.$$

By solving these two equations, we easily obtain the equilibrium values of the instantaneous utilities of the employed and the unemployed. They are given by

$$V_L = w - e - tN + (1 - s)t(N - L), \tag{25.6}$$

$$V_U = b - stN. \tag{25.7}$$

We have solved the urban equilibrium, since we know where workers locate in the city (the employed reside close to jobs, while the unemployed live further away because the former have higher commuting costs than the latter and thus bid them away) and what the price of land is at each location (it is equal to the bid rent of the employed for locations between 0 and L and to the bid rent of the unemployed for locations between L and N).

We would now like to determine the labor-market equilibrium; that is, the wages paid by firms and the level of unemployment in the city. Firms face a problem, since they do not perfectly observe the behavior of workers (whether they work hard or shirk), which affects production and thus their profit. We assume that, at each period, firms can monitor some workers but not all of them, because it is too costly. The rate of monitoring is denoted by θ and if a worker is caught shirking, he or she is automatically fired. The job acquisition rate is denoted by a and δ is the job destruction rate. The lifetime expected utilities of nonshirkers, shirkers, and unemployed workers, I_L^{NS}, I_L^S, and I_U, are given, respectively, by

$$rI_L^{NS} = V_L^{NS} - \delta(I_L^{NS} - I_U), \qquad (25.8)$$

$$rI_L^S = V_L^S - (\delta + \theta)(I_L^S - I_U), \qquad (25.9)$$

$$rI_U = V_U + a(I_L - I_U), \qquad (25.10)$$

where r is the discount rate, and where $V_L^{NS} \equiv V_L$ and V_U are given by equations (25.6) and (25.7), respectively, and $V_L^S = V_L + e$. The first equation that determines I_L^{NS} states that a nonshirker obtains today a utility level V_L^{NS} but can lose his or her job with probability δ (because, for example, the job is destroyed or because the worker decides to live in another city). In that case, he or she obtains a negative surplus of $I_U - I_L^{NS}$. For shirkers, I_L^S, the probability of losing a job, is even higher because either the job is destroyed (with probability δ) or he or she is caught shirking and fired (with probability θ). The last equation for the unemployed has a similar interpretation.

We can see straightaway the trade-off faced by a worker when deciding whether or not to shirk. There is a *short-run gain* of shirking because workers do not provide effort e (the gain is thus $V_L^S - V_L^{NS} = e$) but there is a *long-run cost* of shirking because the rate at which workers lose their jobs is higher ($\delta + \theta$ instead of δ).

Because shirking is very costly for firms (workers do not produce at all while being paid), firms would like to set wages in such a way that no rational worker shirks. These wages are called *efficiency wages* and are determined by the following incentive inequality: $I_L^{NS} > I_L^S$. Since all firms compete with each other to determine this wage, there is no need to pay more than $I_L^{NS} = I_L^S$. There are two ways to justify that $I_L^{NS} = I_L^S$. Either one assumes that when workers are indifferent between shirking and nonshirking, they always prefer to work than to shirk, or one can set an efficiency wage that is infinitesimally above the threshold $I_L^{NS} = I_L^S$. This obviously makes no difference in the analysis.

By using equations (25.8) and (25.9), $I_L^{NS} = I_L^S$ can be written as

$$I_L - I_U = \frac{e}{\theta}. \tag{25.11}$$

This highlights the nature of the (urban) efficiency wage w_e. The intertemporal surplus of being employed, $I_L - I_U$, is strictly positive and does not depend on spatial variables. This is a pure incentive effect (to deter shirking) that increases in effort and decreases in the monitoring rate θ (indeed, if firms better monitor their workers, then wages and thus $I_L^{NS} = I_L^S$ are lower).

In equilibrium, it has to be that the flows in unemployment are equal to the flows out of unemployment; that is,

$$a(N - L) = \delta L. \tag{25.12}$$

In words, the number of unemployed workers who find a job is equal to the number of employed workers who lose their job. By combining equations (25.11) and (25.12) and using equations (25.8)–(25.10), we are now able to calculate the efficiency wage:

$$w_e(L) = b + e + \frac{e}{\theta}\left(\frac{\delta N}{N - L} + r\right) + (1 - s)tL. \tag{25.13}$$

This equation is referred to as the Urban No-Shirking Condition (UNSC hereafter), since it is the wage that firms have to set at each employment level L in order to prevent shirking; that is, $I_L^{NS} = I_L^S$. Indeed, the lower the unemployment level $N - L$ in the city (or, equivalently, the higher the employment level L), the higher is the efficiency wage (see Figure 25.2). This is because unemployment acts as a worker discipline device, since the higher the unemployment, the more difficult it is to find a job and the higher are the long-run costs of shirking. As a result, in downturn economies with high unemployment rates, firms do not need to pay high wages to workers, since they discipline themselves because the cost of shirking is too high.

Interestingly, an increase in the unemployment benefit, b, would induce a rise in the efficiency wage, $w_e(L)$, because the outside option of not working is better and workers are more likely to shirk. As a result, firms have to increase wages to meet the condition $I_L^{NS} = I_L^S$. A similar interpretation can be made for the positive impact on wages of an increase in the job destruction rate δ or the discount rate r, or of a decrease in the monitoring rate θ.

Let us now understand the role of the spatial variables in the efficiency wage (25.13); that is, the commuting cost t and the unemployed CBD-trips s. Firms have to compensate their employed workers for spatial costs. Indeed, when setting their (efficiency) wage, firms must compensate the spatial cost differential between the employed and the unemployed. For the employed and the unemployed who both live at L (which is the border distance between the employed and the unemployed) and thus pay the same land rent, this differential is exactly equal to $(1 - s)tL$. Now, since mobility is costless, all the employed and unemployed workers obtain, respectively, the same utility level whatever their location.

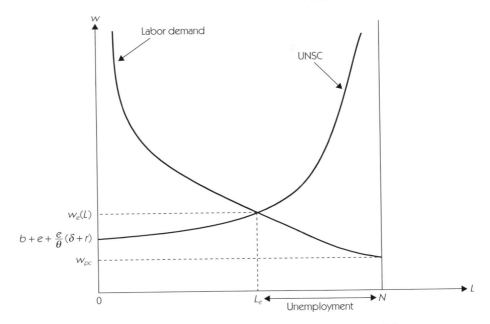

Figure 25.2   Labor equilibrium in the basic model.

Therefore, the spatial cost differential between any employed and unemployed worker is equal to $(1 - s)tL$. In order to see this, we can calculate the spatial costs of each individual, which consist of transportation plus land rent. In equilibrium, using equations (25.6) and (25.7), they are given by

$$SC_L = tN - (1 - s)t(N - L)$$

for the employed and

$$SC_U = stN$$

for the unemployed. We can thus calculate the spatial cost differential between the employed and the unemployed:

$$\Delta SC \equiv SC_L - SC_U = (1 - s)tL. \tag{25.14}$$

It is easy to see that ΔSC is precisely the last term in equation (25.13) and its role is to compensate workers for spatial costs. This implies that the efficiency wage can be written as

$$w_e(L) = b + \underbrace{WI}_{\text{Work Inducement}} + \underbrace{\Delta SC}_{\text{Spatial Compensation}}, \tag{25.15}$$

where

$$WI = e + \frac{e}{\theta}\left(\frac{\delta N}{N - L} + r\right)$$

and ΔSC is given by equation (25.14), so that, compared to unemployment, work-ing gives a wage premium of $WI + \Delta SC$. In other words, the efficiency wage has two roles: to prevent shirking (the incentive component) and to insure that workers stay in the city (the spatial compensation component).

Finally, by maximizing their profit $F(eL) - w_e L$, firms determine the labor demand L_e in the city. The model is closed and the labor-market equilibrium is depicted in Figure 25.2. The intersection between the Urban No-Shirking Condition (UNSC) curve (equation (25.13)) and the labor demand curve gives the equilibrium values of wage $w_e(L)$ and employment L_e. Observe that at $L = N$, there is full employ-ment and the corresponding wage, w_{pc}, is the wage that would be paid by firms in a perfectly competitive environment. Urban unemployment occurs here because wages are too high $(w_e(L) > w_{pc})$ and are downward rigid. Indeed, even with excess supply, firms will not cut their (efficiency) wages because the UNSC curve will not be met and all workers will shirk in equilibrium.

We would now like to adapt this model to deal with the US spatial mismatch, where the unemployment rate is higher in the central part of the city (Table 25.1), blacks live disproportionately downtown (Table 25.1), far away from jobs (Table 25.4), and there are more jobs in the suburbs than in the city center (Table 25.3).

There are several ways in which this model can be adapted to account for the US spatial mismatch. The easiest way is to flip the city so that the CBD corresponds to a suburban business district (SBD) that concentrates all jobs. So, if all jobs are in the suburbs rather than the CBD, all we require for consistency is to define $x = 0$ to be the workplace location, which is in the suburbs. But in fact, jobs are more centralized than residences. Indeed, Glaeser and Kahn (2001) have shown that jobs have been suburbanizing faster than residences, so that, in the large US metropolitan areas, the average job is now only 1 mile closer to the CBD than the average residence. So, even if we flip the city in the above model, there seems to be some inconsistency, since the unemployment rate in US cities is higher at (central) locations that appear to have better access to jobs. However, since most blacks are unskilled, we need to differentiate between skilled and unskilled jobs. Using both the 1994 Multi-City Study of Urban Inequality (MCSUI) and the 1990 Census, Table 25.2 displays the spatial distribution of recently filled low-skill jobs and of people by race and education. This table shows that the distribution of low-skill jobs is similar to that of all jobs, except that *there is a greater share of low-skill jobs in general in white suburbs*. This implies that low-skill jobs are much more decentralized than high-skill jobs. If one compares jobs with people, then the situation is worse: 79.6 percent of the metropolitan areas' lowest-skilled jobs, but only 23.6 percent of the least-educated black people (i.e., those with no high school degree) are located in the suburbs. The access to low-skill jobs is thus quite bad for unskilled black workers. Since unskilled jobs are further on average from the CBD than unskilled black workers' residences, and since unemployment is a problem for the unskilled, then our basic model can be adapted to describe the situation for the *unskilled*, but with $x = 0$ corresponding to a location in the suburbs. But the phenomenon of spatial mismatch is made more complicated by the presence of two modes of transportation – mass transit and the car – along with the relatively low incidence of car ownership among blacks, as well as the asymmetry between commuting inward and commuting outward. This, in fact, reinforces the spatial mismatch problem for blacks, since they are not only far away from (low-skill) jobs but, because of the lack of good public transportation in large US metropolitan areas, they have difficulty accessing these jobs, as confirmed by Table 25.4.

In this essay, we will not focus on the transport issue but, rather, assume a unique transport mode for all workers (whether they are black or white) in the city. Instead, by adapting the basic model of this section to the US spatial mismatch, we propose two different theories that can explain why distance to jobs can have adverse consequences in the labor market for black workers. In both theories, we generate a link between unemployment and a seemingly unrelated phenomenon: racial discrimination in the housing market.

25.3   THE THEORY OF SPATIAL MISMATCH 1: THE FIRMS' PERSPECTIVE

In this section, we adapt the basic model as follows. First, we only focus on low-skill workers (black or white) and low-skill jobs. Also, all workers use the same transport mode (mass transit). Second, $x = x_0$ is now the SBD – that is, the workplace is located in the suburbs, where all low-skill jobs are located – while $x = x_f$ is now the city center (there are no jobs there, only people). To be consistent with the basic model, we normalize the SBD to zero; that is, $x_0 = x$. This means that we take the firms' perspective when calculating the distance to jobs, so that x_f, the city center, is now the longest distance from the job center located at $x_0 = 0$. See Figure 25.3 for an illustration of this city. Finally, there is housing discrimination against blacks (housing discrimination against blacks is a well-documented fact; see, e.g., Yinger 1986), which forces them to live downtown (i.e., close to the city-center x_f) and causes them to have poorer access to unskilled jobs than do whites living in the suburbs.

We focus on the firms' viewpoint to explain the spatial mismatch for black workers. We will show that, even though firms have no prejudices against black workers, it can be rational for them not to hire black workers if they live too far away from jobs (they live downtown while jobs are in the suburbs), because they are less productive than white workers who live closer to jobs.

Based on Zenou (2002), let us show how an extension of the model of section 25.2 can capture this idea. Apart from the modifications mentioned above, we use exactly the same model, but we change only one aspect. There are still only two possible effort levels: either the worker shirks, exerting zero effort, $e = 0$, and contributing zero to production, or he or she does not shirk, providing full effort

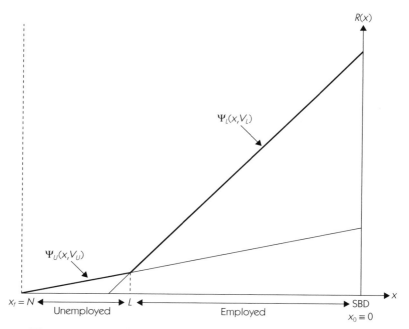

Figure 25.3 Urban equilibrium in the redlining model.

$e > 0$. However, the latter now depends on x, the distance to jobs. That is, $e(x) > 0$ is the contribution to production, with $e(0) = e_0 > 0$. We assume that the greater the distance to work, the lower is the effort level $(e'(x) < 0)$ and, for remote location, the marginal difference in effort is quite small $(e''(x) \geq 0)$.

This assumption, $e'(x) < 0$, aims at capturing the fact that workers who have longer commuting trips are more tired and are thus less able to provide higher levels of effort (or productivity) than those who reside closer to jobs. This implies that commuting costs include more than just money and time costs. They also include these negative effects of a longer commute such as nonwork-related fatigue. Moreover, this assumption can also capture the fact that workers who reside further away from jobs have less flexible working hours. For example, in some jobs (e.g., working in a restaurant), there are long breaks during the day (typically between 2 p.m. and 6 p.m. in restaurants). The worker who lives next door can go back home and relax, whereas the others, who live far away, cannot rest at home. This obviously also affects workers' productivity.

One can question this assumption by arguing that one can take a nap on a train. Indeed, driving 2 hours is tiring, but riding a train isn't. This is true if there is a very good public transport system, which implies, for example, that there is a direct train from home to the workplace. Remember that we are dealing with (low-educated) black workers who are forced to live far away from jobs (housing discrimination). It is well documented that most blacks do not have access to cars and use public transportation. Indeed, using data drawn from the 1995 Nationwide Personal Transportation Survey, Raphael and Stoll (2001) show that, in the USA, 5.4 percent of white households have zero automobiles while 24 percent of black households do not hold a single car. Even more striking, they show that 64 percent of black households have one or zero cars, whereas this number was 36 percent for white households.

It is also well documented that, in large US Metropolitan Statistical Areas, there is a lack of good public transportation, especially from the central city to the suburbs. For instance, *The New York Times* of May 26, 1998, told the story of Dorothy Johnson, a Detroit inner-city black female resident who had to commute to an evening job as a cleaning lady in a suburban office. By using public transportation, it took her 2 hours, whereas if she could have afforded a car, the commute would have taken only 25 minutes. This story illustrates the fact that blacks have relatively low productivity at suburban jobs because they arrive late at work due to the unreliability of the mass transit system, which frequently causes black workers to miss transfers.

The worker's behavior can now be seen as a two-stage decision. First, each worker must decide whether or not to shirk, depending on his or her residential location. Since effort is costly, it is clear that the worker who lives the closest to jobs will be more inclined to shirk than those who reside further away. Thus, contrary to the previous model, *the shirking behavior of workers is here locationally dependent.* Second, once the worker has decided not to shirk (this is the behavior that will emerge in equilibrium), he or she must decide how much effort he or she will provide. This decision is also locationally dependent, since we assume that workers who have longer commutes are more tired and provide less effort than those who live closer to their jobs.

As before, let us first determine the urban land-use equilibrium and then the labor equilibrium. All the locational analysis is exactly the same as in section 25.2, the only difference being that now e negatively depends on x. This creates a new locational trade-off for the employed. They would like to be close to jobs (the SBD located at $x_0 \equiv 0$) to save on commuting costs, but would also like to be far away from jobs to provide lower levels of effort (since effort is costly). However, by assuming that $t > -e'(L)/(1-s)$, we can guarantee that the employed reside close to the SBD, whereas the unemployed live close to the city center (see Figure 25.3). The intuition of this result is as follows. An increase in distance x has offsetting effects on employed workers: they pay higher commuting costs, but lower effort is exerted on the job. The net effect is thus less than the pure commuting cost effect, and the question is whether this net effect is stronger than the shrunken commuting cost effect for unemployed workers, which is smaller than that of the employed worker because $s < 1$. In this context, when the commuting cost t is high enough, the employed workers reside close to jobs by outbidding the unemployed.

Let us now solve for the labor equilibrium. Firms have to set an efficiency wage that prevents workers from shirking. Here, the main difference with the previous section is that the lifetime expected utility of shirkers I_L^S is now a function of x, since $V_L^S(x)$ is now given by $V_L^S(x) = V_L + e(x)$. As in the previous section, the efficiency wage has to be set in order to make workers indifferent between shirking and not shirking. However, *the utility of shirkers is not constant over locations, whereas it is constant for nonshirkers.*

When workers are heterogeneous in terms of location, it is clear that workers' residence matters in the process of wage formation. Firms observe where workers live, but cannot discriminate on the basis of residence or, equivalently, race (i.e., cannot make the wage location dependent or race dependent). In other words, they cannot offer different wages to identical workers who live in different areas of the city (because of housing discrimination, whites tend to live close to jobs, while blacks reside further away from jobs). One reason why firms cannot offer different wages to identical workers is antidiscrimination laws.

It is easy to see that the utility of shirkers increases as x, the distance to the SBD, decreases. The intuition is straightforward. Since the land rent compensates for both commuting costs and effort levels, then shirkers, who do not provide effort, have a higher utility when residing closer to the SBD (since their commuting costs are lower). This implies, in particular, that the highest utility that a shirker can reach is at $x_0 \equiv 0$, the SBD) and the lowest is at L. As a result, because firms cannot discriminate in terms of location or race, the efficiency wage must be set such that workers are indifferent between shirking at location $x_0 \equiv 0$ and not shirking, since if the worker at $x_0 \equiv 0$ does not shirk, then all workers located further away will not shirk. In other words, the condition that determines the efficiency wage is now given by $I_L^{NS} = I_L^S(0) = I_L$. Proceeding exactly as before, we obtain

$$w_e^r(L) = b + e(L) + \frac{e_0}{\theta}\left(\frac{\delta N}{N - L} + r\right) + (1 - s)tL. \tag{25.16}$$

If we compare equations (25.13) and (25.16), the main difference is that, in equation (25.16), the effort function, $e(\cdot)$, now depends on x, the distance to jobs. Two locations are crucial: the SBD, where $x_0 \equiv 0$ and effort is e_0, and the border between the employed and the unemployed, where $x = L$ and effort is $e(L)$.

Our setting thus implies that there is a fundamental *asymmetry* between workers and firms. All workers obtain the same efficiency wage whatever their location. However, they do *not* contribute to the same level of production because their effort decreases with distance to jobs. In other words, even though the wage cost is location independent, the contribution to production is not. This implies that the per-worker profit decreases with distance to jobs, so that firms will determine a red line beyond which they will not hire workers; that is, when the per-worker profit becomes negative. The interesting implication of this model is that it can explain why firms do not hire remote workers. Indeed, if firms *cannot* discriminate in terms of location (make wages location dependent), they do anticipate that remote workers provide lower effort level. So they stop recruiting workers who reside too far away.

To be more precise, all (identical) firms set the same red line $x^r = L$, above which they do not hire workers. The total production (or effort) level provided in each firm is given by $\bar{e} = \int_0^L e(x)dx$. As above, by taking the efficiency wage as given, each firm maximizes its profit to choose the optimal size of the red line (recruitment area L). We obtain $f'(\bar{e}) = w/e(L)$. This equation states that the optimal recruitment area, $x^r = L$, chosen by each firm is such that the marginal productivity of workers is equal to their cost per efficiency unit of labor. This determines the labor demand for each firm.

This model offers an explanation of the spatial mismatch of black workers by focusing on the point of view of firms. If firms cannot offer different wages for the same job, then they can discriminate on the basis of location by setting *higher job rejection rates for those residing far away from jobs*. Since there is housing discrimination against blacks, which forces them to live downtown, they are far away from (low-skill) jobs, which are located at $x_0 \equiv 0$, the SBD. Because firms know that remote workers tend to work less and to be less productive than those residing closer to jobs, they prefer not to hire black workers. In other words, even though firms have no prejudices against black workers, it is rational for them not to hire them if they live too far away from jobs (i.e., beyond the recruitment area determined by firms).

This first model is consistent with the empirical regularities cited in the Introduction. Most unskilled jobs are in the suburbs (Table 25.2) and, because of housing discrimination, most blacks live downtown (Table 25.1). This implies that blacks reside further away from jobs than whites (Table 25.4). As a result, they experience a higher unemployment rate (Tables 25.1 and 25.4), since firms are reluctant to hire them because blacks have relatively lower productivity at suburban jobs than whites.

Let us now investigate the policy implications of this model (Figure 25.2 also describes this labor equilibrium, but for different values of parameters). We focus on unemployment benefit and transportation policies. A reduction in the unemployment benefit shifts the UNSC downward, since at each recruitment area level $x^r = L$, the efficiency wage must decrease to deter shirking. This is the standard outside option effect generated by the unemployment benefit. Because wages are lower, it is less costly for firms to hire new workers, so they increase their recruitment area, which is beneficial for black workers. Similarly, decreasing the unit commuting cost, t, borne by workers or increasing the number of CBD-trips, s, increases the recruitment area $x^r = L$. The intuition is exactly the same as for b, but here the efficiency wage must decrease, not for incentive reasons, but to spatially compensate employed workers (this is the compensation effect mentioned above).

As a result, this model strongly advocates a cut in unemployment benefit and subsidies in transportation costs, since it increases the recruitment area of firms and reduces unemployment among black workers. In particular, these policies lower the negative effect of spatial mismatch, since firms will be more willing to hire black workers living at remote locations.

25.4   THE THEORY OF SPATIAL MISMATCH 2:
THE WORKERS' PERSPECTIVE

In this section, to account for the US spatial mismatch, we adapt the basic model in a different way. First, there are N_B black workers and N_W white workers (with

$N = N_B + N_W$); all workers are *unskilled* and use the same public transport mode (mass transit). Second, there are two job centers, the CBD, located at $x = x_0 \equiv 0$, and the SBD located at $x = x_f$. To be consistent with Table 25.2, we assume that there are more firms and thus more unskilled jobs in the SBD than in the CBD. Finally, there is housing discrimination against blacks in such a way that they cannot live in the suburbs; that is, between $x = x_{BW}$ and $x = x_f$ (where x_{BW} denotes the border between blacks and whites). They can only reside between $x_0 \equiv 0$ and x_{BW}.

Using Brueckner and Zenou (2003), we will show that distance to jobs can be harmful to black workers, because they may refuse jobs that involve excessively long commutes.

Because of the changes made above, the basic model is now quite complicated. So we simplify it as follows. First, we assume that employed and unemployed workers have the same commuting cost – that is, $s = 1$ – but black workers consume less land than white workers (reflecting lower average black income). If h_i denotes the housing consumption for worker of type $i = B,W$ (B and W stand, respectively, for blacks and whites), then we assume that $h_B < h_W = 1$. Second, because we now have eight categories of workers (blacks and whites who can either be employed or unemployed and who can either work in the CBD or the SBD), we assume that relocation costs are so high that people are not mobile at all and are therefore stuck in their location. As a result, people stay in the same location when they change their employment status. We also assume perfect capital markets with a zero interest rate (when there is a zero interest rate, workers have no intrinsic preference for the present, so that they only care about the fraction of time they spend employed and unemployed; as a result, the expected utilities are not state dependent), which enable workers to smooth their income over time as they enter and leave unemployment; workers save while employed and draw down on their savings when out of work. Consequently, there are only four categories of workers defined by their race $i = B,W$ and their workplace $j = C,S$ (C if they work in the CBD and S in the SBD).

Here again, we first solve the urban equilibrium and then the labor-market equilibrium. Since whites have flatter bid rents (blacks and whites have the same commuting costs, but whites, because they consume more land, want to locate in remote locations where the price of land is lower), they reside further away from jobs than blacks. Because of housing discrimination that prevents blacks from residing in the suburbs, the location of workers in the city is as follows. Starting from the CBD, we have blacks working in the CBD (referred to as CBD-blacks), then blacks working in the SBD (referred to as SBD-blacks), whites working in the CBD (referred to as CBD-whites), and finally whites working in the SBD (referred to as SBD-whites).

The equilibrium land rent is described in Figure 25.4, where $x_B(x_W)$ is the border between CBD-blacks (whites) and SBD-blacks (whites), while x_{BW} is the border between SBD-blacks and CBD-whites. If there were no housing discrimination against blacks, then to obtain the urban equilibrium, we would have to juxtapose Figures 25.1 and 25.3. In this new configuration, starting from the CBD, Figure 25.1 would locate first black and then white workers, while, starting from the

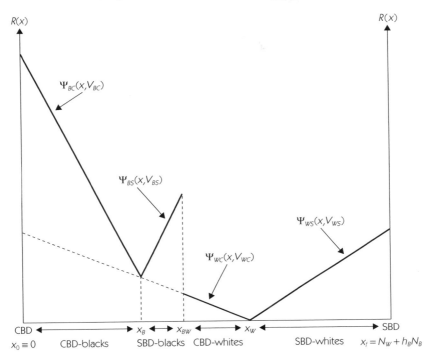

Figure 25.4   Urban equilibrium in the two-center model.

SBD, Figure 25.3 would accommodate first black and then white workers. The border between CBD-whites and SBD-whites would have been at x_f and the urban configuration would have been perfectly symmetric around x_f. Now, because of housing discrimination, the urban equilibrium is depicted by Figure 25.4. To understand this pattern, observe that housing discrimination means that whites face no competition for suburban land. Blacks, however, must still outbid whites for land in the central part of the city. Therefore, the black bid rents in this area must be at least as large as the bids offered by CBD-whites. This, in turn, implies that the minimum point (which occurs at $x = x_B$) of the black bid-rent curves must lie on the extension of the CBD-whites' bid rents (depicted by the dotted line). Figure 25.4 also shows a dramatic bid-rent discontinuity at $x = x_{BW}$, with SBD-black workers offering much more for land in the white area than the white residents themselves. This discrepancy, which would be unsustainable in a competitive market, is a consequence of discrimination by suburban landlords against blacks.

Thus, black workers are skewed toward the CBD and blacks' residences are thus remote from the SBD. For a black worker, working in the SBD involves high commuting costs, which may deter many of them from accepting SBD jobs. As a result, the black CBD labor pool is large relative to the black SBD pool, and the competition among blacks for central jobs is thus fiercer.

We can calculate the efficiency wage for a worker of type ij ($i = B,W$, $j = C,S$). It is given by

$$w_{ij}^m(L_{ij}) = b + e + \frac{e}{\theta}\left(\frac{\delta N}{N - L_{ij}}\right),$$
(25.17)

which is the wage (25.13) when $r \to 0$ and $s = 1$.

As stated above, there are more "unskilled" firms in the SBD than in the CBD. To determine their labor demand, each firm maximizes its profit and the labor-market equilibrium in each center for each type of labor is depicted by Figure 25.2 (for different parameter values). Because of housing discrimination and because there are more unskilled jobs in the SBD, it is then easy to show that, compared to whites, the unemployment rate is higher and wages are lower for black workers, which is consistent with the US spatial mismatch. The intuition is straightforward. Because of housing discrimination, blacks are forced to live in the central part of the city. Because there are more unskilled jobs in the SBD, most blacks have poor access to unskilled jobs and the ones who accept working in the SBD support long and costly commuting costs. As a result, few blacks will accept a job in the SBD and most of them will seek a CBD-job. This leads to a high unemployment rate for CBD-black workers (which encompasses most blacks) and, because in an efficiency wage framework, unemployment acts as a worker discipline device, CBD-firms can set low wages to black workers without fearing shirking behavior. So, even if all workers (black or white) are *ex ante* totally identical, mainly because of housing discrimination, white workers end up with higher wages and lower unemployment rates.

This model is also consistent with the empirical regularities mentioned in the introduction. The unemployment rate is higher downtown than in the suburbs (Table 25.1) because blacks, who are mainly unskilled (Table 25.2), are forced to live around the city center (Tables 25.1 and 25.2), far away from the suburbs where most unskilled jobs are located (Tables 25.2 and 25.4).

Let us now show another interesting result by focusing only on black workers. It has been observed that blacks working downtown tend to have higher unemployment rates and lower wages than blacks working in the suburbs (see, e.g., Brueckner & Zenou 2003, table 3). In other words, let us show that blacks living in the central part of the city but working in the SBD experience lower unemployment rates and earn higher wages than blacks living in the central part of the city but working in the CBD. The argument is as follows. Since, in equilibrium, it must be that all blacks wherever they work (in the CBD or the SBD) must reach the same utility level, then there must be some compensation for those who commute to the SBD. Indeed, because blacks are discriminated against in the housing market, they are forced to live in the central part of the city. Because blacks are forced to live in the central part of the city, the ones who work in the SBD support long and costly commuting costs. So in order for blacks to obtain the same utility level wherever they work, the SBD workers have to be compensated. Because, for blacks, competition in the land market is quite fierce, land rent does not totally compensate them (see Figure 25.4) and thus unemployment rates and the resulting expected income must be higher for the SBD-black workers compared to the CBD-black workers. In other words, *housing discrimination, by skewing blacks toward the city center, increases the number of job applications of blacks for central jobs and decreases this number for suburban jobs.*

In this context, using, for example, Figure 25.2 to determine the equilibrium in each center $j = C,S$, it is easy to see that the unemployment rate of blacks is higher and their wage lower when they work in the CBD than in the SBD. This is because unemployment, acting as a worker discipline device, enables employers to pay low wages when unemployment is high. So the main argument of this model is that suburban housing discrimination skews black workers toward the CBD and thus keeps black residences remote from the suburbs. Since black workers who work in the SBD have more costly commutes, few of them will accept SBD jobs, which makes the black CBD labor pool large relative to the SBD pool. Under an efficiency wage model, this enlargement of the CBD pool leads to a high unemployment rate among CBD workers.

Even though the mechanism is totally different, this model has similar implications in terms of policy as the redlining model of section 25.3. Both a policy that reduces unemployment benefit and a policy that subsidizes commuting costs will reduce unemployment for blacks. However, it is not because the recruitment area (the red line) increases. Indeed, in the first policy, wages are reduced so that labor demand increases in both employment centers. In the second policy, SBD-black workers are more willing to accept more distant jobs so that it increases their labor supply. Both policies, though different, reduce the negative consequences of blacks' spatial mismatch on their labor-market outcomes.

25.5   CONCLUDING REMARKS

Based on urban labor economic theory, this chapter has proposed two models that provide theoretical foundations of the spatial mismatch of black workers. In both theories, there is no labor discrimination or racial prejudice, and it is assumed that, because of housing discrimination, black workers are constrained to reside in remote locations far away from jobs. The impact of the latter assumption on labor outcomes is quite different in each model. In the first model, firms may not want to hire some black workers because they may provide less effort on the job, since workers who have longer commuting trips are more tired and are thus less able to provide higher levels of effort (or productivity) than those who reside closer to jobs. This is particularly true in large US Metropolitan Statistical Areas, where there is a lack of good public transportation, especially from the central city to the suburbs. In the second model, housing discrimination, by skewing blacks toward the city center, increases the number of applications for central jobs and decreases it for suburban jobs. As a result, unemployment increases for black workers who work in the city center. In both models, policies that decrease unemployment benefits and/or that subsidize commuting costs will reduce black unemployment.

So, how relevant are these models? Interestingly, Zax and Kain (1996) have in some sense illustrated the model of section 25.4 by studying a "natural experiment" (the case of a large firm in the service industry, which relocated from the center of Detroit to the suburb Dearborn in 1974). They show that, among workers whose commuting time was increased, black workers were overrepresented, and not all could follow the firm. This had two consequences: first, as in our model, segregation forced some blacks to quit their jobs. Second, the share of black workers applying for jobs to the firm decreased drastically (from 53 percent to 25 percent in 5 years before and after the relocation), and the share of black workers in hires also fell from 39 percent to 27 percent.

It would be interesting to test the redlining model of section 25.3. The popular press often relates stories about firms that do not want to hire workers living in "bad" neighborhoods, which are in general not well connected to job centers. An empirical test to see how policy-relevant this model is would be more than welcome.

Acknowledgments

I would like to thank Richard Arnott as well as an anonymous referee for extremely helpful comments. I also thank the Marianne and Marcus Wallenberg Foundation for financial support.

Bibliography

Brueckner, J. K. and Zenou, Y. 2003: Space and unemployment: the labor-market effects of spatial mismatch. *Journal of Labor Economics*, 21, 242–66.

Glaeser, E. L. and Kahn, M. 2001: Decentralized employment and the transformation of the American city. *Brookings–Wharton Papers on Urban Affairs*, 2, 1–64.

Gobillon, L., Selod, H., and Zenou, Y. 2003: Spatial mismatch: from the hypotheses to the theory. CEPR Discussion Paper Series 3740.

——, ——, and —— 2005: The mechanisms of spatial mismatch. CEPR Discussion Paper Series 5346.

Ihlanfeldt, K. R. and Sjoquist, D. L. 1998: The spatial mismatch hypothesis: a review of recent studies and their implications for welfare reform. *Housing Policy Debate*, 9, 849–92.

Kain, J. F. 1968: Housing segregation, negro employment, and metropolitan decentralization. *Quarterly Journal of Economics*, 82, 32–59.

Kruger, A. and Summers, L. 1988: Efficiency wages and the inter-industry wage structure. *Econometrica*, 56, 259–93.

Neal, D. 1993: Supervision and wages across industries. *Review of Economics and Statistics*, 75, 409–17.

Raphael, S. and Stoll, M. A. 2001: Can boosting minority car-ownership rates narrow interracial employment gaps? *Brookings–Wharton Papers on Urban Economic Affairs*, 2, 99–145.

—— and —— 2002: Modest progress: the narrowing spatial mismatch between blacks and jobs in the 1990s. The Brookings Institution, Washington, DC.

Shapiro, C. and Stiglitz, J. E. 1984: Equilibrium unemployment as a worker discipline device. *American Economic Review*, 74, 433–44.

Stoll, M., Holzer, H., and Ihlanfeldt, K. 2000: Within cities and suburbs: racial residential concentration and the spatial distribution of employment opportunities across sub-metropolitan areas. *Journal of Policy Analysis and Management*, 19, 207–31.

Yinger, J. 1986: Measuring racial discrimination with fair housing audits. *American Economic Review*, 76, 881–93.

Zax, J. and Kain, K. F. 1996: Moving to the suburbs: Do relocating companies leave their black employees behind? *Journal of Labor Economics*, 14, 472–93.

Zenou, Y. 2002: How do firms redline workers? *Journal of Urban Economics*, 52, 391–408.

Zenou, Y. and Smith, T. E. 1995: Efficiency wages, involuntary unemployment and urban spatial structure. *Regional Science and Urban Economics*, 25, 821–45.

CHAPTER TWENTY-SIX

Macroeconomic Analysis Using Regional Data: An Application to Monetary Policy*

Gerald A. Carlino and Robert H. DeFina

26.1   Introduction

Increasingly, macroeconomists have come to recognize that subnational economies, such as those of regions and urban areas, are useful laboratories for examining theory and policy. In part, the advantage of regional analysis is simply additional data. For example, if a researcher wants to examine the effects of changes in interest rates on employment or output, a national economy offers a single set of observations with which to estimate the relationship. To obtain a deeper understanding of macro phenomena, studies often expand the analysis to include data from other countries, such as a selection of industrialized countries. The benefit from the additional observations is partially offset by the lack of comparability across countries with regard to legal, political, and social systems. To some degree, it is possible to control for these differences, but such techniques are far from perfect. An alternative approach is to use data from different areas within a

* This chapter does not necessarily reflect the opinions of the Federal Reserve Bank of Philadelphia, the Federal Reserve System, or Villanova University.

country. These include metropolitan areas, states, and broader regions composed of several states. Within-country regional data provide additional samples where the legal, political, and social environments are quite similar.

A good example of these considerations is the empirical work done by economists during the past decade examining income convergence across countries and regions within countries. The neoclassical growth model predicts that eventually incomes in different countries will converge. The basic idea is that incomes will become increasingly similar as labor and capital move to countries offering the highest returns to these factors. Obviously, the theory cannot be tested using national data from a single country, since the prediction involves cross-country comparisons. But some researchers, such as W. Baumol, found no general pattern of convergence during the period from 1950 to 1980 for a group of 72 countries (Baumol 1986). Other researchers, such as R. Barro and X. Sala-i-Martin, and G. Carlino and L. Mills, point out that it's much harder for labor and capital to cross international borders than to cross states or regional boundaries within a given country. To deal with problems associated with factor migration across countries, macroeconomists have relied on regional data within particular countries. Studies based on data within a given country generally find evidence of convergence as predicted by theory (Barro & Sala-i-Martin 1992; Carlino and Mills 1993). Some other topics for which macroeconomists have employed regional data include Blanchard and Katz's (1992) analysis of local labor-market dynamics, Blank and Card's (1993) examination of the effects of unemployment on poverty, and Ball's (1994) study of sacrifice ratios.

Similarly, regional economists have used the toolkit of macroeconomists to examine growth and change at the regional level. Their motivation for doing so is that particular regions have unique business cycles and growth trends. Local economic fortunes depend on a confluence of national events (e.g., changes in monetary policy), sectoral events (e.g., changes in the auto and financial services industries), and local events (e.g., droughts). Consequently, empirical evidence on economic fluctuations at the national level can have little relevance for subnational economies. The chapter by Edward Coulson in this volume clearly explains some of the basic macro-empiric techniques that are applied to regional analysis and describes a number of applications.

In this essay, we focus on a specific instance for which subnational data are especially helpful in understanding macro phenomena – the effects of national monetary policy actions on subnational income and the ways in which policy actions are transmitted to the economic activity of such regions. Information on these issues is clearly important to policy-makers at many levels. At the national level, for example, monetary policy-makers have access to a lot of information about regional economic conditions through periodic reports from regional Federal Reserve Banks (Beige Book reports) and through the regional business contacts of the presidents of the 12 Federal Reserve Banks, who attend meetings of the Federal Open Market Committee (FOMC). Additional information on how the various regions respond to changes in monetary policy should aid policy-makers in any attempt to more fully and systematically incorporate regional developments into the formulation of national monetary policy. The issue of how policy actions affect different areas also has great relevance to the recently formed European Central Bank (ECB) and its member countries. Differences in the way in which a common monetary policy affects economic activity across countries mean that the cost of disinflation, for example, will be distributed unequally across countries that make up the European Monetary Union, suggesting that setting a common monetary policy might be quite contentious.

26.2   Why Might Monetary Policy Affect Regions Differently?

To be concrete, we will discuss the impacts of monetary policy on personal income growth in US states. We focus on state-level impacts because the best available evidence is for the state level. A more localized unit of analysis, such as metropolitan areas, may respond differently than their states simply because the state data might average out important metropolitan-level variations. For example, suppose that income in the Pittsburgh metropolitan area is much more responsive to monetary policy actions than income in the Philadelphia metropolitan area. Using Pennsylvania's responsiveness to monetary policy changes will tend to understate Pittsburgh's response and tend to overstate Philadelphia's response. Still, a possible reason for the focus on states is the lack of a consistent time series of data for metropolitan areas. That is, metropolitan area definitions have changed through time, making it difficult to isolate the impact of policy. Since metropolitan areas consist of aggregations of contiguous counties surrounding the county containing the region's central city, consistent definitions for metropolitan areas can be constructed using employment data for counties provided by the Bureau of Economic Analysis (BEA), Regional Economic Information System (REIS) CD-ROM. However, the county data series are *annual* and start in 1969. The state data, by contrast, are *quarterly* and date from the 1950s, and thus they add more business-cycle variation for two reasons. Suppose that the Fed unexpectedly raises the federal funds rate by one-half of a percent (50 basis points). Employment in some metropolitan areas may respond almost immediately to the tighter policy, while employment in other states may adjust only one, two, or even three quarters after the change in policy. Thus, the timing of a metropolitan area's response to monetary policy shocks may differ dramatically with any given year. But one will not be able to discern such differences in the timing of a metropolitan area's response to policy if data under analysis are at annual frequencies rather than at quarterly frequencies. Second, the use of state data, which extend back to the 1950s, allows the inclusion of up to nine postwar recessionary episodes, compared with at most six episodes using metropolitan area data, which extend back only to 1969. In any event, the theoretical and empirical frameworks that we describe can be readily applied to data for finer regional disaggregation, such as metropolitan areas, should a researcher desire. In the discussion that follows, we will focus on states.

Regardless of the geographical level of the analysis, monetary theory suggests several reasons why Fed policy actions can have different subnational effects.

These include state differences in the mix of interest-sensitive industries (referred to as an interest rate channel for monetary policy), in the number of large versus small firms, and in the number of large versus small banks (referred to as a credit channel for policy).

26.2.1 Regional differences in the mix of interest-sensitive industries

At the national level, both the timing and impact of monetary policy actions differ across industries. In part, these differences arise because of varying interest sensitivities in the demand for products. Housing, cars, and other durable manufactured goods have historically been more responsive to interest rate changes than, say, consumer services. In a similar vein, differences in an industry's response can depend on whether its output constitutes a necessity or a luxury, and the extent to which demand for the industry's output is linked to foreign trade and, thus, the health of foreign economies.

These varying industry responses, together with differing industry mixes across states, provide a natural way for monetary policy to have differential state effects. As Table 26.1 shows, industry mix differs widely across states. For example, manufacturing, which is thought to be an interest-sensitive sector, accounted for about 34 percent of real gross state product (GSP) in Michigan, on average,

Table 26.1 The percentage of gross state product accounted for by manufacturing (averaged over the period from 1977 to 1990)

Michigan	33.5	Iowa	23.8	Idaho	16.9
Indiana	33.2	Illinois	23.1	Texas	16.7
North Carolina	32.3	Massachusetts	23.1	Louisiana	15.5
Ohio	31.4	Missouri	22.8	Utah	15.4
Delaware	31.1	Maine	22.7	Oklahoma	14.9
Wisconsin	30.4	New Jersey	22.6	Arizona	14.6
South Carolina	28.5	Vermont	22.4	Nebraska	14.0
Kentucky	26.4	Oregon	22.0	Colorado	13.6
Connecticut	26.1	Minnesota	21.9	Maryland	13.2
Rhode Island	25.8	Georgia	21.6	Florida	10.8
Tennessee	25.6	Kansas	19.2	South Dakota	9.0
New Hampshire	25.5	Washington	18.7	Montana	8.8
Pennsylvania	25.1	Virginia	18.5	New Mexico	6.3
Arkansas	24.7	New York	17.8	North Dakota	5.6
Mississippi	24.4	West Virginia	17.8	Nevada	4.5
Alabama	23.9	California	17.5	Wyoming	3.6
				Average	20.1
				Standard deviation	7.7

Source: BEA, *Survey of Current Business*, various years

during the period from 1977 to 1990, but less than 4 percent of Wyoming's real GSP. These state shares can be compared with an overall average state manufacturing share of 20 percent. Compounding these differences are interstate trade relationships, which can transmit localized responses differently across states.

26.2.2 Regional differences in the ability of banks to alter their balance sheets

Recent theoretical work on possible credit channels for the transmission of monetary policy actions to economic activity suggests that state differences in the mix of large versus small firms and large versus small banks could lead to different state responses to monetary policy. Concerning *firm size*, Bernanke and Blinder (1988), Bernanke (1993), and Gertler and Gilchrist (1993) argue that monetary policy affects economic activity by directly affecting banks' abilities to provide loans. Moreover, significant information costs and transaction costs often require small firms to deal with financial intermediaries, primarily banks, to meet their credit needs. Large firms, by contrast, usually have greater access to external, nonbank sources of funds, such as through the issuance of stocks and bonds. Consequently, activity in a state that has a high concentration of small firms could be especially sensitive to Fed policy. It is also possible that the greater uncertainty about the health and prospects of small firms means that they face relatively greater volatility in the costs of *all* forms of finance (bank loans, trade credit, commercial paper, etc.) in light of Fed actions (Gertler & Gilchrist 1993; Oliner & Rudebusch 1995). If so, state-level differences in mix of firm size will imply state-level differences in responses to policy actions.

As Table 26.2 shows, the percentage of small firms (defined as state firms with fewer than 250 employees averaged over the period from 1976 to 1992) varies widely across states. It ranges from a low of about 49 percent in Connecticut to a high of about 89 percent in Montana. The average state share is 72 percent.

A potential role for *bank size* in the monetary transmission mechanism has been developed by A. Kashyap and J. Stein, who suggest that Fed policy actions can have varied effects on different banks' abilities to make loans (Kashyap & Stein 1994). During periods of tight monetary policy, when bank reserves are restricted, some banks can find alternative sources of funding for deposits and loans (by issuing large-denomination CDs, for example) more cheaply and easily than others. Such lending by banks will be less sensitive to monetary policy changes. Some authors propose that bank size largely explains differences in financing abilities, with large banks having more funding options available than small banks (Kashyap & Stein 1994). Thus, states in which a disproportionately large share of bank loans is made by small banks might respond more to monetary policy shifts than states in which a large share of loans is made by the nation's large banks. The effect of the differences in states' reliance on small banks will be diluted if bank-dependent borrowers can obtain credit from sources outside their own states. However, there is evidence that banking markets tend to be segmented along state lines.

Table 26.2 The share of total state employment accounted for by a state's small firms (firms with less than 250 employees, averaged over the period from 1976 to 1992)

Montana	89.1	Iowa	74.1	New Jersey	69.4
North Dakota	87.8	Mississippi	72.9	Rhode Island	69.2
Wyoming	85.9	Arkansas	72.4	Missouri	68.9
South Dakota	84.3	Utah	72.3	Tennessee	67.6
New Mexico	82.1	West Virginia	72.3	Indiana	66.8
Oregon	79.2	California	72.3	Ohio	65.9
Idaho	78.3	New Hampshire	72.0	Illinois	65.8
Florida	77.8	Texas	71.9	North Carolina	65.3
Vermont	77.0	Maryland	71.8	Pennsylvania	65.1
Oklahoma	76.8	Maine	71.7	Michigan	64.8
Kansas	76.2	Kentucky	71.3	Massachusetts	64.6
Nebraska	75.6	Georgia	70.6	New York	64.1
Colorado	75.3	Virginia	70.5	South Carolina	63.4
Louisiana	75.1	Minnesota	70.0	Delaware	62.7
Washington	74.9	Wisconsin	69.9	Nevada	60.7
Arizona	74.9	Alabama	69.9	Connecticut	48.8
				Average	71.9
				Standard deviation	7.3

Source: *County Business Patterns*, various years

Kashyap and Stein (1994) define small banks as those with total assets at or below a given percentile – they use, alternatively, the 75th, 90th, 95th, or 98th percentile. Table 26.3 shows the state distribution of loans for the nation's banks that are at or below the 90th percentile in terms of total assets, averaged for the period from 1976 to 1992. Whether we look at all small banks or only small banks that are *not* members of a bank holding company, the state distribution of loans by small banks appears highly unequal, suggesting that monetary policy could have differential state effects for the reasons proposed by Kashyap and Stein.

26.3 AN EMPIRICAL STRATEGY FOR UNDERSTANDING THE REGIONAL IMPACTS OF POLICY

26.3.1 Constructing a model for the analysis

The starting point for analyzing the effects of monetary policy actions on the US states is the formulation of an empirical model. Several considerations come into play. First, it is well known that changes in economic activity in a state spill over

Table 26.3 The share of total loans made by a state's small banks (averaged over the period from 1976 to 1992)

All small banks[a]				Not in holding company[b]			
North Dakota	73.0	Vermont	28.3	Kansas	63.6	South Dakota	21.9
Kansas	72.7	Florida	25.2	Nebraska	53.4	South Carolina	17.7
Montana	71.1	Illinois	25.0	Oklahoma	50.6	Illinois	17.4
Iowa	69.7	Maine	24.7	Arkansas	47.5	Maine	16.3
Nebraska	64.6	Virginia	20.8	North Dakota	46.7	Utah	15.8
Wyoming	64.2	Michigan	19.1	Iowa	46.3	Virginia	14.6
Arkansas	63.8	South Carolina	18.6	West Virginia	42.4	Florida	12.7
West Virginia	60.8	Utah	17.6	Mississippi	38.1	Connecticut	11.5
Oklahoma	57.6	Ohio	16.6	Louisiana	36.7	Ohio	11.1
Wisconsin	54.9	Maryland	16.0	Kentucky	36.3	Michigan	11.0
Colorado	51.3	Connecticut	12.7	Wisconsin	34.2	Maryland	11.0
New Mexico	48.3	Pennsylvania	12.2	Montana	33.8	Pennsylvania	10.7
Missouri	46.5	Idaho	11.2	Wyoming	32.3	Oregon	9.3
Kentucky	45.7	Oregon	10.4	New Mexico	30.5	Idaho	9.2
Minnesota	44.7	New Jersey	10.4	New Hampshire	29.8	New Jersey	8.6
New Hampshire	43.9	Washington	9.6	Indiana	28.5	Washington	8.6
Mississippi	38.6	Massachusetts	8.3	Tennessee	27.8	California	5.6
Louisiana	37.6	California	6.1	Minnesota	27.6	North Carolina	5.6
Tennessee	36.5	North Carolina	6.0	Colorado	24.2	Massachusetts	5.5
Indiana	34.4	Delaware	4.8	Missouri	23.2	Nevada	4.1
Alabama	33.1	Nevada	4.7	Alabama	23.2	Rhode Island	3.1
Texas	32.9	Arizona	3.6	Georgia	23.2	Delaware	3.0
Georgia	32.3	Rhode Island	3.2	Texas	23.0	Arizona	2.9
South Dakota	29.2	New York	1.2	Vermont	22.2	New York	0.9
		Average	31.7			Average	22.6
		Standard deviation	22.0			Standard deviation	15.5

[a] The percent of loans made by a state's banks that are at or below the 90th percentile in terms of total assets (compared with all banks in the nation).

[b] The percent of loans made by a state's banks that are at or below the 90th percentile in terms of total assets (compared with all banks in the nation) and are not members of a multi-bank holding company.

Source: Compiled from *Federal Reserve Call Reports*, various years

and affect activity in other regions, especially neighboring ones. These cross-state effects arise, for example, from interstate input–output supply linkages as well as interstate demand relationships. Thus, a useful model should account for these interstate spillovers. Second, economic shocks to a state, such as monetary policy actions, generally affect activity with a lag. That is, once the policy change occurs, it takes time for firms and workers to react and adjust to the new circumstances. Finally, once these adjustments begin, they can last for several periods as, for instance, contracts are sequentially renewed in light of the new economic conditions.

An empirical framework that is well suited to incorporating these various features is a vector autoregression, or VAR. The chapter by Edward Coulson in this volume also contains discussion of VARs and their application to subnational analysis. For the present purposes, we offer an abbreviated explanation.

VAR is a widely used modeling technique for gathering evidence on business-cycle dynamics. VARs typically rely on a small number of variables expressed as past values of the dependent variable and past values of the other variables in the model. Each variable in the VAR is considered to be part of a system in which all variables are jointly determined. For example, if a policy action causes income growth in New York to rise, the VAR system allows that increase to affect income growth in all other states. Moreover, after the initial effect, the VAR permits continuing feedback effects among all other states, with the subsequent effects becoming smaller and smaller over time and eventually disappearing.

26.3.2   Specifying the model

Once the VAR methodology is selected for the analysis, the structure of the model must be specified. The VAR ideally would start with equations describing economic activity in each of the 48 states, plus another equation describing monetary policy actions. In practice, such a large system cannot easily be estimated, if at all.

An alternative strategy for measuring the state-specific impacts of monetary policy is to estimate 48 individual VAR systems, one for each state. Within each of the 48 state-specific VARs, a state's economic activity would be allowed to affect and be affected by activity in other broad regions of the country, as well as by policy. For example, the Bureau of Economic Analysis groups states into eight regions. Using these groupings, a given state-level VAR might then minimally include economic activity in the state; economic activity in the state's region less the state (to avoid double-counting); economic activity in each of the other seven regions; and a monetary policy variable. The resulting 10-variable VAR thus would allow for spillovers and feedbacks both because of policy changes and other area-specific shocks to economic activity. The models could be reasonably extended to include additional variables that account for other important macro information that the Fed uses in formulating its policy decisions, such as recent trends in aggregate inflation and unemployment.

It would be preferable to describe economic activity using a measure of a state's total output. The Bureau of Economic Analysis computes gross state product

(GSP) for each state and the eight major regions. However, these data have a major shortcoming for studying the regional effects of monetary policy, since they provide only annual observations. Thus, they smooth important quarter-to-quarter fluctuations due to policy changes and could lead to underestimations of the short-run impacts of policy. Alternative labor-market measures, such as employment or unemployment, are available at a quarterly frequency, but these also have limitations. For instance, output changes occur independently from employment shifts owing to productivity changes. Consequently, employment can be a very imperfect indicator of a state's total economic activity. Another widely used quarterly variable is personal income, which measures individuals' income from wages, rent, interest, and profits plus government transfer payments. Personal income differs from total output because it excludes certain components, such as indirect business taxes, and includes nonearned income (transfer payments such as social security). Another limitation is that personal income is reported in nominal terms and must be deflated using national price indexes, since regional ones are generally unavailable. Given that each of these variables has limitations, it is advisable to try alternative measures of economic activity to gauge the sensitivity of the findings to variable selection.

Which variable best serves as an indicator of monetary policy has been long debated, both inside and outside the Fed. The debates have identified several possibilities, including reserve aggregates (such as nonborrowed reserves), monetary aggregates (such as M1), interest rates (in particular, the federal funds rate and the three-month Treasury bill rate), spreads between certain interest rates, and so-called "narrative" policy indicators derived from the official Federal Open Market Committee minutes. Among the available choices, the case for using an interest rate appears most convincing both in light of actual Fed operating procedures and the most recent empirical evidence.

Should one desire, it is possible to impose more structure on the VAR, aside from the selection of variables and the number of lags, so that the interactions between the system's variables are restricted to conform to theoretical or practical concerns. At times, these restrictions are needed to econometrically identify, or measure, the shocks to certain variables. An example of a useful restriction concerns the speed with which monetary policy actions affect real income. There is a considerable amount of evidence that policy actions do not affect output and incomes until at least one quarter after the policy change. Similarly, one might reasonably expect that changes in economic conditions that are specific to one state do not immediately spillover into other states. One might also want to impose a restriction on the long-run impact of monetary policy. While virtually all economists agree that monetary policy affects real activity in the short run, such as up to 2–3 years following a change in policy, some mainstream macro models suggest that the effect eventually disappears at some longer horizon.

26.3.3 An example applied to US states

Our past work on the state-level effects of monetary policy provides an example of how we might apply the foregoing framework (Carlino & DeFina 1998, 1999a,b).

In our studies, we focused on quarterly data for real personal income at the state level during the period from 1958 to 1992. The VAR for a particular state consists of 13 variables: real personal income growth in the state; real personal income growth in the state's BEA region, less the state; real personal income growth in each of the remaining seven BEA regions; the quarterly change in the federal funds rate (as a measure of the change of monetary policy); and three variables to account for macroeconomic influences on state economies and Fed policy decisions. Concerning the latter three variables, the Bureau of Labor Statistics' "core" CPI (the official index less the effects of food and energy prices) captures underlying trends in the aggregate price level. The BEA index of leading indicators is employed as a parsimonious way of including a variety of macroeconomic real-sector variables. Finally, to account for aggregate supply shocks, we include an energy price variable in the system. This variable is calculated as the Producer Price Index for fuels and related products and power relative to the total Producer Price Index. It is especially important to account for energy price shocks, given the large changes that occurred during the period studied. Our study employs quarterly data for the period from 1958 to 1992. Four lags of each variable are included in each equation to allow for the strong possibility that changes in policy and other variables have prolonged effects on the system.

Studies using macroeconomic time series data such as ours confront a choice regarding how to handle nonstationary data. Typically macroeconomic variables are nonstationary; that is, they have means and standard deviations that change over time. The nonstationarity complicates both estimation and statistical inference. Several approaches have been developed, ranging from simple transformations such as taking the first difference of a variable's natural log (interpreted as a growth rate and which is generally stationary) to the more complicated techniques of cointegration (for a clear exposition of these issues, see Coulson, this volume). A natural alternative is to estimate the model in both levels and log first differences and check for sensitivity of the findings. We did that and found quite similar results. Our discussion therefore focuses on the first-differenced results.

Based on our selection of variables, we employ several restrictions. Each is motivated by practical consideration of time lags in the transmission of economic changes through the regions' economies:

- a state-specific shock affects only the state of origin contemporaneously, although it can spill over into other states with a one-quarter lag;
- Fed policy actions, shocks to core inflation, changes in the leading indicators, and changes in the relative price of energy are assumed to affect state income growth no sooner than with a one-quarter lag; and
- neither state income growth nor Fed policy actions contemporaneously affect changes in core inflation, in the leading indicators, or in the relative price of energy.

We also impose two sets of standard restrictions on the structural variance-covariance matrix:

- structural shocks are assumed to be orthogonal (i.e., the contemporaneous covariance between pairs is zero); and
- the variances of the structural shocks are normalized to unity.

There are several econometric software packages that allow easy estimation of a model such as ours. We used a standard procedure available in the RATS software package.

After estimating the coefficients of the VAR variables, the next step is to summarize the effects of monetary policy changes on state incomes in a way that captures the full dynamics of the system. A typical way to summarize the impact of monetary policy on personal income growth is to show how the level of real personal income in a state changes over time because of monetary policy surprises, or shocks.

Such shocks are measured by unanticipated changes in the federal funds rate; that is, the residuals of the model's federal funds rate equation. Unanticipated policy actions are most relevant in the analysis because anticipated actions will already have been reflected in state incomes, since individuals and businesses tend to be forward looking. Relying on anticipated changes might then lead to the incorrect conclusion that policy actions have no impact, when in fact the impact has occurred in an earlier period. The impact of unanticipated policy changes is measured by the gap between what real personal income in a state would have been without monetary policy action and what it turns out to be with the action. The gap is referred to as a cumulative impulse response.

26.3.4   State impulse responses

Figure 26.1 shows the cumulative impulse responses for each state resulting from a one-percentage-point increase in the federal funds rate. The model treats increases and decreases of the federal funds rate symmetrically, so that an unexpected cut in the funds rate temporarily raises real personal income relative to what it otherwise would have been. Moreover, given data limitations, we ignore any possible structural changes that might have occurred during the estimation period. State responses are grouped by major BEA region, and the weighted average of the state responses, labeled "U.S.," is included in each regional grouping as a benchmark.

Concerning the average response, real income exhibits a slight initial rise, followed by a substantial decline, subsequent to the policy shock. The maximum cumulative, or long-run, response occurs, on average, about eight quarters following the policy shock. Monte Carlo simulations (500 replications) performed on quarterly changes in each region's income growth indicate that these changes are significantly different from zero for the first eight quarters following a policy shock and insignificant thereafter. This result is also evident in the individual state cumulative responses shown in Figure 26.1, in that the effects of Fed actions tend to bottom out between eight and 10 quarters after the shock. This general profile is similar to the estimated impact of monetary policy changes on the US economy as reported in other studies for the national economy.

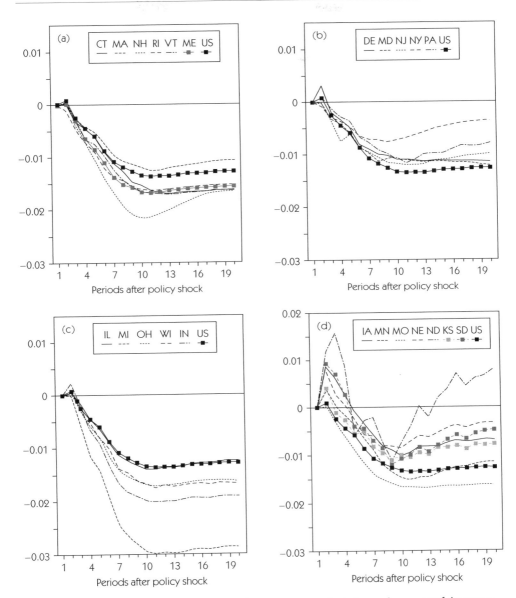

Figure 26.1 The cumulative impulse response of state real personal income to funds rate shock, grouped by major region: (a) New England; (b) Mideast; (c) Great Lakes; (d) Plains; (e) Southeast I; (f) Southeast II; (g) Southwest; (h) Rocky Mountains; (i) Far West.

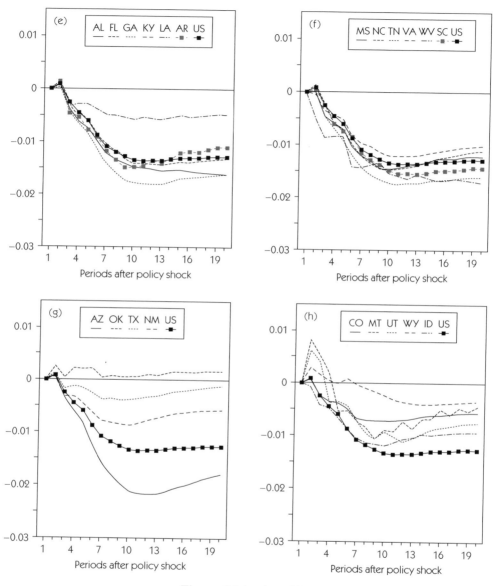

Figure 26.1   (*cont'd*)

The estimated state responses exhibit noticeable within-region and between-region variation at various horizons. For example, in the one to two quarters immediately following the policy shock, many states respond in ways that closely mirror the average response. Still, responses in a number of states, ones mainly located in the Plains and the Rocky Mountain regions, show considerable dispersion around the average. As the period after the shock lengthens, both within-region and between-region variation rise as the dynamics fully work

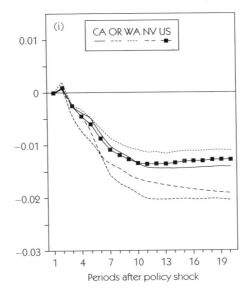

Figure 26.1   (*cont'd*)

through the system. In the long run, the real incomes in individual states gener-ally settle down as they approach their new lower levels.

Because the model treats tightening and easing of the federal funds rate sym-metrically, an unexpected cut in the funds rate temporarily raises real personal income relative to what it otherwise would have been. In our regional study, we found that changes in the federal funds rate have statistically insignificant long-run effects on the level of each region's real income. This finding is con-sistent with the widely held theoretical view that monetary policy actions have no lasting impact on real variables, such as real income and output. We did not conduct a formal test on the significance of the long-run state responses. How-ever, examination of these responses indicates that state personal income behaves similarly to regional income.

While the vast majority of all states' responses follow the general pattern dem-onstrated by the national average, not all states respond by the same magnitude (Table 26.4). Michigan has the largest response: real income fell 2.7 percent (com-pared to what it would have been) eight quarters after a one-percentage-point increase in the federal funds rate. This can be compared with a 1.16 percent decline for the nation. Seven states (Arizona, Georgia, Indiana, Michigan, New Hampshire, Oregon, and Tennessee) respond at least 38 percent again as much as the nation, on average. The standard deviation in the responses is 0.4684, and the seven most responsive states are at least one standard deviation above the aver-age state response.

Possible explanations for this high response include the fact that four of these states (Indiana, Michigan, New Hampshire, and Oregon) have a relatively high concentration of durable goods manufacturing, an interest-sensitive industry. One state (Arizona) has a much higher concentration of construction, another interest-

Table 26.4 Eight-quarter cumulative responses to a one-percentage-point federal funds rate increase (the response is in percentage points; the weight is the state's share of regional personal income)

New England

	Response	Weight
Connecticut	1.2678	0.29
Massachusetts	1.0712	0.47
Maine	1.5099	0.07
New Hampshire	1.9264	0.07
Rhode Island	1.4391	0.07
Vermont	1.4246	0.03

Mideast

	Response	Weight
Delaware	1.0018	0.01
Maryland	0.9174	0.10
New Jersey	1.0607	0.20
New York	0.7176	0.44
Pennsylvania	1.1379	0.25

Great Lakes

	Response	Weight
Illinois	1.2351	0.30
Indiana	1.8345	0.12
Michigan	2.6634	0.22
Ohio	1.5378	0.25
Wisconsin	1.4604	0.11

Plains

	Response	Weight
Iowa	0.8278	0.16
Kansas	0.9653	0.14
Minnesota	1.1982	0.25
Missouri	1.5282	0.29
Nebraska	0.8216	0.09
North Dakota	0.7427	0.03
South Dakota	0.8695	0.04

Southeast

	Response	Weight
Alabama	1.3261	0.07
Arkansas	1.3443	0.04
Florida	1.154	0.22
Georgia	1.6084	0.11
Kentucky	1.1599	0.06
Louisiana	0.4935	0.07
Mississippi	1.3004	0.04
North Carolina	1.3404	0.11
South Carolina	1.2816	0.05
Tennessee	1.5632	0.08
Virginia	1.022	0.12
West Virginia	1.3803	0.03

Southwest

	Response	Weight
Arizona	1.8006	0.13
New Mexico	0.8182	0.05
Oklahoma	−0.0741	0.13
Texas	0.361	0.69

Table 26.4 *(cont'd)*

Rocky Mountain	Response	Weight
Colorado	0.7134	0.50
Idaho	0.9573	0.13
Montana	0.8469	0.11
Utah	1.1396	0.19
Wyoming	0.1109	0.07

Far West	Response	Weight
California	1.1305	0.79
Oregon	1.7168	0.07
Washington	0.9757	0.12
Nevada	1.4356	0.03

Regional summaries

Region	Average response	Weight (% of nation)	Coefficient of variation	Max.–Min. (% average)
New England	1.26	0.06	0.14	0.68
Mideast	0.91	0.21	0.12	0.46
Great Lakes	1.72	0.18	0.09	0.83
Plains	1.14	0.07	0.12	0.69
Southeast	1.23	0.20	0.05	0.91
Southwest	0.52	0.09	0.21	3.60
Rocky Mountain	0.80	0.03	0.15	1.29
Far West	1.16	0.16	0.30	0.64
All regions	1.09	1.00	0.31	2.51

sensitive industry. While Georgia and Tennessee do not have especially high concentrations of interest-sensitive industries, they may have large markets for their products in the other states that are highly responsive to monetary policy shocks; therefore, they would tend to be more sensitive to monetary policy actions than their own industrial structure would indicate.

Seven states (Colorado, Louisiana, Oklahoma, New York, North Dakota, Texas, and Wyoming) are the least sensitive to monetary policy shocks, responding no more than 60 percent as much as the national average, or at least one standard deviation below. Interestingly, the total output of four of these states (Louisiana, Oklahoma, Texas, and Wyoming) includes a high concentration in the extractive industries. Although these states are found to be the four least sensitive to monetary policy actions, they are buffeted by other types of shocks, particularly shocks to the price of energy. For example, a one-percentage-point decrease in the growth rate of the relative price of energy in the four states leaves real personal income between 1.6 percent (Oklahoma) and 3.2 percent (Wyoming) lower than otherwise after 2 years. (Personal income fell 1.9 percent in Texas and 2.8 percent in Louisiana.)

By contrast, New Jersey, an energy-consuming state, experiences a rise in personal income of about 2.0 percent 2 years after a one-percentage-point decrease in the relative price of energy. We also found that Colorado, New York, and North Dakota tend to be less responsive to monetary policy shocks than the average state. One reason is that production in these states involves relatively smaller shares of interest-sensitive industries.

By using a weighted average of the responses of states within a region, we can form an average response for each of the eight major regions (See Table 26.4). The absolute value of these responses ranges from a low of 0.52 in the Southwest to a high of 1.72 in the Great Lakes; in terms of absolute value, the national average is 1.16.

Comparisons of states' responses to monetary policy actions reveal that an individual state's response is often quite different from the average response of its region and from the response of the other states in that region. For example, we found that real personal income in the Far West region fell 1.16 percentage points following a one-percentage-point increase in the federal funds rate, matching the average national response. However, two of the four states that make up the Far West region (Oregon and Nevada) are considerably more responsive to monetary policy shocks, and the other two states (California and Washington) are much less responsive than the average for the Far West region or the nation. Being part of a region that has a low response to monetary policy actions is no guarantee that each state in the region will respond similarly. Arizona responds more than half again as much as the US average despite being part of the least responsive Southwest region. In general, there is much less variation in regional responses to monetary policy shocks than in state responses. The standard deviation of the regional responses is 0.3574; state responses show a considerably larger standard deviation of 0.4684 for the state responses.

We also compared the differences in the responses to monetary policy actions within particular regions with the differences across regions using coefficients of variation. The coefficient of variation is defined as the ratio of the standard deviation of the state responses within a particular region divided by the average response of the states in the region. We found that the variation across regions is generally much greater than that within a region (shown in the penultimate column in the "Regional Summaries" section of Table 26.4). The Southeast region has the least within-region variation, while the Far West region has the most within-region variation.

Finally, it is worth noting that while we report our findings for real personal income, we obtain quite similar findings if we use data on quarterly employment instead of income. In addition, our findings also are robust to whether the data are expressed in growth rates (as discussed in this chapter) or in levels.

26.4   What Causes the Differential State Responses to Monetary Policy Actions?

Earlier, we identified three possible ways in which monetary policy actions could differentially affect state economies, including differences in the mix of industries (interest rate channel), firm size, and bank size (credit channel). How important are these factors in accounting for the different state responses to monetary policy innovations?

To answer the question, we use a standard cross-section regression analysis. The dependent variable is the absolute value of the estimated cumulative responses eight quarters following a policy shock (taken from the "Response" column of Table 26.4). These are regressed on state-level variables that proxy for the hypothesized explanatory factors. Two industry-mix variables are used: the percentage of a state's GSP accounted for by manufacturing (taken from Table 26.1) and that accounted for by extractive industries (not shown in Table 26.1). Recall that a state's share of total GSP accounted for by manufacturing is employed to capture state differences in interest sensitivity to monetary policy actions. The interest sensitivity of a state's industries is likely to rise with the percentage of a state's total output accounted for by manufacturing. Studies have shown that consumer spending on manufactured goods, especially durable goods, tends to be interest sensitive. Spending on services, in contrast, tends to vary little with interest rates. The share of a state's GSP accounted for by the extractive industries was included to reflect the significant dependence of energy-sector production on foreign economic developments. An inspection of the estimated cumulative responses indicates that states with large shares of extractive activity tend to have relatively small responses.

We used two variables to capture state differences in monetary policy actions that may operate through credit channels. The percentage of a state's firms that are small, defined as the percentage of a state's firms with fewer than 250 employees (taken from Table 26.2), captures the possible effects of firm size. To account for the bank size effects, we use two alternative variables: the percentage of a state's total loans made by the state's banks at or below the 90th percentile in assets nationally; and the percentage of a state's total loans made by the state's banks at or below the 90th percentile in assets nationally and not part of a bank holding company (both variables are taken from Table 26.3). The latter variable is used to control for the possibility that a bank can use its parent corporation as an alternative funding source during periods of tight credit. Because the estimated cumulative responses represent average behavior during the sample period, averaging the data for the explanatory variables is appropriate. Data availability limited averaging to the period from the mid-1970s to the early 1990s. Averaging also minimizes the chance that the results depend on the data for a particular year and helps control for business-cycle dynamics. Finally, we included dummy variables to account for region-specific fixed effects.

We find that the percentage of a state's GSP accounted for by manufacturing has a positive and significant relationship to the size of a state's cumulative response to Fed policy shocks, while the percentage of a state's GSP accounted for by its extractive industries has a negative and significant relationship. The importance of manufacturing share can be interpreted as evidence of an interest rate channel for monetary policy.

We find no evidence that cross-state variation in the mix of small versus large firms matters. States containing a larger concentration of small firms tend to be no more responsive to monetary policy shifts than states containing smaller concentrations of small firms. In contrast, we find weaker evidence that a region becomes less sensitive to a monetary policy shock as the percentage of small banks in the region increases. The estimated coefficient is negative and significant when the no-holding-company bank variable is used, but negative and insignificant when all small banks are used. In any event, the finding of a negative sign on the small bank variable is inconsistent with this aspect of the credit channel theory espoused by Kashyap and Stein (1994). If small banks largely make loans to small firms, this relationship would be captured by the small firm variable. There is moderate correlation between the small-firm variable and the small-bank variable (simple correlation of 0.5). This correlation helps to explain the lack of a positive response of the bank-size variable to changes in monetary policy, but not the estimated negative effect. One possibility for the inconsistency is that a bank's asset size may be a poor indicator of its ability to adjust its balance sheet to monetary policy actions. For example, it has been suggested that bank capital is a better indicator – better-capitalized banks have more and cheaper alternative sources of funds available (Peek & Rosengren 1995). It has also been pointed out that regional differences in the types of loans being made might also matter, a factor not controlled for in our study (Kashyap & Stein 1994).

26.5 Conclusion

Increasingly, macroeconomists have come to recognize that subnational economies, such as those of regions, states, and metropolitan areas, are useful laboratories for the examination of macroeconomic theory and policy. For example, recent theoretical work suggests that credit channels may be an important way in which monetary policy actions are transmitted to economic activity, distinct from the generally accepted channel operating through interest rates. Since the variables that proxy for the credit channel differ across states, state-level data provide a useful test of whether a credit channel for monetary policy exists. We find that state differences in the mix of large versus small firms and large versus small banks do not account for the differential state responses to monetary policy actions in the fashion suggested by proponents of a credit channel. Although credit channels may be important at the firm level, they do not appear to be important in the aggregate.

Bibliography

Ball, L. 1994: What determines the sacrifice ratio? In N. G. Mankiw (ed.), *Monetary Policy*. Chicago: The University of Chicago Press.

Barro, R. and Sala-i-Martin, X. 1992: Convergence. *Journal of Political Economy*, 100, 223–51.

Baumol, W. 1986: Productivity growth, convergence, and welfare: what the long-run data show. *American Economic Review*, 76, 1,072–85.

Bernanke, B. S. 1993: Credit in the macroeconomy. Federal Reserve Bank of New York *Quarterly Review*, Spring, 50–70.

—— and Blinder, A. S. 1988: Credit, money and aggregate demand. *American Economic Review, Papers and Proceedings*, 78, 435–9.

Blanchard, O. and Katz, L. 1992: Regional evolutions. *Brookings Papers on Economic Activity*, 1, 1–69.

Blank, R. and Card, D. 1993: Poverty, income distribution, and growth: Are they still connected? *Brookings Papers on Economic Activity*, 2, 285–339.

Carlino, G. A. and DeFina, R. 1998: The differential regional effects of monetary policy. *Review of Economics and Statistics*, 80, 572–87.

—— and —— 1999a: The differential effects of monetary policy: evidence from the U.S. states. *Journal of Regional Science*, 39, May, 339–58.

—— and —— 1999b: Do states respond differently to changes in monetary policy? *Business Review*, Federal Reserve Bank of Philadelphia, July/August, 17–27.

—— and Mills, L. O. 1993: Are U.S. regional incomes converging? A time series analysis. *Journal of Monetary Economics*, 32, 335–46.

Gertler, M. and Gilchrist, S. 1993: The role of credit market imperfections in monetary transmission mechanism: arguments and evidence. *Scandinavian Journal of Economics*, 95, 43–64.

Kashyap, A. K. and Stein, J. C. 1994: The impact of monetary policy on bank balance sheets. National Bureau of Economic Research Working Paper 4821.

Oliner, S. D. and Rudebusch, G. D. 1995: Is there a bank lending channel for monetary policy? Federal Reserve Bank of San Francisco *Economic Review*, 2, 2–21.

Peek, J. and Rosengren, E. 1995: The capital crunch: neither a borrower nor a lender be. *Journal of Money, Credit, and Banking*, 27, 625–38.

CHAPTER TWENTY-SEVEN

Measuring and Analyzing Urban Employment Fluctuations

N. Edward Coulson

27.1 INTRODUCTION

CITIES ARE NOT JUST LITTLE VERSIONS OF THE NATION National economies experience cyclical behavior; they rise and fall, have booms and recessions. From this, we can make the obvious inference that the geographical components of a national economy – regions, states, and cities – must also experience cyclical or other types of temporal variation. After all, the nation is the sum of its parts, and if the sum rises and falls, it logically follows that the parts must do so as well.

However, it does not follow that the parts must rise and fall in concert. Regions, states, and metropolitan areas may rise and fall at different times, with different frequencies, with different intensities, and for different reasons. Therefore, analysis of a nation's geographical subeconomies is of interest, since these regions, states, and cities do not simply follow national trends; each place has its own unique characteristics that manifest themselves in behavior that differs both from that of the nation as a whole, and from that of other areas.

In keeping with the theme of this volume, I concentrate on city – technically, metropolitan statistical area (MSA) – employment, although much of the discussion below could apply to larger or smaller geographical entities and to other measures of city growth, such as total earnings. And as witness to both the similarities and differences in cities' growth and change over time, examine Figure 27.1, which

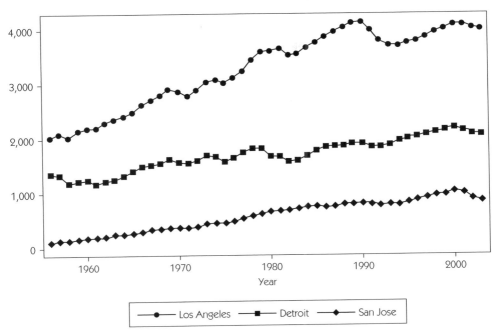

Figure 27.1 The time series behavior of total employment (thousands) in
San Jose, Los Angeles, and Detroit.

merely plots the time series of total MSA employment for three different US
cities: Los Angeles (California), Detroit (Michigan), and San Jose (California),
over the period from 1956 to 2002 (like all of the data used in this chapter, this is
downloaded from the website of the United States Bureau of Labor Statistics;
www.bls.gov). There are a number of facts that can be gleaned from the comparison of these three cities:

1 All three of the areas have employment that is trending upward over time,
   although the rate at which they do so certainly varies across cities and over
   time within cities. This is true even of nominally "no-growth" cities such as
   Detroit.
2 Some cities, such as San Jose, seem almost recession-proof. Unlike Detroit and
   Los Angeles, San Jose experienced no sustained period of job loss until around
   the turn of the millennium.
3 The downward cycles experienced by cities that are cyclically sensitive (such
   as Detroit and Los Angeles) are to a certain extent coincident with each other
   and with what is happening in the nation as a whole. Both cities lost ground
   during the national recessions of the mid-1970s and early 1980s, although the
   severity and timing of the downturns were rather different. The employment
   declines in Detroit from about 1979 through 1983 were not exactly coincident

with Los Angeles' response to the same national phenomenon, since employment in Los Angeles was merely flat during the first part of this period. And all three cities exhibited similar declines in employment beginning in the early months of the year 2000.

4   But the cycles exhibited in Figure 27.1 also reveal substantial differences across cities. A notable difference is that Los Angeles experienced a very substantial fall in employment from around 1989 through 1994. This fall was not particularly experienced by either of the other cities, although neither Detroit nor San Jose had particularly robust growth either. As noted in the above point (3), the three cities had very different reactions to the national downturns of the early 1980s. And Detroit experienced rather strong negative employment changes at the beginning of the sample period in the late 1950s.

Of these four points, the most important one is the last. Cities are worth studying in their own right because they are different from one another. While they are only partly different – because they are certainly influenced by the broad movements of the national economy in which they are situated – it is of interest to delineate the sources of fluctuations that city-economies endure. This question is of importance for many reasons, not least of which is that local policy-makers, faced with a declining local economy, only have local tools at their disposal. If the local fluctuations are merely a reflection of a national phenomenon, there may not be anything they can do. But point (4), and the evidence in more elaborate studies discussed below, inform us that this is not the case.

In this chapter, a couple of different methods are proposed for dissecting, analyzing, and to a certain extent forecasting urban fluctuations. In that effort, I will emphasize the use of "traditional" tools of urban economics, and will also make some mention of more sophisticated statistical apparatus from time series/regression analysis. The literature is large, and the literature on time series modeling is vast beyond all reckoning. I therefore have chosen to concentrate on two issues that are at the center of the study of metropolitan fluctuations: (a) the role of city-industry fluctuations in influencing aggregate city employment fluctuations; and (b) the sources of fluctuations of particular city-industries. The concentration on these two issues is convenient for three reasons:

THE WHOLE (AGAIN) IS THE SUM OF ITS PARTS   Just as national fluctuations can be seen as the sum of what happens in its regions or cities, city employment is the sum of the employments in the individual industries. Thus the topics that are reviewed in this chapter concentrate on the role of city-industries. And because these city-industries do not behave in identical ways merely because they are located in the same area, they are worthy of study as individual entities.

CITIES ARE DIFFERENT FROM ONE ANOTHER BECAUSE OF THEIR INDUSTRIAL MIX   There is one obvious way that cities differ, one that could very well cause all of the differences observed in Figure 27.1, and that is the composition of the city's industrial base. All three cities have economies that rely to a large extent on manufacturing (larger than other major cities, anyway), but manufacturing of very different types. As is well known, Detroit's economy is largely based on manufacture of motor vehicles and their parts, and other enterprises closely related to the auto industry. Los Angeles also has had a presence in a number of manufacturing sectors, particularly aircraft and media. San Jose has benefited from being the location of Silicon Valley and the associated high tech sectors. Thus, returning to Figure 27.1, one's presumption might be that San Jose's uninterrupted growth might be due the strong demand for its product as the "high tech" revolution unfolded. Detroit might be hurt by its reliance on cyclically sensitive industries such as automobiles, in the sense that its employment cycles are more volatile; that is, more responsive to changes in (for example) interest rates. Thus its growth is not uninterrupted.

HISTORICAL PRECEDENT   Much of the earliest work on metropolitan fluctuations emphasized the city-industry, and used models that, while perhaps simple in their technical demands, often proved very insightful and powerful in their analysis. Moreover, all of them provide insight into the two topics on which this chapter concentrates. They include base multipliers, location quotients, and the shift-share decomposition. Moreover, not only do they remain as useful tools, but it turns out that the ideas behind them can be molded into more sophisticated forms using the time series tools at our disposal today.

The chapter proceeds next with a discussion of the relationship between an area's key industries and its total employment, with a discussion of the relationship between the two as described by the base multiplier model. In section 27.3 we then proceed to analyze the sources of fluctuations in those key industries, using the shift-share model as a cornerstone. In both instances, regression and time series based approaches to these two issues are also discussed. Section 27.4 concludes.

27.2 INDUSTRY SOURCES OF METROPOLITAN EMPLOYMENT FLUCTUATIONS

27.2.1 The base multiplier

Figure 27.2 plots three series: total employment in the Detroit MSA, and employment in Detroit's automobile manufacturing and construction sectors. The introduction suggests that cities rise and fall because the industries located there rise and fall – and that this is a matter of arithmetic as much as it is economics. The figure attests to this: there is a great amount of commonality in the business cycle properties of these three series – they all rise and fall at roughly the same time. But conventional wisdom would suggest that Detroit's economy is driven not by its construction sector, but by what happens to Ford and General Motors. What evidence, other than this conventional wisdom, do we have for saying that the Detroit economy depends on the fortunes of the latter and not the former? The answer lies in the timing. Each of the series declines for a short period in the mid-1970s, and then begins to rise out of the resultant employment trough. But

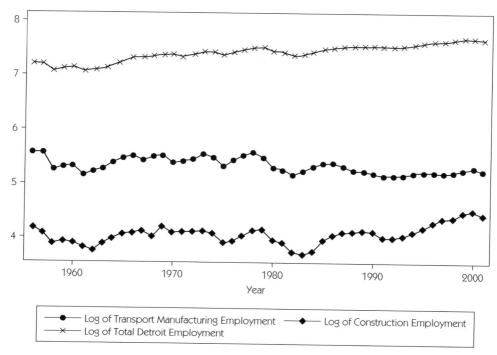

Figure 27.2 The time series behavior of (the logarithm of) total Detroit employment, construction industry employment in Detroit, and transportation manufacturing employment in Detroit.

each hits bottom and begins climbing out of the trough in slightly different months. The auto industry goes first: it hits bottom in January of 1975, and the aggregate employment series only finds its trough in March of the same year. The construction industry in Detroit continues to lose employment until early 1976.

The timing of these three series' troughs is exactly repeated in the downswing of the early 1980s. Employment in the automobile industry is on a broad downward swing through November of 1982, while the overall economy only reaches the bottom in February of 1983, and the construction industry only in March of the same year.

We can therefore see that the automobile industry leads the aggregate metropolitan economy, while the construction industry lags it. Autos are an important "leading indicator" in Detroit, while construction is the "follower." The difference between the automobile industry in Detroit and the construction industry in Detroit is straightforward to discern. The market for the first is largely external (it is an exporter), while the market for the second largely internal to the city – it is a local-serving industry. When someone buys a car from Detroit, the money acts as a stimulus to the local economy: the workers get wages, which they spend mostly in the local economy: on visits to the doctor, or dry cleaners, or on new housing. The construction industry expands in great measure as a result of this demand for Detroit's cars. But it doesn't stop there. The growth in the local economy then re-stimulates demand for all of these other locally produced goods and services, and this income gets spent and re-spent by the doctors and the dry cleaners and the construction workers on more medical services and dry cleaners and housing. The initial stimulus from the auto sector has a *multiplier effect* on the local economy.

If all of this sounds familiar, it is because it is identical in spirit to the most simple of all "Keynesian" models of the aggregate national economy. And the formal modeling of this simple process is nearly identical as well. Employment in a metropolitan area is divided into two parts, one consisting of firms serving the *local* market and another composed of firms which have an export orientation – the word "export" here does not imply international trade, but merely sales to customers outside the metropolitan area. Such firms and industrial sectors are called the economy's *base*, and their employment is called *basic* employment. So we have

$$E = B + L, \tag{27.1}$$

where E is the total employment in a metropolitan area, B is basic employment, and L is local employment. Local employment is assumed to be generated by local demand. A certain percentage of earnings in the metropolitan area is assumed to be spent locally, some is spent on imported items, and some is not spent at all. To simplify the presentation, all spending is assumed to translate at a constant rate to employment, and so

$$L = (b - c)E, \tag{27.2}$$

where b is marginal propensity to consume and c is marginal propensity to import. Again, "import" does not necessarily mean international trade, only the direct purchase of goods and services from outside the MSA. Employment in local-serving industries is a proportion of local employment and that proportion is $(b - c)$, the "propensity to consume from local establishments." Thus we assume that $0 < c < b < 1$. Basic employment, B, is assumed to be exogenous. By exogenous, we may simply mean "determined by forces outside the city," although in more sophisticated setups this may not be a strong enough assumption. In any case, the equilibrium in this model (from combining equations (27.1) and (27.2)) is obviously

$$E = (1 - (b - c))^{-1} B = MB \tag{27.3}$$

and $M = (1 - (b - c))^{-1} > 1$ is the *base multiplier*. The logic is simple. An increase in basic employment (such as auto production) provides an autonomous injection of income into a city from outside. That directly raises E, and this rise in total employment induces an increase in local employment L, but by a smaller amount (since $b - c < 1$). Because of this, a further rise in E occurs, and then additional, though smaller, increases in L, and then E again, and so forth. Thus the original, one-shot rise in B engenders an infinite, though summable, series of increases in E, and the sum of these increases is given in equation (27.3). Every increase in exogenous exports eventually yields an M-multiple increase in the local economy.

This power of exports to stimulate local economies is often cited in the media in reports such as this:

> According to U.S. Fish and Wildlife Service economist Jim Caudill, expenditures by trout fishermen in the Southeast have a tremendous effect on local and regional economies. More than $107 million a year is spent directly on fishing, rising directly from six national fish hatcheries that produce trout. That money, in turn, generates another $212 million a year in related spending. (www.espn.com)

We can see that in the above calculations that Mr Caudill has used a multiplier of 2.98. The initial injection of $107 million is spent in the local economies that host the fisheries, and is then re-spent in such a way that triples the impact on the local areas.

27.2.2   Calculating the multiplier

But how does one know the value of the multiplier? The most common way is not to try to calculate b and c but, rather, to work backwards. Note that $M = E/B$, and that E, total employment, is a known quantity. Thus, if a calculation of B can be made, we can determine M. This is difficult, because B is employment devoted to supplying export demand, and direct data on exports at the local level are hard to come by. We take a sectoral approach, taking B as the sum of basic employments for individual sectors. Then we might ask of each sector whether it is a basic, export, sector or one whose demand arises locally. Such a bifurcation into two categories of demand is, of course, simplistic – many sectors receive significant demand both locally and from outside the city, so we could more generally ask "What portion of the employment in each sector is devoted to export demand and how much to local?" and then add up all those portions to create a measure of the city's basic employment. In equation form, we can write this as follows:

$$B = \sum_i a_i E_i,\tag{27.4}$$

where E_i, $i = 1, \ldots, n$, is the sectoral employment for the ith industry, and a_i is the employment share of industry i that is devoted to exports. Since industry employment for the city is easily available (from www.bls.gov), the problem now becomes one of knowing what the a_i parameter is for each industry. For some industries, such as construction, that are for all practical purposes entirely local-serving, it is zero, and for others such as automobile manufacturing, a_i can usefully be approximated as one. But for some industries it is hard to know whether it is an exporter at all, and if so, to what extent. Take, for example, the financial services sector. In a well-known financial center, such as New York City or Charlotte, North Carolina, financial services might be a strong export sector for the city-economy. But a city such as Detroit might also have a banking industry that is at least a center of regional activity. Its financial service firms might export services to smaller areas such as Grand Rapids or Battle Creek. Location quotients can provide evidence on this issue.

27.2.3 Location quotients

The location quotient for a city-industry is calculated as the relative allocation of labor to a particular industry in the city and in the nation as a whole:

$$LQ_i = \frac{\dfrac{city\ employment\ in\ industry\ i}{total\ city\ employment}}{\dfrac{national\ employment\ in\ industry\ i}{total\ national\ employment}}. \tag{27.5}$$

The idea is that if the location quotient is greater than 1, then the proportion of employment that is devoted to industry i within the city is greater than that in the nation as a whole, and this is an indicator that the city is producing more than its share.

For the example of Detroit, the location quotients for the 10 "supersectors" in the Detroit employment data were calculated for the period 1994–2004. Of these 10, only two, professional and business services (pbs) and manufacturing, have location quotients consistently above 1 (at around 1.4 and 1.3, respectively). Thus we may tentatively conclude that these two industries are exporters for the Detroit MSA.

Having identified these two as export sectors, if we assign each of them an $a_i = 1$ (an option recommended in some cases by Tiebout 1962), we have

$$B = manufacturing\ employment + pbs\ employment \tag{27.6}$$

and we calculate the multiplier as $M = E/B$. This value is remarkably stable over the time period, between 2.80 and 3.05. Taking as a benchmark value for the multiplier of 3, this implies that the marginal propensity to consume locally (i.e., $b - c$) is about 2/3, which seems plausible.

We may not believe, however, that unity is the appropriate value of a_i, particularly in the case of professional and business service employment. Following the logic of the location quotient, we may alternatively reason that only that part of employment that brings the quotient above 1 is export, since that is the part that would seem to be "excess." This suggests that

$$a_i = \frac{LQ_i - 1}{LQ_i}. \tag{27.7}$$

Using this value for professional and business services employment, the definition of Detroit's base employment becomes

$$B = manufacturing\ employment + \frac{(LQ_{pbs} - 1)}{LQ_{pbs}}\ pbs\ employment \qquad (27.8)$$

and a multiplier between 4 and 5.

As can be seen, there can be substantial variability in the way in which the economic base and multiplier are calculated, and only the outlines of the methods have been presented. The researcher will need to particularize the method here to the specific city and purpose of the investigation. For more detailed advice about location quotients and determining an economic base, see Tiebout (1962), Richardson (1985), Brown, Coulson, and Engle (1992), and O'Sullivan (2003).

27.2.4 Causality tests – another way of identifying basic sectors

The base multiplier implies a causal relationship across the various city-industries – that increases or decreases in employment in export sectors cause similar changes in the local-serving sectors. The concept of causality is sufficiently slippery that figuring out whether one variable causes another, using statistical measures, is bound to be difficult. Granger (1969), in attempting to cut, like Alexander, through the Gordian knot of difficulties associated with the concept, provided a definition that is simplicity itself. A variable X is said to cause variable Y if consideration of variable X improves the forecast of Y in a statistically significant sense. Since the emphasis is on forecasts, this amounts to whether or not knowledge of X at time $t - 1$, (X_{t-1}) is statistically significant in a regression model of Y for time t, (Y_t). In practice, Granger causality tests – in this case, *bivariate* causality tests – are usually in the context of a regression equation of the following form:

$$Y_t = \beta_0 + \sum_{j=1}^{L} \beta_j Y_{t-j} + \sum_{j=1}^{M} \gamma_j X_{t-j} + e_t, \qquad (27.9)$$

so that, in words, Y is regressed on lagged values of itself and lagged values of the possibly causal variable, and the test-statistic is an F-test that the γ's are jointly equal to zero. Rejection of this hypothesis leads to the statement that X *Granger-causes* Y. Thus there is a direct connection between the past values of X and the present values of Y.

One must, of course, decide on the lag lengths, L and M. In practice, these are usually the same, and are set so as to eliminate serial correlation in the residual e_t or maximize a model selection criterion, such as adjusted R^2 or the Schwarz information criterion.

We can use Granger causality tests to provide insight on the export orientation of industries. We gather data (of slightly varying time spans) on month-to-month percentage changes in employment for the motor vehicle manufacturing, education and health services, and financial activities sectors. We then perform causality tests, letting each sector be paired with each other both in the role of the causal and caused variables in equation (27.9) – each assumes the role of X and Y with each of the other sectors. We enter this testing sequence in the belief that motor vehicle manufacturing is probably an export-serving sector, so that it has causal influence on the other two but they have no such impact on it. The other two seem like local-serving sectors, and so should be causally influenced by anything that impacts the local economy, including both increases in exports as well as other local-serving sectors.

These prior beliefs about the causal relations between industry employments turn out to be justified. The relevant test is on the F-statistic for the statistical significance of the γ's in equation (27.9). If this is small, then X has no "statistical significance" in predicting Y and we can say that X does not Granger-cause Y; but if the F-statistic is large, then the γ's are large (in a statistical sense) and we can say that X Granger-causes Y. When motor vehicle manufacturing plays the role of Y, it turns out that neither construction nor finance Granger-cause Y, which is consistent with manufacturing being an industry that derives its growth from exports (the probability values of the test-statistics are 0.49 and 0.323, respectively). However, when either finance or education and health services become the Y variable, we find that they are all Granger-caused by the other two local employment variables – the γ's are always statistically significant (at the 10 percent level or less, with probability values ranging from 0.01 to 0.09). This is consistent with their role as local-serving sectors, influenced by any local growth.

27.2.5   Cointegration

Many time series are *nonstationary*, or *integrated*, which means, roughly speaking, that when they move up or down in response to shocks to the economy, the effect is permanent; nothing forces them back to some long-run "natural" level, and they wander pretty freely over time. As Figures 27.1 and 27.2 suggest, such a property seems to be true of regional employment series. For statistical reasons, this makes such series rather hard to analyze, but tests for stationarity (such as the augmented Dickey–Fuller test) have been developed. Simplifying, these tests basically ask whether or not the series in question is a random walk; that is, whether the coefficient h in a regression

$$x_t = hx_{t-1} + \varepsilon_t$$

is equal to one (for a complete discussion, see Enders 2004).

However, Engle and Granger (1987) put forth the idea that while numerous individual series seem to have the property of integration, some series might be integrated in the same way because they are responding to the same shocks over time. Thus, while the series wander about, their *ratios* might be roughly constant over the long run. Engle and Granger call this property *cointegration* in a pair (or more) of time series.

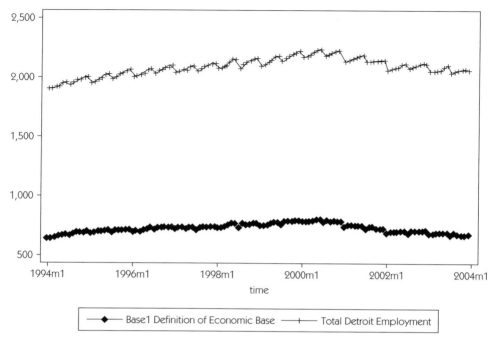

Figure 27.3 The time series behavior of aggregate Detroit employment
(TOTD) and the definition of basic employment (Base1).

Applying this to the issue at hand, Brown, Coulson, and Engle (1992) speculate
that the time series of basic employment, B, is cointegrated with total employment, because the ratio of the two, which of course is the multiplier M, may be
constant over the long run (although Pred (1966) notes that c may rise over the
very long run if a city grows and the range of firm types expands). Thus a test for
whether or not the correct B has been calculated is whether or not it is cointegrated
with E. These authors find, using employment data from the Philadelphia MSA,
that when all manufacturing sectors are assigned $a_i = 1$ and nonmanufacturing
sectors are assigned an a_i from the location quotient formula (27.7), that the
resulting B is cointegrated with E, and this method provides a coherent definition
of the employment base. Figure 27.3 indicates that something like this may be
true in the present example. In the figure, Base1 is the calculation of basic employment from equation (27.8). Note that both it and total employment in Detroit
rise gradually through about the year 2000 and fall in an equally gradual fashion
after that year, suggesting that their ratio might be cointegrated; that is, constant
in the long run. The test for cointegration is to run a regression of E on B and ask
if the residuals from this regression are stationary (as opposed to the *nonstationary*
variables E and B). Such a regression yields

$$Detroit\ Employment = 2.96 * Base\ Employment,$$

which indeed has stationary residuals, and suggesting a multiplier of 2.96. Every change in Detroit's export sectors creates a triple response in the economy as a whole. For further analysis of the relation between cointegration and the base multiplier model, see Brown, Coulson, and Engle (1992), LeSage (1990), and Cutler, Englund, and Weiler (2003).

27.3 SOURCES OF FLUCTUATIONS IN INDUSTRY EMPLOYMENT AT THE CITY-INDUSTRY LEVEL

Having established the link between a city's basic and local sectors, we turn our attention to the analysis of individual sectors. A traditional method for analyzing the trends in employment or earnings is the "shift-share" model (an early source is Dunn 1960), which breaks down employment growth (or decline) using a four-part decomposition (Emmerson, Ramanathan, and Ramm 1975; Coulson 1993):

$$\Delta e_{it} = \Delta n_t + (\Delta i_{it} - \Delta n_t) + (\Delta e_t - \Delta n_t) + (\Delta e_{it} - \Delta e_t - \Delta i_{it} + \Delta n_t), \qquad (27.10)$$

where all of the lower-case symbols represent logarithms, and so the Δ's indicate percentage changes, or growth rates. The notation is as follows: e_{it} is local employment in industry i at time t, e_t is aggregate local employment at time t, i_{it} is national employment in industry i at time t, and n_t is aggregate national employment at time t.

The first component of the decomposition is the *national component*, which predicts employment change in the local industry based only on national factors. If the local industry in question were an average industry in an average city, this part of the component would predict Δe_{it} perfectly. Thus it estimates the contribution of national growth to the growth in the local industry. The second component is the *industry component*. This will be positive or negative according to whether the national growth rate in industry i is greater than or less than that of aggregate national employment, and so measures the (national) industry-specific contribution to local industry growth. The third component is the *aggregate share component*. As it is the deviation of aggregate local growth from aggregate national growth, it measures the contribution of overall local factors (particularly the effect of being in a localized boom or recession) to the growth of the local industry. The fourth component is the percentage change in the *location quotient*, which, as the residual from the other three components, is the contribution to growth that is attributable to factors that are specific to the local industry itself. For convenience, we can now rewrite the decomposition as

$$\Delta e_{it} = N_t + I_{it} + AS_t + LQ_{it}. \qquad (27.11)$$

It is natural, though not completely straightforward, to assign supply and demand interpretations to these components. How you interpret the national component, for example, depends on your views of the sources of national economic fluctuations. If you don't mind a bit of caricature, let's say you're a

Keynesian, and you think that employment fluctuations arise from changes in aggregate demand. Then you will think that the national component measures the effect of demand swings on your local industry. As Keynesianism was the milieu in which the shift-share model came of age, this has meant that the demand-side interpretation has been predominant.

More difficult is the interpretation of the industry component. A demand-oriented interpretation is available if an industry is subject to overall declining or rising demand relative to the aggregate. If demand for financial services has risen over the years (throughout the nation), then a local finance sector may have expanding employment even when other parts of the city-economy are faltering, and the industry component will be expected to measure this. But the deviation between industry and national growth rates may be due to supply-side considerations (as when the national steel industry's rising costs and aging capital stock cause the market to shift overseas).

The AS component is the difference between the city's overall growth rate and the national overall growth rate. Thus it seems to be mainly driven by local demand changes: when a city grows faster than the nation as a whole, this will drive up demand for many local-serving sectors, even if those sectors are faltering at the national. Thus, all sectors in Las Vegas, even anemic ones, are experiencing positive growth, if only because they are located within a fast-growing metropolitan area.

Finally, if the AS component reflects the overall effect of local demand, this implies that the LQ component is mainly supply-side driven. The location quotient is a "difference in difference": it takes the industry component at the national level and subtracts it from a "local industry component"; that is, $\Delta e_i - \Delta e$. The location quotient will be positive whenever an industry outpaces the city-economy by more than its national counterpart is outpacing the national economy or, equivalently, when the city produces an increasing share of output in an industry over and above the city's own growth. It is unlikely that this is a demand-side phenomenon, as this would imply a large shift in local tastes that are not reflected in national taste shifts. A far more likely possibility is that a city is getting more (or less, if there is a negative LQ) productive in that sector.

As an example, consider the manufacturing sector in Detroit over the period June 1997 through June 1998. To provide context, note that the employment change for this city-industry is from 373,400 to 393,600, an increase of 20,200 jobs, or 5.2 percent (as measured by logarithmic differences). The national growth rate over the same year was 2.6 percent. If Detroit manufacturing were only dependent on national (demand) trends, it also would have grown at the same 2.6 percent. If that were all that mattered, this national component would have translated into about 9,600 jobs. But the actual growth is greater than that, so something else must be having an impact. But it is not national trends in manufacturing, since national employment in the manufacturing sector is only about 1.2 percent over this time period, so that the industry component is –1.3 percent. If Detroit's manufacturing sector were an "average" manufacturing sector, it would have exhibited similar trends, and *lost* about 4,900 jobs relative to national trends. Now, since the overall growth rate in Detroit was roughly the same over the

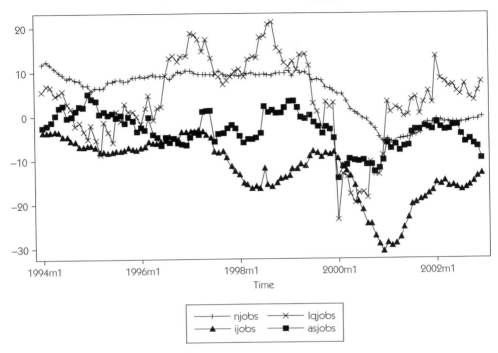

Figure 27.4 The four components of the shift-share decomposition for the Detroit manufacturing sector, in terms of number of jobs created or lost.

year, the aggregate share component is tiny: 0.4 percent, which translates into about 1,500 extra jobs. That still does not fully account for the employment change that is observed. We see that the location quotient is the largest of the four components, at 3.6 percent, which accounts for roughly a 13,400 increase. These add up to the total observed change, as they must. We infer that the growth in Detroit manufacturing can be most attributed to growth in the national economy and factors specific to manufacturing enterprises in Detroit, both of which helped to overcome national downturns in the manufacturing sector and a neutral local economy.

Figure 27.4 plots out the time series of all four manufacturing shift-share components converted (for ease of presentation) to "number of jobs" over the period 1994–2003. As can be seen in the figure, over the decade the national and *LQ* components comprise the strongest contributors to manufacturing job growth in the MSA. The aggregate share component is for the most part unimportant, and the (manufacturing) industry component is a drag on this sector. Thus, the strength of the sector revolves around national demand and local productivity factors.

Note that both of these factors begin to decline in the early part of the new century, when at some moments in time all four become negative. Thus we can view Detroit's decline at this time (as viewed, for example, in Figures 27.1 or 27.3) as resulting from the loss in strength in the national economy and from concurrent, negative supply-side factors in the MSA itself. This then rebounded to the rest of the local economy through the multiplier process, which is manifested in Figure 27.4 in the subsequent sharp decline in the *AS* component (which measures Detroit's total performance relative to the USA). Note, however, that the *LQ* component begins to rise sharply in late 2000; this is a signal of rebound in the local manufacturing sector, which again, through the multiplier process, should have a positive impact on the local aggregate economy. Thus the *AS* component begins a sharp upward movement a number of months later. Note that this is all occurring even as the national and industrial components continue their downward trends through early 2002.

27.3.1   Vector autoregressions

The shift-share model has the fault that it views the four components as arising independently of one another. That may be too naive. There are some indications that they can affect one another. For example, Figure 27.4 seems to exhibit some co-movement between the location quotient component and the national component. This might arise for several reasons; in any case, it is possible that a more sophisticated view is required.

In order to better understand the sources of industry fluctuations within a city, one can set the shift-share decomposition into a vector autoregression (VAR) framework. A VAR is nothing more than the simultaneous estimation of multiple time series models with a few special properties. In our case, the VAR is a set of regression equations:

$$e_{1t} = A_1 e_{1t-1} + B_1 e_t + C_1 i_{1t-1} + D_1 n_{t-1} + v_{1t},$$

$$\vdots$$

$$e_{it} = A_i e_{it-1} + B_i e_t + C_i i_{it-1} + D_i n_{t-1} + v_{it},$$

$$\vdots \tag{27.13}$$

$$e_{kt} = A_k e_{kt-1} + B_k e_t + C_k i_{kt-1} + D_k n_{t-1} + v_{kt},$$

$$e_t = e_{1t} + \ldots + e_{it} + \ldots + e_{kt}.$$

A key element of this system of regression models, and of VARs generally, is that each of the components of the shift-share decomposition is regressed only on *past values* of these same elements. The system above is limited to one lag each, but longer lags are easily accommodated in the model. That the regressors are limited to *lags* of the system variables is key to the structure of VARs, for two reasons. First, this means that each of the equations is ready-made to use as a forecasting model. One can estimate the equation's parameters (α, β, γ, δ) using historical data and then at any point in time, t (say, 2006), use known values of the variables from time $t - 1$ (say, 2005) to forecast ahead the value for time t. Second, the use of lagged values means that one can finesse the problem of *simultaneity.* One does not (usually) need to worry about endogenous regressors when those regressors are lagged values. Also, the fact that the set of right-hand side variables is the same across equations means that no special care need be taken if the residuals on the right-hand side are correlated across equations. Under normal circumstances, one would have to employ the method of *seemingly unrelated regressions* when faced with such correlation, but it turns out that under the circumstance just described, ordinary least squares regressions are numerically identical to the other technique.

So, now one can gather a set of time series data on (say) the Detroit manufacturing sector, and run four regressions. The coefficients are usually too numerous to make sense of, so the information is often displayed in the form of *impulse response functions.* Imagine that, for whatever reason, something shocks the national economy in an unpredictable way so that v_1 increases by one percentage point. Obviously, n_t rises by the same amount. Because all four components are seen to react to the national component with a lag, the next month all four of them rise by the amount of the coefficient – LQ_t by α_4, AS_t by α_3, and so on. And then each of them affects each of the others in the next period, and so on and so on. The summing and tracing out of all these impacts arising from the initial shock is what comprises the impulse response function. For example, Figure 27.5 gives the impact of the shock to N_t on the location quotient factor. As can be seen, the initial effect of a 1 percent rise in N is a 3 percent increase in LQ over the next 6 months. This impact slowly dies off after about 2 years. A thorough examination of the impulse response functions can provide a clear picture of how the various national and local factors combine to affect local employment trends.

Coulson (1993) used a system similar to that of equations (27.13) to analyze local employment growth in various sectors of the Philadelphia economy. In a

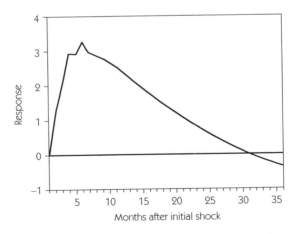

Figure 27.5 The impulse response function of the Detroit manufacturing location quotient to a shock to the national component of the shift-share decomposition.

result that echoes the Detroit patterns discussed above, he found that employment movement is mostly a function of local supply side factors, with national economic factors being the next most important source of local fluctuations. This was especially the case when allowances were made when some of the other restrictions that are embedded in the shift-share framework were loosened in the translation of the shift-share model to a VAR framework. Other studies have used VARs with national and industrial components to estimate the effect of these factors on local industry. Coulson and Rushen (1995) used two measures of technology shocks in order to delineate the role of "high tech" sectors in the Boston MSA. Blanchard and Katz (1992) and Partridge and Rickman (2003) looked at how employment and wages interact with one another at the state and local level in VAR models.

27.3.2   A synthesis of shift-share and multiplier models

Coulson (1999, 2001) proposed a synthesis of shift-share and multiplier models, which followed somewhat similar work for the national economy by Altonji and Ham (1990), Norrbin and Schlagenhauf (1988), and Horvath and Verbrugge (1995). The model is a VAR composed of an equation for each city-industry and an identity that set metropolitan employment as the sum of its industry employments:

$$e_{1t} = A_1 e_{1t-1} + B_1 e_t + C_1 i_{1t-1} + D_1 n_{t-1} + v_{1t},$$

$$\vdots$$

$$e_{it} = A_i e_{it-1} + B_i e_t + C_i i_{it-1} + D_i n_{t-1} + v_{it},$$

$$\vdots$$

$$e_{kt} = A_k e_{kt-1} + B_k e_t + C_k i_{kt-1} + D_k n_{t-1} + v_{kt},$$

$$e_t = e_{1t} + \ldots + e_{it} + \ldots + e_{kt}. \tag{27.14}$$

In this way, each industry employment was modeled with a reworking of shift-share components. Instead of the shift-share components, however, the employment data that enter into the construction of those components are entered directly. (Coulson (1993) established that this made some sense from a statistical point of view.) Then, each industry employment series was allowed to contribute its share to total employment in the city and this in turn provided more impetus to the multiplier process. One interesting output of this model is that it allows a measurement of the importance of each industry to overall growth, at least in the short run. In both Coulson (1999), which studied four diverse US cities, and Coulson (2001), which concentrated on Boston, manufacturing and government employment had the strongest multiplier effects, along with, in some cases, service industries. Carlino, DeFina, and Sill (2001) used a similar model, and added some extra structure to the model by employing insights from input–output analysis (Horvath and Verbrugge 1995). They also found that manufacturing and government employment had a substantial impact on overall employment growth, which is congruent with the idea that external stimulus through exports is important for city employment growth. All three of these papers echoed the earlier theme that local effects matter most strongly in the modeling of local employment.

27.4 CONCLUSIONS

Base multipliers and shift-share models have the important virtue that they are straightforward to implement and easy to understand. Despite, or perhaps because of, their simplicity, they do provide information about the processes that drive local economies and they have been rightly used on that account, and quite extensively, in policy discussions and decision-making. But because of their wide use, their limitations are often forgotten or ignored. Care must be taken whenever these issues are addressed, with the use of more elaborate models and techniques as the need arises. This chapter has attempted to provide an introduction to both.

Bibliography

Altonji, J. and Ham, J. 1990: Variation in employment growth in Canada. *Journal of Labor Economics*, 8, 198–236.

Blanchard, O. and Katz, L. 1992: Regional evolutions. *Brookings Papers on Economic Activity*, 1, 1–61.

Brown, S. J., Coulson, N. E., and Engle, R. F. 1992: On the determination of regional base and regional base multipliers. *Regional Science and Urban Economics*, 27, 619–35.

Carlino, G., DeFina, R., and Sill, K. 2001: Sectoral shocks and metropolitan employment growth. *Journal of Urban Economics*, 50, 396–417.

Coulson, N. E. 1993: The sources of sectoral fluctuations in metropolitan areas. *Journal of Urban Economics*, 33, 76–94.

—— 1999: Sectoral sources of metropolitan growth. *Regional Science and Urban Economics*, 27, 723–43.

—— 2001: Sectoral sources of the Massachusetts Miracle and other turning points. *Journal of Regional Science*, 41, 617–37.

—— and Rushen, S. 1995: Sources of fluctuations in the Boston economy. *Journal of Urban Economics*, 38, 74–93.

Cutler, H., England, S., and Weiler, S. 2003: Determining regional structure through cointegration. *Review of Regional Studies*, 33, 164–83.

Dunn, E. S., Jr 1960: A statistical and analytical technique for regional analysis. *Regional Science Association Papers and Proceedings*, 6, 97–112.

Emmerson, R., Ramanathan, R., and Ramm, W. 1975: On the analysis of regional growth patterns. *Journal of Regional Science*, 15, 17–28.

Enders, W. 2004: *Applied Economic Time Series*, 2nd edn. Hoboken, NJ: John Wiley.

Engle, R. and Granger, C. 1987: Cointegration and error correction: representation, estimation and testing. *Econometrica*, 55, 251–76.

Granger, C. 1969: Investigating causal relations by econometric models and cross-spectral methods. *Econometrica*, 37, 424–38.

Horvath, M. and Verbrugge, R. 1996: Shocks and sectoral interactions: an empirical investigation. Unpublished paper.

LeSage, J. 1990: Forecasting metropolitan employment using an export-base error-correction models. *Journal of Regional Science*, 30, 307–23.

Norrbin, S. and Schlagenhauf, D. 1988: An inquiry into the sources of macroeconomic fluctuations. *Journal of Monetary Economics*, 22, 43–70.

O'Sullivan, A. 2003: *Urban Economics*, 5th edn. New York: McGraw-Hill.

Partridge, M. and Rickman, D. 2003: The waxing and waning of regional economies: the chicken–egg question of jobs versus people. *Journal of Urban Economics*, 53, 76–97.

Pred, A. 1966: *The Spatial Dynamics of US Industrial-Urban Growth*. Cambridge, MA: The MIT Press.

Richardson, H. 1985: Input–output and economic base multipliers: looking backward and forward. *Journal of Regional Science*, 25, 607–61.

Tiebout, C. 1962: *The Community Economic Base Study*. New York: Committee for Economic Development.

PART VII

Quality of Life

Quality of Life

Urban areas both attract and repel people. Cities offer high-paying jobs, parks, museums, nightlife, and a seemingly infinite variety of consumer goods. They also offer crime, pollution, noise, difficult commutes, crowds, a reduced sense of community, and a greater transience of social relationships. Some people love urban life; others prefer to avoid even visiting cities. Even within urban areas, neighborhoods vary dramatically. Poverty-stricken, crime-ridden neighborhoods offer a striking contrast to beautiful, expensive neighborhoods with excellent schools and virtually no crime. It is probably this contrast between wealth and poverty that has led urban economists to be so interested in measuring and analyzing the quality of life both within and across urban areas. One of the most important roles of urban economists is to help design policies that help improve the quality of life for residents of urban areas.

The most common framework used by urban economists to measure urban amenities is the hedonic model. The hedonic approach, which is used to measure the implicit price of the components of a multidimensional product such as housing, has a long and rich empirical tradition. It was used in early studies to measure the implicit price of components of an automobile – weight, engine size, interior room, and so on. The hedonic approach has been used to measure the price of various attributes of a personal computer, and it is used by labor economists to measure compensating differentials for such labor-market characteristics as workplace safety. Urban economists most commonly use the hedonic approach in studies of the housing market. For example, suppose that we want to measure the value that urban residents place on school quality. House prices and rents can be expected to be higher in areas with good schools, because people will pay a premium to live in these areas. Of course, countless other factors also affect prices and rents, including the size and structural characteristics of homes and other characteristics of the neighborhood. After controlling for as many of these other characteristics as can be measured, the hedonic house price function allows us to place a monetary value on school quality, as revealed through the amount people pay for housing.

Sherwin Rosen (1974) developed the underlying theory of the hedonic approach in a classic article. One of Rosen's students, Jennifer Roback, extended his analysis by simultaneously modeling the housing and labor market (Roback 1982). One use of the approach is to develop an index of the quality of life across urban areas. For example, we can expect house prices to be high in cities with good climates, because people will pay a premium to live in an area with good weather. However, migration to these cities can also lower wages by increasing the supply of labor. Roback's model offers a way of combining the housing and labor-market effects of good weather and other amenities into a single measure of the willingness to pay to live in an urban area. Glenn Blomquist's essay, "Quality of Life," reviews this literature and shows how to estimate a quality of life index.

One of the most extensively studied urban amenities is clean air, usually through its opposite, pollution. Urban areas were once associated with dirty, nearly unbreathable, air that soiled buildings and damaged the health of city residents. Environmental regulations and the movement of heavy industry out of many cities have vastly improved the air quality of many urban areas. It sometimes surprises people, however, that the optimal level of pollution is not equal to zero, because it can be extremely costly to reduce pollution levels beyond some point. Matthew Kahn's essay, "Air Pollution in Cities," presents an overview of the economics of pollution in urban areas.

Although crime is a problem throughout the urban world as well as in rural areas, it is a particular concern in American cities. The ready availability of guns in the United States has helped produce an extraordinarily high murder rate. Although murder rates have fallen recently in the USA, they remain high, particularly in low-income neighborhoods with a large percentage of African-American residents. High crime rates have led to large expenditures on crime prevention and prisons. The essay by Stephen Raphael and Melissa Sills, "Urban Crime, Race, and the Criminal Justice System in the United States," documents these trends.

Many observers blame racial discrimination and prejudice for many of the USA's social problems. Race and poverty are closely linked in the USA. African-Americans are heavily concentrated in low-income areas of the inner cities, where crime rates are high, school quality is low, and access to areas of growing employment is poor. Other observers argue that the modern African-American ghetto is similar to the experiences of previous immigrants to urban areas. Immigrants have come to the USA in waves throughout its history. Each group tends at first to live within its own sharply segregated area. These ethnic enclaves offer familiarity and a network of social contacts. However, they also may restrict access to jobs and delay the eventual assimilation into the mainstream community. In some ways, the African-American experience is similar to this traditional pattern. The 1940s and 1950s witnessed a large migration of African-Americans from the rural south to northern cities. At first, these new urban residents were confined to inner-city ghettos. With the enforcement of Civil Rights laws, it no longer is clear how much of the continued segregation of African-Americans is voluntary and how much is a result of white prejudice and discrimination.

In his essay, "Ethnic Segregation and Ghettos," Alex Anas reviews some of the evidence on segregation in American cities. He uses bid-rent theory to analyze the pattern of land rent within a ghetto and across the ghetto boundaries. Anas does not confine his attention to US ghettos, pointing out that France has Algerian ghettos and Germany has Turkish ghettos. Muslim ghettos in India are often thought to arise from exclusion and discrimination. The link between this section and our earlier treatment of the spatial mismatch hypothesis is obviously a close one. Whether a ghetto arises from voluntary or involuntary forces, it may well restrict employment opportunities, because areas of rapid employment growth are likely to be far from ghettos. Prejudice and discrimination on the part of the majority population accentuate the negative effects of spatial concentration by making it even more difficult to exit the ghetto.

With all the attention paid to urban social problems, it should not be forgotten that cities offer enormous benefits as well. With higher wages and much improved employment opportunities, cities offer a much higher material standard of living than most rural areas. Cities offer variety and opportunity. Urban areas help stimulate innovation by bringing together highly skilled people in close proximity. They provide expanded opportunities to exchange ideas and a greater variety of social networks and cultural amenities, while somewhat paradoxically providing a sense of privacy and anonymity that may be lacking in less populous areas. The same agglomerative forces that make cities a good place to locate a firm make urban areas an exciting place to live and work.

Bibliography

Roback, J. 1982: Wages, rents, and the quality of life. *Journal of Political Economy*, 90(1), 257–78.

Rosen, S. 1964: Hedonic prices and implicit markets: product differentiation in pure competition. *Journal of Political Economy*, 82, 34–55.

Measuring Quality of Life

Glenn C. Blomquist

28.1   MONEY, QUALITY OF LIFE, AND URBAN AMENITIES

Life is good when quality of life is high. To many of us, an ideal quality of life index would measure a person's overall well-being; that is, an individual's total utility. An ideal index would depend upon things that money can buy. Traditional economic goods such as food and drink, shelter, clothing, transportation, and entertainment would be included among these things. An ideal index would depend also upon social, environmental, and perceptual dimensions of well-being. Moderate climate, fresh air, clean water, safe neighborhoods, good schools, and good government would be included among these things. Furthermore, an ideal, holistic index would depend on the way in which individuals and households combine marketed goods and services and environmental and community factors with their own time and energy to produce the things, such as happy homes, that give them utility directly and determine overall well-being.

Money income can be used as a metric to measure well-being. The logic is straightforward. More money relaxes the budget constraint and allows a person to purchase more things and achieve a higher level of utility. Not surprisingly, great attention is given to average incomes in different areas, with the underlying notion that households are better off where incomes are higher because they can buy more. For example, in Berger and Blomquist (1988), we used US Census data to compare household incomes, poverty rates, and unemployment rates across urban areas. We made these comparisons for households of different ages and races, and with and without children. Chambers of Commerce, elected officials, and others talk about the importance of jobs, and the accompanying income, to the well-being of individuals who live in the area.

Money income matters, for sure, but it is an imperfect measure of utility. In part, money income is imperfect because it does not measure the satisfaction that individuals and households derive from traditional market goods that are used to produce things that households really care about. In part, money income is imperfect because it does not directly measure the value of the social and natural environment in which the consumption of traditional market goods takes place. It is in this context that Sherwin Rosen (1979) developed an index of urban quality of life. His quality of life index is designed to measure the value of local amenities that vary from one urban area to another and even from county to county. These amenities are features of locations that are attractive, such as sunny, smog-free days, safety from violent crime, and well-staffed, effective schools. This index measures the monetary value of the bundle of amenities that households get by living and working in the area.

To Rosen and many urban economists, a quality of life index should measure the value of local amenities. While information about money incomes in urban areas is readily available, information about the value of amenities that households get to consume in areas is not. Rosen's quality of life index fills the gap. So, a tradition has developed in urban economics that quality of life means not overall well-being or total utility but, rather specifically, the value of the bundle of local amenities in various locations. Such a quality of life index cannot tell us if individuals in Denver, Colorado, at the foothills of the Rocky Mountains, are better off overall than similar individuals in Detroit, Michigan, in the northern Midwest, but it can tell us whether the amenities in Denver are preferred to the amenities in Detroit by the typical consumer/worker.

28.2   A Framework for Valuing Local Amenities

First, think of a simple, bland world in which everyone is the same in tastes, has the same job opportunities and financial assets, lives in similar housing, and consumes the same bundle of local amenities. Strictly, everything should be identical. Few of us would want to live in this dull world, but it will help to illustrate Rosen's framework for quality of life based on urban amenities. For everyone to be satisfied and remain living and working where they are, it must be true that no one has any incentive to move. If moving costs are negligible, so as to make people footloose, then wherever people live they must have the same level of overall well-being, or total utility.

Now, for some spice in our lives, introduce variety in the bundles of local amenities. Let some urban areas have warmer climates, some wetter, others dirtier air and water, some more crime, and other areas better schools. For everyone to be equally well off in this more stimulating world, each household must have the same utility, or someone who is not as well off moves. If there are local labor and housing markets, then when enough people move they affect these markets by changing the supplies and demands in the areas that they leave and the areas that they join. Rosen's fundamental insight is that households will be attracted to areas where there are good buys; that is, better combinations of amenities, wages, and housing prices. Combinations will be more attractive the better are the amenities, the higher are the wages, and the lower are the housing prices. In like fashion, households will be driven away from areas that are bad buys, until all combinations of local amenity bundles, wages, and housing prices everywhere are equally attractive. This concept of spatial equilibrium is central to urban and regional economics. All similar households will have the same total utility. Those who know finance will recognize this spatial equilibrium as a "no arbitrage" condition. In the end, no one can gain by moving from one market to another. Households that choose to live in high-amenity areas will pay for them with combinations of wages and housing prices that make the high-amenity areas more expensive. Households are forced to trade off money for the better amenity bundles. The combination of lower wages and higher housing prices is an implicit premium, or price, that households pay for choosing an urban area with more attractive amenities. It is this value of the local amenity bundle that Rosen and other urban economists call urban quality of life.

The formal framework for analyzing compensating differentials and quality of life was developed by Rosen (1979) and Roback (1982). In this equilibrium model of wages, rents, and amenities, consumer/workers with similar preferences and firms with similar production technologies face different local amenity bundles across urban areas. Spatial equilibrium in the model means that there is no incentive to move, because differences in wages and/or housing prices develop so as to require payments for locating in amenity-rich areas and provide compensation for locating in amenity-poor areas. The full implicit price of a specified amenity is the sum of the housing price differential and the (negative of the) wage differential. In Blomquist, Berger, and Hoehn (1988), we expanded this framework to incorporate agglomeration effects and used this form of the implicit price of amenities to create a quality of life index.

In this model, households derive utility from consumption of a composite good, local housing, and local amenities. Access to local amenities of any given city is through buying housing h in that urban area. Both the composite good and housing are purchased out of labor earnings. For simplicity, households have one unit of labor each, they sell to local firms, and they earn a wage w. Again for simplicity, all labor is alike and all income is labor income. In any given urban area, household well-being is

$$v = v(w, p; a),\qquad(28.1)$$

where $v(\cdot)$ is the indirect utility function reflecting the maximum utility that a household can obtain given the wages and amenities that it gets and the prices it pays. The letter p denotes the price of housing in the urban area, and a is an index of local amenities. The price of the composite good is fixed as equal to one and suppressed. Wages increase utility, $\partial v/\partial w > 0$, and the price of housing decreases utility, $\partial v/\partial p < 0$. An increase in local amenities will increase utility if a is an amenity (good) for consumer/workers, $\partial v/\partial a > 0$. An increase will decrease utility if a is a disamenity (bad) for consumer/workers, $\partial v/\partial a < 0$, and will not matter if a is not an amenity factor.

Firms produce the composite good by combining capital and local labor and production technology is constant returns to scale. For simplicity, the prices of the composite good and capital are fixed by international markets, and wages and prices are normalized on the price of the composite good. Wages and the price of housing are relative to the composite good. In any given urban area, unit production costs are

$$c = c(w;a),\qquad\qquad\qquad(28.2)$$

where c is the unit cost function for a firm and the price of capital is left implicit. If a is a production amenity, then costs to firms are lower to area firms, $\partial c/\partial a < 0$. If a is a production disamenity, then costs are higher for local firms, $\partial c/\partial a > 0$. Also, a may not affect firm costs. Movement of households and firms among urban areas influences wages and housing prices so that labor and housing markets clear. Spatial equilibrium exists when all households regardless of location experience a common level of utility, u^*, and unit production costs are equal to the unit production price. For any area, the set of wages and housing prices that sustains an equilibrium satisfies the system of equations

$$u^* = v(w,p;a),\qquad\qquad\qquad(28.3a)$$

$$1 = c(w;a).\qquad\qquad\qquad(28.3b)$$

Equilibrium differentials for wages and housing prices can be used to compute implicit prices of the amenities, f_i. By taking the total differential of equation (28.3a) and rearranging, the implicit price of any amenity i can be found as $f_i = (\partial v/\partial a_i)/(\partial v/\partial w)$. The full implicit price is as follows:

$$f_i = h(dp/da_i) - dw/da_i,\qquad\qquad\qquad(28.4)$$

where h is the quantity of housing purchased by a household, dp/da_i is the equilibrium housing price differential, and dw/da_i is the equilibrium wage differential. The full implicit price is a combination of the effects in the housing and labor markets. Comparative-static analysis of such a model shows that the signs of the housing price and wage differentials depend on the effect of the amenity factor on households and the effect of the amenity factor on firms. A pure consumption amenity, which does not have an effect on firms, is expected to have a full implicit price that is positive. It is the weighted sum of the differentials in the housing market and labor market that is expected to be positive. It is not necessary that both the housing prices are higher and the wages are lower in cities that are rich in the consumption amenity, but for the situation just described they will be. A variety of combinations are possible.

28.3   Quality of Life, Wages, and Rents
in Different Urban Areas

The variety of possible combinations of wages and rents for some specified quality of life and constant utility for consumer/workers is shown as the upward-sloping curve in Figure 28.1. Rents, the flow from asset values, are shown instead of housing prices. In different cities that have the same quality of life, consumer workers can experience the same overall well-being with high rents and high wages as in the upper right of the curve, with low rents and low wages as in the lower left of the curve, or other combinations of rents and wages along the

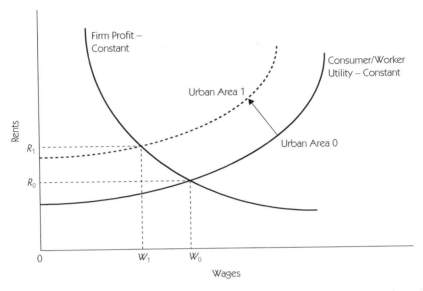

Figure 28.1 A comparison of wages and rents in two urban areas – location 1 has more consumption amenities than location 0.

constant-utility curve. The downward-sloping curve in Figure 28.1 shows the variety of combinations for some specified set of production amenities and constant (zero) profits for firms when rents are added to the cost function. In different cities that have the same set of production amenities, firms can experience the same profits with high rents and low wages as in the upper left part of the curve, low rents and high wages as in the lower right part of the curve, or other combinations along the constant-profit curve. The rent and wage observed for a typical residence and a typical worker is determined by the interaction of consumer/workers and firms and is the equilibrium combination shown as R_0 and W_0.

Now, let us consider comparing urban areas that have different amenity bundles. Figure 28.1 shows what happens when one area has more of a local amenity, such as a spectacular view of a mountain range, that is good for consumer/workers. Assume that the mountains are not amenities in any other way and that they do not affect firms. The presence of such a consumption amenity that increases quality of life is to shift the entire upward-sloping curve for consumer/workers up and to the left, as shown by the dashed curve. Because of better amenities, consumer/workers are now willing to pay combinations of higher rents and lower wages and remain just as well off as they were. In this case of a pure consumption amenity, the equilibrium rents will be higher ($R_1 > R_0$) and wages lower ($W_1 < W_0$) in the urban area with the better views. A comparison of rents for typical housing and wages for typical workers in the two urban areas would show the differences due to the difference in quality of life. Comparisons across many urban areas can be made more readily using a quality of life index.

28.4   A QUALITY OF LIFE INDEX FOR MAKING COMPARISONS

Comparison across a host of cities is facilitated by an index that aggregates local amenities using the differences in rents and wages. In Blomquist, Berger, and Hoehn (1988), the quality of life index (QOLI) for any urban area is as follows:

$$QOLI = \sum_i f_i a_i,\qquad\qquad(28.5)$$

where QOLI is the sum of the endowments of the amenities in the given urban area. Each amenity is weighted by its estimated full implicit price. The full implicit price is based on the wage and housing price differentials. As such, the QOLI is an estimate of the total compensation, or premium, for local amenities made through the housing and labor markets.

The dominant advantage of this type of index is that the weights for each of the amenities in the index are based on consumer/worker preferences, not the preferences of the authors. The weights are firmly grounded in economic theory. What we did in our study was choose a set of amenities that we thought would be salient enough for consumers in the housing market and workers in the labor market that they would affect rents and wages. The weights (f_i) can reflect the preferences of tens of thousands of residents and workers.

An alternative to valuing each of the observed amenities and aggregating to obtain the QOLI is to use the combined, total differences in wages and rents in the urban areas without trying to separate the differences attributable to specific amenities. This alternative does not attempt to estimate the weights for each amenity. Ranking is then based on the effect of the entire group of amenities in each urban area on wages and rents. The idea is that after typical housing characteristics, such as number of rooms, and usual worker characteristics, such as education, are accounted for, the differences in rents and wages must be due to differences in local amenities. Beeson and Eberts (1989) use this approach to identify urban areas that are rich in consumption amenities and production amenities. Gyourko, Kahn, and Tracy (1999) discuss the advantages of the observed amenities and group effects approaches. Their work also emphasizes the importance of local amenities, such as crime control, that are produced by local governments.

28.5   CONSTRUCTING A QOLI – STEP BY STEP

Let's think about how we construct a QOLI such as that shown in equation (28.5), where the index number for an urban area is the sum of the amenity endowment for each amenity (a_i) weighted by the full price of the amenity (f_i) over all the amenities in the index. The first step is to obtain data on housing prices and rents and housing characteristics and wages and worker and job characteristics in various urban areas. The locations of the residences and the jobs must be identified in the data. In Blomquist, Berger, and Hoehn (1988) we used microdata from the 1 in 1000 A Public Use Sample of the 1980 US Census of Population and

Housing. These data are collected from individual residents and individual workers and identify the urban county in which each is located. If someone wanted to update our study, similar data for Public Microdata Areas in electronic form are available from www.census.gov.

The second step is to augment the basic housing price and wage data with local amenities that must be matched to the locations of the individual residences and jobs. Matching these amenities by location is a lot of work. We collected data for 16 different amenity factors from a variety of sources. Urban conditions were represented by three variables. We obtained data on the violent crime rate from FBI crime reports, on the teacher–pupil ratio in public schools from the Census of Governments, and from the Census of Population and Housing we created a central city variable if the individual was located in the central city of an urban area. Crime data are now available at www.fbi.gov/ucr/00cius.htm. Climate was represented by seven variables that were available through the National Climatic Data Center, with one exception. Climate was represented by precipitation, relative humidity, heating degree days as a measure of cold, cooling degree days as a measure of heat, wind speed, prevalence of sunshine, and whether the urban county was on a coast. The last variable was created by consulting maps. If someone wanted to collect similar data for 2000, it is available at www.ncdc.noaa.gov. Environmental quality was represented by six variables that were based on data supplied from various sources at the US Environmental Protection Agency. Environmental quality for each urban county was measured by atmospheric visibility, total suspended particulates in the air, the number of National Pollution Discharge Elimination System dischargers for water, landfill waste quantity, the number of Superfund sites, and the number of Treatment, Storage, and Disposal sites. Environmental data can now be downloaded from www.epa.gov/STORET.

The third step is to estimate housing and wage hedonic regressions. We need to estimate these hedonic regressions in order to obtain estimates of the differences in housing prices due to the local amenities (dp/da_i) and the difference in wages due to local amenities (dw/da_i). If all housing were alike except for the local amenities, then we could easily find these differences by comparing averages, county by county. However, housing differs by living space, age, and other features. Similarly, workers differ in their training, experience, occupation, and other characteristics. Statistically, we control for the nonamenity factors in multiple regression so that we can isolate the influence of the amenities. The hedonic regression for housing is shown in Table 28.1. The dependent variable is monthly housing expenditures with owners and renters combined. Owner's value is converted to monthly imputed rent using a 7.85 percent discount rate. The table shows the coefficient for each of the 16 amenity factors, structural characteristics, and allows for differences between owners and renters. The hedonic regression for wages is shown in Table 28.2. The dependent variable is hourly wage. This table shows the coefficient for each of the same 16 amenity factors, and the characteristics of the worker and the job. Both sets of regression results are reported in linear form rather than for the Box–Cox power transformations that were used in estimation. The linear form is much easier to interpret. Anyone

Table 28.1 Housing hedonic regression: the dependent variable is monthly housing expenditures

Explanatory variable	Units	Mean	Coefficient
Amenities			dp/da
Precipitation	Inches per year	32.02	−1.047
Humidity	Percent	68.22	−2.127
Heating degree days	Degree days per year	4,223.0	−0.014
Cooling degree days	Degree days per year	1,185.0	−0.076
Wind speed	Miles per hour	8.872	11.88
Sunshine	Percentage of days	61.36	2.135
Coast	Yes = 1, no = 0	0.345	32.52
Central city	Yes = 1, no = 0	0.329	−40.75
Violent crime	Crimes per 100,000 population per year	681.60	0.043
Teacher–pupil ratio	Teachers per student	0.080	635.30
Visibility	Miles	15.66	−0.831
Total suspended particulates	$\mu g\ m^{-3}$	73.72	−0.535
Water effluent dischargers	Number per county	1.564	−7.458
Landfill waste	100 million metric tons per county	467.20	0.010
Superfund sites	Sites per county	0.858	13.43
Treatment, storage, and disposal sites	Sites per county	47.59	0.218
Other housing characteristics			
Units at address	Units	2.667	1.375
Age of structure	Years	23.73	−2.363
Height of structure	Stories	2.433	16.52
Rooms	Number	5.395	40.33
Bedrooms	Number	3.510	6.485
Bathrooms	Number	1.486	119.80
Condominium	Yes = 1, no = 0	0.032	−84.82
Central air conditioning	Yes = 1, no = 0	0.313	55.68
Sewer	Yes = 1, no = 0	0.886	10.84
Lot larger than 1 acre	Yes = 1, no = 0	0.062	78.80
Renter	Yes = 1, no = 0	0.410	−58.64
Renter × units at address		1.992	−2.580
Renter × age		9.964	0.899
Renter × height of building		1.220	−17.19

Table 28.1   (cont'd)

Explanatory variable	Units	Mean	Coefficient
Renter × rooms		1.622	−7.189
Renter × bedrooms		1.112	2.014
Renter × bathrooms		0.479	−30.85
Renter × condominium		0.008	126.87
Renter × central air		0.130	50.95
Renter × sewer		0.395	−39.19
Renter × acre lot		0.014	−95.75
Constant			1,256.0

Notes: $R^2 = 0.6624$, $F = 1,823$, $N = 34,414$. All coefficients are statistically significant at the 5 percent level except for four variables: Units at address, Renter × unit, Renter × bedrooms, and Treatment, storage, and disposal sites. The sample mean of monthly housing expenditures in 1980 is $462.93. The dependent variable (p) was estimated in the form $(p^{0.2} - 1)/0.2$ based on Box–Cox maximum-likelihood search. The coefficients reported in this table are linearized by multiplying each coefficient by the mean of p raised to the 0.8 power.

updating this study with more recent data might estimate the housing price and wage equations with the (natural) logarithms of the dependent variables, with a gain in simplicity that would probably outweigh any cost in the less satisfactory functional form of the hedonic regressions.

The fourth step is to calculate the estimated full prices (f_i) in accordance with equation (28.4) above using the estimated coefficients from the hedonic housing equation for dp/da_i and from the wage hedonic equation for dw/da_i. These full prices are then used along with the amenity endowments in each urban county to yield the QOLI value for each county. Before combining the effects from the housing and labor markets, we must adjust the coefficients to make them annual effects for households. The monthly household housing expenditure must be multiplied by 12 months per year. The hourly wage for a worker must be multiplied by the average number of weeks worked per year (42.79), the average number of hours worked per week (37.85), and the average number of workers per household (1.54). An example might be helpful. For the teacher–pupil ratio, the full price per household per year is $(635.30)(12) - (-5.45)(42.79)(37.85)(1.54) =$ $21,217. (The value that we get if we do not round as much as we do in reporting numbers in Tables 28.1 and 28.2 is $21,250.) Estimated full implicit prices (f_i) are calculated for all 16 amenity factors that make up the QOLI.

The fifth step is to calculate an estimated QOLI value for each location. Following equation (28.5) above, we multiply the estimated full implicit price for each amenity factor times the quantity of that amenity in the location, $QOLI = \Sigma_i f_i a_i$. We did this to obtain QOLI values for each of the 253 urban counties in our sample. We can illustrate by calculating the QOLI value for a fictitious county

Table 28.2 Wage hedonic regression: the dependent variable is hourly wage rate

Explanatory variable	Units	Mean	Coefficient
Amenities			dw/da
Precipitation	Inches per year	32.01	−0.014
Humidity	Percent	68.27	0.0072
Heating degree days	Degree days per year	4,326.0	−0.000035
Cooling degree days	Degree days per year	1,162.0	−0.00022
Wind speed	Miles per hour	8.895	0.096
Sunshine	Percent of days	61.12	−0.0092
Coast	Yes = 1, no = 0	0.330	−0.031
Central city	Yes = 1, no = 0	0.290	−0.454
Violent crime	Crimes per 100,000 population per year	646.80	0.00062
Teacher–pupil ratio	Teachers per student	0.080	−5.45
Visibility	Miles	15.80	−0.0026
Total suspended particulates	$\mu g\ m^{-3}$	73.24	−0.0024
Water effluent dischargers	Number per county	1.513	−0.0051
Landfill waste	100 million metric tons per county	477.50	0.00009
Superfund sites	Number per county	0.883	0.107
Treatment, storage, and disposal sites	Number per county	46.44	0.0013
Worker and job characteristics			
Experience	Age – schooling – 6, years	17.44	0.310
Experience squared		513.90	−0.005
Schooling	Years	12.76	0.442
Race	Nonwhite = 1, white = 0	0.153	−0.959
Gender	Female = 1, male = 0	0.452	−0.312
Enrolled in school	Yes = 1, no = 0	0.149	−0.600
Marital status	Married = 1, unmarried = 0	0.586	1.441
Health limitations	Yes = 1, no = 0	0.048	−0.885
Gender × experience		7.598	−0.132
Gender × experience square		221.30	0.0023
Gender × race		0.075	1.102
Gender × marital status		0.237	−1.392
Gender × children		1.118	−0.254

Table 28.2   *(cont'd)*

Explanatory variable	Units	Mean	Coefficient
Professional or managerial	Yes = 1, no = 0	0.232	2.499
Technical or sales	Yes = 1, no = 0	0.336	1.214
Farming	Yes = 1, no = 0	0.012	0.129
Craft	Yes = 1, no = 0	0.113	1.437
Operator of laborer	Yes = 1, no = 0	0.173	0.690
Industry unionization	Percent	23.35	0.038
Constant			2.76

Notes: $R^2 = 0.3138$, $F = 601$, $N = 46{,}004$. All coefficients are significant at the 5 percent level except for: Farming, Humidity, Heating degree days, Coast, Visibility, Total suspended particulates, and Water effluent dischargers. The hourly wage is earnings in 1979 divided by the product of weeks worked and usual hours worked per week. The sample mean for hourly wage is $8.04. The dependent variable w was estimated in the form $(w^{0.1} - 1)/0.1$ based on a Box–Cox maximum-likelihood search. The coefficients reported in this table are linearized by multiplying each coefficient by the mean of w raised to the 0.9 power. The omitted occupation category is Service.

that is also the central city, is located inland and not on a coast, and has the average quantity of each of the other 14 amenities. Following the order of the amenities in Table 28.2 and using the means in that table, we have QOLI (inland, central city, average) = (23.5)(32.01) + (−43.42)(68.27) + (−0.08)(4,326) + (−0.36)(1,162) + (−97.51)(8.895) + (48.52)(61.12) + (467.72)(0) + (645.02)(1) + (−1.03)(646.8) + (21,250)(0.0799) + (−3.41)(15.8) + (−0.36)(73.24) + (−76.68)(1.513) + (−0.11)(477.5) + (−106.07)(0.883) + (−0.58)(46.44) = 429.05. This example turns out to be close to the QOLI value for Sacramento, California. Sacramento County is ranked 80th, and this brings us to the sixth step.

The last step is to rank the areas by QOLI value. Table 28.3 shows the rankings for the top urban counties with a QOLI value more than one standard deviation greater than the mean of QOLI. Table 28.4 shows the rankings for the bottom urban counties with a QOLI value more than one standard deviation below the mean of QOLI. These areas are the best and worst out of the 253 urban counties ranked. The average value of the QOLI is 186, and is less than the value for the fictitious county that we considered in our example above because only 29 percent of the counties are central city. Quality of life as measured by the values of the bundle of local amenities revealed in the housing and labor markets tends to be highest in small and medium-sized urban areas in the Sun Belt and Colorado. Quality of life tends to be lowest in large northern urban areas. The annual premium that the typical household of consumer/workers is willing to pay is $5,146, the difference between the QOLI values for top-ranked Pueblo, Colorado, and St Louis City, Missouri.

Table 28.3 The quality of life ranking for urban counties: the best

Urban county	Metropolitan area	State	QOLI rank	QOLI value ($)
Pueblo	Pueblo	Colorado	1	3,288.72
Norfolk City	Norfolk – Virginia Beach – Portsmouth	Virginia	2	2,105.77
Arapahoe	Denver–Boulder	Colorado	3	2,097.07
Bibb	Macon	Georgia	4	1,599.57
Washoe	Reno	Nevada	5	1,575.37
Broome	Binghamton	New York	6	1,485.63
Hampton City	Newport News – Hampton	Virginia	7	1,444.63
Sarasota	Sarasota	Florida	8	1,430.84
Palm Beach	West Palm Beach – Boca Raton	Florida	9	1,422.54
Pima	Tucson	Arizona	10	1,341.86
Broward	Fort Lauderdale – Hollywood	Florida	11	1,326.91
Boulder	Denver–Boulder	Colorado	12	1,319.47
Larimer	Fort Collins	Colorado	13	1,297.84
Denver	Denver–Boulder	Colorado	14	1,295.25
Charleston	Charleston – North Charleston	South Carolina	15	1,280.21
Monterey	Salinas – Seaside – Monterey	California	16	1,213.97
Roanoke City	Roanoke	Virginia	17	1,129.65
Lackawanna	Northeast Pennsylvania	Pennsylvania	18	1,127.43
Leon	Tallahassee	Florida	19	1,066.51
Richmond City	Richmond	Virginia	20	1,059.96
Fayette	Lexington–Fayette	Kentucky	21	1,055.50
Santa Barbara	Santa Barbara – Santa Maria – Lompoc	California	22	1,025.76
Ventura	Oxnard – Simi Valley – Ventura	California	23	1,022.83
Durham	Raleigh–Durham	North Carolina	24	1,014.01
New Hanover	Wilmington	North Carolina	25	1,000.92
Wake	Raleigh–Durham	North Carolina	26	990.98
San Diego	San Diego	California	27	980.93
Virginia Beach City	Norfolk – Virginia Beach – Portsmouth	Virginia	28	967.70
Lancaster	Lancaster	Pennsylvania	29	965.38
Manatee	Bradenton	Florida	30	958.13
Weld	Greeley	Colorado	31	957.23
El Paso	El Paso	Texas	32	923.02
Racine	Racine	Wisconsin	33	912.83
Guilford	Greensboro – Winston Salem – High Point	North Carolina	34	908.74
Lane	Eugene–Springfield	Oregon	35	884.00
Maricopa	Phoenix	Arizona	36	870.69

Note: The QOLI value for each of these top urban counties is greater than $853, which is more than one standard deviation above the average value of $186.

28.6   QOLI AND *PLACES RATED* RANKINGS

Rankings of urban areas generate an amazing amount of interest. Boyer and Savageau's (1985) *Places Rated Almanac* helped make comparisons popular and *USA Today*, with its national market and proclivity for colorful lists and pie charts, capitalized on heightened interest. The *Places Rated* index was comprised of nine categories for quality of life: climate and terrain, housing, health care and the environment, crime, transportation, education, the arts, recreation, and economics. The authors, using their own judgment, awarded points for characteristics in each category for each of 329 urban areas, ranked urban areas in each category, and added the rankings in each category to obtain an overall ranking. The top-ranked metropolitan area overall was Pittsburgh in Allegheny County, Pennsylvania, and the bottom-ranked area was Yuba City, which is in Sutter County, California, north of Sacramento.

Two distinctive aspects make this procedure different from the one that urban economists use. The first is that economic conditions are included in addition to local amenities, almost as if the attempt is to try to make comparisons of overall well-being. The second is that the authors use their own judgment and prefer-ences. They interject their own preferences in two ways. One is that they assign points in each of the nine categories of quality of life. The other is that they weight the rankings in each of the nine categories equally to calculate the overall score and ranking. This equal weighting means that a one-position difference in climate is equally important as a one-position difference in the crime ranking. In contrast, urban economists use a Rosen index – or something like it – that includes only local amenities, and that aggregates the amenities in each urban area by the values of the amenities that reflect combined individual preferences, which are implicit in the choices that individuals make in the housing and labor markets.

In Berger, Blomquist, and Waldner (1987), we find for approximately the same time period that our QOLI-based, quality of life ranking for metropolitan areas is quite different from the 1981 *Places Rated*. We find that consumer/workers rank the quality of life in the Pittsburgh area 164th of 185 metropolitan areas, far below the top ranking found in *Places Rated*. In fact, we find that the rank cor-relation between our QOLI ranking of metropolitan areas and the *Places Rated* ranking is essentially zero. What is clear is that a preference-based ranking of the value of the local amenities, such as our QOLI, and a ranking based on equal weighting of various local amenities – and some economic conditions – yield vastly different results.

28.7   ONE QUALITY OF LIFE INDEX DOES NOT FIT ALL

The application of the QOLI by Blomquist, Berger, and Hoehn (1988) is based on an analysis of labor and housing markets, and ranks urban areas based on the revealed values of thousands of workers and residents for a bundle of amen-ities in which there is broad interest. The ranking reflects the value of typical

Table 28.4 The quality of life ranking for urban counties: the worst

Urban county	Metropolitan area	State	QOLI rank	QOLI value ($)
Baltimore	Baltimore	Maryland	220	−485.32
St Charles	St Louis	Missouri	221	−486.10
Hennepin	Minneapolis – St Paul	Minnesota	222	−488.20
Camden	Philadelphia	New Jersey	223	−523.00
Saginaw	Saginaw	Michigan	224	−537.30
Clark	Portland	Washington	225	−547.30
Dakota	Minneapolis – St Paul	Minnesota	226	−558.10
Snohomish	Seattle–Everett	Washington	227	−562.70
Allen	Lima	Ohio	228	−585.10
Jackson	Jackson	Michigan	229	−635.30
Will	Chicago	Illinois	230	−676.10
Greene	Dayton	Ohio	231	−681.30
Niagara	Buffalo	New York	232	−682.70
Calhoun	Battle Creek	Michigan	233	−701.10
Denton	Dallas – Fort Worth	Texas	234	−709.90
Peoria	Peoria	Illinois	235	−758.80
Rockland	New York	New York	236	−795.50
Cameron	Brownsville – Harlingen – San Benito	Texas	237	−795.70
Medina	Cleveland	Ohio	238	−823.30
Hidalgo	McAllen – Pharr – Edinburg	Texas	239	−823.80
St Louis	St Louis	Missouri	240	−875.30
Harris	Houston	Texas	241	−916.30
Jefferson	St Louis	Missouri	242	−918.30
Washington	Minneapolis – St Paul	Minnesota	243	−920.20
Kent	Grand Rapids	Michigan	244	−950.90
Kalamazoo	Kalamazoo–Portage	Michigan	245	−976.30
Cook	Chicago	Illinois	246	−979.10
Genesse	Flint	Michigan	247	−1,018.50
Macomb	Detroit	Michigan	248	−1,024.10
Wayne	Detroit	Michigan	249	−1,267.50
Brazoria	Houston	Texas	250	−1,403.50
Jefferson	Birmingham	Alabama	251	−1,539.30
Waukesha	Milwaukee	Wisconsin	252	−1,791.50
St Louis City	St Louis	Missouri	253	−1,856.70

Note: The QOLI value for each of these bottom urban counties is less than −$481, which is more than one standard deviation below the average value of $186.

workers and residents and depends on the distribution of firms and supply of local amenities by nature and local governments. While clamor about the Sun Belt draws attention to climate, products of local governments can be of paramount importance to some groups. Single individuals are likely to be interested in entertainment, recreation, and advanced education opportunities. Married couples with school-age children are likely to focus on school quality and crime control. A QOLI that has these amenity factors will be more relevant for these couples than one that does not. Retirees may be interested in local crime control, but are likely less interested in school quality. A QOLI that excludes school quality may be more relevant for retirees who may not be willing to pay much for the schools. A special QOLI could be constructed for each group.

Numbers can illustrate. Consider again married couples with school-age children. In our study of 253 urban counties, we re-ranked counties based on the teacher–pupil ratio in public schools, the violent crime rate, and central city location. While this ranking may not match exactly what these couples would want in their amenity bundle, comparison to the ranking based on the overall index that includes climate and environmental quality is informative. The comparison is shown in the rightmost column in Table 28.5. Five of the top 15 urban counties remain in the top 15, but others drop. Examples are Sarasota (Florida), which falls to 26, and Hampton City (Virginia), which falls to 48. Palm Beach (Florida), Washoe (Nevada), Pima (Arizona), and Charleston (South Carolina) all drop out of the top 100. Among the bottom 10, all but one move out of the bottom 10. Waukesha (Wisconsin) moves up to 113 and Kent (Michigan) jumps up to 78. St Louis City (Missouri), remains at the bottom.

Using subsets of the QOLI, we ranked the counties by urban conditions, climate, and environmental quality. The correlations of the ranking based on the overall QOLI with the rankings based on subset QOLIs were 0.48 for urban conditions, 0.63 for the climate, and 0.21 for environmental quality. Even with the same weights, the rankings are different because the bundle of amenities varies.

Different groups will be interested not only in different amenity bundles in various urban areas, but in how the price for the local quality of life is paid. A household with two wage earners in the labor market will shy away from urban areas in which most of the premium for a high quality of life is paid for through lower wages. Those households would pay double, in a sense. Retirees, in contrast, will find these urban areas with a large share of the compensation paid in the labor market attractive, because their incomes are independent of local wages. Graves and Waldman (1991) analyzed census data and found that, in fact, migration of the elderly flowed to areas in which the price for the local amenities is paid predominantly through the labor market.

Taken to the limit, each of us could construct a personal QOLI and rank urban areas for ourselves. We would use our own weights and include local amenities that we value. It is possible to tailor an index. Recent editions of the *Places Rated Almanac* by Savageau and Boyer (1993) and Savageau and D'Agostino (2000) offer a short chapter in which an individual completes a preference inventory test that yields weights for each of the factors such as crime, transportation, education, and jobs. These personal weights can be applied to the ratings of the

Table 28.5 A comparison of rankings of urban counties, overall QOLI versus QOLI with only urban conditions, and top 15 and bottom 10 counties

Urban county	Metropolitan area	State	QOLI rank	QOLI urban conditions rank
Pueblo	Pueblo	Colorado	1	1
Norfolk City	Norfolk – Virginia Beach – Portsmouth	Virginia	2	5
Arapahoe	Denver–Boulder	Colorado	3	3
Bibb	Macon	Georgia	4	4
Washoe	Reno	Nevada	5	130
Broome	Binghamton	New York	6	2
Hampton City	Newport News – Hampton	Virginia	7	48
Sarasota	Sarasota	Florida	8	26
Palm Beach	West Palm Beach – Boca Raton	Florida	9	102
Pima	Tucson	Arizona	10	151
Broward	Fort Lauderdale – Hollywood	Florida	11	33
Boulder	Denver–Boulder	Colorado	12	28
Larimer	Fort Collins	Colorado	13	50
Denver	Denver–Boulder	Colorado	14	29
Charleston	Charleston – North Charleston	South Carolina	15	110
⋮	⋮	⋮	⋮	⋮
Kent	Grand Rapids	Michigan	244	78
Kalamazoo	Kalamazoo–Portage	Michigan	245	165
Cook	Chicago	Illinois	246	168
Genesee	Flint	Michigan	247	212
Macomb	Detroit	Michigan	248	231
Wayne	Detroit	Michigan	249	242
Brazoria	Houston	Texas	250	211
Jefferson	Birmingham	Alabama	251	188
Waukesha	Milwaukee	Wisconsin	252	113
St Louis City	St Louis	Missouri	253	253

factors to yield a personal ranking of urban areas. The 1993 edition offered a diskette as a supplement to facilitate personal rankings.

Urban quality of life related to consumption amenities valued by consumer/ workers offers a fascinating perspective on life in different urban areas. Firms, however, need not have the same perspective. As discussed above, production amenities that make firms more efficient in one urban area than another need not be consumption amenities, and vice versa. An implication is that firms will be attracted to high-consumption amenity locations where the price paid by consumer/workers is mostly through the labor market. This attraction will be even stronger for firms that are labor intensive in workers who value local consumption amenities greatly. Holding skill level constant, these locations will be low-wage areas to these firms. Gabriel and Rosenthal (2004) make use of this relationship to rank 37 metropolitan areas by quality of business environment for the period 1977–95. They compare the ranking with a ranking based on a QOLI (using the group effects alternative) and find that many of the areas that are attractive to consumer/workers are unattractive to business. For example, Miami was ranked first for consumers and 34th for firms, near the bottom. Overall, the correlation between the premium for consumption amenities and the premium paid by firms for production amenities was only 0.05, almost zero.

In the end, a QOLI can indicate where quality of life is higher and lower for a bundle of local amenities in which there is broad interest. There is no single index that will serve well for all purposes. Different consumer/workers will value different amenities differently because of their stage in the life cycle and because of different preferences. Firms will value different amenities and have a different perspective and lower wages that compensate for consumption amenities. Quality of business environment need not be the same as quality of life. Urban areas will be ranked differently depending on perspective.

28.8   WHAT HAS BEEN LEARNED FROM STUDYING QUALITY OF LIFE?

Quality of life matters. We have substantial evidence that individuals trade off money for better quality of life as measured by better local amenities in some urban areas. They pay for a higher quality of life through a less attractive combination of lower wages and higher rents. Most of the evidence is for the United States, but in Berger, Blomquist, and Sabirianova (2003) we also find a willingness to pay for local amenities in the large transition economy of Russia.

Local public officials and Chambers of Commerce who ignore local amenities related to environmental and urban conditions may find their areas shrinking as competing urban areas offer more attractive local amenity-tax packages to consumer/workers. As Diamond and Tolley (1982) and Bartik and Smith (1987) demonstrate, these local amenities influence residential location patterns, urban density, and urban development. Governments are crucial to urban quality of life. Crime is influenced by police, courts, social services, and street lighting. Public-school quality is influenced by teachers, facilities, and the ability to attract

good students. Environmental quality is influenced by local policy and implementation of national policy that permits some local discretion. Urban governments that attempt to "race to the bottom" of environmental regulation risk
earning a reputation for a low quality of life.

Quality of life indexes should be tailored to the purpose. While a general QOLI
can be useful, the relevant amenities and values can vary from group to group
and from individual to individual. A household with a married couple who both
work in the labor market and have two school-age children will not necessary
want the same amenity bundle or have the same amenity values as a retired
couple. A tailored QOLI can be used to help forecast changes in urban areas
by indicating how demands for particular amenities are going to change with
demographic and social trends.

There's no place like home. Even if everyone were alike and valued amenities
the same way, we couldn't all live in the same place. With different amenity
bundles in different places, differences in wages and rents will arise to compensate households in areas with a low quality of life and make households pay
in areas with a high quality of life. Households get distributed across urban
areas. Differences in households produce differences in values of amenity bundles
in different urban areas, and the distribution of households across areas will
be systematic, not random. Young couples with children will tend to sort to
high-rent areas with good schools. Retirees will tend to sort to low-wage areas
with pleasant climates. In general, households will tend to sort themselves to
areas that offer the amenity bundle (and price) that they like. The fact that lots of
folks think that the quality of life is good right where they are is no surprise.
Residents stayed in or moved to their current locations because those urban areas
offered the best combination of wages, rents, and quality of life.

Bibliography

Bartik, T. J. and Smith, V. K. 1987: Urban amenities and public policy. In E. S. Mills
(ed.), *Handbook of Urban and Regional Economics*, vol. 2: *Urban Economics*. New York:
Elsevier.

Beeson, P. E. and Eberts, R. W. 1989: Identifying productivity and amenity effects in
interurban wage differentials. *Review of Economics and Statistics*, 71(3), 443–52.

Berger, M. C. and Blomquist, G. C. 1988: Income, opportunities, and the quality of life of
urban residents. In M. G. H. McGeary and L. E. Lynn, Jr (eds.), *Urban Change and
Poverty*. Washington, DC: National Academy Press.

——, ——, and Sabrianova, K. Z. 2003: Compensating differentials in emerging labor and
housing markets: estimates of quality of life in Russian cities. Paper presented at a
session in honor of the memory of Sherwin Rosen at the AERE/ASSA meetings held in
Washington, DC, on January 3–5, 2003.

——, ——, and Waldner, W. 1987: A revealed-preference ranking of quality of life in
metropolitan areas. *Social Science Quarterly*, 68(4), 761–78.

Blomquist, G. C., Berger, M. C., and Hoehn, J. P. 1988: New estimates of quality of life in
urban areas. *American Economic Review*, 78(1), 89–107.

Boyer, R. and Savageau, D. 1985: *Places Rated Almanac: Your Guide to Finding the Best Places
to Live in America*. Chicago: Rand McNally.

Diamond, D. B., Jr and Tolley, G. S. 1982: *The Economics of Urban Amenities*. New York: Academic Press.

Gabriel, S. A. and Rosenthal, S. S. 2004: Quality of the business environment versus the quality of life: Do firms and households like the same cities? *Review of Economics and Statistics*, 86(1), 438–44.

Graves, P. E. and Waldman, D. M. 1991: Multimarket amenity compensation and the behavior of the elderly. *American Economic Review*, 81, December, 1,374–81.

Gyourko, J., Kahn, M., and Tracy, J. 1999: Quality of life and environmental comparisons. In E. S. Mills and P. Cheshire (eds.), *The Handbook of Applied Urban Economics*. New York: North-Holland.

Roback, J. 1982: Wages, rents, and the quality of life. *Journal of Political Economy*, 90, December, 1,257–78.

Rosen, S. 1979: Wage-based indexes of urban quality of life. In P. Mieszkowski and M. Straszheim (eds.), *Current Issues in Urban Economics*. Baltimore, MD: Johns Hopkins University Press.

Savageau, D. and Boyer, R. 1993: *Places Rated Almanac: Your Guide to Finding the Best Places to Live in North America*. New York: Prentice Hall Travel.

—— and D'Agostino, R. 2000: *Places Rated Almanac*. Foster City, CA: IDG Books.

CHAPTER TWENTY-NINE

Air Pollution in Cities

Matthew E. Kahn

29.1 Introduction

Some cities face severe air pollution problems, while other cities of similar population sizes are much cleaner. For example, World Bank data from 1995 indicates that for a sample of major cities where air quality was monitored, the ambient particulate level of the average Asian city was four times higher than that of the average city in Western Europe. In the year 1995, there were at least 25 cities in Asia whose ambient particulate levels exceeded three times the World Health Organization's annual particulate standard of 90 μg m^{-3} (micrograms per cubic meter).

Urban air pollution can significantly degrade quality of life. In polluted cities, time spent outside is dangerous to one's health. Such cities may have trouble attracting footloose high tech firms and their amenity-seeking workers to locate there. A mayor of such a city might wonder: How did this city become so polluted? What cost-effective regulations could be enacted to clean up the city? How much would people be willing to pay to reduce local pollution? This chapter seeks to examine each of these issues by focusing on the supply and demand for urban air pollution.

There are numerous examples of polluted cities, such as Los Angeles, Krakow, and Pittsburgh, that have made dramatic pollution progress. There are other cities whose pollution levels are increasing or are only slowly improving. This diversity of experiences means that researchers can test hypotheses concerning what drives urban air pollution and can investigate what policies effectively mitigate urban air pollution.

A challenge in making progress in understanding the causes and consequences of urban air pollution is that it really requires an interdisciplinary research team. Public health experts focus on measuring the health impacts of air pollution exposure. Atmospheric chemists examine how ambient air pollution is affected by urban emissions increases. Engineers focus on what are the set of feasible technologies that can be used to mitigate a pollution problem. Economists bring two major tools to help study this interdisciplinary policy issue. First, our insistence that incentives play a key role in achieving polluter accountability leads us to focus on certain key details of policy design. Second, our training in empirical hypothesis testing gives us a leg-up over other researchers in establishing the likely causal effects of regulatory interventions.

29.2 THE SUPPLY OF URBAN AIR POLLUTION

Since cities are densely populated areas, it should not be surprising that most cities suffer from air pollution problems. One person who smokes, or drives a dirty car, and one smoke-belching factory will have little impact on overall ambient air quality, but when millions of drivers and thousands of firms each emit pollution in a small geographical area, an unintended consequence is high levels of ambient pollution. It is unlikely that any of these polluters maliciously sets out to pollute. The key reason why air pollution arises in cities is that none of the polluters have an incentive not to pollute. The air is common property that is owned by everyone and the classic "Tragedy of the Commons" problem takes place. If urban air was private property, a polluter would have to buy the right to pollute before he drove a dirty car or lit up a stinky cigar. But this is not the case. Everyone owns the urban air. The cigar smoker pays no "environmental tax" for lighting up, but if this smelly cigar raises pollution levels and this in turn makes a child nearby sneeze, the smoker has imposed social costs on "downstream" victims. This externality was created because the smoker did not face the full social costs of his actions.

Even if property rights for air pollution were privatized, another issue that arises in cities is transaction costs. Such costs preclude the Coasian solution of efficient bargaining to mitigate the externality. If Bill Gates were asthmatic and was willing to pay Seattle polluters money to not pollute, there would still be transaction cost problems of how he would find each of these polluters and bargain with them. The large number of polluters in cities raises the likelihood that effective government regulation is needed to curb urban air pollution.

A further challenge in reducing urban air pollution is that polluting firms have private information about the "toxicity" of their actions. This asymmetry of information is a recurrent theme in popular culture. In the movies *Silkwood*, *Legal Action*, and *Erin Brockovich*, unsuspecting citizens are exposed to environmental risks caused by profit-maximizing firms. These firms are well aware of the environmental consequences of their actions, but keep this information hidden from the general public. A repeated theme in these movies is that big business has a secret agenda and the environment is worse off from the self-interested money pursuit of the capitalist. While no economist would admit that Hollywood movies influence his choice of research questions, leading economists have investigated the consequences of asymmetric information on outcomes in capitalist economies. The Nobel Prize in Economics in the year 2001 was awarded to three economists for their research on this subject.

29.2.1   The sources of emissions

Industry is not the only urban polluter and for some measures of urban pollution, such as ambient ozone and carbon monoxide, it is not the dominant producer of pollution.

To understand what factors cause pollution, imagine two different cities. In "Green City," all 1 million residents of this city spend their day reading the newspaper on their front step, and do nothing else. This would be a clean city! Contrast it with "Brown City," where each morning each of the 1 million smoke a morning cigarette and drive an old clunker car 20 miles to the local factory where they work. This old steel factory uses a blast furnace technology that creates vast levels of particulates and sulfur dioxide. Each person goes home at night and cooks dinner using an electric stove, which gets its power from a nearby electric utility that uses coal to produce power, creating problems similar to those caused by the steel plant. This "Brown City" suffers from severe air pollution because every sector of the economy (transport, industry, power production, home sector) creates more emissions than in Green City.

This "tale of two cities" highlights the three key determinants of local air emissions. At a moment in time, a city can be polluted for three different reasons: because economic activity is high (scale), because the economic activity is concentrated in dirty production (composition), and because the dirty production creates a high level of pollution per unit of output (technique). Intuitively, scale represents how much economic activity is going on within the city's borders. Are there 1 million people or 2 million people living and working in the city? Urban growth increases the scale of economic activity. As the number of mega-cities has grown around the world, this scale effect has increased the likelihood of extremely high levels of air pollution. For example, Buenos Aires, Argentina, is the 10th largest urban agglomeration in the world, with 12.5 million people.

Composition refers to the sectors in which this city specializes. Manufacturing cities will be dirtier than service-sector cities. In the 19th century, Marx and Engels bemoaned the standard of living in British industrial cities. In the twentieth century, the rise of Pittsburgh as a steel capital had the unintended consequence of sharply increasing particulate levels. An unintended silver lining of the US Rust Belt's decline in the 1960s and 1970s has been to sharply improve environmental quality in heavy industrial cities such as Pittsburgh and Gary, Indiana.

Technique is the final key determinant of urban pollution levels. Technique refers to what types of technologies are used within the city. If the average household in a city drives a 2001 model year vehicle rather than a 1974 model year vehicle, then such a city features greener average techniques, because the older vehicles were built before the US Clean Air Act required catalytic converters and thus they emit much more smog inputs (hydrocarbons) per mile of driving. The technologies used in a city depend on a number of factors. A nation such as Argentina that has high import tariffs features an older vehicle fleet in Buenos Aires because new cars are so expensive. Under communism, such cities as Krakow and Budapest featured heavy industry using very dirty technologies because energy was so highly subsidized. Industrialists had little incentive to economize on pollution production. The communist experience highlights the point that techniques used in urban consumption and production crucially depend on the prices of energy. If energy becomes more expensive, urban households and firms will have a greater incentive to green their activities, and if all consumers and producers within a city economize on energy then this will help to "green" the city.

29.2.2 Aggregate emissions and ambient air pollution

Since vehicle transport is a major cause of urban smog, I formalize the above discussion by focusing on the production of urban emissions from vehicles. Suppose that the typical person in a city has a probability equal to P of owning a car. Intuitively, this "P" increases as this person gets richer, if the price of cars is falling, or if public transportation deteriorates. If a person owns a car, he drives it M miles. This level of driving will depend on several variables, such as the person's income, the person's place of residence and place of work, and the price of gasoline. Finally, suppose that the average emissions per mile of driving is equal to E. Under these assumptions, per capita transport emissions equal PME. If there are N people in the city, then aggregate transport emissions in the city equal $NPME$.

This product simply says that aggregate transport emissions in a city will be higher if more people live there, if each person is more likely to own a car, if each person drives more, and if they own a dirty car. It embodies why so many environmentalists support public-transit improvements. Investments in subways and clean buses would reduce P and M. The product embodies why many environmentalists are greatly concerned about suburban sprawl. One brief definition of sprawl is the spread of economic activity such that people are living further away from where they work and shop. In more sprawling areas, people drive more (Kahn 2000).

Of course, transportation is not the only polluting sector with a city. Depending on the pollutant in question, other sectors such as electric utilities and industry may be the dominant supplier of emissions. For example, coal-fired electric utilities are a major supplier of sulfur dioxide, particulates, and nitrogen oxide emissions.

Each urban sector (transport, industry, electric utilities) can be thought of as an input in the production of pollution. In production theory, inputs such as labor and capital are purchased to produce a final output such as pizza. In the case of urban air pollution, no firm is setting out to produce pollution. Instead, urban air pollution is an unintended consequence of activity within the area:

$$\text{total urban air emissions} = \sum_j \text{emissions}_j + \text{net imports.}$$

This accounting equation indicates that an area's total urban emissions is the sum of each sector j's emissions. As described above, the total transportation sector's emissions equal $NPME$. Similar expressions can be created for the industrial sector, the residential sector, and the electric utility sector. Note the new final term added to the expression, called "net imports." This is meant to capture the cross-boundary component through which emissions released in one place can blow down to another city, affecting other people who live nearby. Such "downwind" externalities take place around the world. US electric utility production in Ohio creates acid rain in Canada. Chinese and Indian electric utility production creates acid rain in South Korea.

Total urban air emissions are not equivalent to urban ambient air pollution levels. Ultimately, we care about air emissions if they lower urban resident health capital and lower quality of life. Economists tend to be highly human centric. If all of the urban air emissions simply blew out to sea, most urban economists would declare that this pollution imposed little cost on the urban residents in the city. While urban air emissions are surely positively correlated with urban ambient pollution, the relationship may not be linear. In the following equation,

$$\text{ambient air pollution} = f(\text{local emissions} + \text{imports} - \text{exports},$$
$$\text{climate, geography}),$$

the function f maps local aggregate emissions into local ambient air pollution. Atmospheric chemists can help economists to estimate such pollution production functions.

The same level of urban air emissions can have a very different impact on local air pollution depending on city climate and wind patterns and the city's geography. A city surrounded by mountains will face higher air pollution levels for any given local emissions level relative to a city on a bay. Within cities, air pollution can vary greatly. In Los Angeles, communities closer to the Pacific Ocean feature much lower smog levels than communities inland.

This section has built up a pollution production function, starting with individual household and firm levels of economic activity. Urban air pollution is a byproduct of a city's scale, composition, and technique of economic activity within its borders and of economic activity in nearby cities, whose emissions spillover across political borders.

While this section has sketched an aggregate city-level pollution production function, it is important to note a couple of simplifying assumptions. To keep the algebra simple, I have not explicitly modeled heterogeneity within emissions sectors. As I will discuss below, household emissions will differ depending on such factors as household income. Industry emissions will differ depending on the age of factories and the human capital capacities of the workers who work at the firm.

29.2.3   Government actions to mitigate urban air pollution

So far, in tracing the key determinants of the supply of air pollution, there has been no active government involvement. Government policies, regulations, and laws can affect the scale, composition, and technique of economic activity within a city. For example, if a federal government subsidizes new urban highway construction, then this will increase the number of people who live in the urban area. If government requires that all new vehicles must use unleaded gasoline and have a catalytic converter, then pollution per mile of driving will fall sharply.

Whether a government will take "green actions" depends on the political leader's objectives. Early research in environmental economics assumed that the government chooses policies as if it was a benevolent planner, seeking to achieve a Pareto-optimal allocation of resources. The Public Choice research line has focused economists' attention on politicians' self-interest. If a politician's major election constituency is steel mill union workers who want to see this dirty industry boom, then this politician is unlikely to take strong pollution actions that would raise the cost of producing steel and that might "kill the golden employment goose." Alternatively, if the mayor's political support base is a yuppie highly educated electorate, then he would be more likely to take actions to preserve the city's quality of life and keep it a "consumer city" with rich amenities.

The intention of the Clean Air Act was to improve air quality around the United States. The Act has triggered at least two unintended consequences. Within major polluted cities such as Los Angeles, the regulation has acted to increase environmental justice. At any moment in time, within a city, richer people live in the nicer part of town that features lower crime and pollution levels, while poorer people live in higher-crime, more polluted areas. In Kahn (2001), I document that between 1980 and 1998 in California, the average Hispanic experienced a sharper reduction in ozone smog exposure than the average person. Regulation has helped bring about pollution exposure convergence. A second consequence of Clean Air Act regulation is to push polluting economic activity to less regulated more sparsely populated areas. Cleaner counties with smaller populations face less severe regulation than big cities. An unintended consequence of this differential regulatory standard is to push dirty industries away from highly populated, polluted cities to locate in less populated, unregulated areas.

Until recently, the Environmental Protection Agency focused on command and control approaches to greening urban consumption and production techniques. Command and control requires polluters to take specific actions, such as installing an emissions control device on a piece of capital. Disadvantages of this approach are that it does not provide sufficient incentives for polluters to reduce their pollution and that it forces all polluting firms to take the same actions to reduce pollution. Economists have long advocated the potential gains of adopting a pollution permit system, in which firms that wish to pollute must purchase a permit to cover these emissions. The market price for a permit would be such that aggregate demand for permits equals aggregate supply. This supply could be set with public health goals in mind, to insure that the public is not exposed to too much pollution. The efficiency gains from adopting this flexible regulatory program have been seen in the recent US sulfur dioxide trading permit market (Stavins 1998). Firms with a comparative advantage in reducing their emissions are now rewarded for doing so. Such firms now have an incentive to innovate to economize on pollution and this in turn reduces pollution per unit of economic activity.

The US regulatory experience offers a number of lessons for developing-country cities choosing what anti-air pollution regulations to adopt. The regulatory officials must have the human capital to know how to do their job. They must have the resources to engage in spot audits of polluters to detect which industrial plants are "super emitters," and to credibly commit to fine such companies if they are caught out of compliance. A regulatory authority that is unable to pre-commit to imposing high expected costs on urban polluters will rightly be seen as a paper tiger and its actions will have no effect on urban air pollution. Corruption in such regulatory agencies would increase their ineffectiveness, as polluting firms would recognize that a side payment to an inspector is a cheaper strategy than taking a costly action that would mitigate its emissions. World Bank economists are well aware of the challenges that developing cities face in fighting urban air pollution: "Much of the pessimism about the prospects for environmental quality in developing countries is not about whether a win–win outcome is technically possible for the economy and the environment, but whether these societies have the institutional capabilities necessary for achieving such an outcome" (Dasgupta, Laplante, Wang & Wheeler 2001).

29.3 Empirics on the Supply of Urban Air Pollution

Applied environmental researchers collect city-level databases, ideally observing the same city at several moments in time, to describe basic facts concerning urban air pollution trends and to test hypotheses concerning why air pollution has grown worse in some cities and improved in others. A frustration for environmental economists is that we do not have good ambient air pollution data for cities before the 1970s. Qualitative historians have helped to describe the air pollution problems of the past; for example, the scale of coal burning for home heating and industrial use once played a major role in raising urban air pollution levels (see McNeill 2000; Freese 2003).

In developing countries, urban air pollution has only recently been measured. Around the world, environmental protection agencies focus on six major ambient air pollutants: particulate matter, sulfur dioxide, ozone, carbon monoxide, lead, and nitrogen dioxide. The USA has created the Toxic Release Inventory to measure carcinogenic emissions, but relatively little is known about toxic emissions in cities around the world. Regulators can only take action if they have objective evidence that pollution levels exceed health standards.

One of the most important measures of ambient air pollution is particulate levels. Unlike ozone smog, public health researchers have found that exposure to particulates can kill people through increasing respiratory disease and causing lung damage. In recent years, regulators have focused on a subset of particulates called PM-10 (particulates with a diameter of 10 μm or less). Particulates are produced by diesel vehicles, electric utility plants that burn coal, and heavy industry.

The US EPA has set the ambient National Ambient Air Quality Standard for PM-10 at an annual geometric mean of 50 μg m^{-3}. The state of California features

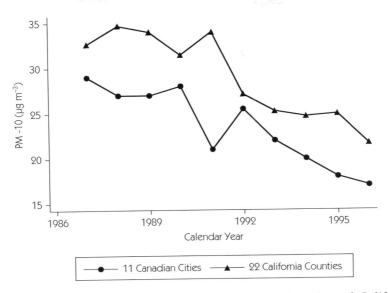

Figure 29.1 Trends in median ambient PM-10 in Canada and California.

some of the most highly polluted locations in the USA and one of the most comprehensive ambient air quality monitoring systems. In the year 1986, 38 percent of California's monitoring stations exceeded this standard, while in the year 1998, only 4 percent of the state's monitoring stations exceeded the same standard.

To provide some evidence on relative progress in reducing urban air pollution across nations, I present trends for 22 counties in California and 13 cities in Canada from 1985 to 1996 in Figure 29.1. To construct this graph, I took the annual ambient PM-10 pollution readings and calculated a median for Canada and California, and I simply graph these annual medians. The California counties include Alameda, Butte, Contra Costa, Fresno, Glenn, Imperial, Inyo, Kern, Kings, Lake, Los Angeles, Madera, Marin, Mendocino, Merced, Mono, Orange, Riverside, Sacramento, San Bernardino, San Diego, San Francisco, San Mateo, Santa Barbara, Santa Clara, Stanislaus, and Ventura. The Canadian cities include Edmonton, Calgary, Halifax, Montreal, Ottawa, Quebec City, Toronto, Vancouver, Victoria, Windsor, and Winnipeg. Canadian PM-10 Ambient Particulate data can be found at www.ec.gc.ca/soerree/English/Indicators/Issues/Urb_Air/Download/default.cfm and the California PM-10 data is from www.arb.ca.gov/adam/welcome.html.

Figure 29.1 shows that California had a slightly higher initial pollution but, perhaps surprisingly, both have a negative slope over time and the lines are roughly parallel. This indicates that PM-10 is declining by the same amount each year in both nations. Given that the economies of both the USA and Canada grew over this time period, scale effects would have predicted that pollution should have increased. This highlights that significant composition and technique effects must have taken place during this time period.

29.4   URBAN AIR POLLUTION AND ECONOMIC DEVELOPMENT

A major research question in environmental economics today asks whether economic development increases or decreases the supply of air pollution. The policy implications of this debate are immediate. If economic growth always raises air pollution, then cities face a trade-off as they develop. Conversely, if economic growth "solves" urban air pollution problems, then the Sierra Club and Greenpeace should advocate that their members vote in favor of Republican plans to eliminate the capital gains tax and other "trickle down" incentives that encourage growth through capital accumulation.

Environmentalists tend to argue that growth degrades the environment through scale effects. Richer people consume a greater quantity of goods. Optimists counter that rich people consume higher-quality goods, such as vehicles that emit less per mile of driving. Clearly, a case can be made that economic development is both a "foe" and a "friend" of the environment. The environmental Kuznets curve (EKC) hypothesis posits a nonlinear relationship between development and environmental quality. As shown in Figure 29.2, the theory asserts that economic development first degrades the environment and then, beyond a "turning point," growth and the environment become "friends." The existence of an EKC within a nation or in a cross-section of nations is in no way a "law of physics."

Interest in this hypothesis began during the debate over NAFTA's environmental consequences for Mexico. Environmentalists argued that NAFTA would raise air pollution in Mexico, because Mexico would become the USA's pollution haven. Under this view, dirty goods would be produced in Mexico and exported back to the USA. Economists argued against the environmentalists' pessimism by positing that if free trade stimulates income growth and if the demand for environmental protection increases as income rises, then in the long run NAFTA would improve Mexico's environmental quality.

Figure 29.2 presents two hypothetical EKC curves; one for the year 1990 and the other for the year 2000. The figure displays the optimistic hypothesis posited in Dasgupta, Laplante, Wang, and Wheeler (2001) that over time the EKC shifts downward.

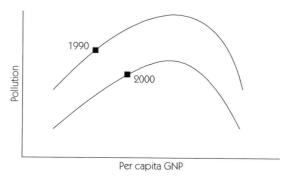

Figure 29.2   An illustration of a shifting environmental Kuznets curve.

The standard explanation for how such a pollution growth path could emerge is that at low levels of economic development, an economy engages in polluting agriculture and manufacturing and invests little in environmental regulation. Consumers in this economy spend their money on dirty goods such as low-quality fuels and older capital (used cars). With economic development, the economy eventually reaches a point at which the growing middle class are willing to pay higher taxes for a functioning government to step in and start addressing the externality. If the economy also makes a transition to services and consumers buy higher-quality capital, the path shown in Figure 29.2 would be observed. Many environmental economists have debated when this "turning point" is reached. The original Grossman and Krueger (1995) paper used cross-national data on urban particulates and sulfur dioxide to conclude that the turning point takes place at roughly $6,500 per capita. To solve for the turning point, a researcher estimates a multivariate regression of the form $Pollution = b_1 \times GNP + b_2 \times GNP^2 + U$, and then uses the ordinary least squares estimates of b_1 and b_2 to calculate the turning point that equals $-b_1/(2b_2)$. This is the level of income such that the marginal increase in pollution for a small change in real per capita GNP equals zero.

One intriguing empirical example is urban ambient lead levels across nations at different points in their economic development (Hilton, Hank & Levinson 1998). Most ambient lead comes from leaded gasoline. Since people in very poor nations drive little, these nations' cities feature low lead levels. As nations develop and urbanites drive more, they drive using low-quality leaded gasoline and urban lead emissions rise. None of this would surprise an environmentalist: economic development is stimulating increased consumption of pollution-intensive goods. But as this nation develops further, government regulation is enacted to require unleaded gasoline. This quality upgrading reduces emissions per mile of driving enough to offset the increased driving and the EKC for lead is observed. An open question in environmental economics is: Why do richer people demand more environmental regulation? Air pollution dynamics in industrializing nations such as China and India hinge on whether the growing middle class will demand more stringent air pollution regulation.

29.5   THE DEMAND FOR CLEAN URBAN AIR

All people seek to have long, healthy, and happy lives. Air pollution is a threat to all three of these goals. Air pollution raises mortality rates, raises morbidity rates, and – through making a city's outdoors less pleasant – lowers quality of life. Air quality is a strange good. If you want a cup of coffee, you can make it yourself or go to Starbucks. But how do you express your demand for clean air? You could move to a clean city. Or in a dirty city, you could move to its cleanest part.

People differ with respect to demand for avoiding air pollution. A person who never goes outside would care little about outdoor pollution, while an asthmatic who loves to jog would care greatly. Cities with more children and senior citizens will be more at risk to damage from urban pollution than a city comprised of professional athletes.

To measure how much people value clean air, we focus on revealed preference methods to learn about their willingness to pay to avoid pollution. Air pollution is a public bad, so if there are 1,000 people who are each willing to pay $1,000 to avoid one more smoggy day a year, then aggregate urban willingness to pay to avoid pollution would be $1 million dollars. This aggregate demand will matter in determining which regulatory policies to mitigate pollution pass a cost–benefit test.

Environmental economists have designed several different tests of how much people value clean air. Here, I focus on two distinct methods, health production functions (HPF) and hedonics. The health production function approach views air quality as a necessary input for being healthy. It essentially asks the following question: For a given demographic group (say, a 37-year-old black male college graduate), if this person lived in a slightly more polluted city, how much more morbidity would he suffer and what increased chance of dying would he risk relative to if he lived in a low-pollution city?

To test for the causal impact of air pollution on health, economists seek "natural experiments," which are cases where there are dramatic unexpected changes in air pollution. Some researchers have used volcanic eruptions, while others have used local economic downturns and labor strikes at local steel mills. In the aftermath of September 11, 2001, in downtown New York City, people were exposed to very high levels of toxics and particulates. There is an ongoing investigation of the health consequences caused by this unexpected shock. These research designs highlight the creativity that economists have demonstrated in attempting to estimate the health consequences of air pollution.

To measure this pollution-induced excess morbidity and mortality requires two types of detailed data. First, it requires individual-level data (such as the National Health Interview Studies) on a random set of urbanites' health levels in a given year and a set of demographic questions to establish what demographic group the respondent belongs to. The data set also needs to provide a geographical identifier, so that the researcher knows what city a person lives in and ideally what part of the city. Even in polluted places such as Los Angeles and Santiago, air pollution can vary considerably within the city. With exact information on where the person lives within the city, the researcher then can merge on ambient air pollution data using geographic information software (GIS). Using GIS software, the analyst would figure out which ambient monitoring station is closest to each person's place of residence and merge on that station's air pollution levels. With a large microdata set, the researcher could estimate how the probability of suffering a sickness related to air pollution, such as bronchitis, is affected by pollution exposure. Several hypotheses could be tested: first, which air pollutants have the greatest impact on raising sickness probabilities; and, second, which demographic groups (i.e., the young, the elderly, the least educated) are most at risk of getting sick from air pollution.

The HPF approach yields an estimate of the excess morbidity and mortality caused by air pollution. Excess morbidity and mortality are measured in probability units (i.e., you are 3 percentage points more likely to get sick and 0.02 percentage points more likely to die if you live in a high-pollution city versus a low-pollution city), while willingness to pay is measured in dollars. To make the leap from such marginal health effects to dollars, economists usually use a person's wage to measure their value of time and an estimate of the value of life borrowed from the labor literature (see Viscusi 1993). This approach raises a series of important philosophical issues. If a retired person is not working, how do we value his or her time? If wages are 80 percent lower in a less developed country than in the USA, are the benefits of reducing urban air pollution in their cities much lower than in the USA?

The second widely used method for measuring the demand for clean air has the fancy name of hedonics. However, this concept is really quite simple. In free-market capitalism, prices adjust until supply equals demand. A really nice house in a really nice community could never have the same price as a lousy house in a lousy community, because people would not buy the bad house and would bid up the price of the nice house. Hedonics is the branch of economics that uses the information incorporated into the differences in the prices of homes to infer how much people value the underlying attributes of the differentiated product.

Suppose that every house in Los Angeles had the same structure and lot size, and suppose that communities within Los Angeles only differed with respect to air pollution. Suppose that you collected real estate data on different homes in Los Angeles, geocoded their addresses, and used GIS software to merge the ambient air pollution of the closest monitoring station. You could then calculated the average home price by community, as follows:

Community	Average home price ($1,000s)	Ambient pollution level
A	250	0
B	100	10
C	50	20

What hedonics boils down to is that the implicit price of purchasing one less unit of pollution, in moving from community B to A, is $(250 - 100)/(10 - 0) = 15$. Given market prices, it will cost you $15,000 to reduce your pollution exposure by one unit. Clearly, anybody who chooses at these prices to live in A over B reveals that his willingness to pay to avoid one more unit of pollution is at least $15,000.

Actual hedonic studies are more complicated than this, because not all homes are identical, and communities differ along many dimensions other than pollution, including crime, school quality, and proximity to other physical attributes. Multivariate linear regression can be used to address such complications.

Capitalization of clean air into land prices creates a political constituency with a stake in keeping an area clean. Landowners in cities have a financial incentive to recognize that deterioration in the quality of life will lower the value of their asset. If the majority of voters in a city are landowners, this creates incentives to enact policies to protect environmental quality.

29.6 CONCLUSION

Is zero urban air pollution Pareto optimal? While the air would be quite clean in such a city, the costs of achieving this strict goal would be Draconian. In cities, there would be no driving, no production, and no smoking. The rational planner would trade off the benefits of clean air versus the costs of achieving this environmental goal. The marginal benefits of further pollution reductions hinge on the health effects and the amenity effects of pollution. This chapter's discussion of hedonic and health production valuation methods provides an overview for estimating the marginal benefits of further pollution reduction. Pollution is a byproduct of economic activity. It is costly to reduce urban pollution. To estimate what are the marginal costs of additional pollution reduction requires a close examination of how firm profitability and vehicle driver welfare would be affected by regulation that affects the scale, composition, and techniques used in the urban economy.

   While the theory of optimal urban air pollution is well understood, there are many open empirical questions. The cities around the world offer a rich laboratory for testing air pollution hypotheses. How does globalization affect air quality in poor nations versus rich nations? How much does suburban sprawl exacerbate US city air pollution problems? Do nondemocracies such as China suffer more or less air pollution as cities boom? The increased availability of new urban air pollution data sets and the importance of the underlying issue guarantee that economic analysis of urban air pollution is a growing research field.

Bibliography

Dasgupta, S., Laplante, B., Wang, H., and Wheeler, D. 2002: Confronting the environmental Kuznets curve. *Journal of Economic Perspectives*, 16(1), 147–68.

Freese, B. 2003: *Coal: A Human History*. Cambridge, MA: Perseus.

Grossman, G. and Krueger, A. 1995: Economic growth and the environment. *Quarterly Journal of Economics*, 110(2), 353–77.

Hilton, F., Hank, G., and Levinson, A. 1998: Factoring the environmental Kuznets curve: evidence from automotive lead emissions. *Journal of Environmental Economics and Management*, 35(2), 126–41.

Kahn, M. E. 2000: The environmental impact of suburbanization. *Journal of Policy Analysis and Management*, 19(4), 569–86.

—— 2001: The beneficiaries of Clean Air Act legislation. *Regulation*, 24(1), 34–9.

McNeill, J. R. 2000: *Something New Under the Sun: An Environmental History of the 20th Century World*. New York: W. W. Norton.

Stavins, R. 1998: What can we learn from the grand policy experiment? Lessons from SO$_2$ allowance trading. *Journal of Economic Perspectives*, 12(3), 69–88.

Viscusi, K. 1993: The value of risks to life and health. *Journal of Economic Literature*, 31(4), 1,912–46.

CHAPTER THIRTY

Urban Crime, Race, and the Criminal Justice System in the United States

Steven Raphael and Melissa Sills

30.1 Introduction

The impact of crime on general welfare is profound. Those most directly impacted are the victims of crime. By one estimate, the combination of direct monetary losses and the costs of pain and suffering among crime victims in the United States amounts to 0.5–0.7 percent of GDP (Freeman 1996). Beyond these direct costs are substantial indirect costs associated with reducing the threat of crime. In 1999, federal, state, and local government criminal justice expenditures amounted to $146.5 billion, or 1.6 percent of GDP (Bureau of Justice Statistics 2003). Many households pay significant premiums, either in terms of housing prices or longer commutes, to live in neighborhoods with lower probabilities of victimization. Many also purchase security devices and insurance to minimize the likelihood and costs of being criminally victimized. Moreover, fear of crime often impacts the most mundane personal decisions, such as whether to walk down a given street or through a particular neighborhood, whether to let one's children play outside, or whether to leave one's home after dark.

In addition to the costs to actual and potential crime victims, our public response to crime affects the lives of an increasingly growing population of male offenders. Over the past three decades, the US has experienced unprecedented increases in the size of the incarcerated population. In 1977, the number of inmates in federal and state prisons was approximately 300,000. By 2003, this figure had increased to 1.4 million. Relative to the US population, the incarceration rate per 100,000 residents increased during this period from 136 to 482.

While all communities are affected by crime and the criminal justice system, residents in large urban areas are particularly impacted. Moreover, within large metropolitan areas, the residents of poor, largely minority neighborhoods suffer disproportionately. The spatial concentration of crime and the residences of criminal offenders have direct as well as indirect consequences for urban neighborhoods. In addition to higher victimization rates and the concentration of unemployed men, crime repels middle-income households, disproportionately burdens the fiscal position of local urban governments, and in general greatly diminishes the quality of life in urban neighborhoods.

The purpose of this chapter is twofold. First, we present an overview of criminal victimization in the USA, with a particular emphasis on crime in urban areas. We begin with an empirical portrait of the incidence of crime. We discuss alternative categories of criminal victimization as defined by the US Federal Bureau of Investigation and document how the likelihood of being victimized differs by the type of city one lives in, where in a given city one lives, and by one's personal characteristics. In general, the residents of relatively poor more urban neighborhoods face a higher risk of criminal victimization than other city residents. In addition, racial and ethnic minorities, African-Americans in particular, are considerably more likely to be victimized.

Second, we present an empirical overview of incarceration trends in the USA, with an explicit emphasis on racial differences in the likelihood of serving time. In addition to being victimized at a relatively high rate, African-Americans are considerably more likely to be incarcerated. These relatively high incarceration rates are often attributed to a higher propensity among African-Americans (males in particular) to criminally offend, to explicit racial discrimination in the criminal justice system, and to criminal sentencing policies that have a disparate impact on African-Americans. We present an empirical overview of what has happened over the past three decades and discuss existing research that attempts to evaluate the relative importance of competing hypotheses concerning racial differences in incarceration.

30.2 AN EMPIRICAL PORTRAIT OF CRIME IN THE UNITED STATES

Felony criminal incidents involving victims are commonly categorized into the following seven mutually exclusive categories:

- *Murder and nonnegligent manslaughter*: defined as the willful killing of one human being by another.
- *Rape/sexual assault*: rape refers to forced sexual intercourse, inclusive of psychological coercion and physical force. Sexual assault is distinct from rape and includes any unwanted sexual contact between victim and offender.
- *Robbery*: a completed or attempted theft directly from a person by force of threat, with or without a weapon and with or without an injury.

- *Assault*: an attack with or without a weapon and with or without an injury. Attack with a weapon or an attack without a weapon resulting in a serious injury is referred to as aggravated assault. An attack without a weapon with no or minor injuries to the victim is referred to as simple assault.
- *Burglary*: the unlawful or attempted or forcible entry of residence; often, but not necessarily, involving theft.
- *Larceny/theft*: the taking of property without personal contact.
- *Motor vehicle theft*: the stealing or unauthorized taking of a motor vehicle, including attempted theft.

The first four felonies are often grouped under the banner of violent crimes, since each felony involves direct coercive or violent contact between offender and victim. The latter three felony offenses are commonly referred to as property crimes, since the objective of each is to unlawfully acquire the property of another without physically encountering the victim. Most official crime statistics focus on these seven crimes (for details, see Rennison 2002).

There are two principal sources of crime data for the USA. The first source is a household survey called the National Crime Victimization Survey (NCVS). The NCVS is a large annual survey of US households that records all incidents of criminal victimization experienced by members of the surveyed households for a given time period. The second source of crime statistics is the FBI Uniform Crime Reports (UCR). The UCR data are based on incidents reported to local police agencies. Total crime rates for cities, metropolitan statistical areas, states, and the nation are tabulated from these reports by aggregating the reports for individual police departments (referred to administratively as UCR reporting agencies). Comparison of crime rates calculated from these two sources of data invariably leads to the conclusion that a substantial amount of crime goes unreported to the police. For example, in 2001 only 39 percent of rape/sexual assault incidents, 60 percent of aggravated assaults, 51 percent of burglaries, and 31 percent of thefts were reported to the police.

We use these two sources of crime statistics to present an empirical profile of crime in the USA. We begin with a simple discussion of the relative frequency of different types of criminal offenses, overall and by the characteristics of the victims. We will also present a simple discussion of recent trends in crime. We then turn to a discussion of how criminal victimization varies across cities and across neighborhoods within cities.

30.2.1 A basic description of criminal victimization in the United States

Table 30.1 summarizes overall crime rates for the year 2001 by type of offense as well as by victim characteristics. With the exception of murder (information on which comes from US vital statistics), the crime rates are tabulated by the Bureau of Justice Statistics (BJS) from the NCVS. The violent crime victimization rates are expressed as the number of incidents per 100,000 people, while the property crime rates are expressed as the number of incidents per 100,000 households.

Table 30.1   Violent and property crime rates overall and by the characteristics of victimized persons and households, 2001

	Violent crimes per 100,000 persons 12 and older	Property crimes per 100,000 households
All	2,510	16,690
Specific violent crimes		
Murder	6	–
Rape	110	–
Robbery	280	–
Assault	2,120	–
Specific property crimes		
Households burglary	–	2,870
Theft	–	12,900
Motor vehicle theft	–	920
Gender		
Men	2,730	–
Women	2,300	–
Race		
White	2,450	16,510
Black	3,120	17,970
Other	1,820	16,360
Hispanic origin		
Hispanic	2,950	22,410
Non–Hispanic	2,450	16,130
Annual household income		
Less than $7,500	4,660	18,460
$7,500 to $14,999	3,690	18,160
$15,000 to $24,999	3,180	17,920
$25,000 to $34,999	2,910	17,040
$35,000 to $49,999	2,630	17,640
$50,000 to $74,999	2,100	17,880
$75,000 or more	1,850	18,000

Source: Rennison (2002)

Table 30.1 thankfully reveals that in 2001 the most serious violent crimes were also the least common. A murder rate of 6 per 100,000 indicates that six thousandths of a percentage point of the US population was murdered in 2001, amounting to more than 15,000 homicides. While this may seem like a large number, the number of people murdered in 2001 is less than 40 percent of the number who died in automobile accidents. In other words, while awful, homicide is a relatively rare event. Rape and sexual assault, on the other hand, occur with greater frequency (110 incidents per 100,000 persons age 12 and older). Moreover, given that the overwhelming majority of rape victims are female, the rape/sexual assault rate calculated explicitly for females is nearly double that reported in Table 30.1. Robbery and assault are the most common forms of violent crime in 2001. In the assault category, 75 percent of victimizations fall under the category of simple assault, while the remaining 25 percent are aggravated assaults. Overall, assault accounts for 85 percent of violent victimizations in 2001.

Property crime is considerably more common than violent crime. The most common property crime is simple theft, with 12,900 incidents per 100,000 households. This is followed by household burglary (2,870 incidents per 100,000 households) and motor vehicle theft (920 incidents per 100,000).

Table 30.1 also reveals considerable variation in the likelihood of being victimized across demographic and socioeconomic groups. In particular, there are substantial differences in victimization rates by gender, race, ethnicity, and annual household income. Men are considerably more likely to be victimized by a violent crime than women, as are members of racial and ethnic minority groups. African-Americans in particular are victimized by violent crime at particularly high rates. The overall likelihood of being the victim of a violent crime is 27 percent higher for blacks relative to whites. For homicide in particular, the racial difference in victimization rates is even larger. During the year 2000, the black homicide rate stood at 20.5 incidents per 100,000, compared with a white homicide rate of 3.3. In other words, in 2000 blacks were 6.2 times more likely to be murdered than whites. Moreover, at the peak of black homicide rates in 1991, blacks were 7.2 times more likely to be murdered than whites.

Table 30.1 also reveals that members of relatively low-income households are more likely to suffer a violent victimization than are members of middle- and higher-income households. Given the geographical segregation of blacks, Hispanics, and the poor within metropolitan areas, these relatively high violent victimization rates translate directly into higher crime rates in poor neighborhoods of urban areas.

For property crimes, we observe similar patterns with respect to race and ethnicity, yet a nonuniform pattern of victimization across household income groups. Both relatively poor households and relatively wealthy households are the most likely to be victimized, while those households in the middle of the income distribution are the least likely. A likely explanation of this U-shaped pattern is that the poorest households live in poor neighborhoods where the risk of victimization of all sorts is the highest, while the wealthiest households are likely to be the most lucrative targets.

A final important dimension along which victimization risk varies considerably is age. The young are the most likely to be the victims of a violent crime, with teenagers 16–19 years of age suffering the highest risk (5,580 incidents per 100,000). The likelihood of victimization drops off sharply as people age, with victimization rates of 2,930 for people aged 25–34, 2,290 for those aged 35–49, 950 for those aged 50–64, and 320 for senior citizens.

30.2.2 Variation in crime rates between and within US metropolitan areas

In addition to differences in criminal victimization rates by race, income, gender, and age, there are substantial differences across metropolitan areas and across neighborhoods within metropolitan areas in the likelihood of becoming a crime victim. In general, large cities have higher crime rates than smaller cities, urban areas have higher crime rates than suburban and rural areas, and poor, largely minority neighborhoods have higher crime rates than more affluent white neighborhoods. Here, we document these differences.

CROSS-AREA PATTERNS   Figures 30.1(a) and (b) present average metropolitan area violent and property crime rates, where the 300 plus metropolitan areas of the USA are stratified along a number of dimensions. The first set of figures presents crime rates for areas separated into four population-size quartiles. The second group of figures presents crime rates by the percentage of metropolitan area residents who are poor. The third set of figures presents crime rates by the percentage of the area population that is black or Hispanic. The final set presents crime rates by the degree of black–white residential segregation in the metropolitan area (where the index of dissimilarity is used to characterize the degree of housing segregation). In Figure 30.1(a), we see a uniformly positive relationship between violent crime and metropolitan area population, the percentage black or Hispanic, and the degree of black–white segregation. While there is not a uniform relationship between violent crime and poverty, low-poverty metropolitan areas generally have lower crime rates than high-poverty metropolitan areas. Similar, yet less pronounced, patterns are observed for overall property crimes in Figure 30.1(b). Property crime is somewhat higher in large areas, poor metropolitan areas, predominantly black and Hispanic metropolitan areas, and segregated areas.

All four of these dimensions are correlated with one another; that is, large metropolitan areas have higher poverty rates, larger minority populations, and generally higher levels of black–white segregation. Hence, an understanding of why crime is higher in large cities is likely to explain the relationship between crime and many of these area-level characteristics.

A recent empirical study by Glaeser and Sacerdote (1999) seeks to answer this question. The authors hypothesize a number of avenues by which city size is likely to influence crime rates. First, they speculate that the density of cities brings potential offenders into relatively closer contact with potential victims, including wealthy victims. This relatively close contact may increase the expected payoff to criminal activity, and thus generate more crime in large, dense metropolitan areas. Second, the authors demonstrate that the likelihood of being arrested conditional on committing a crime is lower in large cities. An increase in the expected payoff to crime through, for example, a reduction in the likelihood of being arrested is likely to increase the number of potential offenders and the amount of offending by a given active criminal. Finally, the authors posit that

(a)

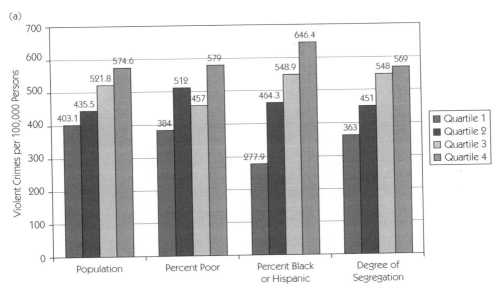

(b)

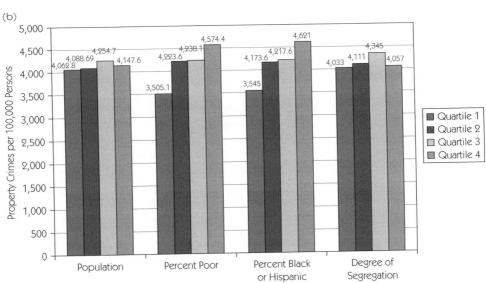

Figure 30.1 Average (a) violent and (b) property crime rates for metropolitan areas stratified by population, percent poor, and percent black or Hispanic, and by the degree of black–white segregation, 2001.

large cities are more likely to be the homes of those who are particularly predis-
posed toward committing crime.

In their cross-city analysis of crime rates, Glaeser and Sacerdote find that roughly
one-quarter of the relationship between crime and city size is attributable to
the relatively higher payoffs to crime in large cities. The lower probability of
being arrested accounts for approximately 20 percent of this relationship. Finally,
the authors conclude that nearly one-half of the relationship between crime and
city size is attributable to a high preponderance of criminally prone individuals
residing in large cities.

VARIATION WITHIN CITIES   Within metropolitan areas, there is a great degree
of variation in crime rates across neighborhoods. Generally, crime is particularly
high in poor, minority neighborhoods. For example, the murder rate in the city
of Oakland, California, was roughly 20 homicides per 100,000 residents in the
year 2001. This is much higher than the national average of 6.1 per 100,000 for
that year, and is at the 91st percentile of the distribution of murder rates for
cities with greater than 100,000 residents. Despite this high murder rate, there are
many neighborhoods within the city where there wasn't a single homicide in
2001. Nearly all of the higher-income residential areas in the Oakland hills and
the more middle-income communities of north Oakland were homicide free
during 2001. Conversely, the poor, predominantly black and Latino residential
areas in the flats of east and west Oakland accounted for nearly all of the city's
homicide count.

Crime rates are generally higher in the central city of a metropolitan statistical
area (MSA) than in the suburbs. Figure 30.2 presents a comparison of overall violent
and property crime rates for 2001 in three geographical areas: urban areas (the
central city of the metropolitan area), suburban areas (areas within the MSA but
outside of the central city), and rural areas (areas located outside of an MSA). These
figures are calculated using victimization data. The violent crime rate for urban
areas is 1.49 times that of suburban neighborhoods and 1.57 times that of rural
areas. Similarly, property crime rates in urban areas are 1.36 times the comparable rate for suburban areas and 1.61 times the comparable rate for rural areas.

In most US metropolitan areas, racial and ethnic minorities reside in central
urban communities, while white households tend to reside in metropolitan
area suburbs. In addition, poverty rates tend to be higher in central urban communities than in residential areas located on suburban fringes. In the light of
these segregated housing patterns, the higher central-city crime rates depicted in
Figure 30.2 would appear to imply that minorities and the poor face higher
neighborhood crime rates than do white households and nonpoor households.
In fact, this is very much the case. Analysis of variation in crime rates across
neighborhoods within a given city tends to find that white neighborhoods have
by far the fewest number of criminal victimizations per 100,000 residents, black
neighborhoods tend to have the highest crime rates, and the crime rates in predominantly Hispanic neighborhoods lie between those for blacks and whites.
Not surprisingly, crime is a particular severe problem in predominantly poor
neighborhoods of urban areas.

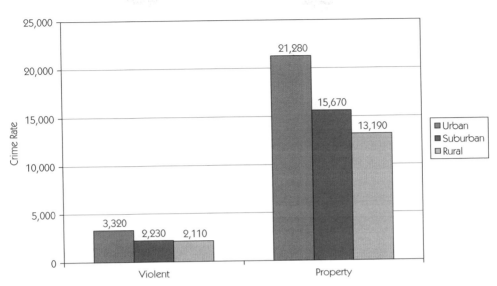

Figure 30.2 Violent and property crime victimization rates by household location within metropolitan areas and for rural areas, 2001.

The disproportionate impact of urban crime on predominantly minority and poor neighborhoods, and the consequent adverse effects on the poor, was recently demonstrated in a fairly stark manner by a housing mobility experiment funded by the US Department of Housing and Urban Development (HUD). The Moving to Opportunity (MTO) housing mobility experiment was designed to analyze the effects of moving predominantly poor, minority, and female-headed households out of central city public housing projects located in high-poverty neighborhoods and into private rental housing in neighborhoods with lower poverty rates and greater socioeconomic diversity. The program enlisted a large group of public-housing households and randomly assigned each household into one of three groups: (1) a treatment group that was given a Section 8 housing voucher, which could be used to rent housing in the private market but could only be used in a neighborhood with a poverty rate lower than 10 percent; (2) a Section 8 only group that was given a rental voucher with no restriction on where it could be used; and (3) a control group that was offered nothing in terms of housing assistance above and beyond what the household was already receiving.

Several teams of researchers analyzed the results of several post-move outcomes, including measures of employment, child educational outcomes, and health status. The research team analyzing MTO in Boston conducted a thorough analysis of the impact of the program on measures of personal safety from crime and the likelihood of being victimized (Katz, Kling & Lieberman 2001). Figure 30.3 presents the average post-program responses to a series of questions regarding exposure to crime and victimization administered to the program participants in the Boston

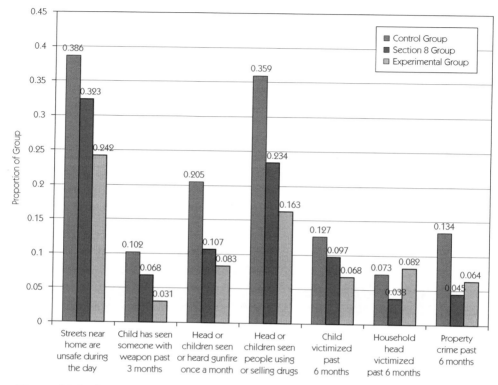

Figure 30.3   Intent-to-treat effects of the Moving to Opportunity program on various measures of exposure to crime for Boston participants.

MTO program. Each bar gives the proportion of the respondents in each group that answered affirmatively to the questions listed along the bottom of the chart.

The results from this study are stunning. While nearly 40 percent of control group households indicated that the streets near their home were unsafe during the day, only 32 percent of the Section 8 group and 24 percent of the experimental felt unsafe. Members of the Section 8 only group and the experimental groups were less likely to have seen someone carrying a gun, heard or seen gunfire in the past month, or witnessed drug dealing. Treatment group households were also considerably less likely to have been victimized by crime in the recent past.

30.3   Race and the Criminal Justice System

Crime in the USA has a disproportionate effect on African-Americans. As we have already seen, African-Americans are victimized by crime at higher levels than members of other racial and ethnic groups. As we will soon see, African-Americans are also incarcerated in prisons and jails at rates that far exceed the incarceration rates of other groups. Explanations of the relatively high incarceration rate for black males usually fall within one of two categories: explanations based on a relatively high black rate of participation in criminal activity, and explanations based on the differential treatment of blacks by the criminal justice system. While these are enormous topics of research in criminology, economics, and the social sciences more generally, about which volumes have been written, here we will highlight a few elements of this debate and some key empirical research.

In this section, we will first document incarceration trends over the past three decades, with a focus on two measures of incarceration. We will then turn to a broad discussion of the explanations of these trends. Our assessment is that both a greater propensity to commit crime as well as differential treatment by the criminal justice system are important contributors to the relatively high rate of incarceration for African-Americans in the USA.

30.3.1   Documenting trends in institutionalization from the US Census

The decennial Census of Population and Housing enumerates both the institutionalized as well as the noninstitutionalized population. The Public Use Microdata Samples (PUMS) for each census includes information on whether an individual is institutionalized as well as micro-level information on age, education, race, and a number of other demographic characteristics. Within the institutionalized population, one can separately identify individuals residing in nonmilitary institutions. This category includes inmates of federal and state prisons, local jail inmates, residents of inpatient mental hospitals, and residents of other nonaged institutions. Here, we document trends in male incarceration rates using these data.

Table 30.2 documents employment and incarceration trends for men by race and educational attainment using data from the 1970, 1980, 1990, and 2000 US Censuses of Population and Housing. The table presents the proportion of non-Hispanic black and white males aged between 18 and 65 that are employed, that are not working and yet not institutionalized, that are in the armed forces, and that are institutionalized. For all black men, the proportion employed declines markedly over this 30-year period, from 0.73 in 1970 to 0.57 in the year 2000. This decline occurs within all education groups, although the drop is largest for black high school dropouts (from 0.71 to 0.34). Employment rates decline slightly for white males overall, and decline substantially for white high school dropouts. However, these changes are small in comparison to those observed for blacks.

Over the 30-year period, the proportion of black men that are institutionalized increases considerably, especially for less educated black men. For all black males, the proportion institutionalized increases nearly threefold, from 0.03 in 1970 to 0.08 in 2000. For black high school dropouts, the institutionalization rate increases nearly fivefold. At the end of the century, roughly one-fifth of black men with less than a high school degree are institutionalized. There is no increase in institutionalization among black males with at least a college degree. Among whites, changes in institutionalization rates, overall and within educational groups, are considerably smaller by comparison.

Table 30.2 Employment and institutionalization status for non-Hispanic black males and non-Hispanic white males by educational attainment, 1970–2000

	Black males				White males			
	1970	1980	1990	2000	1970	1980	1990	2000
All								
Employed	0.73	0.64	0.63	0.57	0.82	0.80	0.80	0.79
NILF	0.20	0.29	0.30	0.33	0.13	0.17	0.17	0.18
Armed forces	0.04	0.04	0.03	0.02	0.04	0.02	0.02	0.01
Institutionalized	0.03	0.03	0.04	0.08	0.01	0.01	0.01	0.01
Less than high school								
Employed	0.71	0.57	0.46	0.34	0.80	0.69	0.63	0.59
NILF	0.23	0.38	0.44	0.47	0.17	0.28	0.34	0.37
Armed forces	0.01	0.01	0.00	0.00	0.01	0.01	0.00	0.00
Institutionalized	0.04	0.05	0.10	0.19	0.02	0.02	0.03	0.04
High school graduate								
Employed	0.75	0.66	0.63	0.56	0.85	0.81	0.80	0.77
NILF	0.15	0.25	0.28	0.35	0.10	0.15	0.17	0.20
Armed forces	0.08	0.06	0.04	0.02	0.05	0.03	0.02	0.01
Institutionalized	0.02	0.03	0.05	0.08	0.01	0.01	0.01	0.02
Some college								
Employed	0.71	0.69	0.68	0.66	0.77	0.81	0.81	0.80
NILF	0.22	0.25	0.23	0.26	0.18	0.17	0.16	0.17
Armed forces	0.06	0.04	0.05	0.03	0.04	0.02	0.02	0.02
Institutionalized	0.01	0.02	0.05	0.05	0.00	0.00	0.01	0.01
College plus								
Employed	0.87	0.84	0.85	0.81	0.89	0.91	0.90	0.89
NILF	0.09	0.13	0.11	0.16	0.07	0.07	0.08	0.10
Armed forces	0.04	0.02	0.03	0.01	0.04	0.02	0.02	0.01
Institutionalized	0.01	0.01	0.01	0.01	0.00	0.00	0.000	0.00

Source: Figures are tabulated from the 1970, 1980, 1990, and 2000 Public Use Microdata Samples from the US Census of Population and Housing

Table 30.3 presents similar tabulations by age. For black men, the proportion institutionalized increases within every age group, with the most pronounced increases for the young. In 2000, roughly 11 percent of black men aged between 18 and 40 are institutionalized. Again, while there are slight increases in the proportion institutionalized among young white men, the changes are small in comparison to what we observe among African-Americans.

Tables 30.2 and 30.3 indicate that both age and educational attainment are strong predictors of current incarceration. Table 30.4 explores the interaction between these two dimensions for black men only. The table presents comparable

Table 30.3 Employment and institutionalization status for non-Hispanic black males and non-Hispanic white males by age, 1970–2000

	Black males				White males			
	1970	1980	1990	2000	1970	1980	1990	2000
18–25 years								
Employed	0.55	0.48	0.46	0.43	0.63	0.69	0.68	0.68
NILF	0.32	0.40	0.41	0.43	0.26	0.26	0.25	0.27
Armed forces	0.08	0.08	0.06	0.03	0.10	0.04	0.05	0.03
Institutionalized	0.05	0.04	0.07	0.11	0.01	0.01	0.01	0.02
26–30 years								
Employed	0.80	0.69	0.64	0.61	0.89	0.86	0.86	0.85
NILF	0.13	0.22	0.23	0.25	0.07	0.10	0.10	0.11
Armed forces	0.04	0.04	0.04	0.02	0.04	0.02	0.03	0.02
Institutionalized	0.04	0.05	0.09	0.12	0.01	0.01	0.01	0.02
31–40 years								
Employed	0.82	0.76	0.70	0.64	0.91	0.90	0.89	0.87
NILF	0.11	0.18	0.21	0.23	0.05	0.07	0.08	0.10
Armed forces	0.04	0.03	0.03	0.02	0.03	0.02	0.02	0.01
Institutionalized	0.03	0.03	0.06	0.11	0.01	0.01	0.01	0.02
41–50 years								
Employed	0.83	0.77	0.74	0.65	0.92	0.90	0.90	0.86
NILF	0.14	0.21	0.21	0.28	0.06	0.09	0.10	0.12
Armed forces	0.01	0.01	0.01	0.01	0.01	0.01	0.01	0.00
Institutionalized	0.02	0.02	0.04	0.06	0.01	0.01	0.01	0.01
51–65 years								
Employed	0.72	0.61	0.58	0.53	0.81	0.72	0.69	0.70
NILF	0.26	0.37	0.40	0.44	0.18	0.27	0.31	0.29
Armed forces	0.00	0.00	0.00	0.00	0.00	0.00	0.00	0.00
Institutionalized	0.02	0.01	0.02	0.03	0.01	0.01	0.01	0.01

Source: Figures are tabulated from the 1970, 1980, 1990, and 2000 Public Use Microdata Samples from the US Census of Population and Housing

tabulations for the subset of relatively young (under 40) and relatively less educated (dropouts and high school graduates) black men. For young high school dropouts, the declines in the proportion employed are considerably more drastic than the declines in employment for black male high school dropouts overall. For dropouts aged between 18 and 25, the employment rate declines from 0.50 to 0.27. For those aged 26 to 30, the proportion employed declines from 0.76 to 0.30, while for 31–40 year olds, employment rates decline from 0.81 to 0.35.

Similarly, increases in the proportions institutionalized are much larger than those observed for dropouts overall. For dropouts aged between 18 and 25, the

Table 30.4 Employment and institutionalization status for non-Hispanic black males aged 40 and under with a high school education or less, 1970–2000

	High school dropouts				High school graduates			
	1970	1980	1990	2000	1970	1980	1990	2000
18–25 years								
Employed	0.50	0.38	0.30	0.27	0.62	0.52	0.49	0.44
NILF	0.38	0.51	0.55	0.50	0.23	0.32	0.36	0.44
Armed forces	0.04	0.04	0.00	0.00	0.13	0.13	0.10	0.04
Institutionalized	0.08	0.08	0.15	0.23	0.02	0.03	0.06	0.09
26–30 years								
Employed	0.76	0.58	0.40	0.30	0.83	0.70	0.64	0.58
NILF	0.16	0.32	0.38	0.36	0.09	0.21	0.24	0.29
Armed forces	0.01	0.01	0.00	0.00	0.06	0.05	0.04	0.02
Institutionalized	0.06	0.10	0.22	0.34	0.02	0.04	0.08	0.12
31–40 years								
Employed	0.81	0.70	0.52	0.35	0.82	0.76	0.69	0.62
NILF	0.13	0.25	0.34	0.37	0.08	0.17	0.24	0.27
Armed forces	0.01	0.00	0.00	0.00	0.08	0.04	0.02	0.01
Institutionalized	0.05	0.05	0.13	0.28	0.02	0.03	0.06	0.11

Source: Figures are tabulated from the 1970, 1980, 1990, and 2000 Public Use Microdata Samples from the US Census of Population and Housing

institutionalization rate increases from 8 percent to 23 percent. For those aged between 26 and 40, the institutionalization rates increases from approximately 5 percent to 30 percent. For all dropouts less than 40 years of age, the institutionalized population is only slightly smaller than the population of employed men from this demographic group. For black dropouts aged between 26 and 30, there are actually more institutionalized than employed. Comparable, although somewhat muted, patterns are observed for black high school graduates.

Tables 30.2 through 30.4 demonstrate the relatively high rate at which black men are incarcerated. If we turn our focus to the proportion ever having served time, the racial disparities are even larger. This is due primarily to the high turnover rates in state and federal prisons driven by relatively short median sentences. For example, the median sentence for new prison admissions in the USA in 1999 was roughly 3 years for the maximum sentence and 13 months for the minimum sentences. Moreover, many inmates will serve considerably less time than their maximum sentences (see Raphael & Stoll 2004).

Gauging the population of former prison inmates is difficult, due to the fact that none of the major household surveys in the USA ask respondents whether they have served time. Thus, estimating the size of this population requires indirect methods. The BJS estimates the number of former inmates by combining population data, birth cohort estimates of the likelihood of entering prison for the first time at each age (often separately by race and gender), and cohort and age-specific mortality rates (Bonczar 2003). Based on this methodology, the BJS estimates that in addition to the 1.3 million current inmates in 2001, an additional 4.3 million noninstitutionalized persons had served a prison term in the past. Combined, current and former prison inmates account for 4.9 percent of the adult male population in 2001.

Of course, there are large differences by race and ethnicity. The same set of estimates indicate that 2.6 percent of non-Hispanic white males, 16.6 percent of non-Hispanic black males, and 7.7 percent of Hispanic males have served prison time (figures that are roughly double the institutionalization rates listed in Table 30.3). The comparable figures for whites, blacks, and Hispanics for 1974 were 1.4, 8.7, and 2.3 percent, respectively (for more detailed calculations by age and educational attainment, see Raphael 2006).

The BJS also uses this methodology to calculate lifetime probabilities of entering either the state or federal prison system. Given that the risk of incarceration has increased over the past three decades, lifetime probabilities should exceed the current proportion of a specific population that is either currently incarcerated or formerly incarcerated. For white males, the lifetime likelihood of going to prison for men born in 1974 is estimated to be 2.2 percent. For those born in 2001, the risk increases to 5.9 percent. For black males, this likelihood increases from 13.2 percent to 32.2 percent, while for Hispanics the likelihood increases from 4 percent to 17.2 percent.

Thus, institutionalization rates for black men have increased considerably since 1970. These increases have been largest for the young and the relatively less educated. We now turn to a discussion of possible explanations for these patterns.

30.3.2 A differential propensity to commit crime

There are several patterns that strongly indicate that black males offend at higher rates than other groups. Perhaps the most persuasive empirical evidence supporting this proposition comes from victim accounts of the perceived race of the offender and the high rates of intraracial homicide. Concerning victim accounts, 14 percent of white victims of violent crimes involving a single offender reported that the offender was black in 2001. Black victims of comparable violent crime reported that the offender was black in 83 percent of all cases. Together, these two rates imply that for black and white victims of violent crime, the likelihood that the offender is black is roughly 25 percent.

These figures have several implications. First, one should emphasize that black offenders commit only a fraction of the total amount of violent crime in the USA (roughly 25 percent). However, given that African-Americans account for roughly 13 percent of the population, the patterns evident in victim reports suggest that blacks offend at a relatively high rate. Moreover, once one accounts for the fact that most crimes (especially violent crimes) are committed by males, the disproportionate presence of black male offenders becomes even more pronounced.

The relatively high homicide rates for blacks coupled with the high proportion of homicide that is intraracial (i.e., black-on-black or white-on-white) also indicate that blacks offend at a relatively high rate. We have already noted that blacks are roughly six times more likely to be murdered than whites. What we have yet to discuss is the characteristics of those who commit murder in relation to homicide victims. Roughly 86 percent of white homicide victims are murdered by a white offender. Roughly 94 percent of black homicide victims are murdered by a black offender. Given the high murder rates for blacks, these figures translate directly into a relatively high rate of offending (for this particular crime) for African-Americans.

An alternative measure of criminal involvement that is, perhaps, the most frequently cited is the arrest rate. Black offenders are certainly overrepresented among the pool of those arrested in any given year. Black offenders constitute 28 percent of those arrested, yet only 13 percent of the general population in 2000. Assuming that arrests are a valid proxy for criminal involvement, then these figures, like the victimization and homicide reports, suggest that higher levels of criminal involvement explain some part of disproportionate incarceration rates.

Blumstein (1982) presents the first evaluation of the relative culpability of the high black arrest rate in explaining the high black incarceration rates. Using national data for 1974, Blumstein finds that differential arrest rates explain roughly 80 percent of the racial difference in incarceration rates. However, arrest rates explain a larger share of this differential for more serious offenses. For example, arrest rates explained 97 percent of the disproportional incarceration for homicide and 95 percent for aggravated assault, but only 46 percent for auto theft and 49 percent for drug offenses. Blumstein hypothesized that where there is more discretion at the various stages of the criminal justice process (when the offense is less serious), there would be more opportunities for bias and racial prejudice to influence the decisions of agents of the criminal justice system.

More recent studies using various methodological approaches generally confirm the finding that the relatively high rates at which blacks commit crime explains much of the difference in incarceration rates. These latter studies also find that the seriousness of the offense and the prior record of the arrestee are also important indicators of incarceration and sentencing. However, this research finds tremendous variation across states and offense categories in the ability of racial differences in arrest rates to explain racial differences in incarceration. Moreover, there are those who would argue that arrest rates in themselves reflect the differential treatment of African-American by the police and are therefore poor measures of a differential propensity to commit crime. This brings us to the next topic of discussion.

DOES THE CRIMINAL JUSTICE SYSTEM TREAT BLACKS DIFFERENTLY? The implementation of criminal justice policy may result in blacks being treated differently for a number of reasons. Perhaps the most obvious source is the influence of racial prejudice and bias on the decisions made by police, prosecutors, judges, and juries. The process leading from arrest for an offense to conviction and incarceration is loaded with decision points at which agents of the criminal justice system exercise broad discretion and at which personal beliefs concerning race and criminality may come into play. The police decide whether to stop a car or question someone in the street, prosecutors decide whether to prosecute an offense and, in some instances, whether to charge the offender in state or federal court where the sentences are likely to differ substantially, juries ultimately weigh the evidence and assess guilt, while judges often have great influence over the ultimate punishment. To be sure, police, prosecutors, judges, and juries must exercise discretion in order for the criminal justice system to function. However, to the extent that beliefs concerning race and crime (whether or not they are accurate) that are prevalent among the general population also influence the cognitive process and decisions of these agents, discriminatory treatment may adversely affect African-American defendants.

There are many who contend that the police "racially profile" blacks, in that they stop, question, and search minorities solely on the basis of race or ethnicity. Even if blacks and whites commit crimes at the same rate, stopping blacks more frequently than others will result in a higher black arrest rate and, ultimately, incarceration rate. With respect to traffic stops, there is empirical evidence that the police stop black drivers at a relatively high rate. Using data from the NCVS, the Bureau of Justice Statistics estimates that while the police stopped 10.4 percent of white licensed drivers at least once during 1999, the comparable figure for blacks was 12.3 percent (see Schmitt, Langan & Durose 2002). Moreover, on average, African-American drivers travel 2,200 fewer miles per year than white drivers, a fact that renders the higher stop rates more surprising. Moreover, African-American households are considerably less likely to own a car, and own fewer cars on average than white households (Raphael & Stoll 2001). The BJS also found that of those drivers stopped for speeding, 76 percent of blacks were ticketed compared with 67 percent of whites. The survey also revealed that only 74 percent of blacks stopped by the police felt that they had been stopped for a legitimate reason, compared with 86 percent of whites, and that the vehicles of black drivers were significantly more likely to be searched.

Racial profiling, however, may extend beyond traffic stops. For example, Fagan and Davis (2000) examined New York City police stop and arrest data, and found that police stopped 22.6 black residents per 1,000, while stopping only 4.8 white residents per 1,000. There were 7.3 black stops for every black arrest and only 4.6 stops for every white arrest. This latter pattern indicates that police are either worse at predicting criminal activity when they stop blacks or that they target blacks for stops more broadly and indiscriminately.

To the extent that the police scrutinize the behavior of African-Americans at a higher level than others, then part of the racial disparity in arrest rates and ultimately incarceration rates will be accounted for by explicit differential treatment. In addition to the behavior of the police, however, differences in treatment may occur during the adjudication process after an arrest. As we have already mentioned, differential treatment may occur in the decision to prosecute, where to prosecute, what charges to bring, jury deliberations, and sentencing. While we will not review the large body of research investigating this question, research findings generally support the contention that blacks are treated differently during the post-arrest phases of a criminal prosecution, and to their detriment (for an excellent entry into this body of literature, see the study by Mustard 2001).

30.3.3 Sentencing policies that have racially disparate impacts

The discussion in this section thus far has focused on how the differential treatment of black defendants and black citizens more generally is likely to influence arrest rates and incarceration rates independently of any racial differences in the propensity to commit crime. The discussion has emphasized avenues that are based on the discretionary behavior of agents of the criminal justice system. An alternative path that may lead to a relatively high black incarceration rate concerns the race-neutral application of criminal justice policy that has racially disparate impacts. For example, to the extent that poor urban drug users consume drugs outdoors while wealthier suburban drug users consume in the privacy of their homes, police strategies that crack down on visible drug use will disproportionately net urban, poor, and largely minority drug users.

Alternatively, policy-makers may target police enforcement efforts on certain kinds of drugs and enhance the penalties for drug violations accordingly. To the extent that black drug users consume different drugs than white users, and that blacks consume the more heavily penalized narcotics, race-neutral applications of public policy will result in higher arrest and incarceration rates for blacks.

Black drug users are surely disproportionately represented among drug arrests in the USA. While African-Americans account for only 17 percent of drug users nationwide, they represent 37 percent of those arrested for drug use. The opposite is true for whites, who account for 82 percent of drug users yet only 62 percent of drug arrests.

The disproportionate representation of blacks among drug arrests is linked to the increased law enforcement focus over the past two decades on fighting the use of crack cocaine. The "War on Drugs," which officially began in the mid-1980s, redirected law enforcement resources toward illicit drug markets. Among the policy changes, crack was criminalized at a much higher level than powder cocaine or other drugs, funding for the anti-drug activities of police departments was increased, and arrest rates and prosecutions for drug offenses were enhanced. As a result, the proportion of federal prisoners incarcerated for drug offenses skyrocketed from 23 percent in 1980 to about 60 percent in 2000. While arrest rates for white drug offenders increased slightly, the majority of the increase in drug incarceration was born by blacks (Tonry 1995). This latter fact was driven nearly in its entirety by the fact that blacks consume crack at a higher rate than whites. Figure 30.4 shows the racial composition of drug offenders sentenced in federal courts by type of drug, and indicates that blacks are far more likely to be sentenced to prison for crack cocaine than whites.

Those who possess or sell crack cocaine are currently subject to a punishment in terms of sentence length that far exceeds the punishment for being caught with similar quantities of powder cocaine. For example, a drug offender apprehended with 5 g of crack cocaine will face the same mandatory sentence as a drug offender with 500 g of powder cocaine (an illustration of the 100:1 rule). Thus, lower-level users and sellers are likely to be sentenced for crack cocaine

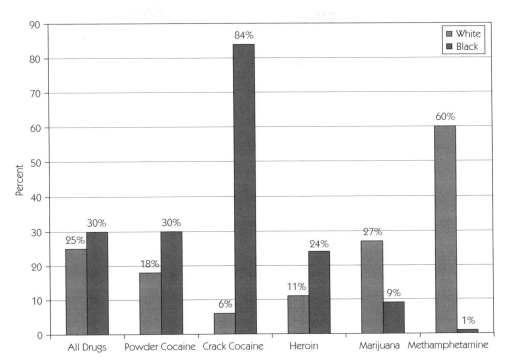

Figure 30.4   The percentage of drugs offenders that are white or black, by drug type, 2000.
Source: US Sentencing Commission

than for powder cocaine or any other drug. Moreover, black offenders are clearly differentially impacted.

30.3.4   Summary

The empirical research that we have reviewed indicates that higher rates of incarceration for African-Americans is likely linked to both a high rate of offending as well as differential treatment by the criminal justice system. In addition, certain policies that fall under the title of the US War on Drugs, while perhaps racially neutral in their implementation, have had racially disparate impacts to the detriment of African-Americans.

High rates of incarceration have economic, social, and political implications for black men, black families, and black communities. Criminal records tend to negatively impact employment opportunities and wages, thus reducing the attractiveness of legal work relative to criminal activity. Incarceration rates are highest for African-American men aged 20–39 years, the ages during which men are most likely to begin families and have children. These high rates of incarceration are socially devastating for black families and communities, as fewer black males are available to fill fatherhood and leadership roles. Disproportionately high incarceration rates may also be politically damaging for black communities, as felons are disenfranchised for the duration of their incarceration in most states, and permanently disenfranchised in some. Addressing the high rate of black incarceration is a terribly pressing policy problem that the USA must grapple with for many years to come.

30.4   Conclusion

The importance of crime control and the impact of criminal victimization on cities nationwide are self-evident. As we have reviewed, in the USA crime imposes enormous costs on society, especially for the most marginalized and fragile communities in the nation's urban areas. We have also seen that those who commit crimes tend to be from the same groups that are most likely to be victimized. This carries serious implications for poor urban communities and for the offenders themselves. Being officially branded an ex-felon is likely to hamper future employment prospects and one's general ability to function as a law-abiding, noninstitutionalized citizen.

Of course, systematic studies of crime and the motivations behind criminal activity are likely to shed light on new possibilities for controlling crime, diverting potential offenders to more productive activity, and lessening the burden on society.

Bibliography

Blumstein, A. 1982: On the racial disproportionality of United States prison populations. *Journal of Criminal Law and Criminology*, 73(3), 1,259–81.

Bonczar, T. P. 2003: *Prevalence of Imprisonment in the U.S. Population, 1974–2001*. Bureau of Justice Statistics Special Report, NCJ 197976.

Bureau of Justice Statistics 2003: Key facts at a glance: direct expenditures by level of government; www.ojp.usdoj.gov.bjs/glance/tables/expgovtab.html

Fagan, J. and Davies, G. 2000: Street stops and broken windows: Terry, race, and disorder in New York City. *Fordham Urban Law Journal*, 28, 457.

Freeman, R. B. 1996: Why do so many young American men commit crimes and what might we do about it? *Journal of Economic Perspectives*, 10(1), 25–42.

Glaeser, E. L. and Sacerdote, B. 1999: Why is there more crime in cities? *Journal of Political Economy*, 107(6), S225–57.

Katz, L. H., Kling, J. R., and Liebman, J. B. 2001: Moving to Opportunity in Boston: early results of a randomized mobility experiment. *Quarterly Journal of Economics*, 116(2), 607–74.

Mustard, D. B. 2001: Racial, ethnic, and gender disparities in sentencing: evidence from the U.S. Federal courts. *Journal of Law and Economics*, XLIV, 285–314.

Raphael, S. 2006: The socioeconomic status of black males: the increasing importance of incarceration. In A. Auerbach, D. Card, and J. Quigley (eds.), *Poverty, the Distribution of Income, and Public Policy*. New York: Russell Sage Foundation, forthcoming.

—— and Stoll, M. A. 2001: Can boosting minority car-ownership rates narrow inter-racial employment gaps? In W. G. Gale and J. Rothenberg Pack (eds.), *The Brookings–Wharton Papers on Urban Affairs*, vol. 2. Washington, DC: The Brookings Institution, 99–145.

—— and —— 2004: The effect of prison releases on regional crime rates. In W. G. Gale and J. Rothenberg Pack (eds.), *The Brookings–Wharton Papers on Urban Affairs*, vol. 5. Washington, DC: The Brookings Institution, 207–55.

Rennison, C. 2002: Criminal victimization 2001: changes 2000–01 with trends 1993–2001. Bureau of Justice Statistics National Crime Victimization Survey, NCJ 194610.

Schmitt, E. L., Langan, P. A., and Durose, M. R. 2002: Characteristics of drivers stopped by police, 1999. Bureau of Justice Statistics, NCJ 191548.

Tonry, M. 1995: *Malign Neglect: Race, Crime, and Punishment in America*. New York: Oxford University Press.

Ethnic Segregation and Ghettos

Alex Anas

31.1   INTRODUCTION

In *The Republic*, Socrates describes income segregation in the Ancient Greek *polis* and goes on to prescribe policy:

> For, indeed any city, however small, is in fact divided into two, one the city of the poor the other of the rich; these are at war with one another; and in either there are many smaller divisions, and you would be altogether beside the mark if you treated them as a single State. But if you deal with them as many, and give the wealth or power or persons of the one to the other, you will always have a great many friends and not many enemies. (Jowett 1999, pp. 137–8)

Later, in ancient Rome, integration of the rich (the patricians) and the poor (the plebeians) was apparently enforced by urban design:

> First of all is the close juxtaposition of the houses of the wealthy and the single-room high-rise apartment dwellings of the poor. As this and many other plan fragments show, there was no significant economic segregation in Rome . . . In our present example of imperial Rome, it is interesting to consider the reality of close physical mixing of social classes against the literary image of the distinct separation of those classes in many social practices. (Reynolds 1997, p. 16)

Although segregation by income need not imply ethnic segregation, the two are correlated, and evidence of this abounds from later periods. For example, in Constantinople, the capital of the Eastern Roman Empire for 11 centuries and the world's largest city for a long time, the majority of the population was Hellenic, but certain areas were settled by European traders and Jews. After the conquest by the Ottoman Turks in 1453, Greeks, Armenians, Jews, and Levantines dominated parts of the city and were, on average, wealthier and more highly taxed than the ruling Turks.

The causes of ethnic segregation in contemporary cities are varied. Many large central cities on all continents have vibrant Chinatowns. Under South African apartheid, blacks and whites were required by law to live in separate areas. Black ghettos in the large cities of the American Midwest and Northeast emerged as freed slaves moved north to seek a new life within a white majority that was racially prejudiced. Although there were no laws restricting location by race, privately initiated racial and religious restrictive covenants operated well into the 1950s. In today's Europe, Algerian ghettos in France or Turkish ghettos in Germany have emerged much like black ghettos have in the United States, as immigrants were injected into a society with a different culture, language, or religion.

The ghettos of large Asian cities, the *favelas* of Brazil, or the *gecekondu* settlements around Turkey's large cities are informally built settlements, often on the outskirts of large cities because poor migrants from the rural areas cannot find affordable formal urban housing. *Gecekondu* translates as "night-perched," referring to an informal dwelling inconspicuously and quickly constructed on public land by the squatter in one night, as it were. In most cases, this is sufficient to afford the squatter a legality of tenure unless the government decides otherwise. The impoverished settlers are often of distinct regional or ethnic origin.

Asia's largest slum, Dharavi, sits on 427 acres (0.67 square miles) sandwiched between two major north–south railways, near the center of Mumbai (Bombay), India. Estimates of Dharavi's population range from one-half to a million people, "crammed into rows of makeshift shanties, cobbled together with nothing more than asbestos sheets, plastics, bamboo sticks, discarded canvas bags, wooden planks and old car tires" (Katyal & Lengade 2004). Dharavi's gross population density implied by such estimates – if they are correct – is 1,171 people per acre or higher, or at most an incredibly low 37 square feet of land per person. The chief occupations are leatherworking, embroidering, and pickle-making. The land is swampy, lacking toilets and water supply. Although many ethnicities mix in Dharavi, 37 percent of the population, the largest group, is Tamil speaking.

The word "ghetto" derives from the medieval *borghetto*, meaning a "settlement outside the city walls," more like today's suburbs than an American ghetto in an inner city. I will use "ghetto" to mean not a *slum*, but significant and contiguous ethnic concentrations, including economically vibrant ones. The politically correct definition has evolved. The 1979 unabridged edition of *The Random House Dictionary of the English Language* gives two definitions. The first echoes Europe's anti-Semitic past: a ghetto is "a section of a city in which in former times, in most European countries, all Jews were required to live." The Warsaw ghetto of World War II is the last example of this. The second definition reflects US reality. Accordingly, a ghetto is "a section of a city, especially a thickly populated slum area, inhabited predominantly by Negroes, Puerto Ricans, or any other minority group, often as a result of social or economic restrictions." By contrast, the paperback pocket edition of *Webster's New World Dictionary*, published in 1995, reiterates the first definition but adjusts the second as "any section of a city in which many members of a minority group live."

Does ethnic segregation emerge from voluntary decisions or from social restrictions? Often, both aspects are present. Chinatowns may be largely voluntary, while the African-American ghettos of the USA and the Muslim ghettos of India are thought to have been caused, in part, by exclusion or discrimination. We will see that ghettos that emerge due to external coercion and those that self-organize voluntarily have observable economic differences.

Segregation can be measured at many levels of resolution. Nationwide in the USA, about 55 percent of blacks and 22 percent of whites reside in central cities, while 55 percent of whites and 31 percent of blacks live in suburbs. No matter what the resolution, segregation exhibits enormous variation among urban areas. In Table 31.1, I list 43 US primary metropolitan statistical areas (PMSAs) with over 1 million population in 1980. I compare the spatial segregation of non-Hispanic African-Americans by dividing their percentage of the central-city population by their percentage of the suburban population. I refer to this ratio as the metropolitan *ghettoization index*. This index, for the year 2000, varies from a high of 21.5 for the Milwaukee–Waukesha MSA to a low of 0.8 for Miami. The year-2000 index for the USA is 2.6. Virtually all of the 23 PMSAs that score higher are

Table 31.1 Ghettoization trends for non-Hispanic blacks in the 43 PMSAs with more than 1 million population in 1980, ranked by year-2000 ghettoization index

| | Percentage non-Hispanic blacks | | | | | | | | |
| | Central city | | | Suburbs | | | Ghettoization index | | |
Primary MSA	1980	1990	2000	1980	1990	2000	1980	1990	2000
Milwaukee–Waukesha, WI	21.0	27.7	34.4	0.5	0.7	1.6	42.0	39.6	21.5
Buffalo – Niagara Falls, NY	24.1	27.9	34.8	1.2	1.4	2.4	20.0	19.9	14.5
Indianapolis, IN	20.9	22.0	25.4	1.0	1.4	2.2	20.9	15.7	11.5
Rochester, NY	25.4	30.7	39.1	2.1	2.5	3.5	12.1	12.3	11.2
Detroit, MI	55.9	66.0	71.4	3.4	4.3	6.6	16.4	15.3	10.8
Cincinnati, OH–KY–IN	33.4	37.8	43.5	4.2	4.5	5.7	7.9	8.4	7.6
Kansas City, MO–KS	24.6	26.1	27.4	1.5	2.2	3.7	16.4	11.9	7.4
Boston, MA–NA	16.5	18.6	20.3	1.0	1.8	2.8	16.5	10.3	7.3
Minneapolis – St Paul, MN–WI	6.4	10.4	17.0	0.5	1.1	2.9	12.8	9.5	5.9
Columbus, OH	19.1	20.2	23.4	1.8	3.0	4.4	10.6	6.7	5.3
Pittsburgh, PA	5.5	6.2	6.6	3.8	4.1	5.3	6.3	6.2	5.2
Hartford, CT	27.9	30.1	31.4	2.5	3.6	6.1	11.2	8.4	5.1
Portland–Vancouver, OR–WA	5.5	6.2	6.6	0.4	0.6	1.3	13.8	10.3	5.1
Cleveland–Lorain–Elyra, OH	37.5	39.6	44.1	6.4	8.0	9.7	5.9	5.0	4.5

Table 31.1 (cont'd)

Primary MSA	Percentage non-Hispanic blacks								
	Central city			Suburbs			Ghettoization index		
	1980	1990	2000	1980	1990	2000	1980	1990	2000
Philadelphia, PA–NJ	38.3	40.1	43.8	6.9	7.8	9.7	5.6	5.1	4.5
Baltimore, MD	53.7	57.8	63.1	8.4	10.4	14.9	6.4	5.6	4.2
Providence – Fall River – Warwick, RI–MA	4.2	5.2	7.5	0.6	1.1	1.9	7.0	4.7	3.9
Chicago, IL	36.8	35.8	33.8	4.6	6.4	8.8	8.0	5.6	3.8
Oakland, CA	35.7	33.2	29.0	6.4	7.4	8.4	5.6	4.5	3.5
St Louis, MO–IL	39.8	40.0	42.1	8.1	9.7	12.5	4.9	4.1	3.4
New Orleans, LA	52.6	59.0	64.6	13.9	17.7	21.0	3.8	3.3	3.0
Newark, NJ	57.3	55.8	53.0	13.1	15.6	17.8	4.4	3.6	2.9
Denver, CO	11.9	12.4	11.6	1.8	3.0	3.9	6.6	4.1	2.9
USA	**22.5**	**22.1**	**22.8**	**6.1**	**6.9**	**8.8**	**3.7**	**3.2**	**2.6**
Atlanta, GA	66.0	66.8	61.6	13.8	18.7	25.6	4.8	3.4	2.4
Dallas, TX	25.4	25.1	23.1	5.3	7.3	9.7	4.8	3.4	2.4
Houston, TX	26.3	26.2	24.7	6.1	8.9	10.7	4.3	2.9	2.3
San Francisco, CA	12.5	10.5	8.2	5.0	4.7	3.7	2.5	2.2	2.2
Seattle–Bellevue– Everett, WA	7.6	8.1	7.9	1.0	2.0	3.9	7.6	4.0	2.0
New York, NY (excluding suburbs in Long Island, New Jersey, and Connecticut)	23.9	25.2	25.5	9.6	11.0	12.6	2.5	2.3	2.0
Washington, DC	55.8	50.4	45.2	16.2	18.8	22.9	3.4	2.7	1.9
Tampa – St Petersburg – Clearwater, FL	9.1	8.8	10.4	3.4	4.0	5.8	2.7	2.2	1.8
San Diego, CA	7.9	8.3	7.8	2.7	3.7	4.6	2.9	2.2	1.7
Norfolk – Virginia Beach, VA–NC	29.5	30.0	35.2	23.7	21.3	21.1	1.2	1.4	1.7
San Jose, CA	3.7	3.9	3.4	2.1	2.5	2.2	1.8	1.6	1.5
Fort Lauderdale, FL	20.4	27.3	31.0	9.2	13.2	20.6	2.2	2.1	1.5
Los Angeles – Long Beach, CA	16.1	13.1	12.1	9.1	8.3	8.2	1.8	1.6	1.5
Phoenix–Mesa, AZ	3.6	3.8	4.4	2.0	2.2	3.1	1.8	1.7	1.4
Orange County, CA	2.3	2.2	2.0	0.9	1.4	1.7	2.6	1.6	1.2
Riverside – San Bernadino, CA	8.2	8.3	9.0	3.9	6.1	7.9	2.1	1.4	1.1
San Antonio, TX	7.0	6.7	6.7	5.2	5.8	6.7	1.3	1.2	1.0
Miami, FL	18.7	20.4	17.8	15.8	18.7	20.4	1.2	1.1	0.8

in the Northeast or the Midwest, and almost all that score lower are in the South or the West. The index has come down in each of the 43 PMSAs since 1980, as the percent-black of the suburbs has increased faster than has the percent-black of the central city. In Milwaukee, the most ghettoized PMSA, the index came down from 42 in 1980 to 21.5 as the suburbs changed from 0.5 percent to 1.5 percent black. For virtually all PMSAs that are more ghettoized than the nation, the percentage of the central-city population that is black has increased, while for PMSAs that are less ghettoized than the nation, the central cities are stable or becoming less black. Table 31.1 does not tell the whole story. There are suburban ghettos where middle- or lower-income blacks reside. A part of the growing suburbanization of blacks seen in Table 31.1 is due to growing black ghettos in the older suburbs of large cities. In Atlanta, for example, 25.6 percent of the suburbs are black, and this concentration lies in the inner southern suburbs. Thus, as a whole, Atlanta is more segregated than its ghettoization index shown in Table 31.1 implies.

According to the US Census Bureau, among the same 43 PMSAs in 2000 with at least 1 million people and at least 3 percent African-Americans, the most segregated was Milwaukee–Waukesha, Wisconsin (Figure 31.1), and the least

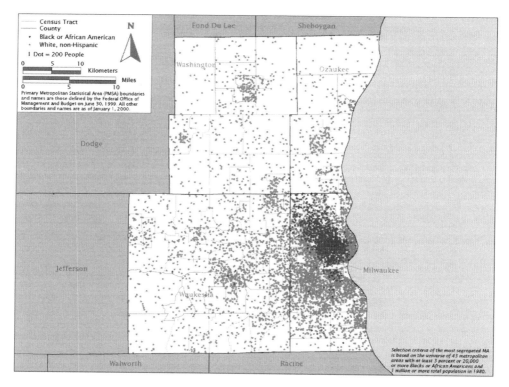

Figure 31.1   Milwaukee–Waukesha, Wisconsin, the most segregated large metropolitan area for African-Americans in 2000.
Source: Iceland and Weinberg (2002)

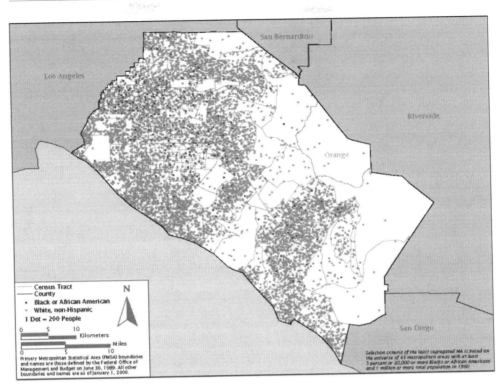

Figure 31.2 Orange County, California, the least segregated large metropolitan area for African-Americans in 2000.
Source: Iceland and Weinberg (2002)

segregated was Orange County, California (Figure 31.2). In each figure, a dark gray dot is a concentration of 200 African-Americans, while a light gray dot is a concentration of 200 white Americans. In Milwaukee, the dark dots are thickly clustered and cover a large section of the inner city, signifying a ghetto. In Orange County, the dark dots appear randomly dispersed: there is no ghetto. Concentrations of African-Americans are much smaller and isolated.

What accounts for the sharp contrast between Milwaukee–Waukesha and Orange County? Perhaps the most clichéd and *passé* explanation is that Midwesterners are far more racially prejudiced than are Californians. Accordingly, Milwaukee blacks reside in a more hostile environment than do Californian blacks and would find it too costly to relocate out of the ghetto. But Los Angeles and San Francisco, two other California PMSAs, contain swaths of African-American and Hispanic neighborhoods. Why, then, is Orange County different? Blacks, not whites, may be prejudiced. Then, African-American ghettos are due to *self-segregation*: not exclusionary prejudice by whites, but inclusionary prejudice by blacks. A third explanation, the one I favor the most, is that the racial segregation is driven by income differences that induce self-selection. Choices depend on a durable land use and housing pattern that is inherited from the past. Residential densities in Orange County are lower and housing values higher than in Los Angeles, and much higher than in Milwaukee. Income differences between white and black Americans have diminished, and about 30 percent of African-Americans now live in the suburbs (Mills & Lubuele 1997). Higher-income African-Americans can afford to live in Orange County. If, for blacks, living in a ghetto is an inferior good and living in the suburbs a normal good, then those who move to Orange County have no interest in forming a ghetto. Whites are also probably less prejudiced against blacks of similar incomes. High-income blacks who move to the suburbs are rarely clustered in ghettos and are accepted in predominantly white neighborhoods. The dispersion of Orange County blacks reflects these observations.

I will show how urban economic theory *can* explain ghettos and ethnic segregation. In section 31.2, I use agglomeration and externalities to explain the formation of voluntary ghettos, Chinatowns being examples. In section 31.3, we see how involuntary ghettos form due to prejudice, discrimination, or exclusionary policies targeting an ethnic minority. In section 31.4, I turn to bid-rent theory and ghettos. What is the pattern of land rent within a ghetto and across the ghetto boundary and how is it different for voluntary and involuntary ghettos? In section 31.5, the central question is whether ghettos are efficient. The answer need not be that involuntary ghettos are inefficient. The segregation of ethnic populations in voluntary or involuntary ghettos can generate net social benefits. In section 31.6, we briefly see how policy and politics in the world has responded to racial and ethnic segregation with bewildering complexity.

31.2 The Voluntary Ghetto

Spatial agglomeration explains how virtuous ghettos can form by voluntary atomistic decisions. But although the concept of urban agglomeration has been used to explain the spatial concentration of firms, it has not been used well to explain ethnic or racial concentrations of people. An agglomeration economy exists when the proximity of economic agents reduces costs. Suppose that members of an ethnic group have a strong taste for sharing a church or temple, preserving customs, trading with each other, borrowing from or lending to each other, speaking their language and teaching it to their children, or enjoying each other's company in day-to-day affairs. Then, many costs are reduced when a sufficiently large number of such individuals, families, and businesses locate in a contiguous area, forming a ghetto.

In a Chinatown, businessmen find it more profitable to set up Chinese food markets, families feel secure that their children will speak Chinese, and business dealings can be conducted in the native tongue, avoiding the less familiar customs of the majority. Tourists come to enjoy authentic Chinese food or to view Chinese New Year parades. Such exportable cultural activities are made possible by the scale of the ghetto. The ethnic ghetto is also an entry point for immigrants, easing their cost of transition. After living or working in the ghetto, the immigrant becomes adjusted. At a later stage in the life cycle, he or she moves out to set up a suburban business or, with some luck and perseverance, becomes a CEO. Ghettos also generate negative intra-ethnic externalities. Growing up in a purely ethnic environment may slow down assimilation, putting the residents at a disadvantage. Positive peer effects may be absent in segregated schooling. Spatial isolation can have adverse economic effects, such as difficulty in acquiring jobs. Ethnic organized crime networks may flourish in large ghettos but become inoperable when the population is dispersed. Cutler and Glaeser (1997) claim statistical evidence that American blacks achieve lower outcomes in schooling and employment and are more prone to single parenthood if they reside in more segregated areas.

The rise and fall of economically vibrant ethnic ghettos was an ongoing backdrop in American cities in the late nineteenth and early twentieth centuries. Jewish parts of town, Little Italies, and Little Dublins were quite common. Eventually, as American-born and English-speaking generations replaced the old, these ethnic gems all but vanished as populations became assimilated and affluent, dispersing to the suburbs. Unless there is a continuing influx of new immigrants, the ghetto is depopulated or filtered down to another less-affluent ethnic group. The once vibrant Greektown near downtown Chicago has lost most of its Greek population. Suburban Greeks still maintain some businesses there. Some cater to ethnic Greeks and others to tourists. But with increasing assimilation and fewer immigrants, it becomes harder to save costs by clustering together. Meanwhile, Greek churches with dispersed congregations have been built in Chicago's suburbs. Astoria in Queens continues to have a considerable but reduced residential and commercial presence by ethnic Greeks. Other ethnic groups of Hispanic and Asian origin are now equally dominant. Today's Astoria has the character of a *multiethnic ghetto*: an agglomeration of diverse groups and immigrants who find it cheaper to deal and live with each other than to disperse into the broader society.

31.3   THE INVOLUNTARY GHETTO

A reason for involuntary ghettoization is that people join a ghetto to find safety. Amartya Sen, the 2001 Nobel Laureate in economics, has alleged possible Indian state involvement in the 2002 anti-Muslim Gujarat riots that started after the Gohdra carnage, in which Hindu worshippers were burned inside a railroad car. After these riots, India's 13 percent Muslim minority of about 150 million has reportedly swarmed to existing Muslim ghettos at an accelerated rate. This is induced by animosity toward Muslims by the Hindu majority, as well as by the Muslim's demand for safety. Ethnic violence against Muslims is alleged to be highest where they are least concentrated. According to some reports, Muslims in Ahmedabad, Delhi, and other cities have flooded to ghettos, complete segregation being prevented only by skyrocketing ghetto rents.

While ghettos may offer safety, they may also facilitate wholesale destruction by accident or design. In 1928, a huge fire destroyed the centuries old and exclusively Greek Tatavla district of Istanbul, known for its ethnic vibrancy. The Greeks of Tatavla were known for the efficiency of their volunteer firefighting force. Was the fire set by the Turkish authorities, as is widely claimed in the folklore of survivors, and did the Turkish police prevent the Greek firefighters from operating, while the public firefighters arrived too late? The surviving Greek population became dispersed and the district was renamed "Kurtulush" (liberation), allegedly to signify "liberation" from Greeks. In contrast, during the pogrom of September 6–7, 1955, the Turkish authorities had to organize mobs that rampaged and sowed destruction through scores of large and small Greek residential neighborhoods and business districts dispersed within Istanbul (Ioannides 1991; Vryonis 2005). The direct cost of this, including the blow to Turkey's reputation, was enormously higher than that of the deliberate or accidental fire of 1929. The pogrom of 1955 targeted only Greeks but could not distinguish between Greeks, Armenians, or Jews where they were spatially mixed. Hence, these other groups suffered "collateral damage."

Why are large concentrations of African-Americans persisting in many American cities? And why are African-American ghettos less vibrant than the ethnic ghettos of the past? One view is that the African-American ghetto is not voluntary but results from *prejudice, racism, discrimination*, and *exclusion* on the part of the white majority. *Prejudice* refers to a negative externality that a member of a group feels when it is residentially mixed with members of another. *Other things being equal*, a prejudiced white prefers an all-white neighborhood to a partially black one. Similarly, a prejudiced black prefers the ghetto. We have already argued that a Chinese immigrant may prefer to locate in Chinatown rather than outside, because the ghetto offers economic advantages. The prejudiced immigrant prefers the ghetto even if the same or better economic advantages exist outside.

Many authors use residential prejudice as implying *racism*. Racists believe that other races are inferior. A prejudiced person may dislike interacting with members of another ethnic group, without implying racism. If a Christian does not like to hear Muslim prayers voiced from minarets or a Muslim does not like to hear church bells, these prejudices do not mean that they hate each other or view each other as inferior, only that they may prefer to live separately. Some white Americans may prefer neighborhoods that have no blacks, because they perceive that if blacks moved in, property values would fall. During previous decades, as poorer blacks moved into predominantly white areas, white flight ensued and values fell. A few who flee initially can spark a wave of white flight. This can occur even if no one white is a racist, but many falsely believe that there are some among them who are and who *will* flee. With such beliefs, a cumulative process ensues as a vicious self-fulfilling prophecy.

Discrimination means treating other groups differentially, often in circumvention of existing laws. American real estate brokers have, for decades, discriminated against blacks by not showing them houses in white neighborhoods or have urged whites to sell when blacks moved in. There has been evidence that some mortgage bankers are less likely to approve home loans to African-Americans. The term *redlining* refers to refusing loans to people in certain neighborhoods often of an ethnic make-up, because they are perceived as risky borrowers. Discrimination in labor markets can also indirectly affect residential location (Becker 1957). Prejudice, or racism, is not necessary for discrimination to occur, although it clearly plays a role. Yinger (1995) has suggested that discrimination by American brokers was economically motivated. Such agents feared that should they not discriminate, they might be penalized by lower pay or job loss.

Exclusion is an institutionalized policy that prevents minorities from locating in specific places. South African apartheid and the Warsaw ghetto are legalized exclusion. Ethnic segregation in Cyprus was imposed in 1974 by the invading Turkish army. Prior to the invasion, the 80 percent Greek majority and 18 percent Turkish minority were mixed in all cities and most villages. The invading army seized 37 percent of the land and ethnically cleansed nearly 200,000 Greek Cypriots (a third of the total Cypriots) from their homes in northern Cyprus, later distributing their properties to Turkish Cypriots who moved north voluntarily and to an estimated 100,000 illegal settlers from Turkey. Israeli settlements inserted into the West Bank and Gaza are another example of exclusionary policies. Since the 1967 war, the occupied territories have become more integrated by the insertion of Israeli Jews, while becoming extremely segregated at the micro level, as each such settlement is purely Jewish and interacts little with its Arab neighbors.

Exclusionary policies also abound in both North America and Europe. Western European governments build housing projects in the suburbs that often house minorities or immigrants. These are, in effect, small distributed ghettos. US suburbs often institute large-lot zoning: houses must sit on private lots of at least a certain size. This results in only expensive homes being built, which remain unaffordable for many minorities. One view is that these ordinances are the result of residents' preferences for low densities. Another view is that poorer residents share the schools offered by the suburban community but would reside in a smaller house and pay lower taxes, since schools are funded by *ad valorem* property taxes. This *free riding* by lower-income residents is prevented by the act of disallowing smaller houses. The policy seeks to exclude by income, not race or ethnicity, which is illegal. However, African-Americans or Hispanic Americans are on average poorer and are indirectly excluded. Suburban schools are segregated and schooling benefits of integration remain unrealized.

Back in 1968, John Kain provided a forceful argument that African-American ghettos are involuntary. He observed that whites controlling hiring excluded blacks from suburban jobs. Because suburban residential zoning also excludes blacks, many don't apply for suburban jobs or cannot commute to them. Kain argued that the resulting exclusion cloisters blacks in inner-city ghettos and is responsible for the high rates of black unemployment. This is exacerbated by many blue-collar jobs having moved out of central cities to suburban and exurban areas. This separation of inner-city minorities from suburban jobs is known as *spatial mismatch*. A vicious cycle ensues. As the ghetto economy becomes isolated, unemployment, poverty, crime, and social problems increase, while political power and public expenditures decline. This feeds the perception that the ethnic group is dysfunctional, increasing prejudice.

A questionable aspect of Kain's 1968 argument was that the exclusion of minorities caused a land limitation, preventing ghetto expansion while population grew. If this were true, rents and densities in the ghetto would rise and blacks, on average, would pay a higher quality-adjusted unit price for housing than would whites. This observation jars with prejudiced whites fleeing expanding ghettos. Flight causes a demand reduction, expanding the housing stock that filters down to blacks. Blacks in ghettos would then pay a lower, not higher, price for housing. Which version is true? It may be conjectured that in the initial stages of white flight, blacks benefit from lower housing prices. Later, if the ghetto population increases but blacks are excluded from surrounding neighborhoods and suburbs, the land limitation may become binding. King and Mieszkowski (1973) and Galster (1977) have found some statistical evidence that blacks pay more, but not much more, for comparable housing. Using my model of city and suburban land and labor markets, I can show that white prejudice lowers ghetto rents paid by blacks and benefits blacks in the housing market, while exclusion raises rents and hurts blacks (Anas 2002).

31.4   GHETTOS AND RENTS

Martin Bailey (1959) thought about how equilibrium rents must vary across the ghetto border. Figures 31.3(a) and (b) depict his analysis. Assume a narrow linear city of unit width. All locations are *a priori* identical. Land must be divided between blacks and whites. Bailey assumed that whites are prejudiced and would regard proximity to the border of a black ghetto as a bad, while blacks would like to reside with whites, regarding proximity to the border as a good. Suppose that distance to the border becomes unimportant beyond 1 mile. Assuming that blacks and whites are identical in income and in other-than-racial preferences, land rent around the ghetto border of a segregated city would be as shown in Figure 31.3(a). The slopes of the rent lines within a mile of the border need not be the same, since they reflect how much blacks (whites) value marginal distance to (from) the border.

If each piece of land is owned by a different landlord, the pattern of Figure 31.3(a) is unstable. *Blockbusting* ensues, where arbitrageurs buy houses from whites just to the right of zero, renting or selling them to blacks. Equivalently, white owners sell to blacks and flee. The border moves to the right, expanding the ghetto. For arbitrage to be unprofitable, black and white bids on a unit amount of land must be equal at the border or, if housing conversion is required, then black and white bids on land will differ by the cost of conversion per acre (ignored in Figure 31.3(b)). In Figure 31.3(b), whites pay a premium for being prejudiced, thus keeping the ghetto from expanding, and the outcome shown is an equilibrium. The premium motivates whites to institute exclusion. If whites exclude blacks from locating on the white side of the border, either by discrimination or by zoning, then Figure 31.3(a) is sustained because arbitrageurs cannot operate. Rents in the white area fall and the premium vanishes. Without arbitrage, rents at the border remain discontinuous.

Figures 31.3(c) and (d) are my extensions of Bailey's thinking. These depict how prejudice and exclusion affect the equilibrium rents on land in voluntary ghettos and involuntary slums. The length of the city is fixed at 2*a*. This allows us to see how land rents might be altered by the demand shifts induced by prejudice

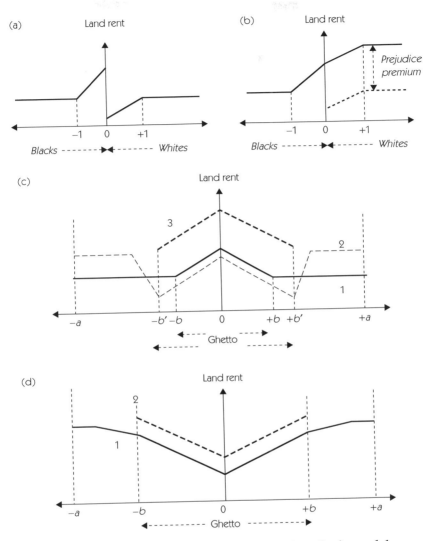

Figure 31.3   Rents and ghettos: (a), (b) Bailey's model;
(c) voluntary ghetto; (d) slum.

or exclusion. Figure 31.3(c) is the voluntary ghetto. The ghetto is $2b$ long. The ghetto center is the most attractive location. Imagine that the ethnic temple, shops, or schools are there. The two groups are identical in income and preferences. Curve 1 is the profile of land rent assuming no prejudice by either group. What would happen if the host group were prejudiced and regarded distance to the border as a bad? This is the case of curve 2. Host residents flee away from the border and the ghetto expands to $2b'$. Ghetto rents are lowered, with the arbitrage condition holding anew at b'. Population density within the ghetto falls. Outside, the same people squeeze into less land, raising average densities and rents. The prejudiced group pays for its prejudice in higher average rents and densities, while the ethnic group benefits. Curve 3 shows what happens if the population in the ghetto increases but the border cannot expand beyond b' due to exclusion. Then, ghetto rents rise and ethnic residents eventually pay more for land than the host group, as was assumed by Kain (1968).

Figure 31.3(d) is the case of a slum. The ethnic amenities of the voluntary ghetto are not present. As in Bailey, residents prefer to be interspersed with the majority, regarding distance to the ghetto border as a good or distance to the ghetto center as a bad, while the majority is prejudiced and regards distance to the border as a bad. Curve 1 depicts the equilibrium rent profile. Curve 2 shows an increase in ghetto rents if the ghetto population increases but the border cannot expand due to zoning. At the border, the ethnic group pays more for land than does the majority. But this may not be true on average, when rents through-out the ghetto are considered.

Figure 31.3(d) (curve 1) leaves one thing unanswered. To my knowledge, it has remained unnoticed in the literature. Rents in the ghetto are lower than outside. The border is established by arbitrage in the *intensive margin* (the areas just by the border). Why is there no arbitrage at the *extensive margin* (throughout the ghetto) also? A developer could buy all the ghetto land by paying a little more than the equilibrium price of land and sell it to members of the majority who would come in from other cities. The developer would make a windfall gain on each parcel of ghetto land. Ghetto residents would have to move out to other cities. Such a giant land assembly would take so long to complete as to yield a subnormal investment return, especially because ghetto rents would rise as the developer's intent became apparent. Also, if ghetto residents who are bought out can only relocate to the ghettos of other cities, then there would be no place for them to go on the net. This brings up the interesting question of why blacks and whites are not completely segregated in different cities. The complementarities between low and high skills in production may be an important reason for the co-location of rich and poor and, indirectly, of ethnic groups in the same city.

31.5   THE EFFICIENCY OF SEGREGATION

Are ghettos and ethnic segregation efficient? Since voluntary ghettos exploit con-centration, ghetto formation has socially desirable aspects. But the question of the size and number of ghettos requires the balancing of the complex positive and negative externalities from ethnic concentration. An optimal ghetto size implies that the ethnic population should be organized into a number of ghettos, possibly in the same city. Optimal ghetto size is reached when adding one more person to the ghetto creates social marginal benefits and costs that are equal. In considering the benefits and the costs, we must add those of the majority and those of the ghetto population. But since the negative and positive externalities are unpriced, it is doubtful that real ghettos are optimally sized.

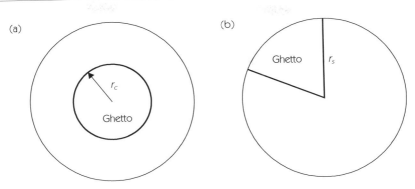

Figure 31.4 Concentric (a) and sectoral (b) ghettos.

Hoyt (1939) noted that most ghettos are not centered on downtowns in a roughly circular or *concentric* pattern, but tend to jot out toward the suburbs, looking like a roughly cut pie slice, a *sectoral* pattern like the Milwaukee ghetto of Figure 31.1. I will present my own simple model encapsulating Hoyt's idea. Imagine that the ghetto is designed by a racist planner who minimizes the points of contact between whites and blacks, known as the *minimum border-length hypothesis* (Loury 1978). Since contacts happen along the border, the objective is achieved by minimizing the length of the border. For a concentric ghetto (Figure 31.4(a)), the length of the border is the perimeter $2\pi r_c$. For the sectoral ghetto, it is $2r_s$, twice the radius (Figure 31.4(b)). Ignoring the possibility that the racist planner wants to allocate smaller lots to blacks, assume that each person is allocated one unit of land. There are N_b blacks and N_w whites. In the concentric case, the length of the border will be $B_c = 2(\pi N_b)^{1/2}$. Suppose that the pie shape covers a fraction ϕ of the circle extending to the rural fringe. The ghetto land is $N_b = \phi \pi r_s^2$ and $N_w = (1 - \phi)\pi r_s^2$ remains for whites. Solve for ϕ from the first equation and substitute this in the second. Then, solve the second for r_s and multiply that by 2. The length of the border is $B_s = 2[(N_b + N_w)/\pi]^{1/2}$. The sectoral ghetto is preferred if $B_s < B_c$. Doing the algebra, this requires

$$\frac{N_b}{N_w} > \frac{1}{\pi^2 - 1} \approx 0.113.$$

The racist planner will prefer a sectoral ghetto if the black population amounts to more than 11.3 percent of the white population. Otherwise, he will prefer a circular ghetto. Real ghettos are not the work of racist planners, but of a myriad of actions by individuals, developers, and local governments. It is not clear why the sectoral shape emerges.

Complete segregation can be Pareto optimal, though it is repugnant to many. Schelling (1969) proposed a simple but fascinating way of thinking about the relocation behavior of prejudiced individuals acting independently and myopically, but ignored whether or not such behavior led to optimal allocations. I will

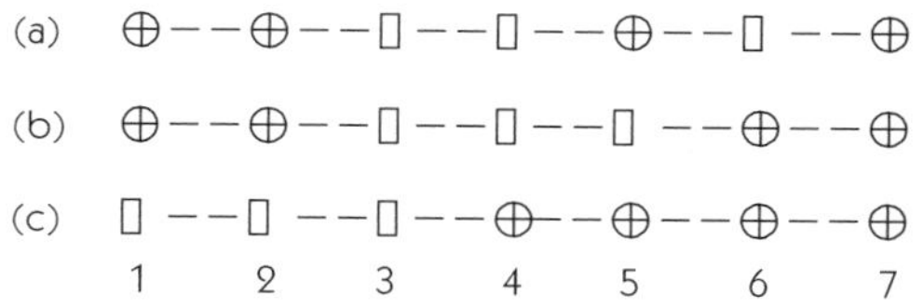

(a) ⊕ − − ⊕ − − ⧠ − − ⧠ − − ⊕ − − ⧠ − − ⊕

(b) ⊕ − − ⊕ − − ⧠ − − ⧠ − − ⧠ − − ⊕ − − ⊕

(c) ⧠ − − ⧠ − − ⧠ − − ⊕ − ⊕ − − ⊕ − − ⊕

    1   2   3   4   5   6   7

Figure 31.5 Unstable allocation (a), a ghettoized equilibrium (b), and a Pareto-efficient ghetto in a Schelling-type model (c).

show here that his idea extends to optimal segregation. Figure 31.5 illustrates Schelling's model for a linear array of an arbitrary seven locations. Imagine them to be seven adjacent houses on a street. Other locations are not available. There are four persons denoted as ⊕. Three others are shown by a ⧠. Each is prejudiced in the sense that his utility is highest if both neighbors are of his type. Utility is lower if only one neighbor is of one's own type and lowest if one is surrounded by the opposite type. Suppose that an agent wants to relocate if he is so surrounded. If at least one agent wants to relocate, the arrangement is not in equilibrium. Arrangement (a) is not in equilibrium because 5 and 6 want to move. If they swap places, they improve their own utilities and those of 4 and 7. Swapping results in (b), an equilibrium in which the ⧠ are ghettoized: (b) Pareto dominates (a). The highest social welfare occurs under the Pareto-efficient arrangement (c). This minimizes the points of contact between the two types, so that there is only one individual of each type experiencing an externality and no swaps will improve welfare. A planner is needed to achieve (c), since (b) is in equilibrium and no voluntary swaps will be initiated between a ⊕ and a ⧠. The racist planner could insure that the socially optimal pattern (c) emerged. Another mechanism for transitioning from pattern (b) to (c) is for persons 1 and 2 to form a coalition and persuade the pair 4 and 5 to swap places with them. Only one person in each pair improves his utility; therefore the coalitions will work only if the gainer in each pair gains enough to compensate his partner. The reader is invited to make up some numbers and create examples where this either is or is not possible.

What if prejudice varies with the fraction of persons of the opposite type in one's neighborhood? Assume N_b blacks and N_w whites. Land consists of two islands. Coincidentally, island one has N_b units of land and island two has N_w units. Each person's demand for land is unity. The utilities are $U_b = k_b a_w^\theta$ for a black and $U_w = k_w a_b^\theta$ for a white. a_b is the fraction of an island's residents that is black and a_w is the fraction of an island's residents that is white. Assume that $0 < \theta \leq 1$. Assume that populations *within* an island contact at random. Then, the higher the proportion of the other type on one's island, the higher is the probability of contact. The parameters k_b and k_w measure prejudice toward the presence of the other group on one's island. If $k_b = k_w = 0$, persons could be allocated to islands in any way that one pleased, without detriment. Consider $k_b \geq 0$ and $k_w < 0$. This, as in Bailey's model, means that blacks like having more whites on their island, while whites dislike having more blacks on theirs. Suppose that people are allocated to the islands according to their proportion in the total population. Hence, $a_b = N_b/(N_b + N_w)$ and $a_w = N_w/(N_b + N_w)$. This is the *perfectly integrated allocation*. Another outcome is the *perfectly segregated allocation*, under which all whites are allocated to island two and all blacks to island one. Then, $a_b = a_w = 0$. Under complete segregation, welfare is zero since there are no externalities. Under integration, aggregate welfare is $W_I = N_b k_b a_w^\theta + N_w k_w a_b^\theta$. If $W_I < 0$, segregation is socially preferable to integration. This reduces to the following:

$$\frac{k_b}{|k_w|} < \left(\frac{1 - a_b}{a_b}\right)^{1-\theta}.$$

If blacks are indifferent toward whites ($k_b = 0$) but whites are prejudiced ($k_w < 0$), then segregation is preferable. For any positive k_b, segregation is preferable if whites are sufficiently prejudiced; namely, $|k_w|$ is sufficiently large. The larger the percentage of blacks in total, the more prejudiced whites would have to be for segregation to be preferable. That is because the utility gains from segregation accruing to the few whites need to be balanced against the gains from integration accruing to a large number of blacks. In South Africa, whites were a minority but they imposed apartheid on blacks. In the USA, blacks are a minority but have been largely segregated in ghettos. The above inequality implies that both outcomes may be socially preferable to integration. The inequality would hold for both cases as long as South African whites were much more racially prejudiced than were American whites, something that fits the stereotype.

Socially optimal segregation is rendered more complex if intra-ethnic and inter-ethnic externalities are intergenerational. For example, it is arguable that growing up segregated and attending segregated schools causes new generations to remain prejudiced, whereas integration improves inter-ethnic understanding and cross-cultural fertilization. Fostering more integration may impose costs on prejudiced current generations who dislike it, but should have benefits for future generations, since children will be less prejudiced as adults. Ghetto children can be educated more cheaply when mixed with children of the majority, who may be better learners, whereas the cost of educating the majority increases when they share schools with the children of ghettos. Still, integration by income and ethnic background can increase average school performance through peer effects, and boost human capital accumulation. Benabou (1993) showed that spatial segregation with separate schools is often the equilibrium outcome, while residential and school integration often the optimal outcome.

31.6 PUBLIC POLICY AND POLITICS

Socrates's advice (see the Introduction) was to deal with inequality and segregation by some form of redistribution. It has been particularly difficult to heed such advice. The public policy response to ethnic segregation has varied enormously and has gone to bewildering extremes. Recently, "the government of Rio de Janeiro State proposed to build a [3 meter tall concrete] wall around its sprawling

favelas in an effort to help control rampant crime in the picture postcard city"
(Colitt 2004). Similarly, Israel is having to wall off the Palestinian Arabs to protect itself from terrorist attacks. The wall was endorsed by Israel's highest court,
provided that its alignment considered Palestinian rights. The International Court
of Justice declared the wall illegal.

India's recent policy toward Dharavi, Asia's largest slum (see the Introduction), is to rehabilitate it with multistory buildings at a cost of $1.3 billion. This
contrasts with India's slum removal policies of the 1970s and 1980s, in which
demolitions were, in some cases, followed by residents being packed into buses,
driven to city fringes, and told to return to their rural homes. Indian police
are often accused of harassing Muslims. Perry (2003) claims that the "Gujarat
authorities even went so far as to price Muslim lives below those of Hindus,
offering $2,050 in state compensation for Muslims killed but double that for the
riot's 58 Hindu victims."

Despite many United Nations resolutions since 1974 calling for the withdrawal
of troops and the restoration of the free movements of people in Cyprus, Kofi
Annan, the secretary general of the UN, recently proposed a system of governance that would legitimize the military-imposed territorial and ethnic partition of
Cyprus, with only limited rights to Greeks to resettle and reclaim their looted
properties, while allowing illegal Turkish settlers to remain. The Turkish government even demanded that these apartheid measures become part of the primary
law of the European Union in advance of Cyprus's admission into Europe on
May 1, 2004. While some have naively defended the Annan Plan, others have
pointed out that it ghettoizes Greek Cypriots in their own country, in violation of
the European laws of free settlement. The Annan Plan required its ratification
through separate referenda by both Greek and Turkish Cypriots, including the
illegally imported Turkish settlers. Not surprisingly, 76 percent of Greeks voted
against, while 60 percent of Turks voted in favor of Annan's plan.

The right to locate freely wherever one wants within a country is fundamental
to all modern societies. Free movement of people among member countries is
one of the most basic tenets of the European Union. A Europe with a low fertility
rate and high wages induces immigration from the poorer countries in the Union
and elsewhere to the richer ones, causing international ethnic integration while,
at the same time, ethnic ghettos emerge and grow within European cities, causing intra-urban ethnic segregation. A trend of growing segregation and social
exclusion in European cities is already established. In the new post Cold War
era of civilizational tensions, the growth of ghettos, especially Muslim ghettos, is
becoming an issue. As Johnson (2004) puts it, "Germany has an estimated three
million Muslim immigrants. Elsewhere in Europe are millions more. Many live
in large cities' immigrant ghettos, speaking the local language poorly, dropping
out of school at high rates and making up an outsized share of prison populations.
So the broader issues . . . are who represents these people, and how – or whether
– they are to be fully integrated into European society."

Immigration can be controlled indirectly. It has been advocated that immigrants
to the USA (e.g., from Mexico) not be given public assistance for a number of
years after entry. This amounts to a tax on immigrants because they add to social

costs in the host country. The policy would slow immigration toward its optimal level. But subsidizing Mexican economic development would also slow immigration (Anas 2002). In the spirit of the Coase Theorem (Coase 1960), the two approaches should yield roughly equivalent outcomes: the externality imposed by an immigrant can be mitigated either by admitting him and taxing him for the marginal social costs that he imposes, or subsidizing him to stay out by paying him the marginal benefit of foregoing to immigrate.

Slowing immigration aside, what should public policy do about ghettos where the racial or ethnic concentration appears to have detrimental effects? American social policy has experimented with a variety of measures, with minor effects. These include the busing of children to achieve racially balanced schools, and the Section 8 and other housing subsidies to increase the supply of low-cost housing outside low-income areas and ghettos. In the historic Mt Laurel decisions in New Jersey in the 1970s and 1980s, the courts concluded that suburban land-use controls violated the state's constitution, but these decisions had only some effect in New Jersey. Although suburban zoning remains the chief obstacle to the suburbanization of ghettoized black and Hispanic minorities, current public policy is limited to subsidizing inner cities. Such income redistribution may be politically justified as compensation to ghetto residents for the prevailing exclusion.

The growing concentration of black voters in central cities (see Table 31.1) has resulted in the election of more black mayors and local politicians. Increased control over central-city politics may provide blacks with an incentive to stay ghettoized. Some black politicians are among the loudest opponents of metropolitan governance or low-cost housing programs that would scatter blacks in the suburbs, since this would dilute their base of voters. It would also stand to reason that the growing proportion of minorities in central cities helps to extract a bigger stream of subsidies from Washington and the state governments. But it is unclear whether these political economies of scale have improved the welfare of African and Hispanic Americans.

Acknowledgments

Feng Qian helped with the construction of Table 31.1. A conversation with Tara Shankar Shaw improved my understanding of Indian ethnic issues.

Bibliography

Anas, A. 2002: Prejudice, exclusion and compensating transfers: the economics of ethnic segregation. *Journal of Urban Economics*, 52, 409–32.

Bailey, M. 1959: Notes on the economics of residential zoning and urban renewal. *Land Economics*, 35, 288–90.

Becker, G. S. 1957: *The Economics of Discrimination*. Chicago: The University of Chicago Press.

Benabou, R. 1993: Workings of a city – location, education, and production. *Quarterly Journal of Economics*, 108(3), 619–52.

Coase, R. 1960: The problem of social cost. *Journal of Law and Economics*, 3, 1–44.

Colitt, R. 2004: Rio de Janeiro state plans to wall off *favelas*. *The Financial Times*, April 13, p. 3 of print edition.

Cutler, D. M. and Glaeser, E. L. 1997: Are ghettos good or bad? *Quarterly Journal of Economics*, 112(3), 827–72.

Galster, G. C. 1977: A bid-rent analysis of housing market discrimination. *The American Economic Review*, 67(2), 144–55.

Hoyt, H. 1939: *The Structure and Growth of Residential Neighborhoods in American Cities*. Washington, DC: Government Printing Office.

Iceland, J. and Weinberg, D. H., with Steinmetz, E. 2002: *Racial and Ethnic Segregation in the United States*: 1980–2000. Census 2000 Special Reports, US Census Bureau, US Department of Commerce, Washington, DC. Retrieved from www.census.gov/prod/2002pubs/censr-3.pdf

Ioannides, C. P. 1991: *In Turkey's Image*: *The Transformation of Occupied Cyprus into a Turkish Province*. New Rochelle, NY: A. D. Caratzas.

Johnson, I. 2004: Decried in Germany, Islamic group sues to clear its name. *The Wall Street Journal*, March 30, p. 1 of print edition.

Jowett, B., with Knight, M. J. 1999: *The Essential Plato*. New York: Alain de Botton.

Kain, J. 1968: Housing segregation, negro employment and metropolitan decentralization. *The Quarterly Journal of Economics*, 82(2), 175–97.

Katyal, S. and Lengade, J. 2004: Asia's largest slum to get $1.3 billion face-lift. *World Environment News*, February 17. Retrieved May 13, 2004, from http://www.planetark.com/avantgo/dailynewsstory.cfm?newsid=23844

King, A. T. and Mieszkowski, P. 1973: Racial discrimination, segregation and the price of housing. *Journal of Political Economy*, 81(3), 590–606.

Loury, G. C. 1978: The minimum border-length hypothesis does not explain the shape of black ghettos. *Journal of Urban Economics*, 5(2), 147–53.

Mills, E. S. and Lubuele, L. S. 1997: Inner cities. *Journal of Economic Literature*, 35(2), 727–56.

Perry, A. 2003: India's great divide. *Time Asia Magazine*, August 4. Retrieved April 28, 2004 from www.time.com/time/asia/magazine/printout/0,13675,501030811-472904,00.html

Reynolds, D. W. 1997: The lost architecture of ancient Rome: insights from the Severan Plan and the regionary catalogues. *Expedition*. *Special Issue*: *Topics in Late Roman Life*, 39, 2.

Schelling, T. 1969: Models of segregation. *The American Economic Review, Papers and Proceedings*, 59(2), 488–93.

Vryonis, S., Jr 2005: *The Mechanism of Catastrophe: The Turkish Pogrom of September 6–7, 1955, and the Destruction of the Greek Community in Istanbul*. New York: Greekworks.com.

Yinger, J. 1995: *Closed Doors, Opportunities Lost*. Washington, DC: Russell Sage Foundation.

Index

Made in the USA
San Bernardino, CA
30 August 2014